KARL BRANDT: THE NAZI DOCTOR

Also by the same author

Medical Films, Ethics and Euthanasia in Nazi Germany

Justice at Nuremberg. Leo Alexander and the Nazi Doctors' Trial

Karl Brandt: The Nazi Doctor

Medicine and Power in the Third Reich

Ulf Schmidt

hambledon
continuum

Hambledon Continuum is an imprint of Continuum Books
Continuum UK, The Tower Building, 11 York Road, London SE1 7NX
Continuum US, 80 Maiden Lane, Suite 704, New York, NY 10038

www.continuumbooks.com

First published 2007

British Library Cataloguing-in-Publication Data
A catalogue record for this book is available from the British Library.

ISBN 978 1 84725 031 5

Typeset by Egan Reid, Auckland, New Zealand
Printed and bound by MPG Books Ltd, Cornwall, Great Britain

Contents

Karl Brandt and Adolf Hitler on the Berghof during Hitler's holiday,
1–3 September 1938 (BSB, Fotoarchiv Hoffmann, hoff-20063)

Illustrations

Plates

For Katia and Bella

Acknowledgements

This book has been a long time in the making. After eight years of research and writing, I understand why it needed that amount of time, no more and no less. A book on a subject such as this has its own history and also its own natural progression and life, yet scholars today are rarely able to take this sufficiently into account: external pressures and the expectation to publish or perish, as the saying goes, often do not allow scholars to 'listen' to the nature of a book project, or to 'hear' what a book demands of them. I am glad to say that I was fortunate enough to enjoy the unfettered luxury of developing this project in my own time and at my own pace, rewrite certain passages and chapters, and research individual aspects in the depth and breath which I felt was necessary. I am grateful to all those who made this possible and who supported this project over the years. Their encouragement and constructive criticism were essential in bringing this project to a successful conclusion. They all deserve my gratitude, and I hope that those whom I have not mentioned by name will forgive me.

From early on, the book was an attempt to go beyond the established literature on Nazi Germany and write a fair and balanced account about one of the leading medical men of the Third Reich, Karl Brandt, Hitler's escort physician. For years, his life and the historical context in which he operated became part of my own daily routine, the letters and photographs and the tiny pieces of information from all quarters serving as the building material for this book. I owe special thanks to his son, who generously sent me selections of his father's papers and photographs. When I met him for the first time in April 1999, we had a substantial discussion; while it is probably inevitable that we are unable to agree on a number of key issues, nevertheless I am grateful to him for having engaged with me in a discourse over the years.

I am grateful to the organizations which generously supported this book project, in particular the German Historical Institute in Washington, D.C., United States, which granted me a Senior Visiting Fellowship in 2003. I am also indebted to the Leverhulme Trust for having supported the work with a six-month Research Fellowship which enabled me to conduct essential research in the United States and Europe, and gave me the necessary time to complete the book. I would also like to thank Mark Connelly, my head of department, who was a great support in the final stages of the book. Some of the findings of this study have previously been presented to the German Historical Institutes in London and Washington, D.C., and to the Universities of Oxford, Birmingham, Penn State and Erlangen, and I am grateful for all the feedback which I received. My colleagues and friends in the

School of History at the University of Kent provided me with an excellent academic environment for the sharing of ideas and material. It is thanks to them that I had the confidence to pursue this project and bring it to completion. In particular, I would like to thank Philip Boobyer, Antony Copley, Kenneth Fincham, Robin Gill, Richard Norman, Charlotte Sleigh and David Turley who all, in their own ways, contributed to this book.

I am greatly indebted to the many archives and their staff who helped me discover relevant sources. I am especially grateful to the staff of the Archive of the Albert-Ludwigs University in Freiburg; the Archive of the von Bodelschwingh Asylum Bethel, especially to Kerstin Stockhecke; the Archive of the Humboldt University in Berlin, especially to Winfried Schultze; the Archive of the Ludwig-Maximilians University in Munich; the Archive of the Ruhr University in Bochum; the Archives de la Ville de Mulhouse in France; the Bergmannsheil clinic in Bochum; the City Archives in Bochum, Chemnitz, Dresden and Velbert; the City and District Archive in Schmalkalden; the German Swimming Association in Kassel; the Federal Archives in Berlin and Koblenz, especially to Gregor Pickro; the Holocaust Memorial Museum, especially to Patricia Heberer; the Imperial War Museum, London; the National Archives, London; the National Archives and Record Administration, Washington D.C.; the Saxon State Archive in Dresden; the Schmalkalden City Council; the State Archive, Nuremberg, especially to Gunther Friedrich; and the Thuringian University and State Library in Jena. I would also like to thank Reinhard Horn from the State Library of Bavaria in Munich who helped me gain access to over 500 photographs of Brandt in the collection of Heinrich Hoffmann, Hitler's official photographer.

A book of this nature and scope would not have been possible without the support of an extended network of scholars and friends, and I am grateful to all of them for their ideas and critical comments. I would especially like to thank Winfried Süß for his help and for sharing his tremendous knowledge on the subject. I am also very grateful to Markus Henneke for having given me access to his extensive collection of primary and secondary sources; his readiness to discuss and exchange archival material has been in the best of scholarly traditions. I am also greatly indebted to Margaret Pelling for having supported the project in the early critical stages with all her knowledge and skill. She, more than anyone else, knows how difficult this book has been at times. I would also like to thank Robert Baker, Richard Bessel, Christopher Browning, Florian Bruns, Richard Evans, Mark Harrison, Uwe Kaminsky, Brigitte Leyendecker, Anthony Nicholls, Gert Niedl, Robert Proctor, Alice Riccardi (von) Platen, Karl-Heinz Roth, Hans Safrian, Dirk Schumann, Gitta Sereny, Christopher Wheeler and David Willcox for their invaluable insights and discussions about the subject.

The original idea for this book was conceived in close collaboration with Tony Morris and Martin Sheppard from London Books and Hambledon Press, now Continuum. I am extremely grateful for the trust and support which they have given this project over the years. Whereas Tony's professionalism and diplomatic skill were essential during the production process, Martin's editorial suggestions were important in turning this book into the first full-scale biography of Hitler's doctor. I am also greatly indebted to Sarah Patey, who did an outstanding job in proof-reading and editing the manuscript, to Ben Hayes from Continuum for his excellent editorial work, and to Barbara Ball for her perceptive copy editing.

Finally, I wish to thank those people who have provided me with the necessary strength and confidence in tackling such a difficult subject. I am especially grateful to Jo Fox, Andreas Frewer, Jonathan Moreno and David Welch for their unflinching support of this book project; their perceptive observations have been a constant source of encouragement and inspiration. I am particularly grateful to them for having proof-read what was barely a manuscript, and I hope I have shown myself worthy of their friendship.

My greatest thanks of all go to Katia Mai, my long-time partner, who has supported me in this endeavour despite the eccentricities of academic life. Her love has been a sanctuary and source of strength in my attempt to understand those aspects of human behaviour which can be deeply troubling and sad. I wish to dedicate this work to her and to our rescue-dog Bella, a Border Collie Saluki cross, whose daily ration of fresh air and need for open spaces gave me the necessary distance. Without the two of them the book would not have been written in the way it has.

Ulf Schmidt
Canterbury, 2007

Abbreviations

AHtA	Archiv der Hoffnungtaler Anstalten Lobetal
AP	Alexander Papers, Boston, Mass. (in possession of Cecily Alexander-Grable)
BAB	Bundesarchiv Berlin
BA-BDC	Bundesarchiv, Abt.III, Außenstelle Zehlendorf
BAFA	Bundesarchiv-Filmarchiv, Berlin
BAK	Bundesarchiv, Koblenz
BA-MA	Bundesarchiv Militärarchiv Freiburg im Br.
BIOS	British Intelligence Objectives Sub-Committee
BSB	Bayerische Staatsbibliothek, Munich
CIOS	Combined Intelligence Objectives Sub-Committee
DUMC	Duke University Archives, Depository for Medical Center Records, Durham, N.C.
DUPA	Duquesne University, Pittsburgh, Penn., Archive
FCLM	Francis A. Countway Library of Medicine, Boston, Mass.
HBAB	Hauptarchiv der von Bodelschwinghschen Anstalten Bethel
HHStA	Hamburg Staatsarchiv
HUA	Humboldt Universität zu Berlin-Archiv
IMT	International Military Tribunal
IWM	Imperial War Museum
LoC	Library of Congress
NARA	National Archives and Records Administration, Washington D.C., United States
NDT	NDT-Records and NDT-Documents, in Dörner and Ebbinghaus 1999
NLM	National Library of Medicine, Bethesda, Md.
NYPL	New York Public Library
OCCWC	United States Office of Chief of Counsel for War Crimes
RGB	Reichsgesetzblatt
RJM	Reichsjustizministerium
RMdI	Reichsministerium des Inneren
RmfVuP	Reichsministerium für Volksaufklärung und Propaganda
RPA	Rassenpolitisches Amt
RSHA	Reichssicherheitshauptamt
SA	Sturmabteilung
SD	Sicherheitsdienst

SHAEF	Supreme Headquarters Allied Expeditionary Forces
SPD	Sozialdemokratische Partei Deutschlands
SS	Schutzstaffel
StaNü	Staatsarchiv Nürnberg
TNA	The National Archives
UNWCC	United Nations War Crimes Commission
USSBS	United States Strategic Bombing Survey
ZSL	Zentrale Stelle der Landesjustizverwaltungen in Ludwigsburg

Prologue

Late at night, on 5 November 1946, Hitler's former doctor, Karl Brandt, was sitting cross-legged on his plank bed in his Nuremberg prison cell. He had that day received and read the indictment against him and his twenty-two co-defendants in the Nazi Doctors' Trial, and had been mulling over the meaning of the document. He decided to use his notebook as 'a kind of diary' for his family. Five days later, at 8.15 a.m., Brandt noted: 'I thought that perhaps this or the other would be of importance to you, that you would realise, in particular, how I myself coped with my journey'.[1] Tall, dark-haired, brown-eyed and good-looking, at the age of forty-two, Brandt realized that he would not see his wife and his eleven-year-old son for years to come, if indeed ever again, if he was to be sentenced for the crimes he was alleged to have committed during the Second World War. The diary was intended to communicate with an imagined world outside his prison wall, and to rationalize the enormity of the charge levelled against him. It was written to console himself and his family during the long prison sentence which Brandt was expecting, or even as long-term moral support for them if he were to be sentenced to death. He wanted them to take part in his forthcoming struggle, to tell them about his daily activities, how he shared his fate with like-minded 'comrades', who silently greeted each other on the metal staircase in the morning. He also wanted to say how he felt in the days when he stood accused in front of the world: 'I just want to calmly open my heart to you once more, without any inhibitions, without any fuss [*ohne Zier und Klausel*]'.[2] Brandt, in short, was trying to remain sane and controlled. But the diary also served another, more profound, purpose. Brandt wanted to portray himself as an idealist, as someone whose conscience was clear, who had followed orders, not just anyone's, but those of Hitler, the head of state and Reich Chancellor; he knew that the trial would decide his life, but it also gave him a platform from which he could take the initiative, justify his role in the regime, and create an idealized image of himself for posterity.

Brandt knew that it would be extremely difficult to justify his role in the regime, particularly his involvement in the 'euthanasia' programme – the killing of tens of thousands of mentally and physically handicapped children and adults: 'However much diligence I spend on this, indeed all I can muster, I am not convinced of the external success. That may be a mistake, given that one should tackle this problem with a feeling of a "definite victory", but then again I am probably too much of a realist for that'.[3] He had also recognized that almost the entire medical elite of the Nazi regime had evaded trial by committing suicide, a fact which did not help his situation since all attention was now focused on him. Given that he had spent twelve years, from the age of twenty-nine to the age of forty-one, in Hitler's immediate vicinity as his 'escort physician' (*Begleitarzt*), Brandt believed that the Allies would want to punish him.

Brandt not only felt wrongfully accused, but believed that he would be forced to shoulder the blame for acts which others had committed.[4] In the evenings, he sometimes turned to his books, Shakespeare among them, in which he hoped to find passages which would help to explain his downfall or forthcoming fate. On Sunday 17 November, at 9 p.m., Brandt felt that Shakespeare's Cleopatra was speaking about himself, and quoted the passage in his diary: 'Be it be known, that we, the greatest, are misthought / For things that others do, and when we fall, / We answer others' merits in our name, / Are therefore to be pitied'.[5] Dreading the 'horrible' weeks to come, Brandt nonetheless studied every piece of evidence which friends and colleagues had unearthed, hoping that some of it would be useful for his defence. 'It might be completely uninteresting for this drama here,' he remarked, 'but I am also just a human being and I shall be content if the image others have of me becomes balanced [*wenn sich mein Bild rundet*]'.[6] He was shocked, or so it appeared, to discover that Philipp Bouhler, the head of the Chancellery of the Führer (*Kanzlei des Führers*, KdF), had been involved in the Holocaust, and feared that the prosecution would assume that he had been involved as well, or at least had been informed about it: 'From documents etc. I can now also see that Bouhler has obviously on his own initiative [*von sich aus*] carried out the extermination of Jews. Today (!) I find out about this.'[7] His main concern was how to disconnect the murder of millions of Jews from the 'euthanasia' programme. 'How shall I now separate this from this honest euthanasia?' he noted in his diary.[8] Without his personal and administrative files, and lacking witnesses, Brandt was struggling with the realization that there was irrefutable evidence which linked Bouhler, and by implication himself, to the Holocaust. At the same time, he felt that his moral conscience had been strengthened through this revelation – if, indeed, it had been a revelation – 'and that must be my best comrade – apart from you, of course!'[9] For Brandt, it was of paramount importance, during his time in prison, or even in death, that his conscience as a man, and as a doctor, had been and would remain clear, whatever incriminating evidence were placed before him and whatever the outcome of the trial. It gave meaning and a sense of direction to what was left of his life.

Born in 1904 in Mülhausen, Alsace, Brandt played a major role in the organization and implementation of the first mass-killing programme of the Third Reich, the so-called 'euthanasia' programme.[10] Later, as General Commissioner for Health and Sanitation (*Generalkommissar für das Sanitäts- und Gesundheitswesen*), Brandt became the foremost medical authority in the Nazi regime during the Second World War.[11] He was also put in charge of biological and chemical warfare research. Allied prosecutors clearly recognized Brandt's significance in the regime as a whole, and put him on trial as defendant number one in the Nuremberg Doctors' Trial in 1946/47.[12] Yet, to date, no comprehensive biography of Karl Brandt has been written. This book intends to fill the gap in the literature.[13]

Brandt's character combined elements of the rational medical scientist and efficient organizer with a fascination for ancient civilizations, mysticism, racial eugenics and romanticism. It is exactly the combination of political and ideological radicalism with a specific form of rationality, medical ideology and world view (*Weltanschauung*) which needs exploration, and also explanation, if we want to understand how a rational, highly cultured, literate, young professional and medical expert, who was not easily blinded by ideological fanaticism or party politics, came to instigate, and become responsible for, mass murder and criminal human experiments on a previously unimaginable scale. Brandt's biography sits uncomfortably with the image of the drunken, ruthless Nazi hordes, who vented their pent-up aggressions, as well as social and professional frustrations, on Jews and political opponents in the aftermath of the Nazi takeover of power, or burned and vandalized hundreds of synagogues in the wake of the 'Crystal Night' (*Reichskristallnacht*), or with some of the fanatical ideologues, SS-Einsatzgruppen and mass murderers who organized the systematic extermination of European Jews in the eastern territories, or indeed with most of the medical and administrative personnel involved in the planning and execution of the 'euthanasia' programme. Brandt was neither a party ideologue who, like Himmler and Rosenberg, called for the annihilation of an entire people and the expansion of German 'living space' (*Lebensraum*), nor did he represent the kind of technocratic 'desk perpetrator' (*Schreibtischtäter*) who, like Eichmann, planned and organized an efficient deportation system which ferried hundreds of thousands of Jews and others to the death camps. For Hannah Arendt, the political philosopher, a man like Eichmann represented the 'banality of evil', a desk murderer, who conscientiously obeyed nothing but orders. Yet the subsequent historiographical and public debate on totalitarianism, fascism, intentionalism and functionalism which scholars have held since the 1960s may have helped to classify and stereotype Nazi perpetrators, rather than enhance a prosopographical and contextualized understanding of the Nazi elite.[14] We need to recognize that Brandt was an integral member of the German intelligentsia, who in the 1930s and 1940s were willing, and empowered, to conceive and support an oppressive, militarist, racist and colonial government policy, and ultimately turn its exterminatory potential into reality.

One of Brandt's closest friends was Albert Speer, Hitler's personal architect. Both belonged to a generation of young professionals, born between 1900 and 1910, who experienced the First World War as children or adolescents, and later advanced to key executive positions in the regime, a young 'expert élite' (*Funktionselite*), as Michael Wildt has pointed out, often highly ambitious and competitive, but also with little empathy for the suffering of others.[15] Like Speer, who managed to create a post-war narrative of himself as an idealistic, conscientious and apolitical expert, Brandt wanted to portray himself as a genuine believer in the moral legitimacy of 'euthanasia', as someone who had reluctantly carried out Hitler's directives, but who had otherwise been ignorant of the crimes of the regime. Both established for themselves an image mirroring that of the millions of Germans who, after the war, wanted the world to believe that they had fallen victim to Hitler's political movement. 'He strung us all along', the writer Joachim Fest recently admitted, after historians discovered that Speer was personally involved in the Holocaust, that his ministry provided the building materials for an extension of Auschwitz, that he made a substantial fortune with Aryanized property, denounced uncooperative competitors, initiated the construction of concentration camps, and supported the draconian measures used against forced and slave labourers in some of Germany's most horrific underground production facilities.[16] If only a part of this had been known during the International Military Tribunal in 1945, which preceded the trial against Brandt and others, Speer would probably have been sentenced to death. The fact that most of it was unknown at the time gave Speer the possibility of creating his own carefully constructed, but also greatly biased, post-war narrative of himself and the regime, a convenient and plausible story, which scholars and journalists either took for granted or were unable to refute. Whereas much has been written about Speer in the last decades, most notably by Gitta Sereny in her study *Albert Speer: His Battle with Truth*, published in 1995, scholars have only fairly recently turned their attention to Brandt as one of the key architects of Hitler's murderous policies.[17]

In Robert Lifton's analysis *The Nazi Doctors*, published in 1986, Brandt represents the type of an 'élitist, highly educated, and dedicated healer', who participated in medical killings. His almost mystical aura of 'elegance and purity' apparently made him the perfect advocate of the 'euthanasia' programme, and an ideal representative of Hitler's wishes. Brandt was the embodiment of the 'decent Nazi', Lifton argued, a scientifically trained, reliable and moral doctor, the prototype of an idealist.[18] Young, elegant and from a middle-class, bourgeois background, Brandt apparently developed what was regarded as an 'adopted son' relationship with Hitler, whom he saw not only as a father figure, but as a 'prophet and saviour'. One doctor in Lifton's narrative described Brandt as 'a highly ethical person … one of the most idealistic physicians I have ever met during my career'. Another noted, however, that Brandt had also been attracted to 'the feeling of possessing power', and was guilty of war crimes.[19] Brandt was 'brutalised and numbed' by the 'euthanasia' programme, stated Lifton, who claimed: 'Brandt's religious-romantic involvement in the Nazi project contributed to his extensive numbing towards mass killing and to his extraordinary capacity to continue to see virtue in the total Nazi programme.'[20]

Other writers took a similar approach. In *The Last Days of Hitler*, published first in 1947, the late Hugh Trevor-Roper felt no repulsion at the sight of Brandt as he did for Hitler's other doctor, Theodor Morell, a pompous quack who apparently had the hygienic habits of a pig.[21] Although Brandt was not among 'the first flight of surgeons', owing his success primarily to chance and nepotism, he was, according to Trevor-Roper, at least 'not altogether disreputable'.[22] It is quite possible that it was the similarity of their academic background and cultured interests which influenced Trevor-Roper's perception of Brandt, but class did matter in 1945, when proof was needed that Hitler was dead. Such people listening to Brandt during the Nazi Doctors' Trial were often left with a feeling of discomfort on realizing that he had truly believed in the 'euthanasia' programme. For Countess Alice von Platen, one of the three German trial observers, who perceived 'with horror the ordinary faces' of the Nuremberg defendants, Brandt was the representative of an 'idealistic type' of Nazi who, in the name of National Socialism, the state, and the Aryan race, had devoted his entire being to a greater ideal.[23] Brandt's longing for a new and better community had, according to von Platen, led him to believe that life was of no more than 'biological value', and that doctors, as the guardians of the health of the nation, were morally obliged to support the 'euthanasia' programme.

Most contemporaries who commented on Brandt in Allied interrogations and witness statements after the war would probably have agreed with this assessment. Speer regarded him as a 'very decent man'. He described him as someone who was 'widely appreciated' and 'very conscientious about his life – whatever he was doing'.[24] After learning that his friend, 'an excellent man in every way', had been involved in the 'euthanasia' programme, Speer was apparently puzzled. According to Speer, Brandt had such integrity that 'he must have believed in it'.[25] The clergyman Erwin Sutz, who had met Brandt in the Swiss mountains in 1930, was convinced that Brandt believed in the 'National Socialist faith ... with the conviction and enthusiasm of a true idealist'.[26] Winifred Wagner, the wife of Richard Wagner's son Siegfried, was shocked to learn that the Allies had sentenced Brandt to death for his beliefs: 'What a nice, decent fellow he was, and how he now has to pay for things which he had to support.'[27] One of Brandt's assistants apparently remembered Brandt as being furious after realizing that some psychiatrists had condemned patients to death 'who should not have been'. He described Brandt as the kind of Nazi who wanted to carry out the programme as 'fairly' and 'humanely' as possible.[28] Eugen Gerstenmaier, who was arrested for his alleged participation in the assassination attempt on Hitler in July 1944, could not have agreed more. Brandt had apparently not only saved him from the gallows, but had 'behaved in a personally decent and understanding way towards the head of the Bethel Institution, pastor Friedrich von Bodelschwingh'.[29] Von Bodelschwingh, whose secret talks with Brandt may have helped to save patients' lives in Bethel, described Hitler's doctor as a man with a certain measure of idealism. He had been particularly impressed by Brandt's willingness to listen to opposing arguments and improve the formal procedures in the 'euthanasia' programme, albeit always resisting the idea that the programme was in itself criminal and amoral. In 1945, von Bodelschwingh told a BBC radio programme: 'You must not picture Professor Brandt as a criminal, but rather as an idealist.'[30]

Such a coherent assessment by scholars and contemporaries of Brandt as the 'decent Nazi', the 'idealist', the 'devoted doctor', who followed his beliefs for the greater good of the national community, the state and the health of the race, warrants substantial historical scepticism, although there are numerous statements from Brandt, which he made during the Doctors' Trial, to support some of these views.[31] The characteristics mentioned above were certainly, to some extent, part of Brandt's overall personality – I once described him as a 'staunch idealist' – but, at the same time, they do not adequately explain the broader motives and rationalization strategies which led Brandt to implement a central plank of Hitler's eugenic policy.[32] Scholars examining the role of Brandt and the Nazi medical elite have in the past relied heavily on sources which were generated by Brandt and others after the war, mostly within the context of post-war trials. Yet Allied interrogations, witness statements, trial testimony, and prosecution and defence documents, are notoriously difficult to examine, and need to be treated with considerable caution as far as their historical and interpretative value is concerned. The aim of this book is to fundamentally challenge the historiographical interpretation of Brandt as a 'decent Nazi', and to provide a critical analysis of one of the most powerful medical figures of the Third Reich.[33]

I want to link the personal history of Brandt's life with the social and political history which shaped the character of the Third Reich. One of my key objectives is to reconstruct and better understand the complex culture of communication and decision-making at the heart of the Nazi regime through a synthetic study, in this case a biography of Karl Brandt. A study of his life may also help to chart the development, distortion and, arguably, the inversion of modern medical ethics in one of the most advanced nation states in the twentieth century.[34] Nazi medicine raised profound questions about medical and research ethics. How was it possible that men and women sworn to the Hippocratic tradition, and trained as professionals in one of the most advanced scientific cultures in Europe, could disregard the dignity of human beings, ignore principles of informed voluntary consent, beneficence and care, and ultimately commit crimes of previously unimaginable proportions? A study of Hitler's doctor needs to explain how Brandt, and others involved in medical crimes, managed to overcome their traditional education and socialization, with its moral norms and humanist values, and also how they defined their relationship with the political ideology and reality of the regime, as well as with powerful interest groups and with the leader himself. Did they know that they were committing a crime? How did they justify their role, to themselves, to colleagues and party comrades, or in public? The history of medicine under Nazism strongly conflicts with traditional views of professional medical conduct. How can we explain the fact that most of the doctors, including Brandt, did not value the life of an individual more highly than their duty towards the state, the community, the party or the Führer?

At Nuremberg, Brandt portrayed himself as a responsible and moral doctor by drawing attention to the underlying idea of the 'euthanasia' programme. He believed that the quality of the idea was sufficient to justify the killing operation, however well or poorly it might have been implemented. Brandt wanted to take full responsibility for the 'honest ideal' of the 'euthanasia' programme, but denied any detailed knowledge of or involvement in the crimes which were committed by those who turned the programme into reality, and did not accept responsibility for any other medical atrocities. As an adolescent, Brandt had experienced the First World War, military defeat, the Versailles Treaty, Allied reparation demands, inflation and economic hardship. As a medical student in Jena, Berlin, Munich and Freiburg im Breisgau, he followed the political debates on racial hygiene, eugenic abortions, reform psychiatry, compulsory sterilization and euthanasia, which dominated the medical ethics discourse in the Weimar Republic.[35] These discourses shaped his general knowledge on patient rights, medical ethics and human experimentation – especially in times of national crisis – the role of doctors in society, and the meaning and purpose of the state. Apart from wanting to explore Brandt's political activities, I want to emphasize the importance of these formative years which shaped Brandt's basic understanding of social Darwinism, eugenics and the concept of the body politic, the *Volkskörper*.

Brandt seems to have believed that 'delivering' the patient from pain at all costs was the doctor's task, even if it resulted in the patient's death. The erosion of Brandt's moral identity partly explains such a distorted view of humanity. Whereas physicians generally perceive the preservation of life as their primary goal, death had become a core value in Brandt's overall moral belief system. The death of the weakling, the frail and the incurably sick, the ones who 'groan' and 'plead to be delivered', appeared to be of intrinsic value for the greater good, for the community and, above all, the race. Their death not only 'delivered' them from suffering, but freed doctors and society from a financial, emotional and even aesthetic burden. Challenging Brandt on the logic of his argument that the 'euthanasia' programme had been a form of 'help' to end the suffering of humans, the Canadian medical officer, Wing Commander John W. R. Thompson, remarked in 1947: 'This very phrase is like a jewel of distortion in which so many mistakes are concentrated that it attracts by the mere shining of untruth. To help another person requires the existence of a person, who should be helped, but in the same moment where the "help" of euthanasia is apparently being received, the alleged recipient ceases to exist'.[36] After reading Thompson's analysis in July 1947, Brandt remarked that Thompson had completely missed the point and that his conclusions were too 'ridiculous' to warrant any comment.[37] Brandt never saw the 'euthanasia' programme as a killing operation, but as a new form of 'medical treatment'.[38] By following Brandt's argument to its logical conclusion, Thompson had intended to show how mistaken Brandt had been in his beliefs, and in doing so, he revealed a core element of Nazism: its obsession with race, myth, and above all, death. As already indicated, for Brandt life in itself, and the life of the individual, was only of biological value. Starting with the assumption that all the actions of a doctor needed to be directed towards improving and safeguarding the biological quality of the community, Brandt, and many Nazi doctors, eventually lost sight of the individual. For Brandt, there was also no meaning for the individual in the 'euthanasia' programme, nor was there any meaning for the individual in human experimentation:[39] there could be no meaning for the individual, unless the person's death was considered to have meaning as a kind of 'sacrifice' for the sake of the community. The Nazis believed that the death of the defective person would improve the life of the community and the race as a whole. An idealized understanding of 'sacrifice' (in the German language the word *Opfer* means both 'sacrifice' and 'victim') may have enabled Brandt and others to genuinely believe that he had acted in a morally responsible way. To speak in this context of Nazi medical ethics or 'Nazi conscience' can cloud a critical understanding of Brandt's particular mindset, unless we link his moral belief system to his political actions as Hitler's doctor.[40] Rather than exploring how 'rational' or 'irrational' this form of medical ideology might have been, how plausible it might appear in retrospect, or whether the system itself represented a kind of 'political religion' and 'totalitarianism', I am interested in examining the extent to which this moral belief system served Brandt in making sense of his immediate reality, how it underpinned his social, professional and political activities, and, last but not least, how it provided him with a theoretical framework with which to justify his actions after the war.[41]

Readers interested in the history of the Third Reich will find libraries full of books on almost every aspect of Nazi medicine and medical science before and during the war: on medical institutions and professional disciplines, eugenics and human experiments, the health and welfare system, and the 'euthanasia' programme, yet they will have to look long and hard to find even a handful of biographies on the leading medical personalities of the regime. Apart from a few isolated articles, no comprehensive biographies exist of Leonardo Conti, the Reich Health Leader (*Reichsgesundheitsführer*), Ernst Robert Grawitz, Reich Physician of the SS and Police, Philipp Bouhler, the head of the Chancellery of the Führer, or Herbert Linden, the senior official in charge of German state asylums in the Reich Ministry of the Interior.[42] These men were of central importance in organizing, monitoring and shaping the nature of the 'euthanasia' programme, in initiating and supporting criminal medical experiments on concentration camp inmates, or in setting up the machinery for the killing of tens of thousands of Jews in the occupied eastern territories. Yet the existing literature about these men is sketchy, at best. Why is this the case? With the exception of Brandt, all these men committed suicide before they could be put on trial after the war. As a result, scholars wanting to examine their role in the regime have searched in vain for Allied interrogations, trial transcripts or psychological assessments of these men. The scarcity of post-war records, coupled with a limited number of contemporary and readily available documents, has made research on these personalities particularly difficult. Consequently, our understanding of the higher echelons of the Nazi medical hierarchy is heavily fragmented. The paucity of literature and sources about the leading medical officials and administrators of the Third Reich also highlights a more general methodological problem which has preoccupied scholars for decades. To this day, largely because of the peculiar nature of governance in Hitler's regime, and because of the wave of destruction of evidence which accompanied the collapse of the Third Reich, we know relatively little about the decision-making processes and culture of communication at the highest levels of the German government.

A lack of post-war records and trial testimony can hardly explain the absence of a biography on Brandt, who was, after all, the key defendant in the Nuremberg Doctors' Trial, which lasted from December 1946 to August 1947. The official name of the trial was 'The United States of America *versus* Karl Brandt'. The pre-trial war crimes investigations by Allied experts, and the trial itself, generated an enormous amount of material. Given that the Allies sentenced Brandt to death in 1947, and hanged him a year later, observers and scholars have widely accepted that he had been criminally responsible for medical war crimes and crimes against humanity. Those who might have wanted to challenge or question the role of a convicted mass murderer not only broke a taboo, but exposed themselves to the accusation of revisionism with the intention of exonerating Brandt. At the same time, the existing trial evidence needed to be treated with considerable caution because of its inherent bias. An even more pressing problem in tackling a biography of Brandt was the difficulty in locating a body of contemporary sources which might have warranted a reassessment of Hitler's doctor. Finally, the historical literature on National Socialism is, like any other discipline, subject to changing trends and academic debates. Historians of the Third Reich have for years been rather cautious, not without reason, about the biographical genre as a feasible approach to enhancing our understanding about the regime, not least because some of the literature was written by the perpetrators themselves in the 1950s and 1960s to justify their role. A significant amount of the biographical and autobiographical literature was apologetic.[43] The role of the individual as an actor in history was often greatly overemphasized, and not adequately contextualized within the development of ideas and institutions, or embedded in national and international economic, political and strategic power structures.

A book about a single individual in the context of the Third Reich and the Nuremberg war crimes trials obviously involves a number of methodological and conceptual risks. There is, after all, no shortage of literature and published material on the Nazi regime. Recent biographical approaches, however, have proved to be fruitful in enhancing our understanding of the leadership structure, generational patterns, ideological driving forces and rationalization strategies. Ian Kershaw's extensive treatment of Hitler's life, Ulrich Herbert's compelling analysis of Werner Best, and David Cesarani's study on Eichmann's life and crimes have all shown the value of examining a single individual who shaped the character of Nazi genocidal policies and culture.[44] Their work has demonstrated that a biographical approach can overcome the tension between depicting 'everyday normality', on the one hand, and unprecedented levels of violence and 'political criminality' in the Third Reich, on the other.[45] A study of Brandt as one of Hitler's trusted commissars can help us to improve our understanding of the inherent contradictions of Nazi health and medical policy, in which the care for wounded civilians and soldiers existed side by side with the murder of tens of thousands of unwanted people. As Winfried Süß has pointed out: 'Few things reveal the inhumane ambivalence of Nazi health policy, in which normality and criminality were closely intertwined, better than the fact that the authority in charge of medical care for the civilian population and the responsibility for the murder of patients came together in one person.'[46]

The extent of available secondary material in the form of short articles and edited collections on individual aspects of the regime, and the publication of new primary sources, make a synthetic study, in this case through the medium of a biography, particularly relevant. The microfiche edition of the entire trial transcripts, edited by Klaus Dörner and Angelika Ebbinghaus in 1999, includes previously unpublished documents of the prosecution and the defence, as well as material related to the background and consequences of the trial.[47] This material also includes relevant sources about Brandt, but it seemed insufficient for a biographical study alone.

When the idea for this book was first conceived, almost a decade ago, I was not fully aware of the conspicuous lack of sources and published material relating to Brandt's family and childhood, or of the limited information about his life as a young adult and student of medicine during the Weimar Republic. It only gradually dawned on me that the available evidence provided relatively little information on why Brandt became a leading personality of the regime, let alone a major war criminal. There appeared to be almost no published material available for the first thirty years of his life, apart from a few isolated, recently published, accounts.[48] There were also few sources, if any, which could shed light on the political and social environment in which Brandt was brought up, or on the networks of friends and colleagues who helped to shape his professional and moral belief system. A biography on Brandt needed not only to attempt to explain how he had become Hitler's doctor, and why he had sanctioned and supported certain policies of the regime, but also to reconstruct his life within the political and ideological climate of his time. To research this period in Brandt's life, I realized, might turn out to be a difficult and fragmented task. However long this would take – and here I must thank an extremely patient publisher ('come back when you're ready') – I also realized that it needed to be examined if one were to hope to better understand Brandt's role in the Third Reich.[49]

A distinct lack of contemporary sources for the early and mid-1930s presented another methodological and practical problem. I managed partly to resolve this issue by turning to a different kind of source, one which, I believe, has been under-utilized by social and political historians in the past. At the State Library of Bavaria in Munich, I discovered, among the archival collection of Heinrich Hoffmann, Hitler's official photographer, more than 500 photographs picturing Brandt.[50] The importance of the collection lies in the fact that the photographs contain detailed information about dates and places, and about the personalities with whom Brandt had regular social and professional contact. Organized in chronological order, the photographs enabled me to reconstruct, to some extent, Brandt's whereabouts at certain points in time, and link his presence with the unfolding of particular political and military events. Most of Hoffmann's images were, as is well known, shot as part of a concerted propaganda campaign to present Hitler as a charismatic leader, the 'architect' of a more powerful German Reich. Photographs of Hitler provided the 'day-to-day contact between leader and people'.[51] Some of the images, however, were never published, perhaps because Hoffmann had selected other images, or because they had been censored.[52] There are also dozens of images which originate from Hoffmann's contact prints. In all likelihood, not even enlargements were ever made. Hoffmann's photographs of Brandt and others thus allow us an insight into a more personal realm of Hitler's court.

Overall, the body of sources for this study is relatively satisfactory, although it cannot be compared with biographies of some other personalities where scholars have had access to a wealth of well-organized private and professional papers.

Sources of this quality were available, for example, for my biography of the Austrian émigré-psychiatrist and war crimes investigator, Leo Alexander, who played a major role in the formulation of the Nuremberg Code.[53] As Herbert has pointed out, the paucity of records is not the exception, but the rule for most biographies of leading Nazi personalities.[54] The correspondence among some of the official government papers is certainly better, but nowhere near complete.

After years of research, especially while I was writing the chapter on 'Detached Leadership', I gained the impression that the paucity of written sources which might have provided somewhat more 'colour' to Brandt's personality was not part of the problem, but a central part of the answer.[55] Not unlike some of the leading SS men, who largely repressed their own feelings and sentiments in exchange for a rather detached rationality, personal discipline and coldness, Brandt had cultivated a certain hardness and rigidity.[56] After the war, someone described Brandt as a 'cold and unapproachable intelligence'.[57] On the basis of the available material, it was occasionally possible to speculate about Brandt's personality and psychological make-up, but not much more. A more in-depth psychological study of Brandt will have to await a scholarly analysis of more of Brandt's private papers, if they exist, and even then it is doubtful whether this assessment of Brandt would have to be dramatically revised. The aim of this book, then, lies more in reconstructing Brandt's political role in intervening in, controlling and coordinating, first as Hitler's escort physician and later as General Commissioner, the state of German medicine and medical science in the 1930s and 1940s.

The period of Brandt's official position in the regime was not only relatively brief, but largely confined to the Second World War. Unlike some of the other Nazi leaders and functionaries of the Third Reich, Brandt's rise to power was not preceded or accompanied by party political activities in the 1920s and 1930s. There are also no memoranda or statements from before 1945 in which he laid down his political and ideological world views. What makes his biography particularly relevant is the gradual process by which his influence on the German health and medical system increased, first in small, incremental steps, mostly through informal, direct assignments by Hitler, and away from the public eye, then through a secret killing operation which rapidly became public knowledge, and needed management, then as General Commissioner, and finally as Reich Commissioner, with the ability to wield extensive executive power.

Few would doubt that Brandt followed with all his energy the man whom he thought had been chosen by providence to lead Germany on the path to national strength and glory.[58] However, the existing character descriptions of Brandt say little about his role as a major political player in the Nazi regime, nor do they reveal anything about Brandt as a manipulative force at Hitler's court of servants. To unravel the role of Brandt in the killing of tens of thousands of handicapped people, and in initiating, ordering and abetting the plans and enterprises of Nazi medical atrocities, we must look at what Brandt actually *did*, and not only at what he *said*, whether before, during or after the war. What kind of orders, instructions and directives did he give? How did he give them? In what fashion and setting did he give his orders, and to whom? Did he communicate his orders directly and orally, or indirectly, by letters and messengers? How did he influence vital policy decisions? How did he manage to stay immune from being implicated in most of the crimes? To what extent can the notoriously poor paper trail, which is symptomatic of the correspondence among Hitler's closest allies – apart from Goebbels' diaries, perhaps – tell us something about the culture of communication, plausible deniability and detachment at the heart of the regime? These are some of the questions which arise when we look at Brandt as a political figure, rather than as an idealistic believer and follower of Hitler.

This brings me to another, more general purpose of the book. Through a critical biography of Brandt, I intend to re-evaluate the system of communication at the centre of Hitler's government, and hopefully contribute to our understanding of the culture of detachment on the part of a regime that was geared towards total destruction and a government that was almost totally removed from its people. As in all modern societies, the quality and quantity of information for decision-making, and the nature of communication, is of fundamental importance for effective government. The flow of information to and from the centre of power, whether this is a head of state, a prime minister, or a dictator trying to wield absolute power, influences not only how decisions are made but, once they are made, how they are relayed, interpreted and ultimately executed by the relevant agencies. For Hitler, as for any other head of government, it was impossible to know, and control everything that was going on around him. The number of decisions which needed to be taken on a daily basis to keep a modern state machinery running was exceedingly high. No one human being could have taken all these decisions, let alone one who was so hesitant and indecisive as Hitler sometimes was. As Jeremy Noakes has pointed out, this is nothing unusual in a modern government, but it means that

> excellent channels for and filters of information are necessary to select, process, and feed in those pieces of information which the head of government needs to know and convey those decisions which he needs to take. And the less work the head of government is prepared to put in himself, the more he is dependent on those channels and filters. Finally, even after a decision has been taken, it has to be implemented and this requires an administration which is efficient and whose performance can be monitored.[59]

A number of trusted individuals were those 'channels' and 'filters', through whom information was communicated to and from Hitler. These channels and filters are 'notoriously difficult to chart', because no record survives, and indeed it is possible that none existed in the first place, but this phenomenon is nonetheless an essential part of the history of the Third Reich.[60] My interest, therefore, lies not so much in the role of Hitler and his personalized dictatorship, although this is also key to the argument, nor with the mass movement and the historical forces which brought him to and kept him in power, but with the 'communicators' and 'translators' between Hitler's political ideology and visionary ideas on the one hand, and the cold reality of German society in the 1930s and 1940s on the other. They were the tools which determined policy-making at the centre. But who were these men and women who shaped the politics of communication? The communicators and translators of Hitler's wishes were the people in his immediate vicinity, who at different times and in different situations, and for specific areas of policy, enjoyed 'Hitler's ear'. Some of them were special commissars, like Brandt and Speer, whose offices were superimposed on existing administrative structures. The commissars allowed Hitler to bypass the bureaucratic apparatus that was traditionally charged with the business of governance, overcome internal ministerial conflicts and deadlocks over responsibilities, and ultimately redirect power and resources to those areas which he regarded as having strategic, political or ideological importance at any given time.[61] They also enabled Hitler to interfere in and influence decisions at a local, regional and national level of government. Without paying much attention to the daily business of governance which is the duty of a head of state in a differentiated modern society, Hitler employed a system of special commissars who extended his political will and power to almost every place and agency in Germany. Hitler was not a weak dictator who lacked the ability for decision-making – his power was real and it was extensive, if he decided to use it. He was, as Kershaw has pointed out, the most central legitimizing force in the Third Reich.[62] The commissars mediated between Hitler's ideological claim for charismatic leadership and the need to solve day-to-day problems; in doing so, they managed to integrate on the one hand a feudal and highly politicized system of governance with, on the other, the executive demands placed upon the bureaucracy of an economically powerful and highly complex modern nation state.[63]

The commissars were an essential part of Hitler's charismatic leadership and of his ability to wield power, but they also had a life of their own. Rather than being an accurate channel of information between Hitler and the administrative machinery, the commissars in the Third Reich acted as filters and gatekeepers of information, and this allowed them to determine the need for decision-making and action at the highest level of government. As a result, this group of people acquired, maintained, and wielded real political power which was independent of the status of their office, but which depended on their access to Hitler. They enjoyed 'ascribed power', as Richard Overy calls it, not so much the power of high office and tradition, but the power that others attributed to certain men and women around Hitler.[64] Rightly or wrongly, it was power which others believed these men and women had. Given the projection of power onto some of Hitler's commissars, 'ascribed power' could sometimes turn into real power, as in the case of Brandt.

Not unlike a medieval or early modern court physician, a personal doctor, who, as Brandt did, accompanied Hitler on almost all his travels, and who belonged to the inner circle of what the dictator called his 'family', could have access to the centre of power at almost all times. Brandt's power was essentially dependent on his access to Hitler, because it solidified his position in the eyes of those who had little or no access. Those who had access to Hitler and lost it, also lost their power, immediately and often permanently. Everyone around Hitler was acutely aware of this fact. Power could be lost in a split second; a slight misjudgement, a critical word too much at the dinner table, a comment which displeased Hitler, all these were sufficient reasons to send a once all-powerful servant into the wilderness, not by stripping him of his rank and office, but by prohibiting him from further access to the Führer. To remain in good standing with Hitler was essential for those running huge empires in the state, like Himmler, Göring and Goebbels, but also for those with superimposed offices like Speer or Brandt. To fall from Hitler's grace, on the other hand, could be deadly.

There is another aspect of Hitler's personalized form of government which needs mentioning. Although evidence for men like Brandt is often extremely fragmented, biased or non-existent, there seems to be sufficient reason to suggest that they constituted in many respects a distorted mirror image, and in some cases an outright copy, of Hitler's style of leadership. By examining the correspondence of people and institutions with no, or limited, access to Hitler, but with direct access to those believed to have the ear of the Führer, we can detect a number of similarities and differences in the way information was being processed and decisions were being made. Like Hitler, Brandt was averse to paperwork. He disliked committing himself in writing, especially during the later years of the war. Like Hitler, Brandt exercised his influence mostly through face-to-face encounters, often on a one-to-one basis, by telephone, and with a limited paper trail as a result. If a record was produced by one or more of those attending a particular meeting, the issue could easily be denied, or presented to Hitler in a different light later. This gave Brandt significant leverage to shape the nature of the German health system, and secure his position. The more Brandt's charismatic authority increased, the more he communicated his instructions in the form of veiled hints, general comments and innuendoes. Sometimes, as in the case of Friedrich von Bodelschwingh, he resorted to ambiguous imagery.[65] This then left his counterpart in the position to gauge, or sense (*ahnen*), what Brandt might have wanted. At the same time, people had little alternative but to assume that this was what Hitler wanted, and that Brandt's wishes, so to speak, represented Hitler's wishes as well. Finding out what the German government wanted was guesswork of monumental proportions. Sometimes, it resembled the art of tea-leaf-reading. Like a Russian Babushka model, Hitler's intentions were covered by layers upon layers of innuendoes and comments made in passing by members of his court. Whether these really conveyed his will, or that of his servants, is far from clear, except that the overall policy direction was largely shaped by the dictator himself. It was a system of government in which the Nazi leadership was increasingly detached from the execution of government and, above all, from the German people.

On a more theoretical level, the principle of 'detached leadership' which I propose in this book has evolved as an attempt to find a middle ground between two concepts. One is Max Weber's widely applied concept of 'charismatic leadership', which attempts to explain this form of governance in the perceivers of 'charisma', as well as through the 'charismatic power' of Hitler and the Nazi leadership in controlling the masses.[66] The other is the recently developed concept – or metaphor, as some scholars prefer to call it – of 'working towards the Führer', which attempts to argue that the process of cumulative radicalization was largely shaped by initiatives, directives and pressures from below.[67] In 1998, Kershaw remarked: 'In the Darwinist jungle of the Third Reich, the way to power and advancement was through anticipating the "Führer will", and, without waiting for directives, taking initiatives to promote what were presumed to be Hitler's aims and wishes.'[68] Both concepts provide important explanatory potential in examining various layers of politics and society during the Third Reich, including the genesis of the Holocaust, but they seem to lack interpretative force in explaining why and how the regime managed to control the pace and nature of illegal activities while the Nazi leadership could both rely on and maintain mass support from a wide spectrum of society over a prolonged period of time.

One of the key characteristics of this form of governance and extraordinary dominance was the particular distance which the head of state and his ministers developed, and kept, from the people from the mid-1930s. As David Welch has pointed out: 'The nature of Hitler's position as charismatic leader, as the Führer of the German people, rested on his continuing ability to detach himself from day-to-day politics with the result that he was never personally associated with the worst extremes of the regime.'[69] Often, the widely proclaimed people's community (*Volksgemeinschaft*) appeared to be leaderless, a regime in which the leadership was far removed and aloof from the day-to-day lives of ordinary German people. Far from being a rudderless regime, I am arguing, however, that a detached Nazi leadership was able to exploit the perceived power and 'charisma' which had been projected onto them, in order to steer the nature of genocidal policies. Throughout the years of political turmoil and opposition, the Nazi leadership cultivated a system of largely oral communication which relied heavily on generalized instructions and veiled hints to safeguard its detachment from a range of criminal activities.[70] Given that this system of communication was far from precise and unambiguous, it is hardly surprising that certain instructions and directives were misunderstood and radicalized by the Nazi rank and file from below, but it was a system of communication and control nonetheless. To unravel this peculiar system of communication, and the way in which Brandt had mastered the culture of detached leadership, is one of the aims of the book.

By looking at the culture of communication, we may also explain the scarcity of records at the centre of government which has given rise to sometimes hair-raising speculations about the degree to which the Nazi leadership knew of mass exterminations and the Holocaust. There can be no doubt that they did. The fact that relatively few records from the heart of the regime have survived can tell us, of course, many things, for example that the leadership was particularly efficient at destroying incriminating documents at the end of the war. It can also tell us something about the nature of the regime itself. Hitler and his court of servants became increasingly detached from the people and from reality. Decisions which had been taken either by Hitler, or by the conduits themselves, were relayed to the agencies in charge of implementing them in an often contradictory and ambiguous fashion. Any kind of administrative supervision of how, and by whom, the decisions had been executed rarely took place. The conflicts and confusions that were generated by this form of government were, in a quasi-social-Darwinist sense, left to sort themselves out. Only occasionally would the Führer interfere from his visionary heights through one of his messengers. It was a recipe for administrative chaos.[71]

Hitler's Berghof epitomized a court better than any other imagery of the Third Reich. Removed from reality, high up in the mountains in the Obersalzberg region on the Austrian–German border, the Berghof and its surrounding buildings were a self-contained high-security complex to which ordinary mortals had little or no access. Surrounded by the Untersberg, the Kneifelspitze, the highest of the mountains, and the Watzmann, the Berghof was in the midst of unparalleled scenery. This place was the obvious choice for a national redeemer, a man chosen by providence, who needed to be close to the skies, if not to God, since he himself felt god-like. The Obersalzberg was Hitler's 'magic mountain'. In many ways the Berghof resembled the imagery of the Greek Olympus, accessible only to gods of different seniority, who rarely communicated with the people directly, preferring to do so through messengers and oracles. When in 1944 the press announced Brandt's promotion to Reich Commissioner for Health and Sanitation without mentioning the name of Conti, one of Conti's colleagues told Brandt that 'he [Brandt] would be unable to imagine what consequences such an announcement, which failed to mention Conti's name, would have outside on the periphery, because he was living on Olympus'.[72] To foresee what the gods might wish, and work towards these projected goals, became standard practice for many to secure and enhance their position. For Hitler, the Berghof was his mountain retreat. It was a place where he felt he could lead life as a private individual, one which was boring and trivial to an extent most people could hardly have imagined. Like a kaleidoscope, the Berghof reflected and combined a whole range of multiple images of the Third Reich, a space where it seems that destructive energy, and apparently wilful ignorance of human suffering, was the unseen iron fist, hidden in a velvet glove of monumental sentimentalism and utter shallowness.

Here, in a quiet atmosphere, Hitler looked for inspiration for what he believed was his mission. The Berghof represents the mystification of ordinary government. Many of the decisions taken at these lofty heights, it would seem, had no sound basis whatsoever, nor was there any expert knowledge available or consulted. Decisions shaping German society were taken at random and on a whim of the moment. Like bolts from the blue, the mass bureaucracies of contemporary German society were jolted this way and that. There was no programme or goal, other than the expulsion, persecution and extermination of European Jewry and the repression of all forces hostile to the regime, the re-establishment of German national pride and glory, the acquisition and expansion of *Lebensraum* for the German people, and the total destruction of Bolshevism. Beyond this, arguably, there was no plan. This form of rule, arbitrary and totally uncontrolled, may have struck a particular chord with a country whose philosophical and historical tradition was shaped by notions of romanticism, salvation and fatalism. Another people might not have taken it that seriously.

In March 1947, after hours spent discussing Brandt's personal history, the Jewish émigré neurologist and medical expert at the Nuremberg Doctors' Trial, Leo Alexander, attempted to sum up Brandt's life. The discussion had ranged not only over Brandt's childhood and youth, his medical studies and professional career, but also over his rise to power at Hitler's court, first as his escort physician and special envoy, and later as the man in charge of the 'euthanasia' programme, empowered to run the health and sanitation system, control Germany's biological and chemical weapons programme, and make decisions about whether experimental subjects in concentration camps lived or died. Alexander concluded: 'You are surely a man who has a deeper understanding and have sided with *one* side only. That is perhaps your personal tragedy, that you were committed to *one* idea'.[73]

2

The Ambitious Idealist

I. CHILDHOOD AND YOUTH

The subject appears to have an extremely rich and complex personality, more instinctive than reflective. In spite of being brilliantly gifted he is unable to follow the strict discipline of the rules of traditional morality, but all he can show is exceptional obedience. Paradoxically, he is, at the same time, easily influenced, undisciplined and child-like. Finally, he has no real intellectual culture, nor has he sufficient self-control to clarify, analyse, classify and channel the exitable nature of his instinct. Signed: Dr Bayle, 1946/47 Nuremberg.[1]

Karl Brandt belonged to a generation uprooted by the economic and professional uncertainty of the interwar period, which was exacerbated by the political instability of the Weimar Republic, yet there were no obvious signs that he would become a leading proponent of the Nazi state, least of all one of the major war criminals. His family line on his father's side came from the Saar region, which before the First World War had been divided into Prussian and Bavarian districts. Coal and other major industries had traditionally shaped the economic and cultural landscape. The region was a vital part of Germany's rapidly expanding economy. Plans to occupy Alsace-Lorraine, located on the border of the Saar region, and annex it from France, had been driven by industrial and military objectives as well as by nationalist sentiment. The population of the Saar region was predominantly Catholic and loyal to the Reich, although a large proportion of left-leaning factory workers and miners regularly voiced their discontent with government policies.[2]

Brandt's grandfather, Wilhelm Peter Julius Brandt, was born in 1838 in Auersmecka. He was a railway secretary (*Eisenbahnsekretär*), and later became a district civil servant (*Kreisregierungsrat*) in Strasbourg. Brandt's relationship with his grandfather was close and caring. Brandt took up a position as a trainee doctor at the local city hospital in order to be near his grandfather when he fell ill in Weimar in the late 1920s. His grandfather died in December 1933. Brandt's grandmother, Katherina Grandpair, born in 1849 in Homburg-Saar, died in June 1914 in Strasbourg, Alsace, shortly before the outbreak of the First World War. Little else is known about her, except that she was of the Lutheran faith, like her husband. Their son, Karl Julius Brandt, Brandt's father, was born in 1877 in Homburg-Saar. In May 1901, he moved from Strasbourg to Mülhausen where he became an inspector with the local police.[3] After the war, he continued to work for the police in Chemnitz until his retirement in 1932.

On his mother's side, Brandt came from a family of medical doctors from Thuringia. His grandfather, Karl Bernhard Johannes Lehnebach, who passed his first name to Brandt, was a district doctor (*Kreisarzt*) in Steinbach-Hallenberg in Thuringia.[4] Born in 1847 in Nauenburg in the state of Hessen, Karl Lehnebach received his approbation as a medical doctor in August 1870. Two years later, in 1872, he was offered a position as the first state-employed physician in the small village of Steinbach-Hallenberg in Thuringia. A contemporary service record lists him as a doctor for the poor (*Armenarzt*) and vaccination doctor (*Impfarzt*).[5] Brandt's grandmother, Maria Luise, née Werner, was born in 1849. She lived with her parents, Mathäus Werner and his wife, Maria Magdalena, née Nothnagel, in Steinbach-Hallenberg,[6] which is probably where they met. Full of energy and vision, Karl Lehnebach gained prominence in the district by introducing sanitary measures and promoting personal hygiene in nearby towns and villages such as Schmalkalden, near Steinbach-Hallenberg. In 1886, for example, he purchased a swimming pool as the head of a consortium of local notables who wanted to improve the health of the population.[7] It was this environment of conservative, middle-ranking civil servants and state-employed physicians, dutiful towards the monarchy and the authorities, which inculcated in Brandt from very early on a sense of loyalty and responsibility towards the state and the nation.

Brandt's mother, Catherina Emilie Elisabeth Brandt, née Lehnebach, was born in Steinbach-Hallenberg in April 1879.[8] She was the only girl and the youngest of four children in the family. Her eldest brother, Franz Ludwig, was born in June 1873, shortly after Karl Bernhard Johannes Lehnebach had moved to Steinbach-Hallenberg.[9] In July 1896, at the age of twenty-three, Franz Ludwig, a student of medicine, drowned in Marburg. Whether he committed suicide is not known. Catherina's next brother, Karl, was born in November 1874.[10] Her third brother was Georg Richard, born in January 1877.[11] Catherina's two remaining brothers both became involved in medicine. One became a doctor, the other an apothecary: one of the reasons why Brandt always wanted to become a doctor himself.[12]

In 1888, Brandt's grandmother died at the age of only thirty-eight. Rather than raising his children alone, Karl Lehnebach remarried. His second wife was Mathilda Lehnebach, née Brack.[13] Lehnebach later moved with his family to a house at the Lutherplatz in Schmalkalden, where he died in January 1901. Catherina Lehnebach's extended family in Steinbach-Hallenberg, Schmalkalden and the surrounding villages gave her the necessary security and stability, and explains why she returned to her birthplace after she and her fifteen-year-old son, Karl Brandt, fled from French-occupied Alsace in 1919.

We do not know where and how Catherina Lehnebach, Brandt's mother, met Karl Julius Brandt, her subsequent husband, or whether it was a romantic relationship. We do know that on 25 March 1903 they married in Mülhausen, Alsace. Brandt's father was twenty-six and his mother twenty-four. The marriage was witnessed by August Kayser, a forest warden, who was fifty-eight years old and lived in Riedisheim, Upper Alsace, and by Professor Adolf Lehnebach, Catherina's uncle. He was fifty-three years old and lived at 13 Gutenbergstraße in Mülhausen. Adolf

Lehnebach is likely to have been the key family focus for Catherina after the death of her mother in 1888, when she was just nine years old, and the death of her father in 1901. It is quite possible that she moved to Mülhausen to live with her uncle, and that she met Brandt's father there. Three weeks after they got married, on 14 April, the couple moved from 4 Franklinstraße to a flat at 62bis Straßburgerstraße in Mülhausen. The reason for this change of address was obvious: Catherina Brandt was pregnant and the couple needed new and larger accommodation. On 8 January 1904, shortly before midnight, Karl Brandt was born at this address. His birth certificate, dated 11 January 1904, stated:

> The inspector Karl Julius Brandt … who lives in Mülhausen, Straßburgerstraße 62-bis, of protestant faith, appeared today before the undersigned registrar, and declared that from Katharina Emilie Elisabeth Brandt, née Lehnebach, his wife, of protestant faith, who lives with him, a boy had been born in his flat in Mülhausen on 8 January 1904 at around 10.45 p.m. and that the child had received the christian names Karl Franz Friedrich.[14]

It was thus in Mülhausen, Alsace, that Brandt spent his youth, and his formative years as a young man. Since 1871, Alsace-Lorraine, one of the most fertile and densely populated regions in Europe, consisted of three districts: Lorraine, Lower Alsace, formerly known as *Bas-Rhin*, and Upper Alsace, formerly known as *Haut-Rhin*, to which Mülhausen belonged. Of the four largest cities, three were administrative and military centres rather than focal points of industrial production. Metz, Colmar and Strasbourg had been garrison towns of the French army, and served as military posts for the German Reich thereafter. Located in the northern part of Alsace, with a largely Protestant population since the time of the Reformation, Mülhausen developed a flourishing textile, chemical and mechanical industry in the late eighteenth and nineteenth centuries. In 1888, for example, the electrical company Siemens established a plant there. Good trade and cultural links with Luxembourg and the Palatinate shaped the character of the city as much as its close connection with France. The textile industry, in particular, provided the impetus for a booming manufacturing industry that attracted capital and technical innovation, even though historians have calculated that the industry suffered a slump after the annexation by Germany. Since the start of the nineteenth century, Protestant and Jewish businessmen, including the family of Alfred Dreyfus, who was unjustly convicted in the notorious Dreyfus affair, had set up mills around Mülhausen, which provided economic prosperity for some, but which also created a whole range of social and political problems that accompanied rapid urbanization.[15] Child labour, and high levels of illiteracy caused by irregular school attendance, were endemic in a city known as the 'French Manchester'. Improvements in transport and infrastructure through the Rhone-Rhine canal and railways transformed the town by the turn of the century into a prosperous business centre in which tens of thousands of both skilled and unskilled workers found employment. Trade schools, hospitals and charities, as well as innovative housing developments, were established to guarantee social peace and order. Local entrepreneurs from Mülhausen funded the creation of schools, sickness funds, and leisure organizations to improve the health of the workforce. Such initiatives strengthened the relationship between employers and employees but did not prevent the emergence of a strong Social Democratic movement, much to the astonishment of the local establishment. In February 1890, Charles Hickel from Mülhausen was elected to the Reichstag, the first socialist deputy from Alsace-Lorraine.[16] Little more than a month later, Mülhausen saw the largest and best-organized strike the region had witnessed since the annexation, involving more than 15,000 workers. By 1902, the Social Democratic Party of Germany (*Sozialdemokratische Partei Deutschlands*, SPD) secured an absolute majority on the city council, prompting the building of public housing and new schools and the taking of control over the local electricity company. By the time Brandt was born, Mülhausen was a city in which workers enjoyed more rights, better pay and living conditions, and were better organized than in most industrial centres of the German Reich. Scholars such as Werner Wittich, a professor at the University of Strasbourg, noted that 'socialism was the only product of the German spirit that won the free sympathy of a large segment of the Alsatian population.'[17] This environment is likely to have contributed to Brandt's interest in occupational health and accident issues, and may well have informed his decision to become expert in bone fracture surgery during his time at the Bergmannsheil hospital in Bochum, a city which was renowned for its mining and steel industry. Mülhausen was, above all, a town in which most inhabitants spoke French and German after it had been annexed in 1871 by the newly founded German Reich. In general, the population felt strong ties to both France and Germany; at times, though, the people experienced a divided sense of identity and dual loyalties, given that the border region might well become the battleground in any future conflict between the two powerful nations.

To further integrate Alsace-Lorraine into the Reich, and to boost the national economy, the German government used language and science education as central elements of nation-building. Shortly after 1871, Alsace-Lorraine saw the emigration of large numbers of French teachers and the immigration of a loyal and dedicated teaching corps that was determined to educate a new generation of Germans.[18] One of the central priorities was to curb irregular school attendance in rural areas, where the need for child labour was greatest during the harvest season, but also in industrial centres such as Mülhausen, where parts of the textile industry relied heavily on the young workforce. From April 1871 onwards, school attendance was compulsory for all girls aged six to thirteen and for all boys aged six to fourteen. German inspectors not only monitored the introduction of compulsory schooling and German language lessons but also ensured that German textbooks and maps were widely distributed and used as uniform teaching material. A nationally oriented school curriculum, modelled on the Prussian one, was likewise meant to encourage loyalty to the monarchy and a shared understanding of the new German Empire. Despite a strong and vocal French-speaking minority, concentrated primarily in the bigger cities, German became the dominant language. In certain cases, French lessons were banned from the school curriculum, except for those cities that had traditional trade links with France, such as, for example, Mülhausen,

Colmar and Guebwiller.[19] When the first census was taken in 1900, more than 86 per cent of Alsace-Lorrainers considered German or one of its many dialects to be their native language. Geography and history lessons were seen as important subjects in the education of the population in the 'knowledge and love of the *Heimat* (hometown or home region), as the first step towards love of the fatherland. Overall, however, instruction in practical subjects and training in religion and morality far outweighed overt national indoctrination, at least until the outbreak of the First World War'.[20] Brandt attended school in Mülhausen from around 1910 until the end of the war, and the German-dominated educational system would have left its mark on his sense of pride and national identity. Schools were surely not solely responsible for promulgating loyalty to the emperor, nor were they the sole places where pupils learned about morality and religious beliefs, but they certainly made an important contribution.

Until the age of nine or ten, Brandt attended one of the *Volksschulen* in Mülhausen before he transferred to a secondary school.[21] The *Volksschulen* had the advantage that children from a bourgeois background mixed with commoners, a system which Albert Schweitzer, educated for eight years in Mülhausen in the late 1880s, believed to have had a positive effect on his outlook and understanding of society. In his autobiography, written in 1924, Schweitzer described his life and education as a young boy in Alsace, how he had competed against some of the village boys, and how he had realized that they were at least as intelligent as he was: 'I never had the arrogance of those many boys who immediately join the secondary school (*Gymnasium*) where they come to believe that children from educated families are somehow better than those children who walk in ... trousers and wooden shoes'.[22] Despite the common experience of going to the *Volksschule*, Schweitzer remained the son of a Lutheran minister and Brandt the son of a police officer. Schooling in Alsace was hardly the place to overcome the social and professional divide, but it provided children with a sense of national identity, one that was admittedly divided and uncertain at times, though pervasive among the population as a whole.

For Schweitzer the climate was one of optimism and national pride. When he passed his *Abitur* in 1893, he was grounded in two rather different worlds, one that was deeply religious and conformist, and in which organ music, prayer services and private tuition in the rules of priesthood played an important part, the other rational, reflective and deeply critical. Schweitzer's pious agnosticism later turned him into what he saw as a 'rational Christian dedicated to action' (*rationalistischer Tatchrist*). It is well worth exploring these divided worlds: they not only allow us to gain insight into the religious and philosophical climate of the time, particularly in a place like Mülhausen, but they throw into relief certain similarities and features in Brandt's own split personality. Brandt, not unlike Schweitzer, grew up bilingual, fluent in German and French, and with a divided sense of identity similar to that of Schweitzer, not so much in terms of nationality, where he felt largely attached to the German cultural tradition, but more in relation to the inherent tension between, on the one hand, the rationality and objectivity inculcated by years of medical studies, and on the other, his highly emotive and somewhat irrational personality.[23] Asked after the war whether he had considered the possibility of a spiritual afterlife, Brandt said that he had to give two answers, because he distinguished between himself as a 'human being', a person with feelings, who assumed that there was an afterlife, and himself as a natural scientist, for whom death meant the 'absolute end'.[24]

Little is known about Brandt's life as a boy or how he performed in school. Brandt later told Leo Alexander, the medical expert at the Nuremberg Doctors' Trial, that his childhood had been 'very calm' and 'undisturbed', except for the experience of the war.[25] He played and ran around like other children, but was conscious of the fact that his mother was alone 'in this war period', and he tried to help her as best he could. At the beginning of his school years, Brandt was apparently one of the best pupils: 'Well, in the first years, until about lower *tertia*, I was the first, second in the class and later I was about the fifth, sixth, seventh.'[26] Most of his friends came from the same school. He suffered from all the usual children's diseases such as measles, scarlet fever and whooping cough, but not much more. At the age of fifteen, shortly after the war, when he had to change school, and was lagging behind in his studies, he suffered from pneumonia. It confined him to bed for a prolonged period.[27] Until he was four, Brandt's family lived at 62bis Straßburgerstraße. In October 1908, they moved to 28 Salvatorstraße and, in February 1913, they moved yet again within the city. Given that from the age of four to the age of nine Brandt lived in the Salvatorstraße, it is likely that he went to one of the *Volksschulen* in the vicinity, for example to the *Kleine Kinder Schule* or the *Nordfeld Schule*. More detailed information about Brandt's early school years is scarce, however.

Brandt described his relationship with his parents as 'completely balanced'. Corporal punishment was apparently non-existent in his family – 'no never,' he told Alexander. He loved animals, especially dogs, cats and mice. 'Why mice?', Alexander queried. 'I enjoyed playing with small animals', Brandt replied.[28] One of the most unpleasant memories of his childhood also related to animals. At the age of four or five, he and his father visited the zoological garden in Basel where the snakes were fed with living cats. Witnessing this gruesome spectacle must have frightened the young boy: 'There I made such a fuss and screamed until my father bought the cats from the warden, so that they came out of the cage and I have taken them home; I had them for years ... I still see myself standing in front of the cage.'[29] Brandt's overall relationship with his father must have been good. He recalled that he was grateful to his father, who had introduced him to the wonders of antiquity, which clearly fascinated Brandt in later life.[30] In 1913, at the age of nine, he joined the *Wandervogel* youth movement which promoted traditional values and a natural lifestyle in young people as a way to counter the negative effects of urbanization and modern society. Brandt remained a member of the movement until 1919, when his family moved to Germany.

Family life may well have faded into the background in the years leading up to the war. Given that the ongoing labour disputes stretched the resources and manpower of the Mülhausen police, it is likely that Brandt's father was working long hours as an inspector in his workplace, Police Station IV at 3 Karl-Hack-Straße.[31] During the summer of 1913, for example, the police had to mount a complex operation to escort strike breakers from the old railway station to the new construction site of the *Nordbahnhof*. In July 1913, strikers clashed with the police; bottles and stones were thrown. The police eventually opened fire, first with blank shells, then with live ammunition. In the end, two workers were killed. Public criticism of the police was fierce. Under the headline 'Police and Gendarmes in the Service of Capital', the *Mülhauser Volkszeitung* attacked the police for protecting the interests of the employers. In the same year, Mülhausen had to come to terms with the Zabern affair, in which a young Prussian officer, a man called von Forstner, had apparently insulted the local population and incited his staff to use violence against Alsatians. Despite public outrage and government intervention, German military officials protected von Forstner from punishment.[32] For many Alsatians, incidents of this kind not only reinforced their objections to 'Prussianism', the expression of the autocratic and militarist nature of the German Reich, but left them with mixed feelings on the eve of the war as far as their loyalty towards the German state was concerned. In August 1914, a priest from Strasbourg noted: 'With their intellect the Alsatians wish for a German victory and lament a French defeat with their heart.'[33]

Whereas the outbreak of war in the summer of 1914 was greeted with mass demonstrations of public support in places like Paris and Berlin, there was little enthusiasm for the war in Alsace. As Harvey has pointed out: 'Living in a frontier province likely to bear the brunt of war and a bicultural society with ties to both France and Germany, all classes of Alsatians were greatly worried by the possibility of war.'[34] Anti-war demonstrations were nonetheless few and far between and, when they did take place, the demonstrators were often dispersed by the police. Because Alsace was a potential battlefield in the forthcoming conflict, the area was placed under martial law. Anyone wanting to travel within the province needed special authorization. Public assemblies were prohibited from one day to the next, and constitutional rights suspended. On 2 August, all healthy men between the ages of seventeen and forty-five were called into the Imperial army. This included more than 220,000 Alsatian men, among them Karl Julius Brandt. Within days, the fears of the local population that the war would bring nothing but deprivation and misery were confirmed. Trying to recapture Alsace-Lorraine, the French army launched a major offensive, occupying Mülhausen from 8 to 10 August and, after further fighting, again from 19 August to 24 August. It may well be that Brandt's father was taken prisoner by the French army in the very first days of the war. In some parts of the city, the soldiers were greeted as liberators, especially in the working-class districts, with bottles of wine and shouts of '*Vive la France!*' leaving those loyal to Imperial Germany feeling isolated and desperate for a reversal of fortune. Soon the French army had to retreat far behind the lines to prevent the German army from reaching Paris. Those who had betrayed their country now had to pay for their actions. In Mülhausen, the police were asked to place pro-French sympathizers under 'protective custody' (*Schutzhaft*), a measure later used by the Nazi regime against socialists and communists. We do not know whether Brandt's father was asked to carry out these orders, but we do know that he was eventually taken prisoner of war, leaving his wife to be the sole breadwinner of the household amid food rationings, unemployment and inflation. Brandt vividly remembered these early days of the war: 'We were stuck in the middle of the war action. The front was relatively close. Shelling, and a somewhat restless school period. Forced migration from Alsace in 1919.'[35]

By the end of the war, Mülhausen was occupied, yet again, by the French army. This time, however, the majority of the population greeted the French soldiers with cheers and music. One observer noted that 'all of Alsace was covered by tricolour flags ... patriotic songs and military marches floated in the air, sung, whistled, and hummed'.[36] Things sometimes turned ugly. At the end of November 1918, local residents turned their pent-up aggression against prominent Germans and German-owned stores, leaving families like the Brandts in fear for their lives. In August 1918, Brandt stopped going to school in Mülhausen. At the age of fourteen, with his father a prisoner of war and his mother struggling to survive, Brandt experienced first hand what it meant to live in a border region that had become the central battleground in a war of attrition.

In March 1919, after Alsace had been annexed by France as part of the Versailles Treaty, Brandt and his mother moved to temporary accommodation in Thuringia, perhaps to Schmalkalden where Brandt's grandparents on his mother's side had lived or, more likely, to Steinbach-Hallenberg, five miles east of Schmalkalden, where his mother had been born.[37] Schmalkalden and the nearby villages had been strong supporters of the war. Hundreds, if not thousands, of local young men had been called to arms to fight for the fatherland. When the total number of men who were awarded the Iron Cross reached a thousand, the residents of Schmalkalden celebrated the occasion by laying a wreath. The town was also known for its prisoner of war camp, where soldiers from all over Europe and the world were kept behind barbed wire, as well as for its thirty or so cigar factories, which some locals described as 'war-important' industries.[38] This was clearly not a place where the population was critical of, or opposed to, the war effort. On the contrary, towns and villages in the area believed in the Imperial monarchy. The experience of military defeat, coupled with the collapse of the monarchy, left the people of Schmalkalden and Steinbach-Hallenberg in a profound state of shock and disbelief.

Like many young men of his generation, Brandt felt uprooted and in need of orientation and perspective after having experienced the horrors of war. In the aftermath of the war, he tried to compensate for his sense of social dislocation and displacement with study of the Bible and his attachment to the Lutheran Church. In particular, he felt attracted by the charitable work of Gottfried Rade, the Lutheran priest of the parish church of Steinbach-Hallenberg from 1915 to 1923. In 1917, Rade had protested against the confiscation of the last remaining parish bell.[39] Later, he established a parish choir for both men and women, and promoted the building of an old people's home in the small village. Rade must have been influenced by his father, Martin Rade, professor of theology at the University of Marburg, who had examined the religious world of industrial workers and had studied the difficult relationship between Christian beliefs and the horrors of war. Significantly, Rade's father had shown a particular interest in the 'Alsatian soul', something his son might also have absorbed. Here, in the small community of Steinbach-Hallenberg, Brandt also came into contact with Rade's youthful wife, Eva Rade, whom he befriended.[40] Brandt seems to have found in the young woman someone whom he trusted and in whom he could confide, and talk to about his religious beliefs, his feelings and his professional ambitions. We know that Brandt and Eva Rade corresponded with one another.[41] Brandt, it seems, was searching for his place in the world. He wanted to know if there was a God. In a letter to his son in 1947, Brandt recalled how he had struggled with his religious belief system in the years after the war, and had eventually become a 'devout heathen':

> My years as a youth saw me strongly attached to the parish church in Steinbach. Perhaps Eva Rade even has some letters from these, my young, searching years. I took the examination of myself and my God very seriously. I pondered for many hours in my childhood, and as a doctor I often sat next to the dying, searching for the wonder of eternity. I saw humans, who peacefully fell asleep in their Christian belief, I saw many, who parted from life in such a composed manner that it was distressing in its sacrificial greatness. But I did not see one Christian who happily armed himself for the last march. Not one! Only the heathen dies happy. One thing the heathen knows, that there is no dying and no end. He knows that everything comes in a circle …[42]

In the spring of 1920, Brandt enrolled for a year in the *Unter-Secunda* at the secondary school (*Oberrealschule*) in Eisenach, forty kilometres from Schmalkalden. The period in Eisenach must have been very difficult for Brandt because he had to repeat the *Unter-Secunda* in a new and unfamiliar environment. Having only been taught French, Brandt now had to take part in English lessons and catch up in mathematics, physics and other natural science subjects. 'It was an enormous burden for me at the time, a very heavy burden,' he later recalled.[43] Brandt's headteacher in Eisenach, a Professor Dr Gentsch, introduced Brandt to the Old Testament, and instructed him to read *Tell* and *Minna von Barnhelm*, as well as poems such as the *Lied von der Glocke* and *Siegesfest* by Schiller. Brandt also had to translate Caesar's *De Bello Gallico* in his Latin lessons and read Marryat's *The Children of the New Forest* in his English lessons.[44] What impact this kind of literature and post-war education had on Brandt's political outlook and ideology is difficult to ascertain, but it may well be that the experience of national upheaval and profound uncertainly left him searching for a new home, a native soil, or *Heimat*, to which he and his family belonged.[45] Brandt certainly loved his native country, the places where he had grown up and had been socialized and educated. In 1947, he told his son:

> The soil which absorbed our youth should be and should remain holy to us. Our parents and ancestors walked this earth before us, breathed the same smell of the earth, saw the same hills and woods and valleys and heard the same wind blowing. How could one leave this behind? The mountains, the castles, the murmur of the rivers and the springing of the streams! *Heimat*! Oh, when the days draw to a close and time has passed, one longs to come home.[46]

In 1920/21, the family moved to Dresden where Brandt eventually passed his *Abitur*.[47] For a prolonged period after the war, Brandt's family was struggling with the financial and psychological consequences of the defeat. For Karl Brandt, especially, the experience meant a decisive loss of security and the need to adapt to a new, unfamiliar social and educational environment. The forced move away from Alsace had a traumatic effect on Brandt's family, especially on his father, who was released from a French prisoner of war camp as late as 1921.[48] Brandt later made the laconic comment that his family 'had experienced a bit of an interruption through the war'.[49] Having served his country as a captain and later as a major in the reserve army, Karl Julius Brandt belonged to the mass of demobilized soldiers of the Imperial army who felt humiliated and betrayed by their government. The myth that socialists and communists had stabbed the army in the back fell on fertile ground with a whole generation of soldiers, and found broad support in society as a whole, particularly among legal experts and civil servants, who had been trained and socialized under the Imperial monarchy. The forced migration from Mülhausen to Dresden undermined the family's social status and eroded Karl Julius Brandt's sense of identity and self-esteem. This may explain, in part, why he decided to send his son to a former cadet school, the *Landesschule*, located in the Marienallee in Dresden-Klotzsche in the north of the city. Perhaps he was hoping that this environment would instil a certain sense of discipline and loyalty in his son. Another reason may have been that schools such as the *Landesschule* were catering for Germans who had fled from areas such as Alsace and Lorraine. In October 1920, the former cadet school had been incorporated into the educational system of the state of Saxony. The *Landesschule*, one of the largest boarding schools in the state, educated up to 250 pupils from around the city, and about fifty pupils from Dresden, mostly from poor and modest family backgrounds, according to humanitarian principles. The aim was to provide pupils with a comprehensive, non-specialist, holistic education. Children of former cadets, as well as needy children of war veterans, were given priority in the allocation of places. The authorities also wanted to allocate some of the places to talented and needy pupils from other backgrounds, as long as places were available. Most significantly, however, the school was meant to provide educational facilities to 'foreign Germans and Germans from annexed and occupied territories'.[50] Brandt's family clearly fell into the latter category and he was given a place at the *Landesschule*. The city also granted annual stipends to twenty-five pupils to cover school fees, board and lodging. Each stipend was of 2,500 Reichsmark, twenty-five stipends were for board only, and fifty for so-called 'external' pupils, to cover school fees only. The evidence shows how the city and state authorities battled against a total breakdown of civil society while the German economy was spiralling out of control. Tens of thousands of families suddenly found their hard-earned savings devalued or were unable to pay for bread and butter or their monthly rent. Food prices increased a thousandfold, so much so that the city authorities decided by 1922 to raise the stipends to 5,000 Reichsmark per year for those students who were granted free school fees, board and lodging, and to 400 Reichsmark for those who were granted free board only.

The provisions of the *Landesschule* must have appealed to Brandt's father after forced migration, military defeat and inflation left the family's financial situation in disarray. Karl Brandt, student number 21b, is mentioned in a list of pupils who in 1921 received one of those twenty-five stipends. The city authorities did not waive the school fees for Karl Brandt, but they granted him free board from January 1921 to March 1921, another indication that the financial situation of the Brandt family might have been under some strain at the time. From April 1921 to September 1921, Brandt's father only had to pay half the cost for board. Perhaps even more significantly, Brandt is listed as one of the students who lived and slept at the *Landesschule*, even though the family had a flat at 22 Jägerstraße in Dresden at the time. There is no obvious explanation for this other than that the family might have been struggling to survive. Perhaps they felt that the boarding school would give young Karl the necessary stability and security in order to flourish in his studies while his father was searching for a job.[51]

In 1923, at the age of nineteen, Brandt passed his *Abitur* at the *Landesschule*.[52] He was not a brilliant or exceptional student but he was certainly hard-working and conscientious, a studious pupil, who wanted to make a good impression on his teachers. He seems to have had a particular interest in religion in which he scored a first-class mark. Another of his favourite subjects was German, and he gained good marks in geography, history and sport. His marks in French and English, in contrast, were rather poor. He was also not particularly strong in chemistry, Latin, physics or mathematics. Without stretching the interpretative value of this source too far, what we note is a young man who was interested in religious theory and practice, who had a strong interest in German history and culture, and was knowledgeable in geography and good at sport. At the same time, Brandt was less interested in other cultures and languages, such as French, Latin or English, and showed no particular strengths in subjects which required a systematic approach and a high degree of logical thinking. He passed his *Abitur* with an average mark of IIb which was, leaving aside the problems of conversion, a fairly average performance.[53] Brandt, in short, did not stand out from the crowd.

By the end of 1922, at the height of the inflation crisis, Brandt's father had found a new position as an officer with the district police in Chemnitz. In December he moved to 103 Planitzstraße, the headquarters of the commando of the Saxony state police for the district of Chemnitz, while Karl Brandt and his mother stayed behind in Dresden at 3 Wormserstraße for another year.[54] In early January 1924, mother and son finally joined Karl Julius in Chemnitz, and the family moved into number 9 Franz-Seldte-Straße (today Henriettenstraße). Brandt's father remained registered at this address until 1942. Brandt later told the Nuremberg court that it had been a difficult time.[55] The forced migration from Mülhausen to Dresden, via Thuringia, perhaps even the personal experience of poverty and the unemployment of his father, exacerbated Brandt's sense of frustration about the Versailles Treaty and his disillusionment with the existing democratic system. He later told Alexander that the Versailles Treaty had contributed to the militarist and nationalist character, and the 'love of war', of his generation.[56] During the Weimar years, Brandt's sense of nationalism and loyalty to the German Reich grew, leaving him with a deep-rooted resentment against France. Years later the 'expulsion of the French', as he called it, still triggered highly emotive reactions. The years of poverty and professional insecurity of his father may also explain why Brandt opted for medicine to secure his living and enhance his social and professional status.

II. STUDENT YEARS

Brandt was, above all, an ambitious young man who wanted to make a career as a physician. He was also idealistic, a strong believer in a better and healthier future in which class divisions and social injustice would be overcome.[57] His choice of profession allowed him to pursue his career ambitions, and the regime that came to power in 1933 provided the perfect breeding ground for men with visionary ideas, however fanciful they might be. Brandt's medical expertise and great ambitions on the one hand, and the regime's radical political ideology on the other, provided a potentially dangerous combination. Brandt may not have been a strong supporter of a new Great German Reich which was reserved only for strong and healthy Germans, free from Jews and communists, nor was he necessarily happy with some of the policies which Hitler and his regime implemented in the 1930s, but he had all the necessary character traits which allowed those in authority to exploit him for their cause. Ranking foremost among these traits was his acceptance and, at times, admiration of authority. Brandt possessed the ability to integrate himself into a strict professional and administrative hierarchy and follow orders. He showed, as one observer noted, a 'tendency for extraordinary obedience'.[58] At the time same, he was eager to climb the professional and social ladder and gain executive power. In short, he was the perfect servant in a regime that was based on the principle of charismatic leadership.

According to Brandt, the decision to study medicine was an obvious one. Since his youth, it had always been assumed that he would one day study medicine. 'Any other question with regard to a choice of profession was not up for debate,' he recalled.[59] After the war, he told the court: 'On my mother's side my family was one of doctors. So that it was a fairly obvious thing to me to study medicine.'[60] Apart from his grandfather, one of his uncles became a medical doctor, and worked as a psychiatrist. He trained with the Swiss psychiatrist and expert on the social life of ants, August Forel, who had been a mentor for Germany's leading racial hygienist, Alfred Ploetz, and his group of health zealots and visionary world improvers.[61] How influential his uncle was in Brandt's education as a young man is not known, but he seems to have made his decision to become a doctor relatively easily. After he had passed his exams in 1923, Brandt told the school that his future professional career would lie in medicine.[62]

From May 1923 to April 1925, Brandt studied medicine at the University of Jena, a hotbed of nationalistic and anti-Semitic currents at the time. Few sources give an indication as to whether Brandt became involved in political activities during that period. He remembered that the political climate was shaped by social tensions and inflation, leading to occasional street fights and beatings which were alien to his character.[63] He also recalled siding with the workers' movement during a dispute between student corporations and workers from the Zeiss factory in Jena, because he disagreed with the 'somewhat traditional relationship' which the student corporations had with the pre-war system of society in Imperial Germany.[64] There is little evidence to corroborate Brandt's version of events, however. According to Brandt, he had no contact with the student fraternities. Studying among only thirty-five to forty medical students, many of whom came from Poland and Bulgaria, Brandt seems to have concentrated his mind on his medical studies.[65] In Jena, Brandt also came into contact with Georg Magnus, who taught as a senior physician (*Oberarzt*) at the surgical clinic. For a young man in Brandt's position, with no apparent professional network and limited family support, studying medicine was difficult. He lacked the necessary connections and financial means which would have allowed him to advance quickly up the social and professional ladder. During his pre-clinical studies, he began to have doubts about his choice of career. Believing that he would 'now get access to the patient', Brandt was frustrated to have to study botany and zoology instead:

> My studies at Jena did not proceed altogether smoothly. Since I was studying medicine and was intending to become a doctor, I was lacking the necessary experience with actual patients during the pre-clinical part of my studies. As soon as I completed the fourth term, I attended the clinical lectures and thereby got in touch with my subsequent boss, Professor Magnus.[66]

In 1925, after four terms, Brandt successfully completed the first medical exam, the *Physikum*: 'I owe it to him [Magnus] that after four terms I succeeded in passing my *Physikum* … so that I actually arrived at the clinic[al part of my medical studies] prematurely.'[67] Brandt was probably not a high flyer when it came to his medical studies, but he was hard-working and keen to make a career as a doctor. From early on, he knew that he wanted to become a surgeon.[68]

Changing universities quite frequently had the added advantage of exposing him to a variety of medical experts, schools and professional networks, but it also introduced Brandt to some of the elder statesmen of the German racial hygiene movement. For the summer semester of 1925, Brandt joined the University of Freiburg im Breisgau, where he attended, for example, lectures in pathology by Ludwig Aschoff, himself a member of the board of the German Society for Racial Hygiene. He also studied pharmacology and toxicology with Wilhelm Trendelenburg, who in 1933 joined the National Socialist German Teachers' Association,[69] and was taught by Erich Lexer, one of the pioneers of plastic surgery and a former assistant to the famous surgeon Ernst von Bergmann.[70] In 1919, Lexer became a professor in Freiburg where he laid some of the foundations for bone transplantations. Lexer, however, was also an ardent advocate of sterilizing the mentally and physically handicapped. After the Nazi sterilization law came into force in 1934, Lexer wrote the chapter on 'The Operation for the Sterilisation of the Male and Castration' in the official commentary of the law. According to Brandt,

Lexer was one of the 'decisive personalities' who had a significant influence upon his medical training. Hitler later honoured both Aschoff and Lexer with the Goethe medal for art and science. Whether Brandt had any influence in recommending two of his former teachers for one of the most prestigious prizes awarded by the Third Reich is not known, but certainly not beyond the realm of possibility.

Between October 1925 and March 1926, Brandt lived in Berlin in order to attend a series of lectures on infectious diseases, tuberculosis, practical medicine and clinical surgery.[71] Studying surgery under August Bier and Wilhelm His, two of Germany's leading experts in the field, gave Brandt the necessary expertise and credentials to advance his career.[72] He then worked for six weeks, in March and April 1926, as a trainee at the city hospital in Weimar, before he spent the summer term studying at the Ludwig-Maximilian University in Munich, from the end of April 1926 to the beginning of October 1926.[73] One reason for his move to Munich is likely to have been the opportunity to hear the lectures of the famous surgeon Ferdinand Sauerbruch (1875–1951).[74] Another was the possibility of studying with Oswald Bumke (1877–1950), an internationally recognized expert in the field of psychiatry and Ernst Kraeplin's successor in Munich.[75] Bumke's political outlook was strongly conservative – he was a German nationalist to the core – and yet he was critical of some of the proposals that were put forward by racial and eugenic fanatics at the time. Except for hereditary feeblemindedness and some psychotic disorders, Bumke questioned the scientific value of sterilizing large numbers of schizophrenics, epileptics and manic depressives. After all, these illnesses were inherited according to a recessive pattern which made it difficult to completely eliminate them from the gene pool of a given population. After the introduction of the Nazi sterilization law in 1934, Bumke apparently offered his resignation in protest, but the regime at that point was unwilling to dispense with a man of his international stature.[76] Bumke, unlike many of his fellow German psychiatrists, foresaw the potential dangers in the debate about reforming the German asylum system on economic grounds. In 1932, he wrote, concerning this, that 'economic perspectives are not just inappropriate but dangerous':

> One only needs to take the idea to its logical conclusion – that one should do away with all those people who at the time seem dispensable for financial reasons – in order to arrive at the rather monstrous result: we must kill not merely all the mentally ill and the psychopaths, but every cripple, including wounded war veterans, all the old maids who are not working, all the widows who no longer have children to raise, and all the invalids and old-age pensioners. That would certainly save us money, but I suspect we would not do it.[77]

Bumke was mistaken. The Nazi regime did indeed take the argument to its logical conclusion, and Brandt helped them to do so. What is more, both Brandt and Bumke stayed in contact throughout the Third Reich. Bumke became a supporting member of the SS after Hitler had come to power, and joined the National Socialist German Teachers' Association (*Nationalsozialistischer Deutscher Lehrerbund*, NSDLB). From 1940 onwards, he served in an advisory capacity as the military psychiatrist for Defensive Zone VII in Munich. Two years later, in August 1942, Hitler appointed him as an extraordinary member of the scientific senate of the Army Medical Service (*Heeressanitätswesen*). Finally, in 1944, he became a member of the scientific board of the General Commissioner of the Führer for Health and Sanitation and was thus, de facto, subordinate to his former pupil Karl Brandt.

So, during his training, Brandt studied with some of the leading experts in the field of German medicine and psychiatry in Munich and elsewhere, and was introduced to the current debates on evolutionary biology, racial degeneration and eugenics. One of his fellow students of the period remembered Brandt as an enthusiastic and intelligent student, but relatively shy. Though anti-Semitism was widespread among his fellow students, Brandt does not seem to have voiced his opinion against the Jews, at least not publicly, except apparently on one occasion. During a demonstration of right-wing students at the University of Munich, a Jewish student by the name of Hirsch was given a book by another fellow student. On the last page of the book someone had drawn a gallows and a hanged man in black ink with a caption which read: 'The end of Hirsch: 19–?' A witness of the incident recalled in 1972 that the student who had made the drawing was apparently Brandt. The available evidence surrounding this incident, however, is questionable and needs to be treated with great caution.[78] Given that Brandt was eager to climb the professional ladder, it is more likely that he was following his studies with great discipline and enthusiasm than that he was engaging in anti-Semitic diatribes, racial hatred or party politics.[79] In August and September 1926, Brandt returned to the city hospital in Weimar to gain further medical training. Once again, he must have shown initiative and motivation. According to the head physician of the city hospital, a Dr Knopf, Brandt had 'worked with great zeal and conscientiousness.'[80]

III. EARLY MEDICAL CAREER AND EUTHANASIA

Brandt's next and final place of study was the southern city of Freiburg im Breisgau, where he lived at 3 Josefstraße. Not far from his native Alsace-Lorraine, Brandt studied in Freiburg from October 1926 until February 1928, and gained further expertise in nearby medical institutions. In the spring of 1927, for example, Brandt stayed in Scheidegg, near Bregenz on the Austrian–German border, where he worked at the children's clinic, Prinzregent-Luitpold, during March and parts of April.[81] The director of the clinic, a Dr Klare, certified that Brandt had gained further experience in the field of tuberculosis: 'The rich material of all forms of tuberculosis in children provided Herr Brandt with the opportunity to gain expertise in the diagnosis and therapy of children suffering from tuberculosis.'[82]

Freiburg not only improved Brandt's medical skills but introduced him to the contentious issue of euthanasia. At Freiburg, he studied, and later took his exam, with the psychiatrist Alfred Hoche, then sixty-one years old and one of Germany's leading voices advocating the killing of severely handicapped people during the Weimar Republic.[83] Brandt and Hoche not only agreed when it came to the legality and moral justification of euthanasia, the two men also shared a special relationship with Alsace and showed a similar dislike of France after it had annexed Alsace-Lorraine as part of the Versailles Treaty.[84] For about ten years, throughout the 1890s, Hoche had worked at the University of Strasbourg. In his autobiography, written in 1936, he recalled the extent to which the area 'felt' German – how the people, their houses, villages and gardens looked the same as in neighbouring Baden, how they were speaking, singing and drinking (!) in German. 'How German Alsace must have always been could be seen by the fact that 200 years of political affiliation to France – an enormous time span to change a *Volk* – had not made the country French,' he recalled.[85] Strasbourg, in particular, was the most German town one could imagine, he felt. But he also noted that the German, and in particular Prussian, influence had created a significant level of tension among the local population, not only about being stereotyped as sloppy and inefficient but about a certain arrogance that was displayed by members of the German Reich, and in some cases by military personnel stationed in and around the garrison cities. Some Alsace-Lorrainers, on the other hand, showed a certain contempt for Germany, and gave Germans the feeling that they were masters in an occupied land. Hoche's autobiography displays a certain sense of his perceived victimization: he describes how his career stalled in the late 1890s because of institutional infighting, how he decided to leave academia to become a local psychiatrist, frozen out by colleagues and universities, in Hamburg and Bremen especially. A change of direction as a political journalist and the attempt to complete a doctorate in law both ended in failure. His career was clearly going nowhere until he was given a chair in Freiburg im Breisgau in 1902. For the next thirty or so years Hoche would not leave the university. He retired from his position in 1934.

Since the end of the First World War, Hoche had argued his case in favour of euthanasia. On 6 November 1918, only days before Germany was thrown into revolutionary turmoil, Hoche gave a talk on 'dying' at the University of Freiburg. His understanding of death was that of a natural scientist: he argued that the human body was in a constant process of dying and in a constant process of renewal, where harmful and useless body parts and cells died and others were created anew in order to sustain the balance of life. Hoche linked this process with the fate of mankind as a whole, and deployed statistics aimed at underpinning his argument that hundreds of thousands of dead people – a reference to the enormous casualties of the war – were little more than the ebb and flow of waves in a permanent cycle of life. As far as the issue of euthanasia was concerned, Hoche was of the opinion that it was the duty of the doctor to ease the pain of those who were dying and prevent the prolonged suffering of the patient. Whilst recognizing that medical ethics did not allow doctors to shorten the lives of patients, at least not at the time, he questioned whether those performing euthanasia should be prosecuted: 'Who wants to be the judge over he who, for the most noble of motives, spares an incurable human being agonising pain?'[86] The ground on which he would make the case for euthanasia was laid.

In 1920 Hoche, with the lawyer Karl Binding, published the famous tract entitled 'Permission for the Destruction of Life Unworthy of Life'.[87] The book was by far the most important contribution to the debate on euthanasia. An expert in constitutional and criminal jurisprudence, Binding had retired to Freiburg after a distinguished career at various German universities, but he died in the course of publishing the book. Hoche, in contrast, does not seem to have attracted much attention for academic brilliance prior to the controversial two-part tract.

Binding first outlined the legality of assisted suicide, starting with the assumption that each individual had full powers to commit suicide, unless, this being the only exception, it involved the loss of a potentially valuable member of society. While he first used the term 'euthanasia' in its original meaning as 'support in the process of dying without the shortening of life', he later included assisted suicide and the elimination of 'life unworthy of life', thus obfuscating the issue of euthanasia, rather than clarifying its legal and ethical limitations. Questions of valid consent seem to have been of little relevance to Binding. Medical and legal ethics were nevertheless at the centre of his argument. He asked the reader whether there is 'human life which has so far forfeited the character of something entitled to enjoy the protection of the law that its prolongation represents a perpetual loss of value, both for its bearer and for society as a whole?'[88]

The book had clearly been written under the influence of the First World War: Binding invited his readers to compare the 'battlefields littered with thousands of dead youth' with asylums and their apparent care for their inmates, whom he saw as 'not absolutely worthless, but in fact existences of negative value'.[89] Binding then moved on to advocate the 'permission for the destruction of life unworthy of life' on the condition that the measure would be a 'deliverance' for the persons in question. Three groups of people were to be targeted. First, the terminally ill or mortally wounded with the ability to express their desire for euthanasia. Second, those considered as 'incurable idiots', and unable to voice their view on euthanasia. Since these people had the ability neither to live nor to die, killing them would not infringe their will. 'Their life is absolutely useless, but they do not regard it as being unbearable. For their relatives as well as for society they are a terribly heavy burden. Their death does not create the smallest gap – except perhaps in the feelings of the mother or nurse.'[90] The final group was made up of mentally healthy people who were in a state of unconsciousness, resulting from accident or battle. Taking for granted that their condition would appal their relatives, legal guardians or doctors, Binding suggested that these people should instigate proceedings on their behalf. For all three groups of people, a state body consisting of doctors, lawyers and psychiatrists would make recommendations to the effect that the person could be killed by a doctor with the aid of drugs. Overstepping the boundaries of generally accepted legal argument without hesitation, Binding judged patients according to their apparent economic value to society and applied rigid cost/benefit criteria to human beings.

Hoche was no less radical in his views on euthanasia. He applied the same preconceptions held by Binding in a discussion on medical ethics and practice. Hoche was interested in 'incurable idiots' and the 'mentally dead', who apparently placed a financial and emotional burden on relatives, the community and the state.

The Freiburg psychiatrist believed that in times of national crisis there was little or no room for persons considered to be 'ballast existences'. No money should be spent on 'inferior elements', he argued. Their being a financial burden for society apparently justified their being killed. Both Binding and Hoche brushed aside the possibility of error in the introduction of such radical measures. While Binding argued that mankind would lose so many on account of other errors that 'one more or less hardly counts in the balance', Hoche claimed that doctors would be in no doubt there was 'one hundred per cent certainty in selection'.

Hoche, and later Brandt as well, applied the concept of the social organism developed by the British sociologist Herbert Spencer to the mentally ill. He saw the state as an organic entity in which the mentally ill were parts of the 'body politic' (*Volkskörper*) that had become damaged, useless or harmful, and needed to be eliminated. The concept of the *Volkskörper* enabled those who advocated, and later actually carried out, the 'euthanasia' programme to place their actions in a wider biological and socio-philosophical context. Leaving logical argument aside, the language of Binding and Hoche's book showed an exceptional disregard for the rights of individuals and little, if any, respect and sympathy for human life.

The book triggered off an intense debate on the question of euthanasia. Legal and medical circles commented on what they perceived as the 'problem on the elimination of life unworthy of life'. Theologians joined the debate on an issue that had previously been of relatively minor importance in the German racial hygiene movement. From 1922 to 1933 a total of eleven dissertations on the topic were produced, seven in jurisprudence, three in medicine and one in philosophy.[91] Some lawyers agreed with Binding's account on assisted suicide, but criticized his proposals to actually kill people, arguing that doctors could not be permitted to kill a fellow human being, even if that individual was unable to express his or her will. They also openly rejected the notion of killing patients for economic reasons.[92] Others were more ambiguous about the issue, supporting the underlying economic rationale which apparently justified such measures, especially at times when the country was hit by hyperinflation and mass unemployment. In 1922, a city official from Liegnitz published a proposal for a law on euthanasia which demanded the elimination of the 'mentally weak' because of the costs to mental institutions. The proposal never got to any serious stage.

The medical profession, by and large, was not impressed by Hoche and Binding's book. Though eugenic sterilization was favoured by many doctors, killing patients was another matter. Binding's assumption that the mentally ill had no will to live, or to die, and that their life was pointless, was almost always seen as unacceptable. Challenging the notion of excessive expenditure in the asylum sector, doctors suggested that much larger savings could be achieved for the national economy by prohibiting alcohol and tobacco consumption to reduce the number of patients. In 1921, the German medical profession unanimously rejected the proposal to legitimize the 'destruction of life unworthy of life' during its annual conference in Karlsruhe. The debate showed, however, that members of the medical and legal professions had placed the issue of euthanasia on their agendas. Here it remained until Hitler decided to implement the 'euthanasia' programme through his personal physician, Karl Brandt.

Hoche's teachings on life and death and on the process of dying, which he discussed with a certain candour, provided the intellectual and moral basis from which Brandt would later argue his case, after Hitler had asked him to implement such a programme, and also during the Nazi Doctors' Trial. Hoche's experiences with dying patients, his understanding of pain and human suffering, and his suggestions on how life could be painlessly shortened, resemble Brandt's position, which he subsequently advocated so forcefully. Hoche also felt that the life of one human being could be sacrificed for the greater good of society or the advancement of medical science. Every member of society was only of importance as long as he or she was a 'reliable part in the chain which linked the past with the future'.[93] In one instance, Hoche recalled how he was tempted, for scientific purposes, to kill a nine-year-old girl suffering from a mysterious brain disease, something that is strangely reminiscent of how Brandt later justified experiments on human subjects during the war:

> The child was completely unconscious; from the pulse rate etc. it was clear that the end was to be expected in the next couple of hours. There was a pressing scientific interest in the possibility to find out through dissection the kind of disease progression [in this case]; then the father appeared and requested that the small girl be handed over … If she was still alive when he returned in the next hour, I had to surrender her; if she died beforehand, we could carry out the autopsy. I was young and passionate and considered completely extinguishing the flickering light of life through a small injection of morphine, more would not have been necessary. While the sister was having lunch, I was sitting by the bed with a filled syringe in my hand and pondered – shall I – shall I not. Later I discussed the problem with which I was faced here for the first time with Binding in a much-criticised tract; I reject the position that the doctor has the unquestioning duty to prolong life; I am convinced that the higher view will prevail against all those who are self-confidently representing morality; there are circumstances in which killing is not a crime for the doctor. In this case I did not kill; our legitimate scientific desire to enlighten an unknown medical case was not sufficient for me to silence the counter-arguments. It would have been something different, if, by shortening this one lost life, one could have obtained immediate knowledge which would have saved other better lives; but that was not how things were. The child died on the train journey home.[94]

For Hoche, dying was not difficult, nor was it something one had to be afraid of. Humans suffered pain and agony throughout life, though not in death, he argued. The 'dentist's is worse than the guillotine' when it comes to the personal experience of pain, Hoche told his critics, mainly because the guillotine killed so quickly; before any information from the nerve endings could stimulate pain in the body, the person was dead. Unnatural processes of dying through drowning, hanging or gas poisoning were 'not unpleasant', Hoche remarked, if one believed those who survived the experience.

Brandt may well have remembered Hoche's writings on the processes of dying in the late 1930s when he had to decide on a killing method that was both efficient and cheap, and also, most importantly, 'humane'. He also remembered that he had once become unconscious without any pain after inhaling fumes from a stove: 'That was the reason why I thought that this coal-oxide [carbon monoxide] death would be the most humane form of death.'[95] For Brandt, the Nazi 'euthanasia' programme was part of a eugenic project and a necessary wartime measure to save on food rationing and bed-space in military and civilian hospitals. The intellectual and philosophical roots of the programme, however, go back to the writings of Hoche and a handful of other radical scholars: their literature opened up the possibility of exterminating the lives of those who were considered to be of no value or use to society. Above all, the specific understanding of what euthanasia was and why it should be carried out in certain cases goes back to Brandt's training as a medical doctor in the 1920s.

In June 1928, Brandt completed his medical studies at the University of Freiburg im Breisgau after submitting his dissertation on 'Congenital Occlusion of the Gall Bladder Ducts'.[96] More than a year later, on 19 October 1929, the university conferred the degree of doctor on Brandt.[97] Like many of his fellow students, Brandt had chosen a topic which was relevant for hereditary research and eugenics and which could advance his professional career. He wrote his dissertation under the supervision of the American-born Carl Noeggerat, professor of paediatrics at the university from 1926 and co-editor of the *Zeitschrift für Kinderheilkunde*.[98] On 27 June 1928, Brandt passed his exam in internal medicine, surgery and paediatrics with the accolade 'good', another indication that he must have possessed a relatively sound knowledge in a number of medical specialties.[99] The previous day, 26 June, he had passed his general medical exam in front of a board of examiners. Brandt kept a small photo album of each member of the board, among them the psychiatrist Alfred Hoche. We can see the white-bearded, slightly bald, and bespectacled Hoche talking to a colleague in what seems to be a lecture hall. Both are dressed in dark suits rather than in the traditional white coat, to distinguish themselves from general practitioners, surgeons or technical staff. The image seems to have been taken in secret, perhaps from behind a student bench. The caption reads *Psychiater Hoche*. On the first page of the album Brandt had written: 'Exam Freiburg i/Br. March–June 28 (26.6.28) K.'[100] Brandt was proud to study with what he believed were distinguished men of science and medicine. He was not only well qualified medically, and had trained with one of the most hardened advocates of the idea of euthanasia years before the Nazis came to power, but had gained first-hand experience of the enormous mental and physical suffering of patients. His years in Freiburg and Bochum, in particular, must have strengthened his belief in the moral and ethical justification for euthanasia.

IV. THE APPRENTICE

From the beginning of 1928, Brandt specialized in surgery at the Bergmannsheil hospital in Bochum, where he lived at 93 Hattinger Straße. Working under Magnus, the head of the surgical department at the Bergmansheil hospital, Brandt wanted to make his mark as an expert in head and spinal injuries as well as in fractured legs and arms.[101] Bochum, a leading industrial centre in the Ruhr region, and the Bergmannsheil hospital in particular, gave him ample opportunity to gain first-hand experience of severe casualties in the coal and steel industry. 'Work in that hospital had the particular characteristic that the medical department was closely connected with the places of work where the actual accidents had occurred,' Brandt later recalled.[102] The human cost of pit accidents was truly enormous. Patients suffering from serious and complicated fractures, and the treatment of seriously ill, often unemployed, workers were a common occurrence at the Bergmannsheil hospital. Writing in the *Deutsche Zeitschrift für Chirurgie*, Brandt told fellow doctors that miners were 'exposed to extraordinarily powerful forces' which explained 'the great number of severe injuries that are being treated in the hospitals of the mining area'.[103] He also drew attention to the 'large number of spinal and pelvic fractures or complicated fractures' which he had witnessed in his work.[104] During this time, Brandt was constantly surrounded by seriously ill patients, some of whom approached him to end their lives. In 1947, he recalled how the experience of attending to the suffering patients had produced the most profound ethical dilemma which doctors in general, and he in particular, ever had to face, namely whether to administer a deadly drug to end the patients' misery:

> During this accident surgery, injuries to the skull played a particularly important role … and … injuries to the spine … Every assistant doctor at the [Bergmannsheil] hospital … found that the most difficult task was caring for patients with spinal injuries. These patients were generally paralysed in the lower organs of their bodies. And they meant to us the greatest human demands. Every one of these patients knew there was no help for him, and that his fate would be decided within a period of weeks, months or, in exceptional cases, years. There was a tremendous neuralgic pain, never leaving the patients a moment of peace, day or night. And to all of us it was a great effort, time and time again, having to visit these patients, having to step up to their beds, and having to say a few words of greeting, which practically were nothing but just words. After a while, time and time again, these patients would make the same request: 'Doctor, give me an injection! I cannot stand it any more'. I think that any description of the situation, however extensive it might be, would always fail to live up to reality.[105]

The whole experience left Brandt convinced that in severe cases it was in the patients' best interest to die rather than to continue to live a life of misery that was of no apparent benefit to society. He later told the Nuremberg court that doctors involved in the 'euthanasia' programme were given an enormous responsibility, one which very much reflected the responsibility which he had experienced during his time in Bochum: 'It was not only a responsibility in view of [the doctors'] right to decide about life and death, but he was also burdened by the fact that he was responsible for the continued suffering of this human being.'[106] Bochum, above all places, turned Brandt into an unequivocal believer in the idea that euthanasia was justifiable.

As an ambitious young doctor of twenty-four, Brandt felt the need to help others by sacrificing part of his private life. A number of colleagues later described him as exemplary in dealing with patients. He devoted time and effort to establishing a good doctor–patient relationship, sometimes even donating blood to save the lives of patients in medical emergencies.[107] On the whole, senior colleagues were fully satisfied with Brandt's work. In January 1929, Georg Magnus, his mentor at the Bergmannsheil hospital, stated:

> Herr Brandt has assisted in examining and treating a great number of patients in this period [1928], especially those suffering from recent injuries and fractures. He assisted with substantial surgical operations, has independently carried out less substantial operations, has given anaesthetics and, in particular, written extensive and complicated medical reports. He has fulfilled all his duties conscientiously, with skill and speed, and he has shown a good understanding of the duties and responsibilities of the medical profession in every respect.[108]

Professor Reichel from the city hospital in Chemnitz, where Brandt worked for two-and-a-half months, probably to be close to his family, was likewise satisfied with his trainee. In March 1929, he noted that Brandt had carried out his medical duties with 'great zeal and a very good understanding'.[109] In April 1929, Brandt moved to Weimar for another four-month stint at the local city hospital. He was thus able to look after his ailing grandfather. The head of the medical ward for internal diseases, a Dr Faber, noted that Brandt had 'deepened and developed his practical knowledge and skills at the bedside, as well as in the diagnosis of internal diseases in the X-ray department and during the standard examinations in the laboratory ... He has been a competent, dutiful and in every respect reliable colleague for me.'[110] In August 1929, Brandt returned to Bochum to start a full-time position as Magnus' assistant in the surgical department of the Bergmannsheil hospital.

One of Brandt's closest colleagues at the hospital was Paul Rostock, whom he met around 1928. Brandt and Rostock developed a friendship that lasted twenty years, until Brandt was hanged at Landsberg. Born in 1892 as the son of a farmer in the district of Meritz in Pomerania, Rostock first studied medicine at the University of Greifswald before he transferred to the University of Jena, where he became more involved in national-conservative party politics. In 1919, for example, he founded the student group of the German National People's Party (*Deutschnationale Volkspartei*) which recruited, among others, Werner Haase, one of Brandt's colleagues in Berlin, who later became his deputy as Hitler's escort physician. From 1922 to 1929, Rostock worked as an assistant at the Jena surgical clinic under Nicolai Guleke, professor of surgery from 1919 to 1951, and from 1933 onwards participated in the Race Political Seminars at the State School for Leadership and Politics of the Thuringian State Department for Race in Egendorf. In 1927, Rostock became the senior physician (*Oberarzt*) at the Bergmannsheil hospital, specializing in casualty surgery and in the treatment of accidents that occurred in the regional mining industry. For more than four years, from 1929 to 1933, both Brandt and Rostock worked under Georg Magnus at the Bergmannsheil hospital. Although Magnus presented some of Brandt's work during the Annual Meeting of German Surgeons in 1932, Brandt's research activity was at best modest. He certainly was not a prolific writer. 'It would be wrong to say that I had played any leading part at all in any scientific field,' Brandt acknowledged after the war.[111] In 1933, Brandt published his 'Results in the Treatment of Thigh Fractures' in the *Deutsche Zeitschrift für Chirurgie* after he had examined the case histories of more than 800 patients with thigh fractures. In 1947, while imprisoned at Nuremberg, Rostock remembered Brandt as a conscientious and caring physician who would spend time and effort in improving the well-being of his patients in Bochum. But he also recalled that Brandt was not a born researcher:

> His scientific productivity was small. I recall a publication about the results in the treatment of thigh fractures in the mining industry from the time when he was an assistant in Bochum. It was [a] systematic follow-up examination of a large group of injured [workers] from a particular period and the interpretation of the findings ... Brandt constantly cared for his patients, in Bochum as well as later in Berlin, and not only looked after them medically and in an excellent fashion, but especially from a human perspective. Patients liked him more than they liked the average physician. He was available for them at any time. I also remember that he donated blood, eight to ten times, for [the] severely injured in Bochum where there was no organisation for blood donations at the time, thus saving the injured from dying.[112]

There is also some second-hand evidence that colleagues may have been less than impressed by the young surgeon. Sauerbruch apparently saw Brandt as 'too young, too inexperienced and too stupid to talk about surgical matters'.[113] Given that the statement was obtained by the Allies at the end of the war during the interrogation of Fritz Bleich, the registrar at the Chancellery of the Führer, who was keen to distance himself from Hitler's doctor, it needs to be treated with caution. Sauerbruch later submitted a petition on behalf of Brandt to save him from the gallows, something a distinguished surgeon such as Sauerbruch would probably not have done had he not had a certain respect for Brandt's professional abilities.

What becomes clear from these documents is that Brandt developed his professional career in a methodical and competent manner by gaining theoretical knowledge and practical experience in a variety of universities and institutional settings. He clearly possessed significant medical expertise and skills and developed a good rapport with patients, patients' relatives and colleagues. Unlike other Nazi physicians, he knew what to do in a medical emergency. As Hugh Trevor-Roper remarked after the war: 'If Brandt and his friends were not, technically, among the first flight of surgeons; if they owed their success to that element of chance which, after all, determines the majority of personal appointments; they were nevertheless not altogether disreputable. At least, under Brandt's treatment, Brückner [Hitler's adjutant] recovered from his motor accident; and if Hitler had been similarly injured, he would doubtless have received competent attention.'[114]

V. KARL BRANDT AND ALBERT SCHWEITZER

Around 1932, Brandt toyed with the idea of going to Africa to help those in need. The daily routine of mining accidents, child labour and disease had brought him into contact with local communities stricken by unimaginable poverty and unemployment, a powerful reminder of how life had been for himself and his family after the First World War. He wanted to be a man of action who would not shy away from hard work and personal sacrifice. What better than to follow the charismatic Albert Schweitzer to Lambarene in Africa – under French rule at the time – and support his missionary work. Given that Brandt was genuinely interested in religion, he might well have read Schweitzer's work as a young adult. Schweitzer's life as a selfless jungle doctor, a devout Christian and a rational thinker provided the perfect role model for many young doctors of Brandt's social background and professional qualifications. Doctors from Switzerland, in particular, followed Schweitzer to Lambarene, mainly because visa requirements and work permits seem to have been less stringent than they were, for example, for German doctors, for whom the French authorities required additional proof of loyalty.

During the First World War, Schweitzer had developed a new ethic which placed respect for life at the centre of his philosophical and theological discourse. According to Schweitzer, the ethic of respect for life (*Ethik der Ehrfurcht vor dem Leben*) placed individuals in spiritual relation to the universe and changed their lives by creating an ethical culture. Schweitzer's philosophy was based on the principle 'I am life that wants to live in the midst of life that wants to live.'[115] In Schweitzer's new ethic, the preservation of life and its development to its highest potential was seen as positive and *good*, as opposed to the desire to destroy or damage life or to suppress developed life, that was seen as negative and *bad*. For Schweitzer a clear understanding of *good* and *bad* behaviour towards life was the most fundamental principle of everything ethical. He had come to realize that the traditional understanding of ethics, which looked at the behaviour of human beings towards other human beings, was incomplete because it neglected the relationship between human beings and other life forms. Human beings were only ethical, according to Schweitzer, if life as such was seen as sacred. This applied to the lives of all other creatures in the universe as well as to the lives of humans. His philosophy was truly holistic.

But Schweitzer also acknowledged the dilemma which humans and other life forms faced in the struggle for their existence: the fact that life could only be preserved by damaging and destroying other life forms. As ethical beings, he argued, humans tried to avoid the problem as far as possible. Ethical human beings always aimed to preserve their humanity and deliver others from pain and suffering (*Erlösung von Leiden bringen*). It is exactly at this point in the understanding and application of ethical behaviour that we can see a fundamental dichotomy between Schweitzer's ethic, on the one hand, and that of Brandt and many Nazi physicians, on the other. Schweitzer's understanding of delivering humans and other life forms from pain and suffering was substantially different from Brandt's. For Schweitzer, delivering humans and other species from suffering translated into medical care and cure, but it did not necessarily mean death. Nazi physicians, including Brandt, on the other hand, believed that delivering the patient from pain at all costs was the doctor's task, even if the patient lost his life as a result. Death became a core value in their overall belief system. The death of the weakling, the frail and incurably sick was believed to be of intrinsic value in relation to the greater good. Death not only 'delivered' them from suffering, but freed society from a financial, emotional and even aesthetic burden. A whole set of social problems – homosexuality, gypsies, Jews, crime, alcoholism, prostitution, the handicapped and so on – were transformed into surgical problems. Like 'surgeons of the Volk', as Karl Brandt stressed, Nazi physicians believed that they were 'cutting out' the 'infected' and 'unhealthy' elements of the social organism.[116] After the war, one Nazi doctor said that German physicians wanted to 'eliminate sickness by eliminating the sick'.[117]

In the world view of Brandt and other Nazi physicians, the murder of tens of thousands was a medical operation. At the same time, they genuinely believed that their actions could be justified on the basis of what they perceived as their noble motivation. In 1947, Brandt stated that the introduction of the 'euthanasia' programme had been 'dictated by purely human considerations'.[118] It was never intended to merely remove people from society but 'designed to free [the patient] from his suffering', he said.[119] 'Human beings who cannot help themselves, and whose tests show a life of suffering, are to be given aid', he said as he later defended his actions at Nuremberg. 'This consideration is not inhuman. I never felt that it was not ethical or was not moral.'[120] Whatever the relation between Schweitzer and Brandt might have been at the time, their understanding and application of ethical behaviour remained worlds apart.

It was an almost naive sense of charity that made Brandt want to become the 'assistant' of the man with a mission. He wanted to be the right hand of the great man. Perhaps he was hoping that the glory of the famous philanthropist would shine on him and provide him with a stepping stone for his professional ambitions. Perhaps it was the missionary appeal which attracted him to Schweitzer. Be that as it may, Brandt's decision to follow Schweitzer was an attempt to discover himself in an increasingly complex world that was shaped by economic and political instability. Other medical visionaries who followed Schweitzer to Africa had similar reasons for leaving the European continent behind in exchange for a simple life in the jungle, where their expertise was needed every day of the week. Schweitzer was surely aware of the romantic appeal of his hospital in Lambarene, a place which combined medical duty and notions of charity with a sense of adventure and untouched wilderness. In July 1928, for example, Schweitzer wrote to the Swiss-born Hans Stalder in Bordeaux, who was about to embark on his journey to Africa:

You will not recognise yourself when you return from Africa, where you will receive something from your independent work and from the experience of nature that Europe can never give you. What is wonderful about Africa is that every day one has the feeling of being absolutely necessary. In Europe, one can be replaced by someone else. In Africa, one is indispensable, indispensable among poor people – and you will come to like these people.[121]

Brandt seems to have established contact with Schweitzer some time during his medical studies, perhaps during his time in Bochum in the late 1920s. Although no correspondence between the two can be discovered,[122] scholars are able to draw upon a fair amount of circumstantial evidence as well as upon Brandt's recollections of the contact, which he recounted to members of the Nuremberg court in 1947. Given that Brandt was accused of orchestrating the murder of tens of thousands of patients in the 'euthanasia' programme during the war, there is, of course, a possibility that Brandt may have used Schweitzer as a convenient icon in order to present himself as an idealistic believer whose moral and ethical values were shaped by a deeply rooted respect for life, similar to that advocated in Schweitzer's teachings.

But Brandt's recollections have a certain ring of truth about them. According to Brandt, Schweitzer had agreed to send him to Lambarene, but the plan was ruined by political reality and by Brandt's national pride. Permission to immigrate into the Congo was apparently granted only under the condition that Brandt served in the French army, which might have meant that he would have had to acquire French citizenship. Both conditions were unacceptable for Brandt, given that his father had been a French prisoner of war. In November 1946, while imprisoned in Nuremberg, Brandt told one of his interrogators:

I can only say for myself that my medical studies grounded me in the natural sciences without turning me into an enemy of the Church. As far as this is concerned – this might perhaps be of importance – in 1932 I tried to go and join Professor Schweitzer in Lambarene after I had completed my surgical training. I had established contact with Schweitzer in 1932 and wanted to join him as a surgeon. This failed because I would have had to have French nationality and, furthermore, would have had to serve in the French army for two years before I could have gone there. That, of course, was not possible.[123]

A couple of months later, in February 1947, he told the Nuremberg court:

Brandt: During the period of my studies I had already made contact with a doctor known not only in Germany, but beyond the borders of this country, Albert Schweitzer. And I intended, trained as a surgeon, to assist him with his medical work in Lambarene, in the French Congo; when, in 1932, I was ready, it was no longer possible to carry out this plan, because it was required that I should serve in the French army, which probably would have meant having to adopt French citizenship.

Servatius [Brandt's defence lawyer]: So you dropped the plan?

Brandt: Yes, that was the reason why I abandoned that plan.

Servatius: So, one could say there was a national consideration.

Brandt: Yes.[124]

There is a possibility that Brandt might have met Schweitzer during one of his European lecture tours, especially those between 1927 and 1929 or during the one in 1932. Brandt might even have visited Schweitzer in Strasbourg or in his home in Günsbach. Brandt would surely have been aware of Schweitzer's achievements and popular appeal, given that Schweitzer's work was increasingly recognized in the arts and sciences and by the German public, not only in speeches and radio interviews, but, more importantly, through the Goethe prize which he received from the city of Frankfurt am Main in August 1928. In March 1932, Schweitzer also gave a much-publicized speech in commemoration of Goethe in Frankfurt am Main. It is also possible that the two men had only an oral agreement about Brandt's relocation to Africa after he had completed his studies. In 1972, one of Brandt's fellow students recalled:

> Karl Brandt had profound admiration for Professor Schweitzer's work – Schweitzer was also Alsatian. I know Brandt visited him several times while we were in Bochum. The professor's intelligence, dedication, and knowledge of science seemed to have an incredible influence on Karl, for he talked about him as if here was a man from whom he had everything to learn.[125]

There is a fair amount of evidence which suggests that Brandt was well qualified as one of Schweitzer's potential candidates. As mentioned earlier, both men had grown up in Alsace and had gone to school in the same town, Mülhausen, where Ludwig Schweitzer, half-brother of Schweitzer's grandfather, was the director of all primary schools. Even though Schweitzer had lived in Mülhausen some twenty years earlier than Brandt, it is almost certain that the schoolchildren of Mülhausen would have been familiar with the name of Schweitzer throughout, and after, the end of the First World War. Both men also shared a similar experience of the First World War and had witnessed the enormous destruction of towns and villages by the French army and the starvation of the Alsatian population, something that may have created a mutual bond. Indeed, in 1917, Schweitzer and his wife were imprisoned in a French prisoner of war camp, not unlike Brandt's father. During the planning phase for his hospital in Lambarene, it became apparent that Schweitzer needed well-qualified doctors who were fluent in French and loyal to Germany because many of his donors came from Germany, among them numerous German professors from the University of Strasbourg. Lambarene also seems to have been a place which attracted a fair number of Alsatians, among them missionaries, craftsmen and doctors. If we are to believe Brandt, the two men established contact in the late 1920s, between 1927 and 1929 perhaps, precisely at the time when Schweitzer needed to replace a number of doctors and nurses in Lambarene. In his autobiography 'My Life and Thoughts' (*Aus meinem Leben und Denken*), published in 1931, Schweitzer recalled: 'There was a lot of disquiet and work because I had to find a replacement for doctors and nurses in Lambarene, and send them off, because they could not cope with the climate or because I had to return home early because of family matters. I managed to recruit Dr Mündler, Dr Hediger, Dr Stalder and Dr Schnabel, all from Switzerland.'[126] When another Swiss doctor suddenly died from a heart attack in October 1929, Schweitzer replaced him with a doctor from Alsace, a Dr Meyländer. Brandt not only came from Alsace, was medically qualified and fluent in both German and French, but he was willing – after completing his medical studies at the Bergmannsheil hospital – to go to Africa and help the poor. It is therefore quite probable that Schweitzer might have considered Brandt a worthy candidate for his hospital in the early 1930s, and that the plan did not materialize for reasons which might lie in Brandt's nationalism and feelings of German patriotism.

If Brandt could not follow Schweitzer, he would follow another religious 'healer', someone who also had a mission to change the world into a better place. That man was Adolf Hitler. 'Schweitzer and Hitler were the two most influential figures in Brandt's life. They were his two role models, his two mirrors', according to one of Brandt's fellow students.[127] In 1947, Erwin Sutz, a clergyman and lifelong friend of Dietrich Bonhoeffer, the German theologian, who was killed for his opposition to the regime, submitted a petition on Brandt's behalf at the Doctors' Trial. Sutz became acquainted with Brandt in 1930 while he was hiking and climbing through the Swiss mountains, one of Brandt's passions.[128] Although Brandt did not share his Christian faith, Sutz felt a 'true and deep friendship' for Brandt, whom he described as the embodiment 'of the ethical, noble and desirable. I was convinced that he was one of those very rare humans one had to have great luck to meet on this earth.'[129] Sutz first realized that Brandt supported the Nazis after Hitler had become Reich Chancellor:

> When in May 1933, on the occasion of one of those rare meetings which we had in the course of the years, Dr Brandt explained to me his National Socialist faith, he did so with the conviction and enthusiasm of a true idealist. At that time Dr Brandt understood the slogan 'Common good comes before personal advantage' in its noblest of meanings and was glad that there was now a community of the rich and the poor which bridged all social classes. Having been under the influence of my revered teacher Professor Karl Barth, [I] received a different picture of National Socialism i.e. that of an anti-Christian and inhuman power; I sharply criticised it in my letters to Brandt on the occasion of the persecution of the churches and Jews. The latter could however not take up this subject, saw then only the good in National Socialism and could never confide to me his real attitude because we did not meet.[130]

Whether Brandt's move away from Schweitzer's Christian mission as a jungle doctor to Hitler's National Socialism signified his longing for authority, or, as someone with low self-esteem, his need for a father-figure, is perhaps best left to psychologists. But whatever the emotional and psychological reasons for Brandt's decision, the Nazi movement certainly appealed to those with subaltern mentalities, from romantics and neo-conservatives to believers in a mystical past and dreamers of a racially pure future. They could all find hope in the 'great German leader' who promised a people's community, a *Volksgemeinschaft*, in which class divisions and social injustices would be overcome. Why such very different men, Schweitzer and Hitler, appear to have played such pivotal roles in Brandt's life, can only be understood in the context of the political climate in Germany in the early 1930s.

During the economic depression, Hitler was hammering home to the masses an almost religious message, which resembled that of a missionary. Indeed, the Nazi movement as a whole, with its rituals and reverence of the leader destined to save the German people from national humiliation and political chaos, had all the key elements of a religious movement, and that appealed to Brandt and his generation.[131] Hitler's message was clear. Skilfully applying religious rhetoric, Hitler and his party created the image of the coming leader, the national redeemer, who would rescue Germany from sliding into chaos, throw off the shackles of Versailles, heal the wounds of inflation and lead the country to a prosperous future. Germany, Hitler's supporters argued, would once again be a country that was united and powerful. In a society in which moral fibre and confidence had been eroded by the military defeat of the First World War, and in which almost all classes and professions had been affected by the unemployment and political chaos that followed, the yearning for such an authority was magnified by visions of a social and racial utopia. Brandt eventually signed up to the Nazi cause, as did hundreds of thousands of young men and women of his age and social and educational background. He was clearly not exceptional nor unusual for his generation, nor were there any signs in his biography which would have suggested that he would become one of the leading personalities of the Third Reich.

VI. ADOLF HITLER

Whether Brandt became a follower of Hitler and the Nazi movement as early as 1926, or only from about the time when he entered the Nazi Party in 1932, cannot be clarified with certainty. By the mid-1930s, when hundreds of thousands of Germans were attempting to show their allegiance to the regime, Brandt claimed to have been a supporter of the Nazi movement as early as July 1926, apparently after he had witnessed Hitler during a party rally in Weimar.[132] The event had been of great significance for the Nazis. After years of infighting and political setbacks, the party displayed a new-found unity. It became well organized and based on a strict principle of leadership. A total of 8,000 attended the rally, including over 3,000 'stormtroopers' (*Sturmabteilung*, SA) and, for the first time, members of the SS. Every stormtrooper had to swear a personal oath of loyalty to Hitler, and, as a sign of establishing a new elite organization, the SS was handed the 'blood flag' from the 1923 putsch attempt. Designed for maximum propaganda effect, the rally left participants overflowing with emotions. Goebbels described its impact as 'deep and mystical. Almost like a gospel'.[133] After 1933, many Germans were only too eager to be seen as 'Old Comrades' and long-time followers of Hitler's movement. Whether Brandt attended the party rally by way of curiosity or genuine support remains unclear. He may have just been in Weimar to visit his ailing grandfather over the summer. After all, Brandt was scheduled to start work as a trainee doctor at Weimar city hospital in August 1926.[134] It is quite possible that he might have combined his duty with the opportunity to attend a grand spectacle.

To understand Brandt's political and ideological outlook, his *Weltanschauung*, and explain why he became a member of the Nazi Party, it is important to recall the socio-economic and political reality which Brandt experienced as a young adult after the First World War and during his time as an assistant doctor at the Bergmannsheil hospital in Bochum in the late 1920s. The economic hardship which many of his patients had to endure during the depression amplified his sense of injustice, made him antagonistic towards the existing democratic system of the Weimar Republic, and drew him closer to nationalistic and *völkisch* party politics. The need to safeguard the existence of the social community, the *Gemeinschaft*, and the biological life of the body politic, the *Volk*, became central to Brandt's thinking during these critically important, formative years. It was during this period that he joined the Nazi Party. When asked about his Nazi Party membership after the war, Brandt stressed that the decision had not been difficult, given that he came from a nationalist, anti-democratic family environment and supported a socialist political agenda during his time in Bochum. For Brandt, the social element, or as he called it at Nuremberg, the 'socialist' element, was an essential part in his political thinking:

> I was [an] assistant [doctor] at the time in the Ruhr region, and everyone who remembers these years will recall the hopeless situation which existed, the unemployment and misery. The prospect for the future was unclear. There were divisions and no sense of reliability, all of this stood in a demanding fashion in front of us in this land of the red earth. Because of my family context, and family acquaintances … I was close to the circle of Friedrich Naumann. Given this context, it was not a difficult decision for me to join the Party.[135]

Brandt acknowledged that his nationalist upbringing and socialization, together with his belief in social and economic justice, had attracted him to political movements which advocated a 'national' or 'German' socialism. Through family connections, he had become acquainted with the circle of largely Protestant reformers around the liberal pastor, Friedrich Naumann, who in the 1890s had founded a 'National-Social Association'. Naumann's aim was to free industrial workers from the Marxist idea of an ongoing class struggle, and turn them into the pillars of a new national community.[136] In May 1896, he declared: 'As politicians we are national socialists and as Christians we are searching for an evangelism which is true and alive …'[137] Naumann's attempt to establish a German socialism, however, had failed shortly after the turn of the century. After the First World War, the concept of a German national socialism became associated with the extreme right-wing and anti-Semitic politics of the *völkisch* movement. Brandt may not necessarily have been a great supporter and believer in a political party which pursued an extremely anti-liberal, anti-Semitic and *völkisch* political agenda during the Weimar Republic but, given his social and educational background, it comes as no surprise that he would have been attracted by a quasi-religious, political movement which claimed to reconcile nationalism with socialism.

Brandt's relationship with the Naumann circle also highlights some of the central factors in his becoming a devoted follower of the Nazi movement. It explains why he focused upon and searched for a quasi-religious leader, a *Führer*, rather than a party political programme and, last but not least, why he supported the concept of charismatic leadership as a means of exercising power from above and receiving 'ascribed' power from below. As numerous studies have articulated, 'charisma' is central to understanding the dynamics of quasi-religious movements such as National Socialism, but it also applies to the inner workings of the Naumann circle. His circle developed its strength from a milieu which revolved around the religious and political charisma of Naumann and other loyal personalities. Charisma served as the integrating factor. It connected Naumann and his inner circle with the expectations and projected beliefs of his followers and established the idea of a 'mission' among them in times of crisis. It enabled the leader to promise his followers that he would 'deliver' them from all feelings of insecurity and inaction. At the same time, the followers could see themselves as the 'chosen ones' by redefining their own position, which is characterized by a sense of inferiority and submissiveness.[138] In short, Brandt first learnt to 'follow' a charismatic leader in the social political milieu of the Naumann circle. It was here that he discovered that his status could be enhanced through submission, obedience and loyalty, and where he saw, perhaps for the first time, how religious charisma was transformed into political charisma. Brandt's early exposure to the dynamics of a quasi-religious movement may explain his tendency to follow different kinds of leaders throughout his life. His shift from following Naumann in the 1910s, to following Schweitzer in the 1920s, to following Hitler in the 1930s, was probably less radical or surprising than it may seem. Indeed, the principles which governed the cohesion of the group and the relationship between the leader and his followers were rather similar. From early on, Brandt was on the lookout for a strong personality whom he would want to follow with total obedience and loyalty. By 1933, and in the years before, he was easy prey for all kinds of religious missionaries and political reformers who promised national salvation and social justice. If Brandt had not followed Hitler and the Nazi movement, he would surely have followed another political missionary.

Brandt joined the Nazi Party in February 1932, and the SA in February 1933.[139] In 1933, he also took over responsibility in the matter of gas warfare and of air raids in the SA in Westphalia and, as such, became the director of the regional group of the Reich Anti-Aircraft Federation (*Reichsluftschutzbund*, RLB) in Bochum. Brandt probably met Hitler for the first time in the summer of 1932 in Essen.[140] It is possible that he was wavering for some time at the beginning of the 1930s as to whether or not he should actively support the Nazis. Brandt does not seem to have been fully convinced that the Nazis were the party which would help him to advance his career. In fact, he was concerned that any support for the Nazis, if given too prematurely or in public, might damage his work as a doctor. In February 1932, when he applied to become a member of the National Socialist German Doctors' Association (*Nationalsozialistischer Deutscher Ärztebund*, NSDÄB), he asked that his name should not be published on a register of known Nazi doctors. He wanted to preserve a 'politically neutral stance *vis-à-vis* the outside [world]', as he called it, whilst positioning himself in case the Nazis came to power. At the same time, he agreed to serve as a medical doctor for the SA and SS formations, and become actively involved in the work of the Association. In particular, he volunteered to give talks about organizational matters and accident insurance issues.[141] However, when asked about his involvement in the organization in 1947, Brandt stated that he had insisted in writing that he would not serve on active duty in any of the SA and SS formations, because as a doctor he did not want to give the patient the impression that he was in fact a politician who was pursuing a 'misleading political agenda'.[142] Brandt's selective memory on this occasion was probably designed to portray himself as an ethical physician for whom the interests of the patient ranked more highly than national politics, and to distance himself from the Nazi regime.

Brandt only became a party member after he had met Anna Rehborn, his future wife, who seems to have been in contact with Hitler and his movement for some years. According to a story circulating at the time, Anna Rehborn had injured her nose and forehead on a sharp rock while diving. She was brought to the Bergmannsheil hospital, where Karl Brandt attended to her injuries, and they fell in love.[143] The narrative has a romantic appeal: a couple brought together by a fateful accident, their lives choreographed by providence. But scepticism remains, given that 'accidents' and chance apparently played a dominant role in Brandt's personal and professional life, and indeed in that of many leading Nazis as well. We do not know when and how Brandt met his future wife, but it is almost certain that they met in Bochum, probably at the end of the 1920s.

Anna Rehborn was one of Germany's finest backstroke swimming champions in the mid-1920s, and later became a swimming instructor. This is perhaps not altogether surprising, given that she was the daughter of the swimming pool attendant (*Bademeister*) Julius Rehborn, himself the son of a baker,[144] and his wife Anna Rehborn, née Voss. Both were of Protestant faith and were born in Elberfeld, Julius in June 1869 and Anna in June 1872. In March 1899 the family moved to 24 Vogteistraße in Langenberg, Rhineland, where in December 1899 their son Karl Julius was born. Five years later, on 25 August 1904, Anna Rehborn was born in the same village. But the family did not stay for long. Little more than a year later, in January 1906, the Rehborns moved to Bochum, where Julius Rehborn took over the management and administration of the swimming pool of the city of Bochum.[145] His official title was *Badeverwalter* (swimming pool administrator) and *Inspektor* (supervisor).

Together with his wife Anna, who was in charge of the swimming pool for women until 1919, Julius Rehborn lived with his children Julius, Anna, and then, born in November 1907, Johanna, in a flat at 13 Marienstraße, in the building adjacent to the city's swimming pool. For more than twenty-five years, until his retirement in April 1934, he served as the *Badeverwalter* of the pool. But Julius also had political ambitions. In August 1932, he became a member of the Nazi Party. A couple of years later, in 1936, he was listed as a supportive member of the SS and, in 1942, he became deputy block leader, or *Blockwart*, of the district. Brandt married into a family environment in which the role of physical health and beauty figured quite prominently, something that obviously appealed to him, and which supported the Nazi regime.

The two sisters, Anni and Hanni, as they were called, were members of the swimming club *Blau-Weiß*. Anna, in particular, had a meteoric career as one of Germany's best freestyle and backstroke swimmers. In 1923 and 1924 she became the German champion in the 100-metre freestyle swimming and in the 100-metre backstroke. Between 1925 and 1928 she won four further titles in backstroke, eight championship titles and broke seven German records. In 1926 she also won the title for the 200-metre backstroke, and in 1928 Anna and her sister Johanna took part in the Olympic Games in Amsterdam. Their elder brother Julius, called Jülle, was a professional high jumper and one of three German athletes who participated in the 1928 Games in Amsterdam. In short, the entire family was present during the Olympic Games in the Netherlands.

Given the publicity surrounding the Rehborn family, with photographs of Anni and her siblings appearing in weekly magazines, it is perhaps not surprising that the family attracted the attention of Hitler and his advisers. For some, she was more than just a sport celebrity and represented simplicity, humour and courage.[146] According to Karl-Adolf Brandt, Brandt's son, contact between Anna Rehborn and Hitler was established after Hitler, whilst imprisoned at Landsberg, congratulated her on one of her swimming victories. There seems to be no evidence to corroborate the story, however plausible it may be. Apparently, Brandt and Anni Rehborn met Hitler for the first time through a Bochum-based family by the name of Gröppel, and were subsequently invited to spend time with Hitler in the mountains of the Obersalzberg. Others, such as Henriette von Schirach, the daughter of Hitler's official photographer, Heinrich Hoffmann, and wife of the Reich Youth Leader, Baldur von Schirach, recalled that Hitler had seen a photograph of Anni Rehborn during one of his visits to Hoffmann's photo atelier. The photograph showed her dressed in the black swimming costume of the German national swimming team, and Hitler is said to have remarked: 'This face could originate from one of the temple friezes of Olympia.'[147] He then apparently asked Hoffmann to invite Anni Rehborn to spend a weekend on the Obersalzberg, where she and Karl Brandt were introduced to Hitler's inner circle. Given that she was not a witness to these conversations, Schirach's account needs to be treated with caution. Some of it may have been little more than second-hand gossip. What seems to be certain, though, is that Anni was one of those women whom Hitler welcomed into his presence, especially during times of relaxation. In a photograph of 1933 or 1934, we see Anni Brandt, Hitler, Eva Braun and Johanna Wolf, one of his secretaries, sitting together in a pub garden at a table.[148] Anni, like her fiancé, became a Nazi Party member in the early 1930s and was given the party number 1264305.

Brandt's relationship with the Nazi movement was shaped as much by tactical as by opportunistic moves, but after January 1933 the decision was easy. He swiftly signed up to the SA, joining the ranks of tens of thousands of so-called *Märzgefallene* who turned with the tide after Hitler had been appointed Reich Chancellor. His conversion from a passionate follower of Schweitzer to a passionate supporter of the Nazi movement was complete. Now he only needed to meet the man whom he wanted to serve with total devotion. For more than ten years Brandt was to serve Hitler, whose style of leadership, rather than reflecting the need for effective governance in a powerful, militarized, modern nation state, in fact resembled that of a feudal monarch surrounded by loyal servants.

3

Becoming Hitler's Doctor

I. BRANDT ARRIVES

On 15 August 1933, while Hitler was spending a brief holiday at the Berghof, his adjutant Wilhelm Brückner, travelling behind Hitler, lost control of his car and drove into a ditch. Coming from Berchtesgaden, the entourage was on its way back to the Berghof when the accident happened near Reit im Winkel. Brückner suffered multiple serious injuries, including a fractured skull, a broken leg and an eye injury. Hitler's half-sister, Angela Raubal, and her two female friends only suffered minor injuries directly to their faces.[1] The car behind Brückner was driven by a young surgeon: Karl Brandt. His fiancée, Anni Rehborn, had been personally acquainted with Hitler since the mid-1920s.[2] They were on holiday near Berchtesgarden, and spent their time in close proximity to the newly elected Chancellor, as many Germans had chosen to do in that year.[3] They had been invited to lunch with Hitler and his party at a hotel in Berchtesgaden when the accident occurred. Brandt immediately provided first aid and drove Brückner and one of the women to the nearest hospital in Traunstein. Clearly excited by their visitors, the hospital staff readily assisted Brandt while he operated on Brückner's fractured skull and removed one of his badly injured eyes.[4] Sacrificing his holidays, and neglecting his professional duties, Brandt spent the next six weeks at Brückner's bedside until his condition had clearly improved.[5] After the war, Brandt assigned an air of destiny to the incident, mystifying the circumstances which had brought him to Hitler's attention.

The incident proved to be a watershed in Brandt's life. After Brückner had recovered, Brandt returned first to Bochum and later, in November, to Berlin, where he was due to take up a position as an assistant to the traumatologist, Georg Magnus (1883–1942), at the surgical clinic in Berlin-Ziegelstrasse. Without taking the views of the medical faculty into consideration, the Prussian Ministry of Culture had appointed Magnus as the successor to the famous surgeon August Bier, based in Berlin.[6] Given that Magnus and his assistants were known supporters of the Nazis, it is likely that his appointment to Berlin in November 1933 was politically motivated. Apart from three of his former assistants, Brandt, Rostock and Hanskarl von Hasselbach (1903–1981), Magnus took Werner Haase (1900–1947), whom he knew from Jena, as an assistant to Berlin. Hitler later appointed Magnus a member of the academic senate of the Army Sanitary Inspectorate. When his mentor died in December 1942, Brandt attended the funeral as a representative of the regime and a friend of the family. One of Hoffmann's photographs shows Brandt walking with Magnus' widow behind the coffin, which was buried with full military honours.[7]

Brandt must have known that the move to Berlin opened up new career prospects, bearing in mind that the regime had stated its objective to remove Jews, socialists and communists from their academic positions. It is inconceivable that Brandt did not understand the profound implications for the German academic community of the nationwide boycott of Jewish businesses, of doctors and other professionals. Further discriminatory measures such as the introduction of the 'Law for the Restoration of the Professional Civil Service' of 7 April 1933, which dismissed all political opponents and 'non-Aryans', had been publicly announced. Only those who had fought in the First World War were exempt from the law. Jews were barred from entering the legal profession, Jewish physicians were prohibited from treating patients covered by the national insurance scheme, and the number of Jewish schoolchildren permitted in schools was limited. The months following the Nazi takeover of power saw the Jewish community exposed to routine discrimination and savage violence, measures which affected all aspects of life, including notably the medical profession and the health care system. Brandt's willingness to spend his holiday in the summer of 1933 in the vicinity of the party leader responsible for such state-sponsored violence might be seen as an indication of Brandt's overall support for such radical measures in times of national upheaval. The dismissal, expulsion, or even suicide, of Jewish colleagues at the surgical clinic in Berlin, and throughout the medical profession, can hardly have escaped his notice.[8]

Even assuming that Brandt did not approve of such outright injustice being done to fellow colleagues, there is no sign that he voiced any objection or opposition to the new regime. On the contrary, friends and colleagues described his mood after the encounter with Hitler as upbeat and positive, and he threw himself into a frenzy of research work. And there was more good news. By the end of March 1934, he had married Anni Rehborn, and knew that he would be promoted to senior physician (*Oberarzt*) a fortnight later.[9] Among the guests attending the wedding ceremony were Heinrich Hoffmann and his wife, Wilhelm Brückner, Hermann Göring and, as the guest of honour, Hitler himself.[10] A black and white photograph of the ceremony, which incidentally took place in Göring's flat in Berlin, shows the tall, dark-haired Brandt, dressed in a tailcoat, arm in arm with his bride, Anni, in her long white wedding-dress. Just behind Brandt stands Brückner and, further to the left, Göring in full *Reichsmarschall* uniform with white-striped trousers, his right hand hidden in his pocket, his left hand positioned imposingly on his hip. On the right, close to Anni, but separated from her by a certain physical distance, stands Hitler, dressed in a greyish jacket, stiff and statesman-like, his hands folded in front of his body. Brandt probably knew that his encounter with Hitler could signal a breakthrough in his professional career.

Brandt's prompt medical intervention following the motoring accident may also have made an impression on Hitler, who was notoriously anxious about his own personal health and safety. With tensions growing amongst the party faithful, some of whom were waiting to 'cash in' their previous support for rewards and influence, Hitler was looking for young and loyal servants as his political and personal advisers. He needed young and experienced men to place between himself and the hotheads in the party, and to pursue his ambitious plans for the future of Germany. The young and level-headed architect, Albert Speer, soon became one of his closest personal advisers, and Brandt became another.[11]

After Brückner's accident, the possibility of having a doctor in attendance, who would accompany Hitler on all his national and international travels, was discussed. Hitler was receptive to the idea and is reported to have said: 'Let's take one more, it doesn't matter whether we are twenty-one or twenty-two.'[12] A decision as to who that person would be was delayed until the day before Hitler was to travel to Venice to meet the Italian dictator, Mussolini. While travel plans were being finalized, the question came up as to who would be able to provide the medical care in case of an assassination attempt. Brückner proposed Brandt. Brandt was medically trained and highly motivated, and he was absolutely loyal to Hitler – probably the most important criterion for Hitler, amongst several, in deciding on his personal appointments.

Questioned about the incident by members of the US Strategic Bombing Survey in one of his first interviews after the war, Brandt recalled that he had not heard from Hitler for months. Then, without warning, he received a telephone call from Brückner on or around 13 June 1934, requesting him to come immediately to Munich to accompany the Führer on his trip to Italy as his 'escort physician' (*Begleitarzt*).[13] From what we know about how the administrative machinery around Hitler functioned, and how decisions were often made at extremely short notice, Brandt's recollection seems plausible. After his return from Italy it was decided that, in future, Brandt would accompany Hitler whenever and wherever he travelled. Like all of Hitler's personal staff he was subordinate and responsible to Hitler directly and to no one else; this put Brandt in a privileged position from the moment of his appointment.[14] Speaking to one of his interrogators at Nuremberg, Brandt attempted to downplay his role in Hitler's court:

> From 1934, I was the escort physician of the Führer, as it was called; that meant that if he was away from Berlin, when he was travelling, doctors should accompany him. There were mostly three to four cars, also planes. If something happened, for example a car accident, a surgeon had to be there and so I was just there. Later I was in Munich ... often I just travelled only to Munich and then back to Berlin.[15]

Trying to cloud the issue, Brandt relayed only part of the truth to the Allies in 1945. His position in the Nazi regime certainly involved considerably more responsibility than 'just being there': it included a substantial degree of political power. His connection with Hitler was also more personal and frequent in the period before the incident. The accident which helped Brandt to become a member of Hitler's court was less accidental than it may seem. Indeed, Brandt had waited for the right moment to attract the attention of the Führer. By the time of the accident, Brandt knew full well that his fiancée could provide the key to Hitler's court. In 1925, Hitler's first chauffeur, Emil Maurice, while serving a prison sentence with his master at Landsberg, had seen a photograph of Anni Rehborn on the title page of the *Berliner Illustrierte*, after she had won the national swimming championship. He had begun a regular correspondence with her. Later, after his release from prison, Maurice had invited her to drinks and parties in Munich or to the Berghof, aware that Hitler enjoyed the company of beautiful young women. Anni probably met Hitler for the first time around 1927 or 1928.[16] On one of these occasions, probably at the beginning of the 1930s,[17] Anni introduced her new fiancé, Brandt, to Hitler. It was, therefore, through Anni that Brandt first made contact with the inner circle of the Nazi regime, some time before the actual car accident occurred.[18] After the accident, Brandt attempted to draw attention to himself, in case Hitler suddenly needed a personal physician. Brandt applied for membership of the SS on 30 April 1934, almost three months *before* his first assignment as Hitler's escort physician.[19] He knew that all bodyguards and drivers in Hitler's entourage had to be members of the SS. It appears that Brandt expected to become, or at least anticipated the possibility of becoming, Hitler's doctor.[20]

II. LIFE ON THE BERGHOF

Since the late nineteenth century, the Obersalzberg region had been a place much loved by holidaymakers and health enthusiasts; farming was hardly sustainable in an area where the ground was covered in snow for five months of the year. The existing infrastructure was primitive and only remotely connected to the railway system in Berchtesgaden. This changed after Hitler became Reich Chancellor. A regular bus service was introduced which then operated throughout the year. In October 1934, the government airport Reichenhall-Berchtesgaden was opened in Ainring, where large passenger planes could land. Based on Hitler's own architectural designs, Haus Wachenfeld disappeared in a series of extensions in what became the Berghof. 'It wasn't good, but it wasn't bad either' was how Speer felt about the design.[21] In July 1936, the Berghof was officially opened. The female designer, Gerdy Troost from Munich, wife of the architect Paul Ludwig Troost, who had rebuilt the Reich Chancellor's apartment in Berlin, created the interior design. The Berghof represented an oversized image of an alpine house. It had more than thirty rooms to make sure that Hitler's adjutants and guests could accommodate their wives and to prevent unwanted intermingling between party and state officials; the large conference room, called the 'hall', had a huge retractable window from where the dictator could watch the magnificent panorama of the nearby mountains.

The Berghof was a self-contained world. Hitler wanted to turn the whole of the Obersalzberg region into his power base. Martin Bormann, Hitler's financial administrator and later private secretary, was assigned the task of remodelling the area. House owners had to sell their houses to the party; those attempting to resist faced intimidation and repression and, in some cases, imprisonment in a concentration camp. When the owner of the hotel, 'The Turk' (*Zum Türken*), Karl Schuster, got into an argument with a gang of drunken Nazis, he was arrested and his hotel was closed. Although he sold the house, rumours that he had been imprisoned by the regime continued to spread far and wide in the region. In January 1934, the *Berchtesgadener Anzeiger* finally printed an advertisement from the local Nazi Party, warning its readers that the distributors of such rumours would be seen as 'enemies of the state'. Consequently, 'these pests would have to be brought into Dachau concentration camp'.[22] There was nothing secret or clandestine about the draconian measures of the new regime: it was obvious to anyone reading the papers.

Once Bormann had seized a property, it was generally destroyed to make way for new ones. About fifty farms and buildings were demolished with great speed in order to spare Hitler the ugly sight of the demolitions, as Bormann explained in 1941.[23] The Obersalzberg became one enormous construction site. Up to 6,000 foreign, and probably also slave, labourers were employed at any one time. Security became tight. Hitler was paranoid about assassination attempts. Part of the SS-Leibstandarte and Department I of the Security Service (*Sicherheitsdienst*, SD) looked after Hitler's personal safety in this top-security compound, with armed guards and flak batteries stationed all around the mountains, and constant checks were made on those who arrived and left the Berghof. These applied to everyone. When Margarete, Albert Speer's wife, once returned from a trip to Munich with Eva Braun, Hitler's mistress, and realized that she had forgotten her identity card, she was permitted into the compound only after the Security Service had been consulted.[24]

Around the Berghof, a three-kilometre fence was erected. Another fourteen-kilometre fence surrounded the entire area, which measured more than seven square kilometres. Finally, the entire region, including the city and county of Salzburg, the Thalgau, Hallein and Golling in the south, Reichenhall in the west, Wolfgangsee in the east, and Seekirchen and Freilassing in the north, was declared out of bounds for ordinary citizens and classified as 'Protective Führer Region' (*Führerschutzgebiet*).[25] For the Security Service, the office in charge of Hitler's personal safety, the entire region constituted a security risk; anyone living in the Obersalzberg area was a potential assassin. Those with a communist past had to fear the worst. By 1938, for example, a Jewish entrepreneur named Kral from Hallein was investigated for allegedly 'supporting' the communist party in the past. For Himmler this was sufficient reason for imprisonment. 'For security reasons,' he ordered, 'Kral and his family are to be arrested during every one of Hitler's visits.'[26] Anyone caught stealing at the Berghof was dealt with by the highest police authorities. When it transpired that one of Hitler's maids had stolen goods from some of the guests, Himmler personally ordered SS-Obergruppenführer Ernst Kaltenbrunner, head of the much-feared Gestapo, to punish the woman with a dozen blows from a stick, to be carried out by 'particularly discreet men of the Reich Security Service'.[27] Any publicity or legal proceedings was to be avoided at all costs. Around the Obersalzberg region, the right of freedom of movement and individual autonomy had ceased to exist; 'protective custody' and physical violence had become the arbitrary tools to disseminate fear and political oppression nationwide.

Shortly after Hitler had become Reich Chancellor, the peaceful atmosphere at the Obersalzberg came to an end. Thousands of well-wishers and Nazi supporters wanted to see their idol, the man of the people, who had promised to eradicate mass unemployment and overcome the shackles of Versailles. Spontaneous, unorganized mass rallies were snaking up the narrow mountain road – supporters wishing to see the Führer with their own eyes. They waited for hours, sometimes days, until Hitler would briefly appear by the entrance of his house. Visiting the Obersalzberg in the summer of 1933, as Brandt had done with his wife, became the obvious pilgrimage for thousands of people supporting National Socialism and, of course, for those going with the times, the *Märzgefallenen* (turncoats after the March election). For the residents of the Obersalzberg region, life was totally transformed: suddenly there were 'swarms of people … coming, by train, bus, car, to tramp up the mountain and stand as close to Hitler's house as they could get, chanting rhythmically, "We want to see our Führer!" until he came out. And then they would scream, applaud, sob, laugh hysterically, even fall to their knees.'[28] By July 1933, the authorities had banned all kinds of unorganized mass pilgrimages and semi-religious chanting along the mountain road. The levels of adoration had reached worrying proportions. Himmler, as chief of the Bavarian political police, also banned the use of binoculars in the region after it had been reported that holidaymakers were monitoring every move of the Reich Chancellor from afar.[29]

Like Brandt, many people hoped that the Führer would cast his eye on them, and invite them into the inner sanctum of his court. One such incident occurred in the summer of 1933 when Hitler spotted a blonde girl from Munich in the crowd. Her name was Bernile. When it turned out that Hitler and the girl had the same birthday, regular visits and correspondence between the two ensued. Photographs of Hitler and Bernile, taken by Hitler's official photographer, Heinrich Hoffmann, became the best-marketed images of the Führer with children. It was a propaganda strategy to portray himself as the man caring for the nation's children and its future. Although the secret police found out that Bernile's grandmother was a Jew, Hitler continued to use the images as powerful propaganda material up until 1938, when the adjutant office of the Führer stopped further visits of Bernile to the Berghof, for fear they could lead to public embarrassment. The distribution of the photographs was discontinued through the head of the Chancellery of the Führer, Philipp Bouhler, who, with Brandt, was later put in charge of the 'euthanasia' programme, the killing of handicapped infants and adults.

Images of Hitler with children were frequently exploited by the Nazi propaganda machine and distributed as postcards, on stamps and in cigarette albums.[30] In one of the earliest photographs in which Brandt can be seen together with Hitler, taken around 1933, a smiling new Reich Chancellor, dressed in his beige-coloured trench coat, is shaking the hand of a small girl. The caption reads: 'Youth congratulates the Führer.'[31] Right behind Hitler, a number of Nazi functionaries are looking on, including members of the SA and the SS, and a young man carrying a portable camera in his right hand: Karl Brandt. Dressed in an ordinary suit, he stands upright and smiles proudly. In another photo, shot in August 1935 during the opening festivities of the Adolf Hitler Koog in Schleswig-Holstein, North Germany, we see Brandt looking on while Hitler talks to two blonde German girls.[32] From the beginning, Brandt became part of the propaganda image of the Third Reich.

This was especially apparent in those images which pictured Hitler's daily life. In one of Hofmann's cleverly constructed images of the Führer as a modest man of the people, we see Hitler having supper with Brandt, Brückner, Erna Hoffmann and Sophie Stork. The picture was taken by Hoffmann on 15 January 1935 at Haus Wachenfeld during one of Hitler's holidays. Reminiscent of early modern paintings of peasants and their families, the image conveys a sense of intimacy. Given the enormous publicity surrounding the Obersalzberg, the viewer is introduced into a space which is public and private at the same time, but also removed and detached from ordinary German citizens. The context appears to be one of family and friends, who are having a well-earned meal after a long day in the field. We see Brandt, slightly out of focus, helping everyone to fill their bowl with *Eintopf*, a rustic German stew made of potatoes, sausages and cabbage. Hitler, sitting by the window on the right and opposite Brandt, seems to be handing bread to the group. He is the central focus of the picture. All attention is directed towards him. He is the host, the first among equals. Through a window behind him, light floods into the small, alpine room, and shines onto the table where the bread is broken. The careful composition and ambience gives the picture its quasi-religious message: Hitler, the man chosen by providence, has gathered a group of followers around a table for the evening meal, a brief interlude in his and his followers' mission. Indeed, those belonging to Hitler's intimate circle, like Brandt and Speer, were often referred to as his 'apostles' while he was called 'the saviour' of the German people.[33]

The Nazis knew that the Obersalzberg had excellent propaganda potential. What had started with sudden and unorganized expressions of support for Hitler was increasingly controlled and monitored by the party. Groups of Hitler Youth (*Hitler Jugend*, HJ), the League of German Girls (*Bund Deutscher Mädel*, BDM), representatives of the SA and the SS and other Nazi organizations regularly marched past the Berghof. The Obersalzberg scenery allowed Hitler to represent himself as the 'People's Chancellor' (*Volkskanzler*), who was totally committed to the concerns of the people and the nation. Images of Hitler at the Berghof showed him in a private, modest capacity, caring for children and animals in what appeared to be a life in harmony with nature. Photography and film conveyed the message of Hitler as the man rooted in the German romantic tradition, studious and simple, who was leading an ordinary and abstemious life with colleagues, friends and, of course, with his German Shepherd. The marketing of these images reached enormous proportions. In books and magazines, and through the sale of souvenirs, the Nazis presented themselves as a people's movement, with a leader who had risen from the people for the people. Hoffmann's photo books 'The Hitler no one Knows' (*Hitler, wie ihn keiner kennt*, 1932), 'Hitler in his Mountains' (*Hitler in seinen Bergen*, 1935) and 'Hitler away from Everyday Life' (*Hitler abseits vom Alltag*, 1937) were best-sellers.[34] The Munich-based film company, Arnold & Richter, even proposed shooting a documentary film entitled 'Visit to the Führer on the Obersalzberg' (*Besuch beim Führer auf dem Obersalzberg*).[35] Combining political propaganda with product marketing, cigarette companies used the Führer cult to boost their sales by including cards with images of the 'life of the Führer' in cigarette packets.[36] The collection of cigarette cards was one of the most popular hobbies among adolescents. From being a haven for ramblers, holidaymakers and mountaineers, the Obersalzberg was transformed into an orchestrated propaganda platform from which a popular and sanitized image of Hitler and the regime was propagated. It had little or nothing to do with reality.

III. SETTING UP RESIDENCE

Hitler's courtiers were composed of three main groups.[37] The 'outer circle' was made up of the regional party leaders, the *Gauleiter*, and other government officials, who in peacetime often attended lunches at the Reich Chancellery.[38] Their primary point of contact to gain access to the Führer was either Bormann, for the party bosses, or Heinrich Lammers, head of the Reich Chancellery, for all other government ministers. Then there was an 'intermediate group' of courtiers, consisting of individuals of major political influence such as Göring, Goebbels and Himmler. Their enormous power base allowed them direct access to Hitler at almost all times. Finally, there was Hitler's 'family', his 'innermost circle', those specially selected individuals who permanently attended the Führer on his journeys inside Germany and abroad: men like Brandt, who kept him company during the hour-long film screenings and nightly tea parties at the Berghof, who stayed with him at the various field headquarters during the war, and who accompanied Hitler on his special train 'America'. Ernst (Putzi) Hanfstaengl, a German-American art publisher, once called them Hitler's 'chauffeureska'.

Membership of this intimate circle of flatterers and servants was based on a number of factors, foremost of which was that each of the members of the court met a particular personal need of Hitler's, such as his need for a doctor in case of a medical emergency. The second precondition was that Hitler needed to feel at ease with the person, and to be sure of his or her loyalty. All these factors made his relations with his personal staff relatively stable. While close proximity to Hitler could be important in wielding essential political power, it was insufficient in itself. Unless the individual courtier could establish some form of *Hausmacht* (claim and responsibility for a department or area of government), he or she was excluded from any kind of power. In fact, most members of the intimate circle had little or no power. However, those on the fringes of the court, such as Goebbels or Himmler, wielded extensive political power because of their essential role in the regime. Hitler surrounded himself with men and women who did not question or argue over what he said and why he said it. This meant, in general, that he enjoyed the company of amateurs and novices, never of intellectuals, whom he distrusted, or civil servants, whom he loathed. He was looking for people who affirmed his radical political views, did not question his inflated self-image, and were ready to join him in his bid for world domination.

Hitler often discussed important matters only with those in his inner circle, with 'old comrades' and cronies, some of whom were key in gaining access to the Führer.

But who were those people to whom Brandt was introduced in the early 1930s? First there were his personal adjutants and servants: Fritz Wiedemann, chief adjutant from 1935 to 1939, had been Hitler's superior in the First World War. Ironically, he had not recommended Hitler for promotion because of 'lack of leadership qualities'. Brandt sometimes discussed Hitler's health and other medical matters with Wiedemann and once told him that Hitler, who had just starved himself of 40 pounds and was suffering from some of the consequences, was perfectly well but needed to lead a more balanced life and eat more healthy food.[39]

Then there were his two adjutants, Wilhelm Brückner, head of the Munich SA during the putsch in 1923, and Julius Schaub, another figure from Hitler's time as a beerhall agitator. Both Brückner and Schaub were tall, ignorant, not particularly bright, and totally loyal to their master, the kind of characters who provided a perfect sounding-board for Hitler's never-ceasing monologues. Allied interrogators regarded Schaub as 'a pretty stupid individual, who was not entrusted with any important assignments'.[40] Yet these men were absolutely crucial to anyone wanting to gain access to the chambers of the Führer. Whenever Winifred Wagner, for instance, wanted to get in contact with Hitler, she would do so through Hitler's adjutants rather than through Bormann, who wanted to control access to Hitler. Another way of getting messages to Hitler was through Brandt. Since Winifred's intimate and long-standing contact with Hitler was public knowledge, her large circle of friends tried to use this channel when they or their friends were in difficulties. Numerous petitions on behalf of Jews and other people oppressed by the regime reached Brandt, who forwarded them to Hitler.[41] Brandt could hardly claim that he was not aware of what was happening in Germany.

On other occasions, Hitler's adjutants first discussed a matter with Brandt before forwarding the relevant paperwork to one of the government agencies. In some cases, they would ask Brandt to become involved and examine a matter of concern. This was especially the case where informal petitions were submitted to Hitler directly, for instance where people petitioned on behalf of their family and friends. In the spring of 1935, for example, the wife of a medical doctor, Klease Dierks of Jena, visited Wiedemann in Berlin to petition on behalf of her husband, whose application for Nazi Party membership had been rejected. After consulting Brandt, who 'had gained the impression that the case of Dr Dierks deserves to be looked at in greater detail', Wiedemann requested an explanation from the office of the deputy of the Führer as to why Dr Dierks was not permitted to join the Nazi Party. The case illustrates that Brandt, from early on, was able to influence decisions that were in one way or another related to medicine, and function as a kind of gatekeeper for the flow of information to and from the centre of power.

Other members of Hitler's entourage included Julius Schreck, his long-time chauffeur, who was allowed extensive liberties when talking to Hitler in the car; Heinrich Hoffmann, his official photographer and intimate from early Munich days; Sepp Dietrich, head of the SS bodyguard; Hans Baur, his personal pilot; and Otto Dietrich, his Press Chief. All these people enjoyed privileges and status because of their close relationship to Hitler. Then there were Hitler's secretaries who were both observers and actors at court. Like Brandt, they accompanied Hitler on his journeys and witnessed the unfolding of major historical events first hand. Before key speeches, the secretaries would wait for hours and hours until the dictator had talked himself into a frenzy whilst racing up and down the room, then suddenly, as inspiration seemed to strike the genius, one of them would be called in and take notes from Hitler at frantic speed. But the secretaries were also part of Hitler's intimate circle, which permitted them to socialize with other guests at the Berghof. This dual function enabled some of them to gain considerable insight into the psychology of the Führer, and influence him, if they chose to do so. Others enjoyed the freedom to express their views on all sorts of public and political matters. The eldest of the secretaries, and in many respects the most experienced, was Johanna Wolf, former secretary to the *völkisch* writer, Dietrich Eckart. Her position at the centre of decision-making in Germany did not change Wolf. She led a modest life, spending all her spare time caring for her eighty-year-old mother or mediating between conflicting parties at the Berghof in a quiet and unobtrusive manner. Then there were Christa Schröder, Gerda Daranowski and Traudl Humps.[42] Brandt described Schröder as an intelligent and persistent character who never hesitated to express her views, even when these stood in contrast to Hitler's. Sometimes this would lead to tension, as Hitler could hardly bear anyone disagreeing with his sense of mission. When Schröder objected to Hitler attacking young soldiers for smoking, she was ignored for several weeks. Yet Schröder also organized Hitler's periods of relaxation at the Berghof: on one occasion she supplied him with twenty-two folders of photographs of artwork 'rescued' – for this read 'confiscated' – from occupied France, to entertain him during his regular tea break.[43] One who certainly would never disagree with Hitler was Gerda Daranowski: with her servility and pleasing manner she hoped to gain some privileges for herself and her husband. This put her on a collision course with Eva Braun, who disliked Daranowski becoming the centre of attention.[44] Although the knowledge and potential influence of the secretaries was substantial, none of them appears to have played any significant political role or altered the course of events. Those who might have changed the course of history were the cooks and dieticians.

Relations between Brandt and members of the court were at first distant. In the early years of the regime, Brandt had no real power base, nor any influence on the key personalities around Hitler, nor on any of the events unfolding in Germany. Brandt had essentially no *Hausmacht*. Given that he stayed constantly in the vicinity of Hitler, he had the ear of the Führer, but not much more. Goebbels, for example, did not take much notice of Brandt. A meticulous diary writer, Goebbels first mentions Brandt in connection with a cancer scandal in Nuremberg in July 1936, more than two years after Brandt's appointment as Hitler's escort physician.[45]

To ensure that he would always be within Hitler's reach, Brandt rented part of the Bechstein Villa, close to Hitler's Berghof. The house had been bought in 1927 by Edwin Bechstein, grandson of Carl Bechstein, founder of the piano-manufacturing company. Both Edwin Bechstein and his wife Helene were passionate admirers of the Nazi movement and had introduced Hitler to their circle of well-to-do friends in industry and politics in the 1920s. Helene Bechstein even wanted to buy Hitler a luxury car. 'Wolf [Hitler's pseudonym],' she told Hitler, 'you have to have the most beautiful car there is. You deserve it.'[46] She thought of buying him a Maybach, but Hitler wanted a Mercedes, the biggest, which cost a total of 26,000 Reichsmark. As a sign of gratitude, Helene Bechstein received the golden party badge; this was of no help, however, when Bormann wanted to lay his hands on their Obersalzberg property so that he could convert the building into a guest house for the Nazi elite. Residing in the luxurious Bechstein Villa was convenient for Brandt, given that influential Nazis were going in and out of the house all the time. Goebbels, for example, used it as his residence when he visited the Berghof. It was also a fitting place as far as Brandt's affection for classical music was concerned. Yet, for Brandt, the new lifestyle of being constantly at Hitler's side also had its downside. Financing two apartments, one in Berlin at 31 Altonaerstraße, and one on the Obersalzberg, had only become possible after Göring, as Minister President of Prussia, had topped Brandt's modest monthly salary of about 350 Reichsmark with a stipend of an extra 125 Reichsmark.[47] Brandt was beginning to climb the social and professional ladder.

In mid-1935, Albert Speer also moved into the Bechstein Villa. Brandt and Speer and their wives became good friends. They went hiking and skiing together, or talked about art, architecture and philosophy. Anni Brandt, an attractive woman with a boyish figure and haircut, shared a passion for sport and the gossip about concerts and fashion with Margarete Speer. In the mountains these two families and the von Belows, the family of another of Hitler's long-time adjutants, constituted a circle of their own, with little contact with the families of Hitler's personal staff. 'I never like to live in places where I look out on houses or where people can, heaven forbid, drop in,' Speer later told Gitta Sereny, except, of course, when Hitler dropped in to drink cocoa or play with Speer's children.[48] Speer and Brandt were both immensely private men, and deeply imbued by the German romantic tradition of *Sturm und Drang*. Speer wanted to wake up to the smell of grass and a view over the mountains, in solitude and undisturbed peace, man and nature in harmony with one another.[49] Two years later, in 1937, he expanded his realm of influence over Germany's architecture by building a studio close to Hitler's Berghof, but outside the immediate security complex, where he could meet in private with colleagues to discuss the massive building plans for Greater Berlin.

For Hitler, it was incredibly convenient to have his personal doctor and personal architect always within reach. The same applied to Bormann, Hitler's personal secretary, as Brandt remarked after the war.[50] For their unconditional support and loyalty, the leading figures of the Third Reich, including Brandt, were rewarded with previously unequalled salaries, tax exemptions, gifts and paintings, as well as luxurious homes full of artwork and tapestries. When Brandt ran into massive debt because of his lavish lifestyle, Hitler bailed him out with a cheque for more than 50,000 Reichsmark, exempt from income tax.[51] For Hitler, 50,000 Reichsmark was pocket money. From 1937 to 1943, he received more than forty million Reichsmark from the sale of special Führer stamps alone, including more than two million Reichsmark from the sale of stamps in the Generalgouvernement, the occupied Polish territories after the beginning of the Second World War.[52] All this money went into Hitler's 'Culture Trust' (*Kulturfond*), which he used to finance his many pet projects and keep his inner circle dependent through payments in kind. Brandt later admitted that he was never prudent, and though he came out of the war with few debts, he also had neither savings nor capital: 'I have no shares, no property, not a dot, and never did have.'[53] Life before the war must have been expensive for Brandt, with the constant travelling and hotels in which he stayed, spending an average of 800–1,000 Reichsmark per month. By the mid-1930s, however, the Brandts lived in relative comfort. Working for the Führer, and breaking into his circle, was paying off, in financial, professional and social terms.

'Here [on the Berghof]', Brandt recalled after the war, Hitler 'wanted to appear in a private capacity and pursue his private, personal relationships and desires'.[54] Brandt obviously belonged to one of those 'personal relationships' and had to endure the surreal mountain atmosphere. Life at the Berghof was terribly boring. Behind the facade of the statesman there was what many later described as an 'odd emptiness' in the life of the Führer.[55] He would not turn up much before eleven o'clock, and would start the day with an extended breakfast or lunch, leaving little time for any kind of government business to be performed. Lammers and other advisers sometimes only had minutes to report a matter of great importance to him, and hope that he would make a decision, or say something that could be construed as a decision. Shortly after lunch, the entourage would take a leisurely walk down the hill to the tea-house where Hitler loved to hold forth in endless monologues, sometimes falling asleep, leaving those present in a state of limbo in which one could only whisper, and hope that the Führer would wake up in time for dinner. Back at the Berghof, Hitler would retire to his rooms and return two hours later for dinner. This was followed by weekly newsreels or feature films, which Hitler loved. In February 1937, the office of the Führer adjutant listed a total of twenty-two films which were available at the Berghof at all times, the so-called 'iron stock'.[56] Films included, for example, 'The Higher Order' (*Der höhere Befehl*), 'Mother and Child' (*Mutter und Kind*), 'Faust' (*Faust*), 'The Old and the Young King' (*Der alte und der junge König*), 'F.P.1 Does Not Respond' (*F.P.1 antwortet nicht*), 'Girls in Uniform' (*Mädchen in Uniform*), 'Sanssouci' (*Sanssouci*) and the Nazi classic 'SA-Man Brand' (*SA-Mann Brand*).[57] In December that year, Goebbels surprised Hitler with 'thirty classic films of the last four years and eighteen Mickey Mouse films'.[58] Sometimes there would be a brief introduction to the films, though everyone in Hitler's presence tried hard not to lift the level of the conversation beyond mere trivialities. Late at night, at around one o'clock, there would be more tea, or another monologue around the fireplace. More often than not, Hitler's Alsatian would then become the centre of attention.[59] 'In monotonous, tiresome emptiness the evening would then drag on for another hour,' Speer remarked exasperatedly after the war. Any government official present during these tedious days must have been conscious of the amount of pressing administrative problems which needed to be solved. At the same time, officials knew that excusing oneself from the Führer's company without good cause meant professional suicide.

On the *Berg*, as members of the court would say with some affection, it was the golden rule not to bring up anything disagreeable; almost everyone carefully avoided any political conversations or anything which could disrupt the peaceful atmosphere for Hitler during his extended periods of rest. In a culture of ignorance – so vital for Hitler to remain the absolute and unchallenged leader – any form of reflective scepticism about the political objectives or even the morality of the regime needed to be repressed. When, in 1943, Henrietta von Schirach questioned Hitler about whether he knew of the mass arrests and brutal beatings of Jews taking place in Holland, she was banned from any further visits to the Berghof with immediate effect. The inner circle was protective of Hitler to such an extent that they themselves became entrapped in a surreal world, remote from the tragedy unfolding in Europe, blinded by a combination of Biedermeier romanticism and wilful ignorance. While thousands, and later hundreds of thousands, of people all over Europe were discriminated against, intimidated, arrested and killed, this artificial enclave remained shielded from the outside world, removed from the necessity of questioning or even of being aware of political events. Here Hitler's personal staff, and their wives and children, enjoyed extensive walking and skiing tours and attended the rather dull film screenings at night, followed by Hitler's continual hollow monologues. Conversations centred around general gossip, film stars, concerts and plays – and, of course, children. Maria von Below, wife of Nicolaus von Below, Hitler's long-serving and loyal adjutant, recalled that their feeling of isolation drew them increasingly closer to one another:

> We depended entirely on each other, socially and emotionally. Anni Brandt and I went to Salzburg a few times, but even that so rarely that now, after all these years, I remember each occasion. You see, when you stayed at the Berghof, you didn't treat it like a hotel. You were a community: Hitler's cook cooked for you, his maids took care of your clothes, your mending – you lived there and, as in many families, you were never really on your own except in your bedroom.[60]

It was a tight-knit coterie. Whenever von Below and his wife were invited to one of the late-night soirées around the fireplace, whether in Berlin or at the Berghof, they felt deeply grateful and privileged to be part of the private realm of Germany's great leader. In January 1938, after an official state visit had ended at around 11 p.m., Hitler invited a number of intimate guests into the 'smoking room' (*Rauchzimmer*) of the Reich Chancellery, which had served men like Bismarck for informal political talks during his reign. Present during these cosy winter evenings were Brandt and his wife Anni, Goebbels and his wife, state secretary Karl Hanke, and a number of young women, for example the two daughters of the 4711-perfume manufacturer Mühlens from Cologne. 'These late-night sessions around the fireplace … were the nicest, most relaxed and happiest social gatherings which we experienced with Hitler in Berlin,' von Below recalled.[61] Three months later, Hitler invited the von Belows for a four-day Easter holiday on the Berghof together with Brandt and his wife. Present during these days were, among others, Speer and his wife and Bormann and his wife, as well as Heinrich Hoffmann and a personal adjutant. None of them had to wear uniform, underlining the informal nature of the occasion.[62] Members of this close circle developed an extraordinary ability to separate Hitler the man from Hitler the politician. For them he was, and remained, the grand father figure, who apparently would look after their interests and well-being as long as their loyalty was total.

In October 1935, Brandt's first and only child was born, a son, named after his father, Karl, and his godfather, Adolf Hitler.[63] Hitler's baptismal gift to young Karl-Adolf was a black Mercedes sports car.[64] The social pressure on Brandt and his wife must have been significant. In a world where most of the Nazi leaders, including Speer, had up to five children and some had up to nine or ten children, like the Bormann family, Brandt tried to compensate for his single-child family by showing a particular affection to his son.

Talking to Karl-Adolf Brandt in 1999 brought back the time at the Berghof, his recollections slowly unfolding during our conversation. He was very young then, and his memories were slightly blurred by post-war historical accounts, though he remembered individual scenes with conspicuous clarity. One event he could still visualize was Hitler inviting the children of his staff to coffee and cakes.[65] Speer's daughter, Hilde, also remembered these rare and formal occasions when they had to go over to the Berghof dressed in *lederhosen* and *dirndl*, always reminded by their watchful parents to shake hands properly with the German Chancellor.[66] Photographs of Hitler surrounded by happy-looking children were intended to convey the strong bond between the Nazi leadership and the next generation of healthy Germans. They were 'Germany's future', and thus part of the Nazi propaganda machine. On one occasion, Hilde had to hand over a bouquet of flowers for the Führer's birthday. She apparently disliked all the fuss, at least in retrospect.[67] Embedded in kitsch and triviality, this petty bourgeois atmosphere was meant to present the illusion of an ideal world. But the sunbathing and mountain scenery, the Bavarian *dirndls* and Blondi – Hitler's Alsatian – were smoke and mirrors, like so much else in Nazi Germany.

IV. MEETING THE WOMEN AROUND HITLER

Brandt's constant presence around Hitler meant that he gained a good knowledge of Hitler's private life and his relationships with women, something Allied investigators were interested in after the war. Conversations between Brandt and Hitler first centred around personal matters rather than political, for example how Hitler saw the role of women in their relationship with men of destiny – clearly thinking of himself.[68] For Hitler, women were a means to an end, a tool, useful in obtaining, consolidating and expanding his power base, but also a kind of aesthetic relaxation and amusement. From early on he saw women as great promoters of National Socialism: idealistic and devoted to the movement. They persuaded their husbands and friends to join the Nazi Party, organized tea-parties, and supported

Hitler's election campaigns financially and with organizational expertise. Women wanting to belong to the inner circle had to be totally committed to Hitler and accept the deeply reactionary, social-Darwinistic and often contradictory views among the Nazi leadership on the role of women in society. 'The female bird grooms herself for the male and breeds the eggs for him. The male therefore looks after the food. Otherwise he stands guard and wards off the enemy,' was one of Goebbels' statements on the subject.[69]

Nazi Germany never really developed a coherent and uniform set of ideas about the role of women. Behind the verbose propaganda about women as the protector of race and family, and pillar of a eugenically healthy community, stood major economic and geopolitical aims: to reduce and manipulate unemployment figures by replacing women workers with men, and to increase the overall birth rate of the population to make the country ready for war and *Lebensraum* expansion.[70] Traditional conservative family values were mixed with mythical concepts of blood and soil, race and nationalism into an amalgam of *völkisch* ideas. The role of women in German society was a conflict-laden area, difficult for the Nazi leadership to make consistent, especially since their wives, girlfriends and mistresses rarely fitted the image of the much-publicized stereotypical woman, other than, perhaps, that almost all of them showed an extraordinary degree of ignorance of world politics. Any form of reflection about their own role or that of their husbands was almost non-existent. Many of them did not stop wearing designer clothes and make-up, and enjoyed themselves with athletics, skiing or cinema. Anni Brandt had only one child, was a professional swimmer and loved skiing. Magda Goebbels often fought hard and long with her husband about women's rights. Margarete Himmler could not take the megalomania of her husband seriously. As a political activist, Carin, Göring's first wife, belonged to the group of women who were loathed by the Nazi leadership, especially by Hitler. Emmy Göring, his second wife and an actress, lived a life of glamour. Henriette von Schirach was active in reviving the cultural scene in Vienna. These women hardly reflected the image of the self-sacrificing, child-rearing, loving housewife with a large family. In general, they had maids to do the cooking. Rather than sacrificing their expensive fur coats for the country's war effort, these women would not part from their luxury items, and hid them in the cellar of the Berghof.[71] By 1938, the Bavarian Ministry of the Interior even sent a list of 'extremely young and pretty female artists' to the Berghof so that Hitler and his court could select the girls with whom they wished to have social intercourse.[72]

Hitler enjoyed socializing with middle- and upper-class women who shared his passion for art and architecture. Among the guests frequenting the Berghof after 1933 was Marion Schönemann from Austria, the wife of a Munich architect, and a friend of Hoffmann, Eva Braun and Brandt.[73] She was known for her interest in art and art history. Her Austrian charm, coupled with her close connections to the tight-knit circle of Viennese opera, allowed her, as Brandt and others observed, to influence Hitler's opinions. She shared with Hitler memories from their time as adolescents in Vienna. Compared with some of the other Berghof lodgers, she was smart and subtle in her conversations and generally put her points across even when they conflicted with Hitler's known position. She had no hesitation in severely criticizing some of the powerful party leaders and *Gauleiters* who spread terror and intimidation across the German districts; for obvious reasons she was particularly interested in influencing the situation in Vienna and Munich. She could tell the Führer things when others might have paid with their life for doing so. Apparently Hitler did not mind. When her attacks against the regime became too serious, Hitler would shift the debate to less controversial areas. For Brandt, this woman possessed a 'rare gift' in handling conversations with Hitler.[74]

Another of Hitler's female companions was the interior designer Gerdy Troost from Munich, who had worked on the Berghof. At Hitler's wish she was granted the title of 'Professor'. Through her architect husband, who had designed several of the Nazi Party buildings, including the House of German Art in Munich, she had gained entry into the court, and from there she could influence German architecture in and around Munich. According to Brandt, she was quite ruthless in the pursuit of her career as an architect. Yet he also acknowledged that she was competent. 'She has a remarkably well-developed sense of colour,' he told post-war interrogators,

> … in the development of her dead husband's work she has influenced the whole colour scheme of the new public buildings in Munich, and their interior architecture. She understood how to demonstrate to Hitler the effects of colour gradations and, as she cared both for the heavy colours of the Makart period and also for the finer shades of colour, it was easy for her to find complete agreement with Hitler.[75]

And she also found agreement with Brandt's own aesthetic taste, since he learned to share his master's passion for art and architecture. Whenever Hitler visited Munich, the 'Atelier Troost' was his first point of call. Here he would stay for hours and hours talking with Troost and Leonhard Gall, one of the top Nazi architects involved in finishing the House of German Art after Paul Ludwig Troost died suddenly in January 1934. In the meantime, important government business had to wait. Hitler's interest in art and culture obviously left its mark on Brandt's taste for the artistic world, and indeed on his similar disregard for the details of organization and management, which became apparent during the 'euthanasia' programme.

All these women had some form of influence over Hitler in one way or another, but none of them was as important as Hitler's mother. Observers almost uniformly agree that Hitler expressed and showed a unique affection for his mother. Often Hitler would talk with Brandt about his mother on their lengthy journeys across the continent.[76] Once he told Brandt that his mother would have been very unhappy 'if she had seen her son in this position and with this responsibility; probably this little woman would hardly have dared to come to see her son'.[77] Pictures of Hitler's mother were displayed in all his main residences, whether in Berlin and Munich or at the Berghof, where one hung in his study. Even when Hitler went underground in the last days of the Third Reich, he carried a picture of his mother with him into the bunker. But images of her were not displayed publicly. Throughout the regime, Klara Hitler, née Pölzl, remained off limits for party and state propaganda campaigns.

Hitler described her to Brandt as a 'simple and unbelievably good woman' who had raised her children in a responsible and patient manner.[78] This corresponds with the impression she made on Eduard Bloch, the Jewish family doctor, who, after being forcefully expelled from Germany, described her as 'a simple, modest, kindly woman. She was tall, had brownish hair which she kept neatly plaited, and a long, oval face with beautiful expressive grey-blue eyes'.[79] Klara Hitler represents the archetype of the passive and pious housewife: she looked after the household and the rearing of her five children, whilst being submissive and obedient to her cold-hearted and autocratic husband, Alois Hitler. The consecutive deaths of her first three children greatly affected her, so much so that all her emotions were centred on Adolf and his sister, Paula. She also supported Hitler financially and spoiled the idle young man during his days in Linz. It was here that Hitler wanted his parents to be remembered. Like an ancient emperor ordering the building of monuments for the worship and adulation of his power, Hitler commissioned the architect Hermann Giesler to design a huge bell-tower as the basis for a mausoleum for the dead bodies of his mother and father. It was another of Hitler's colossal architectural plans to reshape Europe's urban landscape.

In the end, the Nazis became prisoners of their own ideology. Instead of conscripting the female population into the production of armaments, to put the country on a total war footing, as the Allies did, the Nazis pursued a petty fight against make-up and prohibited women from smoking in public. Smoking was seen as 'lung masturbation' which could lead to 'spontaneous abortions'.[80] One woman who was a notoriously heavy smoker was Eva Braun, Hitler's mistress. She filmed and photographed, wore make-up and expensive clothes, and loved the theatre and cinema. It is, perhaps, for that reason that Hitler could not bring himself to marry her while his regime was in existence. As early as 1934, Hitler had told his confidants that 'the greater the man the more insignificant should be the woman'.[81] Hitler felt that a great man, which he believed he was, had no right to marry an intelligent woman, because such a marriage was doomed: intelligent women, Hitler believed, were simply unable to stay in the background. 'Women with modest homely gifts' were much more suitable for men like him. His image of the ideal woman resembled very much the personality of his mother: a woman who was 'satisfied with the normal everyday fundamentals of home life and yet is ever prepared to welcome her partner'.[82] After the war, Brandt suggested that Hitler might have felt that 'Eva Braun was not quite the proper personage to be presented to the nation as the wife of the head of State'.[83]

'Eva Braun is a disappointment for history,' Hugh Trevor-Roper concluded after the British intelligence service had dispatched him to investigate Hitler's last days in the bunker. Throughout the Third Reich there was a 'wall of silence' surrounding the question of Hitler's love life; publicly there were a few rumours that Hitler was living with a woman on the Berghof. Only a small group of Hitler's inner circle knew of the identity of Eva Braun, who was known to be Hitler's private secretary and officially belonged to the personnel of the Berghof. If we are to believe Brandt, he remained ignorant about Eva Braun's true identity for some time after his arrival at Hitler's court. In June 1945, he told his interrogators that he knew Eva Braun well but that 'he had seen her around Hitler's entourage for several years before he realised who and what she was'.[84]

A central element of the relationship was anonymity. Often they would meet in Hitler's large Munich apartment in the Prinzregentenplatz. The more powerful Hitler became, the greater the secrecy surrounding his love affair needed to be. 'I was surprised,' Speer later recalled, 'that she and Hitler avoided everything that might indicate an intimate relationship – in order to then go late at night to the sleeping quarters upstairs'.[85] Others, like the chambermaids, were in the know from the moment they arrived at the Berghof. Anna Mittlstrasser from Austria was instructed not to talk to anyone about the affair and about what she saw and heard in the compound. Literally on the day of her arrival in June 1941, Mittlstrasser was shown the *Kofferraum* (storage room for suitcases), a small antechamber that provided a connecting corridor between Hitler and Eva Braun's sleeping quarters. 'I don't need to say anything further, do I?' one of Hitler's servants said as they concluded the introductory tour of the Berghof.[86] Perhaps Brandt was not receptive to what was so obvious to everyone else, or perhaps he wanted to remain silent about Hitler's personal affairs after the war, and give the impression of someone who had little knowledge of the dynamics at the centre of German politics. Given Karl and Anni Brandt's close relationship with the Speers and others at the Berghof, it is almost inconceivable that he did not know the true identity of Eva Braun. Photographs from the period suggest that the two also got to know each other quite well. A picture from around 1937, shot by Hoffmann, shows Brandt, dressed in a light-coloured suit and tie, sitting close to Eva Braun on the terrace of Hitler's Berghof. Braun is wearing a traditional Bavarian *dirndl* and is talking to Brandt.[87]

Eva Braun spent most of her time waiting for the man in her life. Braun was available for Hitler at any time when he needed company or relaxation or sex; she also looked after the sales of Hoffmann's postcards which helped Hitler to get a (rather crude) sense of which Nazi figures were rated the most highly among the public. She was his 'Hascherl', the Austrian colloquialism for 'dimwit'; in no sense was she his partner. 'Very intelligent people', Hitler told others in her presence, 'should find themselves a primitive and dumb woman … In my spare time I want my peace … I could never marry!'[88] According to Brandt, Hitler 'wanted to preserve the mystical legend in the hearts of the German Volk that, as long as he stayed single, millions of German women could believe in the illusion that they would one day become the woman at his side.'[89] Hitler saw this as 'sound psychology' which apparently ensured political support from a vital section of German society.[90]

Eva Braun increasingly joined Hitler on his travels. The historic and political events surrounding these travels with Hitler never seemed to have entered the mind of this unspeakably apolitical and naive woman. In autumn 1935, for example, Hitler invited Braun to join him at the Nuremberg Party Rally, where he announced the notorious Race Laws which excluded Jews from citizenship and prohibited marriages and sexual relations between Jews and non-Jews. No reflection, no comment and no criticism by Eva Braun has been recorded. In March 1938, she followed Hitler to Vienna to hear him announce the *Anschluss* of Austria to the Reich. Unlike Brandt, who had to stay at Hitler's side all the time, and who can be seen in one of Hoffmann's photographs standing next to Hitler during his entry into Austria, Braun enjoyed going shopping with her mother whilst staying at the luxurious Hotel Imperial. For her it was another political event, but nothing else. Her filming on the streets of Vienna was highly selective, radically ignoring the beatings and intimidations of Jews and political opponents, or cases of violence. While thousands of Jews tried to flee the country, Braun recorded another lovely holiday with her amateur camera. Two months later, she attended Hitler's state visit to Italy as his private secretary. Again, Braun separated from the entourage and made film recordings of Ravenna, Rome and Capri, which she later screened at the Berghof. Travels became ever more lavish and frequent. In early 1939, she boarded the passenger ship *Robert Ley* for a tour through the fjords of Norway. In August 1939, when Europe was on the brink of war, she visited the Venice film festival before returning to the Reich Chancellery, where Hitler was about to unleash the Second World War. Her photo-series of the days in the Chancellery are documents of great importance, conveying the nervous atmosphere surrounding the making of the Hitler–Stalin pact. Her captions are not. The series is called '… and then Ribbentrop travelled to Moskau'. One of the captions reads: 'But still, Poland does not want to negotiate.'[91] She honestly believed that Hitler was attempting to save the peace in Europe.

Despite her obvious naivety, Eva Braun was another factor no one at court dared to underestimate, especially the wives of the leading Nazis. This also included Anni Brandt. Sometimes Eva Braun would see herself as the mother of the country (*Landesmutter*), and befriend some of the empire-builders of the regime. Her social intercourse included regular Berghof guests, such as Brandt, Speer, Goebbels and Hoffmann, and she engaged with Hitler's adjutants, doctors and secretaries; rarely, though, would she come into contact with Himmler or Heydrich. Artists, film actors and actresses were more to her liking. But Eva Braun had no real political influence. Whenever visitors came to the Berghof she was barred from appearing in the corridors of power. She would stay in her room and compensate for the lack of attention by inviting Anni Brandt, Margarete Speer and the wife of Hitler's photographer, Hoffmann, for coffee and cake.[92] Anni Brandt and Margarete Speer enjoyed her company so long as the hierarchy was kept intact, with Eva Braun being the hostess, the others her guests. If she wanted to go swimming and the others preferred sightseeing, the group would go swimming.[93] When Emmy Göring invited the entire staff of the Berghof over for tea, including Eva Braun, Hitler intervened; the two women apparently never got to know each other. After the war, Brandt indicated that 'certain guests', that is to say the wives of the Nazi elite, had to suffer under Eva Braun's 'changing moods'.[94] 'My first impression of Eva', Brandt told the US Army after the war,

> was that she was a woman who had been suddenly transplanted into the whirl and scurry of world society – with it went the fine clothes, luxury and jewels and her changing

moods under which certain guests had to suffer. As years went by, particularly during the early war years, Eva's character seemed to undergo a complete change, she grew more serious, and busied herself more with domestic affairs at the Berghof and the Führer's flat in Munich. In this period, she tried to understand and perhaps to share the mind and thoughts of the Führer.[95]

And Brandt continued:

Eva Braun herself would not have been justified in doubting Hitler's loyalty, for as long as she remained the chosen one at his side, she had very little to fear. After all Hitler had done much for Eva in discovering her as an almost nonentity and moving her to prominence by his side.[96]

In examining the role of Eva Braun, Brandt unintentionally revealed his own position to his interrogators. He, like Eva Braun, believed that he had been chosen by the most powerful man in the country. As long as he stayed at Hitler's side, he had nothing to fear. Brandt's loyalty was absolute. Eva Braun refused to become involved or interfere in cases of untold human suffering. Whenever someone approached her in the hope that she would use her intimate relationship with Hitler to save a human life, she would put her finger on her mouth like the archangel Gabriel to indicate that she did not want to hear it. Only once did she interfere, successfully, in the case of the Jewish physician, Dr Bloch, who had treated and cared for Hitler's mother until she died. He was spared the concentration camp. The reason for her interference seems to have been sentimental rather than anything else. Eva Braun, like many others of Hitler's court, including Brandt, were not ignorant because of lack of information or because they had no access to the necessary intelligence, but because they chose to be so. She, like Brandt, wanted to remain ignorant for as long as possible. Ignorance was at the core of their relationship with Hitler. It secured their place at Hitler's court.

V. TRAVELLING WITH HITLER

Although Hitler loved to be seen as the modest politician whose only mission was to overcome the shackles of Versailles and restore Germany's national pride and glory, the way he travelled and the accommodation he chose reflected the dictator's taste for showiness and luxury. Throughout the 1920s and early 1930s, Hitler had been constantly on the move with his cronies in his luxurious Mercedes Benz, travelling from one mass rally to the next. After 1933, an entire pool of cars and a special train with eleven coaches, a bathtub and sleeping compartments was added to a vastly inflated entourage. From 1935 onwards, Hitler's entourage was exempt from paying rail fares.[97] Some of the leading Nazis were later given their own special trains, fully equipped with a telegraph, a wireless and office facilities. This enabled them to be kept informed of all important developments. Himmler, for example, shared the special train 'Heinrich' with Ribbentrop and Lammers.[98] There were also three planes at Hitler's disposal for long-distance journeys and, of course, a number of specially assigned apartments, hotels and houses.[99] By 1940, for example, he purchased more than 26,000 square metres of land on Schwanenwerder, a small island located on the outskirts of Berlin.[100] Speer was commissioned to draw up plans for another of Hitler's massive building projects, this time for a huge house which he wanted to use whenever he stayed in Berlin. In the process, Schwanenwerder developed into another centre of the Nazi elite. Hitler, Goebbels and Speer all had large estates on the island with direct access to Lake Wannsee, protected by heavily armed guards positioned by the only access road leading to the island. Behind the facade of modesty and tranquillity, the Nazi leadership created a whole range of different courts and castles, accessible only to a small circle of trusted paladins.

When accompanying Hitler during his travels, there was little time for Brandt to pursue independent medical work or research. Most of the time the work was 'not to his liking,' Brandt would tell his American interrogators after the war, 'for it took him away from his surgical work in Berlin, and all he did on the various trips was to sit about and at the most administer some minor first aid.'[101] Brandt, therefore, arranged for two of his classmates, Werner Haase and later Hanskarl von Hasselbach, to be appointed as additional escort physicians to Hitler.[102] Both were colleagues of Brandt at the surgical clinic in Berlin-Ziegelstraße. All three belonged to the notorious circle of Nazi doctors who surrounded Professor Magnus and transferred to Berlin when their mentor was appointed to a chair in November 1933.[103] In 1923, Haase had attempted to take part in the Hitler putsch, and had been imprisoned in Probstzella as a result. Both Brandt and von Hasselbach joined the Nazi Party in 1932 and the SS in 1934. All three doctors were willing to serve the regime with determination and expertise. Sharing what essentially appears to have been a rather dull duty, the three surgeons ensured that, during trips, one of them was always on hand for Hitler, and that none of them would be away from their surgical work in Berlin for prolonged periods.

On 14 June 1934, Brandt travelled for the first time with Hitler's group of paladins. Hitler was scheduled for talks with Mussolini in Venice to air the Austrian question. It was his first visit abroad, carefully orchestrated by the Reich Chancellery and the Foreign Office to boost Germany's foreign relations with Italy, which had publicly backed the Dollfuss government. Violent attacks by Nazi activists in Austria meant that Hitler was walking a tightrope, as he could not risk alienating Italy. The journey turned out to be a major embarrassment for Hitler, one which he remembered for years afterwards. Hitler, wearing the civilian dress of the German Chancellor, was upstaged by the Italian dictator, who flashed his pompous military uniform to the world's media. It made Hitler look like a junior partner in international politics. It was on the return from Italy that Brandt was officially appointed Hitler's escort physician.

At the end of June 1934, a crisis in the SA leadership came to a head. On the evening of 28 June, apparently at *Gauleiter* Terboven's wedding in Essen, the decision was taken to strike against the SA leader, Ernst Röhm, and the SA. Hitler, racing back to his hotel, decided that no time could be lost. Travelling from Essen

to Bad Godesberg on the afternoon of 29 June, he was joined by Goebbels and Sepp
Dietrich, who arrived from Berlin to coordinate the nationwide purge of SA leaders.
On the night of Saturday 30 June, Hitler's entourage boarded a plane to Munich,
accompanied by Brückner, Schaub and Schreck together with Goebbels, Lutze and
Dietrich. Upon Hitler's arrival in Bavaria, Röhm and his men were immediately
arrested at a hotel on the Tegernsee and sent to Stadelheim prison in Munich.
Goebbels, meanwhile, phoned Göring with the password *Kolibri* (humming bird),
which set in motion arrests and killings across the country. Hitler returned to Berlin
the same night, exhausted, still hesitant to liquidate Röhm, one of his 'old fighters'.
On Sunday, 1 July, he changed his mind: an order to kill was given during a garden
party at the Reich Chancellery. Röhm was shot the same day.

There is no evidence to suggest that Brandt was part of Hitler's entourage during
this frenzied weekend. But by the summer of 1934 it would have been difficult not
to notice something of the true nature of Hitler's government, even if we assume
that Brandt was essentially tied up in his surgical work in Berlin, or 'just there'
in Hitler's entourage, as Brandt recalled. Among the few who kept their critical
faculties, and perceived with rare clarity what was happening inside Germany, was
Victor Klemperer, one of the country's leading philologists. On 14 July, the day
after Hitler had given his notorious Reichstag speech in which he accepted full
responsibility for the shooting of those SA leaders most guilty of treason, Klemperer
noted in his diary:

> Yesterday Hitler put on a big show in front of the Reichstag. A loudspeaker was mounted
> on a statue in the fountain at Chemnitzer Platz; I heard a few sentences of Hitler's speech
> as I went to get a taxi in the evening … I almost feel pity for Hitler as a human being.
> The man is lost and feels it; for the first time he is speaking without hope. He does not
> think he is a murderer. In fact he presumably did act in self-defence and prevented a
> substantially worse slaughter. But after all he appointed these people to their posts, and
> after all he is the author of this absolutist system … The dreadful thing is that a European
> nation has delivered itself up to such a gang of lunatics and criminals and still puts up
> with them.[104]

Klemperer was a lonely voice in a sea of silence, swept away by thousands of young
enthusiasts who, like Brandt, saw the dawn of a new era on the horizon with a
proud, strong and healthy German nation. Such an ideal seemed to warrant individual and national sacrifice, and maybe even plain murder.

Hitler probably did not yet take Brandt into his confidence about his more
sinister political and ideological plans. Brandt, like Speer, belonged to Hitler's
intimate circle. This meant that they were to be shielded from any detailed knowledge of Hitler's involvement in mass murder or from anything that might upset
the harmony of their relationship with him.[105] For Hitler it was central that the
members of his court remained as ignorant as possible, so that none of them would
ask any searching questions or challenge his leadership. He wanted them to be happy
and cheerful so that he could pursue his political plans undisturbed. A culture of
distributing presents and gifts evolved where everyone felt immensely grateful

– and dependent – for money, pictures, flowers, houses, or whatever privilege they had come to enjoy as a result of their intimate relationship with Hitler. On the last day of the Nuremberg Party Rally in 1938, while the Sudeten crisis was coming to a head, Hitler handed von Below's wife a large bouquet of flowers in front of hundreds of guests at the hotel *Deutscher Hof* in Nuremberg. To exploit the image of the gentleman was one of Hitler's oldest theatrical ploys, used to keep his closest followers sweet, especially their influential wives. Brandt and his wife were party to this incident and certainly heard Hitler's speech in which he announced to the German public that he would bring the three million Sudeten Germans 'back into the Reich' by 'one way or another' (*so oder so*).[106] Germany's expansionist aims were hardly secret from those who were so close to the man who shaped these policies; in fact, they cannot have been unknown to the wider German population, nor indeed the international community as a whole.

Brandt's presence was often requested during periods of relaxation, when Hitler retreated to the Berghof, visited building sites, attended exhibition openings, balls and concerts in and out of Berlin. In November 1935, for example, he accompanied Hitler and Goebbels to a concert by the Italian singer, Benjamino Gigli, which had been organized by the *Winterhilfswerk*. Brandt also travelled with Hitler to party rallies and was part of his personal bodyguard, the *Begleitkommando*, during state and other official visits. Brandt was at Hitler's side when he made his routine walks through the forest of the Obersalzberg, or when he rambled on in never-ending monologues at the Kehlsteinhaus, the small chalet built on top of the Kehlstein mountain at above 1,800 metres.

At the end of July 1934, Brandt accompanied Hitler to the Bayreuth Festival, where he was introduced to the Wagner family.[107] The Wagner opera festival became one of the high points of the year for Hitler's entourage, 'a special interruption of the year's activities', as Brandt remarked after the war.[108] Hitler generally stayed in a building next to Haus Wahnfried in Bayreuth, together with one of his adjutants and a servant. There, on the ground floor, Hitler had access to a large dining hall seating twenty-five to thirty people, a large lounge and an extensive veranda overlooking the old garden of the estate. Hitler's residence in Bayreuth was a truly luxurious environment.

An insight into the atmosphere at the Wahnfried home can be glimpsed from an unpublished report of one of the guests, who recorded his impressions of Hitler during a summer evening in 1937. The Bayreuth musician, Carl Schlottmann, was so overwhelmed by the presence of the Führer that he asked the authorities to publish his account of an evening at Bayreuth in the Nazi press. Permission to do so was refused because Schlottmann had recorded some of Hitler's views that were not destined for the national and international press. Schlottmann described how Hitler was beginning to talk to a small group of guests, and how it became clear to all those present that Hitler was not talking but that 'it was talking out of him'. No one dared to interrupt Hitler's flow of words which were so full of 'liberating humour' and 'incredible serenity', and represented such enormous generosity and modesty, and so forth. Hitler, the national redeemer, the man with a mission, he who would save Germany from doom, is in every one of Schlottmann's sentences. But then, unintentionally and without noticing, the musician makes some revealing observations about the triviality at the very top of one of Europe's most brutal regimes: 'When someone speaks of the inhibitions of those in his presence, [Hitler] laughs and says, "I want to see the person who is afraid of me."'[109] Hitler then continues to ramble on about his visits to the theatre:

> Rather than being late, I cancel the visit. I cannot put a sign around my neck which says 'this and that idiot has delayed my arrival for a matter which was very important to him' – in fact I love those 'important visits' late in the day! – the doormen in front of the box would probably still let me in, as they do in the case of the president of the police and others for fear that they otherwise will find themselves in 'Oranienburg' [concentration camp]. Here the Führer laughs.[110]

Anyone who witnessed Hitler during one of these trivial, albeit deeply cynical, monologues was in the know. It can have needed little critical reflection to grasp that the man who was laughing about people's fear of concentration camps was actually creating this fear with his regime, with systematic intention, and what can only be described as an utter disregard for individual rights and liberties.

In Bayreuth and elsewhere, power politics was never far away from Hitler. On 25 July 1934, while Brandt was in Bayreuth, Hitler was found to be in an almost hysterical state of mind when it transpired that the Austrian Nazis had embarrassed his government by attempting single-handedly to overthrow the Dollfuss regime. It was a political blunder of grand proportions, which gnawed at Hitler's mind for some time. Seven days later, on 2 August 1934, President Hindenburg died. All of a sudden, policy decisions of enormous importance were taken. Hitler secured total power by combining the office of Reich President with that of Reich Chancellor. The Führer state was about to begin. Securing total control of government during the crisis-ridden summer of 1934 set in motion a process of 'cumulative radicalization' which was characteristic of Nazi Germany. Hitler's personalized style of government fragmented and distorted the state administration and established a 'panoply of overlapping and competing agencies', dependent only on the 'will of the Führer'.[111] This form of rule was a great opportunity for people working in Hitler's inner circle to accumulate power and prestige inside the Nazi regime.

The autumn saw Hitler's prestige rise to unknown heights; members of his entourage, such as Brandt and Speer, now experienced what it meant to travel with the man who was seen as Germany's leader sent by providence. Travelling from Weimar to Nuremberg in Hitler's car on one occasion, Speer recalled the atmosphere on the streets. Speer sat right behind Hitler, and Brandt was travelling with five of Hitler's bodyguards in a second, open, dark-blue seven-litre supercharged Mercedes.[112] As soon as the cars had passed the Thuringian Forest, people in the villages began to recognize Hitler; local party leaders were quick to telephone their colleagues in the next village, so that by the time Hitler's entourage arrived, the entire village was on the street to greet the Führer, waving and cheering 'Heil Hitler!'. Sometimes the railway barriers were used to slow down the convoy even further. Exhausted by this reception, the travellers stopped at an inn in Hildburgshausen. The streets soon filled with 'thousands of people' and, under a 'rain of flowers', the convoy eventually reached the medieval gate. Children and adolescents were running after the cars and were asking for autographs. Once the cars had left the town, Hitler leaned over to Speer and said: 'Until now only one German has been hailed like this: Luther. When he rode through the country people gathered from far and wide to cheer him. As they do for me today!'[113] Hitler's belief in his own self-importance and his quasi-religious mission to the world seemed to be stronger than ever before.

September 1934 saw Brandt accompanying Hitler to the Nuremberg Party Rally where he was drawn further into the realm of party politics and propaganda. Leni Riefenstahl's *Triumph des Willens* ('Triumph of the Will', 1935), shot during the rally, glorified Hitler as the leader who had come from the skies to save Germany.[114] The rally and the film marked the transition to the Führer cult and was one of the regime's greatest propaganda coups. Another way of winning over the masses was the regime's attempt to establish places of worship and remembrance; these allowed tens of thousands of people to channel their emotions into a state-sanctioned narrative of the Nazi movement that was characterized by sacrifice, obedience and heroism. On 8 October, for example, Brandt travelled with Hitler and his chauffeurs, Emil Maurice and Julius Schaub, to Landsberg to visit the prison complex in which Hitler had written his book *Mein Kampf*.[115] On 22 November, Brandt was back in Berlin. As a civil servant, he was now obliged to take an oath of loyalty to Adolf Hitler, previously sworn to the Weimar Constitution.[116] The clinic administration in Berlin-Ziegelstrasse had requested his presence a number of times, but he had always been out of town, accompanying the Reich Chancellor on his journeys. Travelling for the first six months with Hitler seems to have been less dull than Brandt wanted others to believe. It must have felt like a prolonged holiday for Brandt. Photographs from the period, shot by Hoffmann at around 1934 and 1935, show Brandt, dressed in shorts, sitting with Erna Hoffmann and Anni Brandt on the terrace of the Berghof.[117] In others, taken in August 1935, he and his wife sit outside Haus Wachenfeld together with Hitler's personal staff, including Otto Dietrich, Willy Kannenberg, Christa Schröder, Johanna Wolf and Albert Speer.[118] These pictures were probably not for publication, but they do seem to suggest that Brandt was enjoying his new assignment at the heart of government. True, the work itself may have been 'not to his liking', but his personal enthusiasm and pride at being at Hitler's side was unconcealed.

On 4 May 1935, Brandt was present when Hitler visited the battleship *Scharnhorst*. Again, he found himself among the top Nazi leaders who were pressing for more radical policy measures against communists, socialists and Jews. Brandt and Rudolf Heß are pictured listening to Hitler, dressed in uniform and riding boots, while Hans Baur, Hitler's pilot, is taking pictures.[119] In another image we see Hitler talking to Himmler. And in yet another picture we see Hitler and Goebbels. From the beginning, Brandt was never far from the centre of power. During May and July 1935, he went on an eight-week training course at the Reserve Battalion (*Ersatzbataillon*) of the 12th Infantry Regiment at Blankenburg in the

Harz mountains. Even during that time, he was asked to accompany Hitler on his
vacation. On 24 July 1935, he was present when Werner von Blomberg, the Reich
Army Minister, visited Hitler's Berghof chalet. Photographs of Blomberg's visit
show Brandt dressed in a neatly ironed white shirt and tie and wearing cream-
coloured riding trousers.[120] To his right we see Göring sporting traditional German
lederhosen, and Hitler wearing a traditional Bavarian jacket. These images were
not an accidental snapshot of the head of state enjoying a day out with some of his
closest political allies, but part of a carefully orchestrated propaganda campaign
which aimed to reach a wide cross-section of German society. Hitler and the Nazi
leadership were shown to be in touch with the romantic tradition of the Bavarian
landscape, with its scenic mountains and cosy peasant houses. These images were
meant to convey a sense of the calmness and order of a government that was rooted
in national tradition, folklore and local custom. The portrayal of Nazi leaders in
an atmosphere of peace and tranquillity had little in common with the system of
surveillance and political intimidation that had descended on Germany. However,
it enabled Nazi propagandists to detach the image of the Führer from a regime that
was bent on unlimited aggression, and for which the segregation, discrimination
and expulsion of minorities, and political murder, were legitimate means of governance. Brandt's medical expertise may not have been needed, certainly not often
and at the beginning, but he was part of the backdrop in the image of National
Socialism as a national conservative and *völkisch* movement, a pawn on the stage
to deflect attention away from the culture of fear and terror which the Gestapo and
other Nazi military units were spreading throughout Germany.

VI. ON THE ROAD TO 'EUTHANASIA'

By late 1934, the Nazi leadership was beginning to react to pressure from the grass
roots of the movement to ban relations between Germans and Jews, and exclude
Jews from German society. Wherever the leadership travelled, local party leaders
were erecting anti-Jewish noticeboards by the roadside and in villages, which stated
'Jews Not Wanted Here'. It is inconceivable that Brandt would not have understood
the overall policy direction of this regime. By mid-1935, at the latest, he must have
been aware that he was in the service of one of the most ruthless and brutal regimes
in Europe. Prior to this, the regime had shown its true nature on all matters related
to the mentally ill and physically handicapped. Brandt must have agreed with the
regime's policy of racial hygiene, which advocated marriage advice for hereditary
healthy Germans and the compulsory sterilization of the mentally ill. In Brandt's
mind there existed a conceptual link between the successful implementation of
eugenic measures and the need to carry out a 'euthanasia' programme. In 1946, he
remarked about the German sterilization law:

> The more decisive eugenics, that is the prophylaxis and prevention of hereditary ill
> offspring, is being carried out in a comprehensive and consistent fashion, the less the
> whole problem of euthanasia needs to be debated.[121]

In August 1933, Walter Schultze, health officer in the Bavarian Ministry of the Interior, had made it clear that he wanted minor cases of the mentally ill and criminals excluded from the German community on a compulsory basis, and placed in working camps: 'This policy has begun already in our present concentration camps.'[122] Others thought that the opportunity should not be lost to exclude Jews from the German *Volksgemeinschaft*. At one of their annual meetings in Nuremberg in December 1934, doctors sent a telegram to Wilhelm Frick, Reich Minister of the Interior, demanding the 'heaviest punishment' for any kind of sexual contact between a Jew and a 'German woman'. They saw this as the only option in order to maintain German racial purity and prevent 'further Jewish racial poisoning and pollution of German blood'.[123] Reacting to such radical views among the grass-roots supporters of the movement, Gerhard Wagner, the Reich Physicians' Leader, took up the issue less than a year later and helped to establish the Nuremberg Race Laws. Until his sudden death in 1939, Wagner remained one of the most powerful competitors in the struggle over who would be placed in charge of German health and medicine. After Wagner's death, however, things changed. His death meant that the question over who was in charge of German medicine was to be renegotiated and fought over, a battle which was eventually decided in favour of Brandt.

Sterilizing the mentally defective was only the first step in the regime's campaign to improve the human race. The aim was to eliminate 'useless eaters' and 'hopeless cases' from the German body politic. While discussions on the sterilization law were under way, Lammers later recalled, Hitler had contemplated killing mental patients, but had dropped the idea because he feared resistance from the Catholic Church.[124] In 1947, Brandt confirmed that such ideas seem to have been discussed and were in Hitler's mind long before the 'euthanasia' programme was put in place. The initiative for these discussions and proposals, however, did not originate with Hitler himself, but from local party leaders and radical forces at the grass-roots level of the movement.

Brandt recalled that Wagner apparently took up the issue of euthanasia during the Nuremberg Party Rally in 1935, after he had announced in his speech on 12 September that a 'Law to Protect German Blood' was imminent. While Nazi lawyers were preoccupied with drafting the notorious Nuremberg Laws, more sinister plans were in the making. Wagner may have raised the issue of euthanasia with Hitler during these hectic days in order to obtain one of the famous 'Führer decisions' (*Führerentscheidung*), an oral instruction which operated like a written government decree on a certain policy measure. Quite often there was no witness to the conversation and no protocol. It was a form of informal government which became increasingly the norm, but which also created enormous potential for the misunderstanding and misrepresentation of what Hitler had said or wanted. The possibilities for confusion and chaos were infinite. At the same time, this style of governance left the options open for Hitler to change his mind at a later stage, and to stay aloof from having to take responsibility for certain policy measures.

To prepare the ground for killing patients, Wagner had commissioned the shooting of the racial propaganda film 'Hereditarily Ill' (*Erbkrank*), which was intended to criminalize, degrade and dehumanize the mentally and physically handicapped. The film depicted mentally and physically handicapped patients as a burden on society, people for whom there could be no room in what the Nazis envisioned as a racially pure society.[125] Brandt later recalled that Hitler had been 'deeply impressed' after watching the silent black-and-white film, and commissioned a more elaborate sound version from Goebbels' Propaganda Ministry. Hitler felt, however, that the timing was not right for the actual introduction of such radical measures. He believed that the leadership of the party had to proceed with caution until the domestic situation permitted such an unprecedented government programme. In 1947, Brandt told the court:

> I have to assume that the Führer was of the opinion that such a problem would be easier and smoother to carry out in wartime, since the obvious resistance which one could expect from the churches would not play such a prominent role amidst the events of wartime as it otherwise would ... He [Hitler] is supposed to have told the former Physicians' Leader Wagner in 1935, that if war should break out, he would take up these euthanasia questions and would want to implement them.[126]

Less than a fortnight earlier, one of the elder statesmen of the German racial hygiene movement, Alfred Ploetz, had highlighted the theoretical link between the issue of euthanasia and war. On 1 September 1935, Ploetz gave a talk on 'Race Hygiene and War' at the International Congress for Race Hygiene in Berlin, in which he juxtaposed the effects of the Nazi sterilization law with the negative selection process during times of war: 'From a clear racial hygiene point of view we would have to strive to balance the counter-selective effects of war by increasing the number of eliminations,' he told the audience.[127] Hitler must have been well acquainted with the argument, given that he accepted the necessity of introducing radical measures in time of war in order to balance the deaths of 'valuable national comrades' with the elimination of 'ballast existences'.[128]

In 1936, Wagner discussed the question of euthanasia again among a 'small circle of friends' who included Walther Gross, the head of the Race Political Office (*Rassenpolitisches Amt*, RPA). During the discussions, the conceptual link between war and the killing programme was always upheld.[129] Hermann Boehm, who attended some of the discussions, recalled that Wagner told his supporters that Hitler would launch such a programme during a forthcoming war, to rid Germany and the German people of the burden of looking after the mentally ill. A programme to eliminate the handicapped and mentally ill was also easier to introduce in times of war, Wagner told his colleagues, because life was generally worth less. He attempted to dispel Boehm's concerns by telling him that his supporters were beginning a nationwide propaganda campaign against mentally and physically handicapped patients. Schoolchildren were subjected to crude utilitarian ideas of health and welfare in books and classes, and told that extensive expenditure on 'useless eaters' was better spent on healthy 'national comrades'. Medical students were educated by means of dehumanizing teaching films which often depicted patients as mere objects of scientific curiosity.[130] Educators saw 'war-neurotics' as 'deaf, worthless idiots', and promoted the elimination (*Ausscheidung*) of all Jews, Africans and Asians.[131] Combining religious rhetoric with an economic rationale, Nazi magazines presented the mentally ill as a financial and emotional burden on society, and called for their 'deliverance' from suffering. In April 1937, for example, the SS magazine *Das Schwarze Korps* ran the headline 'What is More Humane?' in order to advocate the elimination of mental defectives.[132] Officials responsible for cure and nursing homes were also discussing the killing of asylum inmates as early as 1938 in order to solve some of the problems in the sector. During a conference in the summer of 1938, one of the officials told those attending that 'the solution for the asylum system would be easy if one were to eliminate the people'. Brandt was not party to the discussions on compulsory sterilization and euthanasia, nor was he actively influencing the policy direction of Hitler's government at this point. But it stretches credibility to its limit to suggest that Brandt would not have been aware of the violent nature and geopolitical aims of the Nazi regime.

VII. MANAGING HITLER'S HEALTH

For almost two years, until the arrival of Theodor Morell, Hitler's personal physician (*Leibarzt*) and a former ship's doctor, Brandt remained the unchallenged authority and first point of call in all questions relating to Hitler's health and well-being and that of his staff. In practical terms this had little meaning, because there was hardly anything to do in the early years of Brandt's assignment, except that Hitler became increasingly concerned with his own mortality. Hitler must have felt a sense of exhaustion after those frantic years in opposition, and the need to press on if he wanted to achieve his monumental goals. Despite an unhealthy diet and lack of physical exercise, his health remained relatively good, except for the stomach spasms which plagued him for years. In December 1934, Hitler poisoned himself with neo-Ballistol, a kind of oil hunters use to clean their rifle barrels. A medical variant of this oil existed, and Hitler must have been under the impression that it would help him to overcome his constant gastrointestinal troubles. His symptoms were headaches, double vision, dizziness and tinnitus. The SS physician, Ernst Robert Grawitz, who later became the President of the German Red Cross, diagnosed neo-Ballistol poisoning. In total secrecy, Hitler was rushed to the Westend Sanatorium, where he was X-rayed and his stomach was emptied.[133] It was one of the few instances where Hitler readily complied with his doctor's advice.

Hitler generally exhibited an extraordinary shyness when it came to undressing in front of physicians. To be examined by Brandt or any other of his doctors became a major undertaking; he, the man in charge of Germany's future, could hardly bear the idea of being the 'object' of a medical examination. Whenever Hitler fell ill, Brandt and his colleagues needed all available diplomatic skills to rescue a situation which could easily develop into a national crisis. By 1942, the health of Hitler had reached such a level of strategic importance that every person who came into direct contact with the Führer, or was working in his immediate vicinity, needed to prove themselves absolutely free of illnesses or disease-causing agents.[134]

Hanni Morell, the wife of Theodor Morell, compared his eccentricities in all matters concerned with his body with those of an old virginal spinster.[135] To conduct a thorough medical examination was almost impossible; X-ray pictures were out of the question. Morell had enormous difficulties in fulfilling his medical duties. Comprehensive neurological or internal examinations were never carried out. Hitler's lungs and abdomen were never examined. Until the last days of the Reich, Morell tried persistently, but unsuccessfully, to persuade Hitler to have a full X-ray of his body. Whenever Hitler was in pain, Morell would arrive with his doctor's bag in Hitler's sleeping quarters, the only place where examinations were permitted, and felt or touched the area of Hitler's body where it hurt. Further chemical and radiological tests could only be carried out after persistent persuasion. To a limited extent the measuring of blood pressure, pulse, heartbeat and temperature were possible, as were standard reflex tests. Yet Hitler disliked finding himself in a potentially compromising position, for example when he needed to vomit. The administration of drugs by injection (because parts of his body had to be exposed) needed great diplomatic skill. Even being measured by a tailor produced major problems because Hitler hated to be touched.[136] All such eccentricities suddenly had no meaning when parts of his head or face were injured, especially those organs such as his voice or eyes which Hitler regarded as instrumental in controlling the people and the masses. He was hypersensitive to the slightest idea that these organs might be defective – and undermine the popular image and impact of the Führer cult – so the best experts in the country would be ordered to treat him with all available skills. At these times Hitler made no fuss.

One such incident occurred in May 1935, during the negotiations for the Anglo-German naval treaty, when Hitler suddenly developed problems with his speech. For months he had been coughing so much that ordinary people were beginning to notice it when he was speaking on the radio. Only Goebbels seems to have had his mind on other matters. By the end of April, he recorded that Hitler was in 'brilliant health and mood'.[137] But Brandt and others realized that Hitler was not well. Lacking the specific medical expertise, Brandt called in Carl von Eicken, director of the ear, nose and throat clinic at the Charité in Berlin, who had first been introduced to Hitler's inner circle after Brückner's car accident in 1933.[138] On 13 May, von Eicken examined Hitler in the presence of Brandt in the Reich Chancellery. Together with Professor Rössle from the Pathological Institute, von Eicken diagnosed an unusually large vocal polyp, but reassured Hitler that this was a 'very slight matter which an operation would remove'.[139] Hitler, distrusting his doctors, believed that his advisers were concealing the full facts from him. His reaction cannot be described as anything other than paranoid. He immediately saw himself dying in agonizing pain from cancer, like the Emperor Frederick III who had died of cancer of the throat. Losing his speech, and therefore his ability to reach out and manipulate the masses, would be a disaster for Hitler. Brandt and von Eicken eventually managed to calm him down after it turned out that the polyp was benign.

The operation on Hitler's throat took place on 23 May 1935 in the Reich

Chancellery, where all the necessary equipment had been installed to ensure the greatest level of secrecy. Brandt, who was present during the operation, also attended von Eicken's follow-up examination the next day. After a month of slight discomfort, Hitler recovered fully. Brandt and the other medical experts cancelled the famous speech therapist and actor Professor Nadolesny, who had been scheduled to give Hitler a number of speech lessons after the operation. As it turned out, Nadolesny's services were not called for.[140] Other medical experts were similarly unsuccessful in offering their expertise to Hitler. Georg Rosina Kalkum, for example, offered Hitler a special training course for his 'talking tools', to overcome the illness. According to Kalkum, the operation had only eliminated the immediate symptoms but not the cause, which lay in the unsophisticated use of the organ.[141] Although medical experts were discussing the case, the German public hardly took any notice of the incident.

Years later, at the end of 1944, Hitler suggested that the treatment had not been successful. 'These morons and idiots', he told Morell, 'should have treated my troubles with the larynx instead ... My dear doctor, you have no idea how furious I was at the time.'[142] It was one of many incidents for which Hitler would rewrite history. Since Brandt and all the other doctors involved in the former treatment had lost Hitler's confidence by 1944, there was no need for him to express any sign of gratitude. It is more likely, however, that Hitler was exceedingly grateful to his doctors at the time. Von Eicken apparently received such a rich reward for his service that he was genuinely embarrassed.[143] In the same year, 1935, von Eicken returned to treat Hitler for a slight discomfort of the throat but could not diagnose anything. Then Hitler remembered that he had removed a thorn from his finger with his teeth and had accidentally swallowed it. Brandt and others managing Hitler's health slowly came to realize that the leader of the Nazi revolution was, at times, somewhat clumsy.

Several months later, on 20 May 1936, Brandt needed to call for von Eicken yet again. This time Hitler was suffering from tinnitus, a high-pitched and metallic sound in his ears, especially at night. Again no medical complications could be found. Von Eicken suggested that the symptoms were probably due to lack of sleep, too much work and depression over the death of one of his drivers. He recommended walks, alternating hot and cold baths, and mild sleeping drugs.[144] When the tinnitus continued to irritate him during the Wagner Opera Festival in Bayreuth, Hitler swallowed large amounts of lecithin, which Winifred Wagner had recommended to him. Apparently, the symptoms then ceased. In many respects Hitler showed signs of being a hypochondriac.

In 1935, Brandt became aware that Hitler, then forty-six years old, started to have problems reading his daily pile of government papers. His doctors diagnosed presbyopia and gave him a pair of glasses. He disliked wearing them in private and never wore them in public. They changed his outward appearance which was so central to the image of the Nazi movement. Only a few photographs show Hitler wearing his glasses. In 1939 the Ruhnke company in Berlin was granted permission to supply Hitler with three pairs of gold-framed glasses.[145] Until 1944, the prescription remained more or less the same. What did change, however, was the way in which papers were presented to Hitler. A special 'Führer-typewriter' (*Führerschreibmaschine*) was built, with letters 12 mm in size. All government letters and briefing papers had to be written on this machine. In July 1942, Hitler started complaining about pain and bad vision in his right eye; within days the symptoms disappeared and only recurred two years later, in February 1944. After two weeks of bad vision, the Berlin ophthalmologist, Walter Löhlein, was called to the Berghof to conduct a full examination. Löhlein diagnosed bleeding in Hitler's right eye, which needed treatment and rest. A month later, Hitler was advised to rest for two months, something that was totally impossible for him in the midst of the military campaign which was going so badly. However, Löhlein's medical diagnosis allowed Hitler to indulge in self-pity and to exaggerate his state of health. On 22 March 1944 he visited the palace of Kleßheim, where Speer was recovering from physical exhaustion, and told him that his (Hitler's) health was in such a serious condition that 'he would soon lose his eyesight'.[146] It was little more than another theatrical exaggeration on Hitler's part to win back his minister's trust. He needed Speer's expertise to continue the war. It was a tactical device which Hitler had used time and time again. In October 1937, for example, after two years of minor health complications, he had told a meeting of senior propaganda officials that it was likely that he would not live long since both his parents had died young, and that therefore Germany needed to tackle the problem of living space while he was still alive.[147]

The most important clue in identifying Hitler's body after the war was his teeth. Allied and, in particular, Russian investigators spent an enormous amount of time and resources interviewing Hitler's dentists and locating his dental records. In addition to health problems resulting from natural ageing, Hitler's teeth were in a permanently bad condition as a result of his unorthodox eating habits. Since his childhood and youth, Hitler had eaten large amounts of sweets and chocolate cakes, which had ruined most of his teeth. Christa Schröder, Hitler's secretary, confirmed the bad state of the Chancellor's teeth; she, like many others who met the dictator, commented on Hitler's bad breath. At the end of 1933, the Berlin dental surgeon Johannes Blaschke was called to see Hitler for the first time. He found Hitler's teeth in a dire state; many of them were either infected or loose, and part of the jaw was diseased. Blaschke's step-by-step treatment was long and troublesome. A special dental studio was established within the Reich Chancellery to ensure that the German people could continue to believe in the immortality and superhuman nature of their leader. The evidence is conclusive, though, that from 1933 onwards Hitler needed constant medical and dental provision. Brandt never seems to have become involved in these treatments other than, perhaps, monitoring access to Hitler's body.

In 1936, Brandt's monopoly was increasingly challenged when a second doctor was introduced at court. Brandt and his assistants might not have belonged to the medical elite of the country, but they had enjoyed a sound medical training. They were not entirely disreputable, as was the man who for the next nine years held the health of the German Reich Chancellor in his hands: Theodor Morell. His arrival at Hitler's court led Brandt to consider his position, because he felt that he was being pushed 'completely against the wall'.[148] Coming from a family of peasants in Hesse, the more favourable descriptions of Morell range from a charlatan to a greedy, pompous quack. Yet Hitler was impressed. Throughout the politically tense year of 1936, Hitler exhibited increasing signs of stomach cramps which were accompanied by eczema on his legs, making him feel uncomfortable and irritated. In December, he asked Morell to treat him with some of his vitamin pills, but progress was slow. In late 1937, the stomach cramps suddenly disappeared, and Morell was credited with this apparent medical success. Hitler would believe in this 'quack doctor' until the Third Reich was in ruins. By then most men at Hitler's court had realized that the Führer had become dependent on Morell's drugs and secret injections, if he wasn't, indeed, addicted to them. When the Allies captured Morell, they could not believe their eyes; war crimes investigators were appalled by his character, questioning in total disbelief how such a caricature of a man could have become one of the leading physicians at Hitler's court. Those who saw him, Hugh Trevor-Roper remarked in his intelligence report about Hitler's last days, saw

> a gross but deflated old man, of cringing manners, inarticulate in speech and with the hygiene habits of a pig, [and] could not conceive how a man so utterly devoid of self-respect could ever have been selected as a personal physician by anyone who had even a limited possibility of choice.[149]

Despite holding no rank in either army or party, Morell wore a self-designed pale grey uniform which resembled that of Göring. Many German physicians, including Brandt, realized that he knew little about medical science or medical practice, but was full of half-educated knowledge and mystical beliefs. 'He was a businessman, not a doctor,' Brandt claimed after the war, 'greedy for money and mean; he also treated his staff badly'.[150]

As a 'specialist' in venereal diseases, Morell was introduced to Hitler by his official photographer, Hoffmann. Brandt recalled that Hoffmann had consulted Morell because he, Hoffmann, had contracted gonorrhoea. When Hitler requested that Hoffmann return to Berlin, Hoffmann asked if he could bring his personal physician with him. 'Morell accompanied Hoffmann to Berlin and lived at Hoffmann's home where he had frequent contact with Hitler. Thus he soon became physician to Hitler too,' Brandt remembered.[151] Morell had treated film and theatre stars since 1918 on the Kurfürstendamm in Berlin, but his appetite for influence and money drove him to want more. He first became known as one of the doctors at the Berghof, later as the personal physician to Hitler. Once allowed entry into court, he and his greedy wife, who wanted him to be the director of a pharmaceutical company, skilfully exploited their contacts to build factories and produce patent remedies.[152] During the war, the purchase of some of these drugs was made compulsory. For example, with Hitler's personal approval, Morell's lice-powder was made compulsory under the name of 'Russia' for the entire German army. For others, he secured a monopoly. His 'vitamin chocolates' made him a fortune. Another successful venture was the production and sale of the sulphonamide, 'Ultraseptyl', by his company in Budapest. Despite the warning from medical experts that the drug was harmful to the nerves, the SS and Hitler insisted on believing that sulphonamides were a 'miracle drug' (*Wundermittel*) which could prevent all infections if only correctly administered.[153] Some of the regime's most horrific medical experiments on humans later proved that they were wrong.[154] In the end, Hitler himself became a guinea-pig for Morell's financial ambitions. He literally tested dozens of unknown drugs on Hitler. Opinions on proper medical treatment among Brandt and his colleagues were diametrically opposed to Morell's ideas of fancy nostrums and pills. It therefore came as no surprise when, after years of simmering tensions, Brandt and his colleagues seized the chance to expel Morell from the Führer's headquarters in 1944. The plan backfired, and Brandt was dismissed as Hitler's doctor instead.

4

Hitler's Envoy

I. THE NUREMBERG CANCER SCANDAL

Brandt only gradually became Hitler's envoy and 'troubleshooter' for special missions that vaguely related to medicine. In the period after his appointment, he was frequently consulted on issues relating to medical science and the medical profession. Whether as a key person with whom Hitler could discuss his health, as someone who would relay information to and from Hitler, examine and treat members of Hitler's entourage, investigate and assess the conduct of German medical professionals, make representations on behalf of German scientists, wait in attendance in case a visiting official should injure himself, or as someone who would attend to people who by chance had had an accident involving a member of Hitler's court, Brandt was becoming Hitler's factotum. During the New Year reception in 1939, for example, Brandt was waiting in attendance in the New Reich Chancellery with a group of soldiers carrying a stretcher, in case one of the elderly diplomats accidentally slipped on the shiny marble floor.[1] In early June 1941, Brandt attended to a female cyclist who had collided at a junction in Berchtesgaden with the car of Herbert Döring, the manager of Hitler's Berghof.[2] The woman suffered multiple and serious head injuries and was brought to the nearby hospital. Always concerned about his public image, Hitler ordered Brandt to the hospital to look after the woman's injuries, as he had done for Brückner in 1933, and deliver a large bunch of flowers from Hitler.[3] A year later, in May 1942, Brandt and Maximinian de Crinis, director of the psychiatric clinic at the Charité in Berlin, travelled to Oldenburg to attend to Carl Röver, the *Gauleiter* of Weser-Ems and one of the earliest supporters of the Nazi Party.[4] Suffering from paranoia, Röver had become increasingly erratic and irrational in his behaviour. In the end he had to be saved from a lake. Röver died two days after Brandt and de Crinis had visited him, sparking conspiracy theories ever since.[5] In some cases, Brandt was also charged with organizing matters which had nothing to do with medicine, but with film, art and architecture.[6] By the end of the 1930s, Brandt had established for himself the position of Hitler's envoy, charged with investigating, organizing or solving minor and major medical problems relating to Hitler or his staff, or indeed relating to German medicine as a whole.

Summaries of conflicts among party functionaries and individual petitions often reached Hitler's personal desk, requesting him to provide the quarrelling factions with a Führer decision. Before such a decision was taken, Hitler would dispatch Brandt to examine the matter informally and provide him with an oral report.

Given that Hitler had the total monopoly over these informal and often secretive investigations, he could remain detached from events like an ancient emperor, or deny knowledge, and thus responsibility, at any point later. At the same time, it gave Brandt the opportunity to gradually increase his political power in all areas of German medical science.

Apart from a few historical fragments, for example when Goebbels became involved in the discussions and recorded them in his diary, we have almost no record of Brandt's conversations with Hitler. For individual incidents, Brandt reconstructed these conversations during the Nuremberg Doctors' Trial, but these reconstructions are selective and biased and need to be treated with caution because of the context in which they originated. One of Hoffmann's photographs is emblematic of the way in which these conversations would have taken place.[7] It was shot on the Berghof during yet another of Hitler's holidays, lasting from 1 August to 3 September 1938. Brandt and Hitler are standing together on the terrace of the Berghof. Apart from a man standing in the background, the two men are alone. There are no other people in their immediate vicinity who might be party to their conversation. They can talk in confidence. Brandt is presenting a letter or a document to Hitler. Rather than taking the piece of paper in his own hands and reading it for himself, Hitler, arms behind his back, is listening to what Brandt has to say about the matter. If anything, the image shows the extent to which Brandt was able to bring matters of importance to Hitler's attention, and enjoy the ear of the Führer.

In July 1936, Hitler asked Brandt to investigate an apparent cancer scandal in Nuremberg.[8] It became one of Brandt's first assignments as Hitler's special envoy. The 'organic' physician Wilhelm von Brehmer (who was on good terms with the Franconian *Gauleiter* Julius Streicher, one of the country's most fanatical anti-Semites) had suggested that human cancer was an infectious disease which could be cured by blood transfusion in conjunction with a special chemotherapeutic agent. Blood donors had to be of the Aryan race. Given the ideological context in which the research had been carried out, some medical experts were sceptical about von Brehmer's findings. To avoid international embarrassment, they opposed the proposal that von Brehmer should represent the profession at the International Congress of Pathology in Brussels. The leader of the German delegation, Max Borst, eventually wrote to Hitler directly, explaining the controversy and requesting a Führer decision.

Given Hitler's personal interest in all matters related to cancer and smoking, and the possibility that von Brehmer's work had the potential to boost the reputation of German medical science, he commissioned Brandt to investigate the alleged scandal. Backed up by Georg Magnus, his superior at Berlin University, Brandt invited von Brehmer to Berlin to test his hypothesis through a series of laboratory experiments. As predicted by Brandt and others, none of the experiments showed any meaningful results.[9] This did not prevent von Brehmer, however, from persisting that his claims were true, and from carrying out further research at the Paracelsus Institute in Nuremberg, which Streicher had helped to establish. Once again alerted about the potential of von Brehmer's findings, this time by Streicher, Hitler commissioned Brandt to examine the matter once more. On 11 July 1936, he asked Lammers to pay Brandt 4,000 Reichsmark for the continuation of his investigation.[10] Together with a photographer, Brandt travelled to Nuremberg to document von Brehmer's apparent success in treating cancer patients. None of the images, however, showed any positive results. Indeed, it became clear that von Brehmer and Streicher had been forging the evidence. The argument which subsequently ensued with Streicher made Brandt realize that he had trespassed onto political territory. His involvement in the cancer scandal exposed him, perhaps for the first time, to the ruthless nature of Hitler's followers. Not only did the President of the police advise him to avoid Nuremberg in the future, but Hitler himself ordered Brandt never to visit Nuremberg again, except in his company.[11]

The von Brehmer case also illustrates how Brandt exploited his unique position. Rather than being a pawn in the hand of Nazi functionaries, Brandt took the initiative to improve his own position of power. Goebbels' diary entries from July 1936 reveal the extent to which Brandt's informal and outwardly apolitical role as Hitler's doctor became intertwined with policy decisions at the highest level of government. His diary entries also give the impression that Hitler's regime was lacking direction and clear objectives. Rather than prioritizing issues and delegating them to the relevant administrative channels, the small group around Hitler acted on impulse on every bit of incoming information, without reflection or proper consultation. In the case of Germany's involvement in the Spanish Civil War, for example, Hitler took the decision alone, without consulting Göring and General Werner von Blomberg, the Reich Defence Minister, or any other member of the Nazi leadership. Goebbels' diary entries show the permanent and frantic activism which surrounded those in Hitler's immediate vicinity.

On Saturday 18 July 1936, Goebbels left the Berghof at 6 a.m., drove to the airport in Ainring, boarded a plane and landed a couple of hours later in Berlin Tempelhof. From there he was whisked to the official opening of the exhibition 'Germany', followed by a flying visit to his house on the Schwanenwerder island. The next day he took a plane to Bayreuth where he was invited to stay with Hitler and his staff at Haus Wahnfried: 'We live here with the Führer and it is marvellous,' Goebbels noted. It allowed Goebbels to scan the atmosphere for clues about domestic or foreign policy issues. On Tuesday 21 July, Hitler talked about the danger of Jews and Bolshevists: 'He will oppress them in Germany. May the [rest of the] world do what it likes.'[12] The next day, 22 July, Hitler left Bayreuth, together with Brandt, for a flying visit to Nuremberg. Upon Hitler's return to Bayreuth on the same day, Goebbels was briefed and, of course, agreed with Hitler on the need for immediate action: '... later discussed with the Führer question of Nuremberg cancer treatment. That seems to be a fraud. Intervention is necessary.'[13] The next day, Thursday 23 July, Goebbels wanted to hear more about the matter and conferred with Brandt himself: 'I discuss the cancer fraud with Dr. Brandt. Action needs to be taken against it.'[14] Apart from recording the discussions with Brandt and Hitler, Goebbels has a lot to say about the quality of individual artists and plays that had been staged during the Bayreuth festival, such as *Parsival* and *Lohengrin*. He also mentions talks with Hitler about children and discusses Germany's covert military involvement in what would rapidly develop into the Spanish Civil War. Two days later, on 25 July, Brandt told Goebbels that von Brehmer's research findings were fake and his claims nothing but propaganda: 'Dr. Brandt tells me about his visit to the Nuremberg Cancer Institute. That is pure fraud.'[15] On the same day, late in the evening, Hitler took the decision to send aid to General Franco in the form of twenty Junkers JU-52 transport planes, thus committing Germany to becoming involved in the Spanish Civil War. 'We're taking part a bit in Spain. Not visible. Who knows what it's good for,' is how Goebbels recorded Hitler's adventurous foreign policy decision.[16]

These historical fragments, however biased they may be, show the disparate and unorganized flow of information from the centre to the periphery and vice versa. Like satellites, various personalities were constantly circling around Hitler, whose style of leadership had thrown the doors wide open for mismanagement and corruption. In the Brehmer case, Brandt was the obvious choice for the assignment, not because he was particularly qualified, but because he was physically at hand to deal with the matter swiftly, inconspicuously and outside of government protocol. Brandt's findings gave Hitler the necessary information to plan his next move. Hitler now knew the outcome of any inquiry before it had been set up, let alone started. The information was political capital. By September 1936, during the Nuremberg 'Party Rally of Honour', Hitler called for an investigation into the Brehmer incident (much to the embarrassment of Brehmer's ally Streicher). Leonardo Conti, the health officer in the Prussian Ministry of the Interior and future Reich Health Leader (*Reichsgesundheitsführer*), was asked to head the commission and, like Brandt, came to the conclusion that Brehmer's theory could not be upheld. Brehmer was prohibited from attending the Brussels conference and his theory disappeared into oblivion.

The Brehmer cancer scandal was one of the first cases in which Brandt acted as Hitler's special envoy to investigate a matter before an official decision had been taken. Once Hitler had all the information to hand, he acted as head of government. He did not instruct Brandt (who officially was only his escort physician) to lead the official inquiry, but turned to Conti (who should have been in charge in the first place), and thereby gave the investigation an air of government authority. The military authorities and the Reich Health Ministry later conducted their own independent investigations, which came to the same conclusion. Brandt's presence in Hitler's entourage had not only allowed him to sideline Conti, but had given him additional 'clout' at Hitler's court, something he intended to turn into political capital.

Several weeks after the cancer scandal, Brandt publicly supported Henri Chaoul, head of the X-ray department at the Charité in Berlin, in his plan to establish an independent X-ray institute which would carry out X-ray exposures on cancer patients. Chaoul's newly developed method of cancer treatment, however, raised concerns among the German medical establishment. The surgeon, Ferdinand

Sauerbruch, for one, objected that the method was not sufficiently developed to warrant the creation of an independent research institute. His concerns were shared by SS-Standartenführer Werner Zschintzsch, a senior official in the Reich Ministry of Education, who in March 1936 had been appointed State Secretary (*Staatssekretär*) to cleanse German educational resources from non-Aryan tendencies.[17] On 27 October 1936, Lammers eventually reported the facts of the matter to Hitler, who decided that a meeting between Brandt, Zschintzsch and Lammers should be convened to resolve the issue.[18] The first meeting, which took place four days later, on 31 October, showed no tangible result other than that Chaoul's Aryan descent was questioned. The subsequent investigation concluded that although Chaoul was of 'non-German' blood, he was also not of Jewish descent. This opened up the way for Hitler to side once more with Brandt. In 1937, after further representations from Brandt in December 1936, and a specific directive from Hitler, Chaoul was awarded a professorship and put in charge of the X-ray institute of the Robert Koch Hospital in Berlin. Hitler's doctor, on the other hand, benefited from the fact that he had prevailed against one of the leading figures of the German medical establishment. After he had been promoted to SS-Hauptsturmführer in September 1936, Brandt was appointed first physician at the surgical clinic in Berlin. His direct intervention and support for Chaoul's method in the immediate aftermath of the von Brehmer cancer scandal shows that he had gained in self-confidence, and was ready to play a more active political part in shaping the formation of German medical science.[19]

The von Brehmer case enabled Brandt to establish himself more firmly at the centre of government, liaise with some of the highest-ranking members of the regime, and gradually construct a position for himself as Hitler's special emissary. Above all, the episode throws into relief Brandt's successful attempt to position himself as a modernizer, whose aim was to advance German medical research. The German medical establishment, on the other hand, grudgingly came to acknowledge that Brandt's political power could not be underestimated any longer. The outcome suited Hitler. It not only strengthened his own hand vis-à-vis the medical profession, but allowed him to influence – directly and unbureaucratically through his doctor – the state of affairs in the German health and welfare system. Hitler used Brandt as a convenient channel of information so that he could keep himself informed of ongoing developments, without having to consult any official government agency. This allowed him to respond quickly and flexibly, but also unpredictably, to whatever domestic or foreign policy issue caught his attention. His interference in, and management of, matters of political importance was haphazard, uncoordinated and arbitrary. It was a recipe for administrative chaos. It also ensured that no formal record of vital policy decisions was ever produced which, in turn, allowed Hitler – and Brandt as well – to detach himself from decisions or events that were potentially embarrassing. Brandt, in short, was beginning to learn and imitate Hitler's style of leadership.

II. ON A MISSION TO GREECE

When not acting as Hitler's special envoy, Brandt was busy touring Europe with his benefactor, serving in the armed forces or fulfilling his duty as a surgeon in Berlin.[20] At other times, he spent relaxing hours with his young family at the Berghof. According to some post-war testimony, Brandt was allegedly a great womanizer, and apparently had a mistress called Elisabeth Jördens. It is more likely, however, that this was one of many folk tales that were circulating among some of Brandt's staff after the war.[21] When asked about his 'official mistress' in 1947, Brandt did not give the impression of someone who had committed adultery: 'My wife will be very surprised. Only too bad that you cannot tell me the name ... we actually have led a very happy life'.[22] For most of the time, Brandt found himself on an extended study tour, whether attending the Bayreuth festival or visiting exhibitions and party rallies. Another opportunity to act as Hitler's envoy, and represent the Nazi regime, arose when Brandt was invited to accompany Goebbels on an official state visit to Greece in September 1936. The trip was meant to give political support to General Ioannis Metaxas's newly established fascist regime.

Following the re-establishment of the monarchy in Greece, King George II appointed Metaxas as prime minister in April 1936. Only months later, in August 1936, Metaxas dissolved the Greek parliament, thus establishing a de facto dictatorship that increasingly took on a fascist character. Metaxas suspended parts of the constitution, introduced press censorship, banned the communist party and oppressed left-wing political reformers. His government also suppressed freedom of expression, and prohibited the education of Macedonians and other minority groups. They were not allowed to be taught in their own schools, speak their own language or practise their own customs. Given that Metaxas wanted to create a new society which resembled that of the Third Reich, the official visit by members of Hitler's government could not have come at a better time to give his regime much-needed legitimization and international recognition.[23]

Planning for the trip commenced at the end of July 1936, when Goebbels noted in his diary: 'I am considering, with the Führer, Hoffmann and Dr Brandt, undertaking a trip to Greece in September. I am looking forward to that.'[24] Three weeks later, Goebbels finalized plans for the journey.[25] In the end, Hitler did not accompany them. Karl and Anni Brandt, Heinrich Hoffmann and his second wife Erna, and Joseph and Magda Goebbels were nonetheless excited about the trip; for Goebbels it meant a dream come true.[26] On 20 September 1936, the group assembled at Berlin Tempelhof, where they were met by journalists and the Greek ambassador. One of Hoffmann's photographs shows Brandt and his wife standing on the airfield in front of Hitler's private plane. Anni Brandt, dressed in a white overcoat, can be seen in conversation with Erna Hoffmann. Magda and Joseph Goebbels are standing slightly apart; they appear more relaxed and are smiling. Brandt, on the other hand, dressed in suit and tie, stands alone in the middle of the group, clearly at a distance from the others, but ready to step forward at any given moment. He does not appear to be shy, but observant, not unlike a servant in attendance.

Brandt was not idle during the long flight to Greece. Indeed, there was some medical work for him to do; photographs show him vaccinating Erna Hoffmann, and probably the others as well, perhaps with a vaccine against malaria or yellow fever which was endemic in Greece at the time. The group first flew to Budapest where Goebbels and his entourage were warmly received by the state secretary and ambassador to Budapest, Hans Georg von Mackensen, the son-in-law of the foreign minister, Konstantin Freiherr von Neurath.[27] They then travelled to Belgrade for another stopover before heading towards Athens. In his diary, Goebbels expressed his excitement about the landscape he saw from the sky, marvelling at the beautiful sunset over the Mediterranean Sea. Upon arrival, the group was greeted by a jubilant crowd. 'The people are screaming and are full of joy,' Goebbels noted.[28] This was surely not an ordinary journey by ordinary tourists. These were the representatives of Nazi Germany visiting the Greek islands. Upon arrival, a lavish buffet lunch was laid on for the German delegation. In one of Hoffmann's photographs, we see Brandt, dressed in a meticulously ironed white suit, holding a glass of wine;[29] in another, Anni Brandt, Magda Goebbels and Erna Hoffmann are carrying the large, colourful bouquets which they received upon arrival.[30] Members of the group were treated like royalty. Throughout the next eight days, Brandt and his wife experienced a life of unknown luxury, in a land in which a largely poor population made a living from agriculture and fishing. Brandt must have realized that by working as Hitler's physician, and by accompanying leading Nazis on their trips abroad, he could follow his personal interests in art and architecture, and lead a life most people in Germany and elsewhere could only dream of.

The group first drove to Kephissia, where they stayed the night in a hotel. The next day, 21 September, Goebbels and his entourage first visited the king before meeting with Prime Minister Metaxas, whom he described as a 'jovial old man, very German-friendly, but not a dictator'.[31] Then they travelled through Athens to the sound of cheering crowds, arriving at the Acropolis in a state of euphoria, like some ancient conquerors returning victorious from a battle. 'A real castle of the Gods' was how Goebbels recorded his impression. 'That is how she [the Acropolis] sits enthroned, so powerful and imposing. The most impressive monument of nordic creative power,' he remarked.[32] A visit to a temple or two, a trip through the olive groves to a reservoir and, in the evening, after moving to the more luxurious Hotel Grande Bretagne in the city centre, the 'regular dinner for diplomats' as Goebbels called it. Thus, after twenty-four hours, the group had completed the official part of the trip. Now it was time for an extended study tour. The next day saw visits to some of the Greek amphitheatres and temples, followed by shopping and a trip to Kerameikos, where German archaeologists were digging up parts of the old city wall. Here and elsewhere, Hitler was never far away. 'How happy the Führer would be, if he could be with us,' Goebbels remarked after watching the sunset from the Acropolis.

Visiting these ancient places allowed Brandt and the others, Goebbels foremost among them, to see themselves and the Nazi movement as the successors of Greek civilization and ancient mythology. On Wednesday 23 September, the group drove by car to Delphi where the ancient world sought guidance from the gods. Brief stopovers in Eleusis, Theben and Arachron marked the journey to see the amphitheatre and stadium in Delphi. Photographs of the trip picture Brandt as he visits the ancient places of worship; in others we see Anni Brandt relaxing with Magda and Joseph Goebbels on a stone wall.[33] The group then embarked on a ship which brought them to the small port of Nauplia.[34] The atmosphere on board the ship was relaxed and friendly.[35] Photographs show the group disembarking in a small rowing boat.[36] Karl and Anni Brandt are smiling and waving to the photographer. They were obviously having a good time. Back on dry land, the group headed to Mykenae. After visiting the castle and the so-called tomb of Agamemnon, the group travelled to Epidaurus to see yet another ancient theatre. Sailing throughout the night, and into a heavy storm, the ship arrived in Gythion the next day. Whatever the weather, especially the uncompromising heat, or the conditions of the roads, Goebbels enjoyed every minute of the trip. For him, as for Brandt and the others, everything had meaning on this journey, the ancient places, the temples and theatres, the gods and their relationship with pre-industrial society, in which only the fittest would survive. It allowed them to reaffirm their belief in social Darwinism and eugenics.

The ancient city of Sparta was next on the itinerary, a fitting reminder for Brandt that the ancient Greeks had – according to legends – apparently dispensed with their newborn children if they had turned out to be weaklings. For Goebbels, the history of Ancient Greece, with its sense of heroism and religious mythology, represented a powerful narrative that had enormous propaganda potential for the Nazi regime. On Saturday 26 September, after a cruise across the Mediterranean, the group arrived on Aegina, from where they rode on donkeys, accompanied by the local children, to the temple of Aphaia.[37] Hoffmann's pictures show Brandt and the entire delegation thus mounted. Goebbels was given a particularly small animal to take account of his physique. In one of the images, Brandt can be seen, astride his donkey, taking pictures of Goebbels.[38] 'A very funny ascent. The small Greek boys are lovely. A colourful image of a caravan,' Goebbels remarked.

Once back on board the ship, the group sailed back to Athens, where members of the German diplomatic corps and the Greek government were waiting to have lunch with the holidaymakers. Politics, rather than history, determined the final leg of the journey. Metaxas went out of his way to please the delegation with his anti-Semitic and anticommunist diatribes. Meetings with the press and a speech to German expatriates concluded the day. The last day saw Brandt, Hoffmann and Goebbels visiting the National Museum in Athens, where they admired the marble sculptures and ancient treasures.[39] Then, in the afternoon, Brandt accompanied Goebbels to the opening of the Balkan Games in the stadium of Athens. If we are to trust Goebbels' diary entry, the German delegation received a rousing welcome: 'I am greeted by 70,000 with tumultuous cheers. It is wonderful! This love for Germany comes from the heart. The applause goes on for minutes. The whole government is there.'[40]

On Monday 28 September, Brandt and the others boarded the plane to Salonica, where Goebbels gave another speech to the German expatriate community, then travelled to Budapest for a brief stopover, and back to Berlin. Goebbels and his entourage, Brandt included, had skilfully turned an official government visit into a private study trip. Brandt may have developed a general interest in the moral belief system of the ancient world, with its glorification of sacrifice and heroism, before the Nazis came to power, probably as a pupil or student in Wilhelmine and Weimar Germany, but his mission to Greece threw into sharp relief the fact that Ancient Greece provided an ideal role model for Nazi Germany, with its emphasis on the community and the state. Travelling to Greece strengthened his belief that in all civilized cultures the role of the individual ought to be seen in terms of his or her contribution and value towards the greater good. For a society to function, the individual had to be subordinated to the interests of the national community and the health of the race. What Brandt did not realize, however, was the fact that Nazi Germany was moving ever faster towards the segregation and expulsion of Jews, homosexuals, Gypsies and other minority groups. Nazi Germany in the mid-1930s was not developing into an inclusive and open society, one in which the citizens contributed to the welfare of all according to the best of their abilities, but into an increasingly politicized society, in which the gradual process of cumulative radicalization led to the exclusion, and eventual extermination, of ever more target groups.

III. ART, ARCHITECTURE AND AESTHETICS

After his return from Greece, Brandt served as an army doctor at the Hindenburg military hospital throughout October and November 1936.[41] Hitler, however, continued to call on his doctor to accompany him to exhibitions and building sites, or to be part of his entourage during garden parties and concert evenings. On 13 November 1936, for example, Brandt, dressed in his SS uniform, accompanied Hitler and Goebbels to hear the Berlin Philharmonic Orchestra give a concert directed by the London conductor, Sir Thomas Beecham. At other times, he improved his knowledge of art and architecture, literature and classical music. He loved Greek art, especially from antiquity, admired German poetry and studied the history of medicine. Brandt used to attract Hitler's attention with his expertise and sometimes entertained his guests at the Berghof. Once he told – and showed – a gathering around Hitler how the Ancient Greeks had stitched up wounds. In order to do so, Brandt collected a number of beetles which had two small defensive pincers on top of their heads. Brandt explained that ancient Greek doctors would hold the beetle to the suture of the wound until the pincers of the beetle snapped. The doctor would then twist the body of the beetle so that the pincers remained under the skin like a fine thread.[42] After a while, the pincers dissolved and the wound was antiseptically closed. Hitler is said to have been fascinated by stories such as these. On another occasion, Brandt brought along a skull to demonstrate to Hitler how doctors performed an operation on a patient who was suffering from a brain tumour. And on another, he showed him an elegant small leather casing that contained a beautiful set of Roman surgical tools, estimated to be more than 2,000 years old, which archaeologists had discovered in what had been the Roman province of Rhaetia in south Germany.[43] Hitler welcomed Brandt's general knowledge during extended periods of studious relaxation or when he needed information relating to the history of medieval medicine. For example, he consulted Brandt before commissioning a large Paracelsus sculpture from the Nazi sculptor Josef Thorak, whose colossal hero figures placed him on a footing with Arno Breker, one of the most famous sculptors of the Third Reich.

The calendar of one of Hitler's adjutants provides insight into Hitler's daily routine in 1938, and shows his obsession with micro-managing German art and culture through his personal doctor and officials, who accompanied him on his travels. On Friday 17 June 1938, Hitler was woken up at 10 o'clock. An hour later he met with General von Brauchitsch. This was followed by lunch at 2 p.m. with Brandt, Bormann, Otto Dietrich, his press secretary, and Captain Hans Baur, his pilot. At 5.30 p.m., Hitler and his entourage boarded a plane to attend the opera in Dresden. Upon leaving the opera, Hitler told one of his ministers that the plinth of the bust of the composer Richard Strauß had to be altered. The next day, on Saturday 18 June, Hitler visited a Dresden art gallery before boarding a plane to Munich. Here, he visited the Glyptothek to see the famous bronze statue of a discus thrower from 450 BC by the Greek sculptor Myron of Eleutherae, whose bold representations of athletes fascinated Hitler and the Nazi elite. Brandt was instructed to ensure that Leni Riefenstahl's cameramen would make film recordings of the discus thrower. The relevant entry in the calendar of Hitler's adjutant states: 'action through Dr. Brandt'.[44] After having lunch in his favourite restaurant, Osteria, and a brief stopover in his Munich flat, Hitler inspected a number of new paintings in the Museum of German Art (*Haus der Deutschen Kunst*). The next day, he returned to the Berghof to inspect some of the new buildings. At 1 p.m. he had lunch with Brandt and Hoffmann, his secretaries, and with Eva Braun and her sister. Later in the day, at 7.30 p.m., he phoned *Gauleiter* Bürckel to tell him that he categorically prohibited any form of censorship of paintings that were destined for the *Haus der Deutschen Kunst*. Ten minutes later, he took another call. This time it was Hitler's architect, Speer, announcing the birth of his daughter. Two weeks later, on 12 July, Brandt had fulfilled his assignment. Late in the evening, at 11 p.m., Hitler watched the film recordings of Myron's discus thrower.[45] The calendar entries give an indication of the extent to which Hitler took an active interest in German art and culture, and of the way in which Brandt served to create an idealized image of Ancient Greece, designed for mass consumption.

Brandt's wide-ranging classical knowledge, and contacts with artists such as Thorak and Breker, enabled him to influence the development of German art. Brandt often spent his leisure time with Thorak, owned a number of Thorak's sculptures, and may well have been involved in the making of one of Breker's statues for the new Reich Chancellery.[46] The figure, called the *Wäger*, representing the spirit, or *Geist*, was a sculpture of an idealized male nude, whose head and face showed a striking resemblance to Brandt's facial features. Some thought that it was a portraiture of Brandt.[47] The sculpture was part of an ensemble of two male and three female nudes which was meant to stand in the 'round-room' of the new Reich Chancellery.

The aim of Breker's sculptures, and those of other Nazi artists, was the creation of an idealized image of man, who was removed from the worldly suffering of mortal human beings, free to break with tradition and custom, a new man, willing to ignore the existing moral and ethical boundaries of civilized human society without any feelings of guilt.[48] Breker's sculptures represented the artistic creation of a new man and warrior hero, who was unrestrained by religious and moral beliefs, and had no conscience. The ideal was to dominate the image and life of man, not the reality or his or her empirical appearance. Given that some of Breker's sculptures, including the one of Brandt, showed distinct human features, they were meant to be gilded to depersonalize them, and elevate them to a god-like status. Brandt would have been content with the image of himself. Having inculcated fascist ideology and iconography in art and architecture, he believed in an ideal world in which there were no moral boundaries or limitations, and in which man could shape his destiny according to his will.

Art historians, such as Kurt Lothar Tank, provided the Nazis with a suitable iconographic and aesthetic language, one which fitted their ideology. Tank, for example, reinterpreted Jacob Burckhardt's cultural analysis of the classical period by stressing the positive attitudes of the Greek mythological figures of Heros and Prometheus, both of whom became central figures in the fascist iconography. For Burckhardt, the character of Heros was far from being the ideal image of man, given that all his actions and passions were extreme. Respect for the dignity and morality of man was alien to Heros; he represented a naive sense of egoism which existed in all human beings, but was unable to repent of his actions. These, however, were the character traits which Tank and other Nazi theorists cherished, stressing instead the unyielding and merciless character of Heros, his boldness in carrying out an act which destiny had imposed on him, without any feelings of remorse.

These were also the character traits which Brandt valued in human beings, in doctors especially. He admired their boldness and willingness to decide over life and death without any emotional attachment or feelings of guilt. On 21 December 1946, whilst imprisoned at Nuremberg, Brandt reflected in his diary about the ethics of killing seriously ill patients; he quoted passages from the Greek poet Sophocles, a writer of tragedies and a priest to Aesculapius, a famous Greek physician and demigod in Greek mythology:

> Only one sentence belongs here, manly and sincere, a call from a thousand years ago: 'It is not the way of a clever doctor to chant incantations over a pain that needs surgery!' (*kein kluger Arzt singt weinerlich Beschwörungslieder, wenn ein Schnitt das Übel heilt!*) What a thought this is compared to the lamentations of our century! Then there was clear humanity, heroic – and today a disgusting hypocrisy![49]

Brandt was attracted to personalities who took uncompromising and fateful decisions, yet who were unbending and unrepentant if the decision turned out to be wrong. Hardness, not the 'weakness' of compassion, characterized his relationship with, and response to, other humans and also towards himself.[50] Conversely, he disliked humans who were soft and reflective and wavering in their lifestyle and decision-making. After meeting Robert Servatius, his Nuremberg defence lawyer, for the first time, Brandt could barely conceal his disappointment in him. Brandt was not concerned with any form of legal manoeuvring. He wanted a lawyer who would enable him to deliver one last speech to the world. Brandt revered men who followed their ideal and mission in life, who performed heroic deeds and took responsibility, 'manly and sincere', as he called it, even if it meant their eventual downfall or death. Brandt, in short, admired men like Hitler.

Brandt's knowledge of art and art history provided him with the theoretical underpinning to advocate a holistic medical ethic, in which the doctor's duty was to serve the body politic, and ensure the eternal life and health of the people's community (*Volksgemeinschaft*). For ordinary observers, Breker's sculptures represented an idealized image of man. But for Brandt their meaning was deeper. He was striving towards an ideal; he wanted to be like the *Wäger*, the embodiment of spirit and bold energy, a man ready to act for the good of humanity, merciless and without any moral restrictions. Brandt was not an idealist in the ordinary sense, but a doctor who, in the name of humanity and mankind, was willing to sacrifice the individual liberty and autonomy of others.

Brandt also liked discussing some of his architectural ideas with his architect friends: Wilhelm Kreis, who was one of the designers of the regional headquarters of the air force in Dresden, Professor Preger from Greece and, of course, Albert Speer. He enjoyed making small architectural drawings. His friendship with Speer contributed to this passion. In 1937, Brandt and his wife, Anni, enjoyed an eight-day visit to the International World Exhibition in Paris, where they met up with Speer at the luxurious Trianon Palace Hotel in Versailles.[51] Speer had been commissioned to design the German pavilion for the exhibition, which lasted from 24 May to 25 November 1937. Outside the pavilion, visitors were greeted by a large, Heros-like statue which bore the title 'genius'. It was clearly a reference to Hitler: the statue proclaimed to visitors that he himself had shaped every detail of the plans for the German contribution to the exhibition.

A year earlier, in February 1936, Brandt had accompanied Hitler to inspect a model of the German House, which the architect Woldemar Brinkmann had designed for the World Exhibition.[52] Brandt's increasing knowledge in matters relating to design and architecture allowed him to take part in discussions with Hitler and Speer about their building projects. Whilst holidaying on the Berghof in February 1937, Brandt was party to discussions between Hitler, Speer and Hermann Giesler, another of Hitler's architects. One of Hoffmann's photographs shows Brandt, hands in pockets, peering over Hitler's shoulder onto a large table where the Führer inspected, and probably amended, some of the drawings of his pet architectural projects.[53] Weeks later, at the beginning of March, Hitler travelled to

Nuremberg to see how much progress had been made on the new Reich Party Area (*Reichsparteitagsgelände*). Carefully choreographed images show Hitler, dressed in uniform, together with Brandt, Bouhler, Speer and Streicher, on his train journey to Nuremberg. Hitler can be seen discussing architectural drawings with his closest advisers. Published in the *Illustrierter Beobachter* under the heading 'The Great Builder on His Travels,' the images were part of a relentless propaganda campaign to portray Hitler as a selfless, hard-working politician who was tirelessly engaged in creating a more beautiful and powerful nation, a man with a mission, with little or no time for himself.[54] Once again, Brandt played his part as the necessary backdrop. One of the captions of Hitler read:

> That is how we see him here, how he, pencil in hand, impresses upon the drawings his personal touch with the certainty of an ingenious creator, who even commandeers dead stone in the service of his powerful will.[55]

After arriving in Nuremberg, Hitler inspected the architectural models of the new Reich Party Area. A series of photographs show Brandt standing among the group of architects and draftsmen who are discussing the building projects with Hitler. In other images, Hitler is flanked by Brandt, Speer, Bouhler and Bormann. Most of the images show Hitler, arms folded, critically assessing the models, or, leaning forward, taking a close look at specific drawings.[56] Then it was time for a walk-about to inspect the test facade for the new and oversized congress hall.[57] Three months later, at the end of June 1937, Hitler was back in Nuremberg. Again, we see Brandt, dressed in a white jacket, walking behind Hitler, who marches past one of the monumental building sites on the *Märzfeld*, where the Nazis stage-managed their party rallies.[58] On 17 August, Hitler visited Nuremberg yet again. Always present, yet this time more removed from the group, was Brandt. The propaganda message of these images was clear: Hitler, the politician, who had freed the German people from the shackles of Versailles, was elevated to the role of Führer and architect of the Third Reich.

Depending on the occasion, Brandt and others in Hitler's entourage were obliged to follow a particular dress code. During concerts and art exhibitions, which Hitler would attend as the head of state, Brandt would generally wear his black SS uniform and become de facto part of the Führer's personal bodyguard. After the war, Brandt once described the 'act of putting on this SS uniform as purely superficial', but the images taken by Hoffmann convey a different message.[59] In most images, Brandt appears to be proud to wear the SS uniform. In July 1937, for example, Brandt wore his SS uniform when he accompanied Hitler to the opening ceremony of the House of German Art in Munich. Images of Hitler visiting the exhibition *Schaffendes Volk* (A Working People) in October 1937 show Brandt likewise wearing his SS uniform. Interestingly, Speer, standing immediately next to Brandt, can be seen wearing a plain raincoat, perhaps because he was not part of Hitler's official entourage. On 22 December 1937, Brandt also stood guard in his full SS uniform during General Erich von Ludendorff's state funeral, which was attended by representatives of the German armed forces and by hundreds of onlookers.[60] Ludendorff had been one of the most influential personalities of right-wing and *völkisch* politics during the Weimar Republic, and had attempted, but failed, together with Hitler, to overthrow the existing democratic government in 1923. Given the importance the Nazis placed upon elaborate rituals to control the masses, it came as no surprise that the regime exploited his death for maximum propaganda effect. His funeral turned into a choreographed display of national power and military might. In tune with fascist iconography and rituals, two massive torches provided the backdrop for the soldiers standing guard at the Odeonsplatz in Munich. Brandt, dressed in a long black mantle with SS insignias on his collar, was positioned in the middle of the Odeonsplatz between representatives of the German *Wehrmacht* and other military units. His assignment on this occasion, as on many others, was to contribute to the propaganda image which the organizers wanted to create. Standing there on the Odeonsplatz as on a massive theatre stage, Brandt was beginning to play a significant part in the iconography of the Third Reich, not any part, but that of Hitler's doctor, who showed total allegiance to the regime, and as a model whom German doctors were encouraged to follow. In 1947, Brandt told the court: 'I myself, whenever I wore the uniform, have always worn the SS uniform with the idea of having a special moral obligation, and I did not wear it without pride.'[61]

On other, less official, but still formal occasions, for example during one of Hitler's summer parties at the Berghof, Hitler's entourage had to turn up in white dinner jackets and black trousers. A photograph shot by an anonymous photographer, probably a member of Hoffmann's staff, shows Brandt, Speer, Schaub and Hoffmann all dressed in white dinner jackets.[62] On those occasions, even Speer had to follow the etiquette. All four men can be seen standing together on the terrace of the Berghof. Brandt and Speer have their arms folded. Hoffmann can be seen smoking a cigarette, something that Hitler disliked. 'I will lose you from this,' he once told his official photographer, alluding to the fact that smoking was likely to cause lung cancer.[63] Brandt, sporting his SS insignia on his collar, appears to be absent-minded on this occasion. He is not following the conversation. As in some of the other photographs in Hoffmann's collection, Brandt appears to be part of a group, yet strangely removed, on the fringes, like a passive observer. He appears to be withdrawn, and all by himself. None of the men, except for Schaub, perhaps, look particularly excited. There is no sense of anticipation. These men are waiting for the party to begin – or to conclude. They may be waiting for Hitler to arrive; perhaps they are hungry, or reluctant to listen to yet another of Hitler's endless, monotonous monologues. To be part of Hitler's entourage, and enjoy the luxury and privileges, certainly had its appeal for young professionals such as Brandt and Speer, but it could also be mind-numbing and boring in the extreme. Above all, being in Hitler's vicinity gave Brandt little opportunity to learn about medical practice on the ground. Brandt's interest in classical cultures, art and architecture certainly drew him closer into Hitler's inner circle and gradually turned him into Hitler's envoy for special missions, but it also removed him from the suffering and concerns of ordinary Germans.

IV. THE MEDICAL CONSULTANT

The more Brandt established himself as Hitler's escort physician, the more he became part of the intimate group of men and women who constituted Hitler's family. Each member of this group had, to a certain degree, and depending on rank and personal liking, access to Hitler's ear. Whereas formal government and communication structures increasingly dissolved into ever more informal and arbitrary ways, the power of those with access to the Führer increased disproportionately compared to their role within the administrative hierarchy. Brandt's political influence depended primarily on his physical presence in the vicinity of the Führer. Beyond that he had little political power in the early years of the regime. Brandt had no ministry, no *Hausmacht*, or government portfolio, through which he could influence political events. Officially, he was Hitler's escort physician and not a government minister. As long as he was lacking any formal status, his position was open to attack from various rival agencies and empire-builders. For Brandt it was paramount not only to establish close relations with those who had a power base, or who were likely to be given one in the future, such as Speer for example, but also to work towards the creation of his own government department. Brandt's aim was a Ministry of Health. He wanted to be the Reich Health Minister of Nazi Germany.

To achieve this aim was difficult. Although Brandt managed, on occasion, to attract Hitler's attention with stories of medical inventions and ancient surgical procedures, Hitler's passions remained art and architecture.[64] Brandt may have had access to Hitler's ear throughout extended periods of time, as a messenger between the government and German medicine, but his expertise was a necessity, not one of Hitler's true interests. Albert Speer, Hitler's personal architect, *Generalbauinspektor* (GBI), and later Reich Minister for Armaments and War Production, was one of Hitler's most trusted paladins. 'If [Hitler] had been capable of [friendship],' Speer remarked to the Nuremberg court in 1946, 'I would indubitably have been one of his closest friends.'[65] Brandt and Speer joined the inner circle of the court at around the same time, came from the same social background, were about the same age, and had enjoyed a sound professional training. Most importantly, they were both totally loyal and committed to serving the man whom they saw as a national genius. It is hardly surprising that, in an environment full of half-baked intellectuals, party fanatics and permanent intrigues, they became allies and befriended and helped each other.

At the beginning of 1937, Brandt was assigned another long-term 'special task' when Hitler asked him to collaborate with Speer, who had just been appointed *Generalbauinspektor* (Inspector General of Construction) of Berlin. Architectural traces along the city's east–west and north–south axis are telling memorials that the enterprise was not just a pipe dream. Hitler's reconstruction plan of Berlin was a vast project which included the construction of an entire new hospital and university complex. As the 'medical consultant', Brandt was asked to advise Speer in his architectural work.[66] Brandt's first task, as he later recalled, was to design a new surgical clinic, and subsequently the entire university clinic of the city of Berlin. The work offered Brandt the opportunity to engage in studies of the history and design of European hospital buildings, and enlist his mentor, Paul Rostock, in the work. In April 1937, Brandt and Rostock travelled together on a fact-finding mission to Milan, Belgrade, Budapest and Athens, where he consulted resident architects and hospital directors.[67] Brandt later recalled that the aim of the trip to Greece was to inspect a number of modern hospitals which had specialized in the treatment of tuberculosis.[68] In Athens, he also met his Greek architect friend, Professor Preger, and enjoyed extensive discussions about the meaning of Greek architecture and antiquity. Loaded with terracotta and small sculptures, which Preger had given his increasingly influential friend, Brandt returned to Germany. Rather than learning about the lives and suffering of patients, Brandt was spending a considerable amount of time studying the buildings in which they were looked after.

In 1939, Brandt completed his first architectural plan of the monumental hospital project. He used an article entitled 'The Closure of the Clinic Headed by Professor Bier' (*Die Schließung der Bierschen Klinik*), published in the same year, to justify the envisaged expansion and integration of the university clinic into Speer's grand design. Brandt started off by criticizing the medical politics of the Prussian Ministry of Education during the Weimar Republic, and by attacking those who had supported the closure of the clinic at the time. He especially directed his criticism at a certain Jewish professor, who had apparently played an important part in the closure of the clinic in 1932 by collaborating with the left-wing press. Although the article did not mention the professor by name, perhaps because he knew that the academic would suffer serious consequences as a result, or had suffered them already, Brandt's latent anti-Semitism cannot be ignored. In order to juxtapose the statements Bier had made in favour of keeping the clinic open with an opposing viewpoint, Brandt wrote:

> And now, in direct opposition, an 'enlightening' report in the left-wing press from a Jewish university professor in Berlin: '... in the current climate it is not necessary for the state to build clinics in order to preserve tradition,' and furthermore; 'it is irresponsible to preserve incomplete institutions for reasons of tradition alone and thereby withdraw the significant amount of necessary financial means in other places. It is really necessary now to enlighten the public about this!'.[69]

Brandt's statement contains a whole plethora of racial and anti-Semitic stereotypes that were an integral part of the prevailing Nazi rhetoric: the Jewish professor was naturally supporting left-wing, bolshevist politics. He was described as an intellectual who could not be trusted. The general tenor of Brandt's text was that Jewish academics pursued a mean-spirited political campaign against some of Germany's finest institutions of medical learning. Brandt then praised the enormous improvements which the Nazi takeover of power had brought for the surgical clinic in Berlin: 'In the summer [of 1933], the Führer personally ordered the reopening of the First Surgical Clinic at the University of Berlin. He furthermore appointed Professor Georg Magnus as the new head, who transferred from his workplace in the industrial region.'[70] Brandt argued that, despite the positive change which had been achieved, it was now necessary to consider the expansion of the clinic once more. Given the limited building space that was available in the Ziegelstraße, officials had started to examine alternative solutions, one of which saw the transfer of the entire clinic to another location:

> The area of the Heeresstraße in the west of Berlin is being assigned for this. But the new project has grown in the course of the planning process, and this has eventually led to [the decision] that the entire university of the Reich capital will be established outside Greater Berlin in the vicinity of the Grunewald and the sports complex of the Olympia stadium.[71]

Together with Hitler and Speer, Brandt had designed, at a cost of 200 million Reichsmark, a massive hospital and clinic complex in the form of a skyscraper. Dozens of research institutes and laboratories were meant to cater for up to 4,000 patients and train hundreds of students and junior doctors. According to Brandt, the plan for building evacuation hospitals during the war, known as 'special hospitals' (*Krankenhaus-Sonderanlagen*), developed from the original hospital design, which he had produced for the city of Berlin. Brandt did not have to wait long to receive his reward for contributing to Hitler's world capital, 'Germania'. In September 1940, he was appointed honorary professor of the University of Berlin.[72]

V. TERRITORIAL EXPANSION

Following the reoccupation and remilitarization of the Rhineland in March 1936, the popular euphoria and admiration for Hitler and the Nazi regime knew no bounds. It marked the transition from Hitler the Reich Chancellor and head of state, to Hitler the demigod who believed in his own infallibility and myth.[73] 'That you have found me, among so many millions, is the miracle of our time! And that I have found you, that is Germany's fortune,' he declared.[74] Those who had previously been critical of Hitler's actions, and had called for caution, including the Foreign Office and parts of the military, anxious that such action could lead to war, now embraced Germany's newly established sovereignty. Opposition groups were left deeply demoralized after Hitler's domestic and foreign policy successes. Support for the Nazi regime now crossed the political, religious and class divide. The middle-class housewife Louise Solmitz from Hamburg, whose husband and daughter had previously been denied German citizenship under the Nuremberg Race Laws, now praised the boldness of National Socialism and its leader: 'I was totally overwhelmed by the events of this hour,' she remarked, 'overjoyed at the entry march of our soldiers, at the greatness of Hitler and the power of his speech, the force of this man'.[75] Given the enormous popularity and mass support which Hitler enjoyed after the 'election' campaign at the end of March, the Rhineland coup became an extraordinary success story for the regime. Goebbels' carefully orchestrated and deeply cynical propaganda campaign lifted the image of the Führer to new heights. On the Königsplatz in Munich, for example, the Nazis erected a large column which bore the inscription 'With Adolf Hitler for peace, freedom and honour'.[76] Given Brandt's assignment, he became part of the group of officials who helped to establish the image of Hitler as a quasi-religious and messianic leader.

Three of Hoffmann's carefully choreographed and stage-managed photographs show Hitler addressing a group of Nazi functionaries and political allies in the entrance hall of the old Reich Chancellery.[77] In all three of the images we can see Heß, Darré, Frick, Bouhler, Rosenberg, Bodenschatz and Bormann. Brandt is present in two of the pictures.[78] All three photographs were shot on 'election' day on 29 March 1936, but only one of them was later published in the *Illustrierter Beobacher* under the heading 'The Great Victory'.[79] One of the images was taken from behind where Hitler was sitting on the stairs of the old Reich Chancellery, giving the impression that he is talking to his old comrades.[80] In the other two images, Hitler's supporters are assembled on the left of the picture and he is on the right.[81] There are small but important differences between these two images. In one of the pictures, Hitler can be seen sitting on the steps and talking to his followers from below. Given that the shot was taken from the side, the group of officials and supporters is, in a symbolic sense, looking down on Hitler. That is why Hoffmann changed the camera position and took a second picture, the one which was selected for publication. Here we can see Hitler standing. Amplified through the camera angle, Hitler appears to be talking from above to the group of supporters, whereas the men are looking up to Hitler from below. He is the centre of attention, the focal point, as he delivers his missionary message to his loyal disciples.

Brandt was included in these images because he accompanied Hitler. He represented no more than a necessary backdrop; he had no real political power which might have warranted his presence in these photographs. He fitted into Hoffmann's compositions, not as a particular individual, or indeed a member of Hitler's government, but as someone representing the mass of political admirers, who swore total allegiance to Hitler's movement. The image of Brandt and others in Hoffmann's photographs became a symbolic shorthand for the enormous popular support which the Nazi regime enjoyed among all sections of German society. But the inclusion of Brandt in these images also fulfilled another purpose. Slowly, but gradually, Hitler's doctor came to represent the medical profession and their support for National Socialism. Brandt was also young and energetic. The fact that we find the image of Hitler's doctor in scores, if not hundreds, of Hoffmann's photographs – over five hundred in fact – is not only evidence that Brandt was constantly at Hitler's side, but shows how Brandt gradually came to represent the up-and-coming generation of doctors and medical scientists who embraced the underlying principles of racial hygiene and eugenics, and who were bent on changing the world into a healthier and wealthier place. Hoffmann's propaganda images ensured that Brandt, answerable only to Hitler and to no one else, rather than a senior member of the central medical administration, remained in the public eye and became a household name among the medical establishment and the educated public. Given the bulk of the photographic and textual evidence, the suggestion that Brandt's name and image were almost unknown in the public domain before Hitler appointed him General Commissioner for Health and Sanitation in 1942 might be questioned.[82] Popularizing Brandt's image and name did not happen so much as a result of long-term or strategic planning, by Brandt himself or by Hitler or any of his ministers, but because of Brandt's unusual medical assignment in the immediate vicinity of Hitler. Brandt, almost by default, was on his way to representing German medicine as a whole.

Hitler's engagements became ever more elaborate. Throughout 1937 Hitler, and therefore Brandt as well, remained constantly in the public eye during mass rallies and speeches. On 30 January – the fourth anniversary of the Nazi assumption of power – Hitler gave a major speech to the Reichstag, followed by another to the 'Old Fighters' of the movement in February. Then there were the traditional speeches during the Reich Party Rally in September, and yet another on 8 November, the anniversary of the failed putsch in 1923. Parades and celebrations for Hitler's birthday in April also demanded his presence. He attended the 'National Day of Celebration of the German People' on 1 May, the opening of the International Car Exhibition in Berlin in February, and the Reich Food Estates' Agricultural Exhibition in Munich in May. He also participated in 'Heroes' Memorial Day', and, on 18 July, opened the House of German Art in Munich, which had been designed but not completed by the late architect Paul Ludwig Troost, one of Hitler's favourite architects. To a packed audience of party faithful, he relayed his vision of Germany's past and future world domination, which he claimed was visible in the achievements of German art and culture. His opening speech made it plain that he regarded the new building as a 'true monument for this city and – more than that – for German art'.[83] He told his audience that they were living in a 'new age' which was 'at work on a new human type', and that the art of the future would have to reflect the ancient ideal of healthy and strong men and women: 'There is a new feeling of life, a new joy in life. Never was humanity in its external appearance and in its frame of mind nearer to the ancient world than it is today.' Hitler then attacked the artists of the present, those 'art stutterers' whose works of art belonged to expressionism, Dadaism, cubism and Futurism: 'Misformed cripples and cretins, women who inspire only disgust, men who are more like wild beasts, children who, were they alive, must be regarded as under God's curse'.[84] Hitler's speech not only showed that he was willing to ban artistic work which did not correspond with his sense of aesthetics, but it also gave people an indication of how he thought about mentally and physically handicapped people. Hitler's views on art and culture and his subsequent decision to order the 'euthanasia' programme were closely connected.

In September 1937, Hitler played host to Mussolini's state visit, but this time Hitler ensured that it was he who upstaged Mussolini, and not vice versa. The 'Duce' was given a firm idea of the newly awakened German military might, leaving Italy impressed but deeply concerned about Europe's future. Less than a year later, in May 1938, Hitler travelled to Rome to return Mussolini's visit. On 4 May, the two dictators, dressed in their full military uniform, stood guard on the Piazza Venezia by the tomb of the unknown soldier. In the background, each of them had positioned the leading members of their respective regimes and entourage, including Karl Brandt. He can be seen standing right behind Himmler and Heß.[85] Two days later, on 6 May, Brandt and Albert Bormann, the brother of Martin Bormann and the head of Central Office I in the Chancellery of the Führer, accompanied Hitler to the Coliseum in Rome.[86] Hitler's visit was designed for maximum propaganda effect in order to hammer home to Italy, and to Europe as a whole, that German military might was on the rise, and that the country would from now on be the senior partner in the alliance. Back in Germany, Hitler's domestic policy showed a similar drive to turn his radical ideas into reality. In November 1937, he revealed his plans for the entire reconstruction of the city of Berlin into the world capital 'Germania', with a monumental temple-like hall for more than 10,000 people. Hitler's megalomania knew no limits any more. In total, Hitler gave twenty-six speeches in 1937, of which thirteen were given during the Nuremberg Party Rally alone. Here, he announced that racial hygiene and racial segregation would ultimately 'create the new man' in Nazi Germany, more healthy and stronger than ever before in German history. Other speeches were aimed at attacking 'Jewish Bolshevism' and the Jewish world conspiracy in the most severe and savage way. Those accompanying Hitler on this frantic public campaign trail could hardly have ignored Hitler's political intentions, however repetitively they may have been presented over the year.

To be constantly in the vicinity of the head of government was exciting and new, a fitting environment for someone who felt he had a higher calling. Yet for Brandt it was also quite a restless and unsteady lifestyle, with endless social and political engagements, and an ever-increasing security machinery to protect Hitler's life. Added to this, there was Germany's aggressive territorial expansion, which Brandt experienced first hand. Brandt was at Hitler's side when he marched into Austria in March 1938;[87] he witnessed the jubilant crowds during a military parade in Vienna on 15 March;[88] he accompanied the Nazi leadership during the 'election campaign' to annex Austria into the Reich in April 1938; and he went on an inspection tour with Hitler and his advisers after the German army had marched into the Sudetenland in October 1938.[89] Brandt may have turned a blind eye to the widespread discrimination, suffering and emigration of medical professionals in Germany, he may have ignored the obvious signs that the Nazi Party was pursuing a policy of racial segregation, anti-Semitism and political terror against its opponents, or he may have misinterpreted Hitler's domestic and foreign policy intentions as an attempt to rid Germany of the shackles of Versailles and reassert her role in Europe, but he could no longer ignore the aggressive, geopolitical and militarist nature of a regime that was geared to occupy foreign *Lebensraum* (living space) for the German people. What is more, as one of Hitler's trusted envoys, Brandt was increasingly drawn into the dynamics of medical and party politics.

VI. THE *REICHSKRISTALLNACHT*

In November 1938, Brandt was given another assignment after the assassination attempt on the Legation Secretary, Ernst vom Rath, at the German Embassy in Paris.

This time, Brandt's special mission to Paris became the start of an orchestrated attack against the whole of the Jewish community. For the Nazi leadership, the death of vom Rath offered an ideal opportunity to accelerate Jewish emigration through violent intimidation and mass pogroms, an idea which had been proposed by Eichmann as early as 1937. In the wake of 'Crystal Night' (*Reichskristallnacht*), hundreds of synagogues were burned and vandalized while tens of thousands of Jews, including mothers, children and the elderly, were rounded up, arrested, savagely beaten and killed throughout Germany.[90] Pressure by party fanatics to implement more radical measures against the Jews, to drive them out of the economy, expropriate their wealth, and thus accelerate Jewish emigration had been building up for months in the context of the Czech crisis. The 'Jewish Question' had become a powder-keg waiting to explode.

For years, the German Jews had witnessed an ever greater variety of professional discrimination and brutal assault on life and property. Still many decided to stay, believing that they could weather the crisis. Following the November pogrom, however, life became intolerable. On the morning of 7 November 1938, a seventeen-year-old Polish Jew, Herschel Feibel Grynszpan, who lived with his uncle in Paris, decided to take revenge on German anti-Semitic policies, bought a revolver, took the metro to the German Embassy, asked the porter if he could hand over an important document to a legation secretary, and, upon being admitted to the first official, who happened to be vom Rath, opened fire at point-blank range. He then threw away the revolver and allowed himself to be arrested. It was shortly after 9.35 a.m. when the Embassy staff heard shouting and screaming and saw vom Rath tumble out of his room. Vom Rath, still alive and conscious at this point, was immediately driven to the Hôpital de l'Alma in the rue de l'Université, where the French surgeon, Baumgartner, removed his spleen and mended the outer wall of his stomach. Grynszpan had not intended to kill one of the representatives of the Third Reich in France, though evidence suggests that the two might already have known each other. Vom Rath had apparently promised Grynszpan a German visa in return for homosexual services. This would explain why Grynszpan was so easily admitted to vom Rath's office.

Upon hearing the news, Goebbels immediately seized the initiative to press for the most brutal measures against the Jews. The death of vom Rath played right into the hands of the most radical elements within the Nazi movement. Throughout the morning, Goebbels initiated a flood of vicious attacks against the Jews in the Nazi press. His appetite for violent, uncontrolled outbursts of anti-Semitic hatred was insatiable. The Nazi propaganda machine had a field day when it turned out that Grynszpan was a Jew. The assassination of vom Rath coincided with the fifteenth anniversary of Hitler's failed putsch in 1923. This meant that thousands of party members were out on the streets or in bars to celebrate a major event in the Nazi calendar. In Munich, the party leadership was meeting for a conference. Little needed to be organized to mobilize or unleash the full wrath of the party. Grynszpan could not have chosen a worse day for his impulsive murder. Incited by extremist *Gauleiters*, Nazi Germany was soon out in arms to show the world what would happen to the Jews if they dared to challenge the regime. While tensions among regional Nazi hordes were mounting throughout the day, visibly displayed through spontaneous, often unorganized acts of terror against Jews, the Nazi leadership was ready to let loose the pent-up aggression in a systematic and controlled fashion. In the evening, Goebbels noted in his diary: 'In Hessen big anti-Semitic demonstrations. The synagogues are burnt down. If only the anger of the people could now be let loose!'[91] The death of vom Rath would be the signal to act.

Hitler and his entourage, including Brandt, had been in Weimar during the previous two days, where he had spoken to the party faithful as the leader of the Nazi Party, not as a statesman or head of the German government. A photograph shows Brandt standing guard during the *Gautag* of the Thuringian section of the Nazi Party.[92] Hitler's speech was another diatribe against bolshevism and the apparent Jewish threat to the stability of Europe. On 7 November, after reviewing a number of architectural projects in Weimar, he travelled to Nuremberg. Upon hearing the news of the assassination attempt, Hitler knew that no time could be lost. It was an opportunity not to be missed to push for more radical policies against the Jews. And this is where Brandt came into the picture. As usual, he was at Hitler's side. Hitler gave orders to be kept constantly informed by men of his inner circle. It allowed him to act swiftly and outside the traditional administrative bureaucracy.

That same night, Brandt was dispatched to Paris, together with the traumatologist, Georg Magnus from Munich, Brandt's mentor and former boss in Bochum and Berlin.[93] The French authorities waived the necessary visa requirements because Brandt and Magnus travelled in the plane of the head of state, and as Hitler's personal physicians, to attend a member of the German diplomatic corps, effectively granting Brandt and his colleague diplomatic immunity. On the morning of 8 November, at around 5 a.m., they landed in Paris and immediately went to see vom Rath, who had survived the night relatively well. A photograph taken of Brandt and Magnus on the morning of their arrival shows the two men rushing to the hospital to take charge of the situation, after French doctors had performed an operation on vom Rath's spleen.[94] Brandt, after having examined the abdominal cavity, was satisfied that all had been done. As Hitler's special envoy, he transmitted the Führer's best wishes to vom Rath and told him that Hitler had promoted him to *Gesandschaftsrat I. Klasse*. This apparently made a strong impression on the dying patient. What Hitler now needed was the death of a high government official to sanction his next move. Having seen vom Rath's weakened condition and the seriousness of the shotgun wounds, Brandt and Magnus knew that vom Rath was living on borrowed time. The first press bulletin by the two doctors was, nonetheless, uncommitted and hopeful, stating that

> the condition of Herrn Legationssekretär vom Rath has to be judged to be serious especially because of the injury at the entry to the stomach. The significant loss of blood caused by the injury to the spleen and its consequences might be controlled by further blood transfusions. The best possible operative care and the previous treatment through Dr Baumgartner, Paris, gives reason to remain hopeful for further development.[95]

By the end of the day Brandt issued a second press bulletin which stressed the deteriorating condition of the patient:

> The condition of Herrn Legationssekretär vom Rath has not improved towards the evening. Serious concerns still exist. His temperature has remained high. There are now signs of an incipient circulatory disorder.[96]

The promotion of vom Rath, and Brandt's press bulletins, were building up to a climax. At 6.20 p.m., about an hour after vom Rath had died at 5.30 p.m., German time, Berlin received a telegram from Brandt which laconically stated: 'My Führer! Party member vom Rath died today, 9 November, at 4.30 p.m. due to his shotgun injuries'.[97] As it turned out, this was only part of the truth. Vom Rath had been suffering from severe tuberculosis of the stomach and the intestines which he had contracted on his previous diplomatic posting in Calcutta, India, and he had been sent to Paris for treatment and convalescence. Unknown to the German diplomatic corps, Brandt discovered vom Rath's medical condition when he examined the diplomat on 8 November. It soon became clear to all involved, including the French medical team, that if vom Rath were to die, this would be due partly to his tuberculosis, and not simply to the gunshot wounds, which would not necessarily have killed him. Brandt, in consultation with the Nazi leadership, and probably after having spoken to Hitler on the phone in the afternoon, decided not to make this information public because, as he later recalled, it would have 'disturbed' the causal link between the shots which had been fired by a Jew and the death of vom Rath. That is why Brandt's telegram mentions only the 'shotgun injuries' as the cause of death and nothing else. Less than three years later, in July 1941, Brandt told Otto Bräutigam, himself a diplomat in Paris at the time, that it was unlikely that vom Rath would have died from the injuries alone, and that his death had been carefully orchestrated for maximum political effect:

> Despite the injury, vom Rath could probably have been saved if he had not been suffering from severe tuberculosis of the stomach and intestines. I immediately discovered this during the examination of the patient and looked at my two French colleagues in a questioning manner. When they remained silent, I whispered only one word 'Phthisis?' (consumption)? There both of them nodded briefly in agreement and in earnest. It was not in our interest that this would become public knowledge, because it would otherwise have disturbed the causal link between the shots of the Jew Grünspan [sic] and the death of the young diplomat. We felt that it was very proper in the period thereafter, when Dr Goebbels set in motion his action against the Jews (*Judenaktion in Scene setzte*), that the French doctors continued to remain silent.[98]

If we are to trust Bräutigam's recollection of the conversation between Brandt and himself, and there is no obvious reason why we should not – other than perhaps that he wanted to distance himself and the German diplomatic corps from the events – then Brandt had carefully manipulated the medical evidence in order to give Hitler and Goebbels the necessary justification to exploit the death of vom Rath for an unprecedented nationwide pogrom. Moreover, Brandt's telegram not only gave Hitler and Goebbels the necessary rationale for their action, but its arrival seems to have been carefully choreographed in order to coincide with the announcement by the Nazi leadership that action would be taken against the German Jewry. Brandt sent the telegram at 4.45 p.m. from Paris, which was 5.45 p.m. German time, while the party leaders were on their way to the Munich town hall to listen to Hitler's speech.[99] In all likelihood, Brandt would have informed Hitler of the death of vom Rath hours earlier by telephone, and probably agreed on the text that was to be made public. Nicolaus von Below, Hitler's Luftwaffe adjutant, recalled that Hitler was informed during the afternoon in his Munich apartment, but apparently made no comment, so that those present gained the impression that the matter was of little political relevance.[100] Total secrecy and surprise were among Hitler's favoured techniques to introduce radical policy measures. Whatever the precise timing, Hitler and Goebbels had sufficient time to decide on their strategy as to how to unleash a series of violent anti-Semitic riots which would not engulf the Nazi leadership itself. Above all, it was paramount that Hitler remained aloof and could distance himself from events if things got out of hand. By the time Hitler met the party leadership on the evening of 9 November, Hitler knew that vom Rath was dead, but he did not tell any of those present. Witnesses only saw him talking to Goebbels in an agitated fashion. Goebbels' diary entry gives us a good idea what was discussed:

> I go to the party reception in the Old Town Hall. Huge amount going on (*Riesenbetrieb*). I explain the matter to the Führer. He decides: let the demonstrations continue. Pull back the police. The Jews should for once get to feel the anger of the people. That's right. I immediately give corresponding directives to police and party. Then I speak for a short time in that vein to the party leadership. Storms of applause. All tear straight off to the telephone. Now the people will act.[101]

Goebbels' incitement of party leaders had its intended effect. Orders were immediately relayed across the Reich that violent attacks against the Jews had been sanctioned by the party and that all synagogues were to be set on fire. Local and regional stormtroopers started to wreak havoc on the streets. Synagogues went up in flames, buildings and Jewish shops were destroyed, their owners driven onto the streets, beaten and, in some cases, killed. In Munich, Hitler's personal adjutant, Julius Schaub, who later befriended Brandt, led the group of rampaging Nazi hordes; Goebbels was clearly enjoying the spectacle. 'The Hitler shock-troop gets going immediately to clear things out in Munich,' he recorded in his diary.[102] 'Schaub is completely worked up,' he remarked. 'His old shock-troop past is waking up.'[103] The November pogrom, unlike any other government action, provided thousands of 'Old Fighters' and party activists, whose hopes in a National Socialist revolution had not materialized after the Nazi takeover of power, with an opportunity to relive the time of the political struggle, albeit only for one night, and vent their pent-up aggression and frustration on the declared enemy of the regime.

Himmler's police and SS leaders were also gathering in Munich, but it was decided that the uncontrolled and unorganized persecution of Jews was not the style of Himmler's elite organization. Himmler's maxim was that if the Jews were to be eliminated from the German body politic, it would be done in an organized and 'reasoned' fashion. It soon became clear, however, that the regional police departments needed some direction in how to handle the situation, even if the whole 'action' was meant to look like the spontaneous expression of the people's wrath. At 11.55 p.m., Heinrich Müller, Himmler's subordinate and head of the Gestapo, issued written instructions to the German police to prevent looting and 'other special excesses' in the forthcoming pogrom. He also informed the authorities that the arrest of about '20–30,000 Jews in the Reich' was being prepared.[104] At 1.20 on the morning of 10 November, Reinhard Heydrich, the head of the Security Service, issued further directives to allow for the greatest possible acts of violence without endangering German lives and property or damaging Germany's foreign policy relations more than necessary. Tens of thousands of male Jews, especially the wealthy, were arrested and imprisoned in concentration camps. Reports of more than seventy burning synagogues reached Goebbels, who commented in his diary: 'The dear Jews will think about it in future before they shoot down German diplomats like that. And that was the meaning of the exercise.'[105] Goebbels had clearly understood the feelings of many ordinary Germans, who condoned and supported the pogrom. On the morning of 10 November, Melita Maschmann, a member of the League of German Girls, after discovering that almost all of the destroyed shops and buildings had belonged to Jews, said to herself: 'The Jews are the enemy of the new Germany. Last night they had a taste of what this means.'[106]

A report, written in February 1939 by the Nazi Party's Supreme Court, provides a contemporary analysis of the culture of communication and detachment which by 1938 had become established practice between the Nazi leadership and the party's grass roots.[107] This report offers important insights which help to explain how the Nazi leadership managed to control the process of cumulative radicalization, and how the government was able both to rely on, and to maintain, mass support from a wide spectrum of German society, not only in the period before the Second World War but also throughout the war. Scholars of the Third Reich have quite rightly challenged the idea of a 'top-down model' which alleges that Hitler and his government ordered and micro-managed the criminal policies of the regime; they have argued instead that the process of cumulative radicalization, which was an essential factor in the origins of the Holocaust, was largely driven by ever more radical initiatives and actions by the Nazi rank and file from below.[108] The study of the November pogrom shows, however, that acts of violence against the Jewish community were neither instigated from below, although the Nazi leadership retrospectively wanted the German people and the world to believe that they had been, nor were they ordered from above in the traditional sense of the term. Rather, Hitler's government had cultivated, and was able to use, a system of communication which relied heavily on general, often ambiguous, oral directives to instigate and control illegal activities, without implicating the leadership of the regime itself.

Witnesses recalled that Hitler had left the gathering at the Old Town Hall in Munich earlier than usual to return to his Munich apartment. Well aware of what was about to happen in the next couple of hours, he wanted to distance himself personally from organized acts of violence and detach the Nazi leadership from the pogrom. Investigating the extent to which fourteen Nazis were responsible for the crimes they had committed, and whether they had acted upon higher orders, the party's Supreme Court noted:

> The Leader had decided on hearing his [Goebbels'] report that such demonstrations should neither be prepared nor organised by the Party, but that no obstacles should be placed in their way if they took place spontaneously ... The Reich Propaganda Leader's verbal instructions were probably understood by the Party leaders who were present to mean that the Party should not appear publicly as the organiser of the demonstrations, but that it [the Party] should in reality organise them and carry them out.[109]

The Supreme Court was of the opinion that the men should therefore not be held accountable for their crimes because they had followed orders, had received ambiguous or supposed orders, and had carried them out 'on the assumption' that it was the 'will of the leadership' to avenge the death of vom Rath.[110] The men were not wrong in their assessment. Without having received clear and unambiguous instructions, the Nazi stormtroopers and those who had beaten, raped and killed Jews, or burned down synagogues, had understood the intended message of the leadership correctly. That is why, according to the Nazi Party lawyers, the responsibility for the crimes did not lie with the men who had committed them, but with the 'the authority issuing the order' (*Befehlsgeber*), in other words the Nazi leadership.[111] The Supreme Court's examination of the November pogrom revealed the extent to which the traditional chain of command had degenerated into an interactive, highly ambiguous process of communication between the German government and the Nazi rank and file. It was a system of communication which allowed each party to distance itself and deny responsibility for illegal acts later:

> The re-examination of the conditions of command has revealed that in all of these cases there has been a misunderstanding in any one of the chains of command, especially because it is self-evident for the active National Socialist from the period of political battle that actions in which the Party should not outwardly appear as the organiser are not ordered with final clarity and in every detail. He is therefore used to reading more into such an order than what is said. In the same way the authority issuing the order (*Befehlsgeber*) has, in the interest of the Party, developed the custom – especially in relation to illegal political activities – of not saying everything, and only hinting at what is to be achieved by the order.[112]

In line with the leadership principle (*Führerprinzip*), the Supreme Court believed that the responsibility for the November pogrom did not lie with the perpetrators, who had received ambiguous orders, or had misinterpreted them, but with the Nazi leadership. After Goebbels had been informed at 2 a.m. of the death of the first Jew, who happened to be a Polish national, he had commented 'that the man

1. Karl Brandt and his father, Karl Julius Brandt, *c.* 1910. (Source: Karl-Adolf Brandt)

2. Karl Brandt as a student, *c.* 1925. (Source: Karl-Adolf Brandt)

3. Karl Brandt, *c.* 1928. (Source: BA, BDC file)

4. Karl Brandt hiking in Switzerland, *c.* 1930. (Source: Karl-Adolf Brandt)

Top left: 5. Karl Brandt with his mother, Catherina Brandt, née Lehnebach, 14 November 1914. (Source: Karl-Adolf Brandt)

Top right: 6. Karl Brandt as an adolescent, *c.* 1915. (Source: Karl-Adolf Brandt)

Middle: 7. Karl Brandt on a horse, 13 October 1915. (Source: Karl-Adolf Brandt)

Bottom: 8. Karl Brandt with Anni Brandt, *c.* mid-1930s. (Source: Karl-Adolf Brandt)

9. Marriage of Karl Brandt and Anna Rehborn, 17 March 1934.
(BSB, Fotoarchiv Hoffmann, hoff-8917)

10. Hitler greeting a small girl, *c.* 1933. (BSB, Fotoarchiv Hoffmann, hoff-322)

11. Hitler on holiday with his staff, including Karl Brandt, 15 January 1935. (BSB, Fotoarchiv Hoffmann, hoff-10054)

12. Hitler and Karl Brandt, April 1936. (BSB, Fotoarchiv Hoffmann, hoff-12893)

13. Karl Brandt with his son Karl-Adolf Brandt, *c.* 1938. (Source: Karl-Adolf Brandt)

14. Karl Brandt and Eva Braun at the Berghof, *c.* 1937. (BSB, Fotoarchiv Hoffmann, hoff-316)

15. *Above:* Karl Brandt, Hermann Göring, Adolf Hitler, Werner von Blomberg and staff, 24 July 1935. (BSB, Fotoarchiv Hoffmann, hoff-11166)

16. *Left:* Karl Brandt and Adolf Hitler on the Berghof during Hitler's holiday, 1–3 September 1938. (BSB, Fotoarchiv Hoffmann, hoff-20063)

17. and 18. Trip to Greece by Goebbels, Hoffmann and Brandt, 21–28 September 1936. (BSB, Fotoarchiv Hoffmann, hoff-14675 and hoff-14109)

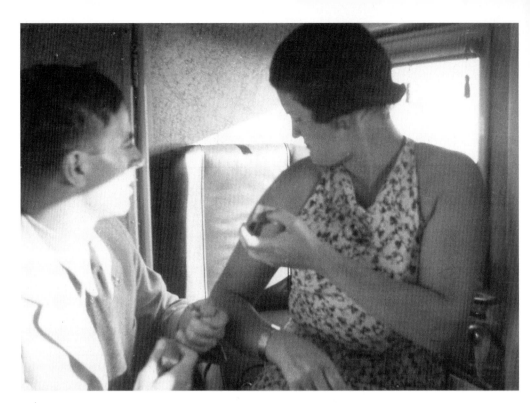

19. and 20. Trip to Greece by Goebbels, Hoffmann and Brandt, 21–28 September 1936. (BSB, Fotoarchiv Hoffmann, hoff-14150 and hoff-14081)

reporting it should not get upset because of one dead Jew; thousands of Jews were going to cop it in the coming days'.[113] Given Goebbels' views on the matter, and because no government directives were issued to prevent the killing of Jews, the Court concluded that 'the eventual success [of killing Jews] was wanted, or at least possible and desired.'[114] Accordingly, the perpetrators had 'carried out not only the apparent wish of the leadership, but indeed also their true intentions, even though these were not at all clearly expressed' [*nicht nur den vermeintlichen, sondern den zwar unklar zum Ausdruck gebrachten, aber richtig erkannten Willen der Führung in die Tat umgesetzt*], for which they should not be punished.[115] In the interests of party discipline and clearly defined areas of responsibility, the Court proposed to terminate the system of communication between the Nazi leadership and the Nazi Party's rank and file which had been based on two factors: first the 'intentionally imprecise' (*absichtlich unklar*) nature of the orders, and second the 'expectation' (*Erwartung*) that the person receiving the order would recognize the intention of the authority issuing the order, and act accordingly. Given the enormous power base of the Nazi Party at the end of the 1930s, there was no longer any need to camouflage its political – and illegal – activities, the Court suggested. After all, the German public knew anyway that the pogrom had been organized by the party: 'Even the public knows to the last man that political actions, such as the one on 9 November, are organised and carried out by the Party, whether this is being admitted or not.'[116] However, rather than reforming the regime's culture of communication, and establishing a clear chain of command between the government and the executive agencies of the party and the state, Hitler's government increasingly detached itself from a whole range of criminal activities which it had initiated, supported or set in train. It was a system of communication which Brandt would learn to apply in his area of responsibility.

On 10 November, Brandt was back in Munich, where Hitler gave a secret press conference in the *Führergebäude* (Führer Building). A photograph shows him standing with Hitler and Otto Dietrich on the steps inside the building.[117] It stretches belief to the extreme to suggest that Brandt was unaware of what his master was doing. Everyone else in Hitler's entourage knew, and some criticized Hitler for permitting things to go that far. The destruction of lives and property was clearly of enormous proportions. Hundreds of synagogues had been burned and at least 8,000 shops had been completely destroyed and looted. The financial cost of the pogrom was estimated to reach several hundred million Reichsmark. Göring, as head of the Four-Year Plan, was enraged. One of the party leaders bitterly complained that it was indefensible that the nation was asked, on the one hand, to 'collect silver paper and empty toothpaste tubes, and on the other hand millions of Marks' worth of damage is caused deliberately.' No matter how hard the Nazi propaganda machine tried to argue that it had all been a spontaneous, uncontrolled expression of people's anger, a large proportion of the people did not believe it.[118] However, this should not distract us from the fact that a large proportion of the population were more upset about the destruction of German property than they were about the persecution of the Jews. It soon emerged that the pogrom had caused irreparable damage to Germany's reputation in the world. Asked in 1941 by Bräutigam about the long-term economic and political implications of the *Reichskristallnacht*, and the enormous damage it had caused to Franco-German relations, Brandt replied: 'You are quite right. This action against the Jews was unfounded and un-German and has caused us a lot of damage.'[119] Brandt was by now identifying himself with the Nazi leadership.

Whereas Brandt had acted as Hitler's envoy during the dramatic days of November 1938, other doctors actively participated in the violence. Doctors from the Düsseldorf local hospital are reported to have taken part in the smashing of windows, looting of shops and burning of buildings. It is hard to imagine how they would have justified their actions. Their sense of medical morality and respect for the dignity of human life must have been corrupted through the years of anti-Semitic propaganda. When it came to racial policies, the German medical profession had traditionally shown an extraordinary degree of loyalty to the regime. To Hitler, the November pogrom had also demonstrated once more that he could totally rely on Brandt, who would fulfil his orders in an informal and professional fashion. Men like Brandt suited Hitler's style of charismatic leadership. They were perfect channels of information for him, allowing him to project his authority and power to areas of policy which had momentarily attracted his attention and which needed, in his view, swift and unbureaucratic action. The way in which Hitler employed Brandt throughout the 1930s as his special envoy anticipated and mirrored in many ways the course of events which led to the introduction of the children's 'euthanasia' programme in 1939. Brandt, in other words, had become an integral part of Hitler's detached leadership.

Brandt must have felt that his role as Hitler's doctor warranted an address to match his status. For a member of Hitler's court, his simple flat on the top floor in the Altonaerstraße in Berlin was inappropriate.[120] By the end of April 1939, Brandt had moved into a six-bedroom apartment in the north-west wing of the Bellevue Palace in Spreeallee, a truly magnificent late-eighteenth-century building which was also used as a government guesthouse.[121] In case a foreign dignitary visited the capital, it was believed to be prudent to have a doctor on site. Both Brandt and State Secretary Otto Meißner, head of the Presidential Chancellery, took up permanent residence in the building. Here, the children of some of the leading members of the regime, including Meißner's son, Hans-Otto Meißner, played with one another and formed a social and professional network. Brandt's access to the centre of government could not have been better. Hitler's doctor had now acquired the social and political standing he believed he deserved. It was in this magnificent architectural environment that Brandt oversaw the Nazis' programme to kill tens of thousands of asylum inmates – a conjuction of two of the many realities which were worlds apart in Germany.

Brandt's ignorance of the real situation in German hospitals and state institutions, and his subsequent ignorance about the potential consequences of certain policies, are important factors in attempting to understand his readiness to carry out Hitler's 'euthanasia' programme. But some people in Germany did know the facts, and took the necessary steps before the programme was actually introduced. 'At the beginning of 1938 I left my job,' the director of the Eichberg asylum, Wilhelm Hinsen, noted in one of the many post-war German trials. 'Euthanasia was on the horizon, it was not yet imminent, [but] I was convinced that it would come.'[122] Hinsen had read the writing on the wall which Brandt and others preferred to ignore. After the *Anschluss* of Austria to the German Reich in March 1938, the notorious Munich Treaty in September of the same year, and the occupation of what remained of Czechoslovakia in March 1939, Hitler had at last started to reveal his true foreign policy ambitions and territorial claims. Now all efforts were geared towards another war. Following the logic of previously stated policy intentions, Brandt and a few chosen men from the Chancellery of the Führer began, in total secrecy, preparations for a programme to kill the mentally and physically handicapped in German institutions. When war eventually broke out, Hitler kept his promise. Brandt and Hitler's chief of staff in the Chancellery of the Führer, Philipp Bouhler, were entrusted with the Nazis' first full-scale, calculated and systematic programme of mass murder.

5

The 'Euthanasia' Doctor

I. THE 'KRETSCHMAR' CHILD

In the autumn of 1939, Karl Brandt and Philipp Bouhler, head of the Chancellery of the Führer (*Kanzlei des Führers*, KdF), were personally entrusted by Hitler to organize and implement the 'euthanasia' programme. The origins of the programme are complex, and scholars are still arguing over how it actually started. However, we have a clear idea with whom it started, namely with the most defenceless and vulnerable members of the population: children. Post-war testimony agrees that around 1939, a severely handicapped infant served as a pretext for Hitler to initiate the programme to kill the mentally and physically handicapped, a policy Hitler had wanted to implement since he had become Reich Chancellor, if not earlier. The precise sequence of events is thus of historical significance, not only with regard to the role of Brandt, but in understanding the mechanisms of decision-making in the high echelons of the Nazi leadership, and the powerful and mostly destructive dynamics which went along with it.

Until recently, the identity of the infant and exactly when it was killed were shrouded in mystery, amplified by the conflicting post-war testimony of those involved in the killing programme. It was believed that the infant, sex unknown, was called 'Knauer', and that the case occurred in the winter of 1938, or at the latest at the beginning of 1939.[1] Testimony seemed to agree that the infant was born blind and with severe handicaps, lacking one leg and part of an arm. Most of the physicians involved in the case diagnosed the infant as an 'idiot', but not all, and some stated that the baby suffered from convulsions. Other sources which could have corroborated the sequence of events were believed to have been mostly destroyed or lost.[2] New research, however, enables us to reconstruct the identity of the infant, and the events which led to its death, with greater clarity.

A German medical historian, Udo Benzenhöfer, has recently found out the name and sex of the child, but he is adamant that he cannot disclose this information because of strict German data-protection laws. He argues that historians should from now on call the case the 'child K' and that the main importance of his discovery lies in its factual value; in other words, that it is now safe to say that this child 'really existed'.[3] Although this approach is understandable and sensitive to the feelings of the parents and relatives of the child, it somehow overlooks the child itself and its individual suffering. Let us be precise in describing the context. The parents of this child wanted the child to be killed. According to the available evidence, they were ardent Nazis, who regarded their child's prospective life as 'not worth living', and saw to it that their child would be killed in accordance with Nazi ideology. By calling the case the 'child K', we would not only medicalize the child's history, but also place the justifiable claim of the parents for anonymity above the personality and suffering of the first 'euthanasia' victim.

I therefore wish to reveal the child's full identity: the child was a boy, born on 20 February 1939 in Pomßen, a small village in the south-eastern region of Saxony. His name was Gerhard Herbert Kretschmar.[4] In the spring of 1939, Gerhard's father, an agricultural labourer called Richard Gerhard Kretschmar of Pomßen, consulted Werner Catel, the director of the University Children's Clinic in Leipzig, with a view to having the child admitted. Catel later claimed that the father had been concerned about the effect the child was having on the mother, Lina Sonja Kretschmar, and had asked him to admit the infant to his clinic with a view to 'putting it to sleep'. Catel apparently declined to do so because he felt it was illegal. The child's parents (probably the father), or a relative, then petitioned Hitler to grant permission to have the child killed.[5] Such appeals were directed to Hitler's KdF, where similar requests had previously been lodged.[6] Brandt later testified that the KdF

> always received such things. I only know that these requests were passed on to the Reich Ministry of the Interior. I myself know of only one request in the spring of 1939 which was sent to the Führer himself through his Adjutant's office. The father of a deformed child approached the Führer and asked that this creature should be killed. Hitler turned the matter over to me and told me to go to Leipzig immediately – it had taken place in Leipzig – to confirm the fact. It was a child who was born blind, an idiot – at least it seemed to be an idiot – and it lacked one leg and part of one arm.[7]

The KdF had been set up to foster the popular image of Hitler as a leader who would listen to the complaints and petitions of ordinary Germans. Headed by Philipp Bouhler from 1934, the KdF functioned as Hitler's private chancellery outside of government and party politics. It was independent of the Nazi Party Chancellery, headed by Martin Bormann, and served alongside, but separate from, the Presidential Chancellery, headed by Otto Meißner, and the Reich Chancellery, headed by Hans Heinrich Lammers. The KdF was a relatively small department with few staff members, and dealt with ordinary people's conflicts in an informal fashion. It was the ideal setting for running a covert operation which was to remain essentially concealed from the public eye.

The KdF was divided into five departments. Central Office I dealt with Hitler's private affairs and was headed by Martin Bormann's brother, Albert. Central Office II handled all matters relating to the government and party and was headed by Oberdienstleiter Viktor Brack[8] and his deputy, Werner Blankenburg; its sub-department IIb, under Hans Hefelmann, was in charge of clemency petitions to Hitler, including those requesting mercy killing. It was through this sub-department IIb that Hefelmann received the petition of the Kretschmar family, who passed it without any further comment to Albert Bormann, who gave it to Hitler.[9] Although, strictly speaking, the petition also fell within the jurisdiction of the Reich Ministry of Justice or the Reich Ministry of the Interior (*Reichsministerium des Innern*, RMdI),

Hefelmann first wanted to gauge Hitler's 'personal' views about the matter before forwarding the case to a government department: 'As, to my knowledge, Hitler had never taken a decision with regard to such appeals, I felt it inappropriate to involve other government departments with it.'[10] The petition of the Kretschmar family was certainly not the only one the KdF had received from German parents since 1933, especially after racial propaganda had stressed that such children were 'ballast existences' for the German body politic, and should be eliminated. Hefelmann, for instance, stated that two thousand petitions reached the Chancellery each day.[11] It is likely, however, that Gerhard Kretschmar's case would have caught the attention of the KdF officials. Given the many disabilities of the boy, they must have realized that the case could serve as a precedent to implement further eugenic measures. It also gave them another opportunity to be seen to be working towards the goals of National Socialism.

They were right. The Kretschmar case interested Hitler, especially after he had seen documents and photographs of the child. He immediately realized the political potential of the case. While Germany was preparing for war, this incident fitted neatly into his racial ideology. He instructed Brandt to travel immediately to Leipzig and investigate the matter in consultation with the Leipzig paediatricians. In case they all agreed that the diagnosis corresponded with the conditions outlined in the petition, Brandt was authorized to allow the child to be killed. In his personal notebook, which he kept in his Nuremberg cell, Brandt recalled that he was sent to Leipzig to talk to the physicians and, if the facts could be corroborated, state the following:

> The doctors were authorised immediately to perform euthanasia. Extra care was to be taken with the mother. It would be ensured that a potential judicial inquiry could not take place.[12]

Brandt apparently discussed the case with Helmut Kohl, the physician on duty, and may have authorized him to 'put the infant to sleep'.[13] Catel later claimed that he was on holiday at the time and did not participate in the decision-making, although his post-war accounts are scarcely credible.[14] It is more likely that Brandt consulted Catel and the leading physicians at the Leipzig clinic, an assumption which is corroborated by Hefelmann. He remembered Brandt telling him that they had first X-rayed the child before holding a conference (*Konsilium*) together with Catel.[15]

Whether Brandt then returned to Berlin to receive his authorization from Hitler before heading back to Leipzig or, as is also possible, to the child's birthplace in Pomßen, is not entirely clear. Brandt may first have travelled to Leipzig to discuss the case with the doctors and, at some later time, travelled to Pomßen, after having received the authorization from Hitler. This would explain why there is a discrepancy between the reports of those who recalled after the war that the case was discussed in Leipzig, and the actual church register, which lists Pomßen as the place of death of the child. Another possibility, which is perhaps more plausible, is that the place of death and the cause of death are fake. Indeed, there is evidence to support this assumption. Brandt knew that it was prudent to conceal the child's identity by inventing a pseudonym, and by keeping the context of the boy's death secret.

At Nuremberg, Brandt elaborated on the circumstances in which Gerhard Herbert Kretschmar was killed, but he never mentioned the child's real name:

> [Hitler] ordered me to talk to the physicians who were looking after the child to find out whether the statements of the father were true. If they were correct, then I was to inform the physicians in his name that they could carry out euthanasia. The important thing was that the parents should not feel themselves incriminated at some later date as a result of this euthanasia – that the parents should not have the impression that they themselves were responsible for the death of this child. I was further ordered to state that if these physicians were to become involved in any legal proceedings because of this measure, these proceedings would be quashed by order of Hitler.[16]

Brandt's testimony of February 1947 is significant in a number of respects. First, he stressed that the parents of the child should not in any way feel guilty or be afraid of being prosecuted at a later date. Second, he told the doctors that any legal proceedings against them would be quashed by the authority of the German Chancellor (who, legally speaking, did not possess such an authority). Brandt's testimony suggests that those involved in the case were not ignorant of the fact that their action was illegal. Hitler, Brandt, the Leipzig doctors and even the parents knew that what they were doing was outside the law and generally accepted medical conduct. In German penal law it constituted a crime. As Ian Kershaw has pointed out, 'even according to the legal theories of the time, Hitler's mandate could not be regarded as a formal Führer decree and did not, therefore, possess the character of law. But an order from the Führer, whatever its legal status, was nonetheless seen as binding.'[17]

The reaction of the doctors involved in the case is also significant. The physicians seem to have agreed to kill the child, although they knew that Brandt's instructions were illegal. They questioned neither Brandt's authority (Brandt was officially only Hitler's escort physician) and the intrusion by the head of state into medical autonomy, nor the legality of such an unprecedented measure. Catel and the Leipzig physicians must have been under the impression that Hitler's authorization was similar to binding law in Germany. They were not entirely wrong about this. By 1939, almost no one in Germany would have dared to question or challenge an authorization given by Hitler, even if it had only been given orally. Hitler's power base at this point was of monumental proportions. Brandt's statement shows that by 1939 any sense of right and wrong had disappeared. Decisions over life and death had literally been handed over to the discretion of Hitler himself.

Brandt's testimony also reflects on the moral attitude of the doctors to mental defectives, and on the general atmosphere in German mental institutions. Asked what the doctors had thought about the Kretschmar child, Brandt remarked:

> The doctors were of the opinion that there was no justification for keeping such a child alive. It was pointed out that in maternity wards under certain circumstances it is quite

natural for the doctors themselves to perform euthanasia in such a case without anything further being said about it. No precise instructions were given in that respect.[18]

If Brandt is to be believed, and there is no obvious reason why we should distrust him on this occasion, then the killing of infants seems to have been carried out in Germany for some time, informally and independently, before the 'euthanasia' programme actually began.

Following the consultations with the Leipzig physicians, Brandt may have travelled to Pomßen where the family of the infant lived. According to the French journalist Philippe Aziz, who allegedly interviewed the Kretschmars in 1973, Brandt told them that Hitler had authorized 'euthanasia' to be used in the case of their son. Richard Kretschmar recalled that 'it was summer, and the afternoon was hot' when he was called to come home because Hitler's doctor had arrived in Pomßen:

> It was right here. Karl Brandt was standing there near the window. He was tall and impressive. He seemed to fill the whole room. He didn't want to sit down. He explained to me that the Führer had personally sent him, and that my son's case interested the Führer very much. The Führer wanted to explore the problem of people who had no future – whose life was worthless. That's why he had sent his personal doctor to see us. From then on, we wouldn't have to suffer from this terrible misfortune, because the Führer had granted us the mercy killing of our son. Later, we could have other children, handsome and healthy, of whom the Reich could be proud.[19]

Shortly after this meeting with Brandt, the boy was dead. Although Aziz' narrative must be treated with considerable caution, Herr Kretschmar's recollections correspond to the Pomßen church register (*Begräbnisbuch*), which provides evidence about the child's date of death in the summer of 1939. The first 'official' 'euthanasia' victim, Gerhard Herbert Kretschmar, was killed at 10 a.m. on 25 July 1939. Three days later, on Friday 28 July, the body was buried in the cemetery of the Protestant church in Pomßen.[20]

Who exactly killed Gerhard Kretschmar, and where, cannot be established with certainty. Some testimony suggests that the child was killed by the Leipzig doctor Helmut Kohl, who administered a lethal injection while the nurses were taking a coffee break. The account conflicts, however, with the church register, which lists Pomßen as the place of death. Considering that those involved in the case were keen nothing should ever be revealed about it, the reference in the church register makes sense. Anyone looking at the church register would think that the boy had died of natural causes, and in his home village. Significantly, there is no reference to the child in the register of the Leipzig clinic. The child's patient record, if one ever existed, has also never been found and appears to have been lost.

Brandt and the Leipzig doctors wanted the boy to die as inconspicuously as possible. This assumption is further substantiated through the church register, which lists the boy's cause of death as 'heart weakness' (*Herzschwäche*). It is safe to assume that the cause of death was faked. One of the most common killing methods in the children's 'euthanasia' programme was by administering drugs such as luminal or morphium-scopolamin to camouflage an unnatural death. Gerhard Kretschmar may have died from the medical complications of such a drug.[21] In October 1945, Brandt admitted that he and the doctors had not given the parents the true cause of death:

> I had to go to Leipzig where a child was born who lacked either two legs and one arm or two arms and one leg. The father sent a request to the Party Chancellery that this child should be given euthanasia. Then members of the family were told that the child had other weaknesses, that it had some sort of heart disease too so that the parents should not have the feeling that they were responsible for the death of this child.[22]

In 1946, Brandt also recalled in his personal notebook:

> Given that the child was, on the whole, weak, I asked the doctors, according to Hitler's instructions, to present the death of the child in such a way as if the death had been the result of other inherited disorders. This was done in order to relieve the parents from any future psychological burden.[23]

For Brandt, the child had no right to live and deserved to die. On 24 June 1945, whilst imprisoned at 'Ashcan' in Luxembourg, investigators recorded Brandt's recollections about the incident:

> His [Brandt's] own experience of seeing the mother of a blind, legless and one-armed infant in Leipzig was cited. He said that he talked to the mother to show her that she shouldn't mind its death. It was taken away and soon died of natural causes – probably congenital heart disease. He said he wouldn't call the infant an infant because it shouldn't have such a name. It might be called a thing.[24]

Brandt was intricately involved in the death of Gerhard Kretschmar, and it is highly likely that he talked to the parents, especially to the mother, in order to relieve her from any sense of responsibility or feelings of guilt. Another possibility, which cannot be discounted, is that Brandt himself may have killed the boy when he was visiting the parents in Pomßen in the summer of 1939. Hefelmann later told a German court that he could not tell whether it was Brandt, Catel, another doctor or a nurse who had administered the 'tablets', but it is significant that he did not rule Brandt out.[25] That Brandt was capable of medical killing became clear only six months later, at the beginning of 1940, when he administered, together with Conti, the first deadly injections in the adult 'euthanasia' programme. This was to show the participating physicians that the two most senior doctors in the Reich were prepared to become involved themselves in the killing programme. Questioned about the Kretschmar child after the war, Brandt may have transferred the place of events to the clinic in Leipzig – where the first meeting with Catel had taken place – to ensure that it would be almost impossible to trace any biographical information about the child, and thus preserve the anonymity of the parents. This line of argument gains additional weight if we take into consideration that Brandt was not prepared to speak about the matter in greater detail in Nuremberg, because this would have infringed patient confidentiality. Having been criticized by fellow prisoners for violating the Hippocratic oath because he had told investigators about Hitler's medical problems, Brandt seems to have been particularly sensitive about the issue. By shrouding the identity of the child in mystery, he knew that he served everyone involved in the case, including, above all, himself.

We will probably never know the whole story. Nonetheless, two conclusions warrant consideration. Those involved in the first 'euthanasia' case knew that their action was (still) against the law and contrary to medical ethics. As long as there was no official government legislation, they felt that their actions had to remain secret. The second, and perhaps more troubling, conclusion is that those involved in the case had a vested interest that the identity of the first victim should disappear from the historical record. For them, Gerhard Herbert Kretschmar had never existed.

II. HITLER'S WISHES

Scholars seem to have overlooked one key element in the sequence of events: the petition of the Kretschmar family to the KdF in the spring of 1939 coincided with a serious power vacuum in the German health system, following Wagner's sudden death of an undisclosed ailment on 25 March 1939. It was at around the same time that Hefelmann probably received the appeal by the Kretschmars to 'put their child to sleep'. A month later, on 20 April, Hitler appointed Leonardo Conti to the office of 'Reich Health Leader' (*Reichsgesundheitsführer*), apparently because he remembered his name from the time of the political struggle in the 1920s, and did not know who the other proposed candidate was.[26] Conti's mandate officially surpassed that of Wagner in scope and responsibility, but only on paper. Despite his grand-sounding title, Conti was, and remained, politically impotent.[27] His office never carried any real power of its own. He was neither an executive member of the party (*Reichsleiter*), nor did he possess the powers of a Reich Minister (*Reichsminister*). Closely integrated into the RMdI, he had no independent financial budget and no immediate access to Hitler, a vital prerequisite in the constant power struggles in the regime. Within the state hierarchy, Conti was nothing but a ministerial counsellor (*Ministerialrat*), and it was not until August 1939 that the Nazi leadership promoted him to State Secretary (*Staatssekretär*). But even then he was still nominally inferior to all ministers and executives of the regions or the party (*Gau-* or *Reichsleiter*), who could interfere at any given time in his area of responsibility. Conti was a typical 'Old Fighter', and he had instigated a series of intrigues against Wagner after Hitler had assumed power in 1933. In the spring of 1939, however, he was short of ideas on how to neutralize some of his most dangerous rivals, especially Friedrich Bartels, Wagner's deputy since 1936 and, most of all, Robert Ley, the energetic head of the German Labour Front (*Deutsche Arbeitsfront*, DAF).[28] He never managed to gain the same level of influence and respect in the high echelons of the Nazi leadership as his predecessor and rapidly lost what remained of his political influence.

Between February and May 1939, a small group of middle-ranking government officials discussed the question of euthanasia in an informal manner in the KdF.[29] They wanted to ensure that all the necessary technical details had been prepared in case Hitler suddenly wanted to begin such a programme after the outbreak of war. The group at first consisted of only four individuals: Herbert Linden, the man in charge of German state asylums in the RMdI; Viktor Brack, head of Central Office II in the KdF, which was earmarked to run the operation; Brack's subordinate, Hans Hefelmann, head of the central office IIb, which dealt with clemency petitions; and his deputy, Richard von Hegener, a former staff member of the Dresdner Bank.[30] In the spring of 1939, Brack, Hefelmann and von Hegener met on several occasions with senior officials of the KdF, and privately with Linden. His collaboration was essential because he provided Hefelmann and von Hegener with links to paediatricians and psychiatrists, who, Linden believed, were likely to take part in the programme.[31]

Having been informed by Brandt about the Kretschmar child, the group entered into a more active planning phase. Sometime in 1939, Brandt told Hefelmann that Hitler had ordered him (Brandt) to set up an advisory committee which would prepare for and supervise the killing of mentally ill children. For reasons of secrecy, the 'Reich Committee for the Scientific Registering of Serious Hereditary and Congenital Illnesses' (*Reichsausschuß zur wissenschaftlichen Erfassung erb- und anlagebedingter schwerer Leiden*) would serve as a cover.[32] The group around Brandt, Brack, Hefelmann, von Hegener and Linden then approached a number of paediatricians who, they thought, might participate in the programme. To serve on the committee as expert referees, they recruited Catel from Leipzig, the child and youth psychiatrist Hans Heinze from Brandenburg-Görden (later one of the killing centres), the paediatrician Ernst Wentzler from a private clinic in Berlin-Frohnau, and the eye specialist Hellmuth Unger. Brandt and Catel joined the committee because of their handling of the Kretschmar child. Heinze was recommended by Linden, Wentzler was suggested by Conti and contacted by Brandt, and Unger was recommended to Hefelmann by von Hegener's sister.[33]

Wentzler later recalled that one day Brandt had suddenly turned up; he had first outlined why Hitler had decided to tackle this particular 'red-hot iron', and then asked him to join the 'Reich Committee' as an expert referee. Convinced by the arguments of Binding and Hoche, Wentzler phoned Brandt after a day or two to say that he would participate.[34] All particulars of the job were explained to the 'experts' by Brack at a meeting in the KdF. He showed them, among other things, how to complete the registration forms of those children earmarked for 'euthanasia'. These men formed the executive body which decided the fate of the children, who would be transferred to 'special children's wards' (*Kinderfachabteilungen*). They decided about the children's lives without ever actually physically examining the children themselves. For reasons of secrecy, they had also established the fictitious Reich Committee. Letters of this agency were signed with code names, mail was sent to an external post office box, and the entire programme was classified 'top secret' (*Geheime Reichssache*).

In the summer of 1939, planning reached a crucial stage. The small group of KdF officials were by then fully aware of the longer-term implications, and anticipated that the scope of the 'euthanasia' programme would not be limited to children, but would be expanded to include adolescents and adults in state asylums. In their world view, it was only logical, considering that they were working towards Hitler's goals, that they should continue with the planning stages without being officially instructed by Hitler, and without any other official authorization. Bouhler, as head of the KdF, also knew that if he managed to prepare the organization of the programme in advance, there was some chance that Hitler might entrust him with its overall control, especially if the state bureaucracy failed to implement it. Gerhard Herbert Kretschmar's death at the end of July 1939 marked the decisive moment in the regime's decision to go ahead with the children's 'euthanasia' programme. It set off a train of events which led inexorably to the killing of handicapped adults. From that moment onwards, the KdF shifted into high gear.

Throughout the summer of 1939, key Nazi officials ensured that the issue of killing mentally and physically handicapped patients remained on Hitler's mind. Hitler's army adjutant, Gerhard Engel, recalled that Bouhler and Bormann showed a noticeable interest in the issue of euthanasia.[35] On 8 August 1939, for example, they jointly organized a film screening for Hitler which showed the life and living conditions of the mentally ill in a number of German asylums. According to Engel, the film 'Unworthy Life' (*Unwertes Leben*) had been commissioned by Conti to address the suffering of handicapped men, women and children. The film may well have been one of the racial propaganda films which had been produced by the Race Political Office (RPA) in the period between 1935 and 1937.[36] When the film screening was over, Bormann suggested to Hitler that he should introduce the film as a trailer in all German cinemas. Brandt opposed the idea, arguing that it would raise concerns among the population and would upset relatives and friends of handicapped patients. As it happened, Hitler sided with Brandt on the issue, but told the gathering that if he had such a severely handicapped child, he would ask the doctors to 'deliver' the child from suffering. In Hitler's view, it was better for the child to die than to live a life of misery. He also pointed out that the people in the East were far more practical in this regard, because they placed newborn babies in ice-cold water or into the snow, to see whether 'the creature could survive'.[37] For those attending the film screening and the subsequent discussion there could be no doubt that the head of state approved any measure which could be seen as delivering handicapped patients from pain and suffering. For Hitler's loyal servants it was also clear that the Führer would soon take a general policy decision on the matter. Those in his vicinity sensed that it was better to be prepared for the arrival of that moment. Throughout July and August, Brandt, Bouhler and others in the KdF were jockeying for position, in case Hitler chose to tackle the issue of euthanasia through a 'Führer decision' (*Führerentscheid*).

In Nuremberg, Werner Heyde, one of the most notorious doctors of the killing programme, told his interrogators that he had received a telephone call in July 1939 asking him to attend a meeting at the KdF.[38] At this meeting, on or around 10 August 1939,[39] approximately ten to fifteen psychiatrists and asylum directors from all parts of Germany were present. Among those gathered were Maximinian de Crinis (Berlin), a liaison man to the SS secret service, Carl Schneider

(Heidelberg), Werner Heyde (Würzburg), Berthold Kihn (Jena), Ernst Wentzler (Berlin-Frohnau), Hans Heinze (Brandenburg-Görden), Hellmuth Unger (Berlin), Hermann Pfannmüller (Eglfing-Haar), Wilhelm Bender (Berlin-Buch) and Gustav Adolf Waetzold (Wittenau).[40] In addition to these men, the key organizers and administrators of the killing programme attended the conference. These included Brandt, Bouhler, Brack, Hefelmann and Linden. Brandt later recalled: 'I was there when the relevant doctors, who had been proposed by the Ministry of the Interior, were informed about the whole situation. They were also informed through Bouhler.'[41] During the conference, the psychiatrists were told that the 'euthanasia' programme would soon commence:

> We were told that the euthanasia of the mentally ill should in practice be put into reality and we were asked to offer our support as experts and advisors. This meeting was followed by a series of meetings from September 1939 onwards. During these meetings Brack, Karl Brandt, Bouhler, Conti, and Linden were present, among others. The attendance of the aforementioned was not regular. At the meeting in September or October 1939 it became very clear to me and also for the others that Philipp Bouhler and Karl Brandt were the men in charge of the so called euthanasia programme.[42]

Testimony therefore seems to suggest that Brandt and Conti were present during some of the preliminary discussions. Events were now taking their course. On 18 August 1939, only three weeks after Gerhard Kretschmar had died, the 'Reich Committee' introduced the compulsory registration of all 'malformed' newborn children. All forms had been prepared months in advance and sent to the relevant expert referees.[43] Doctors were told to report all cases of idiocy, Down's Syndrome, microcephaly, hydrocephalus, physical deformities such as the absence of a limb, and all forms of spastic paralysis. The decision to kill the children was taken by Catel, Heinze and Wentzler, who marked the registration forms with a '+' if they wanted the infant to die, a '−' if the child was to live, and a '?' if the case had to be reviewed.[44] Depending on the judgement of midwives and doctors, their 'verdict' relied entirely on what had been stated on the forms. The referee receiving the form last had the advantage of knowing what the first two had decided. Once a decision on the child was taken, it was transferred to one of a series of paediatric clinics, where special children's wards were established. These clinics were first established in Brandenburg-Görden, Leipzig, Niedermarsberg, Steinhof and Eglfing-Haar. By the end of the war, the total number of clinics was around thirty, located all over the Reich. Here the children were meant to be monitored for some time, and if no improvement in the overall condition was obvious, the infant was 'put to sleep', generally with an overdose of a common drug such as morphium-scopolamin or luminal. Although Brandt and Bouhler believed that they had sufficient 'fail-safe mechanisms' in place to ensure that only severely handicapped children would be affected, the entire programme amounted to bureaucratic murder.

While the preparations for the killing of handicapped children were put in place, the much larger and more complex programme to kill handicapped adults produced considerably more logistical, judicial and administrative problems.

These were further amplified by the ongoing power struggle between Bouhler and Conti over who would be responsible for the operation. Having been put in charge of the administrative side of the killing of children, Bouhler wanted to centralize control over the 'euthanasia' programme in the KdF. Given that Conti was weakened by party infighting, Bouhler had a good chance of success, if Hitler could be persuaded.

At the end of September or at the beginning of October 1939, Hitler summoned Conti, Bormann and Lammers to a conference at Führer headquarters in Zoppot, near Danzig, shortly before the capitulation of Poland.[45] Lammers recalled that it was the first time that Hitler discussed the euthanasia question in his presence, but this does not rule out the possibility that it had been discussed previously with Conti. Hitler told them that he thought that it was right to eliminate certain mentally ill patients by means of 'euthanasia' in order to deliver them from suffering. Using the example of patients so handicapped that they constantly soiled themselves and 'put their own excrement in their mouth as if it were food', Hitler proposed that the life of such creatures should be ended. To bolster his rather feeble example, probably the only one he knew, and give these officials some justification for his policy decision, he added that the killing of adult patients would also have the 'practical effects that buildings, doctors, and nursing personnel could be made available for other purposes'.[46] Hitler then instructed Conti to look into the actual implementation of the problem, and consult Lammers regarding all judicial questions which might arise. Conti seems to have voiced only his general consent.

Lammers, however, was made of different metal. His reaction to such an outrageous and criminal order has been recorded. His response is typical of what Hitler could expect from a member of the conservative elite working at the top of the state bureaucracy. Although totally unprepared, he realized that Hitler's plan created an enormous number of problems. Given the legal, domestic and foreign policy problems involved, Lammers stressed that the matter was extraordinarily sensitive. He also took church-political factors into consideration and drew attention to the religious and ethical dimensions of such an unprecedented programme. Lammers emphasized not only that the whole question required a comprehensive investigation, but that it was unsuitable to be tackled during the war (which is another indication that the war had already begun at the time of the talks). He felt that he had to advise Hitler to postpone the matter until after the war. Hitler obviously did not like what he heard. Lammer's assessment of the matter was diametrically opposed to his own racial ideology, which required that the death of 'valuable' soldiers needed to be compensated for by the elimination of 'worthless' elements in the body politic. Although Hitler was extremely flexible in his political and strategic decisions, and could rapidly adjust to unforeseen developments, he showed an extraordinary degree of rigidity when matters touched on fundamental elements of his racial ideology. The 'euthanasia' question was one of these elements. Realizing that Hitler would not consider waiting until after the war, Lammers suggested that, at the least, a relevant Reich law should be published to give the programme the necessary legality. Hitler did not respond to Lammers' proposal, but instead insisted that Conti should carry out his instructions. Both were then asked to take their leave.[47]

While they were leaving the conference, Lammers told Conti that he would consider the legal aspects and contact him. He drafted a law which included some legal protection in case the programme could not be postponed. Lammers' protections included, for example, the requirement that the law would only be applicable to the most severe cases of the mentally ill, only to those of German nationality, and only after a period of thorough observation. Lammers also wanted to ensure that proper legal procedures would be followed and that doctors and judges would decide each case on an individual basis. Lammers felt that it was important to protect the interests of those affected and their relatives. He hoped that Hitler would shelve such a programme, because it created too many bureaucratic problems, or that he would dismiss Conti and him from dealing with the issue. Lammers never got around to discussing his proposal. A couple of weeks later, Conti phoned Lammers and told him that Hitler had released him (Conti) from handling the matter. 'I thought the matter was closed,' Lammers later conveniently stated.[48] But the matter was far from closed. The murder of tens of thousands of handicapped adults was just about to begin.

Word of the meeting between Hitler, Conti, Lammers and Bormann triggered a power struggle over who would eventually be responsible for this unprecedented full-scale killing programme. Wagner's former press officer, Hellmuth Unger, seems to have passed the information to Hefelmann, knowing full well that this would prompt an immediate reaction by the KdF to secure its place in the programme. Unger had good reasons for doing this. His disloyalty resulted from his close relationship with his former chief, Wagner, whom Conti had once tried to bring down. Hefelmann immediately told Brack, who raced hotfoot to Brandt and Bouhler. In the subsequent intrigue, Brandt and Bouhler allied themselves with Göring, Himmler and Frick to outmanoeuvre the group around Conti and Bormann. There was a truly odd mixture of people in this power struggle. Brandt and Bouhler probably feared that Conti's assignment would in the long run ensure that Bormann would be in control of the 'euthanasia' operation, something even Göring and other high-ranking Nazi leaders wanted to avoid at all costs. While Bouhler and Bormann had jointly organized a film screening in July 1939 to draw Hitler's attention to the 'euthanasia' issue, Bouhler must have seen the possibility that Bormann could outmanoeuvre him and the KdF if Conti and the official state bureaucracy were to be put in charge of the 'euthanasia' programme. According to Brandt, both were also concerned that Conti would be unable to ensure centralized control over the operation. Bouhler, in particular, was concerned that the *Gauleiter* would implement the 'euthanasia' programme independently and at random, without any centralized administrative machinery supervising and monitoring their actions.[49] Bouhler then drafted a report for Hitler, which probably not only outlined the KdF's ability to organize such an operation, but also, to start with, gave details about the experience which had been gathered in the killing of handicapped children. Seeing that Conti and Lammers produced nothing but problems, Hitler decided to regard the euthanasia question as his 'personal' matter, which he would implement through his 'personal' staff. Now it was time for Brandt to move centre stage.

In retrospect, Brandt attempted to distance himself and Bouhler from any suggestion that they had actively sought the assignment to implement the 'euthanasia' programme. In 1946, he recalled in his Nuremberg notebook – which largely outlined his defence in the matter of the euthanasia charge – that the assumption that Bouhler wanted to establish a 'special' area of responsibility for himself was absurd. Brandt conceded, however, that Bouhler wanted to prevent others, especially Bormann, from taking a lead role in the programme. Bouhler, Brandt noted, expected Bormann's motives 'in carrying out such thoughts [the "euthanasia" programme] to be anything other than humane. This he feared and wanted to stop.'[50] For Brandt, the main reason why Bouhler got involved in the discussions on euthanasia was that he felt that he and his department were uniquely positioned as a 'link between the population and AH [Adolf Hitler]'.[51] Bouhler's motives for taking an active role in the programme were governed by 'absolute human feelings and a sense of pity and empathy', Brandt noted.[52] He painted Bouhler, like himself, as a calm, outwardly pleasing personality whose moral integrity was beyond question, and whose primary aim in the 'euthanasia' operation was to help those unfortunate 'creatures' to end their suffering. 'He could also be described as an idealist,' Brandt remarked.[53] Brandt, in short, attempted to create an image of himself and Bouhler as two selfless and idealistic individuals who had supported the 'euthanasia' programme for purely humanitarian reasons. The historical reality, however, looked somewhat different.

On 27 September 1939, Warsaw capitulated. On 6 October the last Polish troops surrendered near Kock. Shortly afterwards, Brandt was summoned to see Hitler at the Obersalzberg where, according to Brandt, the following conversation took place:

> I was called to him for some reason which I can no longer remember, and he told me that because of a document which he had received from *Reichsleiter* Bouhler, he wanted to bring about a definite solution in the euthanasia question. He gave me general directives on *how he imagined it* [emphasis added], and the fundamental instruction was that any insane persons who were in such a condition that they could no longer take any conscious part in life were to be given relief through death. General instructions followed about petitions which he himself had received, and he told me to contact Bouhler himself about the matter.[54]

In his personal notes about the conversation, made at Nuremberg, Brandt recalled that Hitler wanted to put the KdF in charge of implementing the 'euthanasia' programme but that he, Brandt, would also have to become involved in order to keep Hitler briefed on the progress of the operation:

> I would also have to get involved, because he wanted to be directly informed etc. The central issue was to grant these poor creatures peace and quiet once and for all ... Then

AH [Adolf Hitler] gave me a description of eu[thanasia] which I cannot repeat in detail today. The fact is, however, that [the description] was based on the idea of a *good* death, and anything else that may have been said was of secondary importance.[55]

It was only during the conversation with Hitler that Brandt realized the enormous scope of the 'euthanasia' programme. 'I first related this question to the work of the *Reichsausschuss*, and only realised the size of the problem during the course of the conversation,' he later noted.[56] According to Brandt, Hitler dictated a draft text. Brandt then discussed this with Bouhler on the phone on the same day, and reported back to Hitler about his conversation with the head of the KdF.[57] According to Brandt, it was only after the conversation with Hitler that he discovered that Bouhler had previously informed Hitler of the fact that certain *Gaue* had apparently carried out 'euthanasia' independently, and without any official government sanction, and that these cases had led him, Bouhler, to ask Hitler to carry out the operation through the KdF. According to Brandt, Bouhler was concerned that the 'euthanasia' programme would otherwise have been arbitrary, and lacking medical expertise and centralized control.[58] Although Brandt's account has to be treated with caution, given that he assigns responsibility to Bouhler for wanting to control the programme, it is quite possible that Bouhler had brought individual petitions to Hitler's attention, as in the case of Gerhard Kretschmar, and was hoping that Hitler would commission him with the central organization of the operation, and thus expand his responsibility and influence in the regime.

We do not know exactly when the conversation between Brandt and Hitler took place, nor can we say with certainty that it occurred after the meeting with Conti and Lammers. It is highly likely, however, that it did, because Bouhler did not initiate the approach to Hitler until after he had heard about the meeting between Hitler, Conti, Bormann and Lammers. The fact that the first meeting took place at Führer Headquarters, and the second at the Berghof, also suggests that Hitler saw Conti and Lammers probably around the end of September or at the beginning of October 1939 (as Lammers stated in his testimony), and Brandt shortly after 6 October 1939. Brandt later remembered that the conversation had occurred 'after the Polish campaign, around October'.[59]

What we know about Hitler and his personalized rule – his informal decision-making, his reluctance to commit himself on paper, his preference to provide his loyal servants with the 'general gist' of his 'wishes' which would give them an idea of *how he imagined* certain policy measures – all this makes Brandt's statement plausible and credible.[60] In dealing with Hitler, it was important to know, or at least to sense, what he wanted in any given situation. His orders and instructions were often ambiguous and extremely vague. He communicated his orders as 'opinions', as general views on how he 'wished' to have things done, but he expected to have them carried out as orders with military precision. Most of his advisers initially had great difficulties with such an informal approach to government.[61]

Members of the court would recall after the war that Hitler would think aloud (*laut denkend*) about individual problems, examining them from all angles, so that those who were not used to this would find it hard to know what he wanted. He strayed from the subject matter, focused on minute and often irrelevant details, and confused those who tried to follow his argument. To work out the important points, the 'weights' (*Gewichte*), as one of his adjutants called them, was left to the listeners, who were expected to know what was relevant and what was not.[62] As Ian Kershaw has pointed out in his biography of Hitler, one of the key driving forces in Nazi Germany was that the people were, as he calls it, 'working toward the Führer', in other words, they tried to carry out those ideas which they imagined to be in the interest of their Führer.[63] Brandt and Bouhler had clearly sensed the 'wishes' of their leader. For Brandt a 'wish' of the Führer was synonymous with an order.[64] And Hitler's order had to be carried out, whatever the cost.

Brandt may have anticipated that Hitler would talk to him about the 'euthanasia' issue, or ask for his advice. Further evidence seems to suggest that Brandt was trying to assess the popularity of the regime at the beginning of October, and may well have wanted to gauge the religious and moral objections to euthanasia among Germany's leading clerics. On 4 October 1939, Gerhard Engel, Hitler's army adjutant, noted that Brandt had visited Bishop Galen in Münster and that they had discussed religious and other problems. It is quite possible that they also discussed the issue of euthanasia. It is not clear, however, why Brandt met Galen and whether he also consulted other church leaders at around the same time. Galen was outspoken in telling Brandt about the general mood among the population and how the German people felt about the war; he also criticized the regime for its anti-Semitic policies and for its treatment of prisoners. Galen must have left a deep and lasting impression on Brandt. According to Engel, Brandt appeared to be somewhat withdrawn after the meeting with the bishop. When asked by Engel whether he would report Galen's views to Hitler, Brandt replied: 'If I tell the Führer everything that Count von Galen has said to me, he will imprison both the Bishop and myself.'[65] The conversation, if it took place, shows not only that Brandt was aware of Hitler's ruthless nature and his inability to accept criticism but, perhaps more importantly, that he established a confidential channel of communication to one of Germany's most important religious figures who was vehemently opposed to the killing of handicapped and mentally ill patients. Although Brandt knew that Hitler was unwilling to engage with Galen and other critics of the regime, which is why he may have feared certain repercussions from his conversation with the bishop, he agreed nonetheless to meet Galen again. However, it is probable that no other meeting between the two men ever took place. When opposition to the 'euthanasia' programme increased in 1940 and 1941, Brandt asked Hitler several times whether he could contact Galen as the representative of the Catholic resistance against the 'euthanasia' programme. Each time, Hitler turned down Brandt's request.[66]

Brandt established his contact with Galen at a time when the planning for the 'euthanasia' programme had entered its final phase. Key personalities at the centre of Hitler's regime were waiting for the Führer to give the final go-ahead. Brandt, it seems, wanted to have the best possible intelligence at his disposal in case he became involved in implementing the programme. It is unlikely that he expected, or knew, that he would be put in charge of the programme, together with Bouhler, but he also does not seem to have been as 'unprepared' as he later wanted the world to believe.[67] He must surely have been aware of the potential consequences of introducing a state-sanctioned programme for the killing of tens of thousands of handicapped patients.

Probably in the late autumn or winter of 1939, Hitler signed the only surviving document which clearly links him to the killing operation. The euphoria of military victory may have pushed Hitler's belief in his own infallibility over the line of caution, so that he felt he could press ahead with such a programme. For a brief moment he acted rashly. It was one of the few instances, in fact, where Hitler committed himself on paper with regard to one of the regime's major crimes. The document is more an authorization than a formal government order, written on Hitler's personal stationery, an indication that he saw this programme as part of his 'personal' affairs. The text was dictated by Hitler, and further amended by the KdF staff, Brandt and Bouhler having first discussed the wording with Conti in the RMdI.[68] Conti's collaboration in the programme was still vital for Brandt and Bouhler because they needed to secure access to Linden's authority over state asylums, and Linden was directly subordinate to Conti. Without Conti's collaboration, Brandt and Bouhler would not have had a government machinery to implement the programme, a fact which will not have escaped Conti. During a meeting in October, the three men must have agreed the text.[69] Brandt wanted to stress that there was no absolute certainty in determining who was incurably ill and who was not, and he suggested including a sentence such as 'probability that borders on certainty' (*Mit an Sicherheit grenzender Wahrscheinlichkeit*). Unaccustomed to such medico-legal terminology, Hitler also included, on Brandt's suggestion, the caveat that patients should only be killed 'after the most careful assessment of their condition'.[70] The authorization reads as follows:

> Berlin, 1 Sept. 1939. Reich Leader Bouhler and Dr. Med Brandt are charged with the responsibility of enlarging the powers of specific physicians, designated by name, so that patients who, on the basis of human judgement, are considered incurable, can be granted mercy death after the most careful assessment of their condition. (signed) A. Hitler.[71]

According to Brandt, the wording that both were 'charged with the responsibility' had a double meaning. Brandt and Bouhler were not only responsible for seeing that the programme was actually implemented, but also responsible for how the programme was carried out. The wording 'after the most careful assessment', which Brandt had proposed, was apparently meant to function as a kind of 'textual safety precaution' [*textlich festgelegte Bremse*] for the doctor who was charged with carrying out Nazi 'euthanasia'.[72] In view of what was to follow, the wording of the authorization appears to have been extraordinarily cynical. The original was given to Bouhler, who put it in his safe at the KdF. Copies were shown to those doctors collaborating in the programme, or given to those who questioned Bouhler's authority – among others, to the Reich Minister of Justice, Franz Gürtner, in August 1940. His copy is the only one which has survived.

In order to emphasize the fact that the 'euthanasia' programme was closely intertwined with the outbreak of war, and to suggest that Hitler, the national redeemer 'following providence like a sleep-walker', who thought of nothing but the good of his country, had mapped everything out for the German people, Hitler backdated the document to 1 September 1939, the outbreak of the Second World War. This was meant to ensure maximum propaganda effect after the war. Hitler would seem to be a genius, one who had led the German nation onto the path to racial purity, living space and power. The authorization was never published in the official legal gazette and there is debate about whether or not it had the force of law. For Brandt, it certainly had. 'For us, who were involved, there was no doubt that [the authorization] had the force of law, and there was therefore no question that our responsible actions were also formally legitimate,' he recalled in 1946.[73] He also stressed that in an authoritarian state it was part of natural law (*Gewohnheitsrecht*) that the head of state should sign such a decree himself and thus take full responsibility: 'For those who were involved in euthanasia there was no doubt ... that their action was morally and ethically legitimate and legally secure. Without this assurance and the conviction of this fact, none of the doctors would have acted in the way they did'.[74] For Brandt, it was crucially important after the war that his conscience was clear and that his actions and those of his fellow doctors had been legal. Irrespective of whether or not the authorization had the force of law from a legal perspective, what is important here is to note that Brandt and many others, including state, medical and legal officials, *perceived* any oral or written expression of Hitler's will, or any utterance of his wishes, as having the force of law in Nazi Germany. In Hitler's Germany, especially during the war, the authorization served to sanction the 'euthanasia' programme, and dispel the remaining doubts of those who questioned its legality.

Engel, Hitler's army adjutant, also recalls that Hitler was contemplating tackling the 'Jewish problem' in a more systematic and radical fashion at around the time that he commissioned Brandt and Bouhler with the responsibility for the 'euthanasia' programme. On 8 October 1939, Hitler discussed the 'Jewish problem' and the creation of large ghettos in Lublin and Lodz among a small circle of press and party officials.[75] His visits to Poland had convinced Hitler that the 'Jewish problem' was not a religious but a racial problem, which needed to be resolved in the German-occupied territories. Hitler questioned why he had been so 'humane' and 'generous' in the introduction of the Nuremberg Race Laws at the time. The identification of Jews was insufficient, Hitler told the gathering. Germany had missed an opportunity to solve the 'Jewish problem' in the Reich territory by not concentrating them in ghettos with their own administration, police and workforce. Engel then recorded a statement by Hitler which, if he did make it, gives an indication of the cumulative radicalization process which led the regime to oppress ever more target groups and deport large numbers of Jews to the occupied territories, where they were crammed into ghettos before being sent to one of the concentration or extermination camps: 'He [Hitler] would consider with Himmler and Heydrich how one could, in this way, after one had the Polish territory, deport the majority of the Jewish population to this place or to the protectorate.[76] These fragments about Hitler's policy intentions are important in a number of respects. Hitler's decision-making process with regard to Germany's anti-Semitic and racial policies seems to have been influenced by imminent foreign policy or military successes (or indeed foreign policy failures), which emboldened the dictator to 'solve' some of the outstanding problems in a more radical and uncompromising fashion.[77] The euphoria of military victory gave Hitler the opportunity to press for the implementation of more radical measures, and he wasted no time in informing some of his closest advisers that the war had changed the regime's policy towards Jews as well as towards handicapped and mentally ill patients.

III. THE START OF THE 'EUTHANASIA' PROGRAMME

Brandt and Bouhler never established for themselves a clear division or demarcation of individual areas of responsibility in the 'euthanasia' programme.[78] Their work and role in the programme evolved haphazardly and arbitrarily, without any guidance from state, legal or supervisory bodies. It would seem that they made the programme up as they went along. Brandt later recalled that individual areas of responsibility resulted from the expertise each of them possessed and the degree to which they had access to Hitler's ear. 'I had to inform AH [Adolf Hitler] about medical matters which arose, or advise him [on medical matters] if these remained unclear to him', is how Brandt described his role after the war.[79] Brandt also recalled that it was important to Hitler to have a doctor involved in the programme.[80] Brandt's role was also to provide Bouhler, whose primary role was the management and organization of the operation, with direct access to Hitler. Before making representations to Hitler about matters which concerned the 'euthanasia' programme and gaining his authorization, Brandt and Bouhler generally attempted to find a compromise or come to a mutual agreement.

Delegation was of key importance. Brandt and Bouhler first charged the head of Central Office II in the KdF, Viktor Brack (a bicycle enthusiast with no medical expertise whatsoever), with setting up and running the organization of the adult 'euthanasia' programme. It was a much larger operation than the killing of infants, requiring additional and trained personnel, logistical facilities and a sophisticated bureaucratic machinery. Although the murder of adults was directed from the KdF, the size of the organization exceeded its available space and facilities. Brack, therefore, moved the office to Columbus House on Potsdamer Platz, but soon realized that the estimated murder of 70,000 people required even more office space. The staff running the 'euthanasia' operation moved into the previously confiscated villa of the German expressionist painter, Max Beckmann, at 4 Tiergartenstraße. It was because of this address that the secret operation became known as 'Aktion T-4,' or simply 'T-4'.

Brandt was not concerned with the day-to-day running of the adult 'euthanasia' programme, especially after Bouhler gradually took over almost the entire administrative side of the operation. Bouhler was the man implementing and overseeing the programme, but even he delegated most of the work to Brack, who in turn delegated it to his deputy, Blankenburg, who passed directives on to Hefelmann, who delegated them to von Hegener. Others included Brack's cousin Reinhold Vorberg, Gerhard Bohne and Dietrich Allers, to name but a few members of staff.[81] Although Hefelmann and von Hegener were directing only the children's 'euthanasia' programme, they also participated in meetings and decision-making in Aktion T-4. At the beginning, Brandt and Bouhler often discussed specific guidelines at weekly meetings, and problems which had occurred. They would appoint new medical collaborators, or talk about the most effective and inconspicuous way to kill the patients. At the KdF, Bouhler would also introduce and sign up new doctors, who would carry out the actual killing of patients after Brandt had agreed to their assignment on the basis of information he had received from the RMdI. According to Brandt, the doctors were given a certificate which was signed by both Brandt and Bouhler.[82] What exactly these certificates said is not known. Not one has ever been found. Brandt also needed to liaise with Bouhler on a regular basis to keep Hitler briefed on the progress of the operation. Brack later recalled: 'It is true that after such meetings between Brandt and Bouhler I received a number of orders, more often from Bouhler than from Brandt directly.'[83]

Brack and Blankenburg were the men ultimately running the killing operation. They recruited ever more staff through personal connections and Nazi Party contacts. None of those involved in the killing programme was forced, or joined the programme under duress; they all participated voluntarily, apparently believing in the humane nature of such policy measures: 'We welcomed it,' Brack said, 'because it was based on the ethical principle of sympathy and had humane considerations in its favour.'[84] Brack admitted that there were some minor 'imperfections' in the actual execution of the programme, 'but that does not change the decency of the original idea, as Bouhler and Brandt and I myself understood it'.[85] The statement reveals elements of the underlying rationale of those directly connected with the organization of the killing operation. Brack, Bouhler and Brandt seem to have been under the impression that as long as the original idea was 'decent', it did not really matter too much *how* the programme was implemented in practice, and whether thousands of vulnerable individuals died. As long as these persons died for the 'idea' of improving the race, these men believed that any form of negligence or 'imperfections' on their part could apparently be tolerated. What seems to have mattered was the grand vision, not the individual patients in state asylums, whom they never saw face to face.

While Bouhler was responsible for the administrative side, Brandt was in charge of all the medical aspects of the programme. This included the selection and appointment of medical expert referees, and the decision about the actual killing method. He appointed the psychiatrist Werner Heyde from Würzburg as his deputy for medical matters and put him in charge of T-4's medical office (*Medizinische Abteilung*), which evaluated the condition of the patients and selected them for the 'euthanasia' programme.[86] Born in 1902 in Forst in Lusatia, Heyde had come to the attention of the KdF in the mid-1930s as an expert referee for sterilization cases. He also worked as a referee for the Gestapo and in concentration camps, whose inmates apparently provided him with 'wonderful research material'.[87] Until he was replaced by Paul Nitsche in December 1941, probably because of his homosexuality, Heyde was one of the most enthusiastic advocates of the killing operation.

To ensure that the operation remained secret, the KdF established a number of cover organizations (*Tarnorganisationen*). These fictitious organizations were meant to hide the identities of the various T-4 agencies, especially the KdF, in order to avoid implicating Bouhler and Brandt, and ultimately the Reich Chancellor himself. Four cover organizations were set up to serve this purpose: The Reich Working Committee for Cure and Nursing Homes (*Reichsarbeitsgemeinschaft Heil- und Pflegeanstalten*), known as RAG, liaised with all health offices and government agencies and sometimes with the relatives of patients. The Charitable Foundation for Institutional Care (*Gemeinnützige Stiftung für Anstaltspflege*), known by the staff as *Stiftung*, represented the killing operation in all its official dealings with government and party agencies, including the recruiting, payment and privileges of T-4 killing personnel. The Charitable Foundation for the Transport of Patients, Ltd. (*Gemeinnützige Kranken Transport G.m.b.H.*), known as *Gekrat*, ferried the patients to one of many killing centres. And, finally, there was the Central Accounting Office for State Hospitals and Nursing Homes (*Zentralverrechnungsstelle Heil- und Pflegeanstalten*), which was in charge of financial matters, including correspondence with relatives, who were paying for the patients, sometimes even after they had been killed.[88]

It was a truly conspiratorial set-up. The men and women involved in the operation used fictitious stationery and post-boxes, fake addresses and pseudonyms. Brack, for example, called himself 'Jennerwein' (referring to a famous eighteenth-century poacher), his deputy Blankenburg found the name 'Brenner' (meaning stoker) attractive, and Vorberg, head of the *Gekrat*, included a little joke in his pseudonym, calling himself 'Hinterthal', which means 'behind the valley' – the opposite of his name 'Vorberg', which means 'in front of the mountain'. It all sounds like an Al Capone movie, and to some extent the comparison warrants consideration. The group organizing and implementing the adult 'euthanasia' programme could after all be described as professional dropouts and second-rate criminals.

Asylum directors, physicians and nurses participating in the programme needed to be instructed on how to perform their job. Such a large operation also needed sophisticated statistics on the number of patients in individual state institutions and killing centres, and on those patients who had already been evaluated by one or more of the expert referees. All this was done primarily at the RAG, which served as another cover for the T-4 medical office. This was meant to ensure that Brandt would not in any way be implicated in the programme, because his name stood in direct contact with Hitler. At first run by the business manager Gerhard Bohne, the organization was taken over by Heyde once Brandt had appointed him chief physician at T-4. Any problems arising were discussed with Brandt on an informal but regular basis, generally at lunch time. In 1941, Heyde was succeeded by the psychiatrist Nitsche, the director of the state asylum Sonnenstein near Pirna in

Saxony, who since 1920 had supported occupational therapies and active treatment for the mentally ill. Like Heyde, Nitsche was a stern advocate of racial hygiene and euthanasia. He also participated in some of the early experiments at the beginning of 1940 to establish the most effective methods of killing the patients.[89] He later told the German courts that he regarded his participation in the 'euthanasia' programme as a 'service to humanity' (*Dienst an der Menschheit*).[90]

Following Hitler's authorization, Brandt and Bouhler and all the other members of the programme had to decide on the method by which the patients were to be killed.[91] Brandt later claimed 'credit' for having influenced the decision about the killing method. Since leading T-4 officials anticipated that they would have to deal with thousands, if not tens of thousands, of people, the method had to be inconspicuous, fast, easy to handle and not too expensive. Ideas of train accidents and other fantasies were quickly abandoned. Some doctors suggested the use of narcotics in connection with barbiturate acid, but this was soon dropped, because it would have taken too long for the patients to die. Tests had shown that although the person quickly lost consciousness, death only occurred a few hours later. Such a method was considered not to be 'humane'.

Some psychiatrists proposed the use of carbon monoxide gas 'as a different kind of medicament'. Brandt at first seems to have opposed such a technique because for him the 'euthanasia' operation was a 'medical programme', and killing people by means of gas was not, in his 'medical understanding', a proper procedure.[92] He eventually changed his mind after he had remembered that he had once become unconscious without any pain, after inhaling fumes from a stove:

> In this connection it was suggested that we use coal oxide [carbon monoxide]. I did not like the idea, because I said to myself that this whole question can only be looked at from a medical point of view. In my mind coal oxide had never been an instrument of medicine. I myself had learned about it a few years ago and had experienced a little coal oxide poisoning when I was in a room where there was something wrong with the stove. Then I remembered that at that time when I went to the door, I had fallen out of the room without feeling anything and had simply passed out. So on reflection I thought that coal oxide death might be the most humane form of death. I did not come to this conclusion quickly, because it was clear to me that the moment I accepted this idea I would be bringing into being a wholly new medical concept. I thought very hard and earnestly about all this, in order to put my own conscience at rest.[93]

For Brandt the essential question was not whether the programme was legitimate, morally and ethically justifiable, or in itself humane, but whether the method of killing was humane. But he realized, at the same time, that he was on uncharted territory and outside generally accepted medical morality. Why would he have struggled with the issue of euthanasia in the way he did, if he had felt that the programme was beyond reproach and accepted by the laws of medical ethics and human decency? There would have been no need to put his own conscience at rest. But as things stood, medical doctors were about to begin a programme of medical murder of unprecedented proportions, one that had never before been put into practice in a civilized society. Brandt knew that there was no precedent for this project. This explains why he wanted to have a clear conscience, and why he wanted to make sure that the head of state would take full responsibility for the programme.

When Brandt phoned Hitler to discuss the matter, he not only wanted to find out what the best killing method or Hitler's preferred choice would be, but to place the moral and legal responsibility on his shoulders as head of state. Hitler apparently was not interested in any medical details, and just wanted to know 'which is the more humane way', whereupon Brandt suggested the use of gas. In his personal notebook from 1946, Brandt recalled:

> AH asked me which method, based on current considerations and experiences, was the mildest, that is to say the safest, quickest and the most effective and painless one. I had to concede that this was death through the inhalation of carbon monoxide gas. He then said that this was also the most humane. I myself then took on board this position and put to one side my medical concerns for external reasons ... I am convinced that the procedure with carbon monoxide was right.[94]

While physicians were using an overdose of a common drug to kill handicapped infants, the use of carbon monoxide gas became the standard technique in the adult 'euthanasia' programme. After Brandt had given his account to US investigators in October 1945, he prided himself on finding such an effective method of killing: 'This is just one case of a major leap being made in medical history.'[95] Whether this off-hand remark betrayed his real understanding of progress is hard to tell.[96]

Others involved in finding the best possible killing method told a somewhat different story. The leading chemist at the Technical Institute for the Detection of Crime, Albert Widmann, recalled after the war that it was Conti who had objected to the use of medical injections and had proposed gas. Before any final decision was made, all technical details were discussed between Widmann and Brack, who pondered such questions as whether one should bring the gas to the patients, or the patients to the gas. Although they decided that the latter would be more practicable, they still needed to conduct a series of tests to find out about the overall feasibility of the technique, and 'teach' those physicians participating in the operation how to use a gas valve. A former prison in Brandenburg-Görden was quickly transformed into history's first operational killing centre, with ready help from Himmler's central construction office. The next need was to find some experimental subjects. Where exactly these first patients came from is unknown. They were divided into two groups, one to be killed by injection, the other by gas.

A couple of days before the tests began, Brandt travelled to Brandenburg-Görden and discussed with some of the technicians the advantages and disadvantages of each killing method.[97] It is likely that only after he had been informed by the 'experts' that gas would be more efficient did he brief Hitler, and tell him that this would be the method he would prefer. Such a sequence of events would certainly fit his profile as a medical scientist, and as Hitler's personal doctor. For Brandt it was now clear which of the methods would be used. A comparison between the two killing techniques was meant to serve as final proof. The procedure is that used by experimental scientists conducting serious research in a laboratory, and using control groups to compare findings.

All of those participating in the first killings of patients in the adult 'euthanasia' programme remember that the day was cold and wintry, and that it was either in December 1939 or in January 1940. The latter date seems more likely, if we consider the time needed for the extensive remodelling of the prison building into a killing centre, and to build the team of chemists, of other technicians at the Technical Institute for the Detection of Crime (*Kriminaltechnisches Institut*, KTI), and of doctors and staff participating in the programme. We have a good idea of who was present: Brandt, Bouhler, Conti, Linden and the KdF staff (Brack, Blankenburg, Hefelmann, Vorberg, von Hegener and Bohne) were there. A number of T-4 doctors, such as Heyde, Nitsche, Eberl, Schumann and Baumhard, and the KTI chemists, Widmann and August Becker, were also present. Christian Wirth, a police officer from Stuttgart, had also come along to witness the event. He later played a key role in the killing operations in the East, and became commandant of Belzec concentration camp.

Brandt and Conti began the test by administering deadly injections to the patients in the first group. Like an initiation rite of some unknown tribe, the presentation was meant to show all those present that two of the most senior doctors in Germany were willing to be directly involved in the 'euthanasia' programme. The patients did not die immediately, and in some cases the drugs had little effect. They later had to be gassed too. The gruesome scene reached its climax when a group of eight handicapped men was brought forward to test the effectiveness of gas. When they entered the gas chamber, which had especially been built for the occasion, the chemist Widmann turned the valve, while his colleagues stood to attention to record intensity and duration. Outside, through a peephole, the senior administrators, asylum directors, psychiatrists and others involved were watching the spectacle, genuinely believing that the new age, in which the German race would be purified, had dawned. It is all hard to believe, so few years later.

Von Hegener remembered the sequence of events rather differently. In his narrative there were about thirty patients, who were led into the room to sit on some kind of bench. They were calm and showed no resistance. Once the door was closed, the chemist August Becker turned the valve to let the gas enter the room. After two to three minutes, von Hegener observed that individual patients had lost consciousness. After about five minutes all the patients had fallen into 'a kind of sleep'. Becker, however, was keen on keeping the gas running for another ten minutes to make sure that the patients were dead. Hefelmann even insisted on leaving the gas running for half an hour before a physician, protected by a gas mask, entered the room, examined the bodies and announced that they were all dead.[98]

It was time for speeches. Apparently the occasion seems to have merited it. Brack was first, then came Brandt. Brack told those dignitaries present that he was satisfied with what he had seen, and stressed that the 'euthanasia' operation should be carried out only by doctors, in accordance with the motto 'the syringe belongs in the hand of the doctor'. Then Brandt addressed them, emphasizing once again that only doctors were meant to perform the gassing operation.[99] Brandt and his colleagues viewed the killing of tens of thousands as a 'medical' operation, aimed at balancing the deaths of valuable national comrades in times of war. For a moment in human history, reason had given way to such irrationality. The 'euthanasia' programme had begun.

IV. DETACHED MANAGEMENT OF THE 'EUTHANASIA' PROGRAMME

The bureaucratic machinery, the setting up of killing centres, the recruiting of killing personnel, the remodelling of buildings, the financing and coordinating of the operation, all this was left to others. If he had wanted to, Brandt could have supervised, monitored, checked, investigated or amended the programme. He was certainly entitled to, and had the power to do so. But he felt he had other things to do. He needed to accompany Hitler on his travels and catch up with his surgical work in Berlin. Brandt kept a low profile, informed by Bouhler of how things were going. Detaching himself from the actual operational running left him, of course, exposed to manipulations on the part of Bouhler who, as time progressed, did not tell him of all the extremely dubious projects his men had become involved in, including the setting up and running of concentration camps in the East for the murder of the Jews. Bouhler is ultimately the person who was the most accountable for the 'euthanasia' programme, though nominally Brandt had the same share of responsibility. If nothing else, Brandt was guilty of criminal negligence.

The whole set-up of the operation was so obviously flawed that it is unlikely that Brandt did not know where the programme was heading. He may well have thought it better not to know too much, and not to become involved in every aspect. That way he could always claim that he had not known. Brandt not only wanted to remain detached from the programme, but he *had* to. His name, like the name of the KdF, was directly linked with the Reich Chancellor; any public knowledge that Hitler might have approved such illegal measures was to be avoided at all costs, at least in the initial stages of the programme. Like a mirror image of Hitler, Brandt saw his role as initiating developments, giving the first push, and then leaving things to develop for themselves, intervening only if the situation interfered with key ideological goals, or if it threatened his own power base. For the moment, this was not the case. As Süß had pointed out, Brandt's handling of the 'euthanasia' programme, his detached decision-making and coordination of conflicting interests, as well as his distance from the day-to-day operations, reflected and anticipated in many ways his subsequent work as General Commissioner.[100]

For Hitler, finding a solution to the 'euthanasia' programme which could legally, or semi-legally, be carried out by government agencies was still an issue of concern. He was perfectly aware of the criminal nature of the enterprise for which he had given his written authorization. For most of 1939 and the first half of 1940, however, he did not concern himself with the programme. Sometimes Brandt briefed him on the latest situation, but nothing further seems to have been discussed. Everything seemed to go according to plan. Hitler's attention at the beginning of 1940 was focused almost entirely on his military campaign in the West. By the spring, the German conquest of Europe appeared to be unstoppable. Waging an unprecedented *Blitzkrieg* offensive, Hitler's armies had overrun Denmark, Norway, Luxembourg, Holland and Belgium in less than six weeks. Only after France was signalling defeat at the end of May, and intoxicated by one victory after another on the continent, did Hitler and some of his more ruthless officials feel that the time had come for vital decision-making. For the Führer and his staff, the western campaign was almost over. France would soon capitulate; England was on her knees.

The start of the military offensive against France had been shrouded in complete secrecy. It is almost certain that Brandt had no prior knowledge of the start of the campaign. Not even Hitler's closest advisers and members of his entourage knew that the German armed forces would soon turn westwards. Shortly after midnight, on 10 May, Hitler's special train, coming from Berlin, left its northbound track to travel west. Most of his staff believed that they were travelling to Hamburg or to Denmark or Norway to boost the morale of the troops. The next day they found themselves at Hitler's field headquarters, 'rock eyrie' (*Felsennest*), in the Eifel massif south-west of Bonn. In the midst of the military operation, Brandt had little time to concern himself with other things. Besides, the sleeping quarters, which Brandt had to share with the Chief of the Army's Directional Department, Alfred Jodl, and Hitler's adjutants, were overcrowded and rather spartan.[101] The 'euthanasia' programme was probably not on Brandt's mind when Hitler declared with great drama: 'Gentlemen, the offensive against the Western powers has just started.'[102]

At this time, Hitler's court was in what Speer described as a 'state of rapture', genuinely believing that this man was the 'greatest conqueror of all times'.[103] Brandt was constantly at Hitler's side. It not only allowed him to experience at first hand history in the making, but incidentally made him part of the propaganda image of Hitler's historic mission. On 11 May, Brandt was at the Führer headquarters in the Eifel massif.[104] Two days later, he and Bormann enjoyed some time in the countryside near the headquarters, while numerous Nazi leaders, including Admiral Raeder, the head of the German navy, received medals of honour.[105] Throughout May, Brandt attended the military briefings, which sometimes took place outside in the sun, with Hitler sitting in a deckchair and talking to his military advisers.[106] In general, the atmosphere was jovial and relaxed, at times euphoric. Many of the photographs of Brandt show him smiling.[107] Given Germany's successive victories, Hitler's doctor and those around him were in a good mood.

On 1 June 1940, Hitler decided to inspect the First World War Western Front and visit the places where the Germans had fought, suffered and died. Captured on photographs and film, Brandt was, once again, an integral part of the propaganda image of the Third Reich and its military leadership. Visits to Werwick, Langemarck and Ypres were designed to create the image of a national leader who had returned to the battlefields and places of remembrance of the First World War.[108] In Lille, Hitler set up his Führer headquarters in the castle of Annapes. A photograph taken on 1 or 2 June shows Brandt standing with Hitler, Keitel and others on the steps at the front of the castle.[109] The Nazi leadership was satisfied with itself. The next day, 2 June, Brandt was part of Hitler's entourage visiting the memorial on the Loretto Heights and the command posts on the Vimy Ridge, where German soldiers had fought an embittered battle. For Nazi propagandists, it provided another opportunity to create the image of a charismatic leader who had triumphed over his adversaries.[110] Later, on the evening of 2 June, Brandt, Hoffmann and, probably, Speer celebrated the total evacuation of the encircled British and French troops from Dunkirk with champagne in their room.[111] Throughout these weeks, Brandt made every effort to befriend as many of the leading Nazis as possible, perhaps to establish a network of supporters who might be useful at a later stage in his career. Earlier, Morell had noted: 'Dr. Br[andt] currently keeps the best of friendship with each and every one.'[112]

By June, it became clear that France would soon surrender. On 15 June, twenty-four hours after German troops had entered Paris, Heinrich Hoffmann and members of Hitler's entourage, including Brandt, were instructed to travel to the forest of Compiègne. Brandt and Hoffmann were especially interested in inspecting the train in which the German government had signed the armistice in 1918. Weeks earlier, on 20 May, Hitler had decided to stage the peace negotiations with France in the same place, and to have Marshal Foch's railway carriage brought back from a museum. For Hitler, it was a fitting place to humiliate the French.[113] Brandt and Hoffmann continued their sightseeing tour by visiting the Palace of Versailles and the Opéra.[114] The next day, 16 June, Brandt was back at the *Wolfsschlucht*, Hitler's field headquarters in Bruly-de-Pêche, near Brussels. Hitler was in an exuberant mood, slapping his thigh in an expression of joy after hearing the news that the French government was suing for peace on 17 June 1940.[115] Total victory over Europe was now within Hitler's grasp. Only Britain needed to surrender. Brandt was also present when Himmler visited the Führer headquarters on 20 June.[116] The next day, he accompanied Hitler and the Nazi leadership, including Göring, Raeder, Brauchitsch, Keitel, Ribbentrop and Heß, to Compiègne to witness Pétain's government sign the armistice with Germany.[117] Brandt returned with Hitler to Bruly-de-Pêche the same day to greet the arrival of Hitler's architects and artists, Speer, Giesler and Breker, in particular.[118]

Breker later recalled that he had been woken up on 22 June at 6 a.m. by the Gestapo in his house in Berlin, telling him to get ready for a short trip. No further information was given. An hour later, two SS men drove him to Staaken airport, on the outskirts of Berlin, where he boarded a JU-52 transport plane. Not knowing the destination of his journey, Breker was more than surprised when he landed three hours later on French soil, six kilometres from Bruly. 'You were scared, were you?' Speer asked, as he greeted him at the entrance to Hitler's Führer headquarters. Shortly afterwards he was welcomed by Hitler, who, in the presence of Brandt, Jodl and Engel, told him that he wanted to travel to Paris with Speer, Giesler and himself to assess the urban architecture of the capital, but that it had not been possible to give him advance notice.[119] After having accomplished a complete military victory, Hitler wanted to visit the French capital with members of his inner circle. Tight security around Hitler's headquarters and his whereabouts meant that, for those who were brought in from the outside and had no permanent place on the inside, such as Brandt and Speer, a mystical air was often attached to what would otherwise have been a blunt invitation to see the head of state.

On the morning of 23 June 1940, at 5.30 a.m., Hitler, dressed in a white trench coat, landed at the Le Bouget airport with his entourage, Brandt included.[120] Hitler's three-hour sightseeing tour started off with a visit to the Opéra. The group then drove along the Boulevard de La Madeleine, along the Champs Elysées, looked at the Tomb of the Unknown Soldier below the Arc de Triomphe, visited the Eiffel Tower and the Panthéon, and stopped at Les Invalides to see the tomb of Napoleon.[121] Hitler must have felt elated, and compared himself to Napoleon. After concluding his whistle-stop tour with a visit to the Church of Sacré-Coeur in Montmartre, Hitler immediately left the French capital, and never returned. He had found a lot of the architecture 'disappointing', and told Speer that Paris would 'only be a shadow' once his plans had been put into reality in Berlin. When the armistice was officially announced on 25 June, Hitler was back at the *Wolfschlucht*, carefully stage-managing the way in which the historic moment would be captured for posterity.[122]

Brandt spent the end of June travelling with Hitler, Max Amman and Ernst Schmidt – two of Hitler's comrades from the First World War – to the battlefields of Flanders where they had once been stationed.[123] A couple of Hoffmann's photographs show Brandt sitting in the back of one of the accompanying cars.[124] On 28 June, Hitler's entourage visited the cathedral in Strasbourg.[125] Two days later, Hitler returned to his Führer headquarters *Tannenberg*, near Freudenstadt, where he and a small group of confidants, including Brandt and Morell, went for a long walk through the woods.[126] On 1 July, Brandt used the opportunity to chat to some girl labourers (*Arbeitsmaiden*).[127] To the outside world, it looked as if the dictator was taking a break after having successfully conquered almost the whole of Western Europe, but for weeks his mind had concentrated on matters which would reshape the map of the European continent, and the composition of its inhabitants, for a long time to come. Another issue which needed resolving was the fact that the 'euthanasia' programme lacked official legitimacy.

In the spring and summer of 1940, the time had come for Hitler and his closest advisers to plan for the future, and implement some of their other far-reaching ideas. Hitler himself felt confident enough to provide the 'euthanasia' programme with a certain legitimacy, but he held back from a fully fledged law. He instructed Bouhler to get in touch with Lammers and liaise with the relevant government agencies. Whether Brandt was involved in these talks is not known, but not impossible, given that he saw Hitler almost on a daily basis during these weeks of frenzied activity. In the late spring of 1940, probably at the end of May, Bouhler contacted Lammers. The meeting took place in Lammers' special train in Belgium, where he was preparing all the necessary details for the Belgian capitulation, which was signed on 28 May 1940. Bouhler must have been in a hurry. Having just come from Hitler's headquarters, *Felsennest*, where Hitler stayed from 10 May to 5 June 1940, Bouhler told Lammers that Hitler now wanted to give him (Bouhler) an order (*einen Auftrag*) for the 'solution of the euthanasia problem'.[128] Realizing that this might put him in overall charge of the programme, Bouhler was impatient to move on. Lammers, however, once again stonewalled and told Bouhler that euthanasia could not be carried out unless there was a law: 'In discussing this problem I drew Bouhler's attention to the serious concerns which I had and said that the matter could only be carried out on the basis of a published law'.[129] Lammers then showed Bouhler his draft proposal for a law on euthanasia. Bouhler was not impressed, realizing that a law would take too much time to be introduced, and might cause significant political tensions, especially at a time when the actual killing of patients had already started. Lammers also got the impression that Bouhler wanted to rush things to ensure that he would be given the Führer order (*Führerauftrag*), and then implement it. Although Lammers was supportive of the overall government policy, Bouhler knew that he would not agree to the wholesale killing of patients – unless there was a law which permitted the state to do so. The meeting was adjourned. Before Bouhler headed off, Lammers told him that he needed to report the matter back to Hitler.

We know the approximate timing of the meeting between Bouhler and Lammers, because Lammers remembered that it occurred in the 'late spring of 1940' in his 'special train in Belgium'.[130] This places their conversation in the period between the end of May and probably not later than 14 June, when German troops occupied Paris and when Lammers left Belgium. This assumption is supported by the personal correspondence of Morell, who on 28 May wrote to his wife, Hanni, that Bouhler had survived a plane crash: 'The adjut[ant] Bouhler really got away with his life despite the burning plane crash. He is in the military hospital in Maastricht,[131] where the son of Werlin (left arm amputated) also is. Dr. Br.[andt] has visited both of them (without my knowledge)'.[132] We can safely assume that Bouhler's plane probably crashed *shortly after* the meeting with Lammers, probably on the way back from Brussels to Hitler's headquarters near Bonn; it is thus likely that their conversation took place on or around 28 May 1940.

Why is the chronology of the various decision-making meetings between Hitler, the two plenipotentiaries for the 'euthanasia' programme and other government officials of significance? The meetings tie Hitler's plan to kill the mentally ill much closer to his overall foreign and genocidal policy, especially to major turning points during his military campaigns. A pattern seems to emerge from what we have seen. Whenever Hitler had gained a major foreign policy success (or later suffered a major foreign policy setback) in his military campaigns, he was emboldened to push for his other longer-term ideological goals, especially with regard to his racial aims. Key decisions or attempts to implement certain policies seem to have been made at exactly such focal points. Hitler's first 'push', as it could be termed, to implement the 'euthanasia' programme came *after* it had become clear that Poland would capitulate. His second major push seems to have occurred in the period *after* it was clear that France would soon capitulate, and that the western campaign had been a stunning success. What is more, the various meetings at the end of May 1940 in Hitler's headquarters are also linked with decisions of even greater importance: the future enslavement and expulsion of large populations in the East, especially of the Jews.

By the end of May, Himmler had drafted a secret memorandum which specified that the former Polish state and its individual nationalities – Poles, Jews, Ukrainians, White Russians and others – should be broken up into 'innumerable small parts and particles' so that they could build up no national consciousness and culture. The racially valuable elements should be fished out from the 'hodgepodge' and brought to Germany for assimilation.[133] In ten years, Himmler suggested, the people of the Generalgouvernement would be reduced to a remnant of an 'inferior population … a leaderless labour force at our disposal which will provide Germany annually with casual labourers and workmen for special projects (streets, quarries, buildings)'. Eventually 'the concept "Jews" will be completely eliminated, I hope, by a major emigration of all Jews to Africa or otherwise into a colony'.[134] On 25 May 1940, only days before the 'euthanasia' programme was discussed, first between Hitler and Bouhler, and later between Bouhler and Lammers, Hitler received Himmler at his headquarters. The pedantic Reichsführer-SS later recorded the conversation in one of his pencilled office notes:

> I handed the Führer my report on the treatment of people of alien races in the East. The Führer read the six pages and considered them very good and correct. He directed, however, that only very few hard copies should exist, that it should not be copied and that the report is to be treated with utmost secrecy. Minister Lammers was present as well.[135]

After listing the officials who were to be informed, Himmler adds: 'Everyone has to confirm that he has been informed that this is to be considered as a directive, but that it shall never be laid down in an order of one of the Main Offices, neither in the form of a mere excerpt nor from memory.'[136] The evidence suggests that by the end of May 1940 Hitler had pushed for the introduction of his racial and anti-Semitic policies, although neither he himself nor any of his key officials were supposed to commit themselves, ever, on paper. For Hitler the 'euthanasia' programme was an integral part of his policy of racial cleansing, and it is therefore only logical to deduce that the discussions about implementing such a policy in the Reich and in the occupied eastern territories were conducted at or around the same time.

Lammers did, in fact, report back to Hitler about the conversation he had had with Bouhler about the 'euthanasia' programme. Hitler did not *expressis verbis* reject the proposal, which would have had to be presented to all Reich ministries, but he did not agree with it either. Hitler told Lammers that he did not want a law for 'political reasons'.[137] Lammers recalled that he did not hear about the matter for a long time, believing that Hitler had finally dropped it. The next time he apparently had to deal with it was at the end of 1940 or at the beginning of 1941, after the

Reich Chancellery had received several complaints about the murder of patients from concerned citizens and members of the Church. It was only then, Lammers told the Nuremberg court, that he discovered that Hitler had authorized Brandt and Bouhler to pursue the covert killing operation, and that the 'euthanasia' programme was being carried out. Although Lammers is generally a fairly reliable witness, he conveniently forgot to mention a number of documented conversations about the 'euthanasia' programme and its criminal nature.

By the early summer of 1940, Lammers definitely knew that crimes were being committed, and that an increasing number of protests had reached the government, but he tried to blame other agencies, for example the Reich Ministry of Justice (*Reichsjustizministerium*, RJM). On 23 July, he met Franz Gürtner, the Reich Minister of Justice, and informed him that the Führer had prohibited issuing a law, whereupon Gürtner wrote back the next day, telling Lammers that the killings had to be stopped. As an appendix, Gürtner attached copies of the reports which had reached the RJM from concerned justices and the public.[138] On 27 July, Lammers referred Gürtner's letter and the attached reports to Bouhler, who at this point was de facto in charge of administering the killing operation. Frenzied exchanges of letters between the KdF, the Reich Chancellery, the RMdI, and the RJM followed, the result of which was that Bouhler eventually handed over a copy of Hitler's authorization to Gürtner. He obviously wanted to end the debate about the legality of the programme and assure the Reich Minister that the programme was carried out on the highest order of the Führer. It is the only surviving copy, and was discovered among Gürtner's papers. As a reliable government official, he jotted down the date when Bouhler had given him the copy: 'Given from Bouhler to me on 27.8.40 (signed Dr Gürtner).' In order to alleviate the ongoing tensions with the judiciary over the 'euthanasia' issue, Gürtner attempted to introduce specific rules and regulations which would govern the 'euthanasia' programme, something that was stopped nine days later through Bouhler's intervention: 'Based on the authorisation of the Führer, and as the only one responsible for the implementation of the requisite measures, I have issued any directives to my staff which I deem necessary. Beyond this, there is in my view no longer any need for any special regulations [*Ausführungsbestimmungen*] to be confirmed in writing.'[139] Gürtner now readily accepted the will of the Führer as the 'supreme source of law'.[140]

At the same time, an increasing number of complaints from individuals, the Church and other agencies flooded the German state administration. Some of the complaints reached Brandt. Hitler's personal doctor, who had detached himself from the actual day-to-day running of the operation, was told by the Nazi rank and file about the effects of Hitler's policy. Brandt was undeterred, but agreed that a legal sanctioning of the operation would have suited him better. The main worry for Brandt and many others involved in the programme was that there was no official law. If the murder of patients could be legalized, these men believed, there would be no cause for concern.

V. PUBLIC AND RELIGIOUS CONCERN

Although the 'euthanasia' programme had been classified 'top secret', all attempts to preserve a sufficient level of secrecy failed miserably. The sudden death of large numbers of people inside the Reich posed huge problems, and could not be explained away. In some cases, relatives received two urns, both alleged to pertain to the one family member. In others, the cause of death was so obviously false that people became suspicious. Large sections of the public sensed that something was being done outside of law and order (*es geht was nicht mit rechten Dingen zu*). Relatives and local authorities were beginning to search for asylum inmates who had been transferred without their knowledge and then suddenly died. Locals living in the vicinity of the killing centres had witnessed the grey buses from T-4, which transported the handicapped from train stations to the killing centres, but generally returned empty. They saw smoke rising from the crematoria, and sometimes smelled the burning flesh. Children living in the vicinity of Hadamar, one of the killing centres, would shout to their friends upon seeing the T-4 buses: 'There goes the murder box.'[141] Other children, if they fell behind in their studies, would be told by their peers: 'You're not clever, you'll go to the Hadamar oven.'[142] Old people became scared if they were referred to a state hospital, believing that they would be next in line after the killing of 'idiots' (*Schwachsinnigen*). Rumours were now linking the government to a programme of mass murder. At the end of 1940, public knowledge about the killing centre at Grafeneck had spread to such an extent that Himmler proposed its closure, and that popular disquiet be defused by screening racial propaganda films.[143]

Opposition from the Church increased in the late summer of 1940 after the full extent of the 'euthanasia' programme became public knowledge. Protestant charities such as the *Innere Mission* or the *Caritasverband* attempted to delay the registration and transfer of patients. In most cases this form of resistance was ineffectual and could easily be overcome through government pressure. More problematic were rumours and detailed information from hospital directors, who passed their information to the leaders of the Church. Only a few church leaders, however, felt compelled to protest against the government policy. Among those taking a stand was the Protestant bishop Theophil Wurm of Württemberg, who in July 1940 sent a letter of protest to the Reich Minister of the Interior, Wilhelm Frick, and copied it to the Reich Minister of Justice, Franz Gürtner. Like other men of the Church, Wurm had received his information from members of the laity whose relatives had been killed. Using national and religious rhetoric, Wurm appealed to the authorities to end the operation. For him the sanctity of human life had to be preserved above all else. Any departure from this would, according to Wurm, brutalize society and lead to a general decline in morality and in the authority of the state. The government had a duty to prevent such a potentially disastrous development.[144] On 5 September 1940, after realizing that he would not receive an answer, Wurm once again wrote to Frick, asking him rhetorically: 'Does the Führer know, does he approve?'[145]

The Catholic Church had also received detailed intelligence about the killing of handicapped children and adults through some of its priests, who had passed on information from the diocese or what they had heard during confession. As early as 1940, some of this intelligence was passed to the Vatican, and subsequently channelled to the British Foreign Office through the British Embassy in Bern.[146] Alerted by reports from the Holy See, an official from the British Foreign Office noted in October 1940 that 'this question is doubtless connected with [the] story current[ly circulating] that in Germany mental defectives are being liquidated'.[147] A month later, intelligence sources reported that the inmates of a Viennese asylum had recently been 'transferred to Germany without consulting relatives and destroyed, only urns being returned'.[148] In Munich, rumours were circulating that '80,000 had been disposed of in this manner'.[149] In March 1941, the British Embassy in Zagreb reported that there was 'definite evidence of liquidation of insane persons. Reliable sources state that cripples, severely wounded, and aged poor are being removed'.[150] Half a year later, in September 1941, a German railway guard, who had been sworn to secrecy under penalty of death, confirmed to the British Legation in Bern that severely wounded soldiers were being 'gassed', and that his conscience had not permitted him to withhold the secret from the world any longer:

> Guards and superintendents of trains containing wounded soldiers from the eastern front are ordered at certain places to put on their gas-masks. The trains then enter a tunnel where they remain for upwards of half an hour. On leaving the tunnel, all of the wounded soldiers are disposed of in the same manner in so-called emergency hospitals … The guard who furnished this information is stated to have been on duty on one of the trains in which wounded soldiers were 'gassed'.[151]

The leaking of secrets about state-sanctioned murder was beginning to get out of hand. The damage to the reputation of the regime, if it had not suffered already, was incalculable. Leading officials of the Catholic Church now lodged a formal protest to the German government. In August 1940, the chairman of the Fulda Conference of Bishops, Cardinal Adolf Bertram, wrote to Lammers, objecting to the secret transfer and killing of handicapped patients. Others, such as Bishop Heinrich Wienken, executive of the Fulda Conference, seem to have developed a rather cosy relationship with T-4 officials during some of their backstage negotiations. Church leaders such as Cardinal Faulhaber from Munich, like the Catholic Church as a whole, eventually called for an end to such accommodating talks and began distancing themselves from Wienken. On 6 November 1940, Faulhaber sent a robust letter of protest to Gürtner, pointing out that the murder of patients would seriously undermine the trust of the German people in their government and health care agencies. Although negotiations for a law on euthanasia were still under way (and continued throughout 1941), it now became clear to Brandt and the T-4 operation that the Vatican was opposed to any kind of compromise. On 2 December 1940, the Holy Father, Pius XII, unequivocally condemned the murder of handicapped patients in the Nazi 'euthanasia' programme.

One person who confronted Brandt with the effects of the 'euthanasia' programme was Hermann Boehm, head of the teaching division at the Nazi Physicians School in Alt-Rehse in Mecklenburg.[152] In November 1940, Boehm had heard from Kurt Klare, a prominent physician who openly opposed euthanasia in the 1930s, that relatives of the mentally ill had been informed of their deaths in an unacceptable manner. Boehm was not so much concerned about the killing of patients per se, but about the manner in which the relatives were informed. Klare had asked Boehm to support a more 'humane implementation' of the 'euthanasia' programme and to bring this to the attention of the government. Boehm first approached Bormann to get an audience with Hitler, but Bormann referred him to Brandt as the man in charge of the 'euthanasia' programme.[153] Some time at the end of 1940, Boehm met with Brandt in Boehm's hotel room in Berlin.

Boehm expressed his concern about the secrecy and mismanagement of the 'euthanasia' programme. His main objections were as follows (note the order of priority): first, he disagreed with the 'unpleasant way' (*unschöne Art*) in which the relatives were being informed; second, he criticized the fact that no attempt was made to obtain the consent of the relatives of the patients; and third, he was critical of the fact that the relatives were given a fake cause of death. For Boehm, this constituted 'indecent' behaviour. Brandt replied that all these three issues had been decided and introduced on the direct order of Hitler.[154] But Boehm was persistent. He argued that the 'euthanasia' programme should be carried out under an appropriate law, and not in a secretive and conspiratorial fashion. Brandt conceded that he himself would have preferred a legal ruling in this matter, and that Reich Minister of Justice Gürtner had strongly supported such an initiative. Brandt also agreed that it was necessary to obtain the consent of the relatives whose family members were identified for inclusion in the programme. As if to reassure Boehm of the scientific nature of the programme, Brandt told him that the selection of patients to be killed was done by medical experts, who apparently examined the patients personally, something that was untrue.[155]

It was not the first time Brandt had been approached about the issue. On 27 September 1940, Adolf Freiher von Oeynhausen, government president of Minden, who had played host to Hitler during his election campaign in 1932, and Beyer, the head of personnel in the state of North Westphalia, who had been sent on instructions of *Gauleiter* Alfred Meyer, met with Brandt and Bouhler in the Reich Chancellery. On the agenda was the growing concern about the 'euthanasia' programme among large sections of the clergy and the German population. It also transpired that the killing of patients had caught the attention of Swedish and American journalists, who had reported on it in their respective countries.[156] The information, only the tip of the iceberg, had been furnished to Oeynhausen and Meyer by two influential priests from the Bodelschwingh asylums, Paul Braune, head of the Lobetal asylum, and Friedrich (Fritz) von Bodelschwingh, director at Bethel, a Protestant asylum near Bielefeld.[157] Both had refused to fill in the registration forms supplied by the T-4 organization, and called for opposition to the 'euthanasia' programme. Braune had already been arrested. Brandt sensed the seriousness of the matter, and agreed that he should visit the Bethel asylum and speak with von Bodelschwingh to quell potentially harmful criticism.[158] The previous month had been one of the worst for the managers of the 'euthanasia' programme, given that secrecy surrounding the operation had almost completely broken down. It had been extremely embarrassing for the T-4 organizers to admit that the head of state was involved in illegal activities. Dissent from sections of the public was mounting, putting Brandt and Bouhler onto the defensive, and ultimately forcing Hitler to change tack.

Since the early summer of 1940, Braune and von Bodelschwingh had inundated Oeynhausen and Meyer with letters of complaint about the ongoing killing opera- tion. Having compiled irrefutable evidence that the regime was involved in the wholesale murder of patients, the two men approached state secretaries (Conti) and Reich Ministers (Gürtner, Lammers), and contacted the intelligence service of the high command of the armed forces (Hans von Dohnany).[159] They also forced Brack and Linden to admit that the withdrawal of food in cure and nursing homes was meant to be an inconspicuous method of killing patients by cheap means. In July, Braune had gone on the offensive by submitting a well-researched and damning report about the 'euthanasia' programme to Lammers and Göring. According to the Reich Chancellery, Hitler was informed about its content. The reaction to such treason was swift. On 12 August 1940, Braune was arrested by the Reich Security Main Office (*Reichssicherheitshauptamt*, RSHA), and kept for three months in 'protective custody'. The document ordering his arrest, signed by Heydrich, stated that he had 'sabotaged measures of state and party in an irresponsible fashion'.[160] Brandt and others agreed that such a repressive policy was not helpful. Since his arrest, Braune had been included in the daily prayers of people in his region, a subtle way of spreading the news that patients were killed on an unprecedented scale. A number of senior clerics now began to send letters of protest to the authorities. Nothing was more counterproductive than producing a martyr, especially at a time when Brandt and most of the Nazi leadership still believed that they would eventu- ally be able to implement the programme on a legal basis. Compromise rather than confrontation was Brandt's strategy, a view which most of the T-4 managers did not share. They were heading towards a full-scale power battle between the state and public opinion, with potentially disastrous effects for the regime.

On 26 July, Brack and Linden travelled to Bethel to pressure von Bodelschwingh and his physicians into compliance with the programme.[161] Von Bodelschwingh refused, however, to fill in the necessary registration forms which were needed in the selection process of patients. One of the doctors, Karsten Jaspersen, also reported a murder at the police station in Bielefeld, to them and to the Gestapo in Berlin, and attempted to persuade other clinics and doctors to refuse to hand in their registration forms. Such measures had no immediate effect, but they disconcerted the organizers of the T-4 operation and made them feel less sure of managing a smooth implementation of Hitler's policy. Following the bombardment of Bethel by the British air force on 18 and 19 September, which led to the death of a dozen epileptic children, and caused an instant outcry by the German press against such barbarity, von Bodelschwingh wrote a furious letter to Oeynhausen on 28 September 1940. Oeyenhausen had just returned from the meeting with Brandt and Bouhler the previous day in Berlin. Von Bodelschwingh told Oeyenhausen: 'Shall I in fact condemn the action of the British only to turn around and support the murder of children in Bethel on a much larger scale?'[162] Rather than condemning the British, von Bodelschwingh or one of his colleagues seems to have passed on their information about the killing of handicapped patients to a source who was in contact with the British Consul-General in Zurich, hoping, perhaps, that international pressure might force the regime to reconsider its policy. On 10 December 1940, the British Legation in Berne, after having received a memorandum from the 'ultra cautious' Consul-General, reported to the Foreign Office in London:

> The source got it from an informant who lives at Bethel near Bielefeld, the Bodelschwing [sic] institution for the crippled and deformed. According to this information, many thousands of the inmates of the institutions have been secretly murdered in the last few months. The decisions are taken by the Directors of certain homes and sanatoria in Baden … Patients are removed in grey-coloured vans without knowing their destination and for their destruction they are sent to Grafeneck, near Münsingen in Württemberg or to Linz in Upper Austria.[163]

In the meantime, Brandt wanted to take a back seat and see how events developed, interfering only at crucial points in the process, if at all. As the 'euthanasia' programme fell nominally into the area of responsibility of the RMdI, most of the requests and complaints had to be dealt with by Linden and Conti, both of whom were experienced in stonewalling techniques. By the end of 1940, pressure was mounting on Bethel to comply with the government's wishes. A number of Jewish patients had already been transferred by the T-4 organization, and were probably later killed.[164] Von Bodelschwingh was now increasingly convinced that he would not be able to prevent the transfer – and subsequent killing – of non-Jewish patients from Bethel for much longer. Support from Nazi officials was rapidly ebbing away. On 6 January 1941, von Bodelschwingh approached Göring to enlist his support. After outlining the extent to which mental patients, especially those suffering from epilepsy, were working and living as 'valuable citizens' in Bethel's community, in which different forms of occupational therapy brought them 'happiness and honour', von Bodelschwingh told Göring that the work of the asylum was threatened by the 'measures of the Reich Ministry of the Interior to exterminate "life unworthy of life"'.[165] No limitations as far as the patient groups were concerned had apparently been drawn. Von Bodelschwingh regarded the government's utilitarian and materialistic approach to the current shortages in supply, hospitals and personnel as a painful misfortune: 'The saving in foodstuffs, space and personnel stands in no relation to the blow to the trust and legal conscience (Rechtsbewußtsein) among wide sections of our people.'[166]

Von Bodelschwingh's attempt to enlist Göring's support failed. On 29 January, Lieutenant General Karl Bodenschatz told von Bodelschwingh that his information about the killing of patients was 'partly imprecise and largely wrong', and that

Göring had asked Brandt to provide him with the 'necessary enlightenment'.[167] On the same day Gürtner died of natural causes, and with him the futile hopes that some senior government official would interfere in the killing operation. Things were looking increasingly bleak. Von Bodelschwingh began contemplating that he might have to 'hand over' the Bethel patients to the T-4 organization. The only question which remained was how many he could save. On 19 February, a 'medical commission' (*Ärztekommission*) of eighteen T-4 physicians, headed by Heyde, finally arrived at Bethel to fill in the registration forms.[168] Von Bodelschwingh was left with no choice other than to buy time. His stenographic notes reveal that Bethel's line was not to participate actively in the 'euthanasia' programme, but also not to oppose it (*Nicht aktiv handeln, aber auch keine Opposition*).[169] He told the members of the commission that the directorship of the Bethel asylum was of the opinion that the patients should share the burden and misery of the German people during the war, and that the institution had taken the necessary consequences, but that they could not 'actively help with another step', even more so because there was no legal basis for the killing of patients. He appealed to the T-4 doctors to show consideration for the patients of the asylum, and conduct the examinations in an inconspicuous manner: 'The patients know what's going on.' Von Bodelschwingh made it plain that the commission would be fully responsible for the selection of completed registration forms, that is to say the selection of patients who would be killed; he also hoped to exclude certain patient groups from the programme, for example 550 patients who had been assigned to the asylum in the last five years, and educated patients: 'It would be the greatest social injustice if they were to be penalised with death, because they had previously not learned to do agricultural labour.'[170] The leading members of the commission did not like what they heard. Brack asked to see von Bodelschwingh alone, ironically in the small prayer chamber next to von Bodelschwingh's study room, where Brack told him that there was an arrest warrant against him, but that his arrest had been postponed in view of the ongoing negotiations. Calling Brack's bluff, von Bodelschwingh replied that this would not change his position that Bethel would not fill in the registration forms.[171]

What the commission did not know, however, was that Brandt had visited the Bethel asylum on the same day as the T-4 doctors had begun their work in Bielefeld.[172] In the subsequent conversation with Brandt, which took place in von Bodelschwingh's study room, von Bodelschwingh defended Bethel's position with regard to the 'euthanasia' programme out of Christian and patriotic motives. He told Brandt that the killing of mental patients had led the German people to distrust their government. Given that the programme was carried out in secret, and without a legal basis, it was affecting Germany's standing in the world. 'Is it worth it? We will have to pay for it' (*Lohnt sich das? Es wird uns heimgezahlt*), von Bodelschwingh told Brandt; he also stressed the specific situation of the Christian asylum, which was not only well known both inside and outside Germany, but which cared also for 1,500 private patients. Von Bodelschwingh asked Brandt to work towards the discontinuation of the operation, or at least guarantee that some of Bethel's patients would be excluded from the programme. In the end, von Bodelschwingh agreed to cooperate as far as possible with the government, still hoping that this would allow him to save specific patient groups. Although von Bodelschwingh's and Bethel's role has in the past been criticized for its lack of open resistance against the regime, and for the fact that von Bodelschwingh tried to save his patients by establishing close links with Brandt and the regime, one needs to acknowledge the degree of moral courage of men like von Bodelschwingh.[173] The Bethel institution certainly did not make things any easier for the Third Reich.

After having turned down the invitation to stay for supper, Brandt left Bethel on the same day, but agreed to return to continue the conversation with von Bodelschwingh and some of the Bethel doctors.[174] On 28 February, two days after the commission had completed the work, von Bodelschwingh told Oeynhausen about his meeting with Brandt. His notes record that Brandt must have emphasized a new medical doctrine and image (*Bild*), according to which incurable patients would not be killed as a punitive measure, but as a form of 'salvation' (*Erlösung*).[175]

The reality of the killing operation could not have been further from the truth. Whereas von Bodelschwingh managed to prevent any further transfer of Bethel patients to one of the killing centres up until September 1941, when the programme was temporarily stopped, other asylums were less successful in postponing the ruthless execution of the operation in Westphalia. Between July and August 1941, almost 3,000 patients were ferried from Westphalia in twenty-seven transports to the gas chamber in Hadamar. At the end of July, the authorities were satisfied that the killing programme was 'speedily progressing' and would be completed in two to three weeks.[176]

Von Bodelschwingh's persistent reference to international public opinion was nonetheless of concern to the regime. Hitler and the T-4 organization knew that the Allies would exploit public knowledge of the 'euthanasia' programme as a powerful propaganda weapon. While top-secret preparations for 'Operation Barbarossa', the German attack on Russia, were under way, the regime carefully monitored Allied propaganda plans. Hitler wanted to avoid allegations by the Russians or the Western Allies that Germany was violating the laws of war, in particular the claim that Germany was including foreign nationals in a domestic killing programme. Any notion that Germany was killing other than German nationals or stateless persons in the 'euthanasia' programme had to be avoided at the beginning of 1941.

VI. SECRET EXPANSION

At around the same time, and despite growing concern among the general public, various agencies were making secret plans to expand the killing of the handicapped to other population groups outside the Reich territory. Whereas Himmler commissioned T-4 to conduct research into the sterilization of Jews through the use of X-rays, Brandt and Bouhler discussed new selection criteria for potentially new target groups in the 'euthanasia' programme. On Monday 13 January 1941, Himmler met with Victor Brack at 6.15 p.m. to discuss the 'euthanasia' programme.[177] It is likely that their forty-five minute conversation addressed the circumstances which had led to the closure of the Grafeneck killing centre and to the transferral of T-4 personnel to Hadamar where, on the same day, the first group of patients was murdered by means of gas. Himmler asked Brack to initiate research into the sterilization of large numbers of people through X-rays. On 28 March, and again on 19 May, Brack reported his findings to Himmler.[178] It is unlikely, given that Brack regularly reported back to his superior Bouhler, and also to Brandt, that Brandt would not have known about the plan to sterilize the Jewish population. Brandt's post-war claim that he had no knowledge of the expansion of the 'euthanasia' programme stretches credibility to its limits, given that he himself, together with Bouhler, laid down the general guidelines.

Apart from the actual 'euthanasia' decree, few documents have survived which directly concern the two plenipotentiaries, Brandt and Bouhler, or talks between these two men and Hitler. Two such records, however, were produced at the beginning of 1941 in conjunction with modified assessment procedures for persons who were to be included in the killing operation. One of the documents records the results of a meeting between Brandt, Bouhler and Hitler at the Berghof. Both documents, hitherto largely neglected by scholars, suggest that the killing of foreign nationals had been under consideration for some time, but that Hitler and his advisers eventually decided against it, with some exceptions. They knew that the killing of foreign nationals would have provided the Allied press with useful propaganda material. The two documents also highlight the degree of ruthlessness with which T-4 was pursuing its policy of racial cleansing, and link Brandt with some of the planned murders in the East.[179] Most importantly, however, they provide insight into how the Nazi leadership broadened the scope of the killing programme and thereby increased the initial target figure.

The first document records the discussions between Brandt and Bouhler about the 'euthanasia' programme, which happened at the height of the debate about Bethel, but before Brandt had personally visited the institution. On 30 January 1941, an official from the KdF, probably Hefelmann, recorded the basic decisions (*Entscheidungen*) of the 'two euthanasia representatives', that is Brandt and Bouhler, about new assessment procedures for 'euthanasia' victims. According to the notes, all war veterans and those with decorations, and also all senile persons (apart from 'senile criminals' and 'senile asocials') were to be excluded from the killing operation. T-4 was prohibited from 'working' in Alsace-Lorraine, where Brandt had been born, in Luxembourg, in the Eupen-Malmedy protectorate and in the Generalgouvernement. Czech citizens outside the Protectorate of Bohemia and Moravia with German nationality could be killed, whereas Czech citizens with Czech nationality would be expelled to the Protectorate. Jews outside the Reich were to be transferred to Jewish institutions unless they could be deported. Relatives of Jews from overseas would not be notified of such deportations.

The proposed guidelines then stated that Polish and other prisoners of war were not to be included in the killing operation, but that Polish male and female workers could be killed. Realizing that this amounted to a permission to murder foreign and slave labourers, the official crossed out the second half of the sentence. Poles in mental institutions in Silesia, Warthegau, Danzig-West-Prussia and in other areas should *for the time being* [emphasis added] not be killed in the T-4 operation, but it was planned to concentrate them in Polish asylums, where they were later to be killed. 'Aliens' and 'enemy aliens' were to be excluded from the 'euthanasia' programme, but there was an exception to the rule. The guidelines stated that so-called 'unknown foreigners' could be killed, because no one seemed to care about them. Children up to the age of fourteen were to be transferred to the *Reichsausschuss*, which handled the killing of infants and adolescents. The first document from January made no specific reference to the Bethel asylum.[180]

The notes show that Brandt was both informed about, and played an integral part in, the planning stages for a gradual expansion of the 'euthanasia' programme. These notes were the basis for an oral report which Brandt and Bouhler delivered to Hitler about the progress and difficulties of the 'euthanasia' programme less than two months later. But the new guidelines also served to inform other members of the government. On 31 January 1941, the day after Brandt and Bouhler took the decision to increase the target figure, Bouhler met with Goebbels and briefed him about the meeting. Goebbels noted in his diary: 'Discussed with Bouhler the quiet liquidation of the mentally ill. 80,000 are gone. 60,000 still have to disappear.'[181] Goebbels is, as we know, not necessarily the best witness when it comes to factual accuracy, especially because of his tendency to exaggerate, but he appears to have been correctly informed by Bouhler on the basis of the new guidelines. Scholars have been unsure for some time as to how Goebbels arrived at a figure of 80,000, when an internal statistic had calculated that about 38,000 people had been killed at that point. Given that the latter figure did not include those patient groups which had been killed outside the Reich and those which had died from malnutrition and deliberate starvation, Bouhler probably had more accurate figures at hand, and was able to provide Goebbels with an updated target figure, from the original figure of 60,000 to 70,000 people to about 140,000 persons.

On Monday 10 March 1941, Brandt and Bouhler met with Hitler at the Berghof to discuss the new guidelines.[182] The notes of the meeting largely include the same points as the first (January) document, except that it had been slightly modified after Brandt had met von Bodelschwingh at the end of February. Brandt seems to have accommodated some of the concerns which the Bethel case had raised. Hitler now placed the murder of handicapped patients in a greater foreign policy context and considered the situation on the home front. This became even more apparent after the start of the Russian campaign, when growing public disquiet about the lack of success, and Allied air raids made Hitler sensitive to criticism from the Church of the 'euthanasia' programme. For the time being, however, the regime attempted to rid the nation of as many 'useless eaters' as possible in and outside the Reich. Whilst making concessions to institutions like Bethel on the one hand, Brandt and Bouhler, with Hitler's consent, broadened the scope of potential 'euthanasia' victims on the other.

During the meeting with Hitler, Brandt and Bouhler decided in favour of the 'elimination' (*Ausscheidung*) from the German body politic of all those persons who were incapable of productive work in institutions. The new criteria were meant to include all patient groups, and not only those who were 'considered mentally dead'.[183] Although war veterans were to be excluded on principle, the final decision rested with Brack, alias Jennerwein. The following guideline was meant to help Brack in his decision-making process: 'Besides, participation in war does not protect from inclusion in the operation,' the notes stated. Patients who were considered senile were not included in the operation unless they exhibited symptoms of schizophrenia or epilepsy or another mental disorder. Given that Brack had no medical training whatsoever, it is quite astonishing that Brandt and Bouhler entrusted him with the responsibility to decide in special cases on the basis of the patients' medical records. T-4 was authorized to kill only German nationals from the Reich; the guidelines stated, 'that means also no Poles', but Czech citizens with German nationality could be killed. As in the first document, it was agreed that 'enemy aliens' were definitely excluded, but, contrary to the first document, there was an additional reference to the Bethel asylum in the section which dealt with the children's 'euthanasia' programme. It stated: 'The children in Bethel shall be treated with special care.'[184] Von Bodelschwingh's persistent representations to Brandt had apparently paid off.

The above discussions at the highest level of the Nazi hierarchy reveal both the arbitrary nature of the programme and the amateurish approach which Brandt and Bouhler adopted in implementing it. The documents show how Brandt and Bouhler modified and widened the target population almost at random as the programme progressed. The evidence also shows how the regime temporarily adjusted its policy in the face of public concerns and external pressures. Whenever public disquiet had subsided, however, Brandt and others showed their true colours and pressed for the murder of all those whom they considered to be a 'burden' to the state. The above guidelines provide compelling evidence that the Nazi leadership, and Brandt and Bouhler in particular, had thrown the door wide open for the programme to be mismanaged, and for patient populations to be selected on the basis of racial and social prejudices. Both men must have known that as soon as the military situation changed, individual members of the T-4 operation would, on their own initiative, expand the 'euthanasia' programme, and kill those whom they deemed 'unfit' for the future of the German Reich. The 'euthanasia' programme was moving closer to those elements of the regime who pursued an ideologically driven cleansing process against Jews and 'useless eaters' in the occupied territories by the most brutal means. Two days after the meeting, on 12 March, Brandt accompanied Hitler on a visit to the cemetery and town hall in Linz, near Hitler's birthplace.[185] Few in Hitler's entourage would have known that two days earlier the 'euthanasia' programme had been broadened to include even more target groups.

After the war, Brandt maintained that there had been an order which 'exempted non-German nationals' from the 'euthanasia' programme.[186] He was probably referring to the above guidelines. Yet under cross-examination, Brandt was unable to explain how this order had worked or who had received it. He could not tell the court why the T-4 personnel had to fill out questionnaires for foreign nationals, if they were apparently to be exempted from the operation. His ignorance corresponds to the general approach which Brandt took towards the programme. He saw his role as laying down the general framework and deciding, in consultation with Bouhler, the overall policy direction. But he left the execution of the operation to others. He never exercised any meaningful level of supervision or control over the programme.[187]

VII. FRIEDRICH VON BODELSCHWINGH

Despite his ignorance of the overall scale and nature of the killing operation, Brandt continued to engage in discussions with von Bodelschwingh. On 31 March 1941, while Bethel was visited again by T-4 managers, Brandt, Bouhler, and probably Oeynhausen as well, met with von Bodelschwingh to see how far the registering of mental patients had progressed.[188] Von Bodelschwingh, on the other hand, wanted to use the opportunity to show Brandt and Bouhler some of the work they were doing. Although von Bodelschwingh had hoped to show Brandt the *Hermannsheide*, a group of what were, originally, three farms where young adults were working as part of the Voluntary Protestant Work Service (*Freiwilliger Evangelischer Arbeitsdienst*), he only managed to show him Patmos, one of the nursing homes for severely handicapped children, perhaps because Brandt and the other visitors had to leave Bethel the same day.[189] The name 'Patmos' derived from a small island, located on the eastern border of the Aegean Sea, which was significant in the early history of the Christian religion. In Nuremberg, Brandt recalled what he saw in Bethel:

> I conducted with Herrn [von] Bodelschwingh in Bethel joint visits to the patients. We went to the children's ward, and subsequently talked about individual children, not with regard to whether or not one should assign each child to the 'euthanasia' programme, but whether such a creature actually feels a human existence. I remember children of 8 to 10 years of age, who were really not anything more than a wretched and pitiful piece of creature. Children with an enormous hydrocephalus, who could never be in a position to straighten up for a moment, given that a tiny torso hung on a massive head. Herr [von] Bodelschwingh also had the feeling that it would be a blessing if such pitiful creatures were to meet their end. In principle, it was not that we were both of the same opinion and shared the same position, but it was possible to respect and understand each other's views. Herr v. Bodelschwingh believed that if a legal solution [*gesetzliche Regelung*] is publicly known, then these reasons of state [*Staatsräson*] obviously have to be decisive for all. It had nothing to do with the fact that Bodelschwingh, who was deeply attached to the Church, saw always in the most pitiful creatures still something special as human beings.[190]

Whether von Bodelschwingh really agreed with Brandt that it was 'a blessing' for certain children to die remains doubtful, but also not impossible, considering von

Bodelschwingh's complex personality. In November 1946, Brandt noted: 'When I visited Bethel, during which there was a tour of the facilities, von Bodelschwingh admitted for about 250 to 300 patients that for these death would mean an absolute delivery. If there were to be the legal force of a decree even he, if not immediately, but finally, gave up his reservations. According to my knowledge, these patients were also included in the "euthanasia" programme.'[191] Brandt's notes need to be treated with caution, given that they were taken in anticipation of his trial defence, but his overall recollection has a ring of truth, especially as far as von Bodelschwingh's strong emphasis on the value of life was concerned. In February 1943, when the two men talked again about Brandt's visit to the children's ward, von Bodelschwingh highlighted the fact that the children were invaluable for the community and helped people to learn something about humanity.[192] Later, in October 1945, Brandt told his interrogators: 'Pastor Bodelschwingh maintained the point of view that those weaknesses and faults had been brought into the world by God so that man could exercise his love towards them and put it into practice.'[193] Seeing the actual patients and the way they lived must have left a deep impression on Brandt, given that he vividly remembered them in February 1943, when he met von Bodelschwingh in Berlin, and during the Nazi Doctors' Trial.

Twenty-four hours after Brandt's visit, Bethel was attacked by Allied bombers; eighteen people were killed. On 25 April, in an attempt to buy more time, von Bodelschwingh told Brandt that he was concerned that Bethel's patients should be transferred before another meeting between him and Brandt had taken place. Von Bodelschwingh was anxious that Brandt and the T-4 managers applied different categories to patients who were to be included in the programme. Whereas Brandt wanted those patients included whom he regarded as 'life that has become extinct' (*erloschenes Leben*), the T-4 managers used the categories 'incurable' (*unheilbar*) and 'hopeless' (*hoffnungslos*) as selection criteria. Any reasonable man must have realized at this point that the categories which the state applied to take away the life of humans were extremely vague and totally arbitrary. Von Bodelschwingh also told Brandt that the 'euthanasia' programme had become public knowledge through the arrival of the medical commission in Bielefeld. Even the staff in the hotels of Bielefeld, having overheard the conversations of the T-4 doctors, knew about the killings; rumours were spreading far and wide. Some of the peasants in the area had asked the patients who were working in the field: 'Do you know that the murder commission has arrived in Bielefeld?'[194] Von Bodelschwingh respected Brandt's 'idealistic perspective', which had shaped his view on the matter, but felt that the way in which the programme had developed had 'caused more harm than benefit to our German people'.[195] Finally, he invited Brandt to suggest to Hitler that he should postpone the programme until it was possible to put it on a 'clear legal footing' (*eine klare gesetztliche Grundlage*) after the war.

Brandt's response to von Bodelschwingh's letter has not been recorded. Perhaps he had no time to reply. Throughout the spring and summer of 1941, while the Nazi leadership was preparing the attack on the Soviet Union, one of the most destructive and barbaric military onslaughts in modern history, Brandt spent most of his time accompanying Hitler from one place to another. On 20 April, he celebrated Hitler's birthday in his special train *Amerika*, which had been stationed in front of a tunnel.[196] At the end of April, he travelled with Hitler to Marburg an der Drau, then to Graz and on to Klagenfurt.[197] On 5 and 6 May, he accompanied Hitler to Danzig to inspect the latest generation of battleships and submarines.[198] Von Bodelschwingh was nonetheless undeterred. On 23 May, he wrote yet again to Brandt in order to foster good relations, and to ensure that the petitions which von Bodelschwingh's brother had made to the authorities, among others to Bouhler, would not reflect badly on the Bethel asylum. He also wanted Brandt to understand that the population was well informed about the killing centres in Bernburg and Grafeneck. The 'euthanasia' programme, in short, was undermining morale and public support for the regime at a critical moment in the history of the country.[199] Brandt, however, was far too busy with other things. At the beginning of June he travelled to Munich, where Hitler received the Romanian leader, Ion Antonescu, to inform him of the imminent military campaign against Russia.[200] Hitler made it plain to his Romanian ally that he would wage a war of annihilation; he anticipated that the German army would be victorious in about six weeks. Hitler's misjudgement of Germany's military superiority, and of Russian and Allied weaknesses, was of truly historic proportions.

Twenty-four hours after Germany's attack on the Soviet Union had begun on 22 June, and after over three million German soldiers had crossed the borders into Soviet territory, Hitler left Berlin with his entourage to go to his new field headquarters in Lützen, near Rastenburg, in East Prussia. The plan was to spend a couple of weeks at the headquarters while the German armies were advancing into Russia, then visit the newly conquered territories in the East, and return to the German capital. It became Hitler's new 'home' – and by default Brandt's as well – for almost three and a half years until he returned to Berlin. Brandt was thus forced to spend a considerable amount of time at field headquarters, where he attended presentations about the latest military hardware and military briefings, the so-called 'situation discussion' (*Lagebesprechung*), with Keitel, Göring, Todt, Bormann and Himmler.[201] Later, on 6 August, he attended Hitler's visit to the Army Group South in Berdicev in the Ukraine, which had been captured by General Rundstedt's troops in mid-July.[202] At the end of August, he accompanied Hitler and Mussolini on their propaganda tour of the eastern battlefields, for example to Brest-Litowsk and Uman.[203] It is unlikely that he visited or showed much concern for about 20,000 wounded Russian soldiers who had been imprisoned in a camp in Uman without any medical supplies or personnel.[204] Instead, Brandt not only used the opportunity to be pictured next to a destroyed Russian aircraft, but provided urgently needed medical aid and transportation to wounded German troops in Smolensk.[205] Back at home, the German public could see that Hitler's doctor was personally engaged in looking after the health of the troops.

For Brandt and others in Hitler's entourage, it soon became clear that their lives were confined to the rather oppressive atmosphere at field headquarters. At the end of August, Christa Schröder, Hitler's secretary, told a friend: 'We are permanently cut off from the world wherever we are – in Berlin, on the Mountain [the Berghof], or on travels. It's always the same limited group of people, always the same routine inside the fence.'[206] Some, like Jodl, later described the place as half-way 'between a monastery and a concentration camp'.[207] Cut off from the world of normal human beings, Brandt left the day-to-day organization and supervision of the 'euthanasia' programme to others. As far as the Bethel asylum was concerned, however, he continued to be kept informed, perhaps more so than he might have wished.

On 28 August, von Bodelschwingh wrote one of the most powerful letters which he had ever written to a leading member of the regime, and probably one of the most difficult that Brandt had ever received about the 'euthanasia' programme, and about Hitler's Germany, more generally.[208] Cleverly targeted at Brandt's complex personality, the letter was both frank and subtle at the same time. Given that von Bodelschwingh had met Brandt on two occasions, he had formed an impression about Hitler's doctor and about his value system, but also about his personal weaknesses. He wanted to see in Brandt a 'creation of God' (*Geschöpf Gottes*) who, he hoped, could be influenced through the power of his arguments, but who also was a fallible human being. Throughout the letter, von Bodelschwingh stressed his own patriotism and love for the fatherland, which left him with no choice but to tell Brandt about the appalling consequences of some of the regime's policies. He told Brandt that, since his last visit to Bethel, a new chapter in world history had opened. Apart from the ongoing military campaign, the German people would have to face challenges in the East which were of enormous proportions. To 'overcome bolshevism inside the people', and achieve a permanent peace in Europe, the nation needed to use all her energies, maintain steadfast unity and be ready to make great sacrifice. Knowing that Brandt was likely to share a strong sense of nationalism and feelings of patriotism, von Bodelschwingh's opening remarks ensured that he argued from a position of like-mindedness. At the same time, von Bodelschwingh wanted to keep Brandt's moral conscience alive and remind him of his own compassion for human beings.

Von Bodelschwingh regarded some of the demands on the people as 'superfluous' and 'outright dangerous' in the current situation. He was concerned, for example, about the fact that the regime had reduced the use of paper by the general press to about 60%, but to about 2% for Christian newspapers and journals, which catered for large sections of the German public. The journal 'Missionaries of Bethel' (*Boten von Bethel*) alone had a distribution of 340,000. The radical suppression of Christian print media, von Bodelschwingh argued, had 'cut off untold channels' which formerly had provided the home front and the soldiers in the field with the necessary strength to do their duty. He questioned whether such acts were 'politically sound'. Another concern related to the closure and takeover of confessional day-care centres for children (*Kindertagesstätten*) and kindergartens by the National Socialist People's Care (*Nationalsozialistische Volksfürsorge*, NSV), which affected tens of thousands of families in Westphalia. Although the regional authorities had admitted that the measures constituted an unnecessary waste of resources and personnel, and were bad for morale, they were unable to change things because 'the directives which have been given from above have to be fulfilled'.[209] The German public was gaining the impression that the regime wanted to use the war to resolve the 'religious question'. Given that the hope that pre-Germanic cults would establish genuine religious feelings had not materialized, and no alternative to Christian belief had so far been found, the regime was uprooting the population. As a result, von Bodelschwingh told Brandt, the German people were not only losing their 'moral decency' (*sittlichen Halt*), but were inevitably becoming a 'materialistic atheist movement' (*materialistische Gottlosenbewegung*), which was what had led the Russian people into the abyss. Von Bodelschwingh's use of powerful imagery and innuendos was a clever piece of rhetoric, designed to impress upon Brandt the need to reflect about the nature of the regime, and his role within it.

Finally, von Bodelschwingh addressed the 'euthanasia' programme, or as he put it frankly, the 'killing of patients' (*Krankentötung*). He admitted, and was grateful, that the programme had become 'more cautious' through the use of 'transit centres' and the exclusion of certain patient groups. His principal concern had only increased, however. The extermination of patients was affecting almost every parish. People from far and wide had received, and were talking about, the urns sent by T-4. Fake death certificates from Hadamar were passed around among the people and were causing alarm. The programme was far worse for people's morale than propaganda by the enemies of the state. State documents obviously contained untruths. Given that the loss of trust among the German public was immeasurable, and the consequences incalculable, von Bodelschwingh issued a veiled threat:

> In the great spiritual struggle of our days, it is critically important what kind of face the German state shows to the world. Many people see in these intrusions into life and family context, which are carried out without a legal basis and in secret, a fearful pattern of unscrupulous brutality. The people around us are gaining the same impression. Our actions are handing to the enemies of our fatherland welcoming weapons; and a measure which might have resulted from an extreme form of racial idealism (*hoch gespannten rassischen Idealismus*) leads to a deepening of hatred among the people and to a lengthening of the war. That is why I fear that many German mothers will have to pay the bill for the guilt which has been placed upon our people with the blood of their sons.[210]

If Brandt had hoped to claim that he had not known what was going on in German asylums, if he had wanted to pretend ignorance in the face of mass murder, or if he had wanted to overlook the enormous suffering which the 'euthanasia' programme had caused to the spiritual health of the nation, here was the information, in black and white, which prevented him from doing so. Von Bodelschwingh's letter prevented Brandt from ever saying that he had not known. It forced him out of reservation, away from a position of detached leadership, to one where he had to face the fact that he, together with Bouhler, was ultimately responsible for the deaths of tens of thousands of human beings. No one, von Bodelschwingh believed, could be so callous as not to feel any sympathy for the enormous suffering of patients, especially someone who had been trained to care for patients, and cure them.

Appealing to Brandt's moral conscience, von Bodelschwingh told Brandt: 'I know that you have placed a heavy burden upon your heart in the patient matter.' He had realized this after Brandt had talked with him about the great sense of responsibility which he bore for the death of so many people. Von Bodelschwingh reminded Brandt about a remark which he had made in passing during his last visit to Bethel: '... you commented that sometimes, in the evening, when you went to bed, you would think: "Today there have again been so and so many ...".'[211] However hardened, idealistically stubborn, and in many ways ignorant, scholars may over the years have judged Brandt to be, the 'euthanasia' programme had apparently not left him completely untouched. 'Please do not permit this warning voice in your heart to fall silent!' von Bodelschwingh pleaded. Given that the German people faced another harsh winter at home and on the front, von Bodelschwingh wanted Brandt to reconsider, together with Bouhler, the 'euthanasia' programme, propose a termination of the operation to Hitler, and postpone any continuation of the programme until a legal ruling had been found. Von Bodelschwingh knew that the frankness of his letter was potentially 'ambiguous and dangerous', and he was willing to meet Brandt 'at any time and at any place' to discuss the issues in person, but he explained that he needed to say these things because he did not want to reproach himself later for having been silent for reasons of lethargy and cowardice at a fateful hour, when the existence of the German people was being decided. Von Bodelschwingh's letter was a piece of rhetoric which could not easily be ignored.[212] What von Bodelschwingh did not know, however, was the fact that four days earlier, on 24 August 1941, the 'euthanasia' programme had officially been 'halted'. Eighteen months later, in February 1943, Brandt admitted to von Bodelschwingh that the letter had made quite an impression on him. During the conversation, von Bodelschwingh acknowledged that his letter had been 'very frank'. 'One could truly say that,' Brandt replied.[213]

VIII. THE HALT OF THE 'EUTHANASIA' PROGRAMME

By August 1941, the pressure on the regime from various sections of society critical of the 'euthanasia' programme was mounting. Public knowledge of the programme and the growing disquiet among the churches, the judiciary and the state bureaucracy were among the key factors in bringing to an end the first phase of the killing operation. The idea that the T-4 organization had somehow reached its initial target figure does not seem to have been the overriding reason for the interruption.[214] Hitler and his advisers were constantly kept briefed on the mood of the population through secret reports from the Security Service; these stated that the German public was concerned about a whole range of issues; foremost among them the fact that the Russian campaign had turned out to be less successful and swift than many had anticipated. At the end of July, the people were desperately waiting for one of the 'special reports' (*Sondermeldungen*) which were issued after major successes in the war. Yet no such report was forthcoming. Germans were also worried about Allied bombing raids which turned medical supplies and hospital space into a rare and important commodity. When public criticism about the killings came to a head in August, Hitler and his inner circle decided to defuse the situation by ordering an official halt to the programme, especially after the bishop of Münster, Clemens August Graf von Galen (1878–1946), had made it internationally known that Nazi Germany was killing handicapped children and adults on an unprecedented scale. Hitler's decision to halt the programme and his decision to shift the focus to the creation of more hospital space in what became known as the 'Aktion-Brandt' are intricately connected.

Opposition from the Church to euthanasia had been anticipated by Hitler from the early 1930s. He had good reasons to postpone its introduction until the outbreak of war, when it was thought that resistance among the clergy could be muted. The Church did not prevent the murder of 70,000 handicapped people in the first phase of the killing operation, nor the deaths of thousands of patients from 1942 to 1945. But some of its leaders caused a major domestic and international embarrassment to Hitler's government, and steered the situation towards open confrontation. A sermon by Bishop von Galen probably had the greatest public impact. When, in July 1941, the local Gestapo office decided to expel Jesuits (the order which had trained him) from property which they occupied in Münster, Galen decided it was time to act. On 3 August 1941, he delivered his powerful sermon to a crowded Lambertikirche, openly attacking the underlying hypocrisy of the 'euthanasia' programme and the economic rationale for the killing of the handicapped:

> If you establish and apply the principle that you can kill 'unproductive' human beings, then woe betide us all when we become old and frail! If one is allowed to kill unproductive people, then woe betide the invalids who have used up, sacrificed and lost their health and strength in the productive process. If one is allowed forcibly to remove one's unproductive fellow human beings, then woe betide loyal soldiers who return to the homeland seriously disabled, as cripples, as invalids.[215]

Galen's sermon was immediately repeated from the pulpits in his diocese. His words did not miss their target. The Nazi leadership was furious. The Nazi rank and file called for the arrest and execution of Galen as a traitor who openly challenged the regime at the height of its power. With all the attention on his military campaign in the East, and after having launched the most ruthless attack against the Soviet Union in June 1941, Hitler refrained from following his first and perhaps most violent instincts, and postponed a final reckoning. The priests and people who had disseminated Galen's sermon, however, lost their jobs or were sent to concentration camps. Brandt later stated that he had wanted to mediate between Galen and the regime and that he had intended to speak to Galen on several occasions, but that Hitler had forbidden him to do so.[216] Although his intentions might have been good, Brandt continued to support the 'euthanasia' programme.

Only a couple of weeks prior to the halt in the 'euthanasia' programme, Brandt put his weight behind the operation vis-à-vis the executives of the regions (*Gauamtsleiter*) and leading physicians of the German Medical Council (*Ärztekammerleiter*).[217] The meeting took place in the summer of 1941 in

Munich. Brandt did not turn up alone, but brought reinforcements from the T-4 organization: Brack, Bouhler and Conti were all present, ready to answer questions in case Brandt's authority were to be challenged. Brandt confirmed that he had been personally entrusted with the programme by the Führer, and that all the necessary fail-safe mechanisms had been put in place to ensure that only serious and incurable cases would be eliminated. He told the participants that he knew that the Church and sections of the public were opposed to the programme, but that there was also substantial agreement among the population (which was true). To dispel concerns among his audience, Brandt showed them a legal text, signed by Hitler, about the 'euthanasia' programme, which was meant to be published after the war. It was a ploy which worked for the moment. The German medical profession was not only being heavily implicated in the programme, it could also hardly claim that it had no knowledge of state-sanctioned murder.

While public protest had a great effect on Hitler's decision to halt the operation, scholars have since also suggested other factors. By January 1941, the organizers of the 'euthanasia' programme anticipated that their initial target figure would be met in about half a year, and consequently issued only six-month contracts for new staff. Allers, for example, was given an assignment specifically 'for half a year', because Brack and the T-4 organization expected 'to have finished by July at the latest'.[218] In the late summer of 1941, a T-4 statistician had also compiled a summary of the number of people killed in the 'euthanasia' operation. His report, which was later discovered in the safe at Hartheim, listed the monthly figures for each killing centre and arrived at a total: 70,273 persons had been 'disinfected'. It turned out that by August 1941 the T-4 operation had slightly exceeded the original target of killing one chronic patient per thousand inhabitants, that was about 70,000 persons. According to the report, this apparently saved the German Reich 885,439,980 Reichsmark over a period of ten years, or, 13,492,440 kilograms of meat and wurst. Whether Brandt had such crude utilitarianism in mind when he signed up for the programme may be doubtful, but it seems to have been the logical outcome of Nazi policies of racial cleansing.

We need to acknowledge the limitations of the above argument.[219] When the programme was halted in August 1941, many T-4 protagonists were apparently surprised, mainly because hundreds of patients were still waiting to be transferred from one of the 'transit centres' to places like Hadamar, where they were scheduled to be killed. The existence of these patient populations and their survival, even though only temporarily, shows that the programme had not been completed at that stage. As we have seen, the overall target figure seems to have been increased in early 1941 from between 60,000 and 70,000 to about 140,000 people. New patient populations in and outside the Reich had been assigned as part of the killing operation, but were not necessarily included in the Hartheim statistics. Be this as it may, the organizers of T-4 could certainly claim that they had achieved, and somewhat exceeded, the initial target figure of killing one per cent of the German population, or, as Brandt had calculated, about ten per cent of an estimated 700,000 –800,000 mentally ill patients.[220]

The circumstances of the halt of the 'euthanasia' programme are important because it coincided with the beginning of 'Aktion Brandt', the creation of hospital space through the building of new hospitals and the evacuation of asylum populations to institutions in less endangered air-raid areas. The discussions at Hitler's headquarters in August 1941 show that the regime was able to react flexibly to growing discontent among the population, and attempted to defuse rumours about the 'euthanasia' programme that had circulated in certain regions. Instead of imprisoning and punishing Bishop Galen, as many of the leading Nazis were demanding, Hitler decided to stop the killing operation. He knew that the imprisonment of Galen and the continuation of the 'euthanasia' programme would have dampened the public mood further, which might have destabilized an already tense and fragile situation in the Reich. Compared to the need to have a stable home front at a critical juncture in the war, the 'euthanasia' programme appears to have been of secondary importance. The extent to which the killing of mental patients impacted on the mood of the German people was also on Goebbels' mind. On 15 August 1941, he noted in his diary:

> I must ask the Führer whether he currently wishes a public debate about the euthanasia problem. We could perhaps link the debate to the new film by Liebeneiner 'I accuse' [*Ich klage an*]. I myself am opposed to it at this time. One would only arouse the emotions of the people once more [*Gemüter aufs Neue erhitzen*] with such debates. That is exceptionally unhelpful in a critical period of the war. One should keep all inflammatory matters away from the people at the moment. The people are so occupied with the problems of the war that other problems would only give rise to worry and exhaustion.[221]

Upon arrival at the *Wolfsschanze* on 18 August, Goebbels found Hitler in an exhausted state, both physically and mentally. Hitler was apparently suffering from another bout of dysentery and from the stresses and strains of the last four weeks which, as Goebbels noted, had 'given him a hard time'. The military developments on the Eastern Front, the high number of German casualties and the ongoing food and fuel shortages had made the German population weary and the Nazi leadership tense and nervous. 'That was a difficult time for all of us,' Goebbels noted. 'We had not expected military problems to that extent'.[222] Hitler asked for a detailed report from Goebbels about the mood in the population and about the situation in Berlin. Goebbels' report made it clear that the Germans were unhappy about the progress of the war, especially about the prospect of spending yet another winter in air-raid shelters. The constant British air raids gave reason for widespread concern among the general public. On 13 August, a severe bombing raid had hit the capital; on 16 August more than 300 bombers had attacked the cities of Hanover, Braunschweig and Magdeburg.[223] The air raids demonstrated to the Germans that the enemy could reach far into the German hinterland and cause significant damage to morale, material and people. Goebbels' diary notes also indicate that the Nazi leadership was well informed about the mass murder of tens of thousands of Jews in the eastern territories which was carried out behind the lines by members of the *SS-Einsatzgruppen*, backed by the Germany army:

We also talk about the Jewish problem. The Führer is convinced that his prophecy in the Reichstag at the time, that if the Jews were to manage to provoke a World War once more, it would end with the annihilation of the Jews, is becoming a reality. His prophecy turns out to be true in these weeks and months with a certainty which feels almost eerie. In the East, the Jews have to pay the bill.[224]

Another point of discussion between Goebbels and Hitler was the question of whether Jews should be deported to the East and whether German Jews, like those in Poland and in the Czech Protectorate, should be forced to wear a special star. Hitler agreed that the German Jews should be easily identifiable for future deportations, but that these could only take place if the Russian campaign had successfully been completed.[225] Hitler's reluctance to agree to Goebbels' request for deportations at this point, a position he changed only weeks later, is another indication that the scarcity of resources and material must have been on his mind at this time.[226] A proposal to create additional bed spaces through the building of extra hospitals and through the transferral of asylum populations probably fell on fertile ground.

On the same day that Goebbels reported to Hitler, the *Gauleiter* of Westphalia, Alfred Meyer, who six months later attended the Wannsee conference, wrote a letter to Bormann, asking him for a decision from the Führer about the continuation of the 'euthanasia' programme.[227] Given that rumours about the killings were circulating in Münster and Westphalia, regional officials had been asking Meyer to decide whether to continue with the killing operation or halt the programme temporarily. Meyer had heard from

> party member B. (…) that the Aktion shall be continued. I would see this as the right course of action, if the Bishop of Münster is to be imprisoned; if not, it is to be feared that he will continue to spread rumours in the churches, especially about this programme. May I ask you to come to a decision on the issue.[228]

Whether Meyer was referring to Brandt as the 'party member B.' is not known, but what becomes clear is that Meyer gave the Nazi leadership two options: either to imprison Bishop von Galen and risk alienating the population further, or to stop the programme in Westphalia, if not altogether. We know that Bormann, to whom the letter was addressed, attended the meetings on 24 August during which the decision to halt the programme was taken. It is quite possible that Bormann may have relayed Meyer's either/or options to the Führer, and thereby may have forced a decision on the issue. Hitler was, as we know, particularly susceptible to situations which presented themselves in black and white and which required a clear course of action in one way or the other.

On Sunday 24 August 1941, Brandt had several meetings with Hitler. During the first meeting, Brandt, together with Bormann, discussed the continuation of the 'euthanasia' programme with Hitler. Himmler was not present. He was ill and was unable to attend any meetings.[229] Some chroniclers have alleged that the discussions were heated, but there is little evidence to sustain these claims. Hitler eventually told Brandt to halt the programme. Brandt then telephoned Bouhler, who passed on further instructions to Brack. Somewhere down the lines of communication, however, one KdF official wanted to know the precise nature of Hitler's order. Hefelmann inquired from Brandt whether the halt of the operation included all target groups, or whether children would be exempted. Brandt reported back to Hitler who said 'no', it did not include all groups. Until the end of the war, the killing of children and adolescents continued.

Later on the same day, another discussion took place which was indirectly connected to the first. We know that Brandt, Bormann and Fritz Todt, the Reich Minister for Armaments and Munitions, were present during the second meeting with Hitler.[230] On 24 August 1941, Brandt recorded the content of the conversation in a letter to Bormann, in order to document the fact that Hitler had tasked him with another area of responsibility:

> The Führer has ... suggested that certain cities vulnerable to air raids (Hanover, Hamburg, Bremen etc.) shall receive additional buildings for damaged hospitals; furthermore, these additional hospitals shall be of a size that they are able to admit a significant number of additional patients ... As far as [it] is possible, the cure and nursing homes which are located in the region of the relevant cities can serve as a basis for such hospitals. The use [of these hospitals] ... occurs with the agreement of the special representative (Dr Linden) in the Reich Ministry of the Interior.[231]

Brandt made it clear that the new hospitals would be built by the Todt Organization (*Organisation Todt*, OT) in liaison with himself. Cure and nursing homes that were located near cities vulnerable to air raids could be used as a basis for these new buildings. Linden from the RMdI, who had previously coordinated parts of the 'euthanasia' programme, was instructed to oversee the evacuation of cure and nursing homes. Brandt promised Bormann that the regional *Gauleiter* would be consulted about the buildings, and that he, Brandt, would keep close contact with Alois Poschmann from the department of sanitation of the OT.

The two meetings were followed by a series of frantic telephone calls to some of the regional asylums in the north of Germany that were to be evacuated. Who exactly made these calls is not known, but it is possible that Brandt or Linden may have made them. At the end of August, or at the beginning of September, a caller, who withheld his identity, instructed the asylum in Oldenburg, on the basis of an order of the Führer, to evacuate the building within a fortnight so that it could be transformed into a hospital. The Rotenburg asylum near Bremen and the asylum in Lübeck-Strecknitz, as well as smaller institutions in Rickling and the monastery of Blankenburg, near Wehnen, received similar anonymous calls asking the staff to evacuate the patients to other places. If Brandt made these calls, it is likely that he made them from Führer headquarters in East Prussia, where Hitler was waiting impatiently for news from the Eastern Front. To provide the German public with the image of a leadership in charge, Hitler started to do some sightseeing. On 10 September, Brandt accompanied Hitler to the Tannenberg Memorial, the place of Hindenburg's military victory in the First World War.[232] After having stage-managed

Hindenburg's funeral at the Memorial in 1934, Hitler returned to the scene with his entourage to promote the image of a victorious warlord amidst growing fears that the German army had underestimated Russian resolve and resources.

Defusing rumours about the 'euthanasia' programme turned out to be extremely difficult. The transfer of patient populations by the T-4 organization to other institutions in the eastern parts of the Reich fuelled concerns that the murder of patients was shifting to regions which had previously been unaffected by the programme. The evacuation of asylums was carried out by the same transport organization which had hitherto been used in the killing programme. By now most relatives of patients knew the meaning of the grey buses from the T-4 organization which ferried patients to their death. Brandt and others involved in setting up the new hospital building programme were using the same administrative structure that had previously served the 'euthanasia' programme.

On 8 October 1941, Brandt wrote a letter to the Party Chancellery to stem the rising tide of concerns among the Nazi rank and file. The letter was to be circulated to all party offices in the Reich.[233] Brandt repeated Hitler's directives to create additional buildings for damaged hospitals and extra bed spaces through the transferral of asylum populations. He also hinted that there was no underlying intention to kill the patients, although certain sections of society might think that there was such an intention. To quell potential rumours, the Nazi Party was asked to engage in a concerted propaganda campaign:

> This purposeful measure will cause a certain concern in some circles of the population because of the transferral of patients from cure and nursing homes into other institutions. Yet since the patients are really only transferred for the period of the war, the relatives will also be informed about the residence in advance. Moreover, it shall be made possible that the patients can be visited to a reasonable extent ... It would seem appropriate that the reasons for the entire programme should be discussed in a propagandistic fashion in the local press of those cities concerned ... Under these circumstances it will be possible to reduce any existing concerns and defuse rumours through this explanation, because the public can completely control the above-mentioned measures.[234]

Within a short space of time, Brandt had reinvented himself from being Hitler's plenipotentiary for the 'euthanasia' programme to becoming Hitler's representative in hospital and asylum matters. We should not forget that Brandt, at this point, had no official position. He was Hitler's escort physician, who had been charged with organizing the 'euthanasia' programme, but who had otherwise no government portfolio or power base. Knowing that a halt to the 'euthanasia' programme would reduce his sphere of influence, Brandt managed to persuade Hitler to give him a new assignment with potentially wide-ranging powers. It allowed him to encroach further into the administrative realm of the RMdI and transform his image from that of Hitler's 'euthanasia' doctor to that of a leading official in charge of civilian medicine. Shortly after Brandt had written to the Party Chancellery, the Hamburg senator Kurt Struve proposed that the programme for the creation of new hospitals should be called 'Aktion Brandt', 'in honour of Karl Brandt'.[235] Struve had read between the lines and was contributing to Brandt's advancement.

IX. PREPARING GENOCIDE

Whereas Brandt was reinventing himself in the autumn of 1941 as the man in charge of hospitals, the regime was moving further towards the systematic murder of the European Jews. The question is whether Brandt either knew of, or was connected with, any of the killing operations which required the use of T-4 personnel and expertise. We need to be cautious in the absence of conclusive evidence, but we also need to realize that Brandt, given that he was constantly in the vicinity of Hitler and Himmler, and in regular communication with the KdF, could hardly have remained ignorant of what was happening in the occupied eastern territories, since the staff of the KdF was in touch with the development of the killing machinery. On balance, however, Bouhler and Brack were more clearly involved in the implementation of genocidal policies. Brandt, it seems, kept his distance when the fateful decisions were made on the road to the Final Solution.

Despite the stopping of the 'euthanasia' programme, T-4's technical expertise and organizational skills turned out to be a great asset in the extermination of the Jews. The murder of large numbers of people caused enormous logistical, technical and also psychological problems which required the use of experts. Most of those involved in the organization of the Final Solution witnessed mass shootings. On 15 August 1941, Himmler attended a mass execution of Jews near Minsk. Later, on the same day, he visited the hospital at Nowinki, where he instructed officials to kill the patients through a method that was less gruesome than shooting, for example through gas.[236] Over the next two days, 16 and 17 August, Himmler lunched with Hitler and probably told him what he had seen.[237]

Since the first gassing of mental patients in January 1940, the men and women of T-4 had learned a great deal. Some of them were sent to Riga and Lublin to help in the construction and use of gas vans, and collaborated in the murder of Jews by Odilo Globocnik, organizer of the 'Aktion Reinhard'. In 1946, Brack recalled:

> In order to preserve the personnel which had been freed up through the halt [of the 'euthanasia' programme], and in order to make it possible to organise a renewed euthanasia programme after the war, Bouhler ordered me to transfer this personnel to Lublin, and place it at the disposal of Brigadeführer Globocnik.[238]

From early 1941, Brack was also secretly drafting plans on behalf of Himmler on how to sterilize large numbers of people while at the same time preserving their potential as slave labourers. On 28 July, Brack and von Hegener approached the military economic administration to enlist its support in carrying out a 'special assignment of the Führer' (*Sonderauftrag des Führers*), which apparently was unrelated to the 'euthanasia' programme.[239] From April 1941, T-4 physicians were sent to concentration camps, where they transferred prisoners who were classified as 'sick' or a 'burden' to one of the 'euthanasia' facilities.[240] Men such as Werner

Heyde, Paul Nitsche and Friedrich Mennecke began their work in Sachsenhausen and moved on to select 'asocials' in Buchenwald, Auschwitz and Mauthausen. Later, they expanded their selection criteria to so-called criminals, Jews, and political prisoners in Ravensbrück, Flossenburg and Neuengamme. This programme was code-named 'Aktion 14f13'; fifteen to twenty thousand prisoners eventually died in the gas chambers of Bernburg, Hartheim and Sonnenstein.

In the autumn of 1941 it became increasingly clear that the meaning of deportations to the East had gradually become code for mass murder. On 23 October, the emigration of Jews from the Reich was stopped. Two days later, on 25 October, Hitler told Himmler and Heydrich that the Nazi leadership could show no mercy to the Jews: 'Let no one say to me we cannot send them into the swamp! Who takes any interest in *our* people? It is good if your advance is preceded by fear that we will exterminate Jewry. The attempt to create a Jewish state will end in failure.'[241] On the same day, Erhard Wetzel from Rosenberg's Ministry for the Occupied Eastern Territories wrote to the Reich Commissioners for the Ostland, suggesting that T-4 personnel should be employed in the killing of Jews through gas.[242]

After the war, the registrar at the KdF, Fritz Bleich, told Allied interrogators that Brandt had been informed about the use of T-4 personnel for killing operations in the East.[243] Although his testimony is far from conclusive, and needs to be treated with caution, it may provide some insight into how T-4 personnel were used after August 1941. In the winter of 1941/42, Bleich was sent to Cholm in Russia with the Todt Organization to work as a medical orderly and return convoys of wounded German soldiers to the rear. There is corroborating evidence which suggests that T-4 personnel were in fact on active duty in the occupied territories, although it is unclear what exactly they were doing there. On 12 January 1942, Friedrich Mennecke, one of the 'euthanasia' doctors, wrote to his wife:

> Since the day before yesterday a large delegation from our organisation, headed by Herr[n] Brack, is on the battlefields of the East to help in saving our wounded in the ice and snow. They include doctors, clerks, nurses, and males nurses from Hadamar and Sonnenstein, a whole detachment of twenty to thirty persons. This is top secret.[244]

Mennecke's letter suggests that Brack had arrived with the 'T-4 delegation' on or around 10 January 1942. The question arises as to whether the transferral of wounded soldiers was the only assignment of the group, or whether Brack had been charged with a rather more sinister task. Two days prior to the arrival of Brack's delegation, Himmler had carried out an inspection tour which brought him into the vicinity of Belzec concentration camp around 7 or 8 January. On 12 December 1941, Himmler had met with Brack to discuss the possibility of killing the European Jews by means of poison gas, commenting that 'for reasons of camouflage one had to work as fast as possible'.[245] Later, on the same day, Himmler met with Hitler, Rosenberg and Bouhler. Bouhler was probably instructed to send personnel from the KdF to the Lublin area in order to help in the establishment of the extermination camp, Belzec. By the end of December 1941, Bouhler was complying with Himmler's wishes by sending T-4 personnel to the Belzec extermination camp.[246] In June 1942 Brack reported to Himmler:

> On the instruction of Reich-Leader Bouhler, I placed some of my men – some time ago now – at the disposal of Brigadeführer Globocnik to execute his special mission. On his renewed request, I now transferred additional personnel. On this occasion Brigadeführer Globocnik stated his opinion that the whole Jewish project should be completed as quickly as possible so that one would not get caught in the middle of it one day if some difficulties should make a stoppage of the action necessary. You yourself, Reichsführer, have already expressed your view, that work should progress quickly for reasons of camouflage alone ...[247]

Seen in this light, it is likely that the work which the staff of the T-4 programme carried out for the Todt Organization had become a cover to camouflage the rapidly evolving Final Solution. Bleich also stated that he was stationed in Minsk, where he witnessed the maltreatment of Jews in concentration camps.[248] This would confirm the presence of T-4 personnel at newly established killing centres, but it leaves open the question as to whether Bleich was involved in the killing programme. If he was, his testimony needs to be treated with caution since he might have wanted to shift responsibility for the programme to his superior, that is to Brandt.

As the man in charge of opening the post, Bleich recalled that Brandt had received a letter which came directly from Himmler.[249] Brandt was told temporarily to suspend the activities of the T-4 operation and 'concentrate on Jews and political offenders instead'.[250] Bleich did not remember the exact date of the letter, stating that it might have been in mid-1943 when Brandt had received it. Bleich also remembered that Brandt had received another letter from Himmler, shortly after the first. This time Himmler requested that Brandt select specific members from the T-4 operation for service in Russia. Brandt seems to have complied with Himmler's request, given that shortly afterwards about thirty people were sent on a mission to gas Poles and Jews at the Treblinka concentration camp. One of the key selection criteria was whether the men had experience of the 'euthanasia' programme.[251] Bleich called them *praktische Leute*, practical people, who were experienced in the routine of the killings. Those sent to the Generalgouvernement and Russia were certainly no desk murderers. They were former guards and police officers, men such as Franz Stangl and Christian Wirth, but also male nurses and stokers (*Brenner*) from the killing institutions and, of course, the doctors who had operated the gas valves.[252] These men were dressed in SS uniforms and sent to the various camps to carry out the killings.

Bleich later talked to the men in Berlin. Some told him about the ongoing murder of Jews and about the killing methods used.[253] Generally, the T-4 personnel were paid in kind with a free trip to Berlin as a reward for their 'achievements'. Bleich recalled that some of them showed off at the KdF with photographs of their missions; the pictures showed them armed with long, heavy, leather whips, torturing and maltreating their victims before gassing or shooting them. A collection of these images was put together in a photo album and given to the personnel director

Friedrich Haus, who used them to boast to a few selected friends at the KdF.[254] With so much information circulating in and around the KdF, it is hard to imagine that Brandt had no idea what was happening in the eastern territories. Since he and Bouhler had drafted the overall framework for an expansion of the programme, he must have known that Jews, Czechs and others would eventually be incorporated into the programme.

Brandt was adamant after the war that the 'euthanasia' programme had absolutely nothing to do with the Final Solution. On 16 December 1946, he recorded in his diary his frustration over one of Brack's incriminating statements:

> This man has testified and underwritten that the euthanasia problem is linked to the extermination of Jews in Poland and that this extermination was carried out with my approval. I still cannot find the right words.[255]

Since Brandt regarded the 'euthanasia' programme as a humanitarian measure to deliver patients from suffering, the two programmes were unconnected from his perspective. His post-war outrage about such apparent 'transgressions' of the 'euthanasia' operation may have been genuine, or perhaps a combination of self-denial, ignorance and an attempt to provide his family with a positive image of himself. In other words, the 'euthanasia' programme was not the prologue, but the first chapter of Nazi genocide. Brandt and Bouhler were the directors of the first act, although perhaps ignorant, at least in part, of its overall plot.

6

The General Commissioner

I. BECOMING HITLER'S GENERAL COMMISSIONER

In the winter of 1941, Hitler's *Blitzkrieg* offensives ground to a halt. The apparent military genius, the leader-strategist led by providence, had underestimated one of the most powerful forces of nature: the harsh Russian winter. Totally unprepared, German soldiers were dragging through devastated landscapes in icy snow, abandoning vehicles, guns and military equipment. Unprotected from the elements, these men lacked almost everything, from waterproof gear to socks, gloves and winter boots. The army high command had simply not anticipated such a scenario. Over-confidence from past victories, and the belief in the infallibility of the Führer, had made them inattentive and careless in military planning. A realistic exit strategy had not been prepared. The effect on the ground was catastrophic; army morale down to an unprecedented level.

Brandt's influence on Hitler, however, was at its zenith. Seeing the Führer almost daily at field headquarters, he was well informed of the overall military situation. Knowing that his professional expertise could make a difference, Brandt exploited the weaknesses in the organizational structure of the army. Upon his return from one of his journeys to the Eastern Front in the winter of 1941–42, the Reich Minister for Armaments and Munitions, Fritz Todt, told the assembled generals that the medical organization of the army was inadequate. Having inspected places such as Viasma, Smolensk and Minsk, Todt had concluded that there was a serious lack of medical supplies and services, which was killing thousands of men in the freezing conditions. Wounded soldiers were not transferred to the rear.[1] Inadequate facilities brought medical care almost to a standstill. Although Todt's description of the situation was met with disbelief at Führer headquarters, Brandt suggested that such conditions could and should be improved.

By January 1942, Brandt was dispatched for eight to ten days on another of his fact-finding missions, this time to the Eastern Front. Brandt recalled that he drove along the road from Smolensk to Moscow. Reports indicated that thousands of seriously injured soldiers were freezing to death without any form of medical care. 'The information [we had] was imprecise and in part entirely incredible,' Brandt remembered.[2] After hours of travel, Brandt arrived in the small village of Viasma. There, along the railway station platform, he witnessed the true horrors of war, a scene which Goya could have created in his etchings entitled 'The Disasters of War' (*Los desastres de la guerra*), which recorded the unimaginable horrors of the Napoleonic invasion at the beginning of the nineteenth century. It was an image

Brandt would never forget:

> Ten big freight trains stood there, closed freight trains, all packed with the wounded. The
> temperature was between 35 and 40 degrees celsius below zero. Some of the bandages and
> dressings of the wounded were actually frozen to the floor of the cars. The boilers [of the
> locomotives] had burst. A small number of medical personnel tried to help the wounded
> as much as they could, but it was, of course, practically impossible. In the ten trains, there
> were approximately 10,000 wounded. At the railway station, there were two medical
> officers with a minimum of medical supplies, and these two officers were hardly able to
> stand any longer. In the village the small buildings which had been converted to receive
> the injured were overcrowded, and the situation for the wounded was similar. Agencies
> of the army, with which I came into contact, attempted to blame these conditions on a
> failure of the medical command. The same attitude was taken by the operational staff
> of the army. The truth was that the medical services were to be blamed for the failure of
> the actual strategic command, especially for the inadequate supplies of winter clothing
> for our troops.[3]

Realizing that there was a serious problem in the organization of medical supplies
and in the management of medical care within the German army, Brandt travelled
further east in order to assess the seriousness of the situation:

> I continued to travel along the road towards Moscow until I came to the central
> bandaging stations for the troops [*Truppen- und Hauptverbandsplätze*], and there I
> learned from those in charge of supplies that there were also complete inefficiencies
> here. About 30 kilometres from Moscow, at a small station by the name of Moschaisk,
> freight trains had arrived with Soda water, all frozen and also completely unnecessary.
> The most urgently needed medical supplies were not on board the trains. Discussions
> with the responsible medical agencies in this area of the central sector showed that the
> army was no longer capable of supplying medical aid. About 10 kilometres away from
> the railway station in Viasma, which I mentioned before, was an airfield. At this airfield
> a medical officer had been stationed who had nothing to do, but who had orders not to
> leave the airfield.[4]

Returning to Hitler's headquarters, Brandt confirmed Todt's impression.[5] He told
Hitler and his advisers that the 'failure in providing for the care and transport of
the wounded was grounded in the main fact that the army alone – after this critical
situation had arisen – was not capable of controlling the situation, while at the same
time large contingents of materials etc. were handed out'.[6] The only feasible way
to alleviate the suffering of the solders, and salvage the situation, Brandt argued,
was to use the personnel, facilities and supplies of the German air force and the
navy. Given the existing military command structure, Hitler was forced to issue
an explicit Führer order to ensure that the different military services gave support
to the army. Within twenty-four hours, and with the support of Hitler's personal
courier squadron, Brandt managed to fly forty-five medical officers from the
medical headquarters of the air force and the navy to the region around Viasma.
Medical supplies were flown in from Königsberg. It was an attempt to stem the

rising tide of a military medical catastrophe. On 20 January 1942, the same day that the Nazi administration organized the systematic extermination of European Jewry at the Wannsee conference, Goebbels noted in his diary:

> Professor Brandt reports to me about his journey to the Eastern front to study the sanitary conditions. He tells me terrible things. Even our sanitary system has pretty much failed. This has been caused also by the lack of supply lines. The care for our wounded is extremely poor. However, the Führer has now taken decisive measures in order to tackle these evils ... Brandt has seen things at the Eastern front which hardly bear any description. One can imagine that therefore the mood among our wounded is particularly bad. We have to be concerned all the more with relieving their severe difficulties, at least at home. We now also have to expect many cases of frostbite and hypothermia. The transport infrastructure is incredibly poor. Sometimes, the wounded have to be transported in open freight cars, without blankets, without straw and exposed to a barbaric cold of [minus] thirty degrees. How much we could have done here, if we had only tackled this problem immediately in the most generous fashion! But I will now become involved and make sure that our medical generals [Sanitätsgenerälen] get a move on.[7]

To stem the acute crisis among the troops, and remedy the shortages of medical personnel, Brandt proposed sending some of the remaining personnel of the 'euthanasia' programme to the Eastern Front. He knew that these men and women were readily available after the 'euthanasia' programme had been halted in August 1941. From December 1941 to April 1942, a group of twenty to thirty doctors, nurses and administrative personnel from the T-4 organization took part in the 'Front Support Centre' (Fronthilfe Mitte), which was organized through the Todt Organization. Their activities were concentrated on the area around Minsk–Smolensk, where they helped to gain control of a catastrophic medical and logistical situation by transferring soldiers in buses supplied by T-4 to rear area hospitals.[8] There is also evidence, as we have seen, that they engaged in more sinister activities, and perhaps killed severely wounded German soldiers to 'deliver' them from suffering. One of the nurses later admitted that she had given German soldiers lethal injections because she believed they were 'mad'.[9] Victor Brack, the head of Central Office II in the KdF, who was leading the group, was also sent by Himmler and Bouhler on a 'top secret' mission, quite possibly without Brandt's direct knowledge or involvement. At the end of 1941, Brack was instructed to use the work they were carrying out as part of the Todt Organization as a cover for the extermination of the European Jews.[10] In the meantime, Goebbels discussed with Bouhler ways to propagate the 'euthanasia' programme to the general public, preparations which would come in handy if Hitler wanted to resume the killing operation. On 30 January 1942, the two men talked about the production of an educational film which 'justified the liquidation methods that were applied to the mentally ill'. Goebbels wanted the film to juxtapose only those cases which were 'absolutely convincing' with those where the patient was curable and should be cured, and not show any ambiguous cases, because the film 'might otherwise have not a convincing effect on the people'.[11]

The 'euthanasia' programme and issues of professional medical ethics also seem to have been on Brandt's mind at the time. Perhaps he was thinking along the same lines as Goebbels, particularly as to how one could better legitimize the 'euthanasia' programme to the Nazi rank and file and the population as a whole, if Hitler decided to resume the programme in the future. From August 1941, at the latest, Brandt was in correspondence with Paul Diepgen, director of the Institute for Medical History in Berlin, and Nazi medical theorist.[12] When Brandt told him about Hitler's interest in vegetarianism, Diepgen replied that the information had triggered in him a 'complete admiration for this unique man'.[13] Probably at the beginning of 1942, Brandt approached Diepgen to gain an overview of the existing literature on medical ethics. On 29 January, Diepgen sent Brandt an annotated bibliography containing about thirty book titles on medical ethics, which included references to John Gregory's *Lectures on the Duties and Character of a Physician* (*Vorlesungen über die Pflichten und Eigenschaften eines Arztes*) of 1778, which Diepgen judged 'reasonable and good in the context of the time'; Julius Leopold Pagel's *Medical Deontology* (*Medicinische Deontologie*) of 1897; Albert Moll's book *Medical Ethics* (*Ärztliche Ethik*) of 1902, judged to be 'extremely liberal'; and Isidor Fischer's *Professional Duties and Professional Questions* (*Standespflichten und Standesfragen*) of 1912. Diepgen told Brandt that Pagel, Moll and Fischer and others were 'Jewish authors', and that some of their work had been 'completely superseded'. Conversely, work by non-Jewish authors, which had been produced largely in the 1930s, was 'to be recommended' by Diepgen, for example Joachim Mrugowsky's book *The Medical Ethos* (*Das ärztliche Ethos*), published in 1939. After the war, Mrugowsky was sentenced to death at the Nuremberg Doctors' Trial for his criminal involvement in concentration camp experiments.[14] Diepgen also recommended Walter Klusemann's *The Medical Booklet* (*Das Ärztebüchlein*) of 1937, Georg Gruber's publication *On Medical Ethics* (*Von ärztlicher Ethik*) of 1937, Erwin Liek's book *The Doctor and his Mission* (*Der Arzt und seine Sendung*), published in several editions from 1926, and, last but not least, his own book *Medicine and the Medical Profession* (*Die Heilkunde und der ärztliche Beruf*) of 1938. After stressing that the contents of the books related to different intellectual periods in the development of the medical profession, Diepgen remarked: 'It is curious how many Jews are among the authors.'[15] On 4 February, Brandt acknowledged that he had received Diepgen's material.[16]

In the absence of other sources, it is difficult to know exactly what Brandt wanted from the information. A number of possibilities should, nonetheless, be taken into consideration. Recent scholarship has shown that Nazi medical philosophers and medical theorists, in collaboration with members of the SS, initiated and supported the establishment of a new Nazified medical ethics and medical history field, which aimed at propagating a new image and culture of the National Socialist doctor and the medical profession.[17] In 1942, Rudolf Ramm, in charge of overseeing the quality of German medical education, and one of the country's leading medical ethicists, declared: 'However, we have to assume, on the basis of our knowledge about the creative performance of the Aryan, which is always present, that *he* has been the sole founder of medical science ...'[18] On the basis of a variety of medical disciplines, including the medical ethics field, Nazi medical theorists attempted to demonstrate that the superiority of the Aryan race in the fields of medicine and medical science was historically determined. The medical ethics field, in other words, had developed into an integral part of Nazi ideology and theory to legitimize not only the discriminatory, anti-Semitic and racist policies of the regime, but also its geopolitical and genocidal policies. Whether Brandt was, or became, part of these discussions is not known, but there is evidence that he was not opposed to the ideas of eugenics and of evolutionary and racial biology. In February 1947, he told the court that one should not interpret the fact that he had declined to give lectures on racial questions to the Nazi Doctors' Association as evidence that he 'would not accept racial aspects as such and [was] not of the opinion that these [racial aspects], seen from a bigger perspective, could play an important role in the life of the peoples [*Völker*]'.[19] However, because of his belief in basic principles of respect and human decency, Brandt later objected to the general treatment of Jews, Gypsies and Poles by the Nazi regime.[20] In other words, issues of race and national community were central categories in Brandt's ethical world view, although he was less radical and ideologically driven than, for example, Conti, or certain members of the SS. For Brandt, the survival and political primacy of the body politic (*Volkskörper*) not only determined the rules and laws of society, but became the sole determining factor in shaping the formation of ethical standards. According to Brandt, the national community 'alone has the right to determine morality'.[21] Seen in the context of the Second World War, which increasingly endangered the very existence of the German people, Brandt's interest in medical ethics seems not only plausible, but necessary under a regime which had decided, in January 1942, on the systematic extermination of European Jewry.[22] Brandt, unlike other Nazi officials, not only showed a certain awareness of the ethical aspect of his actions, even if the ethic to which he subscribed was inverted, but he was also extremely concerned that his conscience as a doctor should remain clear.[23]

Another possibility is that Brandt's interest in the literature of medical ethics was related to the ongoing power struggle at Hitler's court. Brandt happened to express his interest in medical ethics at a moment in his career when his position within the Nazi regime, and within the Nazi medical hierarchy in particular, was relatively uncertain. Brand could, after all, not legitimize his position through his role within the party or the state, but only because of his access to Hitler. After the 'euthanasia' programme had been stopped in August 1941, Brandt was essentially without a major assignment, apart from organizing the evacuation of hospitals vulnerable to air raids, in collaboration with the Todt Organization. Throughout spring 1942, he engaged in discussions with Hitler and other officials, including Conti, about how to reform the military and civilian health system in a comprehensive fashion, most likely with a view to securing another, more official assignment from Hitler. The enormous ethical and moral problems which the 'euthanasia' programme had raised, coupled with severe criticism from the Nazi grass roots of the killing of the handicapped, and the potential prospect of a responsible position within the health system, which Hitler might have promised to Brandt, might explain why Brandt planned to read up on the ethics and history of the medical profession. In short, he might have wanted to prepare himself for the intellectual and professional conflicts to come. As someone who was significantly more knowledgeable and intellectually more capable than, for example, Conti, this would have fitted his personality.

Finally, there is the possibility that Brandt might have toyed with the idea of influencing, or taking responsibility for, the medical education system and expert literature. The Russian campaign in the winter of 1941/42 had not only led to an enormous number of casualties, but highlighted a serious shortage of trained medical personnel in the civilian and military sector. Brandt later recalled that of 85,000 physicians practising before the war, the German army had drafted about 40,000 into service by 1942.[24] Other figures suggest that the civilian population had access to approximately 40% fewer medical personnel than in the pre-war years.[25] Some Nazi officials, taking a distinctly pragmatic approach, accused Conti, whose responsibilities extended to the regulations governing the medical studies and examinations of doctors, nurses, dentists, pharmacists and midwives, of an 'obsession with ideological purity', and proposed that Jewish, female and foreign doctors should be permitted to serve in the German health and sanitation system.[26] Brandt undoubtedly wanted to ensure that medical education at German universities should be continued throughout the war, and to a good standard. After the war, he recalled that he had wanted to put university professors and their assistants in positions where they could deliver proper teaching again: 'One important task was the question of our medical literature more generally – to ensure a good supply of books and journals so that we could at least somehow supply the students with textbooks'.[27] In 1943, a year after Brandt had been receiving guidance from Diepgen on medical ethics literature, leading Nazi officials, including Conti, Goebbels, Speer and Ley, decided to close all German medical schools.[28] Only after Brandt, as he remembered, 'went to each one personally and pleaded with them to reconsider their action', which he considered to be 'a national catastrophe', was it agreed that certain years (*Jahrgänge*) would be permitted to continue and complete their studies. According to Brandt, it had been a 'hollow victory' because it had affected his relationship with Conti, who apparently told him afterwards that he, Brandt, 'was more interested in medicine than in victory'.[29] Brandt's recollections of his struggles to protect German medical education may well have been accurate, but what affected his relationship with Conti and others, more than anything else, was his attempt to gain an official government position which would ultimately place him in charge of the German health system.

In order to regain control over the administrative chaos in the medical sector, Brandt proposed to Hitler that a 'Medical Chief for the Army' should 'somehow [be] put into the picture', someone who would have jurisdiction in all sections of the military: the army, the navy and the air force. The position of Chief of Army Medical Services (*Chef des Wehrmachts-Sanitätswesens*) was created.[30] Colonel

General Siegfried Handloser became the first (and last) to hold this rank. Apart from managing a crisis situation, Brandt's rise to power benefited from the sudden and unexpected death of Todt. When, on the wintry morning of 8 February 1942, Todt's plane came crashing down in flames near Hitler's headquarters at Rastenburg, East Prussia, Brandt happened to be one of the first to know about the tragic accident.[31]

Brandt recalled that Todt had had a major argument with Hitler the day before the accident and, as a result, Todt had been excluded from attending the daily situation conference. On the same evening, Brandt had been sitting and talking with Todt, who appeared depressed for no obvious reason. Only later did Brandt discover that Todt had found himself completely at odds with Hitler. To add insult to injury, Todt had not been invited to join Hitler in his bunker for supper, as he usually was. Shortly after midnight, Todt went to bed. Two hours later, after Hitler had gone to sleep, Brandt accidentally entered Todt's room and found him awake and depressed. A few hours later, at eight in the morning, Brandt received a telephone call from the airport in Rastenburg, telling him that Todt had died in a plane crash. None of the passengers had survived. Brandt was asked to come immediately to the airport in order to identify Todt's body.[32] Later in the day, Brandt raised his hand in a Nazi salute in a mark of respect while Todt's body was transferred to his burial place.[33] Given that Todt had told Hitler for months that the war against Russia could not be won, rumours were spreading far and wide that the head of the the Todt Organization might have been assassinated, or have killed himself. Todt's relationship with Hitler had been problematic since at least 1941. Some suggested that Todt might have realized that his criticism of Hitler's war had gone too far, and that the only way out was to take his own life.

Realizing the significance of Todt's death, Brandt telephoned Speer minutes after the plane crash. Speer had arrived at Führer headquarters the previous evening from Dnepropetrovsk in southern Russia, and was scheduled to take the same plane to return to Berlin. For unknown reasons, he had cancelled the trip, perhaps because he was too tired. Three hours later, Speer was appointed Minister of Armaments as Todt's successor. The day was not only of utmost significance in the life of Speer, but for Brandt as well in establishing his place as a major political player in the Nazi medical hierarchy. It marked a sea-change in Hitler's selection of ministers. At a time when the military situation looked increasingly bleak, Hitler sometimes did not promote people whose party political affiliations and ideological conformity showed an impeccable record, but professionals like Speer and Brandt, who possessed the managerial abilities to run a complex, modern war machinery.

Brandt now had one of the most powerful men of the Reich as his ally. Most importantly, both of them had ready access to Hitler. With Speer's support, Brandt was able to convince Hitler that there was an urgent need to reform the country's health services during the war. Brandt's rise to power cannot be viewed as separate from the enormous and rapid expansion of Speer's empire after 1942. To do so would be to fail to acknowledge the underlying dynamics at the highest levels of the government. The relationship between Brandt and Speer at Hitler's court was mutually beneficial. The more power one of them had, the more secure the position of the other became, and the more likely the accumulation of further influence for each of them and their allies became. Brandt also showed great flexibility in forging new alliances with key members of Hitler's regime, for example with Goebbels, although their relationship was not always without tensions. Speer, Brandt and Albert Saur, Speer's deputy, managed to establish a powerful triumvirate around Hitler. Bormann called the three men 'an efficient mutual admiration society, each of them helps to push the other up the ladder by his praise'.[34] According to Bormann and others, Brandt was acting as 'Speer's agent' who had such burning ambition that it 'almost tore him in two'.[35] 'Just imagine how loathsome I find Brandt,' he told his wife.[36]

Despite an increasing number of powerful enemies, Brandt gained additional confidence and standing with Hitler after he had yet again justified his reputation as a troubleshooter at the beginning of 1942. The reward followed six months later. On 28 July 1942, Hitler issued the first of three published decrees which gave Brandt extensive powers over the German health care system.[37] The decree was an attempt to reorganize the leadership structure and the organization of the German health and welfare system, within both the military and the civilian sector, and to bring order into the chaos of overlapping interests and responsibilities. Brandt had proposed the Führer decree to Hitler after Conti had reported increasing problems on the home front, particularly with regard to the different demands by the German Labour Front, the civilian sector and the military. As a former paediatrician, Conti's more traditional, racial-policy-related understanding of population issues and of health and welfare conflicted with Ley's ambitious concept of introducing so-called 'plant physicians' (*Betriebsärzte*) in all factories, to ensure the maximum use of the existing workforce for the German war industry. Although Conti resisted the idea of viewing the health of the body politic as nothing but 'an appendage of the workforce', Ley was gradually winning the argument in the context of an expanded armaments industry that was geared to supplying the means for geopolitical expansion.[38] One way of putting an end to Ley's power ambitions was a Führer decision.

Exploiting the tension at the top of the medical hierarchy, Brandt told Conti in the spring of 1942, and in strict confidence, that he had managed to persuade Hitler to establish a Chief of Army Medical Services, and that he was intending to ask Hitler to create the post of Chief of Civilian Medical Services for Conti. He himself would ask for an assignment which would allow him to coordinate the demands between the 'two major columns' and perform a range of special tasks.[39] Conti, not realizing what Brandt was up to, largely agreed to his proposal but warned that the new post could not become a 'leading command post' (*Befehlsspitzenstellung*), because it would conflict with his own position as the Reich Health Leader.[40] Conti hoped that by collaborating with Brandt he would gain direct access to Hitler. Rather than organizing a meeting with Hitler, Brandt used the existing shortcomings in the health system to press for greater powers for himself.[41] The decree originated without any meaningful input from the legal experts in the Reich

Chancellery, which is why it was worded in a way which gave Brandt extensive but largely ambiguous and imprecise powers. A leading administrative official later remarked that the first and subsequent decrees were 'administratively impossible. They have not been made by an expert.'[42]

Instead of resolving an already complicated situation, the decree made matters worse in certain areas. The decree divided the medical field into three linked parts: the medical services of the armed forces, the civilian health care system, and a new position of General Commissioner of the Führer for Health and Sanitation (*Generalkommissar des Führers für das Sanitäts- und Gesundheitswesen*), whose official responsibility was to coordinate the demands between the military and civilian sectors. In paragraph 1, Hitler extended the authority of General Handloser, the Chief of Army Medical Services, by putting him in charge of the medical services of the armed forces as whole, effectively subordinating the medical services of the air force and navy under his command:

> 1. For the Wehrmacht I commission the Medical Inspector of the Army, in addition to his present duties, with the coordination of all tasks common to the Medical Services of the Wehrmacht, the Waffen-SS and the organisations and units subordinate or attached to the Wehrmacht, as Chief of the Medical Service of the Wehrmacht … For the purpose of coordinated treatment of these problems a medical officer of the navy and a medical officer of the Luftwaffe [air force] will be assigned to work under him, the latter in the capacity of Chief of Staff. Fundamental problems pertaining to the medical service of the Waffen-SS will be worked out in agreement with the Medical Inspectorate of the Waffen-SS.[43]

The paragraph reflected the overlap and tensions which existed between the different administrative, military and party political empires, particularly between Göring's Luftwaffe and Himmler's SS. These two men, in particular, had amassed such extensive powers that they sought to ensure that the highest official of their organization was not necessarily subordinate to the Chief of Army Medical Services. The decree was in many ways ambiguous and left enormous scope for potential conflict over areas of responsibility. Brandt later recalled that it had taken months 'until most of the difficulties of jurisdiction were resolved, and this decree of 28 July 1942 was issued'.[44] In paragraph 2, Hitler reiterated the fact that Conti was in charge of the civilian health care system:

> 2. In the field of civilian health administration the State Secretary in the Ministry of the Interior and Reich Chief for Public Health, Dr Conti, is responsible for coordinated measures. For this purpose he has at his disposal the competent departments of the highest Reich authorities and their subordinate offices.[45]

Finally, in paragraphs 3 and 4, Hitler appointed Brandt as his plenipotentiary for Health and Medical Services, and placed him in charge of coordinating the demands of the military and the civilian sector:

3. I empower Prof. Dr Karl Brandt, subordinate only to me personally and receiving his instructions directly from me, to carry out special tasks and negotiations to readjust the requirements for doctors, hospitals, medical supplies etc. between the military and the civilian sectors of the Health and Medical Services.

4. My plenipotentiary for Health and Medical Services is to be kept informed about the fundamental events in the Medical Service of the Wehrmacht and in the Civilian Health service. He is authorised to intervene in a responsible manner.[46]

One month later, on 20 August 1942, Hitler appointed Brandt as General Commissioner of the Führer for Health and Sanitation.[47] Given that Brandt had spent most of July and August at Hitler's new, but damp and mosquito-infested, field headquarters, called *Werwolf*, near Vinnitsa in the Ukraine, he might have found opportunity to influence Hitler.[48] Brandt's appointment as General Commissioner substantially increased his authority. He now had an official government position.[49] About three years later, on 20 April 1945, on Hitler's birthday, Brandt's office was dissolved.[50] It was during those three years that Brandt established his place in the Nazi medical hierarchy, and as a force potential enemies had to reckon with in the struggle to control German medicine and medical science. Brandt was poised to become Hitler's medical supremo. Asked in 1947 whether he had been ambitious, Brandt gave the impression that this meteoric rise to power had been an organic development which had stood outside his own control:

> The situation turned out as it did, really, because of the way things were in the relatively small Führer headquarters ... Life was always busy and things led one to another, and from one responsibility to the next. It seemed there was no stopping the train of events.[51]

The appointment of the General Commissioner was meant to overcome existing deficiencies in coordinating the various civil and military agencies, especially their demand for scarce resources and trained personnel. The office was not established to undermine or to abolish the office of the Reich Health Leader. Hitler's decree explicitly stated that Conti remained 'responsible for coordinated measures'. But with the creation of a parallel office with supervisory functions over areas of the health system, frictions and competition were inevitable from the outset. In the social-Darwinistic understanding of Hitler's polycratic regime, the more qualified and competent of these agencies would ultimately succeed. But Hitler's commissioners were more than just another instrument of power to overcome administrative shortcomings: they allowed him to be flexible in channelling vast resources to areas of high priority without actually concerning himself with existing areas of bureaucratic responsibility. His will thereby could be implemented at almost any time and at almost any place under German control, without relying on cumbersome government machinery.

Brandt, who, as Morell had remarked, wanted to be everyone's friend, now found himself faced with powerful opponents. Reactions to Brandt's appointment among Hitler's acolytes ranged from silent approval to open hostility. Conti learned about the fundamental change in medical policy from reading the *Völkischer Beobachter*; others recalled that the news had struck them 'like lightning from heaven'.[52] The journal *Der Angriff* proclaimed that the entire 'health system [was to be] reorganised'.[53] It also transpired that, during the negotiations, Brandt had requested the title of Reich Commissioner, which would have made him superior to Conti.[54] Shortly after the signing of the decree, at the end of 1942, Conti told Brandt that 'if the Führer wished to change the leadership in the health system, his person would not be a hindrance', whereupon Brandt replied that he should never again say anything like that. For the moment, Brandt kept his cards close to his chest. He knew that the army, some of the civil government departments and the Nazi Party were none of them particularly happy about his potential intrusion into their areas of competence.

The Reich Chancellery had not been consulted prior to the issuing of the decree, as they generally were. Hitler's decree created far-reaching powers for Brandt, without actually defining his exact areas of responsibility. The decree was likewise all-encompassing and ambiguous. Most significantly, it did not define the exact power relations between Brandt and Conti. Lammers' attempt to interpret and clarify 'Hitler's will' not only turned out to be rather feeble, but it revealed the arbitrary nature of Hitler's ambivalent decision-making. According to Lammers, Conti was now subordinate to Bormann within the party, to Frick as State Secretary of the RMdI, and to Brandt with regard to the 'state in some sense'.[55] Aware that his position was potentially under threat, and as a way of counter-balancing Handloser's position as Chief of Army Medical Services, Conti wanted to be promoted to Chief of Civilian Medical Services, with his own budget and personnel. Not realizing that Brandt was far too ambitious to be content with his role as coordinator of the agencies of the state and the military, and unaware of the difficulties in containing Brandt's political influence, Conti's allies were under the illusion that the office of the Reich Health Leader could become a superior Reich department, with direct access to the Führer. On 11 September, after having talked with Conti about the current medical situation, Goebbels noted in his diary: 'The recent decree of the Führer, which gives Professor Brandt great powers, has also, on the other hand, made Conti responsible for the entire civilian health system.'[56] Conti's dual positions as Reich Health Leader and State Secretary in the RMdI allowed him to intervene in medical matters that related to both the Nazi Party and the state, but it also made him suspect to the traditional elite. His exaggerated and largely unrealistic demands in the aftermath of the first Führer decree antagonized leading officials in the Reich and Party Chancelleries, and allowed Brandt to establish himself.

II. BRANDT'S OFFICE

The office of the General Commissioner was everything but a government ministry. It was a combination of various small offices which were staffed with a number of experts who dealt with the various assignments which Brandt had accumulated over time. Its annual budget was modest, at best resembling that of a small university institute. With a monthly budget of 10,000 Reichsmark in 1943, about 20,000 Reichsmark in 1944, and approximately 30,000 Reichsmark at the end of the war, Brandt could hardly claim that he was running an impressive administrative machinery. Brandt and his staff were first paid from Hitler's household budget. From September 1944, his office was financed from the budget of the Reich Chancellery.[57] Brandt later claimed that the role of his office was greatly overrated, and that it had developed as a reaction to certain structural deficiencies:

> I have the impression that people think with regard to my agency that a kind of ministerial institution was created in one single act. In reality one assignment followed another as a result of the continuous situation of the war. It was not a development, which occurred organically according to a clear pattern, like in peacetime, but there were deficiencies somewhere, deficiency symptoms …[58]

What Brandt did not say, however, was that the shape and size of an organization said little about its efficiency and political power in the Third Reich. Brandt's office was modelled on Speer's office of the Inspector General of Construction as well as on Todt's agency of the Inspector General of Roads, two of the most efficient and powerful administrative structures that the Nazi regime had established. Hitler had given Brandt the responsibility to coordinate, rather than to administer, a specific area of government policy, not unlike Speer and Todt. Following their example, Brandt superimposed his new agency on an already existing bureaucratic structure.[59] This allowed him to intervene in a flexible and expeditious fashion, and direct existing personnel and resources to priority areas in a constantly changing war situation.[60] Hitler favoured this form of organization, which had proved its effectiveness in the period after the dictator had assumed power.[61]

Soon after the issuing of the decree, Brandt began interfering in the day-to-day running of the health system. He originally concentrated his activities on Germany's pharmaceutical production, which had previously been in the domain of the Reich Finance Ministry. In addition to pharmaceuticals, he managed to take control of first-aid supplies to expand his realm of influence over German medical supplies generally. Brandt initially selected his areas of activity according to their political and strategic importance for a stable home front, and ignored the need for coordination and consultation with other agencies.[62] Since the winter of 1941/42, surveillance reports by the Security Services had indicated that the general population was increasingly complaining about a noticeable shortage of general drugs. In the second half of 1942, a chronic lack of medical supplies and pharmaceuticals led to what officials described as an 'extremely tense supply situation'.[63] Painkillers, vitamin pills and dressings were in particularly high demand. To stem the crisis, Brandt established a 'Control Office for the Supply of Pharmaceuticals' as part of his Department for Medical Planning and Finance. Civilian pharmacies, hospitals and the military were required to submit monthly reports which detailed the use of specific drugs during the last six months, the quantity which had previously been distributed and the quantity that was requested.[64] Shortages in vital medical technology, for example the supply of X-ray machines, further exacerbated the sense that the authorities were unable to coordinate supply and demand. In the autumn of 1942, an official from the RMdI warned that the lack of medical supplies could have a negative impact on the home front.[65] Given that the supply situation improved at the end of 1942, it is perhaps not unreasonable to assume that Brandt's management of pharmaceuticals stabilized the situation for some time. At first, he intervened in an informal and inconspicuous fashion to avoid any unnecessary frictions with Conti. Effusive Christmas greetings to Conti became as much part of Brandt's repertoire for concealing his real ambitions as his increasing tendency to distort information, or deny knowledge, in the ever more frequent negotiations with leading government officials.[66] In the period up until the autumn of 1943, when his trespassing into other areas of government was retrospectively sanctioned by Hitler, Brandt became a key political player in the regime.

Brandt first contacted the various Reich Offices which functioned as subsidiary departments of the Reich Finance Ministry, for example the Reich Office for Precision Engineering and Optics or the Reich Office for Textile Economy. A total of about thirty-five different production offices had to be managed according to military and civilian demands.[67] In October 1942, for example, he met with representatives of the Business Group for Precision Engineering and Optics to find out about the lack of supplies of medical instruments in the military and civilian sector. At the end of October or the beginning of November 1942, Brandt undertook, together with Schaub, a three-week inspection tour of Stalingrad and the Caucasus region to assess the organization of medical supplies on the Eastern Front. What they discovered was chaos and mismanagement on a monumental scale. One of Goebbels' diary fragments suggests that Hitler, upon hearing Brandt and Schaub's report, decided to give Brandt additional powers which allowed him to intervene in the work of leading emergency medical officials. On 7 November, Goebbels noted:

> Schaub has been ... and has partly found rather unfavourable conditions there. In particular, the emergency medical services are very poor. There is very little available in the field hospitals. In the Caucasus conditions are truly dismal. The Führer has, on the basis of the report by Schaub and Brandt, who accompanied him, given Brandt general authority ... against the big shots in the emergency medical services.[68]

Schaub later recalled that he had admired Brandt's resilience and practical approach; despite constant sleep deprivation and the tiring flights they undertook to the Eastern Front, Brandt would generally start operating in one of the front line military hospitals shortly after landing. He described Brandt as a 'practical man of action' (*praktisch zugreifender Mensch*), rather than a manager who organized things from his desk.[69] After returning from Russia, Brandt gave a vivid description of the suffering among the encircled German troops at Stalingrad to a private dinner party at Breker's house.[70] Whether he also talked about some of the atrocities which the SS and the Sixth Army had been committing on the civilian population in reprisals for alleged attacks by partisans is not known.[71] One of Breker's guests that evening was Speer. After a heated discussion about the conduct of the war, Breker is said to have told Speer: 'Either you [Speer and the Nazi government] know how to escape from this terrible catastrophe, and gain control of the situation – or your [Speer's and the government's] actions are criminal.'[72] Although Brandt and Speer knew that the fall of Stalingrad might well be a decisive turning point in the campaign against Russia, they were as yet unwilling to face up to the possibility that Germany might lose the war altogether.

Brandt realized, as Speer had, that some shortcomings had to be overcome as a matter of urgency: first, the production process of medical supplies had to be protected from the arbitrary drafting of experts by the army and armaments industry; second, the requisitioning system of the army had to be reformed to prevent the stockpiling of first-aid supplies by individual army units. Brandt then entered into lengthy negotiations with the Supreme Command of the Army (*Oberkommando der Wehrmacht*, OKW), the Chief of Army Medical Services, the Ministry for Armaments and War Production, the Plenipotentiary of the Work Force, and other leading government officials. Although the various administrative and military organizations eventually met the demands of the economy, Brandt faced increasing opposition from Conti, who frequently attempted to keep Brandt's agency uninformed because he felt that Brandt was trespassing into his area of responsibility.[73] It was this tension between Brandt and Conti which a year later developed into a full-blown crisis.

Flexible, but determined in his approach, Brandt pursued his new assignment with relentless vigour and managerial style. German winter uniforms had to be produced, the production of pharmaceuticals needed to be coordinated, the number of sick workers in essential war production had to be reduced, additional hospitals needed to be built, and asylum beds had to be freed from 'unnecessary use' by the mentally ill. Here was a new field of frenzied activity for Brandt. On 7 September 1942, little more than two weeks after he had been appointed General Commissioner, Brandt informed Göring's office that Conti was representing the RMdI in the Presidential Council, and that he, Brandt, was representing German medicine and the management of German health (*Gesundheitsführung*) in the same government body.[74] The battle lines between Brandt and Conti were drawn from the moment Brandt had taken office.

Brandt's office eventually had about twelve members of staff, mainly working in the surgical clinic in Berlin-Ziegelstraße. He first established the Department for Medical Planning and Finance, headed by the ophthalmologist and *Oberstabsarzt* Alfred Fikentscher, then later the Department for Medical Research and Science, led by his former boss at the surgical clinic in Berlin, Paul Rostock.[75] Brandt first established the administrative structure, and later assigned Rostock and some of his assistants to supervise certain areas of medical science and research. Another member of staff was the lawyer Friedrich Geist, who conferred with the various Reich institutions about matters relating to textiles, mechanical and optical affairs or X-ray equipment.[76] Hellmuth Lüpke was in charge of pharmacy and chemistry.[77] These men had their offices in the surgical clinic in the Ziegelstraße.

For lack of space, the remaining administrative staff were given offices in

Bouhler's KdF, the headquarters of the 'euthanasia' programme. They consisted of Ludwig Weber, Brandt's personal secretary; Jutta Rach, his first secretary; Ms Beiersdorf, one of the general secretaries; and Fritz Bleich, the registrar.[78] Bleich and some of the other members of staff, therefore, came into contact with the day-to-day running of the 'euthanasia' operation, although this had not been intended. Their testimony after the war was crucial in determining the extent to which Brandt had actually been involved in the running of the killing operation, and to what extent he knew or could have known about the mass murders. While Brandt's post was officially delivered to the KdF, the managers of the 'Aktion T-4' operated through a Berlin post box number. Aside from frequent contacts at the highest levels, for example with Bouhler, Heyde or Nitsche, Brandt kept a low profile with regard to direct contact with the staff of the 'euthanasia' programme. There was generally no contact between T-4 staff and Brandt's staff at the surgical clinic, or with his staff at the KdF.[79] There was also not much contact between the staff of Bouhler's office and that of Brandt's KdF office. During office hours, no one at Brandt's KdF office would ever talk about the 'euthanasia' programme. The staff of Bouhler's office had also been sworn to total secrecy.[80] In general, Brandt's office received no correspondence, and did not deal with files which had anything to do with the 'euthanasia' programme, except on a few occasions, as Bleich later recalled.[81]

Despite all the precautions, Brandt's staff knew, to varying degrees, that the 'euthanasia' programme was being carried out. Born in 1909 in Berlin, Bleich had studied sculpture at the art academy in Berlin. Until 1939, he frequently changed jobs, working at times as a decorator, at others as a courier or a nurse in hospitals for children and mothers. Drafted into the army in 1941, he was sent to the Eastern Front to support the 'Campaign for Frozen Soldiers', where he was briefly placed under the supervision of Brandt. With the situation worsening in the East, he was drafted to transport wounded soldiers from the front, but became infected with typhus in May 1942. After recovering from the disease, Bleich eventually began working as Brandt's personal registrar in October 1942. He was one of Brandt's first members of staff.[82] Officially no one in the department was supposed to know anything about the 'euthanasia' programme, but information occasionally leaked out. Whenever someone was ill, or T-4 was short of manpower, Bleich was asked to assist the *Stiftung*, as it was called, in organizing their administration, 'although Professor Brandt did not like to see it'.[83] Knowing that he was operating on the fringes of legality and professional medical conduct, Brandt wanted to compartmentalize his different areas of responsibility. These strict dividing lines were also necessary to protect Hitler from being implicated in the killing operation. They allowed Hitler to stay above criticism and perpetuated the Führer myth.

Staff members often talked about their daily routine, or chatted in the evening over a glass of *Berliner Weiße*. Bleich recalled that he often helped his 'comrade with the post because of our friendly relationship; we always travelled home together'.[84] His colleague, Erich, was in charge of the post in the KdF. They regularly exchanged information and sometimes Erich would show his friend some of the 'top secret' correspondence of the killing operation. Bleich also saw photographs which T-4 physicians handed around in the office after they had returned from the killing fields in the occupied eastern territories. The photographs showed T-4 staff with leather whips in their hands, posing as conquerors of the Greater German Reich.

Jutta Rach, Brandt's secretary and a relative of Brandt, always opened the post before handing it to Bleich. She also knew about the degree to which Hitler had entrusted the 'euthanasia' programme to Brandt and Bouhler. Rach may have seen one of the few copies of the decree, but she was adamant that none of the children discussed in the letters were killed:

> Particular requests [for me] occurred only rarely, and then only in the form of informa-tion for doctors and parents about the birth of physically and mentally handicapped children useless for life, for whom euthanasia was requested. Such requests were dealt with only insofar as specific doctors were asked to comment on the individual case or gain financial means for the preservation of the life of the child. Permission to carry out the requested euthanasia was never given.[85]

Rach's statement may have reflected her limited knowledge of the programme. One of the key principles employed in the Nazi 'euthanasia' programme was the need-to-know principle: each person had access only to the information he or she needed in order to carry out the assigned task. However, given that she was related to Brandt's family, Rach's post-war testimony was probably designed to defend Brandt in the Nuremberg Doctors' Trial.[86] In general, it was difficult to assess what was going on. The staff saw Brandt constantly coming and going, often into Bouhler's office. Their offices were on the same floor. Staff later recalled seeing Brandt three to four times a week in Bouhler's office and assumed that they were talking about Brandt's work as General Commissioner: 'We had, for example, the whole area of People's Gas Masks (*Volksgasmasken*) and transferrals of industries', Bleich remembered.[87] What they did not know was that Brack, the chief organizer of the 'euthanasia' programme, generally received his orders from Bouhler after a meeting between the two plenipotentiaries.[88]

Brandt also had a number of rooms for public-relations purposes, where he would receive leading Nazi officials. All important conferences were held in the KdF and not in the surgical clinic. Every week, sometimes every fortnight, Brandt met for lunch with Heyde and Nitsche, the two principal doctors in charge of the medical side of the 'euthanasia' programme. Bleich recalled: 'Nitsche and Heyde had their office in the Tiergartenstraße, and as directors [of the *Stiftung*] they certainly came over to the KdF. And here I have seen them of course almost on a daily basis.'[89] Although Brandt later claimed that his principal office was at the surgical clinic, which *de jure* was true, Brandt was de facto running his office from the KdF before he and his staff moved to Beelitz, just outside Berlin. The Chancellery of the Führer and the adjacent government buildings certainly matched his status and suited his taste for architectural ostentation.[90]

III. THE SECOND FÜHRER DECREE

Brandt's interventions in major areas of policy did not go unnoticed. In general, the Reich and Party Chancelleries attempted to restrict Brandt's areas of competence as much as possible, and strengthen the role of the Reich Health Leader as the official in charge of the civilian health system. Conti's lack of statesmanship and strategic thinking, however, prevented him from establishing effective alliances which might have contained Brandt's influence. Prohibiting the staff of the RMdI from talking to Brandt, for example, proved counter-productive.[91] With ready access to the Führer, Brandt was able to legitimize his decisions by invoking direct 'orders from Hitler'. This gave his policies a high degree of government sanctioning, but it also exposed him to the combined jealousies of those at the heart of Hitler's government. Some officials believed that tensions between Conti and Brandt had been mounting since 1941.[92] In the summer of 1943, the conflict between the two men finally came to a head.

The more it became impossible to ignore the disastrous effects of the war on all areas of German society and the economy, the more radical the approach of Brandt and others became to finding solutions for an ever greater number of urgent organizational and logistical problems. For some members of Hitler's court the approach to a given problem became a matter of survival in an increasingly hostile environment. Since Stalingrad, any long-term planning was made almost impossible through Hitler's interference in minute military decisions, compounded by the belief in the infallibility of the Führer. To fail to improve matters in one's area of responsibility could result in the instant withdrawal of Hitler's trust, and access to him, and thus in an immediate loss of power. While Germany was in the process of defeat, many sought to introduce the most radical of policies to secure their positions. The power struggle between Conti and Brandt ended disastrously for Conti, but it lifted Brandt to new heights.

Conti had assumed his position after Wagner's unexpected death in 1939.[93] Regarded by many as unimposing, Conti was absolutely loyal to Hitler and devoted to Nazi racial ideology. In no meaningful sense was he less radical and thirsty for power than his predecessor. In a documentary film from about 1942, discovered by the author in 1995 in Goebbels' 'archive of personalities',[94] Conti expresses a crude racial ideology:

> We have identified a decreasing birth-rate, negative selection and race-mixing as the major dangers which can lead a people into the abyss; but this does not describe in full the dangerous influences affecting a civilised people. We must also ask whether our modern life style, which all civilised peoples have, in fact has characteristics which lead to gradual decay and degeneration … The destiny of a people is never at rest, it must either rise or fall; a people must be either hammer or anvil – the value of their blood, the value of their race, is decisive. The German people have proven their value. They have to become the core of a Great German Reich; then we will succeed in proving that although the individual human being is mortal and his or her life ends with death, a

people can renew itself and become more beautiful and stronger from generation to generation, an eternal life.[95]

Conti's ideas of racial superiority did not cut much ice with the German public at a time when German cities were being bombed, yet they seem to have appealed to the Nazi elite in the mid-1930s, when Hitler scored one foreign policy success after another. To call Brandt and Conti enemies would be an understatement. Behind the curtain of Berghof pleasantry and ideological conformity, both men engaged in the art of intrigue. Brandt's main advantage was his presence at Führer headquarters. According to Hitler's chauffeur, Brandt was there at least once a week.[96] All major officials of the regime knew how important it was how often one had access to Hitler. After the outbreak of war, Brandt was among the few with regular access to Hitler.[97] While Hitler gradually withdrew from public sight, and into isolation, Brandt's exclusive access to the dictator became an important instrument in the ongoing power battles. He was thus in a position to distort and manipulate Hitler's perception of events. Speer recalled that it was relatively easy to manipulate Hitler, who it seems had little sense of the ongoing court intrigues, or decided to ignore them.[98]

On 30 November 1942, for instance, Hitler issued a decree which charged Brandt with the reorganization and unification of the medical transport system.[99] This raised grave concerns among top government officials, who alleged that Brandt was using his position for his own benefit. Lammers later told Conti that he had been carrying the decree around for weeks 'without actually knowing what one actually should do with such a Führer decree'.[100] In the end, he had decided to tell Hitler that 'one couldn't do things like that' (*so ginge es ja nun doch nicht*), and that he had repeatedly asked him not to sign such important matters without his involvement. Hitler promised to keep that in mind, but added that the war would always make such 'sudden directives' necessary.

On 26 December 1942, and in response to the November decree, Lammers told Brandt that it was 'unhelpful for a number of reasons if the channel by which the Führer was presented with paperwork, which included directives for the civilian state administration, was different from the one ordered by the Führer himself'.[101] According to Lammers, anyone interfering in the proper administrative process was producing 'additional work' for the Führer, and, of course, for himself. On 3 January 1943, Brandt told Lammers that the 'procedure was new to him' and that he was grateful for the support of the state administration in these cases.[102] A couple of months later, Lammers was beginning to question whether Brandt had actually meant what he had said.

Based on the Führer decree of July 1942, Brandt was empowered to pursue 'special tasks' on the direct orders of Hitler. These 'tasks' were neither defined nor limited to certain areas of policy, but they constituted an integral part of Hitler's charismatic and dictatorial rule. Any criticism of them, or of one of the decrees, was also a criticism of Hitler himself and his personalized rule. Brandt's original brief included the supervision of the building programme for evacuation hospitals in areas vulnerable to air raids in North and West Germany. Emboldened by his promotion to SS-Brigadeführer and Major General of the Waffen-SS at the end of January 1943, Brandt began to claim areas of competence in other government departments, especially those that were subordinate to Conti.[103] A meeting between Brandt and Conti in February 1942 to define the areas of responsibility between Brandt's office, the RMdI and the Reich Work Ministry resulted in no tangible improvement.[104] Nazi officials now started to complain to the regional *Gauleiter* about the confusion which had arisen in the health system as a result of Brandt's appointment. One of the problems which officials encountered was the fact that Brandt was unavailable for extended periods of time, generally because he was accompanying Hitler to the Eastern Front. On 13 March, for example, Brandt travelled with Hitler to Smolensk to visit the headquarters of the Army Group Centre.[105] The trip almost cost Brandt his life.

After weeks of preparation, the German resistance movement had chosen the place for an assassination attempt on Hitler's life. The main challenge for the conspirators around Colonel Henning von Tresckow, the first staff officer of Field Marshal von Bock at Army Group Centre, and their sharp-shooter, Lieutenant Colonel Georg Freiherr von Boeselager, was to breach Hitler's personal security. Constantly surrounded by SS bodyguards and wearing a bulletproof vest and hat, Hitler took no chances wherever he travelled. Prearranged meetings with military leaders were cancelled at the last minute. An attempt at the end of February to arrest Hitler at the headquarters of Army Group B in Poltawa had failed, because Hitler had suddenly decided to visit Zaporozhye instead. The original plan to kill Hitler in the mess of Field Marshal von Kluge, in charge of Army Group Centre, was changed: the dictator was to be shot on his way back to his car. Neither of the plans materialized. In the end, Tresckow decided to kill Hitler with a British 'clam', a small explosive the size of a book. Shortly before take-off, one of the conspirators asked a member of Hitler's entourage, Lieutenant Colonel Heinz Brandt, to take a small package with him in Hitler's plane to Army High Command. Heinz Brandt was told that the package contained two bottles of cognac. In reality, the detonator had been activated moments before, ready to explode in thirty minutes, while the plane was en route to Minsk. For unknown reasons, the British-made bomb never went off. If the device had exploded, it would have destroyed the plane and killed everyone on board, Karl Brandt included. When the conspirators learned that Hitler had safely arrived at his field headquarters, they knew that a major opportunity to stage a *coup d'état* and bring the war to an end had been missed.[106]

Unaware of the assassination attempt, Brandt was looking forward to spending some time with his wife and son at the Berghof during the spring and summer.[107] At the end of March, Hitler returned to the Obersalzberg to breathe new life into his flagging military alliance. He may also have been planning to give Brandt additional powers in order to resolve some of the problems in the medical health system, hoping that this would shore up support at home. Others, however, were not impressed by Brandt's performance. On 20 April 1943, Brandt was told that his assignment to unify the medical transport system had caused such a degree of discontent among party officials that the *Gauleiter* for Pomerania, Franz Schwede-Coburg, had proposed that Hitler's decree of November 1942 be 'generally revoked'.[108] Rather than bowing to party political pressure, Brandt had other things in mind. On 1 April, Lammers informed Conti that there had been discussions about issuing a second Führer decree which would substantially expand Brandt's powers.[109]

Livid with rage, Conti immediately requested a meeting with three of the most senior officials of the regime. On 22 April, two days after Hitler's birthday, Conti visited Göring, Lammers and Bormann at Berchtesgaden, and complained to each of them individually about Brandt.[110] Given that Brandt was about to receive additional powers for the central planning of hospital beds, Göring first enquired whether any plans had been drawn up, because Brandt had told him that none existed. Conti told Göring that a centralized coordination of hospital beds certainly existed, but that Brandt was 'so ignorant that it was not even possible to explain to him even the most urgent problems'.[111] Lammers largely agreed with Conti's accusations, particularly about Brandt's inexperience in administrative matters. He was unable, however, to tell Conti when he would be in a position to report the matter to Hitler, and felt that it was a 'calamity' that Hitler would rarely see important personalities, if at all. For Lammers, the main problem lay in the fact that Brandt was able to inform Hitler in a biased and irresponsible fashion. Bormann thoroughly agreed. He was of the opinion that Hitler had only issued the Führer decree to ensure that he would be informed of, and be able to respond to, important military matters in a more expeditious fashion, but not in order to provide Brandt with an opportunity to establish his own organizational apparatus within the medical hierarchy. Although vaguely reassured, Conti told Bormann that he was feeling a bit like a builder who was 'putting stone upon stone to erect a building while someone was sawing on the scaffolding on which I am standing'.[112]

At the beginning of May 1943, the conflict came out into the open. On 10 May, Lammers and Bormann informed Hitler of the ongoing dispute between Brandt and Conti, and about the fact that Brandt was circumventing the existing administrative channels. Hitler instinctively sided with his officials, at least at first. He instructed Lammers to remind Brandt that any paperwork touching upon the responsibilities of the state bureaucracy had to be brought to his attention by Lammers, and by no one else. Hitler also instructed them to 'resolve' the differences of opinion between Brandt and Conti.[113] Two days later, on 12 May, Conti was invited to have lunch with Hitler and his guests at the Berghof, but in spite of his high hopes, this did not give him an opportunity to raise his concerns with the dictator. Conti's memorandum about the occasion gives us a fairly good idea what was discussed instead.[114]

When he arrived at the Berghof, von Hasselbach led Conti to a small ante-chamber where most of the invited guests and adjutants were assembled. Present were Brandt, Goebbels, Morell, Martin Bormann and Albert Bormann, the permanent liaison man of the Foreign Office at Führer Headquarters, SS-Brigadeführer Walter Hewel, the lawyer and State Secretary, Erich Neumann, who had been present at the Wannsee conference, and SS-Oberführer Benno von Arent, affectionately called

Reibübi, the Reich Stage Creator (*Reichsbühnenbildner*), who was in charge, amongst other things, of designing the party rallies and theatre plays. Hitler welcomed Conti by asking 'How are you?' and Conti replied 'Thank you, I'm fine', and the group then sat down for a rustic German stew made of potatoes and beans. During the meal almost no one spoke. Then, suddenly, Hitler started to talk in a jovial manner about some of the cartoons which had been published in the *Angriff*, before the conversation moved to the role of the press and propaganda. Hewel remarked that the British people were listening to the German news bulletins. Hitler was satisfied with the attitude of the German press and said that the 'Jewish question' should always be highlighted, a subject which started off one of his anti-Semitic diatribes. According to Hitler, only the 'Jewish element' held the two juxtaposed systems, capitalist and bolshevist, together. The ultimate aim of the Jews, he said, was to annihilate the leadership structure in all major countries and establish Jewish rule (*Judenherrschaft*). Hitler was by now in his element. 'The Jews are like parasites,' he told his assembled guests, 'who, by acting instinctively, destroy their fertile soil, but don't realise that ultimately their existence is being destroyed by the fertile soil.'[115]

Like a well-rehearsed theatre group, Goebbels now turned the discussion to the *Protocols of the Learned Elders of Zion*, first published in 1903 in Russia, which allegedly described a plan by the Jewish people to achieve world domination, but which had been exposed as a hoax after the First World War. This was followed by Hitler's comments about Jewish jokes which, in his view, demonstrated that all Jews were liars: 'In general, the Jew acts instinctively, like an animal,' he told the gathering.[116] There could be absolutely no doubt for anyone present, Brandt and Conti included, that the German head of state despised the Jews; they were his mortal enemies. While Conti and Brandt were having their rustic *Eintopf* with the dictator, hundreds of thousands of European Jews were being murdered in extermination camps on a previously unimaginable scale, a fact Hitler himself hinted at: 'As far as the Jewish question is concerned,' he told his guests, 'it has now been proved that it was wrong to claim that one cannot do without the Jews.'[117]

Conti quickly realized that the main thrust of conversation revolved around general subjects. None of the guests raised any specific political or ideological problems. In general, Hitler kept aloof and detached from the realities of the life of the German people. It must have been deeply frustrating for Conti, after having waited so long to gain access to the Führer. Brandt, who sat next to Conti, then started a conversation which focused on the co-founder and first director of the German Hospital Association, SA-Oberführer Ralf Zeitler, whom Brandt wanted to appoint as his special representative to coordinate German hospital space.[118] Conti's response was unambiguous: 'I said that the appointment of such a special representative was actually impossible, and that I felt it necessary, given that I wanted to handle things completely openly, that all these questions should for once be discussed between us in front of the Führer.'[119] Brandt was not given an opportunity to respond, because Conti turned around to listen to what Hitler had to say. After lunch, Hitler excused himself and went for a walk with his dog. Disappointed about the outcome of the meeting, Conti confided to Bormann that one of the *Gauleiter* had told his staff that 'Dr Conti was more or less a dead man'.[120] Conti had certainly not left any doubt in Brandt's mind that senior officials were seriously concerned about his style of governance, but Brandt, on the other hand, must have realized that Conti's position was potentially untenable if Hitler withdrew his support.

While party political opposition to the General Commissioner was gathering momentum, Brandt was exploiting the crisis to expand his own power base. On 20 May 1943, Brandt was given the power to intervene in all unresolved and contentious questions relating to the building of military and emergency hospitals and the admission of hospital patients.[121] The next day Hitler expanded the assignment, which had originally been limited to North Germany, to the whole of the Reich, and put Brandt in charge of the production of pharmaceuticals.[122] Bormann transmitted the news to Lammers, who immediately tried to limit the far-reaching scope of the decree. Once again, the decree had originated behind his back and without prior consultation with any government minister. Brandt, it seemed, had yet again presented Hitler with a draft decree, and had obtained his signature. The decree had been worded in such a general manner, probably by Brandt himself, that it gave him the power, in theory, to confiscate vital government buildings. On 4 June, Lammers told Brandt:

> According to the wording of this decree you would have, for example, the right to confiscate the buildings of the Foreign Office in Berlin or the buildings of the Army headquarters and use them as military hospitals. You would have the right to intervene in differences of opinion with regard to patient admissions in army hospitals. It goes without saying that the decree should not confer this much authority.[123]

The additional assignments, together with a liberal interpretation of his brief as General Commissioner, gave Brandt the necessary power to gain a stronghold in vital areas of the medical industry, something that became of great significance when Allied bombing raids began to reshape the lives of German citizens. At first, Brandt scored some success by making the medical system more effective through the frequent use of 'Führer orders'. These oral, and sometimes written, orders allowed Brandt to bypass the existing regional administration, and establish himself as the leading authority in all questions of air-raid emergencies and hospital matters. Realizing the gradual shift of power in the medical hierarchy, some government agencies began discussing policy issues with Brandt directly, thereby circumventing the existing medical bureaucracy.[124] Brandt's handling of air-raid damage and the efficient mobilization of critical resources had become possible because Brandt did not waste any time over questions of competence. As he put it to Conti, 'these times are hardly suitable for discussion'.[125] In general, Brandt acted directly on behalf of the Führer. His small staff kept administrative frictions to a minimum. To create bed spaces in evacuation hospitals, he used the existing cure and nursing homes which were administered by Linden, with whom he had good contact through the 'euthanasia' programme. Such a radical and swift approach to urgent problems was certainly to Hitler's liking.

On 29 May 1943, while spending time in the pleasant surroundings of the Berghof, Brandt felt that the time had come to confront Conti:

> Dear Leo Conti! For days – indeed weeks – I have been thinking of writing to you. Please do not read this from a formal legal perspective! But the more this letter became necessary, the more difficult it is and has been for me to approach you, especially given your own queries and the manner in which they have been phrased. However now I am writing to you. I could wait. But for what? You have complained about me and my conduct. Some gentlemen, with whom you have talked, have informed me. Others may not have done so. Others have come and offered their help to mediate. I especially do not want to go down that road. After all, we are men, Mr Conti, who have known each other for years, and we have helped each other. Should not [direct communication] be possible, even under difficult circumstances? I say this in particular with concern for our reputation as doctors and therefore also with concern that the necessary work will be carried out. It is difficult to engage in discussion at times like these. You will feel that as I do. We must all be generous! (*Da muss auch das Herz gross sein!*) I generally don't write like this. But I am concerned to find a solution and to pursue the higher goal (*das grosse Ziel*). I am happy with Mr Handloser who – I can describe it at least as a very friendly relationship. Do things really have to be different with us, especially so publicly in the sight of people who have nothing to do with our difficulties? But whatever you may decide in your inner self, dear Mr Conti, you should know one thing: I will pursue my way with a clear goal. Only the order of the Führer can prevent me from doing that. I greet you, Mr Conti and Heil Hitler! Yours Brandt.[126]

Brandt's letter was a clever piece of double strategy. Whilst pretending to be concerned about their mutual 'reputation as doctors' on the one hand, Brandt threatened Conti on the other. By attempting to personalize the whole debate, Brandt painted a picture of two doctors who were seemingly unable to cooperate with one another, stressed his own willingness to collaborate, and shifted the blame for any future problems onto Conti. The question for Conti was: what kind of compromise Brandt was offering. He was left with little room to manoeuvre. By stating that he would pursue his 'way with a clear goal', Brandt made it clear that he was determined to fight; 'only the order of the Füher' would prevent him from carrying on as before. In other words, Brandt was seeking one of the notorious Führer decisions, if not another Führer decree. Brandt's letter was not an attempt to compromise and work together, but a declaration of war. On 1 June 1943, Conti replied:

> Dear Mr. B.! Your letter of 29 of the month is long overdue! I have in no way made things difficult for you. Openly and honestly I have offered you my hand to collaborate after the Führer decree [28 July 1942]. I have been to great pains to inform you about all basic questions and work. For some time I persuaded myself that it would work because it had to. Then your intrusions followed (first by your informing me, but later I found it out by other means), which, when increasingly repeated, brought confusion into my area of

responsibility, an area which for its fragmentation is more than difficult to keep under control. The next consequence was the lowering of discipline. Chaos is reigning. This is one matter. The other is this: to me you often talked in an appreciative way about my work. To others – those in the highest places – you talk very differently! Mr Brandt, it is very very hard to come to terms with this. And simply *because* of my medical reputation and my responsibility, I had to approach Bormann and Lammers. I don't need a mediator in the same way as you. And since the time of total war is unsuitable for 'debate', I have come to my own conclusions: I have to demand, in the interest of the health of the nation, that the current wholly unworkable two-fold structure, which is fractured and lacks any clarity, be abolished. And soon. Because a continuation of the current situation is irresponsible. Until now, you have never said a word about your intentions and your clear goal. What you mean by this remains unclear. It might have been helpful if you had explained to me your clear goal. You have often claimed that you wanted to serve only the idea [*der Sache*] and that for yourself you had no interest. I am an old follower of the Führer, and it goes without saying that his order is the highest law; I made it very explicit at the beginning of our collaboration that I will never get in the way if the Führer wishes to make changes. But you have rejected such a notion, and said that I should never say something like that again. Today the situation is so confused that only a Führer decision will bring order into the current disorganisation. I am happy to join forces with you to ask the Führer jointly for a final clear decision. Heil Hitler. Yours C.[127]

Conti's response shows that he was well aware that Brandt was concealing his political ambitions behind an external servility towards the idea of National Socialism. Brandt's objective remained oblique; the idea [*die Sache*] was an empty linguistic phrase which served perhaps as a cover for professional ambition, status and influence, but little else. Conti wanted to call Brandt's bluff. During the following weeks, each man was busy recruiting allies in what amounted to a serious power struggle at the top of the medical hierarchy. Among Conti's allies were Frick, Lammers, Bormann and, to some degree, Goebbels. On the side of Brandt was one man in particular: Hitler.

In June 1943, Bormann and Lammers criticized Brandt for having repeatedly 'led the Führer into making an expression of his will by informing him one-sidedly'.[128] Since the 'will of the Führer' was considered to be the supreme source of law in the Third Reich, the Reich Chancellery had to honour these changes in policy direction even when they had not been properly consulted. Brandt was circumventing the Reich Chancellery and thereby weakening the position of Lammers and Bormann, if not shifting the balance of power as a whole.[129] Those supporting Conti in the struggle for power wanted to prevent Brandt from further expanding his realm of influence, and to stabilize their own power base. Lammers told Brandt that his (Brandt's) way of handling policy matters was creating major difficulties for the administration. By influencing Hitler in such a way that he would express his wishes or sign certain decrees without consulting the relevant officials, Brandt was creating additional work and confusion at a critical time for the country. Lammers's concerns show the extent to which every word which Hitler muttered could have serious political implications. The decree which gave Brandt responsibility for emergency and military hospitals had been clumsily drafted. As Lammers noted, the wording of the text gave Brandt the right to confiscate the rooms of the Foreign Ministry in Berlin or the buildings of the Army Command and use them as emergency hospitals.[130] Instead of administering important government business, Lammers found himself in a position where he was limiting the scope and potential interpretation of certain decrees. Others were likewise concerned. On 8 June, Oskar Kauffmann, one of Conti's closest allies, told the Reich Health Leader that Brandt's interferences were likely to destroy all their future plans.[131]

Goebbels' diary entries demonstrate his opportunism in trying to ascertain who would eventually have Hitler's support. He knew that to be on the losing side in a battle for power at Hitler's court could affect his own position. Downplaying the seriousness of the conflict, Goebbels at first sided with Conti, who had the backing of the Nazi Party. Once he realized that Hitler might decide in favour of Brandt, he changed tack and supported Brandt. For Goebbels, the problem seemed at first to be more of a technical and administrative nature. On 10 June 1943, he noted in his diary that he had resolved a 'little conflict' between Brandt and Conti, because Brandt had interfered 'a little bit in Conti's areas of responsibility'. This had apparently been necessary in order to coordinate the medical and emergency welfare measures between the civilian and military agencies: 'Conti's powers are not sufficient in this field.'[132] However, to air some of the problems, Brandt was asked by Lammers to come to a meeting in Berchtesgaden. High up in the mountains, the battle for control over German medical services was about to begin.

On 18 June 1943, at eleven o'clock, the meeting took place at the Berghof.[133] Those present were Brandt, Conti, Lammers, Bormann and Gerhard Klopfer, State Secretary in the Reich Chancellery and Bormann's deputy in the Party Chancellery. His brief was to take the minutes of the meeting, something he was used to doing. In 1942, Klopfer had been among the attendants at the Wannsee conference. Although Hitler was in residence at the Berghof, he did not attend the meeting. It had originally been anticipated that he would chair the meeting, but Hitler preferred not to get involved. Brandt started off by expressing his 'outrage' about Conti's attempt to stonewall his relations with the German X-ray Society. The discussion then moved to other matters, most of which revolved around Brandt interfering in Conti's areas of responsibility. Brandt was adamant that all of these interventions had occurred 'without his knowledge'. For some incidents 'he had never given any orders', others he 'denied very emphatically'. Brandt's passionate expression of ignorance and innocence mirror in many ways the testimony he later gave at the Nuremberg Doctors' Trial. To Lammers and Bormann it appeared that Brandt was forcefully evading any admission of guilt or wrongdoing. Both felt that Brandt's style of leadership was 'unusual and improper'.[134] 'Never before', Lammers told Brandt, 'had he witnessed one of Hitler's special commissioners carry out an assignment like Brandt does.'[135] Brandt, it seems, was imitating Hitler's style of leadership.

Bormann had waited for this moment for months. In the presence of some of the most senior officials of the regime, Bormann revealed that Brandt had told

Hitler that the RMdI had given a totally 'stupid' answer to an important question. For a brief moment Brandt was exposed. The record seems to suggest that he was genuinely embarrassed. The fact that he had criticized other government agencies in front of the Führer could hardly be denied, if the information came from such a well-placed source as Bormann himself. It undermined Brandt's position and showed his desire to manipulate Hitler in his own interest. For Conti, the talks at Berchtesgaden were a total vindication as they had ended with a 'destructive criticism of Prof. Brandt's behaviour'.[136] Goebbels began to waver when he heard the outcome of the meeting, and when Frick raised further concerns about Brandt:

> To crown it all, there is a heated argument between Professor Brandt and Dr Conti. Professor Brandt attempts, on the basis of his Führer order, to get his hands on a great many of Conti's competences, against which Dr Frick defends himself. Even if Conti does not operate very cleverly, and has caused most of the difficulties for himself, I cannot lend my hand so that he is squashed against the wall by Professor Brandt, who has only been given a partial order from the Führer. I will therefore side with Conti in this conflict.[137]

Conti's victory was short lived. Brandt quickly regained the initiative by inviting Conti to discuss some of the issues on the train journey back to Berlin that same night. Conti accepted the invitation. Although he had denied any involvement or interference in Conti's responsibilities in the presence of Lammers and Bormann, Brandt now made it plain that he regarded his office as superior in all military and civil health matters, and for all special commissions (*Sonderbeauftrage*).[138] Four days later, on 22 June, during another meeting with Conti and two members of his staff, Brandt argued that sudden decisions at Führer headquarters made rapid interventions necessary, without following the formal chain of command.[139] Brandt maintained that he was still trying to establish the position of a Chief of Civilian Medical Services. Conti was not convinced. Suddenly the telephone rang. Ernst Robert Grawitz, Reich Physician of the SS and Police, was on the line. He told Conti that Brandt had summoned him the previous day, and had given him orders concerning the regional rescue services, orders which differed substantially from those of Conti. This was another interference in Conti's province. Prolonging this cat and mouse game was pointless. Brandt finally handed Conti a drawing in which all departments, including the one of the Reich Health Leader, were subordinate to the General Commissioner. Pushing Conti further onto the defence, Brandt told him that he was intending to present the drawing to Hitler. Conti knew that if Hitler accepted the plan, his loss of power and authority in the civil health system would be immense. Brandt's 'goal', as he called it, was a high-ranking office within health and medical services, maybe even the Ministry of Health.[140] Brandt had finally revealed his true colours. On 23 June 1943, Conti wrote to Bormann:

> The moral defeat of Prof. Brandt during our argument was unambiguous, was it not? How is it possible that this dilettantism is allowed to produce such chaos in my area of work? There are no rational arguments for this. Whereas Professor Brandt is able to talk

to the Führer on a daily basis, so to speak, I have, after four years of work as the Reich Health Leader, not even been able to report to the Führer (except with regard to the euthanasia problem).[141]

Brandt knew that he was untouchable so long as Hitler sanctioned his policies, however arbitrary or confusing they were for those having to execute them. Hitler's style of leadership showed a similar degree of impromptu decision-making which interfered with established administrative lines of communication. He also had a similar disregard for bureaucrats. It is therefore hardly surprising that his trusted doctor was beginning to copy the master's style of leadership. Moreover, on 17 June, one day before the talks at Berchtesgaden, Hitler had placed Brandt in charge of the 'planning and distribution of hospital space, medical personnel, and equipment in all air-raid areas and potential areas of evacuation'.[142] Brandt's new assignment had been given orally and in private; only later was the order confirmed by Hitler, and only after the Reich Chancellery had asked the head of government for clarification. Another of Hitler's 'wishes' had acquired the force of law.[143] While on the one hand Hitler was using Lammers to keep Brandt's ambitions in check, on the other he was encouraging him to pursue his quest for power, all within the space of twenty-four hours. Such ambivalent signals must have strengthened Brandt's belief that the Führer silently sanctioned his style of leadership as long as he delivered efficiency improvements in the health system under the constraints of war.

While Allied bombers were turning almost every German region into either a target zone or an area for evacuation, Brandt was now de facto in charge of the German health care system. On the periphery, however, the ongoing conflict between Brandt and Conti left a somewhat different impression. Regional health officials and medical experts had understood that there were, in effect, two men in charge of the German health system, but they had difficulties in grasping that they were not collaborating with one another in the current national emergency. On 21 June 1943, the regional head (*Landeshauptmann*) of Westphalia, Karl Kolbow, noted in his diary: 'It is interesting, if somewhat sad, to realise that there is absolutely no contact between the two pillars of the medical services [*ärztlichen Machtsäulen*] Brandt and Conti and that each of them works for himself without a plan, and neither of them knows what the other does. There is complete mismanagement [in this area] as well.'[144] Later, in September, the racial hygienist Ernst Rüdin enquired of the T-4 psychiatrist Nitsche whether those who wanted to promote the field of psychiatry in the future had to approach Conti or Brandt. 'In the past,' Rüdin told Nitsche, 'Brandt was really simply a kind of worker between the civilian and military health system', but some kind of change had apparently happened after newspapers had suggested that Brandt had been put in charge of the entire health system.[145] After years of working with a detached leadership, doctors and health officials had become accustomed to the complicated flow of information to and from the centre of government.

Hitler's new directive meant that Brandt would ultimately win the ongoing power struggle at the top of the medical hierarchy. It was the knowledge of being personally entrusted by Hitler which encouraged Brandt to pursue an energetic and sometimes ruthless approach. On 21 June 1943, he told the RMdI and the OKW that he was taking full control of hospital space.[146] The next day, on 22 June, he requested more than 80 million Reichsmark from Lammers for the expeditious building and running of special hospitals as part of 'Aktion Brandt', money which was part of the budget of the RMdI. Once again Brandt was encroaching onto the RMdI's area of competence. Four days later, Conti informed Bormann that Brandt had ordered the transferral of 1,000 mentally ill patients to Saxony without consulting the relevant state and party officials. According to Conti, Brandt had given his orders directly to the transport company. Brandt was no longer concerned about any departmental sensitivities and became increasingly bold in his statements. Brandt, the helper-turned-politician, had finally found his calling. The intensification of Allied bombing raids had given him a good reason to argue that any conflicts over areas of responsibility had to come second to the urgent need to help the German population. On 30 June, he told Lammers:

> If Herr Reich Minister Frick draws attention to the fact that the work complex which I have taken over practically extends to the whole of the Reich, then he is right. There is no distinction any more between the area of air warfare (*Luftkriegsgebiet*) and the remainder of the Reich. I can have no sympathy with any concerns about areas of responsibility, especially in the emergency created by events in the Ruhr area. On the contrary, I am convinced that removing the damage caused by terror raids, and assisting in the war zone in the middle of the Reich, mean that even administrative boundaries and property rights have to be overridden under certain conditions. To do so, does not produce 'total confusion' but instead it helps.[147]

After Lammers and Bormann had made representations to Hitler, Brandt was instructed to collaborate with Conti and not to establish his own administration. The only viable strategy by which Lammers could contain Brandt's power was to ask Hitler for another Führer decree, which he hoped would 'essentially correspond to the anticipated will of the Führer'.[148] Rather than allowing the established bureaucracy to curtail his powers, Brandt used his influence with Hitler to draft a decree which actually extended them. At the end of July 1943, Brandt used a relatively minor conflict with Conti, who had attempted to ambush his relations with the German X-ray Society, as a pretext to push for another Führer decree.[149] Hitler told Bormann that 'urgent matters' (*Wenn Eile nottue*) needed fast interventions which made it impossible to comply with ordinary bureaucratic procedures. What he and other officials needed to understand was that it was not the 'compliance with bureaucratic procedure' (*Einhaltung des Dienstweges*), or some 'minor frictions' (*kleine Friktionen*), that were important, but rather the 'success of the whole' (*Gesamterfolg*), which in Hitler's view was Brandt's achievement.[150] The court understood the message. Bormann immediately warned Conti to cooperate with Brandt 'as closely as possible'. Goebbels, who had previously been highly critical of Brandt, suddenly praised the work of Hitler's doctor.[151] To sense the mood of Hitler in the brief period prior to an 'expression of his will' was of paramount importance for everyone in Hitler's vicinity. Within the space of four weeks, Goebbels had made a complete U-turn in the dispute between Brandt and Conti. On 10 August, he wrote in his diary:

> The Führer is very happy that I have good things to report of Professor Brandt. Brandt has done exceptionally well adapting to his work as General Inspector of the Medical Services. In any case, he is a different kettle of fish from Conti. The Führer also shares my judgement about Conti. Conti is nothing but a successful country doctor. We will not be able to expect very much from him, although Bormann strongly sides with him. However, I cannot suppress my view. Brandt is in a different class altogether (*Brandt ist eine Klasse besser*).[152]

All of a sudden, Brandt was perceived as being in a 'different class'. On 16 August 1943, Conti still hoped that he would be able to make his case, stating that 'Prof[essor] Brandt's continuous encroachments ... have brought about a (complete) annihilation of any authority and any possibility of leadership in my ... field of work.'[153] In a draft letter, Conti requested that Hitler either make a decision in this matter or release him from his duties. Despite having the support of Bormann and Lammers, it was too late. Hitler had made up his mind. On Monday 16 August, at 11.30 a.m., the same day that Conti wrote his letter, Hitler went for a morning walk with Brandt. It gave Brandt yet another opportunity to present his case.[154] Four days later, on 20 August, Goebbels had a meeting with Brandt, followed by a 'long conversation' with Conti. Brandt was undoubtedly superior in the conflict, Goebbels noted, because he enjoyed the 'unlimited trust of the Führer and also seems to be the stronger personality'.[155] According to Goebbels, Conti was embroiled in minute disputes (*kleine Stänkerein*) and was likely to lose his position, whereas Brandt knew exactly what he wanted: 'He is heading straight for his target, and Conti's organisational failures only make it easier for him to achieve his aim. Dr Brandt easily earns sympathy, something that cannot be said of Conti.'[156] Brandt's aim was nothing less than to gain full powers as Germany's Minister of Health.

Things were now moving fast in Brandt's direction after it transpired that Hitler was unhappy with Frick, whom he regarded as 'old and worn out'.[157] According to Goebbels, the Reich Minister of the Interior was spending three-quarters of the year on holiday at Lake Chiemsee in Bavaria. Goebbels criticized Frick for having failed to strengthen morale on the home front. The deposition of Mussolini in Italy, followed by the withdrawal of German troops from Sicily, suddenly focused Hitler's mind on the domestic situation and the danger of rebellion at home. 'And, as usual on such occasions, the mob has forgotten all merits of Fascism and is assaulting the local Party offices of the Fascists. It is "*Jubilate*" today and "*Crucifige*" tomorrow!' Bormann told his wife.[158] At around the same time, Brandt presented Hitler with another decree which expanded his area of responsibility. On Tuesday 24 August, at 12.25 p.m., shortly after breakfast, Hitler had a fifteen-minute meeting with Brandt. Although no record of the conversation exists, it is likely that the matter was discussed.[159] Brandt had in effect written and worded his own promotion.

Hitler agreed that he would 'discuss' the decree with Lammers. This alone was sufficient for Brandt to inform Lammers that 'the Führer agreed with the content and wording of the draft'.[160] The next day, 25 August, it was announced that Frick had been relieved of office and replaced by Himmler. That same day, Klopfer warned Conti about the imminent expansion of Brandt's powers.[161] Shocked at the outcome, Conti told Bormann two days later that the new decree would ensure that 'chaos would become a permanent state of affairs'.[162] When Lammers realized what was happening it was too late. By then all government departments had already been instructed to comply with the new policy.[163] By signing the draft on 5 September 1943, Hitler retrospectively sanctioned Brandt's intervention into all areas of government, and ended the dispute.[164] The decree stated:

> The plenipotentiary for the Medical and Health Services, Commissioner General Prof. Dr. med. Brandt, is charged with centrally coordinating and directing the problems and activities of the entire Medical and Health service according to instructions. In this sense this order applies also to the field of medical science and research, as well as to the organisational institutions concerned with the manufacture and distribution of medical material. The plenipotentiary for the Medical and Health Services is authorised to appoint and commission special deputies for his spheres of action.[165]

Given that the decree gave Brandt the highest authority in the German health care system, reactions by certain government agencies were overtly critical. Attempting to limit the damage that had been caused, Lammers managed to squeeze out a last-minute 'view' from Hitler who now 'wished' Brandt 'not to interfere, except in an emergency, in the regular activity of, and the organisation which is subordinate to, the Reich Health Leader'.[166] Brandt was also asked that extraordinary measures which he might deem necessary would be executed as far as possible by the Reich Health Leader and his administration. In practice, however, it was understood that Brandt had been promoted to be Conti's superior.[167] For Goebbels, the decree gave Brandt a 'supervising authority' (*Aufsichtsrecht*) to exercise control over Conti and his administration. On 15 September, he noted in his diary:

> The Führer has significantly expanded the powers of Professor Brandt. Brandt now has supervising authority over Conti and his organisation. Conti has brought this upon himself through his brusque and undiplomatic character and action. If Conti continues in this way, he will lose a lot of credit.[168]

For Conti the repercussions of this second Führer decree were disastrous. Demoted and humiliated, Conti disappeared as a significant player in Nazi medical politics. Shortly after the decree, he remarked: 'The Führer has unambiguously decided, and one does not question a decision of the Führer. In peacetime, my resignation would be the natural consequence.'[169] Conti now wanted Brandt to tell him openly whether he was still interested in any form of collaboration, because he and his allies were concerned that he might otherwise be demoted to third, fourth or fifth place in the medical hierarchy.[170] Knowing how the regime functioned, their worries were not altogether unjustified. Two weeks after the publication of the decree, the Moscow-based *Deutsche Volkssender* broadcast that the Reich Health Leader had been dismissed from his position as a consequence of Frick's demise.[171] On 20 September 1943, Conti wrote a long letter to Hitler in which he expressed his disappointment that he had not once in four years been given the opportunity to report to him personally. According to Conti, this could only mean that he did not enjoy the support of the Führer any longer. Unless Hitler showed that he still supported him, Conti wanted to serve the Führer in another capacity.[172] Hitler flatly rejected both demands and ordered him to cooperate with Brandt. Adding insult to injury, Bormann advised Conti to keep the letter to Hitler confidential because others might think that he was 'suffering from low self-esteem'.[173] Bormann knew that Conti's resignation could have further weakened the influence of the party in the regime which, in turn, could potentially undermine his own position. By the end of October, one of Conti's closest allies told the Reich Health Leader that the 'loss of prestige' was catastrophic, and 'our effectiveness is devastatingly weak'.[174] Others saw him as a 'king without a kingdom'.[175] Hardly anyone disagreed with these assessments.

IV. PARALLEL EMPIRES

The second Führer decree gave Brandt the authority to direct, monitor and supervise German medical science and research. This had previously been in the domain of the Reich Ministry of Education. The decree allowed him to appoint his own members of staff, and thus establish his own parallel empire. Having gained control over medical supplies in the army, the civil health care system, the medical economy, and medical science and research, Brandt had risen to the position of supreme medical authority in Germany. By the end of 1943, Brandt's office was in charge of five major areas of activity. He was in control of the 'special hospitals' (*Krankenhaus-Sonderanlagen*) of Aktion Brandt, a building programme that provided about thirty hospitals (with approximately 15,000 beds) by May 1944 – about 7 per cent of all new hospital beds that had been created since the beginning of the war.[176] Second, from the spring of 1943, he coordinated, together with the Reich Commissioner for Cure and Nursing Homes, the evacuation and transfer of mentally and chronically ill patients. Third, Brandt's special representative, SS-Untersturmführer Willy Gutermuth, was tasked with reducing the number of sick in the armaments industry through a coordinated use of 'special medical commandos' (*vertrauensärztliche Sonderkommandos*). Fourth, his Department for Medical Research and Science, headed by Rostock, was in charge of coordinating German medical research. Within this context, Brandt's office was also in charge of overseeing and directing the medical expert literature.[177] On 25 September 1943, for example, three weeks after the signing of the decree, Brandt asked Diepgen whether he would be prepared to serve Brandt's office in an advisory capacity in the field of medical history, an invitation which Diepgen duly accepted.[178] Finally, Brandt's Department for Medical Planning and Finance controlled pharmaceutical production, and coordinated the relocation of pharmaceutical plants to more secure sites.[179] He and his office had become the centre of gravity for medicine and medical science within the amorphous power structures of the Third Reich.[180]

The Führer decree gave Brandt *de jure* substantial powers to interfere in the business of almost all government departments, but he had to operate nonetheless within the strict confines of what more powerful empire-builders regarded as their own turf. Himmler's SS camps, for example, were off limits. Following the establishment of the slave labour camp, Dora-Mittelbau, near Nordhausen, in August 1943, Brandt instructed the head of emergency services in the Todt Organization, Alois Poschmann, to examine the general health conditions of the inmates and inform him about the existing medical supplies and the number of qualified physicians. Although Poschmann was able to witness some of the conditions in the camp from a distance, he returned empty-handed. SS-Gruppenführer Heinz Kammler, the ruthless chief of the Works Department at the SS Finance and Administration Head Office, prevented him from inspecting the camp. Brandt later told his interrogators: 'I mention it, because the people stationed there and the people responsible for the care, were SS physicians, and I found out from Poschmann that the accommodation for the workers was bad.'[181]

Kammler's refusal to allow an inspection of the camp was unacceptable for Brandt. He told Himmler about the appalling sanitary conditions which Poschmann had witnessed. According to Brandt, Himmler is reported to have said: 'I know, Dr. Kammler reported to me that Dr. Poschmann was there. I want to point out to you that this matter has nothing to do with you whatsoever. If something has to be put right, it will be done by Kammler himself.'[182] Far from letting the matter rest, Brandt spoke to Hitler, who referred him back to Himmler. Given that Brandt had talked to Himmler already, Hitler realized that he had to take sides in the matter, telling Brandt: 'Leave it; Himmler will put it right.'[183] According to Brandt, he never heard anything about it until after the war, when he learned that barracks had been built through the personal intervention of Albert Speer.

Brandt or Poschmann probably informed Speer, who later gave vivid testimony of what he saw when visiting the camp. The conditions were absolutely outrageous, he told the journalist Gitta Sereny. Having been told that the camp was Dante's 'Inferno', Speer forced himself into the underground production site for V2 rockets. It was probably the most hellish labour camp of them all. Prisoners lived in caves and tunnels in the freezing cold, slaving eighteen hours or more under the most appalling conditions. There was no heat, no ventilation, and no adequate sanitary system. Inmates were suffering from malnutrition, dysentery and a range of other infectious diseases. At least ten thousand inmates eventually died. Speer said that he had never been so horrified, and immediately ordered the building of barracks while he was there. It was one of those instances where Speer showed some emotion: 'Yes, there I was appalled,' he told Sereny.[184] Given that Speer and Brandt were friends, it is almost inconceivable that Brandt was not aware of the appalling conditions in Germany's slave labour camps.

Collaboration between the two men also intensified in other areas. On 15 October

1943, Brandt informed a range of government ministers, including the Head of the SS, the Chief of Army Medical Services, the Reich Labour Minister, the Reich Minister of Education, and the General Plenipotentiary for Chemical Production, that he was now in charge of the central management of building projects in the area of health and medical services: 'In the interests of greatest economy and greatest efficiency it is necessary to centrally control and influence all building projects in the field of health and medicine.'[185] The ministers were asked to submit all applications for building projects falling into Brandt's area of responsibility to him for consideration and approval. Brandt also told them that he would ask them to amend their building plans in certain cases in order to coordinate the limited availability of resources. Finally, they were asked to appoint a representative who would liaise between Brandt's office and their department.[186] Attached to the letter was one of Speer's circulars, which instructed the civilian and military administration to collaborate with Brandt's office. The circular was meant to add political weight to Brandt's requests. However, cooperation between the various government agencies and Brandt's office does not seem to have been particularly successful at first. In January 1944, Brandt felt the need to repeat his demands.[187]

Hitler's decision to support Brandt in the conflict with Conti was part of a wider pattern of Hitler's not to concede any power that could potentially challenge his own authority. Lammers and Bormann's plan to exploit the situation for their own ends, and strengthen their grip over the Nazi administration, failed when it became apparent that Hitler supported one of his trusted servants who himself was totally dependent on him. With Keitel, Lammers and Bormann were the three main executive pillars on which Hitler's power rested. At the beginning of 1943, the three men had been put in charge of a coordinating body, a kind of small 'war cabinet', in order to strengthen centralized control for urgently needed war measures. The coordinating body soon became known as the 'Committee of Three'. Powerful figures with their own administrative empires and vested interests, such as Göring, Goebbels and Speer, had been excluded to ensure that the coordinating body could not become a threat to Hitler's own position. But the 'Committee of Three' soon ran into major difficulties in streamlining the convoluted areas of responsibility in a regime that was almost totally devoid of any systematic and rational form of governance. Conflicting party and ministerial interests at all levels of German society meant that the meetings between the 'Committee of Three' and the heads of other departments throughout 1943 produced almost no results. By early April, Goebbels became concerned that the leadership of the regime was losing control of the situation: 'The entire Reich and Party leadership is on holiday,' he noted in his diary.[188] Shortly afterwards, he told Speer that the country was not only suffering from a leadership crisis but from a 'Leader crisis'.[189] Goebbels and those around him felt that Hitler needed to be 'helped' in this situation, and prevented from giving any powers to men like Lammers whom Göring saw as a 'super bureaucrat'. Goebbels was convinced that losing the war was simply not an option any more, as he told Göring: 'Above all as regards the Jewish Question, we have committed [*festgelegt*] ourselves so much that there is no getting out any longer. And that's good. A movement and a people that have burnt their boats fight, from experience, with fewer constraints than those that still have a chance of retreat.'[190]

At the same time, the leading officials of the Reich knew that, if the war was to be won, the overall structure of the Third Reich had to be reformed. What they did not understand, however, was that any attempt to reform a regime that was built on competing authorities and personalities was, in effect, challenging Hitler's authority, and was therefore doomed from the outset. It was a government system, if it was a system at all, whose very nature was based on oligarchy and, to a large extent, on administrative chaos at the higher levels of government. Hitler's personalized and amateurish style of government led him to support those groups and personalities who did not aim to rationalize and systematize the business of governance, and whose style of leadership resembled very much his own. The creation of bureaucratic chaos was the result of Hitler's and his representatives' eccentric rule. At the same time, it was the confusion around him which ultimately secured Hitler's power and that of men like Brandt as well. Hitler sided almost instinctively with the person who would foster the cumulative process of administrative chaos which, in Hitler's world view, fitted perfectly into the eternal struggle for existence in which the strongest would survive.

7

Detached Leadership

I. AKTION BRANDT

The Third Reich not only thrived on chaos at the higher levels of government: chaos was its very nature and the basis of Hitler's power. Brandt not only ensured continuity for Hitler's leadership, he also functioned as part of a wider group that accelerated the process by which the Nazi system was spiralling out of control. On the periphery, however, strangely detached from the constant power struggles of the Nazi elite, and on a lower hierarchical level, the German administrative and organizational machinery, economy and society, having adapted to a detached leadership after years of upheaval and confusion, and having learned to read their general policy announcements, continued at times to function with astonishing flexibility, independence and efficiency in carrying out the intended aims of the Nazi government. Far from being a leaderless regime, in which the cumulative process of radicalization necessarily came from below, the Nazis had cultured a system of communication in which the Nazi leadership was able to control the extent and pace of illegal operations through veiled hints and euphemisms, and the Nazi rank and file endeavoured to interpret these hints correctly. This system of communication not only allowed Nazi officials to detach themselves from illegal activities, if they had to, but ensured that they could claim that the outcome of certain policy directives had not been the original intention, and that the Nazi rank and file had misunderstood their orders. It was a system of communication which provided enormous potential for misinformation and misunderstanding, resulting at times in administrative chaos, but it could also lead to the execution of an efficient and largely independent programme of mass murder and genocide on a monumental scale. Brandt, it seems, had not only learned to master the language of the Nazi elite, but had learned the principles of detached leadership.

After a heavy air raid on the city of Emden in the second half of June 1941 which destroyed almost all its hospitals, Hitler ordered the expeditious construction of hospitals that would be made available for wounded German soldiers and citizens.[1] In September, the bombardment of the famous Bethel asylum, near Bielefeld, further fuelled German propaganda against Allied attacks and helped to overcome the existing bureaucratic deadlock. The programme was originally confined to the north-west of Germany and administered through the Todt Organization and later, after the sudden death of Todt, through Brandt's office, which is why the programme was called 'Aktion Brandt'. Yet Aktion Brandt is also associated with the second phase of the killing of the mentally handicapped which continued until the end of the war, and in isolated cases beyond that.[2] Scholars have estimated that between 72,000 and 117,000 patients were killed or starved to death.[3]

In contrast to the suggestion that the killings represented part of a 'wild euthanasia', that is the uncoordinated, decentralized and unorganized murder of mental patients, the term 'Aktion Brandt' evokes the idea that behind the continuation of the 'euthanasia' programme stood a centrally directed, coordinated and well-oiled administrative machinery.[4] So far, both interpretations have not gone much beyond the intentionalist/functionalist debate: whereas some see Aktion Brandt as another step in the planning and execution of mass murder, with a central command structure and a clear intention to reduce patient populations to the status of 'place-holders' (*Platzhalter*), others stress the ad hoc nature of the programme, which made any form of organization and coordination apparently impossible under conditions of war. Regional studies, in particular, have emphasized in recent years that there is insufficient evidence to support the idea that Aktion Brandt was a targeted and centrally controlled killing operation.[5] Moreover, the severity of the bombing raids on North and West Germany, particularly in the later stages of the war, apparently made any form of central planning impossible and forced officials into uncoordinated and improvised policy decisions.

There appears to be some truth in the idea that the second phase of the 'euthanasia' programme was decentralized and largely uncoordinated, that there was no underlying intent to kill, at least not at the beginning, that the programme was flexible, and that the transferral and subsequent killing of mentally ill patients happened largely in response to sudden emergencies which required the immediate use of hospital beds for soldiers and the civilian population. What also appears to be true is that the overall structure of Aktion Brandt had little in common with the systematic and centrally organized murder of mental patients in the earlier Aktion T-4. Yet the above interpretations do not seem to take sufficient account of the overall nature of the regime and its representatives, and of the way in which policies were communicated and implemented, particularly in cases where general directives were given orally and through intermediaries.

A closer look at the role of Brandt and some of the officials involved in the programme shows that there was no systematic and orchestrated plan to kill patients in Aktion Brandt, nor were there any specific criteria as to why certain patients should be killed and others not. In some cases, the only criteria used to decide the life or death of a patient became his or her ability to work, and the extent to which an unforeseen emergency required the transfer of patients to another institution. Those two components primarily determined the number of patients evacuated – and killed – in a particular instance. The programme was adaptable to the fast-changing situation of the war and could be executed by the regional authorities on the ground. Hospital directors did not have to wait for specific orders from above in order to act, but could initiate the transfer of patients independently and on an ad hoc basis on their own initiative. Such an independent regional response to a sudden need for hospital beds made the programme flexible and efficient. Yet, it is unlikely that those in authority would have acted in the way that they did, had they not been given the impression, through veiled hints and general remarks, that the 'evacuation' of patient groups was a euphemism for the transfer and subsequent killing of mental patients, and that a revival of the 'euthanasia' programme was in the interest of the regime. Moreover, hospital directors must have received some indication that the killings had been sanctioned in one way or another by Hitler or his representatives.

Mark Roseman's analysis of the Final Solution also applies to a large extent to the killings in Aktion Brandt: a rather general, probably even vague, authorization came from the top, that is from Brandt and others, but the initiative came from local physicians from below, who responded to what they perceived as a regional 'problem'.[6] The available evidence suggests that regional officials and directors of cure and nursing homes adapted and modified their policies towards the mentally ill according to their own needs in the particular geographical area. They seem to have believed that by acting largely independently, and without waiting for any official instructions or authorization for the killing of patients, they were working towards Hitler's vision of a racially cleansed society. The Third Reich was, as we know, in a constant, self-perpetuating process of cumulative radicalization, and in a state of crisis which demanded constant action and improvisation on multiple fronts. Hitler and his regime provided the general public with visionary ideas of a racially pure future and geopolitical expansion on a monumental scale, but left the actual implementation of these ideas largely to the organizations, individuals or groups concerned, without any meaningful amount of control or supervision, and oblivious to the administrative chaos which might result. What the study of Aktion Brandt, and of Brandt in particular, seems to suggest is that the programme was not only a mirror image of the way in which the regime functioned in general, but also reflected its very nature.

From 1937, the idea of creating extra hospital beds and space, in addition to a central registry of available beds, had been part of the mobilization plans in case of war. Military planners allowed for the evacuation of more than half a million people from cure and nursing homes, schools and hospitals. The increase in bombing raids on major northern German cities from early 1942 meant that evacuations had to be carried out more often and more efficiently, especially after it had become apparent that areas of responsibility between the military and the civilian sector overlapped and were not clearly defined. Brandt, as we have seen, exploited this situation to advance himself to the position of Hitler's trusted crisis manager. On 5 August 1942, shortly after Brandt's appointment, the RMdI official Herbert Linden, who had previously been involved in the 'euthanasia' programme, and was now in charge of cure and nursing homes, conducted a survey to establish whether one could use cure and nursing homes as 'evacuation hospitals' (*Ausweichkrankenhäuser*). All relevant institutions were instructed to inform the authorities within ten days how many additional patients they could admit in open wards, common rooms and chapels, and state whether the institution was likely to be evacuated because of being vulnerable to air raids.[7] The idea was to use cure and nursing homes as a reserve for major emergencies, and provide additional hospital beds in case there was a sudden rise in the number of ill and wounded.

At first, there was little support for resuming the 'euthanasia' programme. Medical experts and government officials knew that any programme designed to kill handicapped and mentally ill patients lacked institutional and popular support. Opposition to what many perceived as state-sanctioned murder had previously been significant, especially from the Catholic Church. In July 1942, the former administrative headquarters of the 'euthanasia' programme, code-named the Reich Working Committee for Cure and Nursing Homes (*Reichsarbeitsgemeinschaft Heil- und Pflegeanstalten*), issued a report about the drop in new admissions to mental institutions, and the extent to which the reputation of the field of psychiatry had suffered from the 'euthanasia' programme.[8] Relatives and friends of patients were often 'timid' and suspicious of asylum admissions, and opposed the transfer of loved ones to other institutions for fear that they would be killed. The authors of the report detected, for example, a general lack of trust among the population in Westphalia, Hessen, the Rhine province, Wiesbaden and Brandenburg, and doubts in cities such as Freiburg and Oldenburg. In some cases, families showed a tendency to entrust their relatives to 'confessional institutions', where they were believed to be 'safer'. In Westphalia, 'Care Aktion B' (*Fürsorgeaktion B*), probably a reference to Aktion Brandt, had led to a detectable decrease in hospital admissions. To overcome the crisis, some officials proposed the publication of a law which would make euthanasia legal. Others proposed a separation between 'genuine' institutions, which would treat mental patients who were deemed to be curable, and asylums which would look after patients considered to be incurable, but who were not 'unworthy of life'. Officials from Westphalia hoped to improve the reputation of asylums by prohibiting the widespread 'defamation of the mentally ill and asylums', in conjunction with a concerted medical propaganda campaign.

For T-4 officials, the report highlighted the fact that any future resumption of the 'euthanasia' operation would not only cause disquiet and anxiety among the population, but could damage the reputation of psychiatry for a long time to come. Scholars criticizing the field needed to be silenced, if major damage was to be prevented. On 3 September 1942, the head of T-4's medical office, Paul Nitsche, successor to Werner Heyde, drafted a letter to Professor Zutt, editor of the *Zentralblatt für die gesamte Neurologie und Psychiatrie*, in which he criticized the journal for having published a review article about a paper by a Dr Enge entitled 'The Future of Psychiatry'.[9] The author of the review article had apparently embellished parts of Enge's article by stating that those supporting the 'elimination of severe cases' were committing a 'great injustice'. By doing so, Nitsche argued, the author was defaming a programme which had the support of the government:

> The review article defames a measure which is now supported, for highly ethical reasons, by a number of responsible people, and is clearly accepted, as the success of the film *I accuse* shows, by large sections of the German people; this in spite of the fact that the film was permitted and examined by the Reich Propaganda Ministry, which showed that the state recognised that this was a significant problem.[10]

Nitsche's letter to the journal had been prompted by Linden, who had suggested two weeks earlier that the editor of the journal should be given a 'censure' (*Verwarnung*). On 20 August, Linden told Nitsche: 'It is obviously not helpful that measures carried out by the state should be criticised in public in such a fashion.'[11] Nitsche and Linden believed that the 'euthanasia' programme would be resumed in a different form, and they worked towards that goal. Since the autumn of 1941, when the programme had officially been 'halted', Nitsche had begun to put a system in place that allowed T-4 physicians to conduct research on specific patient groups, prior to the transfer to one of the killing centres.[12] On 18 September 1941, he noted that it was important to examine the existing cases of epilepsy in a research establishment 'before their disinfection'.[13] Two days later, after he had discussed the matter with Blankenburg, alias Brenner, the deputy director of the T-4 organization at the time, it was agreed that the organization would, despite the stop to the 'euthanasia' programme (*trotz Stoppung*), employ a neuropsychiatrist to examine such cases. It was also agreed that while the programme was halted (*während der Stoppung*), a doctor from each of the T-4 institutions would be seconded to a pathological-anatomical institute, probably to ensure that T-4 physicians would be in place in case the programme were to resume on a large scale.[14] On 19 November, shortly after his appointment as Reich Commissioner for Cure and Nursing Homes, Linden met with Nitsche, Allers and Heyde to discuss the future use of some of the T-4 institutions.[15] Nitsche and 'the men from the planning commission' were asked to inform Linden about the work which had been carried out so far. After liaising with the regional authorities, Linden wanted to decide, in consultation with Brack, alias Jennerwein, how some of the asylums would be used. Whereas the 'planning commission', the T-4 organizers, would remain at 4 Tiergartenstraße, one member and a secretary of the T-4 organization would transfer to the RMdI to ensure a more efficient collaboration.[16]

Little more than half a year later, on 11 and 12 May 1942, Linden met with doctors and managers from T-4 for a conference in Heidelberg; these included Valentin Falthauser (Kaufbeuren-Irsee), Otto Hebold (Eberswalde), Hans Heinze (Görden), Rudolf Lonauer (Linz), Friedrich Mennecke (Eichberg), Robert Müller (T-4), Paul Nitsche (T-4), Hermann Pfannmüller (Eglfing), Victor Ratka (Tiegenhof), Curd Runckel (T-4), Gustav Schneider (T-4), Curt Schmalenbach (T-4), Alfred Schulz (Großschweidnitz), Horst Schumann (T-4), Theodor Steinmeyer (Pfafferode), Erich Straub (T-4), and Gerhard Wischer (Waldheim).[17] These doctors and T-4 officials played a critical part in the planning and implementation of the second phase of the 'euthanasia' programme. The correspondence shows that leading government and T-4 officials believed that the halt of the 'euthanasia' programme was only temporary, and that the time could be used to improve the systematic identification and selection of potential 'euthanasia' victims under conditions of war.[18]

By the autumn of 1942, the organizers of the 'euthanasia' programme detected a noticeable shift in government policy, or at least veiled hints which could be interpreted as such. On 23 September, the government official Fritz Cropp, Linden's superior, told the institutions:

Any inconveniences for the mentally ill which occurred as a result of the overcrowding and creation of emergency camps in the individual institutions have to be accepted for a short time. I will try, however, in consultation with the representative of the Reich, to improve the overcrowding situation by transferring the mentally ill to asylums in less endangered states, regions and provinces. Please therefore inform me immediately of any changes in the number of mentally ill who are eligible for transfer.[19]

The phrase 'mentally ill who are eligible for transfer' could mean different things in the Third Reich. It could mean the transfer of those patients who were fit for transport. However, given the prevailing culture of communication, it could also be a euphemism for the identification and selection of patients who were seen as a burden on society in times of war, and who should be killed. In Berlin the message was understood. Only a week after the RMdI had informed the institutions about the 'forthcoming transfer' of mental patients, the group of fully committed T-4 psychiatrists who had met earlier in the year, and whom Nitsche called 'practical psychiatrists', met for another conference in Heidelberg, from 30 September to 1 October 1942, to discuss the administrative implications of a resumption of the 'euthanasia' programme. Those present at the conference were almost the same physicians and T-4 officials who had met in May 1942.[20] We know little of what was said, but we do know that a second conference was scheduled to take place shortly after the first to 'coordinate' the future work of medical experts (*Gutachter*). The two successive conferences suggest that T-4 wanted to ensure that the administrative machinery was put on stand-by and prepared in case the Nazi leadership ordered – or authorized – the resumption of the operation.

On 6 October 1942, Nitsche and senior T-4 physicians met to discuss any changes needed to the organization in the event of such a resumption.[21] The second conference was attended by the T-4 doctors Otto Hebold, Ernst Meumann, Robert Müller, Victor Ratka, Gustav Schneider, Gerhardt Siebert, Theodor Steinmeyer, Erich Straub and Gerhard Wischer. The reorganization included changes to the way in which the patient records would be marked in the future. A '+' sign, for example, meant: 'Unambiguous plus case, who, in case our work is suddenly resumed, can be considered for elimination in our institutions without further examination.'[22] Marking the patient record with '+?' now meant: 'Plus case, but the relevant patient has to be examined prior to the transfer in our institution.' A patient fortunate enough to be marked with a 'Ø' would 'not in any circumstances be treated by us' and would be treated as 'if he had not been identified'. Then there were the patients marked with the letters 'KZ', which meant that 'the examining physician has the discretion to transfer the patient to a concentration camp'.[23] To keep public disquiet about the operation to a minimum, and provide relatives with a false sense of security, T-4 physicians were required to state in every case the institution to which individual patients would be transferred. The minutes of the meeting say nothing about preferred killing methods, but evidence suggests that T-4 physicians anticipated from the beginning that they would kill the patients in the institutions themselves, and not in specially designed killing centres. The idea was to kill those considered to be 'unworthy of living' as inconspicuously as possible.

Three weeks later, on 26 October, the film-maker Hermann Schweninger sent Nitsche his film script for a projected documentary about mental illness and the practical execution of the 'euthanasia' programme. The film was meant to promote the ideology and 'scientific rationale' behind the programme. In section IV, on incurable patients, the film was to tell the audience: 'National Socialism has the courage to commit itself to its principles, views and feelings through action; the courage to give genuine mercy by delivering incurables through a mild death.'[24] Section V, called 'Delivery', dealt with the actual killing process in one of the killing centres. Captions 9 and 10 read: 'Bathing-room' and 'Before – After'. Far from acknowledging that the programme amounted to little more than bureaucratic murder, T-4 planners were convinced that morality and medical ethics had changed in German society, and that their own 'natural feelings' (*natürlichen Empfinden*) and 'views which were close to reality' (*wirklichkeitsnahen Anschauungen*) allowed them to perceive the killing of countless humans as delivering patients from suffering.[25]

The extent to which the resumption of the 'euthanasia' programme was initiated and promoted on the periphery often depended on the regional *Gauleiter* and their respective health departments. Whereas the *Gauleiter* of Saxony and his health officials, including Nitsche as the advisory psychiatrist of the region, were among the most ardent supporters of killing handicapped patients by means of drugs and starvation, the relevant government official in the Rhine area was significantly more critical about the operation. In Bavaria, on the other hand, a number of asylum directors had previously been involved in the 'euthanasia' programme and were now promoting a new 'starvation diet' to reduce the number of handicapped patients, and to free bed space. On 17 November, the Bavarian Ministry of the Interior invited the regional asylum directors to a conference where it became apparent that the aim of the 'starvation diet' was a 'reduction of the number of asylum inmates'.[26] The T-4 psychiatrist Valentin Falthauser, who was responsible for the killing of children and adults in the asylum of Kaufbeuren-Irsee, told the participants that he wanted to use the 'starvation diet' as a way to continue the 'euthanasia' programme by other means. Given that the transport of incurable patients to killing centres had ceased, one 'would be able to continue the thing through a gradual starvation of patients'.[27] Experience had shown, Falthauser said, that patients died within the space of about three months. Two weeks later, on 30 November, the Bavarian Ministry of the Interior instructed the regional cure and nursing homes that those inmates who were 'conducting useful work, or are in therapeutic treatment, and children who still can be educated, war veterans and those suffering from age … should be fed better; this would be detrimental to the other patients'.[28] Over the following months, a number of Bavarian asylums established special 'hunger houses' (*Hungerhäuser*) where patients assigned to die were transferred, for example in Kaufbeuren-Irsee, Eglfing-Haar, Ansbach, Erlangen, Klingenmünster and Mainkofen.

At the beginning, the killings resumed on an isolated basis, largely uncoordinated and in institutions formerly connected to the 'euthanasia' programme in one way or another. In some cases, the T-4 machinery resumed with somewhat unorthodox methods. When it turned out in December 1942 that the sudden death of the mental patient Max P. would be likely to cause major disquiet in the region, because of the patient's extended family connections, the director of the Niedernhardt asylum, Rudolf Lonauer, requested the Reich Criminal Police to transfer the patient to a concentration camp. One month later, on 30 January 1943, Dietrich Allers, the managing director of T-4 headquarters, code-named Reich Working Committee for Cure and Nursing Homes, informed Lonauer, who was also in charge of the Hartheim killing centre, about the transfer of the Russian patient Boris Mirkelo to his institution, and told him: 'The reason for the transfer should be pretty clear to you.'[29] Lonauer knew what he had to do. Shortly after having been transferred to Hartheim, Mirkelo was led to the dressing room and shot in the back. When it turned out that he was still alive, Mirkelo was carried into the gas chamber and killed by one of the male nurses.[30]

Officially, Aktion Brandt was a rapid reaction force which came into operation after heavy air raids had hit West German cities. In May 1943, when Duisburg was seriously hit by Allied bombers, Brandt had used his authority to send a fleet of ambulances and lorries to the area. These were equipped to perform field operations and able to set up evacuation hospital camps. Collaborating with the German Red Cross, headed by Grawitz, and the 'Dredge Regiment Speer', this rapid intervention force was named 'Aktion Brandt' after another bombing campaign had struck Wuppertal.[31] The organization and efficiency of this machinery was impressive. Stationed in the special hospital complex Hösel, near Düsseldorf, the force was on permanent stand-by to respond to major bombing attacks, but it also transferred patients from destroyed hospitals and asylums to other institutions in East Germany. The company Miesen in Bonn had developed extra-large ambulances for the Red Cross headquarters.[32] Traditionally the centre of the German coal and steel industry, the Ruhr area was vital for the continuation of the war effort. Brandt and Speer had been given the task of protecting the resources and manpower of the region in order to provide ammunition, fuel and tanks for the military machinery.

Almost all negotiations with the ministries, as well as with the military and civil agencies, were conducted by Brandt or by some of his top liaison men. The collaboration between Brandt's office and Speer, who by 1942 had taken over the Todt Organization and had become Minister for Armaments and War Production, worked well. Both were constantly in Hitler's vicinity. This made communication swift and informal. When in May 1944 Speer initiated the 'Geilenberg Programme' in order to secure vital industries in areas suffering from heavy air raids, Brandt was asked to provide the factories with sufficient physicians and medical supplies. Due to their organizational talents, Brandt and Speer managed to gain substantial control over these industries. They eventually managed to get a total of approximately 84,000 people released from the army for the 'Geilenberg Programme'.[33] While Brandt, like Speer, was dealing with tens of thousands of human beings on a daily basis, he may have become less concerned about individual human lives, and for mental patients in particular.

As the Allied bombing campaign spread, it became necessary to centralize control of the scarce supply of drugs and medical equipment for German cities. At the beginning of 1943, Cropp was put in charge of air-raid damage. The administrative change allowed the managers of the T-4 operation to return to centre stage. With their contacts with the relevant authorities, such as the RMdI, Speer's ministry and Brandt's office of the General Commissioner, the T-4 managers aimed to restart the 'euthanasia' programme. Access to monthly statistics about patient figures in each institution was ensured through Linden from the RMdI. As Süß has pointed out, Linden became the 'link between the health administration of the RMdI and the euthanasia complex'.[34] In January 1943, the T-4 headquarters in Berlin made the first tentative steps towards engaging the leading health authorities in discussions about the resumption of the 'euthanasia' operation; though, in fact, the asylums of Kaufbeuren, Hadamar and Meseritz-Obrawalde had been killing patients since the late summer of 1942. At the end of January 1943, Nitsche told Schneider in Heidelberg that he was planning to have a meeting with Conti in order to boost the reputation of German psychiatry, but which 'would also be valuable for the euthanasia question'.[35]

II. SENDING MIXED SIGNALS

Plans to resume the 'euthanasia' programme were brought to the attention of von Bodelschwingh and others who had opposed the registering and transfer of patients from their institutions during the first phase of the operation. At the end of 1942, von Bodelschwingh realized that the Bethel asylum might yet again become a target for the T-4 organization, when Linden told him that the RMdI was now insisting on 'registering all patients' in the future, regardless of their illness or length of stay in the asylum. Linden wanted von Bodelschwingh also to report all those patients not previously identified and registered.[36] Attempting, at first, to gauge the situation in other asylums, von Bodelschwingh soon understood that something was afoot. On 17 December, one of his colleagues told him that the 'previous action continues'.[37] Gravely concerned about the 'revival of the old things', von Bodelschwingh asked Braune rhetorically: 'Do people really want to resume the procedure in the current general situation? If not, then I can hardly understand why the asylums are expected to conduct such a laborious task'.[38]

On 2 January 1943, von Bodelschwingh decided to ask Brandt for clarification, because it had come to his attention that the 'registration forms could yet again be used for the execution of planned economy measures [*planwirtschaftliche Maßnahmen*], as they were in the years 1940 and 1941'.[39] He told Brandt that it was completely impossible to keep the processing of the forms secret, and that alarm and disquiet among the patients would result. Relatives would once again be worried that their children and elderly parents would no longer be safe in Bethel. Given that it had been agreed in February 1941 that the processing of the forms would not be expected of Bethel in the future, that if necessary it would happen at the earliest 'after two or five years', and that it would then be carried out by a commission, von Bodelschwingh requested that Brandt instruct the RMdI to exempt Bethel from filling out the forms.

The timing of the letter could not have been worse. Brandt received the letter in the midst of the catastrophe that was unfolding at Stalingrad. In the middle of January, it had become clear that tens of thousands of German soldiers were freezing and starving to death in the city, without any food or medical supplies, and with no logistical support. Ordered by Hitler to hold out or die, the leading officials knew that it was only a matter of time until the Sixth Army surrendered. Brandt and others close to military medical planning knew that every hospital bed would soon be needed for an ever increasing number of wounded German soldiers, and that the civilian health services were already overstretched. Every possibile extra bed space had to be used. Faced with the looming disaster of Stalingrad, in which tens of thousands of national comrades were about to die, Brandt regarded the transfer – and possible death through injection or starvation – of a couple of hundred mental patients as insignificant. Four weeks later he told von Bodelschwingh that, compared to the large number of people who died at Stalingrad, the 'death of all other people ranked second'.[40] Brandt's reply to von Bodelschwingh's letter was frosty, to say the least:

> My dear priest, if you think that the filling out of forms could cause disquiet among relatives and patients in your asylums, be assured that this could only happen if the relatives were wrongly informed or influenced when briefed by those responsible for this task. The filling out of forms does not mean, as you say, that the relatives of the patients should fear that their children and old parents would not be safe with you any more.[41]

Brandt required von Bodelschwingh to process the forms, but indicated that he would be willing, at some point, to discuss the content of his letter in person. At this time, leading members of the regime, Himmler, Goebbels, Speer, Ley and Brandt, especially, and Hitler himself, adopted a more radical approach to resolving the problems of the war and the stabilizing of the home front. 'The shock of Stalingrad was really quite significant,' Brandt told Alexander after the war, 'but then, time and time again we hoped that we still had the capacity to see the thing through'.[42] On 23 January 1943, Brandt told Goebbels that he shared his conviction that something extraordinary had to be done to change the direction of the war.[43] Three days later, he asked Himmler's adjutant, Karl Wolff, whether it might not be possible to conduct nutrition experiments on camp inmates.[44] Later, on 13 February, Goebbels remarked, after having spent the previous evening discussing the subject of total war with Speer and Ley over dinner, 'Speer and Ley are very radical in their views; Ley has indeed become even more radical during his journey to East Prussia.' On the same day, Goebbels noted: 'The Führer is much more radical than people generally assume, if we could only prevent the young hooligans from getting access to him time and time again, and attempting to pull him in a weak direction.'[45] Egged on by each other, the Nazi leadership further accelerated the process of cumulative radicalization which ultimately brought about the self-destruction of the German people. Von Bodelschwingh, who had recognized the destructive and criminal energy within the regime, had told Brandt in 1941 that Germans would pay for the injustices which had been committed 'with the blood of their sons'. Now, eighteen months later, his warning had become a stark reality.

On 28 January, von Bodelschwingh acknowledged Brandt's request, but told him that he did not know how to carry it out 'in good conscience'.[46] He also told Brandt that the 'new Aktion' had already become public knowledge, and that he had written to the RMdI in the meantime, requesting permission not to complete the forms. A couple of days later, on 5 February, Brandt agreed to meet von Bodelschwingh in person, perhaps after realizing that this clergyman was unlikely to give up lightly.[47] By that time, things had changed in von Bodelschwingh's favour. A couple of days earlier, Bethel's head of administration, Johannes Kunze, had learned from Linden that the official request for the processing of the medical forms had been the result 'of an error in the office'. Linden had told Kunze that the agreement, according to which Bethel and the other asylums of the *Innere Mission* were exempt from completing the forms, was still in force. On 6 February, von Bodelschwingh immediately informed Brandt of the turn of events, but accepted the invitation for a meeting nonetheless. Whether Brandt had asked Linden to withdraw the request for the completion of the forms, or whether this was another case of the ongoing administrative chaos in the regime, is not known. He was certainly not particularly concerned about any administrative errors, as long as the right kind of patients were identified in the programme. In 1945, he told his interrogators: 'That all sorts of difficulties arose on [sic] the paperwork connecting [sic] with this problem is natural, when you consider that this was the first time anything like that had been done, it is understandable and excusable.'[48] For Brandt, it was more important to engage in a mutual dialogue with von Bodelschwingh, who was vehemently opposed to the 'euthanasia' programme.

The meeting between Brandt and von Bodelschwingh took place on Saturday 13 February 1943 at Brandt's residence in the Bellevue Palace in Berlin, and lasted from 3.30 p.m. to 5 p.m.[49] Von Bodelschwingh's notes about the conversation provide a unique insight into Brandt's ambivalent mindset with regard to the revival of the killing operation. Von Bodelschwingh started off by taking up the issues he had raised in his frank letter to Brandt in August 1941 – to which Brandt remarked 'you could indeed say that' (*Das könne man wohl sagen*) – and addressed the renewed disquiet among the people. Brandt then asked whether von Bodelschwingh had only 'felt negative effects', whereupon von Bodelschwingh replied: 'Yes, exclusively!' He reiterated that the killing of patients, and the way in which it had been done, with false death certificates, for example, had led to an enormous loss of trust among Germans. Brandt admitted that certain mistakes had been made. For von Bodelschwingh, this was not good enough, and he emphasized the fact that 'such a dangerous instrument, if it falls into careless hands, must cause incalculable damage'.[50] He also told Brandt that a resumption of the programme was currently 'impossible', given the constant bombing raids in western Germany, and stressed the special relationship between the people of Westphalia and their patients. Brandt responded by saying that his viewpoint was 'fundamentally different', but that one could openly discuss the matter without each trying to push the other onto the defensive. That was why he, Brandt, had wanted to talk to von Bodelschwingh in person, and not through an intermediary such as Brack. Brandt then repeated his arguments about the apparent physical and mental suffering of patients, and said that he always had to reflect upon severely ill children, especially those with a hydrocephalus from Patmos, one of Bethel's children's wards which Brandt had visited in 1941.[51] Von Bodelschwingh remained unconvinced, saying that even those children had given young carers something that had been of importance in their career: looking after mentally ill patients had taught them things which were invaluable for their work with mentally healthy human beings.

The discussion then moved onto the question as to whether or not the regime would resume the 'euthanasia' programme. Von Bodelschwingh later noted: 'He [Brandt] apparently will and cannot say anything explicitly about the current intentions.'[52] As far as the Bethel asylum was concerned, however, Brandt agreed, for the time being, that the registration forms did not have to be completed, and that there were no plans to send a commission to Bethel to fill in the forms. 'You do not have to fear a disturbance in the foreseeable future,' he told von Bodelschwingh.[53] Von Bodelschwingh's overall impression was that Brandt was in two minds about whether the killing operation should be revived, and perhaps inclined to decide against it, but that he also considered the possibility that Hitler might force his hand on the issue at some later date:

> I have the impression that he himself will not easily decide in favour of a resumption of the procedure, but that he reckons perhaps with the possibility that it might somehow be ordered from above – in this context he drew attention to the enormous number who died at Stalingrad [*das große Sterben in Stalingrad*]. In comparison, all other deaths are of minor importance [*Demgegenüber sei alles andere Sterben klein*]. I used the opposite argument: the death of many young people was also a result of the injustice which has been committed. One should therefore not burden our people with new guilt. He hesitated to open his mind to this thought.[54]

During the conversation, Brandt struggled to maintain a coherent position, at times wavering and reassuringly undecided about what would happen next, at others more forthright and uncompromising with regard to the fate of Bethel's patients; at one moment, he would tell von Bodelschwingh that it would obviously be difficult 'to make permanent exceptions', the next, that the completion of the questionnaires was difficult anyway because of lack of personnel:

> It seems he is searching for a reason to halt the preparations [for the resumption of the 'euthanasia' programme] temporarily. He seems reluctant to commit himself, perhaps because he cannot decide without Bouhler.[55]

Von Bodelschwingh's remarks suggest that Brandt was waiting for the decision to be taken out of his hands by the development of the war, or by Hitler himself. The remainder of the meeting revolved around the religious situation in Germany and focused on the battle against Christianity by Nazi Party officials. The change of topic revealed Brandt's general lack of knowledge in the field. Von Bodelschwingh told Brandt that it was impossible for 'Germany to fight against the whole world' and, at the same time, against Christians at home. He criticized the suppression of Christians by the state, the pressures on people to leave the Church, and the fact that spiritual care was non-existent in the army. Those openly committed to Christianity were treated as second-class citizens, he told Brandt. In return, Brandt pointed out mistakes that had apparently been made by the Catholic Church, especially the misuse of the pulpit (*Kanzelmißbrauch*) for political purposes. The Christians, Brandt told von Bodelschwingh, should 'also somehow raise a flag'. What exactly he meant by that was not clear – presumably that the Christians were meant to show more nationalistic fervour. In general, von Bodelschwingh gained the impression that Brandt 'obviously knows very little about these things'.[56] Asked to name a mediator for potential negotiations between the state and the Church, von Bodelschwingh mentioned the Protestant Bishop Wurm from Württemberg, who had spearheaded some of the protests against the 'euthanasia' programme in 1940. As it happened, Brandt did not seem to know him: 'He obviously hardly knows him' (*Er kennt ihn offenbar kaum*). Brandt agreed to discuss the matter with Goebbels the same evening, and, if possible, arrange a meeting with him the next day.[57] Brandt also wanted to raise the issue at Führer headquarters and report back to von Bodelschwingh. The conversation was concluded with some light banter about Brandt's work as a doctor – he wanted to perform operations the moment he was in Berlin: 'He does not want to become a paper pusher.' After saying good-bye to Brandt's 'very nice young wife' and his seven-year-old son, von Bodelschwingh felt that Brandt had yet again made a good impression on him: 'Personally the same good impression as before. He conducts himself more freely and openly,' von Bodelschwingh remarked.[58]

Whereas Brandt was showing signs of ambivalence and uncertainty with regard to the resumption of the killing operation in February, others were pressing ahead to find a radical solution to the current crisis in the civilian health services. In the spring of 1943, some Nazi officials and T-4 managers anticipated that the 'euthanasia' programme might soon be resumed. Whether Brandt was party to these talks is not known. What is certain, however, is that rumours were circulating among the Nazi rank and file. In March 1943, the former administrators of the killing centre in Bernburg, Hans and Margot Räder-Grossmann, told the former T-4 doctor Friedrich Mennecke, who was conducting killing operations in the East: 'Nothing has happened here so far. However, there is talk that we will soon get a lot of work, and by the beginning of May we shall know one way or the other. Apart from some men, who have been released for the army, no-one is allowed to leave.'[59] After Essen and the surrounding area had been hit by another wave of heavy air raids in the first days of April, the government responded. On 4 April 1943, Linden approached the central offices in the regions in order to introduce some of the former T-4 staff into the relevant medical institutions. By doing so, he hinted at the possibility that the 'euthanasia' programme might soon be restarted:

Because the Reich itself has no mental asylums ... I am taking the liberty of asking whether your administration might be willing to appoint a psychiatrist of relevant quality to a leading asylum position in that administration ... I certainly believe that the measures of the Reich Co-operative [pseudonym for T-4] will at a given time be revived, though the nature of the procedure may be different; in particular it might be necessary to incorporate the Cure and Nursing Homes to a greater extent into the execution of the measures. The presence of an approving director with regard to these measures would then be of utmost importance.[60]

Hospital directors and directors of cure and nursing homes were given a fairly clear idea of the intentions of the authorities, and of what they themselves had to do to support the government. To revive 'the measures of the Reich Co-operative' was the established code for the killing of mental patients by the T-4 administration. They were also told that the 'kind of procedure' would be different; in particular, that it would be necessary for the staff of the cure and nursing homes to carry out the actual killings, and that therefore the presence of a director who 'approved' and took responsibility for the killings was essential for the execution of the operation. Linden's circular suggested to the regional authorities that the decentralized policy of killing patients by means of drugs and starvation was sanctioned by Hitler and the regime. In contrast to the first phase of the 'euthanasia' programme, patients were now supposed to be killed in their own institutions or in those institutions to which they had been transferred, but not in specially designed killing centres. The transfer of large numbers of mental patients, however, made parts of the German population suspicious. In some cases, relatives took the mentally ill home, and brought them back once the transfers had been completed.[61] Such occurrences had to be prevented if the operation was to be successful.

On 4 April, the same day that Linden alluded to the resumption of the 'euthanasia' programme, Brandt accompanied Hitler, Speer, Giesler and Hoffmann to St Florian near Linz, Austria, to see the winged altarpiece which had been painted for the abbey, *Augustiner-Chorherrenstift*. Hitler and his entourage also travelled to St Valentin to inspect, yet again, the Nibelungen armaments plant, and to Linz, near Hitler's birthplace, where the dictator discussed ongoing and future building projects.[62] Hitler's arrival in St Florian was greeted by jubilant crowds. Brandt, at this point, was significantly detached from the T-4 organization, and hardly available for any of the officials who intended to revive the operation.

Six days later, on 10 April 1943, Goebbels chaired a conference in Essen as the head of the Inter-Ministerial Committee for Air Raid Damage, in order to coordinate rescue and reconstruction operations in the region. He was in no mood for half measures. Having travelled from Berlin to Essen by the overnight train, Goebbels had discussed the dire situation of the German air force with General Field Marshal Milch, who had levelled the most severe criticism against Göring.[63] Arriving in Essen in the early hours of 10 April, he witnessed the enormous destruction which had been inflicted upon the city by the British air force. He acknowledged that a large percentage of the city had to be 'written off'.

The conference started at 10 a.m. and assembled representatives of the ministries in Berlin, including Ley, the Reich Commissioner for Cure and Nursing Homes, the *Gauleiter* of the West German regions, and a number of mayors whose cities had been severely damaged. A number of *Gauleiter*, supported by Goebbels, argued that 'all mentally ill should increasingly be transferred to the East' to free up much-needed bed spaces.[64] Six weeks later, Brandt was invited to become a member of the Inter-Ministerial Committee for Air Raid Damage to coordinate the 'central planning of hospital beds'.[65]

In the Third Reich, a government proposal to send large numbers of people to the eastern territories could mean little else than the systematic killing of those who were considered to be a burden for society in the midst of war. A week after the conference, Linden provided the district of Düsseldorf with 2,500 beds in foreign asylums that were located, in part, in the Generalgouvernement. In the period between May and July 1943, and in tandem with the evacuation of wounded civilians and the elderly, about 4,000 mentally ill patients were transferred from the Rhineland to other regions, where most of them were killed. By the end of the war, an estimated 6,000 mental patients from the Rhine region had been killed in this way.[66]

Hitler was in no mood for compromise. Throughout April 1943, he conducted a flurry of diplomatic activity at the Berghof or at the Palace of Kleßheim to shore up morale among the Axis allies. From 7 to 10 April, Mussolini visited the baroque palace of Kleßheim, near Salzburg, where Hitler and the Nazi leadership attempted to boost the morale of the Fascist dictator. It was one of those occasions where Brandt and others were asked to remain in the background. On at least one occasion, he stood guard for the arrival of Mussolini.[67] For the first time, Hitler used the 'Jewish Question' to pressure the heads of government from Bulgaria, Romania, Hungary, Norway, Slovakia, Croatia and Vichy France to stay on board with the German war machine. In particular, he criticized them for having introduced policies against the Jews which were far too mild. In April, Himmler's SS had informed Hitler that a million and a half Jews had so far been 'evacuated' and 'channelled through' the Polish camps. Alluding to the ongoing Holocaust, Hitler told them that he had 'thoroughly cleaned up' things in Poland. Jews not wanting to work should be shot and 'if they could not work, then they would have to rot'.[68] The more radical their measures against the Jews the better. Reverting to his social-Darwinist outlook, he told Admiral Nikolaus Horty, the regent of Hungary, that the Jews 'would have to be treated like tuberculosis bacilli from which a healthy body could become infected. This is not cruel, if you consider that even innocent creatures, like hares and deer, have to be killed. Why should the beasts that want to bring us Bolshevism be spared?'[69] Although Brandt would probably not have objected to Hitler's biological world view, it is unlikely that he was party to these exchanges. One of Hoffmann's photographs from the time of Horty's visit on 16 and 17 April shows Brandt reading a book in a deckchair outside on the balcony of the palace of Kleßheim, in the presence of a member of Hitler's SS-Leibstandarte.[70] Seemingly unaware of what was discussed inside, Brandt appeared to be enjoying the first rays of sun after spending a long and harsh winter in Hitler's field headquarters in East Prussia.

Around this time, Hitler told his *Reichs-* and *Gauleiter* that the German people would face terrible retribution if the war were lost. They had to understand that boats had been burned and that they were all in it together. There is little doubt that they got the message. Compared with a quarter of a million Axis soldiers captured in Tunis, over half of them German, and North Africa lost to the Allies, the death of hundreds, perhaps thousands of mental patients, who added little to the war effort, was of no relevance to the *Reichs-* and *Gauleiter*. Most of them had already been made complicit in mass murder on a far larger scale. The more radical approach by the *Reichs-* and *Gauleiter* to free bed space was reflected in a change of tack at the centre of government. Amidst the negotiations with numerous heads of government, Brandt found sufficient time to talk to Hitler about the state of German health services. On 16 April, he told Conti that he had discussed with Hitler a centralized plan for the supply of hospital beds, and that he was intending to appoint Zeitler as his representative for this. Significantly, Brandt made it clear that the previous administrative machinery, and officials formerly involved in the 'euthanasia' programme, would play a central part in the operation:

> Having visited north-west Germany, and on the basis of a number of conversations with individual *Gauleiter*, I have become convinced that a large-scale plan for the supply of hospital beds etc. is necessary. I have therefore initiated, after discussing the matter with the Führer, a corresponding central plan (*Zentralplanung*) and have chosen to join me in this task Herrn President Dr Zeitler, whom I have appointed at the same time as a member of my team. The organisation (*Einrichtung*) which has helped us in the registration of the cure and nursing homes through the Chancellery of the Führer will support him. Herr Blankenburg will also collaborate in this.[71]

Brandt's reference to the 'organisation (*Einrichtung*) which has helped us in the registration of the cure and nursing homes through the Chancellery of the Führer' was code for the former 'euthanasia' administration, and Blankenburg was a former member of the 'euthanasia' programme. There could be little doubt for Conti that the Nazi leadership was in the process of reviving the 'euthanasia' programme, even if no official authorization for the renewed killing of patients had yet been given. Government officials had by now become accustomed to interpreting such generalized hints in a way which would not implicate the Nazi leadership itself in the operation.

Four days later it was Hitler's fifty-fourth birthday, celebrated on the Berghof in the presence of his staff and their families.[72] Some of the birthday photographs show Hitler standing in his reception room, flanked by Eva and Franziska Braun, Karl and Anni Brandt, Martin and Gerda Bormann, Theo and Hanni Morell, Albert and Margarete Speer, Marion Schönemann, Gretl Fegelein, Gerhard Engel, and Walter Frentz.[73] Other images show Hitler among the children of members of his entourage, for example among Eva, Maria and Eicke Bormann, Fritz and Albert Speer, Hilde Schramm and Karl-Adolf Brandt, Brandt's seven-year-old son.[74]

Amidst all the flowers and birthday presents, an uninformed observer might have thought that the rustic festivities belonged to a successful middle-aged business man, the director of a company, perhaps, who had gathered his family and friends at his Alpine house. Except for Brandt, few of the birthday guests would have known that the regime was in the process of evacuating thousands of the mentally ill and the elderly to other asylums, where many of them would die as a result of drug injections, starvation and neglect. Perhaps some of the guests had a sense that the war was not going according to plan, but all of them were utterly determined to ignore reality until it was too late.

In the period between 1941 and 1944, an estimated 35,000 patients were evacuated and deported from a range of mental institutions, and thousands were killed.[75] The major evacuation of mentally ill patients began in the spring of 1943 in the Rhineland, continued in Hamburg and Westphalia, and later expanded to Berlin. Almost any patient could be transferred to another asylum. In some instances, patients suffering from chronic or incurable illnesses who could not easily be transferred were selected to make space for wounded civilians. Beds freed by the transfer of mental patients, however, were not available for everybody, neither for prisoners of war, nor for eastern workers or slave and forced labourers.[76] Even ordinary Germans, the frail and sick and those suffering from incurable diseases, were not supposed to have access to these additional hospital beds. Dying patients were not necessarily admitted to hospitals any longer, and only the most essential operations and treatments were permitted. Officials in the RMdI and other agencies tried, but largely failed, to prevent the German army from taking over the additional bed space which had been created through the transfers. The army was one of the greatest beneficiaries of the second phase of the 'euthanasia' programme.[77] In some cases, the German military authorities also initiated the murder of mental patients in the occupied territories to free much-needed bed space.[78] In a largely decentralized fashion, the Nazis were gradually beginning to replace the mental patients in cure and nursing homes with physically ill and wounded civilians.[79]

III. PLAUSIBLE DENIABILITY

Careful to distance himself from any suggestion that a centralized 'euthanasia' programme had been restarted, mainly because of the regime's public relations concerns, Brandt, not unlike Hitler, communicated orders most of the time orally and to messengers. This allowed him to deny responsibility later. It was this level of aloofness which almost all the key leaders of the regime had cultivated as a means of power, and as a means of survival. It is a policy better known as 'plausible deniability': the idea of detaching oneself sufficiently from illegal activities, while at the same time producing evidence that makes it possible to deny involvement later, and blame someone else.[80] After the war, Lieutenant Colonel Leonard A. Scheele from the US Public Health Branch stated that he believed that Brandt had 'withheld information regarding war crimes and that he was always attempting to establish an alibi for himself.'[81] Those who were on the receiving end of Brandt's instructions, however, put pen to paper and shared their information with colleagues and confidants. Their notes not only provide some of the few existing sources which link Brandt with the continued killing programme, but they also tell us something about the prevailing culture of communication which governed the second phase of the 'euthanasia' programme.

Important decisions with regard to the continuation of the 'euthanasia' programme were given at a time when the military situation looked increasingly bleak for Germany. Almost all of Brandt's instructions and assignments for killing handicapped patients were given orally. The idea for the decentralized killings seems to have come from T-4 psychiatrists, who supported the programme, and from some of the regional authorities. But the overall government sanction apparently came from Brandt, who was seen as a direct representative of the will of the Führer. If Brandt sanctioned the programme, then Hitler had given his overall consent, at least that is how T-4 physicians would have read it. Brandt's remarks made in passing, his veiled hints and general instructions had become the extension of Hitler's wishes, which at this point in the war meant an extension of Hitler's will. Innuendoes and comments made by Brandt could be interpreted as having the force of law in Nazi Germany, and doctors in mental institutions acted accordingly. Reading not Hitler's, but his representatives' wishes, became the art of finding out whether Hitler might sanction a particular policy. In the case of the decentralized killing programme, the psychiatrists were not working towards the Führer any longer, but towards Hitler's doctor, who, they believed, had the ear of the Führer.[82] They were working, so it seems, towards Brandt.

Based on Hitler's general directives, Brandt possessed 'charismatic authority' which enabled him to interfere in medical politics in a dynamic and flexible fashion, and adapt to the changing demands of the war.[83] By mid-1943, the increasing number of evacuations from West Germany had led to a situation where the hospitals and asylums in the receiving areas were beginning to show serious signs of overcrowding. The flow of patient populations from one side of the country to the other added additional pressures to a regional administration stretched already to the limits. On 7 July, Linden acknowledged in his Barracks Decree (*Barackenerlaß*) that the asylums in the receiving regions had exhausted, or would soon have exhausted, their ability to admit any further patients.[84] At the same time, the authorities were piling on the pressure to free as many beds as possible in order to ensure that the health services could cope with the rising number of wounded civilians who were expected over the coming months. By the autumn of 1943, the situation had worsened to such an extent that Linden told the regional government authorities that the asylums of all regions (*Gaue*) were so overcrowded that 'evacuations, except for the ongoing special actions (*Sonderaktionen*), are no longer possible'.[85] Linden's remark about the 'ongoing special actions' probably referred to the large-scale transfer of patients from Hamburg and Westphalia which was instigated in the summer of 1943.[86]

On Thursday 17 June 1943, Hitler entrusted Brandt with the organization and distribution of hospital space for the whole of the German Reich.[87] On the same day, Allers told the Ministry of the Interior in Saxony that Brandt had instructed him to evacuate all cure and nursing homes in air-raid areas, beginning with the transfer of 23,000 mentally ill patients from Rhineland and Westphalia to other regions, including Saxony.[88] Allers told the Ministry that he would have to make use of the asylums in Arnsdorf, Großschweidnitz and Leipzig-Dösen. At around the same time, discussions about the evacuation of individual asylums were taking place in Westphalia. On 21 June, regional officials met with members of T-4's transport organization, whom Brandt had authorized to discuss the transfer of patients from Aplerbeck, Münster and Warstein.[89] At around the same time, T-4 planners were producing a statistical overview of the existing bed space in German cure and nursing homes. An internal T-4 statistic from 3 August calculated a grand total of 172,132 beds in thirty-one institutions.[90] Given the rising tensions between the urgent need to free bed space and an overcrowded asylum system, it comes perhaps as no surprise that some medical professionals, especially those previously involved in the 'euthanasia' programme, proposed to relieve the pressure on the health system by killing those patients who were unfit to work and deemed to be incurable.[91]

There is some evidence that Brandt, although generally detached from the operation, wanted to diffuse any rumours about the killings which might be raised by individuals or institutions, and in particular by the Church. In February, Brandt and von Bodelschwingh had agreed to meet again in order to continue their conversation. Whether another meeting took place is not certain, but, contrary to what some scholars have suggested, there is some evidence that it did.[92] A proposed meeting in mid-April failed, because von Bodelschwingh only received Brandt's invitation on the day Brandt was leaving Berlin to attend the negotiations at the palace of Kleßheim, near Salzburg.[93] Brandt was nonetheless still interested in talking to von Bodelschwingh. On 20 April, Brandt told him that he would inform him if another opportunity for a meeting arose.[94] Von Bodelschwingh, on the other hand, said he was willing to meet Brandt in Berlin or in Berchtesgaden in the first half of May.[95] Finally, on 8 June 1943, von Bodelschwingh told Brandt that he would be in Berlin for a long weekend, from Friday 18 June to Monday 21 June. We know that Brandt was at the Berghof on 18 June, but he returned to Berlin on the night train that evening.[96] Both men were in Berlin during the weekend which followed, and were thus able to meet.

Brandt's secretary, Jutta Rach, told the Nuremberg court in 1947 that she was present during one of the meetings between Brandt and von Bodelschwingh, and she confirmed the informality of the discussion: 'In the summer of 1943, Pastor Bodelschwingh once was a guest for a whole afternoon in the private flat of Prof. Brandt in my presence, when they aired the issues in an informal fashion.'[97] Rach might not have remembered the date correctly, although it is difficult to confuse a meeting which took place in February with one which took place during the summer. It is highly unlikely that Rach attended the meeting in February 1943, because she only started working as Brandt's secretary on 1 April. She must have either lied to the court or remembered the date correctly.

Other evidence seems to confirm that another meeting took place. In a letter dated 15 June, von Bodelschwingh told Braune that he would see 'brother Brandt' in Potsdam on Friday 18 June. This referred probably to Wilhelm Brandt, the director of the Reich Women's Aid since 1942. He also told Braune that he would have 'some negotiations in Berlin on Saturday'.[98] The rather vague reference about 'some negotiations in Berlin' is reminiscent of von Bodelschwingh's code for the 'negotiations' which he had previously held with Brandt in Bethel and Berlin. On 16 February, three days after the meeting with Brandt, von Bodelschwingh had told Pastor Nell from Düsseldorf that Brandt had given him the assurance that Bethel and its associated asylums would not have to process the registration forms. Von Bodelschwingh told Nell that he could pass on the information, but he suggested that Nell should do this in a general, roundabout way, if he did it in writing. Von Bodelschwingh proposed the phrase 'I have been officially informed by the relevant office in Berlin'.[99] The fact that von Bodelschwingh did not further specify what he was doing in Berlin, and that he may have met with Brandt on a Saturday, the same day of the week as he had done in February, makes it likely that a meeting between the two men took place during this weekend. So it seems quite possible that von Bodelschwingh saw Brandt on Saturday 19 June at his flat in the Bellevue Palace in Berlin.

Why is it of significance that von Bodelschwingh might have had a second meeting with Brandt in the summer of 1943? It is relevant because it appears that Brandt was seriously considering resuming the 'euthanasia' programme at this point. It would fit what we know of him that he would want to inform von Bodelschwingh of his decision in advance, and discuss a kind of compromise; this would also help von Bodelschwingh, on the one hand, to save some of his patients, and the regime, on the other, to keep opposition against the killings to a minimum. Brandt's post-war statements suggest that this kind of narrative is probably more than speculation. After the war, Brandt recalled the following about one of the conversations he had with von Bodelschwingh:

> When I talked to Pastor Bodelschwingh, the only serious warning voice I ever met personally, it seemed at first as if our thoughts were far apart, but the longer we talked and the more we came into the open, the closer and the greater became our mutual understanding. At that time we weren't concerned with words. It was a struggle and a search far beyond the human scope and sphere. When old Pastor Bodelschwingh, after many hours, left me and we shook hands, his last words were, 'that was the hardest struggle of my life.'[100]

Given that Brandt recalled that von Bodelschwingh 'left me', we must assume that the meeting took place at Brandt's flat in Berlin, and therefore excludes any of the previous meetings, when Brandt visited Bethel in 1941. Brandt's recollection about the end of the conversation, if it is true, does not sound remotely like the end of the conversation von Bodelschwingh had in Brandt's flat in February 1943, when they engaged in some light discussion about Brandt's work as a surgeon. There is no indication from von Bodelschwingh's notes about the meeting in February that it constituted the 'hardest struggle' of his life. If von Bodelschwingh ever said this, it is more likely that he said it at a time when his patients were yet again under threat, that is in the summer of 1943. Earlier, in February, Brandt had been in two minds about whether he should support the resumption of the 'euthanasia' programme, and had assured von Bodelschwingh that he would not have to fear anything from T-4 in the foreseeable future.[101] If there was a threat to Bethel's patients, it is likely to have materialized in the summer of 1943. The fact that Brandt later recorded in his personal notebook, which he kept at Nuremberg, that he was not entirely sure whether von Bodelschwingh was once or twice at his home in Berlin (*Pastor Bodelschwingh ..., der [1mal? 2 mal?] bei mir zu Hause in meiner Wohnung war*), but recalled that he visited him twice in Bethel, is another indication that it is quite possible that the two men met both in February and in the summer of 1943 in Berlin.[102]

Brandt's post-war statement was not only intended to cloud his defining role in the operation, but was meant to stress the idealistic and moral intentions behind his support for the 'euthanasia' programme. Both men probably struggled hard to come to an agreement. They were both experienced tacticians, who knew that they had to concede some of their objectives, and perhaps justify their encounter later. The outcome of the meeting was mutually beneficial for both men, and gave Brandt what he wanted. The regime no longer had to deal with public criticism of the elimination of handicapped patients from the Bethel asylum. In return, Brandt seems to have excluded the Bethel institution from the continued 'euthanasia' programme. The deal, if one was struck one way or another, meant that von Bodelschwingh had to remain silent to save the lives of *his* patients. It was a moral conflict which was clearly of Faustian proportions. One can easily see why, at the end of the talks, the old man may have said that it had been 'the hardest struggle of [his] life', not so much because he and Brandt had struggled over the moral issues, which they had done previously, and might have done on this occasion as well, but because von Bodelschwingh knew that he had sold part of his soul.[103] In short, von Bodelschwingh had implicated himself in the killing operation to save his own patients. Another factor which warrants consideration is the fact that Rach seems to have been present at the meeting, most likely because Brandt wanted to have a witness to the conversation who could implicate von Bodelschwingh if necessary. Significantly, there is no further evidence of any meeting with Brandt in the Bethel archive. If the meeting between the two men took place in the summer of 1943, and if an agreement of such a nature had been struck, it would not be surprising that von Bodelschwingh, who was a notorious notetaker, would not have wanted the outcome of the meeting recorded on paper.[104] Apparently, no further patients were transferred from the Bethel asylum.[105]

Only days later, on 23 June 1943, while the conflict with Conti was coming to a head, Brandt met with the T-4 psychiatrists Paul Nitsche and Maximinian de Crinis in Berlin. The meeting was convened on an ad hoc basis to discuss the future of German psychiatry and the resumption of the 'euthanasia' programme.[106] Nitsche was informed of the meeting only a few hours in advance. He later told the racial hygienist Ernst Rüdin: 'It is extraordinarily difficult to get in touch with Prof. Br[andt] and there was suddenly the rare opportunity, mediated through de Crinis, that we both could talk to him …'[107] In the presence of Brandt, Nitsche and de Crinis reiterated their 'Thoughts and Proposals concerning the Future Development of Psychiatry' which they had laid down in a comprehensive memorandum.[108] A number of eminent German neurologists and psychiatrists, among them Rüdin and the psychiatrist Carl Schneider, had realized that Nazi psychiatry would ultimately make the profession superfluous, and themselves unemployed. By killing tens of thousands of mental patients, German psychiatrists were seriously damaging the reputation of their academic discipline, prompting one physician to ask, 'Who will wish to study psychiatry when it becomes so small a field?'[109] Two weeks earlier, on 5 June 1943, Nitsche and de Crinis had presented the same memorandum to Conti as part of their 'Aktion with the Reich Health Leader' (Aktion beim Reichsgesundheitsführer). Given that it was unclear at the time who was in charge of German health and medicine, the psychiatrists approached the two most senior officials, hoping that one of them, at least, would support their plan.[110]

The central idea of the memorandum was to boost the standing of German psychiatry, which, they argued, fulfilled an important role in the Nazi state. They aimed not only to identify and research hereditary illnesses among the German people, but also if possible to prevent them. Given that the work of the discipline had been undermined, criticized and discredited in the recent past, Nazi psychiatrists had detected a 'serious crisis' in recruiting young doctors to the field. Others who had already trained in the field were 'fleeing' from it. The lay public was apparently badly informed about the discipline and often equated hereditary inferiority with inferiority generally. The aim was to reverse the negative reputation of psychiatry by stressing the scientific importance and practical value of the field. They told Brandt that stressing the importance of somatic therapies, and of other apparent successes of the field, would persuade the population to accept and tolerate the killing of all 'hopeless cases':

> Also, the euthanasia measure will find a more general understanding and acceptance, if in every case of psychiatric illness every effort is made to heal the patients, or at least to improve their condition so that they can work, either in their profession or in some other way for the national economy, and moreover if it becomes widely known that this is what we are doing.[111]

The psychiatrists welcomed the establishment of a central register of all asylums and cure and nursing homes which identified changes in, and movements of, patient populations in a special card index. They saw this as a reliable basis for a uniform coordination of the asylum system in which psychiatrists would continue to serve in leading positions in the future, and also as a basis for the resumption of the 'euthanasia' programme in the future.[112] Nitsche then came up with a 'pretty concrete proposal' on how to organize the continuation of the 'euthanasia' programme, the so-called 'Aktion with Prof. Br.[andt]' (Aktion bei Prof. Br[andt]).[113] We do not know exactly what the proposal entailed, but it is likely that

Nitsche suggested the killing of individual patients by means of luminal injections after they had been on a 'starvation diet'.[114]

There were good reasons why Nitsche approached Brandt and not Conti with the idea. Brandt was widely known as the advocate and plenipotentiary of the 'euthanasia' programme, who had ready access to Hitler – a key factor if the operation was to have the necessary government sanctioning. The idea was to organize the killings in such a way that it would be virtually impossible to link them to any agency of the state and thus implicate the Nazi leadership. The programme would be introduced independently by each of the asylum directors, and according to the specific and changing needs for hospital beds. Whenever bed space was needed, for example after a bombing raid, a certain number of patients would be transferred to specific institutions where they would be killed by means of a 'starvation diet' in combination with drugs. Only the transport of patients would be centrally organized. The operation was far more flexible than Aktion T-4 and was adjusted to the specific conditions of the war. The surviving fragments suggest, however, that Brandt gave the two men no indication of whether or not he would support such a proposal. He only told them that he would be willing to meet them again in the future. Brandt, at this point, remained uncommitted.[115]

We have a fairly good idea why Brandt was so cautious at this point. By the time he met the two psychiatrists, Brandt's position had come under increasing attack from leading government officials. Throughout the last couple of weeks, Conti had criticized him in front of senior members of the regime. Only five days earlier, on 18 June 1943, Brandt had denied his involvement in a number of previous operations. His denials were so obviously stage-managed that Lammers and Bormann had severely criticized Brandt's managerial style.[116] This may explain in part why Brandt was reluctant to appear as the man in charge of another 'euthanasia' programme: it not only interfered with some of Conti's areas of responsibility, but had also previously proved unpopular. He knew that by taking a firmer position in the matter, he could risk losing power altogether. Brandt only agreed to consider the proposal. His subsequent handling of the issue, and the way in which he communicated with Nitsche, also indicated to de Crinis that it was unlikely that Brandt would shoulder much responsibility for any revival of the 'euthanasia' programme.[117] Brandt's general tendency to remain unavailable to Nitsche and de Crinis for more than nine months seems to confirm this interpretation.[118]

Brandt's priority for the time being remained the evacuation of mental institutions, not the killing of large numbers of patients. On 23 June 1943, the same day that he met Nitsche and de Crinis, Brandt discussed the evacuation of asylums with Linden from the RMdI, who had the necessary bureaucratic machinery at his disposal.[119] Although he agreed with the RMdI's overall planning, Brandt suggested that 'it would not in any case be advisable to leave the mentally ill in the asylums', thus alluding to the fact that in cases where hospital beds were urgently needed, it might be better to evacuate the mentally ill to specially designated asylums.[120] The information was probably brought to Conti's attention. On the same day, Brandt discussed with Cropp the issue of evacuation hospitals for patients suffering from infectious diseases. The next day, 24 June 1943, being unable to get hold of Conti, Brandt telephoned Cropp to organize the evacuation of wounded citizens from Mühlheim and Oberhausen. Brandt also told him about his conversation with Linden the previous day. Cropp replied that he had also discussed the matter with Linden a couple of days previously, and that Linden had told him that Brandt's views about the organization of the asylum system corresponded to the measures which had been decided, or were planned, by the RMdI. In other words, Brandt and leading Nazi officials agreed that the evacuation and transfer of patient groups from areas vulnerable to air raids was now accepted government policy.

Assuming that Brandt believed that patients would only be transferred to other asylums, and not killed, it nevertheless stretches credibility to the limits to think that he was unaware of what the renewed use of the T-4 organization and personnel would imply for such an operation. Did he really have no sense of how the physicians on the periphery would perceive the renewed use of the T-4 administration? It may well be that Brandt thought that the T-4 administration could be used for a different purpose, namely just for the transfer of mentally ill patients, but he never monitored how the programme evolved. It soon became clear that doctors and officials on the ground had understood the signals that were coming from the top of the regime in a way which would mean the death of thousands of patients.

Twenty-four hours later, on 25 June, Brandt called Cropp again to order the transfer of healthy babies from air-raid areas, but Cropp told him that healthy babies were formally outside his realm of influence. Brandt and Conti's battle over areas of responsibility had reached another low. Brandt was in no mood to surrender. A couple of hours later, after having spoken to Conti, he phoned Cropp again, telling him that the matter concerned babies and small children who were ill. Then, in the afternoon, it turned out that Brandt had indeed wanted the evacuation of healthy babies. The level of confusion was beginning to obstruct any meaningful emergency planning. On the same day, Linden informed the cure and nursing homes that Brandt had ordered the first transfer of mental patients by T-4's transport organization.[121] About a week later, Brandt ordered the transfer of mental patients from West Germany to East Prussia.[122] German asylum directors and regional officials now learned that all financial and bureaucratic matters for the operation would be dealt with by T-4's Central Accounting Office for State Hospitals and Nursing Homes, at 4 Tiergarten Straße, the former address of the 'euthanasia' programme.

The next day, on 26 June, the whole matter became the subject of another discussion about Brandt's areas of competence. Conti told Bormann that party officials in Saxony had been complaining about the fact that Brandt had ordered regional officials to accommodate a thousand mentally ill patients, and that he had given his instructions directly to the transport company. Although Conti's members of staff, Cropp and Linden in particular, were well informed, Conti told Bormann that he knew nothing about it, probably to emphasize the fact that Brandt had been interfering in his domain. Another possibility is that he was insufficiently briefed by his own staff.[123] The dispute over the transfer of patients to Saxony was part of an attempt by the regional authorities to prevent any further transportation of patients to the region. In June, the regional health leader, the SS-Obersturmbannführer Alfred Fernholz, responsible for the 'euthanasia' programme in Saxony, had been instructed by the *Gauleiter* that 'non-Saxon mental patients' should no longer be admitted to the regional asylums.[124] In the end, the T-4 organization managed to force the regional authorities to accept the transport of patients from other regions, although only after Brandt's intervention. Brandt increasingly interfered in the regional decision-making process and asserted his authority to speed up the large-scale evacuation process of mental patients. T-4, on the other hand, operated more and more on the basis of directives given by the General Commissioner.

In the meantime, the practice of killing specially selected patients had not been affected by the halt of the programme. Any public debate or admission that in certain cases patients were killed was nonetheless to be avoided at all costs. On 12 July, Linden told the racial hygienist and SS-Standartenführer, Karl Astel, in charge of the State Department for Racial Matters in Thuringia, that the Reich Committee for the Scientific Registering of Serious Hereditary and Congenital Illnesses, which served as a cover for the children's 'euthanasia' programme, had alerted him to the fact that medical staff at the University of Jena had repeatedly made entries into patient records which suggested that Nazi 'euthanasia' was being practised: the 'application for euthanasia has been made' (*Euthanasie beantragt*), for example, or 'euthanasia, which has been applied for, has not yet been granted' (*Die beantragte Euthanasie is noch nicht bewilligt*). Astel was asked to ensure that the relevant officials discontinue such entries for fear of negative publicity: 'As you know, the fact that in individual cases euthanasia can be granted shall not become public knowledge.'[125]

One factor, which may have highlighted for Brandt the urgent need to free hospital beds, was the fact that he saw the total destruction of entire regions from bombing raids and the massive human suffering which went along with it. He later recalled that he witnessed between twenty-five and thirty heavy bombing raids first hand which exposed him to 'very shocking images'.[126] On 21 June, Schaub told Sister Treulinde that he had travelled with Brandt through the Ruhr area to inspect the damage that had been caused by Allied bombings.[127] Shortly thereafter, on 30 June, Brandt told Lammers that, having witnessed 'the events in the Ruhr area', he no longer had any sympathy for Conti's concerns about areas of responsibility.[128] What mattered most was that the population was provided with medical aid in an expeditious and efficient fashion.

Brandt was also present during one of the heaviest air raids Germany had ever witnessed. On 24 July 1943, the Allies began their second carpet-bombing of the city of Hamburg in what was termed 'Operation Gomorrah'. Arriving on the second day, Brandt stayed on and experienced almost the entire raid. 'You cannot imagine what I saw there,' he told Alexander after the war.[129] Brandt flew to Hamburg on the morning of 25 July. From 80 kilometres away he could smell the smoke in the cabin of his aircraft and see a massive cloud over the city.[130] After his plane had landed, he was shocked to find the administration on the ground in total disarray. There was virtually no collaboration or coordination between the agencies of army, navy, party, police, city, Gau and state. Brandt immediately placed the chief medical officer in charge of all medical and relief operations. On the night of 27 to 28 July, Allied bombers struck again, the attack more deadly this time: more than 2,000 explosive and fire bombs fell on the city. The resulting firestorm caused unimaginable human suffering and the total destruction of large parts of the town. Brandt recalled that the 'updraft' was so horrific that it overturned cars and trucks; the resulting heat was 'beyond description':

> In Hamburg, I was literally lying on the floor and on my belly and was holding myself onto a broken lamp post with my hand in order not to be thrown across the street and into the fire. I was lying there until others helped me to pull myself away out of the suction. Unimaginable.[131]

Many people were less fortunate and were sucked into the flames, he told his interrogators after the war.[132] About 40,000 people died, among them 7,000 children and young adults. In many cases people were burned alive on the street, or suffocated in the houses or the bunkers to which they had fled. More than 900,000 citizens had to be evacuated.[133] Totally exhausted, Brandt drove to the university clinic in Hamburg-Eppendorf where he organized emergency medical supplies and ambulances to evacuate the patients.[134] The air raid was a stark reminder to the Nazi regime that the existing bunkers and places of safety were totally inadequate, and that the health system was insufficiently prepared for this level of warfare. The attack on Hamburg also highlighted the deadly mix of explosive and fire bombs, which left hundreds of people with severe burns. A couple of weeks later Grawitz, prompted by Brandt, asked Himmler to conduct experiments on human subjects in the Sachsenhausen concentration camp in order to test a new ointment for phosphorous burns.[135] It is quite possible that Brandt's personal experience of the raid, which had destroyed various hospitals and medical supply depots, may also have contributed to his decision to authorize the evacuation of asylums for hospital use, and thus, perhaps, the killing of mental patients.[136] The raid on Hamburg and other German cities may well have dispelled any moral or ethical objections which the leading Nazi officials might have had against experiments on camp inmates or against the transfer and 'elimination' of mentally handicapped patients.[137]

The ever more frequent emergencies also gave Brandt an opportunity to consolidate his position. On 24 July, the same day that the air raid on Hamburg began, Brandt phoned Conti from Führer headquarters and instructed him to inform Poschmann that Hitler had ordered the administrative transfer of all hospitals established as part of Aktion Brandt to the office of the General Commissioner.[138] Poschmann was ordered to complete the transfer by the middle of August, and report back to Brandt. Knowing that the conflict with Conti would soon be coming to a head, Brandt wanted to demonstrate that he would not shy away from difficult decisions, and that he was willing to take a radical approach should any problems arise in providing medical care for German soldiers and citizens. Demoting Conti to the position of a messenger did not go unnoticed, however. A week later, on 30 July, one of Conti's closest allies remarked: 'One can truly say that we have almost no say.'[139] Brandt had successfully exploited the crisis to make an impression on one of Hitler's most trusted lieutenants. On 9 August 1943, Goebbels noted in his diary: 'Professor Brandt has worked very well with regard to the evacuation of the hospitals and military field hospitals. The Army agencies have once again completely failed in this area.'[140]

Officials on the fringes of the T-4 machinery, largely on their own initiative, interpreted the information about the 'imminent evacuation' of mental patients in the same way in which they had previously understood the transfer of patients in the 'euthanasia' operation, in which T-4 managers had used a range of euphemisms to cover for state-sanctioned murder. By attempting to camouflage the killings, Nazi officials had distorted the German language to such an extent that it had become almost impossible for doctors and officials on the ground to distinguish whether 'evacuation' meant the transfer of humans to more secure locations or, in fact, the killing of patient populations. Officials sometimes chose the more radical interpretation, even if this might not have been Brandt's intention. By distorting the flow of information in the traditional channels of administration, the *Lingua Tertii Imperii* further accelerated the process of confusion, and ensured that radical forces in the regime could turn their own policy initiatives into reality.

IV. DETACHED DECISION-MAKING

Always one step ahead, Nitsche and others ensured that the necessary apparatus was put on stand-by to continue the 'euthanasia' programme the moment it was authorized. On 8 August 1943, Werner Blankenburg, alias Brenner, who in the meantime had succeeded Brack as head of T-4, drew up new 'standing orders for T-4 headquarters and Asylum "C"' (*Geschäftsordnung für Zentraldienststelle und Anstalt 'C'*). Asylum 'C' referred to the Hartheim asylum in which patients would be killed.[141] This hitherto largely neglected three-page document is important insofar as it sheds light on the way in which the organizers of the 'euthanasia' programme attempted to maintain a high degree of centralized control despite the enormous practical problems of the war. It also indicates that the organizational apparatus was not dissolved after the 'halt' of the 'euthanasia' programme in August 1941. Given that some departments of T-4 headquarters had been relocated from Berlin to other places to safeguard them from air raids, Blankenburg wanted to establish a particularly rigorous, albeit flexible, organizational structure. Nitsche was officially Blankenburg's deputy, but he and his department were located in Schoberstein, near Lake Atter. In the absence of Nitsche from Berlin, the new standing orders gave Allers, the managing director (*Geschäftsführer*) of T-4, the power to supervise and control all matters related to Asylum C. The organization was divided into three departments. Department I was responsible for the identification and examination of patients to ensure that the continued programme could be efficiently executed.

Department II was in charge of actually killing the patients in the designated asylum. The standing orders stated: 'Asylum C carries out the disinfections.' Finally, Department III was responsible for managing the finances of the organization. A more detailed description of Departments I and II stated:

> Department I creates through identification and examination the basis of the work, which is then carried out by Department II. Department I undertakes the scientific and practical analysis of the work; it is responsible for the medical section of Asylum C, bathing and disinfection. Department II deals with the technical winding up. Should medical matters play a role in the technical winding up, then Department I should participate.[142]

Given that the three departments were in different places, it was decided that certain members of staff should be in charge of all three departments and sub-departments in any given location. In Berlin, the managing director was responsible for Departments I and II. The deputy director of the Central Accounting Office for State Hospitals and Nursing Homes was in charge of overseeing those parts of the T-4 organization which were located in Asylum C and on the Schoberstein. Paul Nitsche was the head of Department I. Gerhardt Siebert, the head of the Charitable Foundation for the Transport of Patients from 1941, was responsible for Department II, and Friedrich Lorent, T-4's business director (*Hauptwirtschaftsleiter*), was in charge of Department III. In the event that T-4 were to be further fragmented and needed to move to more secure locations, Lorent would receive supervisory powers over those parts of the organization which remained in Berlin.[143] T-4's organizational structure and contingency plans show that senior T-4 officials attempted to establish a system of centralized control over the killing programme under conditions of war. What is particularly significant is the fact that the standing orders were laid down shortly before the second phase of the 'euthanasia' programme was authorized by Brandt. Perhaps Blankenburg, who was in direct communication with Brandt about the matter, knew by that point that the killing programme would be resumed, and that the organizational system had to be modified as a result.

Rather than implementing the 'euthanasia' programme on their own, without any official government sanctioning, T-4 psychiatrists went to great lengths to extract some kind of authorization from Brandt, however veiled or rudimentary it might be. On 12 August 1943, after a board meeting between T-4 managers about department IIa, a reference to Hartheim, Nitsche remarked that it was paramount that all asylums continued to report their patients to T-4, so that 'in case the "stop" is lifted we would be able to begin the work'.[144] He also issued special instructions that were to be followed in case there was 'a new start to the Aktion'.[145] This particular source can help to clarify the chronology of Brandt's decision-making. Faulstich, for example, has alleged that Brandt informed Nitsche 'early in July 1943', through Blankenburg, that he was authorized to act according to his 'euthanasia' proposal.[146] Nitsche's note, however, dates from 12 August. If Brandt had authorized him in July, there would have been no need to put T-4 managers on alert 'in case the "stop" is lifted' in August.

The note suggests that Brandt informed Nitsche, via Blankenburg, about his decision some time at the beginning of August, probably between 12 and 17 August 1943, when Nitsche summoned a number of 'specifically selected practical psychiatrists' to tell them that he had been authorized to resume the 'euthanasia' programme.[147] Contrary to what some scholars have suggested, it is unlikely that Brandt would have given his authorization without prior consultation with Hitler, and perhaps even his general approval.[148] In February, he had hinted to von Bodelschwingh at the possibility that the 'euthanasia' programme might, under certain circumstances, have to be resumed, if it were 'ordered from above', which was a general code for Hitler or the Nazi leadership.[149] Brandt certainly had an opportunity to talk to Hitler, given that he spent a considerable amount of time at field headquarters in the summer, and was present during the visit of Boris III, King of Bulgaria, on 14 and 15 August.[150] The next morning, at 11.30, Brandt also accompanied Hitler for a walk which was followed by breakfast and meetings with Bormann, Keitel and Himmler.[151] A general hint or word of approval from Hitler would have sufficed for Brandt to believe that he had the authority to act. Senior members of Hitler's court had realized in the preceding weeks that Brandt had the 'unlimited trust of the Führer', which might have allowed him to propose such a radical measure, and inform Blankenburg by telephone.[152]

There is some second-hand evidence from Brack about a conversation he had had in April 1942 with Bouhler, who told him that Brandt had approached Hitler a number of times to ask about resuming the 'euthanasia' programme, but that Hitler had refused, to avoid causing public disquiet in an increasingly difficult military situation.[153] One should not infer from this post-war evidence, however, that Hitler continued to refuse his permission until the end of the war. It may well be that Brandt had told Bouhler at the beginning of 1942 that the 'euthanasia' programme could not be officially resumed for the above-mentioned reasons, and that Bouhler had passed on the information to Brack and others in the KdF, including von Hegener.[154] In the summer of 1943, eighteen months later, the situation may well have presented itself in a rather different light to Hitler.

The fact that Brandt was extremely cautious in committing himself to the continuation of the 'euthanasia' programme in the summer of 1943, as well as later, in 1944, says little about whether or not Hitler had sanctioned the continued killings, but it says something about the fact that the regime wanted to disassociate itself from the killing operation. Hitler sanctioned almost any removal of 'useless eaters', as long as the killings did not produce any evidence which would implicate the regime in the activities and thus cause negative publicity for the regime at a critical point in the war. Improving morale on the home front was also particularly on Hitler's mind in the middle of August, and one of the reasons why he released Frick from his duties as Minister of the Interior. Furthermore, between the end of June 1943, when Brandt met with Nitsche and de Crinis, and the middle of August, when he authorized the 'euthanasia' operation, developments had taken a turn for the better for Brandt. Since the beginning of August, it had become clear that Hitler was supporting Brandt in his conflict with Conti. The enormous increase in Brandt's power and status, formalized in the second Führer decree at the beginning of September, gave him the additional confidence to sanction the continuation of the 'euthanasia' programme, albeit only through an intermediary and in a generalized, roundabout way. In short, Brandt's veiled authorization to Nitsche was intended to keep a distinct distance between the Nazi leadership and the organizers of the operation. Moreover, according to Süß, it was 'neither imaginable nor possible' that Brandt, who was totally dependent on Hitler's trust, could act against Hitler's will.[155] If this is true, then Brandt must have somehow obtained Hitler's general approval for the second phase of the 'euthanasia' programme in the summer of 1943.

There is also some indirect evidence that Brandt probably consulted Hitler before authorizing the second phase of the 'euthanasia' programme. When asked in Nuremberg whether he believed that Hitler knew about the killing of sick inmates in some of the concentration camps, which had been authorized by Himmler, and which became known as 'Aktion 14f13', Brandt told the court that he did not believe that Himmler had carried out 'these measures' independently and without Hitler's approval, however veiled or general it might have been: 'It is my opinion that he [Hitler] knew about it in some form. The question is whether he gave orders or whether he gave hints so that Himmler carried them out in this form.'[156] Similarly, it is likely that Hitler was informed 'in some form' about Brandt's intention to authorize the killing of patients through the T-4 organization on a limited basis, and that Brandt interpreted some of Hitler's hints in a way which allowed him to assume that the head of state had sanctioned his action. Brandt's statement also reveals the enormous discretion which Nazi leaders had in interpreting and executing Hitler's wishes.

Nitsche's post-war recollections seem to confirm that Hitler had been consulted. After the war, Nitsche told German prosecutors that in August 1943 he had 'managed to obtain Hitler's expressed approval, through the mediation of Professor Brand [sic], to authorise certain responsible physicians to perform euthanasia in individual cases by means of drugs. In Saxony, this concerned the accused Dr Schulz and ... Dr Wischer.'[157] Nitsche's post-war statement is significant insofar as his recollections about the 1943 authorization show a distinct resemblance to Hitler's authorization in 1939, in which he charged Brandt and Bouhler 'with the responsibility of enlarging the powers of specific physicians' so that they could perform 'euthanasia' for patients deemed to be incurable.[158] Just as Hitler had authorized Brandt and Bouhler to authorize other physicians with the execution of the 'euthanasia' programme in 1939, Brandt seems to have authorized Nitsche to authorize other doctors in 1943. In other words, the power to authorize other doctors to carry out 'euthanasia' had been passed on from Hitler to Brandt, and, four years later, from Brandt to Nitsche.

Another possibility is, of course, that Nitsche *assumed* that Brandt's authorization to him could only have been made if Hitler had endorsed and sanctioned the operation, and that Brandt might well have left Nitsche and the other T-4 physicians in the belief that they were acting with the approval of the government. Brandt, more than anyone else, knew that there was almost no evidence which linked Hitler and the regime to the ongoing killing operation.

We do not know for sure who attended the meeting on 17 August, convened by Nitsche in Berlin, during which he transmitted Brandt's general 'killing authorisation' (*Tötungsermächtigung*) to the T-4 psychiatrists, but it is likely that the meeting was attended by a group of doctors similar to that which had discussed the resumption of the 'euthanasia' programme at the end of September 1942.[159] In addition to the staff of T-4 headquarters, there is evidence that about ten committed T-4 psychiatrists attended the meeting, most of whom were involved in one way or another in the children's 'euthanasia' programme and had previous expertise in killing adult patients. The T-4 psychiatrists Dr Beese (Uchtspringe), Hans Heinze (Görden), Valentin Falthauser (Kaufbeuren-Irsee), Hermann Pfannmüller (Eglfing), Victor Ratka (Tiegenhof), Hubert Schuch (Ansbach), Alfred Schulz (Großschweidnitz), Theodor Steinmeyer (Pfafferode, Niedermarsberg and Bernburg), Hilde Wernicke (Meseritz-Obrawalde), Mathilde Weber (Kalmenhof/Idstein) and Gerhard Wischer (Waldheim) were probably present.[160] The T-4 psychiatrists Carl Schneider and de Crinis did not attend.[161] It is highly likely that Nitsche proposed to kill the patients by means of drugs and starvation, as he had done on previous occasions.[162] There is also relatively good evidence that the psychiatrists were authorized to select – and kill – patients according to their own discretion. Wischer later emphasized that the authorization had given those doctors involved in the operation a significant amount of leeway in carrying out the killing of patients.[163] Hildegard Wesse, the wife of T-4 doctor Hermann Wesse, who was herself involved in the killing of patients, recalled that Beese, the director of the Uchtspringe asylum, had told her after returning from the meeting in Berlin in August 1943, that their institution had been instructed to 'euthanise patients who were severely ill. In Berlin there was obviously no longer any order, which is why he said that we would conduct the selection ourselves.'[164] During the following eighteen months, approximately thirty asylum doctors, prompted, in part, by Nitsche and the T-4 headquarters, or encouraged by the regional authorities, carried out the killing of handicapped patients, sometimes independently and without further authorization or instructions by the government.[165]

Given that Nitsche fulfilled a dual role as head of T-4's medical office and chief psychiatrist in Saxony, it is perhaps not surprising that the T-4 psychiatrists in Saxony, Schulz and Wischer in particular, later attempted to shift responsibility for the operation onto the regional government by claiming that the health department of the Saxony Ministry of the Interior had issued them with a general 'authorisation' for the killing of patients, although they had in fact received the authorization from Nitsche directly.[166]

On 20 August, three days after the conference, and after they had spoken on the telephone, Nitsche issued further written instructions to Hans-Joachim Becker, the deputy head of Department III and office manager at Hartheim.[167] Becker was told how the expert reports on patients who were to be included in the 'euthanasia' programme were to be processed in the future. Linden was to monitor and check all '+' cases – patients who were to be killed in T-4 institutions 'without further examination' – as well as all 'z' cases – patients for whom no decision had yet been taken, for example because of being a 'good worker in an asylum', or because of being curable. For patients classified as 'z' cases it was nonetheless not impossible, as the guideline from October 1942 stated, that the patient might be included 'in our Aktion' at a later date.[168] Nitsche stressed that Werner Villinger, who had advised von Bodelschwingh on how to exclude Bethel from the 'euthanasia' programme, and who had, according to Nitsche and others, been too lenient as a T-4 expert referee, would generally not receive any referee forms (*Gutacher-Sendung*). In special cases, Nitsche would issue specific instructions after he had personally selected the relevant forms.[169] Nitsche's letter to Becker shows that he wanted to remain in control of the renewed killing operation and assign work only to those expert referees who were favourably inclined towards the 'euthanasia' programme.[170]

Finally, on 25 August, Nitsche contacted de Crinis from Weissenbach, near Lake Atter, where he was recovering from a medical operation, to say that the killing programme had resumed:

> In the matter of Prof. Br.[andt]'s Aktion, I was unable to speak to him during my fourteen-day visit to Berlin, but he has given me the authorisation by way of Herrn Blankenburg to proceed according to my E.-proposal, which I made to him orally. You can find out the details from Herrn Blankenburg or summon my Berlin collaborator Dr. med Borm (4 Tiergartenstr., Tel. 22 35 42), who can fill you in about all the details.[171]

Deciphering such cryptic communication is important. The letters 'E.' and 'Eu' had been introduced as the standard abbreviations for 'euthanasia'. Nitsche's collaborator, SS-Hauptsturmführer Kurt Borm, was one of the officials at the headquarters of the 'euthanasia' programme. The document shows that Brandt used Blankenburg as a messenger to authorize the second phase of the 'euthanasia' programme. The authorization was neither laid down in a government directive, nor published in the official gazette or written on paper, but it was given orally, indirectly and in a generalized fashion. The authorization was not given to Nitsche directly, but to one of his collaborators, who worked for T-4 headquarters. The way in which the authorization was given, and was understood by those for whom it was intended, reveals the extent to which T-4 and its leading personalities had become accustomed to a detached culture of communication, especially after the regime had initiated the Holocaust. Rather than not acting upon such a vague authorization, they were content to start the operation on a limited, largely regional level, and expand it to the whole of the Reich once they had received a more explicit permission in the future. The authorization for the second phase of the 'euthanasia' programme was neither obtained on a single day, nor was the authorization from August 1943 explicit enough to assume that the government had fully sanctioned the programme. What we have here is not so much a single authorization, written down by the head of state, as for the first phase of the 'euthanasia' programme, but a series of veiled and rather vague hints by Hitler's medical representative, which could be understood as 'partial authorizations'. To understand the way in which the second phase of the 'euthanasia' programme was authorized, we need to take the entire 'authorizing process' into account – and it took more than a year. At the same time, we need to recognize that T-4, Nitsche and de Crinis especially, were determined to solicit an expression of Brandt's wishes which would satisfy them that the programme had the necessary government sanction. They were carrying out mass murder, but the leading personalities wanted to ensure that they were not acting illegally. As long as the government or one of its representatives approved the operation in one way or another, they were satisfied that they were not committing a crime.

Yet in the summer of 1943 Brandt's commitment to the operation remained ambiguous and detached. Only days later, on 31 August, de Crinis told Nitsche that although he had talked to Brandt in the previous couple of days about a number of pressing issues, it had not been possible 'to pin him down for our common cause. Since I will be meeting him again in the near future, I hope to get from him a view about the matter which we have discussed.'[172] De Crinis' comments suggest that he had not yet received Nitsche's letter from Weissenbach, probably because of delays in the postal service. Two months later, on 30 October 1943, Nitsche told de Crinis again that Brandt had accepted the proposal for the secret continuation of the 'euthanasia' programme:

> You remember that I made Prof. Br.[andt] a pretty concrete proposal on the E-question, when we were visiting him at the end of June. I haven't yet been able to tell you that he has accepted this proposal and that I have therefore, in agreement with Herr Blankenburg, summoned a number of specially selected practical psychiatrists to a meeting on 17 August (to which I have already alluded, I realise, in my letter of 25 August). As I wrote then, you can, if you wish, be briefed by Dr Borm (22 35 82 Tel.).[173]

Mentally ill patients were now killed in their own institutions and without any fake transfers. The number of patients assigned for murder was not centrally organized, but was the responsibility of, and at the discretion of, the relevant asylum director. No further orders were required. The above fragments from Nitsche and others show how radical forces in the medical administration took the initiative to push for vital policy decisions which they believed were in the interest of the regime. In the Third Reich, the ability to anticipate the 'Führer's wish' had become a major precondition in advancing one's professional career. Pressure from party fanatics or, as in this case, from over-zealous T-4 physicians, could instigate executive measures which would set in train the killing of thousands. Of course, one did not have to be telepathic to know that any kind of policy of racial cleansing, or one which was designed to free urgently-needed bed space, was sanctioned by Hitler and the regime.[174] What is significant in this particular case, however, is that both men showed a keen interest in receiving the necessary authorization from above, namely from Hitler's doctor, however generalized or veiled Brandt's hints might have been. At the same time, the T-4 psychiatrists could feel confident that their proposal to kill patients by means of drugs and starvation would be favoured by the head of state or his representative. The total breakdown of any checks in the government machinery, the informal decision-making, and the general military and political situation, enabled them to instigate another programme that was aimed at putting the ideas of National Socialism into reality. As in the first phase of the 'euthanasia' programme, the initiatives occurred at a time of heightened tension and confusion at the top of the medical hierarchy.[175] The permanent state of emergency, which in many ways was so characteristic of the regime, together with the need to free bed space, made Brandt appear to be the one person who could provide the killing operation with the necessary authorization. At the same time, due to his official position, he detached himself, and thus the Nazi leadership, from any direct involvement in the continuation of the 'euthanasia' programme.

V. MANAGING THE OPERATION

Brandt soon realized that a number of religious leaders and institutions were strongly opposed to the resumption of the killing programme. On 19 September, for example, Catholic priests read out a 'Joint Letter of the German Bishops about the Ten Commandments as a Law of Life of the People' during the service in Germany's Catholic churches. The second part of the letter, which focused on 'the right of humans to life and limb', was scheduled to be read out a week later.[176] Such activities did not go unnoticed. On 22 September 1943, Brandt informed Himmler that he had talked with Hitler about the fact that the Catholic Church was raising concerns about the transfer of mental patients from air-raid areas, suggesting that the regime's intentions were more sinister.[177] He told Himmler:

> I have recently reported to the Führer that the Bishop of Münster, Galen, has special concerns about the transfer of mental patients from Cure and Nursing Homes in air-raid areas to evacuation areas. In previous letters to the Senior State Official (*Oberpräsident*) of Westphalia, he [Galen] requested information of which the Führer has said that it is none of the Bishop's business. Today I receive a copy of a new letter, dated 28 August 1943, which I enclose for your information.[178]

In his letter of 28 August, Count von Galen had raised concerns about the transfer – and sudden death – of a sixty-year-old businessman, Edmund Northoff, from the Eichberg asylum.[179] In October 1942, the doctor at the asylum of Münster had noted in Nordhoff's patient record that he was 'completely stupid and impassive, unclean and untidy, degenerates physically'.[180] It would hardly be surprising if T-4 physicians had decided to give Nordhoff an overdose of a common drug to hasten the death of a person whose life was regarded as 'unworthy of living'. Brandt supported the idea that patients like Northoff should be granted a 'mercy death', but he also realized that he had to tread carefully in authorizing any kind of centralized and coordinated 'euthanasia' programme which impacted negatively on the home front, and thus on the war effort. He also knew that he had vaguely

21. *Above:* Goebbels on a donkey. Karl Brandt taking photographs in the background. Trip to Greece by Goebbels, Hoffmann and Brandt, 21–28 September 1936. (BSB, Fotoarchiv Hoffmann, hoff-14092)

22. *Right:* Karl Brandt in the National Museum, Athens, during his trip to Greece with Goebbels and Hoffmann, 21–28 September 1936. (BSB, Fotoarchiv Hoffmann, hoff-14005)

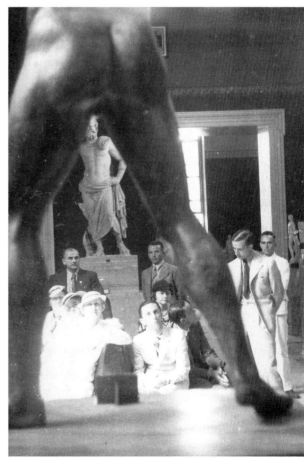

23. Karl Brandt, Albert Speer, Adolf Hitler and Hermann Giesler at the Berghof, 11–19 February 1937. (BSB, Fotoarchiv Hoffmann, hoff-14812)

24. Karl Brandt, Adolf Hitler, Albert Speer and Philip Bouhler, 5 March 1937. (BSB, Fotoarchiv Hoffmann, hoff-14953)

25. Funeral of Ludendorff, 22 December 1937. (BSB, Fotoarchiv Hoffmann, hoff-38729)

26. Albert Speer and Karl Brandt during a summer party at Rudolf Heß' house, 17 July 1939. (BSB, Fotoarchiv Hoffmann, hoff-26235)

27. Karl Brandt, Albert Speer, Heinrich Hoffmann on the terrace of the Berghof, *c.* 1937. (BSB, Fotoarchiv Hoffmann, hoff-317)

28. *Reichstagswahlen*, 29 March 1936. (BSB, Fotoarchiv Hoffmann, hoff-12808)

29. *Above: Reichstagswahlen*, 29 March 1936. (BSB, Fotoarchiv Hoffmann, hoff-12804)

30. *Right:* Hitler's State Visit in Italy. Karl Brandt is part of the entourage, 4 May 1938. (BSB, Fotoarchiv Hoffmann, hoff-18577)

31. *Left:* Philip Bouhler, who organised the 'euthanasia' programme together with Karl Brandt, no date. (Source: BAB)

32. *Below:* Karl Brandt on board a plane, *c.* 1942–43. (Source: Karl-Adolf Brandt)

33. Karl Brandt travelling on a boat, no date. (Source: Karl-Adolf Brandt)

34. Hitler and his staff, Führer headquarters, 10 May–5 June 1940. (BSB, Fotoarchiv Hoffmann, hoff-29873)

35. *Left:* Hitler visiting Paris with his entourage, 23 June 1940. (BSB, Fotoarchiv Hoffmann, hoff-66072)

36. *Below:* Karl Brandt next to a destroyed Russian plane near Smolensk, August 1941. (BSB, Fotoarchiv Hoffmann, hoff-37393)

sanctioned the revival of the 'euthanasia' programme along the lines of Nitsche's proposed plan. People were again asking questions about the deaths of friends and relatives, suspicious that they had died after being transferred from one of the cure and nursing homes. After briefing Hitler about the matter, who commented that the transfer of patients was none of von Galen's business, Brandt submitted the relevant paperwork to Himmler to ensure that appropriate action would be taken. Himmler, after having proposed arresting Galen in 1941, decided to approach the matter in a rather more subtle fashion. He instructed Ernst Kaltenbrunner, the head of the RSHA after Heydrich's death, to discredit the bishop by spreading malicious rumours after one of his parish priests had died in Münster: 'It should be said that the priest concerned was done away with by his [the Bishop's] adherents because he had said this or that against the Bishop at one point.'[181] Brandt may not have been aware of the finer details of Himmler's smear campaign against the bishop, but one cannot avoid the impression that Brandt collaborated with one of the regime's most ruthless henchmen to suppress any discontent among the population against the transfer – and occasional death – of mental patients in Germany.

One person who welcomed the revival of the 'euthanasia' programme was Gerhard Wischer, director of the Waldheim asylum in Saxony. On 13 September 1943, he told Nitsche:

> In all respects, the work in question proceeds without any problems in Berlin; I anticipate a monthly average of twenty to thirty patients; any kind of difficulties have so far not occurred, neither with regard to personnel, nor from relatives … Almost every day there are new admissions, and we have to work speedily to get everything done.[182]

Weeks later, at the beginning of November, Wischer revealed that he concentrated his murderous activities on newly admitted patients to ensure that his asylum would not become overcrowded:

> I … have a lot to do, because almost all new admissions from Leipzig, Chemnitz and Meißen come to me. I could never, of course, accommodate all these admissions, if I did not, in order to free bed spaces, perform the relevant measures, and this is going very smoothly. However, I am very short of the necessary drugs. Herr Allers recently wrote to me that you have also not yet received the drugs that had been promised (probably by the Reich Security Main Office).[183]

Wischer's barely disguised language leaves little doubt that some Nazi doctors were happy with the renewed killing of mental patients by means of drugs. Wischer later claimed that he had received a general 'authorisation' (*Ermächtigung*) for the killing of patients, which had given him a greater degree of discretion and flexibility in comparison with the Aktion T-4.[184] To start with, however, the continuation of the 'euthanasia' programme did not progress according to plan, as Wischer's comments about the lack of drugs suggest. On 2 December 1943, Nitsche asked T-4 headquarters about the date from which the asylum directors authorized to carry out the killing of patients, code-named the 'E-assignment', had started receiving the required drugs. Nitsche wanted to assess 'how long the individuals have been doing the work we have discussed (*wie lange die Einzelnen im bewussten Sinne jetzt schon arbeiten)*'.[185] The drugs were procured through Albert Widmann of the Technical Institute for the Detection of Crime, and distributed by the Reich Committee for the Scientific Registering of Serious Hereditary and Congenital Illnesses, T-4 headquarters and the Reich Commissioner for Cure and Nursing Homes. On 31 January, for example, Nitsche received 5,500 ampoules of morphine and 5,900 ampoules of scopolamine.[186] The asylums of Meseritz, Tiegenhof, Uchtspringe, Großschweidnitz, Waldheim, Ansbach, Görden, Kalmenhof and Stuttgart-Nord were among the institutions which received the drugs. Wischer certainly had sufficient drugs to carry out his work. On 29 December 1943, he told Nitsche:

> There is a lot of work in the asylum, many new admissions, especially after the terror attacks against Leipzig, which caused a lot of confusion. Also many exits (*Abgänge*), which are carried out without any friction.[187]

For the first six months the operation was, nonetheless, haphazardly organized and lacked an orchestrated plan. Nitsche and de Crinis knew that they were operating on a rather weak basis after they had failed to secure a direct authorization from Brandt or the head of state. It was almost a year before Brandt expressed a firmer commitment to the operation. Due to a serious surgical operation with subsequent medical complications, and a long convalescence in Weissenbach, Nitsche was temporarily cut off from the flow of information in Berlin. A lack of leadership at the beginning of the operation, together with Brandt's ambiguous role, explains in part why the operation may have appeared to have been introduced independently by the institutions. As long as no one issued any further directives, the asylum directors carried on with the killings, safe in the knowledge that the policy had been broadly sanctioned by Nitsche and T-4 in August 1943, as well as by Hitler's doctor and probably by Hitler himself.

In 1944 the killing operation intensified. More and more people became victims of the inconspicuous killing operation. Unlike in 1940 and 1941, there was little opposition from the population. It seems that at this point the churches and the judiciary had been forced into submission. Five years of war and eleven years of Nazi rule had made their mark on the German people and its institutions. Far from being content with the situation, T-4 psychiatrists wanted to expand the programme, and exploit the murder of mental patients for scientific purposes. Attempting to enlist the support of Brandt in gaining additional research staff, however, exposed the detached and indirect channels of communication between the T-4 leadership and Hitler's doctor. On 2 December 1943, Nitsche told Allers and Lorent, who had come from Berlin to visit him at Weissenbach, that he wanted to submit an application to Brandt to grant T-4's medical department another research post. Given that he had 'heard' from Carl Schneider that Brandt intended to support German medical research by releasing young scientists from the army, Nitsche wanted to see whether it would be possible to release one of Schneider's researchers, Ernst-Adolf Schmorl, from military duty. The next day,

Nitsche put his request in writing. He wanted Allers to pass on the information to Blankenburg, who would hopefully then pass on the application to Brandt.[188] The flow of information to and from the centre and the T-4 organization was not only convoluted and complicated, but time-consuming, inefficient and insecure. Executive decision-making, if it took place at all, was now rarely laid down on paper. Although Nitsche was doubtful that Brandt would mediate on his behalf, he was determined to develop a research centre in which T-4 physicians could conduct neuropathological work on 'euthanasia' victims.

At the end of January 1944, Carl Schneider told Nitsche: 'At the start of the entire "Aktion", the medical participants were sure that the opportunity should not be missed to research and combat mental diseases and, in particular, to cure and prevent them.'[189] However, the problem for Nitsche and his colleagues was gaining the government sanction they believed they needed. Since he was constantly on the move with Hitler's headquarters, Brandt was difficult to get hold of, and he seemed to be detaching himself further from the operation.[190] Meeting Brandt on several public occasions was by no means a guarantee that one could speak to him in person about sensitive, and largely secret, issues. On 14 January 1944 Nitsche reported to his Heidelberg friend Carl Schneider about the plan to review the killing programme:

> I must also inform you today that I am intending, when I am next in Berlin, to summon again those colleagues whom I gathered in Berlin in accordance with the E.-order of Professor Br.[andt] – I have told you extensively about the whole thing, and you could not come to Berlin at the time – in order to support the matter further and establish its current state of affairs.[191]

To receive the necessary government sanctioning, Nitsche wanted to involve Brandt in the discussions about the resumption, and perhaps expansion, of the 'euthanasia' programme. The next day, 15 January, Allers informed Nitsche that he had talked to Brandt about the matter. Allers' description of Brandt's response provides a good example of the extent to which Brandt had inculcated the principles of detached leadership:

> I have also informed Herr Professor Brandt about it [a conference to discuss the resumption of the 'euthanasia' programme]. He regards the matter as perfectly correct. I have asked him to attend the conference himself. He appeared to be very interested and said, however, that he could not [himself] say anything; rather, because of his official position, [he] could practically really only say the opposite; [he could] express his opinion, albeit hedged in restrictive clauses; he feared, however, that he then would not be understood by all. I think, however, Herr Professor, that you will have the opportunity to talk to Herr Professor Brandt himself when you come here. In any case, Professor Brandt is very interested in the whole problem. He has emphasised especially that the resumption of the work on a large scale must come one day without doubt, but that it would not be expected during the war.[192]

Having recuperated from his health problems, Nitsche needed to regain greater control over the programme. In some cases, asylum directors had misinterpreted their assignment and had killed hundreds, if not thousands, of patients without any underlying plan. On 20 January, Heinze protested to Nitsche against what he called 'wild E.-measures'. For Heinze, the killing of mental patients needed to be properly organized and centrally controlled through the T-4 infrastructure; otherwise the operation, which he knew was illegal, was apparently in danger of becoming pure 'madness':

> Will we still be able to stop any unwelcome actions? Matters will only be brought under control if we learn from the experiences of the Reich Committee during the illegal interim stoppage period, and then introduce some central discipline. Headquarters will need to clean up the operation and introduce sanctions for those who act on their own initiative. If things don't improve, all our efforts to lift the reputation of psychiatry will be wasted.[193]

Establishing a grip on a killing programme which had appeared to be out of control for months was further complicated by Allied air raids and failing communication lines. A conference about the 'euthanasia' programme, scheduled to take place at the beginning of February 1944, had to be cancelled at short notice. Blankenburg, de Crinis, Allers, Borm and Mennecke arrived at the Chancellery of the Führer in Berlin nonetheless. They had not received the cancellation in time. Weeks later, a meeting between Nitsche and Brandt had to be postponed indefinitely when Berlin came under severe attack.[194] The war made central and secretive planning a difficult enterprise. Any line of communication with Brandt, and thus to the centre of government, however remote, was worth further exploration. On 7 February, the T-4 psychiatrist Steinmeyer told Nitsche:

> I do not know whether you are aware that I have recently taken in a large-scale fever therapy department of the air force in my asylum, which Professor Brandt transferred to me through Linden. Through this department, I am directly in permanent contact with Berlin.[195]

On 29 and 30 March 1944, T-4 administrators finally came together to discuss the nationwide expansion of the killing operation at Nitsche's new official residence in Schoberstein, near Lake Atter. The number of doctors involved in the planning of the killing operation now included representatives from Baden and Württemberg and other regions.[196] Apart from Blankenburg and Nitsche, the meeting was attended by the T-4 psychiatrists Hans Bertha, Hans Heinze, Friedrich Mennecke, Victor Ratka, Gustav Schneider, Valentin Falthauser and Theodor Steinmeyer. While Nitsche issued specific instructions to each of the asylum directors in his office, the others started to drink heavily. According to Mennecke's letters to his wife, Steinmeyer finally became so drunk that he found himself lying in the snow. Falthauser, Ratka, Bertha and Mennecke, on the other hand, celebrated their newly found friendship by offering each other the *Du*, the personalized form of address in Germany.[197] Mennecke, in particular, used the opportunity to seek a directorship in one of the asylums in Graz, Klingenmünster or Meseritz-Obrawalde. He obviously believed that the killing of mental patients could be a viable career path.[198] The killing of thousands of handicapped people had, it seemed, completely desensitized these men over the years. Unable to distinguish between right and wrong, their moral conscience had corroded to such an extent that they were willing to continue to commit wholesale murder as long as the operation was loosely sanctioned by the regime. Given that Brandt did not attend the conference, the T-4 psychiatrists attempted to obtain a stronger commitment, however general or veiled, from Hitler's representative through other channels.

With Carl Schneider, de Crinis made another attempt to discuss the expansion of the 'euthanasia' operation with Brandt during the Fourth Meeting of Consulting Physicians, which took place from 16 to 18 May 1944 at the SS hospital at Hohenlychen. De Crinis, however, was brushed aside. Acting as the representative of the Führer, Brandt gave the keynote speech to the leading physicians of the Reich, bestowing honorary medals on, among others, Gebhardt, Handloser and Toennis for their service to the fatherland.[199] At the end of his speech, Brandt made his own re-commitment and exhorted his hearers to be 'Faithful to oneself! Faithful to the people! Faithful to the Führer!'[200] Conti was among the participants. It was a solemn occasion, and for Brandt obviously the wrong context for talking about the killing of mental patients. On 25 May, de Crinis told Nitsche:

> It has not been possible to pin Prof. Brandt down on our matter. He merely gave me the short answer that he was now thinking about the matter in a more relaxed way, by which he meant more generously. I draw the conclusion from this that he means to be able to take greater responsibility.[201]

In the Third Reich, the established channels of communication to and from the government had degenerated to something like tea-leaf reading for those wanting to find out whether the regime would sanction a certain policy initiative. For de Crinis, the veiled hints made by Hitler's doctor were sufficient for him to believe that the expansion of the killing programme had received a greater level of government sanction.

In the meantime, word about the continuation of the killing programme had reached Himmler. On 9 June 1944, he told Brandt that *Gauleiter* Koch had asked him in a letter of 19 May 1944 whether there was a possibility 'of delivering a four-year-old, Rüdiger Poeck, who was suffering from incurable meningitis, from his illness by admitting him to a relevant "clinic".'[202] Himmler must obviously have been aware that asylum patients were being killed, by drugs or other means. Koch had apparently discussed the case with the mother of Rüdiger Poeck, who seems to have agreed that it was better for her son to die. Himmler asked Brandt to get in touch with Koch to see what could be done. We do not know whether Brandt contacted Koch, or whether Rüdiger Poeck was subsequently killed. The correspondence shows, however, that in 1944 senior members of the regime still considered Brandt to be in charge of all questions relating to the killing of incurable patients.

On 2 June 1944, Linden told Allers that asylum doctors had to do everything possible to 'achieve the reduction of mentally ill patients'.[203] The T-4 machinery could not have been encouraged in its activities in clearer terms. However, professional support for the 'euthanasia' operation was not necessarily forthcoming. On 30 June, after having visited dozens of mental institutions, T-4 psychiatrist Curd Runckel provided Nitsche with a comprehensive report about the state of German psychiatry, particularly about the extent to which asylum directors had introduced modern psychiatric therapies, including cardiazol and electric-shock therapies, and supported the 'euthanasia' operation. Runckel's conclusion as far as the 'euthanasia' programme was concerned was disappointing:

> I always find the attitude of numerous asylum directors particularly sad as far as the therapy and the problems tackled by the Reich Committee are concerned. For example, in the asylum of Haina, I saw two children who, apart from having severe physical deformities, were total idiots and were mollycoddled although conditions there were very difficult as far as space and nursing personnel was concerned. I also saw time and time again in a number of asylums that chronically severely mentally ill patients are kept alive through all kinds of substances. It is an attitude for which it is especially difficult to have empathy during a war! I always ask the senior physicians in the asylums about therapy and also about the euthanasia problem, and have so far found no enthusiasm for this, except in those institutions with which we collaborate.[204]

Runckel had realized that some physicians did not even want to talk about the killing of mentally ill patients; others showed noticeable suspicions once they had realized that he was collaborating with the T-4 headquarters. He, therefore, kept his involvement with the operation a secret.[205] He was also astonished about the negative attitude of asylum directors vis-à-vis euthanasia (*Sterbehilfe*) on the one hand, and on the other their willingness to follow a starvation diet for mental patients who were considered incurable: 'They refuse to shorten the suffering of patients through the provision of drugs, but they are in absolute agreement that the patient really starves and dies one day undernourished (*unterernährt eines Tages den Weg geht*), which they could have made easier for him with a little help.'[206] At the end of his report, Runckel asked Nitsche to give him some 'detailed written directives' in the future so that he would know the subjects Nitsche was particularly interested in. Runckel's comment is significant, because it suggests that, even within the T-4 organization itself, the personnel did not necessarily know what was expected of them, and that their initial instructions had been given orally. A few days after his report, Runckel had a chance to clarify his brief with Nitsche.

From 3 to 5 July 1944, T-4 physicians met for a third conference in Vienna to discuss the practicalities of expanding the operation to free further bed spaces in air-raid areas. Among others, the Austrian T-4 psychiatrist Jekelius, Hefelmann and Heinze, as representatives of the Reich Committee for the Scientific Registering of Serious Hereditary and Congenital Illnesses, and the former head of the killing centre in Sonnenstein near Pirna, Horst Schumann, who had been transferred to Auschwitz, took part in the conference. Although Schumann's participation in the meeting has led to the suggestion that one of the subjects for discussion was the murder of slave and forced labourers who were suffering from tuberculosis – and who were subsequently killed in places like Hadamar – the expansion of the 'euthanasia' programme seems to have dominated the agenda.[207] Nitsche and Blankenburg saw the aim of the meeting as 'reviving the T-4 Aktion again in a comprehensive fashion', not as a centrally controlled programme, in which patients were selected and transferred to specially designed killing centres, but as a decentralized operation in which the T-4 organization coordinated the murder of asylum populations by means of sedatives and starvation methods.

Shortly after the conference, on 10 July, Nitsche asked Brandt for a meeting to discuss the continued 'euthanasia' programme, and receive some kind of sanction for its expansion: 'Oberführer Blankenburg has told me in confidence about the conversation he had with you with regard to the "Eu-Matter". I feel duty bound to ask you to grant me a meeting about this as soon as is possible.'[208] Word soon came back from Brandt. As in the summer of 1943, Brandt communicated his decisions by way of intermediaries, and not directly.

While discussing plans for the renewed evacuation of cure and nursing homes with Runckel on 18 July 1944 in Berlin, Brandt made some unmistakable remarks with regard to the continuation of the killing operation, and told him to relay the information to Nitsche. Given that it had proved extremely difficult to reduce the number of 'operations inimical to health' (*gesundheitsfremde Betriebe*) which had been established in evacuated cure and nursing homes, Brandt had summoned Runckel to his office to hear of new plans to remedy the problem. Runckel proposed two lines of action 'to procure space in a different kind of way'.[209] His first plan of action suggested the evacuation of cure and nursing homes through a reclassification of the existing asylums into four categories. Only the first category, the 'cure homes' (*Heilanstalten*), would provide patients with therapeutic and psychiatric treatment. The remaining three categories, the 'nursing homes' (*Pflegeanstalten*), would cater for the mass of incurable and physically weakened patients. Category Two would look after mental patients who were physically fit. Category Three would be responsible for patients with severe mental illness who were physically ill but whose health prognosis was negative. For this category of patients, Runckel suggested the issue of euthanasia would have to be considered, given that the patients would die anyway. The final category related to old and frail patients who were otherwise not mentally ill. Runckel suggested that the identification and selection of patients would have to be carried out by a medical commission in collaboration with the asylum doctors.[210]

Runckel's second plan envisaged the transfer of students of both sexes who had passed their school exams from Nazi educational institutions to large work and military camps, and to prisons and correctional institutions. One obviously had to accept that the policy would result in a 'certain hardship' (*gewisse Härten*) for some of the inmates, Runckel noted in his memorandum, but he estimated that about 60 per cent of the space of former educational institutions could be used for other purposes. He anticipated great resistance to his plan, and asked for

extensive powers from the authorities to carry it out. Brandt largely agreed with
Runckel's proposals and supported them, especially the evacuation of educational
institutions. Given that numerous cure and nursing homes had previously been
transformed into Nazi educational institutions, for example in Thuringia, Saxony
and Württemberg, Brandt wanted to reverse the trend in order to assert his
authority over the regions.[211]

The disadvantage of Runckel's plan was not only that it was time-consuming,
but that it needed the involvement of the RMdI and the support of the regional
and local authorities. Brandt was facing another endless round of wrangling and
negotiations. Tens of thousands of wounded German soldiers were returning from
the front, and the need for hospital beds had increased exponentially in recent
months. Due to the enormous influx of soldiers into the Reich, it is likely that
Brandt decided to use all available means, including the killing of incurable and
mentally ill patients, to free existing bed spaces as fast as possible.[212] Brandt used the
meeting with Runckel to authorize T-4 to become more active in the inconspicuous
killing of incurable patients. On 24 July 1944, Runckel informed Nitsche about his
conversation with Brandt:

> Herr Professor Brandt has asked me to inform you about these things and has at the same
> time hinted that you might want to set in train our specific therapy in an inconspicuous
> fashion (*eine Andeutung fallen lassen, ob es Ihnen möglich wäre, eine Aktivierung unserer
> spezifischen Therapie hierbei unauffällig in die Wege zu leiten*).[213]

Two days later, on 26 July, Brandt told Nitsche that he was now 'available for a
meeting with Professor de Crinis'.[214] Nitsche understood the message. A couple of
days later, on 30 July, Nitsche told Blankenburg at T-4 headquarters:

> Our desire, of which we talked in our telephone conversation on 27 July, to discuss as
> soon as possible with Prof. Br. the E-question and the outcome of our discussions in
> Vienna, is being considered in a positive way. I would like to ask you, in reference to
> Prof. Br's wish, which Dr Runckel transmitted to me, to ask him [Brandt] to convene
> the meeting with Prof. de Crinis I requested about two and a half weeks ago, about the
> E-Matter, as soon as possible.[215]

The available evidence suggests that Brandt was signalling his willingness to agree
to the expansion of the programme. Brandt's standing with Hitler and his overall
influence in the regime was near its peak at the time. A month after he agreed
to meet Nitsche for a discussion about the 'euthanasia' programme, Brandt was
appointed Reich Commissioner for Health and Sanitation, and thus became the
most powerful official in the German health system. On 24 August, Nitsche told
Brandt that he had agreed with Blankenburg to come to Berlin for a fortnight
for a 'comprehensive discussion about the new organisation of the E-Matter in
the presence of those men directly involved'.[216] Nitsche and Blankenburg hoped
that Brandt would be able and willing to attend the conference as well. We do not
know whether the conference took place or whether Brandt attended it. Given that
Brandt was released from his duties as Hitler's escort physician a couple of weeks

later, and that the military situation deteriorated, it may well be that nothing came of the proposed meeting.

The correspondence of Nitsche, de Crinis and others shows that the leading medical experts, who had proposed and largely initiated the resumption of the killing operation, continued to seek the proximity and general approval of Hitler's doctor as a way to legitimize the second phase of the 'euthanasia' programme. As long as some flow of information to and from the centre of government was taking place, however veiled, and through whatever channels of communication, and as long as the hints that these men received could be interpreted in a way which suggested that they were permitted to go ahead with the operation, the executors of the programme were content that the killings had been broadly sanctioned by Hitler's regime.

After the war, Brandt vigorously denied his role in the continued killing operation, but alluded to the fact that he had supported the programme. In October 1945, he revealed, perhaps unintentionally, the underlying rationale of the programme:

> Now I'd like to mention what I might call an excuse for these actions which were carried out on people's own initiative. It is not a legal excuse. It is an excuse which resulted out of the situation. You must remember that during that last year a great number of wounded soldiers came back into the German states. There was a time when inside the Wehrmacht there were over one million wounded soldiers. Added to this, the hospitals in the cities were destroyed. In just one raid all the major hospitals in Hamburg were destroyed, and the air raids meant that there were more wounded persons, so that whatever building was still standing and could be used as a hospital was terribly overcrowded.[217]

Hospital space and beds were the central reasons why Brandt indirectly sanctioned the killings. When asked what had happened to the equipment and questionnaires from the first phase of the 'euthanasia' programme, he replied: 'I believe that the equipment was left where it was … because it was thought that if the occasion arose later, the matter could be taken up again.'[218] During the emergencies of the summer of 1943 and the summer of 1944, Brandt had used his political authority to increase the pace and extent of a killing operation that had continued, on a local and regional level and on a selective basis, after the stopping of the first phase of the 'euthanasia' programme. By broadly sanctioning the killing operation, he hoped to accelerate the process, perhaps only temporarily, by which hospital beds were freed up, and by which the regime could remain in control of the home front, despite an increasingly hopeless military situation elsewhere. To detach the Nazi leadership from the resumption of the killing operation, Brandt only communicated important decisions orally and through intermediaries.[219] Those for whom the information was intended understood his messages. Thousands of murdered patients are proof that communication was functioning in the Third Reich, with or without paper. Anyone looking for explicit written orders which Brandt might have given fails to understand the nature and culture of communication at the highest levels of the regime, and perhaps even the regime itself.

VI. LIVING IN THE TWILIGHT OF KNOWING AND NOT KNOWING

For Brandt and other leading Nazis involved in criminal activities, it was not only important to maintain an outward appearance of propriety and idealism which detached them from the apparent 'excesses' of the Nazi rank and file, but they needed to cultivate a psychological mindset which allowed them to live in a twilight of knowing and not knowing, and in which they could persuade themselves that their conscience was clear.[220] 'In my own mind, my conscience is clear. For me personally that is the most important thing at the moment,' Brandt told Alexander after the war. He was convinced that 'one can only feel responsible for things which one can support with one's medical conscience (*Sie können nur das verantworten, was Sie mit Ihrem ärztlichen Gewissen verantworten können*). There can be nothing else.'[221] A couple of months later, he told the Nuremberg court that his actions in the 'euthanasia' programme had been motivated only by 'human feelings', and that he had not incriminated himself in any way: 'I am convinced that whatever I did in this matter, I can bear responsibility for it before my conscience.'[222]

The use of euphemisms and innuendos not only influenced the culture of communication between the Nazi leadership and the people, but also served them to protect themselves, each other and their own conscience. By not expressing their opinions and decisions directly, but only in a roundabout way, in great secrecy and through intermediaries, Brandt and others managed to create an imagined world in which their instructions and directives had apparently not been said at all, and in which their consciences were somehow elsewhere, in an artificial world that was free from moral corruption. Rather than having to convince himself that he had done nothing illegal, Brandt could fall back upon an image of his personality and himself that had been heavily guarded and that he therefore genuinely believed was free of any moral complicity.[223] Secrecy among the Nazi leadership was of fundamental importance in keeping this illusion alive. Brandt later recalled:

> It was so with many measures. Then there was no reason for more men – other than the very smallest circle of people – to know about such measures. In the circles around Hitler, no one discussed his tasks and assignments with others unless the Führer himself felt it necessary or spoke about it.[224]

At Nuremberg, Speer came to a similar conclusion when reflecting on his relationship with Brandt. Although they were friends for years, they had apparently revealed little to each other about their more sinister activities. They both knew that communicating such knowledge to the other person could both implicate themselves in criminal activities and also damage their moral conscience, and the other person's psychological well-being as well. On 9 December 1946, Speer remarked:

> In our personal dealings, nothing would ever be said about any sinister activities we might be engaged in. I sometimes see Karl Brandt among the defendants in the Doctors' Trial ... Today he waved sadly to me in passing. I hear there is gravely incriminating

evidence of his having engaged in medical experiments on human beings. I frequently sat with Brandt; we talked about Hitler, made fun of Göring, expressed indignation at the sybaritic living in Hitler's entourage, at the many party parasites. But he never gave me any information about his doings, any more than I would have revealed to him that we were working on rockets that were supposed to reduce London to rubble. Even when we spoke of our own dead, we used the term 'casualties' and in general we were great at inventing euphemisms.[225]

We obviously have to be cautious not to overstretch the interpretative value of the source. Written at the beginning of the 1970s, Speer's 'diary entry' may have been written to distance himself in retrospect from Brandt, who was clearly implicated in medical war crimes. If Speer had admitted that he knew about the crimes in which Brandt was involved, he might have drawn attention to his own activities, particularly his apparent ignorance of the extermination of European Jews.

Brandt seems to have enjoyed his role as the medical supremo, charged with looking after the health and welfare of German citizens and soldiers. Perhaps his work reminded him of his early plans to follow Albert Schweitzer to Africa. Now he himself had acquired the image of a holy helper. Apart from Brandt's uncompromising commitment to exploiting all available means to free bed space in a national emergency, we find a certain degree of generosity which he exhibited to people in need, especially when they had some kind of connection with his family. Using the power of his title, Brandt frequently intervened on behalf of people who, for one reason or another, had been arrested and sent to a prison or concentration camp. Numerous people testified after the war that Brandt had saved their lives or had otherwise been of immense importance. Within Brandt's moral universe, such activities helped to eradicate any traces of involvement in illegal activities from his moral conscience, and corroborated the idealistic image which he wanted to have of himself; they helped him to remain pure. To understand Brandt as a person, we need to take a look at one such testimony.

After the war, Louiza Ernwein, a doctor from Alsace, where Brandt had been born, told interrogators that Brandt had saved her life. She was imprisoned in the concentration camp of Schirmeck in the lower Rhine from 1942/43. Schirmeck was essentially a women's camp. Because of her outspoken political views, the camp commander wanted her transferred to the Ravensbrück concentration camp, where she probably would have died from malnutrition or torture, if not from medical experiments. It is unlikely, given what we know today, that Ms Ernwein, aged sixty-five, who was suffering from bad health after eighteen months of imprisonment, would have survived the Ravensbrück ordeal. Her fellow prisoners certainly did not: five out of six died. A couple of days before she was supposed to be transferred, a friend of the family contacted Brandt and asked for help. Overstepping his powers, Brandt requisitioned her from the Gestapo for duty in the city hospital of Mannheim.[226] Whether he did so because the woman came from Alsace, or because she was a doctor, or perhaps as an alibi in case the war were lost, can no longer be established with certainty.

Whereas Brandt detached himself from the continued killings in German institutions, he showed genuine concern for the suffering of civilians and for soldiers on the battlefield. He would suddenly arrive at the front in the Führer plane, out of the sky, so to speak, and disappear in the same way. Some experienced Brandt as someone who was not of this world, a redeemer-like figure, who brought salvation wherever he turned up. After the war, Anton Sebastian Weih, a priest from the Salvatorian Order,[227] provided Allied investigators with a dramatized description of one of Brandt's impromptu visits to the front. It happened on Christmas Eve in 1943. Instead of spending time with his family, Weih described how Brandt gave comfort to German troops in the infinite space of the Russian winter landscape. Weih and the medical unit, to which he was attached, had set up camp in the town of Chodossowitschi, near Bobruisk. In the afternoon, Brandt unexpectedly visited this embattled regiment. He did not expect special treatment for himself or his SS guard, as Weih especially points out, but rolled up his sleeves and assisted the exhausted surgeons, cared throughout the night for the wounded, and performed the most difficult surgical operations under heavy enemy fire. The story sounds almost too good to be true. But whether it is fact or fable, what is significant is that Brandt is presented as a sacred healer, as someone sacrificing himself for the well-being of German soldiers. This was exactly the kind of image Brandt wanted to convey of himself, and which he believed to be true. Weih continued his narrative:

> On the morning of 25 December Prof. Dr. Brandt, without any kind of guard, visited me in my room for the seriously injured, which had been decorated despite the heavy fighting with a Christmas tree and a crib. I informed Dr. Brandt of the condition of some of the wounded and about those recovering from operations. Then he pressed my hand and said, approximately, the following: 'I am happy that you as a comrade and priest stand so loyal and with so much sacrifice side by side with the seriously injured. Does your duty not become a burden?' Upon my answer that, despite all, I still very much liked to do my duty, he said: 'Then I will make you a Christmas present with a piece of personal information. In recent days I was able to ensure that the sisters in your order can continue to do their duty in military and civilian hospitals.' With that he said good-bye.[228]

Weih's narrative portrays Brandt as someone who influenced other people's lives for the better, someone who cared for the wounded and helped those in need. Even if only parts of Weih's story are true, it would suggest that Brandt knew how to construct a certain image of himself. Weih's narrative and its biblical metaphors seem to suggest that Brandt was beginning to copy his master. Throughout the 1920s and early 1930s, Nazi propaganda had managed to create the image of Hitler as a charismatic leader, the national redeemer appointed by providence, who was destined to lead the German people onto the path of national glory and salvation. His descent into the waiting crowd by aeroplane in Leni Riefenstahl's propaganda film *Triumph des Willens* ('Triumph of the Will', 1935) had been one of the devices which had shaped the image of the Führer, who was seen as one with the German body politic.[229] We can be almost certain that Brandt had seen the film and learned the lesson. Whereas Brandt had cultivated the principles of detached leadership as far as his involvement in illegal operations was concerned, he had learned to imitate the principles of charismatic leadership with regard to the German people.

A more sceptical assessment might draw attention to Brandt's intentions. Were his visits to the battlefields perhaps part and parcel of his policy of plausible deniability? By helping certain individuals in concentration camps and by making a good impression on the soldiers at the front, Brandt established for himself useful testimony in case the war was lost. Creating such testimonies was not uncommon among the Nazi elite. As the war drew to a close, senior officials were beginning to look beyond the Nazi pomp and circumstance, and wonder how they could justify their role. Some sought to support a Jewish friend or neighbour in case Hitler's apparent weapons of mass destruction failed to bring about any miracles. His frequent visits to the front also allowed Brandt to argue that he had not been in Berlin when vital decisions with regard to the continuation of the 'euthanasia' programme, human experiments on camp inmates, or the extermination of European Jews had been made. He could claim that he did not know what was going on in the German capital. To some extent this may well have been true, at least as far as his level of ignorance was concerned. But Brandt's ignorance was, it seems, part of a broader strategy to disassociate himself from those executing his directives, and to detach himself from those who had understood his wishes. In other words, his ignorance was deliberately cultivated.

This line of argument is more than speculation. By the end of the war, men like Brandt and Speer were well aware that by being unavailable for prolonged periods of time, and by being away from Berlin and Hitler's headquarters, one could establish a useful alibi to mount a convincing defence after the war. They could argue that they had no knowledge of the crimes which members of the regime had committed. No one had apparently informed them, least of all their own officials. Yet for a convincing post-war defence one needed to stay clear of people who were directly implicated in mass murder and the Holocaust. For men like Gerhard-Friedrich Peters, who supplied the extermination camps with cyanide gas, Brandt was simply unavailable. 'Dr. Brandt avoided me,' Peters told interrogators after the war.[230] Brandt must have known that any contact with a man like Peters, however fleeting or informal, would have turned a policy of plausible deniability into plain denials. Yet Brandt was not always cautious enough; perhaps he was unaware about the extent to which medical officials and administrators recorded the conversations which they had with Brandt at one point or another. After the war, these fragments provided the American prosecution with incriminating evidence which showed that Brandt was involved in, and was connected with, criminal human experiments which Nazi physicians had carried out on concentration camp inmates. It was this evidence, among others, upon which the Nuremberg court sentenced Brandt to death.

8

Human Experimentation

I. MEDICAL ETHICS

Rather than showing a callous disregard for the life and dignity of subjects used for research in concentration camps, as most of the camp doctors did, Brandt was largely indifferent to the ethics of human experimentation. Central issues such as informed voluntary consent, beneficence and care do not seem to have figured predominantly in his medical and ethical world view. In a series of interviews conducted in the autumn of 1945, he explained that human subjects had 'always' been used for experimental purposes 'in one way or another'. According to Brandt, every surgical operation was a form of human experiment. The first time he had come into contact with experiments on humans was during his time at the Bergmannsheil hospital in Bochum in the late 1920s. One evening, Georg Magnus had apparently asked his assistants, including Brandt, whether they were willing to conduct an experiment on themselves to establish the effectiveness of the sedative Evipan. Brandt and his colleagues agreed. Moments after they had taken the drug they were fast asleep. Brandt believed that 'by this trial, a human experiment was actually carried out.'[1] Brandt was correct in believing that doctors had carried out experiments like the one by Magnus for centuries, either on themselves or on members of their family. But these experiments had nothing in common with the experiments that were carried out on concentration camp inmates. Brandt had consented to the experiment in a voluntary and informed fashion. He knew what the potential risks of the experiment were. At any time during the experiment he was able to terminate it. Hundreds of experimental subjects in the camps, however, had no choice. For them, the issue of informed voluntary consent never applied in any meaningful sense of the word. Whether Brandt intentionally conflated the issue to detract from his own level of culpability in the camp experiments, or whether he genuinely misunderstood that the experiments were of a totally different nature, is not known. Brandt was certainly aware that the issue of informed consent played a part in human experimentation, but he did not assign any importance to the concept in deciding whether an experiment was legitimate. Informed voluntary consent was one of many apparently equally important categories which served to decide whether to carry out an experiment. In September 1945, he stated:

> Firstly, there are experiments that are made for, or with, somebody on a voluntary basis, and secondly against the will of the person concerned. Then there is another sub-division, that is, whether experiments are connected with considerable danger or whether they are

comparatively harmless and without any symptoms of danger. Another differentiation is
whether the result of this experiment constitutes some important factor or whether it is
only a ridiculous playing that is being tried out by some scientific person. Out of these
six differentiations, there results a sort of guideline which enables one, from a medical
point of view, to say either 'Yes' or 'No'.[2]

Brandt's categories not only raise a number of ethical issues with regard to human
experimentation in general, but they allow an understanding of how and why he
initiated, sanctioned and supported certain camp experiments on humans.[3] To
what extent was it legitimate, for example, to carry out an experiment against a
person's will if the experiment was classified as 'important', and if the experiment
was likely to procure 'important results'? Was it justifiable to carry out such an
experiment if the life of the experimental subject was at risk? For Brandt, the
answer was 'yes'. According to Brandt, it was legitimate to subordinate the health
of the experimental subject if the experiment was considered to be of importance
to state and national security.[4] Brandt tried to justify 'the ethical consideration of
the German doctor as a whole' by distinguishing between 'medical orders' which
were issued by doctors and scientists, and 'non-medical orders' that were issued by
party officials and political agencies.[5] In Brandt's world view, doctors could not
violate medical ethics, not because they were unable to inflict harm on humans,
but because they were doctors. Their professional status freed them from any kind
of moral and ethical responsibility towards their patients, and gave them immunity
from medical ethics violations.

Asked in 1945 whether he had any information about the camp experiments,
Brandt stated that he had known of some of the Dachau freezing experiments: 'I
had (I cannot give the time) to take it for granted after a conversation that these
experiments were carried [out]; while I didn't know ... what was done and to
what extent and in what various forms things were done.'[6] Brandt also knew of
experiments that had been conducted in other camps and institutions: 'There
were other experiments carried out on human beings. I know that in the military
medical academy in Berlin experiments were carried out [with] Lost [mustard gas],
at an emergency surgery that was one of our sub-divisions.'[7] Realizing that he was
incriminating himself, he backtracked and stated that he had not heard 'anything
of larger experiments ... [E]xperiments, which were outside the limits which were
... generally accepted by the medical profession were not known to me ...'[8] During
the Nuremberg Doctors' Trial, the prosecution was able to demonstrate that Brandt
had not been telling the truth.

At the same time as Brandt was trying to deny responsibility for concentration
camp experiments, the US Army made a sensational discovery. In June 1945,
intelligence officers found most of Himmler's personal correspondence in a salt
mine in Hallain, near Salzburg. The documents showed the enormous extent to
which Himmler's SS, the German army and other agencies had carried out criminal
experiments on humans in collaboration with hundreds of German medical
scientists. Evidence presented during the Doctors' Trial also threw into relief the

extent to which Hitler had sanctioned experiments on prisoner populations. As Brandt pointed out, 'Himmler, on his own initiative, would not have done that without being covered by Hitler.' Following his throat operation in 1935, Hitler is said to have told his entourage that 'it would generally be right to use criminals in order to solve unresolved medical problems with their aid. He did not repeat this for any particular or general case, but it was his understanding that this was correct.'[9] More significantly, Brandt provided the court with an explanation of why no written order from Hitler about human experiments had been discovered among Himmler's papers – because it is highly unlikely that one was ever produced. The informal communications system at the heart of the Third Reich allowed men such as Himmler to interpret Hitler's general utterances within the framework of his own racial and geopolitical ideology, and transform them into concrete policy directives. As Brandt recalled: 'It may well have been that the Führer said something like that quite generally and Himmler then understood it and applied it to some specific case and then on his own initiative continued to deal with it.'[10] Given what we know about the way in which general statements by Hitler were read, interpreted and executed in the Third Reich, Brandt's narrative seems plausible.

Brandt was significantly less helpful as far as his own knowledge, involvement and responsibility for concentration camp experiments was concerned. Among Himmler's correspondence, Allied investigators discovered letters which showed that Brandt had requested from the SS the use of concentration camp inmates for medical experiments. He not only had extensive knowledge of human experiments that were carried out under the auspices of the SS, but had initiated, sanctioned and supported many of the experiments. In October 1946, Rudolf Brandt, Himmler's personal secretary, pointed out:

> A number of people close to Himmler were well informed of these experiments. Karl Brandt, Grawitz and Gebhardt were consulted on this matter by Himmler. The aforementioned were members of the 'SS Gruppenführer Corps,' and often the experiments were topics of discussion in private talks at Gruppenführer meetings. Such a fundamental matter as these experiments on human beings simply could not go on at all without those men knowing of it and taking a position with respect to it.[11]

II. FOOD EXPERIMENTS

In almost all cases, Brandt's involvement in human experiments coincides with a progressively worsening military situation that impacted on the health and welfare of tens of thousands of German soldiers, and undermined morale among the civilian population. While Germany was fighting an embittered war on multiple fronts, with thousands of soldiers suffering from malaria, typhus and other infectious diseases such as viral hepatitis (infectious jaundice, *infektiöse Gelbsucht*), or dying from the after-effects of severe battle injuries and gas gangrene, research in all areas of medical science gained the highest priority. On the Eastern Front, in particular, German soldiers were suffering from severe cases of malnutrition, frostbite and hypothermia. Closer to home, the citizens of western Germany were suffering from the effects of Allied bombing raids which caused third and fourth degree burns. Brandt's promotion to General Commissioner in July 1942, together with his promotion to SS-Standartenführer in August, gave him the necessary power, as well as confidence, to play an active part in shoring up support for the regime at a decisive turning-point in the war. The increasingly bleak military situation, which called for radical measures, austerity and sacrifice from all sections of society, also provided the rationale for initiating experiments on concentration camp inmates.

The major summer offensive of 1942, which ended in the catastrophe of Stalingrad, not only came as an enormous psychological shock to the German people, but it rattled the military leadership to its core. Against the advice of his military advisers, Hitler had taken the high-risk strategy of dividing Army Group South into Army Groups A and B, and ordered the attack on the Caucasus region and Stalingrad simultaneously. The weaker Army Group B was directed to attack, capture and totally destroy Stalingrad. Upon entering the city, the army was instructed to destroy (*vernichten*) the male population and deport all females. As early as July 1942, Halder, the Chief of Staff, had noted in his diary: 'This chronic tendency to underrate enemy capabilities is gradually assuming grotesque proportions and developing into a positive danger.'[12] In the late autumn of 1942, it not only became clear that the Soviets were about to start a massive counter-offensive, but also that the supply lines of Army Groups A and B were stretched to their limits. Medical supplies, food and clothing, and other essential resources such as fuel, were not reaching the front line troops any more. On his three-week visit in November 1942 to Stalingrad and the Caucasus region, Brandt was to assess the organization of medical supplies, boost military morale, and report back to Hitler.

The situation at Stalingrad was worsening dramatically at the time. On 19 November, the Soviet offensive got under way. Three days later, on 22 November, the 220,000 men of the Sixth Army, under the command of General Paulus, were completely encircled. Hitler, believing that logistical support could be organized and sustained from the air, continued to refuse Paulus permission to fight his way out of Stalingrad. Sub-Arctic temperatures made life in the city all but unendurable. At the end of November, Brandt was back at Führer headquarters in East Prussia. On 1 December 1942, Hitler's loyal adjutant, Julius Schaub, who accompanied Brandt on his trip to the Eastern Front, wrote to their mutual friend, Sister Treulinde:

> We visited a number of first-aid stations, army hospitals and field hospitals. The sisters we found nearest to the front were in Solduskaja in the Caucasus. If the weather somehow permits, we want to go back there in the next couple of days in order to supply the people with drugs and blankets. The last journey was really quite exhausting, but very interesting and Brandt will be able to do a lot of good now that he has seen the conditions there.[13]

Shortly before Christmas, it became clear that any attempt to break out of Stalingrad was doomed. Fuel and food shortages, coupled with a total breakdown of logistical supplies, meant that the Sixth Army was left to its own devices, without any form of outside help or military support. In his last letter home, one soldier wrote that there was nothing but 'misery, hunger, cold, resignation, doubt, despair, and horrible dying … I'm not cowardly, just sad that I can give no greater proof of my bravery than to die so pointlessly – indeed all this is a crime.'[14] The final phase in the destruction of the Sixth Army by the Soviet forces began on 10 January 1943. Food now became of vital importance for the survival of the soldiers. On 15 January, Hitler instructed the Luftwaffe to fly 300 tons of supplies a day to the encircled Sixth Army. It was nothing but wishful thinking. The freezing weather conditions often made the take-off and landing of planes impossible. On 22 January, the Sixth Army lost control of the last airfield. Tens of thousands of German troops, exhausted, some injured, and under constant enemy attack, were literally freezing and starving to death. At the end of January 1943, the Sixth Army finally surrendered to the advancing Soviet forces, leaving approximately 100,000 men dead and another 113,000 soldiers captured as prisoners of war. When it eventually transpired that Stalingrad had fallen to the Soviets, the shock to the German people was profound.

The looming catastrophe at Stalingrad sent Hitler's inner circle into overdrive. Total panic that the war could be lost was beginning to grip the regime. Now was the time to introduce radical and uncompromising measures to avoid military disaster and defeat, without regard for any legal, moral or ethical considerations. Some of the initiatives which Brandt and others launched during these frantic days showed a lack of strategic thinking, limited professional expertise and, above all, a dilettante approach to the solving of complex organizational and scientific problems. On 23 January, Goebbels remarked that Brandt was in agreement with him as far as a more radical approach to the war effort was concerned: 'Prof. Brandt especially, because of his deep knowledge of the situation of the wounded, shares my conviction that something extraordinary has to be done in order to give the war a decisive turn.'[15]

Two days later, on 25 January, Himmler told Oswald Pohl, head of the SS Finance and Administration Head Office (SS *Wirtschafts-Verwaltungshauptamt*, WVHA), that he had read in a book that at the time of Genghis Khan the Mongols had developed certain methods of dehydrating meat and conserving milk.[16] It is possible that Hitler, who by this time seemed to be living in a fantasy world, had drawn Himmler's attention to this kind of literature. Whilst staying at 'Werwolf', his headquarters near Vinnitsa in the Ukraine, Hitler had described Stalin, because of his achievements, as a 'latter-day Genghis Khan'.[17] Himmler instructed Pohl, who was in charge of hundreds of thousands of concentration camp inmates, to begin a series of human experiments to test the effectiveness of such methods. He also told Pohl to search for members of Ghengis Khan's and other Mongol tribes among the prisoners of war, and to use them as experimental subjects.[18] Himmler forwarded a copy of the letter to his chief liaison officer at Führer headquarters, SS-Obergruppenführer Karl Wolff, who may have discussed it with Brandt. One day later, on 26 January, Brandt approached Wolff to inquire about the possibility of conducting nutrition experiments on concentration camp prisoners:

Since in the meantime I have received ample material about the development of concentrated food, as a special project for the area of the fortress Stalingrad, for example, I would like to raise again the matter we discussed at the time. Is it possible to carry out relevant nutritional experiments in concentration camps? I think that for this you would need to contact Dr. Luft at the Medical Research Institute for Aviation and *Ministerialrat* Ziegelmayer, the consulting nutritional expert with the *Wehrmacht*, through me. A clear plan of the experiments, which corresponds to the actual conditions, should then jointly be drawn up. I think it is quite possible to eventually obtain new, valuable results in a comparatively short time (a few weeks).[19]

Brandt had previously raised the issue of nutrition experiments with Wolff and other officials, probably after returning from his inspection tour to Stalingrad at the end of November 1942. He later recalled that he had discussed the issue of concentrated food for the army to drop to the encircled troops in the East.[20] Experts had calculated that every soldier needed about 3,500 calories per day through concentrated food, but this seemed to be insufficient under the extreme living conditions at Stalingrad. The problem, Brandt thought, was that the concentrated food which the Ministry of Agriculture could provide contained different amounts of fat and proteins. It was neither known which food was the most suitable, nor whether 3,500 calories were enough to preserve and sustain the fighting capability of soldiers. After discussions with Wilhelm Ziegelmayer, the army's consulting nutritional expert, Brandt told Hitler that there was uncertainty among experts about the most suitable form of concentrated food. According to Brandt, Hitler is supposed to have suggested that experiments on camp inmates would be the fastest way to solve the problem. It was Hitler, and not he, who had proposed the experiments. He was only the messenger, who passed on Hitler's instructions to the SS: 'He [Hitler] said at the time, that this could be solved in the most expeditious way in this form [experiments on concentration camp inmates], and I passed this order on.'[21] Brandt assigned no particular importance to the matter. Under different circumstances, he would have called it a 'troop experiment'.[22] It may well be that Hitler proposed to approach Himmler about the matter, and sort the problem out in one of the concentration camps. Yet, there is no evidence to corroborate Brandt's version of events. This is not altogether surprising, given that Hitler generally discussed and decided matters in an informal and oral fashion. If Brandt's version of events is true, which is doubtful, it raises the question as to why Brandt did not object to experiments on concentration camp prisoners without their consent. He must have agreed with Hitler's suggested plan of action. For Brandt, it was another opportunity to make his mark as the man in charge of coordinating German experimental research – hence he stressed the need for the contact between the SS and the experts in the field to be established through him. In the midst of military defeat and human suffering, Brandt was using his position as General Commissioner to expand his power base at the centre of the German government.

Brandt's first recorded initiative to discuss the possibility of experiments on camp inmates with the SS resulted from the enormous logistical problems and human suffering which he had encountered on the Eastern Front. Another impetus came from the increasingly desperate situation at Stalingrad in the middle of January 1943. His approach to the SS was an attempt to contribute to the ongoing war effort by expediting experimental medical research, and by establishing a collaborative framework with Himmler's SS in all questions pertaining to the testing of substances on people in the future. Brandt's letter shows, above all, that he knew that experiments on humans were and could be carried out on camp inmates without their consent. For Brandt, it was of no concern whether or not the subjects were volunteers. What mattered to him more than anything else was the urgent need to obtain valuable scientific data in the most time-efficient way for some of the most pressing medical issues of the day. In the context of modern military conflict it was seen as legitimate to sacrifice individual human lives in the name of science. For Brandt, and other leading Nazi officials, human experiments on camp inmates were little more than a necessary evil in times of total war. In 1947, Brandt conceded that the war, and the way in which it had been fought, had created a struggle for human existence in which the individual human being played no part any more.[23]

It took the SS almost two months to respond to Brandt's letter. On 20 March, Pohl explained that the daily bombing raids had prevented him from responding to the proposal. He told Brandt that the SS had dispatched SS-Sturmbannführer Ernst-Günther Schenck, the Nutritional Inspector of the Waffen-SS during the military campaigns in the West, South-East, Norway and Russia, where he had gathered data under extreme war conditions. As far as nutrition experiments on camp inmates were concerned, Pohl was of the opinion that the SS had a very good understanding about the 'physiological nutritional needs of soldiers'.[24] This body of knowledge had been obtained through experience in the field and through scientific research on nutrition which Schenck and the Military Medical Academy had carried out. In other words, Pohl was not convinced that Brandt's proposal would produce anything new:

> On the contrary, we cannot expect anything fundamentally new from the investigations on prisoners, which might even distort the actual conditions in relation to the nutrition of the troops because, first, the prisoners can not be compared with the nutritional conditions and training of the troops, even if they are undernourished and, second, because the positive forces of morale, which play such an important part among the troops, are not present.[25]

Brandt's proposal was turned down. Given that the SS had matters under control, Pohl was heard to be saying, there was no need for the General Commissioner to become concerned or involved, especially since his knowledge and understanding of the issues at hand was limited. It was one way of telling Brandt that he should mind his own business. However, since the SS was conducting specific nutrition experiments in one of the camps, Pohl was prepared to use prisoners for medical experiments if these could help to solve 'special questions' (*Spezialfragen*).[26] Although Brandt was asked to submit particular questions to the SS for examination, no further communication seems to have taken place between Brandt and the SS. Pohl's rather terse response raises doubts about Brandt's post-war statement that Hitler had instructed him to propose the experiments to the SS. It is highly unlikely that Brandt would not have mentioned Hitler's instructions in his letter to Wolff, if Hitler had really wanted the experiments to be carried out. Brandt's subsequent silence about the matter is another indication that the initiative for the experiments probably came from Brandt, who may have briefly raised them in the most general fashion with Hitler. For the time being, the SS had put the General Commissioner in his place.

Brandt also seems to have played no discernible part in the nutrition experiments which were subsequently carried out by the SS on 450 'healthy prisoners' at Mauthausen concentration camp. From the summer of 1943, the prisoners were fed with *Östliche Kostform* (Eastern Nutrition), a kind of artificial pâté made of cellulose remnants. The artificial pâté had been developed, among others, by SS-Brigadeführer Walter Schieber of the Armaments Supply Office (*Rüstungslieferungsamt*) with whom Brandt later collaborated on chemical warfare matters.[27] It must have been revolting. As a result, many of the prisoners suffered from severe stomach and gastrointestinal problems. One of them recalled that 'dogs wouldn't touch this pâté …'[28] Pohl and his officials, including Schenck, however, were excited about the prospect of using the cellulose remnants to feed the growing concentration camp populations. In December 1943, he decided to conduct a massive three-months' nutrition experiment on 100,000 prisoners in the concentration camps of Dachau, Buchenwald and Sachsenhausen.[29] At the same time, 370 prisoners were selected for another six-months' nutrition trial at Mauthausen: 150 prisoners were again fed with *Östliche Kostform*, and 220 prisoners were used as a control group. A total of 116 prisoners eventually died.[30] After the war, a West German judicial inquiry concluded that it was no longer possible to determine whether the death of the prisoners had occurred as a result of the experiment, or because the prisoners had been suffering from general exhaustion and malnutrition.[31]

Although Brandt visited Mauthausen to inspect the stone quarries, he does not seem to have been directly involved in the SS nutrition experiments.[32] His request to use camp inmates for similar experiments in January 1943 is, however, proof that he was well aware of the systematic use of concentration camp prisoners for human experiments without their consent. As a member of the working group 'Nutrition of the Army' (*Arbeitsgemeinschaft Ernährung der Wehrmacht*), Brandt seems also to have been informed about the food experiments which military experts carried out, largely on Russian prisoners of war and on the inmates of concentration camps and prisons.[33] As one of the most influential medical officials of the regime, he did nothing to prevent the experiments. On the contrary, he sanctioned and supported them. The same is true for the notorious sulphonamide drug and bone transplantation experiments which were carried out on Polish and French prisoners of war at the Ravensbrück concentration camp. [34]

III. SULPHONAMIDE EXPERIMENTS

Most of the experiments on women at Ravensbrück involved unnecessary suffering, and safeguards were rarely put in place to protect the women from severe and multiple injuries, mutilations, disability or death. There is no evidence that any of the women consented to the experiments. There is also no case reported where the experimental subject was at liberty of her own free choice to withdraw from the trial. Often the experiments were performed by unqualified medical personnel, and at random, for no scientific reason, and under appalling physical and psychological conditions. All the women experienced extreme pain, and almost all of those who are still alive today are suffering from physical injuries and traumas, either as a direct result of the experiments, or because of the total lack of post-operative care at the time. The scars left on the victims are well documented.[35]

Owing to heavy German casualties at the Eastern Front in the winter of 1941/42 from gas gangrene, and the effect on German morale of Allied propaganda about the value of sulphonamide drugs, leading SS authorities had demanded for some time that the quality of these drugs should be examined. Hitler and his inner circle eventually ordered experiments with sulphonamide drugs after the SS-Obergruppenführer and head of the RSHA, Reinhard Heydrich, had died in Prague from a gas gangrene infection which had developed after the attempted assassination in May 1942. The man in charge of these experiments was Karl Gebhardt, head of the SS clinic in Hohenlychen, who was accused of negligence for not having treated Heydrich with sulphonamides. Gebhardt's motive for conducting the experiments was to clear himself of the responsibility for Heydrich's death and to convince Himmler and leading SS officials that his judgement concerning sulphonamide drugs was correct. The experiments were no more than a 'mere medico-political gesture'.[36]

The initial order for experiments on human subjects probably came from Himmler and Grawitz, though Gebhardt was left in charge of the general direction.[37] His objective was to test the efficiency of various commercial sulphonamide drugs, both Swiss and German.[38] Sulphonamide drug experiments began at the end of July 1942, those on seventy-four Polish women at the beginning of August 1942. The first twenty operations were performed on twenty male prisoners from Sachsenhausen. Thirty further operations were performed on Polish women, who suffered much more severe infections owing to the introduction of foreign bodies such as fragments of wood or powdered glass. In one case, a curved surgical needle and twenty centimetres of silk was left in the wound.[39] After completion of the first series of experiments, Grawitz visited the camps and examined the young women. As no deaths had occurred among the experimental subjects, Grawitz gave orders to fire bullets through the legs of the women in order to produce battle-like gas gangrene infections. Gebhardt and his assistant, SS-Sturmbannführer Fritz Fischer, decided against the order but produced severe tissue damage on a number of women instead.[40] Five women died from the effects of the experimental operations, six were later killed.

Experiments on human beings at Ravensbrück were anything but secret in Nazi Germany and were openly discussed at the 'Third Working Conference of Advisory Physicians' from 24 to 26 May 1943, where Gebhardt and Fischer presented their findings to over two hundred army physicians. Fischer's talk on 'Special Experiments on the Effects of Sulphonamide' revealed that the experiments had been carried out on camp inmates without their consent, and that in three cases the outcome had been fatal. Brandt was among the attending guests. He had been given a seat in the front row with Handloser to his right and Conti to his left. Although he arrived late, witnesses remembered him listening to the talk of Fischer, and a photograph was even taken.[41] Gebhardt also recalled after the war that, prior to the meeting in May, he had met Brandt and Rostock on a train station, and had used the occasion to tell them about the results of the Ravensbrück experiments.[42] According to Gebhardt, both 'evidently' knew that the experiments had been conducted on prisoner populations. There is little doubt that Brandt was informed about the experiments.

Brandt and the participants could probably not have known that the experiments were criminal according to the German penal code, because not all the participants had ready access to the information Gebhardt told some of his colleagues in private. But they could have realized that the experiments constituted a marked transgression from previous research practices, and contravened national and international standards of medical ethics, especially after Gebhardt had made unambiguous remarks before the talk, and after Fischer had given a rather graphic presentation. It must have been clear to everyone attending the conference that the experiments had been performed in a concentration camp. On the basis of his subsequent personal experience, Brandt later admitted that 'hundreds of thousands of concentration camp inmates' had been 'improperly incarcerated and condemned to death'.[43] It was the responsibility of leading medical officers such as Brandt and Handloser to ensure that medical ethics standards were maintained, and that any transgressions were properly investigated. If nothing else, Brandt was guilty of gross negligence. After the war, the US prosecution remarked:

> Having acquired knowledge, Brandt was not privileged to remain silent; he was under a duty to act. Brandt did nothing. He did not investigate the experiments; he did not voice any objection at the meeting; he did not ask for a report from the SS; he did not report to the Führer. He took a 'consenting part' in this criminal use of helpless concentration camp inmates.[44]

Brandt's tacit approval of the experiments fitted a general pattern. None of the attending physicians of Germany's medical elite felt it necessary to protest against human experiments which violated every conceivable and existing moral standard of clinical research.[45] Years later, some of the scientists defended their silence by stating that criticism against experiments conducted by the SS was out of the question, 'not least because of military etiquette'.[46] Other scientists involved in the experiments had no qualms about publishing their research findings in established German academic journals.[47] In an environment filled with a strict code of professional conduct, and subservience to higher authority, it comes as little surprise that the voice of Brandt is conspicuously absent.

IV. EPIDEMIC JAUNDICE EXPERIMENTS

Brandt had good reasons not to speak up. Only days before the conference, he had sanctioned and supported human experiments on the causes of viral hepatitis. The subjects of the experiments were concentration camp inmates, who were transferred from Auschwitz to the Sachsenhausen camp. For Brandt, experiments on prisoners performed without their consent were nothing out of the ordinary. This may explain why he had great difficulties in remembering the conference after the war, or what had been discussed.[48] The conference had been of little importance to him. It left no trace on his conscience.

The high rate of jaundice infections with hepatitis epidemica during the Russian campaign made research into the causes of the disease a military priority. Kurt Gutzeit, professor of internal medicine at the University of Breslau, recalled in 1950 that the German army counted approximately five to six million soldiers who had fallen ill from hepatitis in the years between 1941 and 1943. On the Eastern Front, there were 190,000 soldiers suffering from the disease in September 1941 alone. There was also a rising number of hepatitis cases among the civilian population, eventually more than among the army. Gutzeit estimated that the total number of hepatitis cases was over 10 million during the Second World War.[49] Given that Gutzeit had himself been heavily involved in experimental research during the war, it comes perhaps as no surprise that he portrayed the disease as one which was of great military and strategic significance. However, his basic assumption that the disease caused major disruption to military operations seems to have been correct.

In 1939, Gutzeit, who had been appointed to advise the Army Medical Inspectorate (*Heeres-Sanitäts-Inspekteur*) on the disease, established his own department within the Military Medical Academy in Berlin. A central plank of his research was to demonstrate that the jaundice affecting the army was an infectious disease which was caused by the hepatitis virus. In 1942, the bacteriologist and medical officer, Arnold Dohmen, who had previously worked at the university hospital in Hamburg-Eppendorf, joined Gutzeit's department in Berlin. One of Gutzeit's other assistants was Hans Voegt, an expert on hepatitis at the University of Breslau. It was through Gutzeit that Dohmen and Voegt began to collaborate. In October 1941, Voegt had attempted to demonstrate the infectious nature of hepatitis through an experiment on himself, the results of which he published in the *Münchner Medizinischen Wochenschrift*. Shortly afterwards, Voegt persuaded the director of the clinic for nervous diseases in Breslau, Professor Villinger, to use some of the mental patients for his research and infect them with hepatitis without their consent. Having been informed of the experiments, Gutzeit wrote to Voegt: 'I am glad that you have approached the jaundice research in such an active fashion and I agree with the investigations you have initiated.'[50]

One month earlier, in September 1941, Friedrich Meythaler, professor of internal medicine at the University of Rostock and medical adviser to the army, had told Gutzeit that he had conducted hepatitis experiments on British prisoners of war on the island of Crete, which had only recently been occupied by the German army. The numbers of infected German soldiers had apparently reached such high proportions that officials were talking of 'yellow divisions', a pun on the German word *Gelbsucht* (jaundice), which literally translated means 'yellow disease'. On 30 September 1941, Gutzeit wrote to Meythaler: 'I am glad that you have already begun to undertake experiments to transfer hepatitis-infected blood onto prisoners, and I hope that, if you make these blood transfusions once the hepatitis is beginning to show, we will succeed after all.'[51]

After the war, especially at the Nuremberg Doctors' Trial, Gutzeit wanted to portray himself and his researchers as a group of scientists who had come under increasing pressure from the SS and the German medical establishment to conduct experiments on humans in order to verify some of their research data.[52] Eugen Haagen, a professor at the University of Strasbourg, and Grawitz from the SS had apparently attempted to persuade Dohmen to supply them with some of his cultures for their own experiments. In both cases, Dohmen had apparently refused in order to remain in control of his work. Feeling pressured by the SS and other agencies, who accused Dohmen of sabotaging the war, and in order to mend relations with the SS, Dohmen had eventually decided to conduct the relevant research on human subjects himself. Gutzeit's narrative provided Dohmen with a reasonable explanation for why he had conducted experiments at Sachsenhausen, exonerated Gutzeit's own research group from serious wrongdoing, and shifted the responsibility for the experiments to Grawitz and Himmler, both of whom were dead, and onto the organization of the SS, which was on trial at Nuremberg anyway.

Evidence from Dohmen's papers and other archival sources suggests, however, that the initiative for the experiments came from Gutzeit and his research group, and that the professional pressure which Gutzeit applied to Dohmen may have led him to carry out the experiments on concentration camp inmates. Rather than the SS or one of the government agencies ordering the experiments from above, the essential dynamic and initiative for the experiments came from below, from the scientists themselves, who were pressing ahead with their research in order to advance their professional careers. In order to do so, the scientists needed not only the necessary institutional set-up, research facilities and material, but also the support from a key member of Hitler's government, someone like Brandt, who was perceived as the up-and-coming medical supremo. Dohmen's decision to approach Brandt with his proposal for conducting human experiments, and Brandt's subsequent sanctioning and support of the experiments, is yet another example of scientists who, in their desire to work for the benefit of the Führer, were actually working for the benefit of his medical representative. By 1943, Brandt was seen as one of the few personalities who had the political clout to sanction involuntary and non-therapeutic experiments on humans.

Dohmen's correspondence with Gutzeit, recently discovered by Brigitte Leyendecker from Berlin, provides insight not only into how the hepatitis experiments actually started, but into how Brandt became involved.[53] At the end of December 1943, Dohmen wrote a long letter to Gutzeit in which he tried to justify the slow progress in his research, and the fact that he had not yet been able to carry out the hepatitis experiments with the group of children who had especially been assigned for this work at the Sachsenhausen concentration camp.[54] In his letter, Dohmen told Gutzeit that he had originally tried to conduct experiments with infectious hepatitis on the inmates of Wittenau mental asylum, and that he had therefore approached the director of the asylum, probably Gustav Adolf Waetzoldt, in March and April 1943.[55] There are two possible explanations as to why Dohmen might have wanted to conduct the experiments on asylum inmates. Not only had Voegt, Dohmen's colleague, previously carried out hepatitis experiments on mental patients in Breslau, but Dohmen wanted to carry out his work in an institutional environment in which the lives of his research subjects could be strictly controlled, and in which the disease could be accurately monitored and documented.[56] A mental asylum seemed the ideal environment. Waetzoldt, Wittenau's director and author of the standard text 'Hereditary Improvement through Eradication' (*Aufartung durch Ausmerzung*), seems to have agreed to Dohmen's proposal:

> When these discussions [with the director of the Wittenau asylum] led to a result, I informed you [Gutzeit] about this as well. The personal ban by the Commissioner of the Führer for the Health System, Professor Brandt, prevented [me] from carrying out these particular experiments. It was then possible to establish contact with Herr Prof. B. On 19/20 May 1943, I attended a meeting at the Führer headquarters. This was followed by discussions of a different kind which are known to you.[57]

Dohmen's recapitulation of events, if it is true, seems to suggest that Brandt prohibited Dohmen from using the inmates from a mental asylum for human experiments.[58] The flow of information to and from Brandt remains somewhat speculative, however. Dohmen recalled in his letter to Gutzeit that it was only *after* Brandt had banned the Wittenau experiments that it had become 'possible to establish contact' with Brandt. This would suggest that the first time Dohmen himself established contact with Brandt was at the end of April 1943, and that any communication between the two before that date was through intermediaries. Wittenau's director, Waetzold, probably permitted Dohmen to carry out the experiments in his asylum as long as they were sanctioned by a higher government authority. Considering Waetzold's involvement in the 'euthanasia' programme, he probably approached the KdF with the matter in order to obtain Brandt's general approval. In return, Brandt would have communicated his ban via the KdF to Waetzold, who would have informed Dohmen of Brandt's decision.

It is even more difficult to establish why Brandt might have prohibited the experiments on mental patients. There are multiple explanations as to why Brandt turned to the SS for experiments on humans. The suggestion that he wanted to use the vast SS machinery for his own research ambitions is difficult to substantiate.

A more plausible explanation is that he wanted to shift the responsibility for medical experiment from his own area of responsibility to Himmler and the SS. Brandt probably wanted to avoid institutions and personnel which were associated with, and linked to, the 'euthanasia' programme becoming involved in human experiments, and for which he would be responsible if any of the experiments resulted in fatalities. This assumption is further corroborated by the fact that Brandt was in the process of amassing further powers over the hospital sector at the time that Dohmen approached him. On 20 May 1943, the same day that Brandt and Dohmen discussed the hepatitis experiments, Hitler signed a decree which gave Brandt the power to decide over contentious areas relating to the building of military and civilian hospitals and the admittance of patients.[59] Brandt may have been concerned that experiments in any of these institutions or in mental asylums might cause further problems with Conti over their mutual areas of responsibility. Given that Brandt's relationship with Conti was at an all-time low in early 1943, and considering that his own position at the heart of the regime was rather fragile, Brandt probably wanted to ensure that the experiments would be conducted by an organization which was beyond Conti's criticism, especially once they had been signed off and sanctioned by Himmler.

Finally, there was Himmler and his SS empire. Evidence seems to suggest that in 1943 Himmler claimed ownership over human experiments conducted in German concentration camps. Rudolf Brandt, Himmler's personal secretary, recalled after the war how doctors wanting to conduct experiments had to obtain prior permission: 'Before an experiment could be conducted on inmates of a concentration camp, Himmler's permission had to be secured.'[60] In August 1943, Himmler issued a formal directive, stating that he wanted to be personally consulted, as a matter of principle, if anyone wanted to use prisoners for medical experiments.[61] However, given Himmler's interest in medical science, it was relatively easy for physicians to obtain the necessary authorization, especially if the experiments promised to 'aid the war effort'. Rudolf Brandt also remembered the process by which the experimental subjects were selected:

> The people to be experimented on were generally earmarked by Himmler – for instance Jews, Gypsies, Poles or criminals condemned to death. The individuals to be used were selected at the camp out of the groups specified beforehand by Himmler. Later on Himmler no longer ordered that only volunteers condemned to death were to be used, and it is quite obvious that concentration camp inmates normally did not volunteer for the said purpose. They simply were selected and experimented on, their consent was not requested. The physicians and other persons involved in these experiments appealed to Himmler since it was impossible to get volunteers. No one involved in these experiments could fairly believe that only persons volunteering for that purpose were used.[62]

The evidence shows that Himmler authorized human experiments and selected the relevant victim groups. By March 1943, it had become clear that the Reich Research Council granted government funding to Grawitz and the SS on the basis that the research 'can be carried out only with the material [prisoners] accessible to the Waffen-SS and therefore cannot be undertaken by any other agency'.[63] In other words, officials or agencies wanting to conduct government-funded human experiments were required to approach the SS, and obtain Himmler's personal approval. Brandt was certainly aware of this rule. Brandt had approached Wolff about the nutrition experiments in January 1943.[64] He may now have felt that he had to consult Himmler about Dohmen's proposed experiments as a matter of course, and leave the execution of the experiments in the hands of the SS. He certainly did not want to alienate one of the most ruthless and brutal men in modern history. The recollections of Himmler's secretary also leave no doubt that Nazi doctors and other officials, including Brandt, knew that the experiments were conducted on camp inmates without their consent.

Whereas Brandt prohibited Dohmen from using mental patients for his experiments, he ensured that the hepatitis experiments could be carried out in a concentration camp instead. On 30 April 1943, Dohmen approached Brandt with his plan to conduct jaundice experiments on human subjects.[65] This time, Dohmen wrote to Hitler's doctor directly. In order to convince Brandt that experiments on humans were needed, Dohmen told him that it was necessary 'to demonstrate that the causal agent [for jaundice] was in fact the causal agent of human hepatitis epidemica'.[66] Once this question was solved, Dohmen told Brandt, scientists could start developing a possible vaccine against the disease:

> It would therefore be necessary to conduct experiments on humans [*Rückübertragungsversuche*] in order to come up with the final identity [of the causal agent]. The experiments would have to be carried out in such a way that six persons would be infected with the material which had previously been obtained through the animal experiment.[67]

Dohmen's report had the desired effect. On his return from Denmark on 17 May 1943, where he had attempted to organize a sufficient supply of mice for his laboratory work, Dohmen was instructed to attend a meeting with Brandt at Führer headquarters.[68] Leaving Berlin in a sleeper car on the evening of 19 May, Dohmen arrived the next morning at Hitler's headquarters. In a letter to his mother, written at the beginning of June, Dohmen could barely conceal his excitement that he had visited the centre of German military might and power, had seen the Führer from a distance, and had attended a meeting with Hitler's medical representative, Karl Brandt:

> But now I have to tell you about my experiences at Führer headquarters. You can imagine my amazement when one day I received a call from there, and was informed that the General Commissioner of the Führer would like to talk to me about my work. For the journey I received my ticket for the sleeper car here at the Reich Chancellery and was taken by car to the actual Führer headquarters. After reporting to the General Medical Officer Professor Brandt, I had some breakfast. Afterwards I had the opportunity to see the Führer from a tea house from a very close distance, how he went for a walk and played with his extremely beautiful Alsatian ... The whole walk only lasted about a quarter of an hour. It is the only time during the day that the Führer has some air.[69]

Apart from the sense of adulation of Hitler and the Führer image, so apparent in Dohmen's letter, his narrative suggests that Brandt had somehow learned about his work and had decided to talk to the scientists. In reality, Dohmen wanted to talk to Brandt. On 20 May 1943, in the afternoon, Brandt finally met Dohmen and discussed for four hours the prospect of human experiments. Dohmen described Brandt as 'extraordinarily nice from a human point of view', and as someone who was an 'excellent man in all respects'.

> We talked about my work in which he was very interested and for which he promised every support from his side. In case I should have difficulties in any area, I should contact him directly. Completely satisfied and with a sense of having had a unique experience I drove further to Berlin.[70]

The meeting with Brandt had given him the 'drive and the necessary perspective' which one needed during the war to carry out one's work, Dohmen told his mother. In the official report about the meeting, Dohmen stated that he had provided Brandt with a comprehensive report about his work and about the need to conduct human experiments with children who had not yet suffered from hepatitis and who, in all probability, had not yet developed any antibodies:

> Professor Dr Brandt offers his support in order to overcome any problems that might arise, and [he] recognised the need for the concluding investigations; he will arrange the preconditions for this, as far as he deems it necessary. In particular, [we] aired the possibility of transferring [the hepatitis virus] into humans.[71]

Brandt also proposed a meeting with the scientists involved in hepatitis research in order to assess what had been achieved, ensure that unnecessary projects would be avoided, and lay down a uniform research strategy for the future.[72] Back in Berlin, where he arrived on 21 May, Dohmen was asked by his superiors to give a paper to the Third Working Conference of Advisory Physicians, where Gebhardt and Fischer also presented their findings from the Ravensbrück experiments. Dohmen had not originally been due to present his work at the conference, and it may well be that one of the reasons why Dohmen approached Brandt with his proposal was to convince Hitler's personal physician that his and Gutzeit's research warranted additional research facilities and state funding.

Brandt kept his promise to 'arrange the preconditions' for Dohmen's experiments. When exactly Brandt approached the SS is not known, but it is possible that he did so after he had heard Dohmen deliver his paper during the conference at the end of May. According to Dohmen, Brandt seems to have been impressed with his work. What is certain, however, is that Brandt approached the SS with the request that they provide Dohmen with the necessary number of prisoners to carry out his jaundice experiments, and that severe injuries and even the death of the experimental subjects were taken into account. On 1 June 1943, Grawitz wrote to Himmler:

> The General Commissioner of the Führer, SS-Brigadeführer Prof. Dr. Brandt, has approached me with the request to support research investigating the causes of infectious

jaundice (hepatitis epidemica), and which he is greatly in favour of, through the provision of prisoner material.[73]

Before writing his letter to Himmler, Grawitz discussed the matter with Dohmen in person. On 1 June, Grawitz met with Dohmen at 51 Knesebeckstraße to discuss his research proposal. In the same letter, Grawitz told Himmler:

> In order to enlarge our knowledge, which previously was based only on the inoculation of animals with pathogens from humans, it will now be necessary to reverse the procedure and inoculate human beings with virus cultures which have been bred [in animals]. *Cases of death have to be anticipated* [emphasis added]. The therapeutic and especially prophylactic conclusions are naturally dependent on this final experimental step. Eight prisoners would be needed at the prison hospital at Sachsenhausen concentration camp, prisoners who have been sentenced to death, and preferably of a young age.[74]

Grawitz felt that Dohmen's research was important because jaundice had spread extensively among 'the Waffen-SS and police as well as among the army', and in some military units the number of infected soldiers had reached 60 per cent for a period of six weeks.[75] Grawitz then asked Himmler for permission to carry out the experiments in the way outlined, with Dohmen in charge of them. Although Dohmen was not a member of the SS (but SA-Führer and Nazi Party member), Grawitz supported his application 'in the interests of continuity in the experimental process and therefore the accuracy of the results'.[76] On 16 June, Himmler gave permission to use 'eight criminals from Auschwitz who had been sentenced to death' for the experiments. As an afterthought Himmler added in brackets that Dohmen should use 'eight Jews from the Polish resistance movement sentenced to death'.[77] The next day, on Thursday 17 June, Himmler had two meetings with Hitler on the Berghof, a short one for fifteen minutes, at 2.30 p.m., and one after lunch for forty-five minutes, at 3.30 p.m. It is quite possible that Himmler informed Hitler about the experiments. More significant, however, is the fact that Brandt met with Hitler for three-quarters of an hour immediately after Hitler had seen Himmler, at 4.15 p.m.[78] We have no information about what was discussed between Hitler and Himmler or between Hitler and Brandt on this day, but it is likely that Brandt would have briefed the head of state about the forthcoming hepatitis experiments.

A week later, on 23 June, after another meeting with Grawitz, Dohmen was on his way to Auschwitz.[79] The next day, on 24 June, Dohmen stood on the ramp at Auschwitz together with Josef Mengele to identify and select his research subjects. Mengele, sporting a riding crop on the ramp, had arrived in Auschwitz at the end of May to conduct detailed studies on twins which, he believed, would help him 'to advance one step in the search to unlock the secret of multiplying the race of superior beings destined to rule'.[80] Maximilian Rosmarin, one of the few witnesses of Dohmen's experiments, recalled that he had been ferried from Bencin, Upper Silesia, to Auschwitz on 24 June.[81] On that day, the entire transport, consisting of forty-seven boys, was sent to the gas chamber, except for the eighteen children, including Rosmarin, whom Dohmen selected for his research project. Frightened by the atmosphere on the ramp, Rosmarin had 'instinctively' approached Dohmen to see whether he could perhaps be of any use to the doctor, whereupon Dohmen asked him how old he was and whether he had had any jaundice:

> I told him that I was 19 years of age, but that I had not yet had jaundice. Dr Dohmen also said: 'I actually need boys before puberty for my purposes.' I then said that he could use me as an interpreter, because I could speak German and Polish. He then said: 'Alright, come with me.'[82]

Rather than selecting eight members from the Polish resistance movement who had been sentenced to death, as Himmler had originally stated, Dohmen selected eighteen Jewish prisoners who were between nine and twenty-two years old. Emaciated and exhausted from their journey, the children must have appeared younger, which explains why some of the witnesses of the experiments later believed that Dohmen's subjects had been between eight and fifteen years of age.[83] On the day of their arrival, Mengele conducted a medical examination of all the children and set up a card index. The group stayed at Auschwitz until 10 August, when a guard instructed eleven of the children to put on civilian clothes before accompanying them on an ordinary passenger train from Auschwitz to Berlin. Arriving in Berlin, the group took the underground to another station from where another train left to Oranienburg, thirty kilometres north. From there the group made its way to the Sachsenhausen concentration camp. What happened to the remaining seven children of Dohmen's original group is not known, except for the brother of one of the experimental subjects, who was part of the group and survived the war. Rosmarin also recalled that Dohmen left Auschwitz as soon as he had completed his selection, probably on 25 June, and travelled to Giessen.[84] The obvious brutality and criminal nature of a place like Auschwitz, and the experience of seeing dozens of children sent to the gas chamber, probably left Dohmen traumatized. He may have changed his mind about the experiments after realizing that the SS, which, after all, had given him access to his research subjects, was in effect a criminal organization.

At Sachsenhausen, Dohmen's eleven research subjects were housed in Block 2, and were given the label 'Medical Experimental Series Dr Dohmen on the order of the Reich Security Main Office'. Their names were Abraham Singer, Kopel Reitzenstein, Maks Rozmaryn (Maximilian Rosmarin), Solomon Feldberg, Moses Pietrkowski, Simon Rotschild, Fischel Steinkeller, Saul Hornfeld, Bernhard Lemel, Hirsch Litmanowitsch and Wolf Silberglet.[85] Wolf Silberglet, the youngest in the group, was nine years old, but told everyone that he was twelve because his grandfather believed that it would improve his grandson's chances of survival.[86] The children were again medically examined and kept in strict isolation. Their door was kept locked. To talk to other prisoners was strictly prohibited. A couple of weeks later, they were allowed, for the first time, to leave their barracks and go for a walk for half an hour. One of the prisoners, Franz Ballhorn, recorded the arrival of Dohmen's experimental group in his diary:

21 August 1943. Eleven Jewish youths have been transferred to the hospital building. They come from Sosnowiec in Upper Silesia and were for some time in the concentration camp of Auschwitz. The youngest is seven[87], Wolf Silberglet. Their parents, brothers and sister have been burnt in the notorious Jewish extermination camp Auschwitz. They themselves have somehow escaped and shall now serve as guinea-pigs to test new medical discoveries. Wölfchen is still the child; he likes to play and cannot get enough of listening to fairytales. He knows *Rotkäppchen*, *Hänsel und Gretel* and *Hans im Glück* by heart and tells them with fantastic embellishments and extras. Per Roth [a male nurse] from Stavanger [in Norway] tells him from the rich body of Andersen's nordic fairytales which make him whoop with pure joy. Hirsch Litmanowitch is only a little older. Very quiet and very serious. He is stricken with grief. The older ones are more 'cynical.' They are not excited, they are not indifferent. The horrors of the Auschwitz camp have shaped them. They are strictly orthodox.[88]

Some time in September 1943, after having married and been on honeymoon in August, Dohmen visited the Sachsenhausen camp for the first time. He introduced himself to the group and explained that he would carry out a series of medical experiments on them. Saul Hornfeld, one of the experimental subjects, recalled that Dohmen took off his gun and placed it in the hands of Hirsch Litmanowitsch to show that they could trust him: 'He told us that he would try to do nothing which could cause serious damage to our health.'[89] Maximilian Rosmarin recalled that Dohmen told them that he wanted to test a vaccine against hepatitis which had been produced in a laboratory. In order to see whether the drug worked, they would first have to be infected with hepatitis. According to Rosmarin, Dohmen described the experiment as a 'safe and harmless thing'. 'The children did not understand this very well and the mood in the group was certainly not depressed,' he recalled.[90] Some of the boys then asked Dohmen what had happened to their parents whom they had last seen in Auschwitz. Evading the obvious answer, Dohmen told them that their parents had perhaps been transferred to a work camp.[91] In October 1943, Dohmen returned to Sachsenhausen to start his experiments. Each of the eleven children was given an injection in the upper part of their left arm. Some of the children received one injection, others two or three. It is not known whether the subjects suffered any ill effects at this point.[92]

Suddenly the experiments stopped, without notice or explanation. In November 1943, Allied bombers had destroyed much of the Robert-Koch Institute, including parts of Dohmen's research material. This made work in Berlin almost impossible. Dohmen moved to the University of Gießen from where he wanted to pursue his research. At the end of 1943, Dohmen felt he needed to justify himself to Gutzeit after the latter had complained that his work was lacking the necessary impetus. He also tried to explain why he had not yet conducted the experiments on the eleven children.[93] Evidence seems to suggest that Dohmen may have wanted to postpone the experiments at this point. Apart from the external conditions, which made work difficult, Dohmen seems to have been concerned that his experiments contravened established medical ethics standards. Given that he had originally proposed the experiments, he knew that he was ultimately responsible for them, unless he was instructed or ordered to carry them out. This also applied to other work he was asked to do. In February 1944, he told officials at the Military Medical Academy that he could not carry out a liver puncture: 'If I carry out the [liver] puncture, I would have to accept responsibility as a doctor. This would obviously be different, if I had to interpret the "expectation" as an official order.'[94] Dohmen, so it seems, was hoping to shift the responsibility for the experiments to his superiors and the government.[95]

Six months later, at the beginning of June 1944, Gutzeit's research group became the centre of attention during a conference at the Bacteriological Institute in Breslau. Handloser, as Chief of Army Medical Services, had organized the conference to coordinate jaundice research. The conference was chaired by Walter Schreiber, commander of the Military Medical Academy and head of the Department for Science and Health Leadership (*Abteilung Wissenschaft und Gesundheitsführung*) in the Army Medical Inspectorate. Schreiber was also responsible for epidemic research in the Reich Research Council, and thus able to fund research projects that were considered to be of vital importance.[96] Handloser, Gutzeit and Dohmen attended the meeting.[97] From the German air force, the consulting hygienist of the Luftwaffe, Eugen Haagen, who was conducting camp experiments on prisoners in Natzweiler and Schirmeck, had come to Breslau, as had the pathologist Franz Büchner, the specialist in internal diseases Heinz Kalk, and the surgeon Ludwig Zukschwerdt. Johannes Stein, also a specialist in internal diseases, from Strasbourg, SS-Sturmbannführer and a member of Himmler's Security Service, also attended.[98] Others, like the malariologist Gerhard Rose, were annoyed that they had not been invited.[99] In his opening address, Handloser explained that the central aim of the conference was to provide German hepatitis researchers with an opportunity to exchange ideas, and allow them to compare their cultures.[100] Most of those present later claimed that experiments on humans were not discussed during the meeting, except for Haagen, whose testimony was ambiguous.[101] Given that a few weeks after the conference, human experiments were widely discussed by Gutzeit, and planned by Haagen and three air force officials in 'Strasbourg or its vicinity' – a reference to the Natzweiler concentration camp – it is highly unlikely that the issue of human experiments would not have been raised in one form or another during the conference.[102]

Brandt's presence in Breslau, and possibly on the fringes of the conference as well, not only sanctioned the work of the scientists, but raised expectations for measurable progress. Apart from enquiring into the latest hepatitis research, Brandt, Conti and Rostock had come to Breslau to assess how far German penicillin research had developed. Hans Killian, professor of surgery at the university clinic in Breslau, recalled that Brandt and leading medical officials had visited his laboratory in June 1944 in order to inspect their primitive penicillin production in the cellar of his surgical clinic.[103] During the conference, plans were drawn up to establish a collaborative framework between Gutzeit's group and Haagen in Strasbourg. Dohmen, in particular, was instructed to work for Haagen.[104] Responding to the sense of urgency, Gutzeit was now pressuring Dohmen to conclude his experimental research on humans. On 21 August, he visited Dohmen in Gießen to assess how much progress had been made. Two days later, he wrote to a colleague:

> In Gießen, I have once again tried – I don't know how many times – to wake Dohmen up from his lethargy in animal experiments, so that we finally get to a conclusion. It is ironic how difficult the step from the animal to the human being is, but in the end this last [step] is the most important.[105]

By the end of 1944, the professional pressure on Dohmen to carry out the Sachsenhausen experiments had increased significantly. At the same time, the government now accepted responsibility for ongoing hepatitis research, and advocated research on human subjects. On 24 August 1944, one day before his official appointment to Reich Commissioner for Health and Sanitation, Brandt held a staff conference about the future of Germany's medical research.[106] It was decided that essential manpower and supply would only be made available to 'decisive and war important research areas'. Brandt and Rostock defined and selected these areas of research.[107] The minutes of the meeting reveal that hepatitis was identified as an important research area. As a corollary, military officials were advised to ensure the inclusion of human subjects: 'As a final element in the investigative protocol, the experiment on human subjects is needed with the alleged hepatitis virus.'[108]

The professional pressure and government sanctioning had the desired effect on Dohmen. In September 1944, he arrived at Sachsenhausen to carry out his hepatitis experiments.[109] All eleven children were placed in strict isolation. Throughout the autumn, Dohmen visited them six times. Hornfeld recalled that the experiments were significantly 'more intensive than in the previous year', and that Dohmen monitored and controlled all the examinations, injections and blood tests. In October, he wore a medal of honour (*Kriegsverdienstkreuz 1 Klasse*) which he had been awarded in recognition of his research. Despite developing a high fever, the children believed that Dohmen, who always appeared 'polite and correct but somehow more nervous', would do them no harm. For the entire period, the children were locked up in their barracks. According to Dohmen, the children were infected with hepatitis cultures, probably with hepatitis epidemica. On two of the children, Saul Hornfeld and Simon Rotschild, he performed painful liver punctures in order to establish whether they had been infected by hepatitis.[110] The children do not seem to have suffered any kind of mid- or long-term organic effects as a direct result of the experiments. Three of them later complained of gastrointestinal trouble which they linked to the experiments, although this is difficult to confirm, as hepatitis epidemica infections generally do not leave any long-term organic damage.[111]

This does not change the fact that the experiments were highly unethical. The experiments were conducted without any form of consent. None of the children, their parents or their legal guardians, consented to the tests. The children had been forced to Sachsenhausen after being separated from their parents. At no point during the experiments were they in a position to terminate or withdraw from the experiment. It was the uncertainty of not knowing what had been done to them which probably caused severe and long-term post-traumatic – to use the current term – psychological damage. In short, the experiments constituted a gross violation of civil liberties and medical ethics.

In Nuremberg, Brandt noted that he had not received a report about Dohmen's experiments in 1944, suggesting that he had not been informed whether they had been carried out. Brandt must have known, however, that he had provided the experiments with the necessary government sanction and encouraged them through the power of his position. Given that the experiments had been performed during his term of office as Reich Commissioner, it is not surprising that the US prosecution saw Brandt as ultimately responsible, and as someone who would have had the power to stop them. The evidence suggests, however, that not only did he not stop Dohmen's experiments, but he sanctioned and supported them. The more power Brandt was able to amass, the more he became involved in experiments on concentration camp inmates.

V. PHOSPHOROUS BURN EXPERIMENTS

Following the second Führer decree, Brandt wanted to take control of Germany's medical research and scientific industry. This also meant that he had to assume authority over areas of scientific inquiry which had previously been part of Conti's portfolio. In 1945, Brandt recalled: 'It was my aim to take away from Conti everything belonging to science and bring it to Rostock.'[112] Although Brandt also wanted to manage the powerful and internationally recognized Kaiser-Wilhelm Institutes (KWIs) and the Military Medical Academies, he never seems to have gained full control of these organizations.[113] His quest for power reached deep into the SS empire with its concentration camps and ready access to potential research facilities and human subjects.

By 1943, the strategic bombing raids by the Western Allies had not only left tens of thousands of German citizens severely traumatized, injured and homeless but hundreds, if not thousands, of men, women and children suffering from various degrees of phosphorous burns. For the German population, Allied air raids with phosphorus ammunition meant the beginning of 'air chemical warfare'.[114] Although evidence suggests that minor injuries, particularly to the eyes, as well as various kinds of cuts and bruises from falling debris, far outnumbered major injuries from explosives and phosphorous burns, research to find an effective treatment for the burns nonetheless became a scientific and military priority.[115] Brandt recalled that, 'from 1943 onwards, the problem of fire bombs' was all-consuming. Every week the medical literature discussed the latest therapeutic approach. 'During this time, we all dealt with this question of phosphorous burns from a practical and theoretical perspective,' he later remarked.[116] Brandt spoke from his experience of the Hamburg firestorm in July 1943. To alleviate the enormous suffering of the German population, it had become essential to develop new therapeutic drugs and methods of treatment for phosphorous burns and other burn injuries. Days later, on 1 August, Speer allegedly told Hitler that the war would effectively be lost if the Allies launched another six such attacks on Germany.[117] One day later, Bormann told his wife that he had seen 'an enormous number of really horrifying photographs from Hamburg' which made him concerned for the safety of their house if it were hit by 'one of those cursed phosphorous-and-rubber things'.[118] Two weeks later, he told her in confidence that the Western Allies might drop 'gas bombs' on the Obersalzberg complex, and that the regional population would be issued with gas masks as a result.[119] The seriousness of the situation might have convinced Brandt to leave any remaining moral and ethical considerations behind, and collaborate with the SS in this field of research.

Shortly after the signing of the second Führer decree in September 1943, Brandt enquired of the SS whether it was possible to test a new ointment for the treatment of phosphorous burns. According to Brandt, he had received the ointment from a company in Bonn. In order to test its efficacy, he sent it to various anti-aircraft agencies that were responsible for the protection of German civilians. This also included Grawitz's office of the Reich Physician of the SS and Police. On 30 September, Grawitz wrote to Himmler:

> SS-Brigadeführer Prof. Dr. Brandt has approached us with the request to test a new ointment for the treatment of phosphorous burns which is still at the experimental stage. As I consider that the testing of this ointment on German civilians for burns received in terror raids would take too much time, and would be unreliable from a methodological point of view, and as, in view of the importance of the problem, I do not believe that experiments on animals would produce sufficiently conclusive evidence, I respectfully ask you, Reichsführer, to grant permission in principle for experiments to be made in the hospital of the Sachsenhausen concentration camp on individual prisoners and prisoners who are unfit for work on account of illness.[120]

A week later, on 7 October 1943, Himmler informed Grawitz through his personal secretary that he agreed to 'experiments being made with the ointment for phosphorous burns at the Sachsenhausen concentration camp on individual prisoners who have become unfit for work through illness'.[121] During the Nuremberg Doctors' Trial, Brandt vehemently denied that it had been his intention to test the ointment on camp inmates. On the contrary, and according to Brandt, it was Grawitz who had misinterpreted his initial request and, on his own initiative, had proposed experiments on concentration camp prisoners to Himmler:

> I certainly did not give this ointment to Grawitz in order to instruct him to test it on some concentration camp inmates. I gave it to him, as well as to other agencies, for it to be tested in practice. This suggestion did not seem to be right for Grawitz so *on his own initiative* he translated the questions I had asked him and turned them into the need for an experiment, because he thought 'it would take too long to test the ointment on civilians in air raids etc.' I say expressly and unambiguously that I gave it to him to be tested in his anti-aircraft medical stations [*Luftschutzsanitätsdienststellen*].[122]

Brandt's interpretation of Grawitz's letter has a certain ring of truth. A careful reading of the letter suggests that the central initiative for the experiments came from Grawitz. He used Brandt's request for the testing of a new ointment as a prelude to asking Himmler for his general permission to conduct concentration camp experiments in this field. To complicate matters further, Brandt probably did not approach Grawitz directly, or speak to him on the phone, but communicated his request through Wolff at Führer headquarters. As Brandt later recalled: 'If any such matters ever arose, I addressed Wolff, as [I did] in the first letter in '43, and here apparently an appeal went to Himmler through the same channels.'[123] As Grawitz pointed out, Brandt had not approached him personally, but had approached 'us', meaning the SS. Wolff, in turn, approached Grawitz, who, in turn, approached Himmler, and passed on Brandt's request with his own interpretation and view of the matter. The possibilities for misunderstandings and misinterpretations were endless. In the Nazi regime, officials like Grawitz enjoyed enormous leverage in interpreting and executing official requests according to their own ideas. More often than not, these ideas were more radical, uncompromising and ruthless than the sender of the request might have intended. As Kershaw has pointed out, 'distortions of the truth were built into the communication system of the Third Reich at every level – most of all in the top echelons of the regime'.[124] Essential government policy was being initiated, sanctioned and shaped from below, on Grawitz's own initiative, and without waiting for official instructions from above. Other leading Nazi officials, including Brandt, acted in the same way, and he rightly pointed out that Grawitz was doing it. Grawitz was not only attempting to secure and expand his power base within the SS hierarchy, but working towards Himmler and the idea of National Socialism.

Little more than a month after Himmler had sanctioned Grawitz's proposal, incendiary bomb experiments started at the Buchenwald concentration camp. The site for the experiments which Grawitz had suggested was changed from Sachsenhausen to Buchenwald.[125] For six days, from 19 November to 25 November 1943, five prisoners from Germany and the Netherlands were burned with phosphorous material from a British incendiary bomb.[126] According to one of the witnesses, Martinus Johannes Joseph de Wit from Weert in the Netherlands, the experiments were carried out by the SS doctor Erwin Ding-Schuler in block 50. A certain amount of phosphorous material was smeared on the arms of the inmates and then ignited. Witnesses recalled that the research subjects suffered excruciating pain, and some apparently died.[127] 'One of the worst [experiments] was that with phosphorus,' Johannes Franciscus Hees from Amsterdam remembered:

> The phosphorous [material from] bombs dropped by the British was collected and this was applied to the prisoners' bodies. These experiments invariably resulted in death, for if the patient was still alive, the burns were such that he had to be finished off, and that is what always happened.[128]

According to Ding-Schuler's diary, the experiments were carried out in order to test the drug 'R 17' for fresh phosphorous burns and the two ointments, 'Echinacin

Ointment' and 'Echinacin Extern', as a follow-up treatment in cases of phosphorous burns.[129] The drug 'R 17' and the two ointments came from the Madaus company in Radebeul near Dresden. In mid-November 1943, after a trip to the German Healthcare Institute in Riga, Ding-Schuler had met with representatives of the Madaus company to receive the test material, and discuss the forthcoming experiments. On 5 January 1944, he sent his test protocols to Grawitz, with the request to pass them to the Madaus company.[130]

There is a discrepancy between Brandt's recollection that the ointment came from 'a company in Bonn', and the fact that the ointments that were tested in Buchenwald came from the Madaus company in Dresden. As it turns out, the well-known pharmaceutical company was founded in 1919 by the Madaus brothers in Bonn. Brandt probably recalled the place where the company was founded and from where it made its name. He probably did not know the place where the test material came from, but he seems to have known the location where the experiments were carried out. In 1947, he stated that Buchenwald was a suitable place for the tests, because some of the prisoners had suffered from phosphorous burns after Allied air attacks. After the war, Ding-Schuler's assistant, Arthur Dietzsch, also recalled that Ding-Schuler had told him that Brandt had visited the camp.[131] Although Dietzsch's credibility needs to be called into question, because he is known to have maltreated and beaten prisoners, and probably wanted to blame someone else, his testimony may well have been true. It is not known, however, if Brandt visited Buchenwald, whether he visited it in connection with the phosphorous burn experiments, or for some other reason. During the Doctors' Trial, Brandt denied ever having been in Buchenwald.[132]

The evidence suggests that in 1943, shortly after his promotion, Brandt prompted, and set in motion, perhaps unintentionally, a series of human experiments on concentration camp inmates without their consent. Anyone with the slightest idea about the SS and its system of concentration camps must have known that any official request for the testing of drugs and other agents by a leading member of the regime could easily result in experiments on camp inmates. Although Brandt later claimed that he did not believe that 'such experiments should be carried out in a concentration camp', there is no evidence to suggest that he ever inquired about the progress or outcome of the experiments.[133] He also did not check whether the tests were carried out in anti-aircraft medical stations, as he claimed to have proposed to Grawitz. Brandt saw himself as a key coordinating link between various civilian and military government agencies. At the same time, he failed to monitor, inspect, and take responsibility for the experimental programmes which he set in train.

VI. BIOLOGICAL WARFARE RESEARCH

After the war, Brandt claimed that he had no knowledge of biological warfare research, code-named 'lightning conductor' (*Blitzableiter*), and that he was not involved in discussions about conducting human experiments with biological warfare agents. The evidence surrounding Brandt's share of responsibility in biological warfare activities is largely circumstantial and needs to be treated with a certain degree of caution. Brandt certainly discussed the issue of biological and chemical warfare with Hitler a number of times, but Hitler was of the opinion that the Germans 'would not be the first' who would start this kind of warfare.[134] Hitler had suffered from mustard gas exposure in the First World War, and believed that the use of chemical agents was of little strategic use in modern warfare. On several occasions, he also prohibited the development of offensive biological weapons, and opposed their use.[135] A number of biological scientists and military experts were nonetheless convinced that biological warfare research was important to ensure Germany's defensive capability. The bacteriologist Heinrich Kliewe, director of the Department for Biological Warfare in the Military Medical Academy and head of the section for special investigations in the Army Gas Protection Department, had received dozens of secret intelligence reports, some more trustworthy than others, which suggested that the Allies were preparing for extensive biological warfare.[136] The discovery of an apparent biological weapons store in a flat in Warsaw in December 1942, where the Gestapo had found typhus pathogens, and the information that the Polish resistance movement had allegedly killed more than four hundred people in the space of four months by posting seventy-seven typhus-infected parcels, further fuelled the belief that an Allied attack with biological agents was only a matter of time.[137] From 1943, military officials therefore argued for greater research activity in the field.

On 9 March 1943, officials in the Army High Command established a working committee to further the development of defensive measures, and improve collaboration between military and civilian scientists. The committee was code-named 'lightning conductor' (*Blitzableiter*). Chaired by Walter Hirsch, head of the Army Gas Protection Department, it consisted of about twenty members, including the malariologist Gerhard Rose and the cancer researcher Kurt Blome, who in 1942 had been asked to coordinate biological warfare research in the civilian sector.[138] At the end of April 1943, Blome was formally instructed by Göring to coordinate biological warfare work under the cover of a new committee for cancer research. Whereas Conti expressed reservations, Brandt strongly supported Blome's nomination, believing that 'the choice was particularly good'.[139]

Whether Brandt was aware that the working committee for cancer research was a cover for biological warfare work, and that Blome was a member of the *Blitzableiter* committee, is not known for certain. It may well be that he supported Blome's appointment to the cancer committee, and was not aware that it served another purpose. This is rather unlikely, however, given that Rostock, as the Chief of the Department for Medical Research and Science under the Reich Commissioner for Health and Sanitation, was informed of Blome's biological warfare work during a meeting on 18 May 1943.[140] Moreover, a week later, on 26 May, Brandt met with Kliewe himself, who informed him about the kind of chemical and biological warfare which might be launched on German soil.[141]

Another possibility is that biological and chemical warfare research may have been kept as separate fields to ensure a greater level of secrecy. During the initial discussion to establish a 'chemical working committee' that would have been responsible for investigating water poisoning, it was suggested that the members of the new committee, including Brandt, should 'not come into contact' with the *Blitzableiter* committee because the former was also looking into the offensive possibilities of water poisoning. Until the end of the war, the *Blitzableiter* committee and Blome's cancer research committee existed side by side.[142] When one of the defendants in the Doctors' Trial was asked whether he regarded Blome as the highest official with regard to biological warfare, he replied: 'For cancer research yes. For biological warfare agents one cannot say that in this way, because centralised work did not exist in this field in Germany.'[143] German biological warfare research was largely shaped by competing civilian and military agencies and personalities, and by an ineffective, often chaotic, administrative system that was unable to consolidate and concentrate the scarce resources in an extremely specialized field of research.

Blome recalled after the war that he had met with Himmler a total of five times. In each of the meetings they discussed biological warfare issues, and on some occasions experiments on camp inmates. According to Blome, he turned down the offer because a concentration camp did not provide a secure environment against infections. What Blome wanted was to establish a new institute in Posen-Nesslestedt to conduct biological warfare research. In their first meeting in July or August 1943, Himmler instructed Blome to develop an effective vaccine against plague and methods for the distribution of plague. If Blome's recollections are true, it would suggest that, contrary to Hitler's ban on the use of such weapons, Himmler was preparing for an offensive attack with biological warfare agents. Later, in September 1944, Himmler asked Blome whether it was possible to halt the Allied invasion through offensive biological warfare against humans and animals, for example through an influenza epidemic. Some military officials agreed with Himmler's approach. On 21 September 1943, Erich Schumann, head of the Department of Science in the General Army Department (*Allgemeines Wehrmachtsamt*, AWA), an expert in plant diseases, suggested that Hitler was not sufficiently informed about the potential military benefits of biological agents, and needed to be 'won over' to support offensive biological warfare against the Allies:

We cannot play the part of the indifferent spectator; we must also prepare for the mass deployment of bacteriological materials. Especially America would have to be attacked simultaneously with different human and animal epidemics as well as with plant parasites. The Führer must be won over to the plan. For this purpose officials are to submit a brief but complete paper on enemy preparations and on sabotage activity of the enemy with bacteria and poisons. Furthermore, they are to indicate which agents and methods of introduction would be feasible, and the requisite number of personnel, laboratories, instruments, airplanes, submarines, etc. that would be needed for the preparation and the attack. The Chief of the Armed Forces Medical Corps, Veterinary Inspector, Chief of the General Army Department, the Reichsführer-SS and deputy Reich Health Leader should then jointly present these documents first to the Reichsmarschall, and then to the Führer.[144]

Schumann's proposal coincided with Allied preparations for a similar kind of warfare. While German military officials were discussing plans to persuade Hitler to employ biological warfare agents, American and Russian scientists were meeting in Cairo to discuss the level of preparedness for offensive and defensive bacteriological warfare.[145] Three days later, on 24 September, the *Blitzableiter* committee, for the first time, it would seem, discussed the issue of human experiments with biological warfare agents. Kliewe noted: 'Since it is not known under what conditions inhaled aerosols or dispersed droplets of certain pathogenic germs cause disease in man, Prof. Blome suggested experiments on human beings.'[146] In the subsequent discussion, officials from the Military Medical Academy objected to the idea that experiments on man would be conducted in their laboratories. A decision about the matter was postponed.

Brandt, it seems, was not party to the discussions of the *Blitzableiter* committee, but was kept well informed about Allied biological and chemical warfare activities. In November 1943, the head of the Army Medical Service submitted a full report to Brandt about known acts of sabotage with bacteria and poisons. The report had been drafted as a result of Schumann's proposal.[147] The relevant army departments and Himmler's SS also received copies of the report. By late 1943, Brandt also supported the establishment of a research institute for the production of vaccines against plague and other potential biological weapons.[148] On 22 November 1943, Walter Schreiber, commander of the Military Medical Academy and plenipotentiary for epidemiology in the Reich Research Council, told Brandt that it was planned to establish a top-secret institute for microbiology in the *Sachsenburg*, a medieval castle near Chemnitz.[149] The aim of the institute, Brandt was told, was to 'research and combat particularly dangerous [*gemeingefährliche*] diseases'.[150] Central areas of work included the 'production of plague vaccines; animal experiments to diagnose plague and test the efficacy of vaccines; other research with plague and plague-like material'.[151] In short, the institute was designed to conduct research with some of the most potent biological agents known to man. The main problem in the establishment of the institute was that it needed extensive refurbishment. To expedite matters, Brandt wrote to the relevant building department in the Armaments Ministry in December 1943, asking for special permission to renovate the derelict castle.[152] Although planning permission was granted within weeks, work on the castle and the institute progressed slowly. The building project was not given military priority, because raw materials and personnel were needed elsewhere in the Reich.

A couple of weeks later, in February 1944, Kliewe met Blome to enquire about the level of progress which had been made since the *Blitzableiter* committee had convened in September the previous year. Blome told Kliewe that experiments had successfully been conducted with potato beetles which had been dropped, and had remained alive, from aeroplanes from a height of 8,000 metres. Other experiments with 'plant parasites' were planned. He also told Kliewe that he had not yet conducted experiments on humans. 'These, however, are necessary, and he plans to do them,' Kliewe later recorded.[153] Blome's immediate task was the establishment of a new research institute in Posen-Nesselstedt:

A new institute under his control is being built near Posen, in which biological weapons are to be studied and tested. Field Marshal Keitel has given permission to build; Reichsführer-SS and Generalarzt Prof. Brandt have assured him of vast support. By request of Field Marshal Keitel, the armed forces are not to have a responsible share in the experiments, since experiments will also be conducted on human beings.[154]

After the war, the US prosecution alleged that the 'vast support' which Brandt had promised included the support for experiments on concentration camp prisoners. Brandt denied this charge. He told the court that Blome had telephoned him to tell him about the plan to establish a new institute. According to Brandt, his support related to 'construction' problems, and not to the issue of biological warfare: 'A question of biological warfare and possibly any further resulting human experiments were certainly not discussed by telephone.'[155] Like his previous intervention to support the renovation of the *Sachsenburg*, Brandt sent a letter to the construction office and 'asked that Mr Blome might be helped to establish his institution'.[156] Brandt's narrative seems plausible. It is likely that Blome contacted Brandt to speed up the foundation of his institute in Posen-Nesselstedt, and that, at a later stage, he wanted to get permission from him to carry out biological warfare experiments on humans. In February 1944, Kliewe noted:

> Prof. Blome is of the opinion … that biological weapons … can become a very serious hazard to us. Therefore this field must be examined more extensively and intensively than before. Especially necessary is an examination of our vaccine, the pestilential virus [plague] vaccine in particular. Experiments must accordingly be made on human beings. Furthermore, certain misconceptions concerning the effect of maximum doses of several poisons can be corrected only by experiments on human beings. As soon as Prof. Blome has conferred with the Reichsmarshal and Generalarzt Prof. Brandt, he will notify me.[157]

Blome, it seems, had not yet asked Brandt for permission, but was planning to conduct experiments on human subjects. Whether Brandt was ever asked by Blome to give his consent to such experiments, or whether he ever authorized them, is not known. It appears that leading officials from the army, including experts from the Military Medical Academy, were concerned about Blome's proposal. Keitel, in particular, did not want to be associated with experiments on humans.[158] The US prosecution alleged that the conversation between Blome and Kliewe showed that Keitel, and therefore Brandt as well, must have had 'some knowledge of previous experimentation on concentration camp inmates and that he knew that these biological warfare experiments were something of the same sort'.[159] The existing evidence does not support this conclusion. We also do not know whether Blome actually carried out biological warfare experiments on humans, though there is some evidence that he attempted, but failed, to destroy 'the arrangements for human experiments' in his institute by the end of the war.[160] Blome was undoubtedly the main driving force behind the proposal to conduct human experiments with biological warfare agents, and he was willing to carry them out. According to the

International Military Tribunal, experiments with bacteriological agents were carried out on Soviet prisoners of war. However, the extent of Blome's responsibility in the experiments remains ambiguous. Blome was acquitted in the Nazi Doctors' Trial because of lack of evidence. The overall extent of Brandt's knowledge of the biological warfare research and experimentation also remains unclear. He seems to have shrouded his involvement in mystery.[161] What appears certain, however, is that by 1944 Brandt was increasingly drawn into, and took part in, the world of chemical warfare research and experimentation.

VII. CHEMICAL WARFARE EXPERIMENTS

Brandt's active involvement in chemical warfare experiments started at the time when his Department for Medical Research and Science, headed by Paul Rostock, became fully operational in the spring of 1944.[162] Rostock, who had followed Brandt's meteoric rise to power since the late 1920s, wholeheartedly supported the newly appointed General Commissioner and advised him on hospital planning and the Aktion Brandt.[163] By the end of 1943, probably by September or October, Rostock had set up office at the surgical clinic in Berlin with a team of assistants and secretaries. He was unaccustomed to large-scale bureaucratic operations, so work at first progressed slowly. A major improvement was the 'research index' (*Forschungskartei*), which comprehensively detailed almost all scientific research projects in Germany, except those conducted under the auspices of the SS. By February 1944, Brandt's office moved for security reasons from Berlin to barracks in Beelitz.[164] These were located in the 'special hospital' (*Krankenhaus-Sonderanlage*) which Brandt shared with some of the offices of Speer's powerful ministry. Housing some sensitive and top-secret plans, the place was extremely well camouflaged by means of wire-netting, spread over artificial trees, which extended over the entire building complex. The roads leading to the barracks were painted with a special brown colour in order to mimic cart tracks. As a result, the complex was never bombed, although Allied bombers used to fly at zero-height over it.[165] Brandt must have had a special relationship with the place, given that he seems to have written a poem about it.[166]

Rostock used the extensive amount of discretion and power which Brandt had given him to overcome certain structural problems within German medical science. In March 1944, the department was fully operational. Issues relating to chemical warfare were apparently dealt with by Brandt himself: 'These things belonged to questions of warfare agent protection, and were dealt with by Mr Brandt himself,' Rostock recalled at Nuremberg, when asked why he apparently had no knowledge that human experiments had been conducted in this field. Rostock's statement seems hardly plausible, given that he was Brandt's right-hand man in all questions relating to medical science and research.[167] Brandt also discussed issues of chemical warfare with Speer. Like Hitler, they both thought that Germany should not start this kind of warfare, especially after Germany had lost air supremacy over its territory:

Speer was of the opinion that chemical warfare, which the German side would begin, had to be prevented. We were well aware that if any agency of the German military were to try to use chemical warfare agents or order their use, the practical use had to be prevented. There were certainly discussions with Speer on this specific question in the autumn of 1944, and also in the spring [of 1945].[168]

It is not known whether Brandt and Speer also talked about human experiments with chemical warfare agents. However, while the Third Reich was engulfed in a Teutonic struggle for survival, it had become an 'approved military medical practice' among the Nazi medical elite to use concentration camp inmates for the testing of certain drugs, poisons and biochemical agents.[169] Human experiments with chemical warfare agents, especially with Lost, a poison gas commonly known as mustard gas, were primarily conducted at the concentration camps of Sachsenhausen and Natzweiler.[170] In 1947 the US prosecution pointed out: 'Wounds were deliberately inflicted on the victims, and the wounds were then infected with mustard gas. Other subjects were forced to inhale gas, or to take it internally in liquid form, and still others were injected with the gas.'[171] Rudolf Brandt recalled that the experimental subjects were generally non-German nationals, often Poles, Russians, Jews or Gypsies.[172] Officials such as Brandt, Grawitz, Sievers and others believed that it was the most expeditious and efficient way of obtaining reliable data for a whole plethora of medical problems. They believed that by solving these problems they could alter the course of the war. Given that tens of thousands of German soldiers were dying on the battlefields, the rights and dignity of individual human subjects ceased to exist. In Brandt's world view, the testing of substances on prisoners of war was a necessary evil to protect German citizens, especially as rumours were circulating that the Allies were stockpiling chemical warfare agents in preparation for a large-scale gas attack on Germany. Whether it concerned nutrition or hepatitis experiments or the testing of ointments for the treatment of phosphorous burns, Brandt knew whom to approach in order to test new drugs or biochemical agents on camp inmates. His post-war claim that he was ignorant of the large-scale exploitation of camp inmates for experimental purposes runs contrary to the evidence. On 4 February 1944, Rudolf Brandt, Himmler's personal secretary, sent a secret teletype to SS-Obersturmbannführer Paul Baumert, a member of Himmler's personal staff:

> SS-Brigadeführer Prof. Dr. Brandt called and requested the approval of the Reichsführer-SS that ten prisoners from Oranienburg should be made available as of tomorrow for two days, to test a certain drug. Nothing would happen to them. The tests have already been discussed and must be started tomorrow morning, 5 February. SS-Gruppenführer Dr Grawitz is only waiting for permission from the Reichsführer-SS. Please obtain the decision and pass it on immediately to Dr Grawitz. Signed: Yours Rudi.[173]

For Brandt, the pattern of obtaining camp inmates for experimental purposes was by now well established. Either directly, or through Himmler's liaison man Wolff, Brandt had discussed and arranged the experiments with Grawitz, who consented to them. The only thing Grawitz needed was the 'permission from the Reichsführer-SS'. In this case, Brandt must have been under time-pressure to test the drug, and wanted to speed things up. He telephoned Rudolf Brandt, probably on 4 February, who in turn sent a secret cable directly to a trusted colleague ('Yours Rudi') on Himmler's personal staff. Baumert was able to obtain Himmler's permission. On 8 February, SS-Sturmbannführer Werner Grothmann, Himmler's adjutant, sent a top-secret teletype from Himmler's field command post to SS-Gruppenführer and Generalleutnant of the Waffen-SS, Richard Glücks, who was in overall charge of the concentration camps:

> Hereby confirm approval of Reichsführer-SS, for ten prisoners from Oranienburg to be placed at the disposal of SS-Brigadeführer Professor Dr. Brandt (SS-Gruppenführer Professor Dr. Grawitz).[174]

Himmler granted his permission to use camp inmates for human experiments to both Brandt *and* Grawitz. As far as experiments on humans in concentration camps were concerned, the boundaries between the General Commissioner for Health and Sanitation and the Reich Physician of the SS and Police had become blurred. It was no longer clear who initiated the experiments or requested a certain number of inmates for particular tests. From Himmler's perspective, both men were responsible for the tests. That is why he granted the permission to both of them.

Earlier, at the end of 1943, Brandt learned that Otto Bickenbach, medical professor at the University of Strasbourg, was carrying out chemical warfare experiments in collaboration with August Hirt and the SS Research Foundation, Ancestral Heritage – *Ahnenerbe* for short. It was the start of Brandt's involvement in chemical warfare experiments on humans. Bickenbach was ambitious, competitive and strongly anti-Semitic, and his managerial style was known to be that of a 'cleansing commissar' who had helped to expel Jews from the University of Munich.[175] Allied investigators called him an 'extremely suspect character', who had apparently worked for the Security Service.[176] From the summer of 1942, the SS-Ahnenerbe provided Hirt and Bickenbach with financial and logistical support to conduct phosgene experiments on animals and humans at the Natzweiler concentration camp.[177] In early 1943, Hirt reported that their experiments with mustard gas had finally produced the desired results: 'Our L[ost]-Experiments at Natzweiler are now at last making good progress. After three fatalities, the applied therapy is producing a good healing process.'[178] The fact that three people had died as a result of the experiments did not concern Hirt and his co-workers. Encouraged by these reports, the SS-Ahnenerbe planned a large-scale experiment on 240 prisoners, but advised Hirt to keep his research data confidential for fear that the Waffen-SS might otherwise claim credit for the experiments. As the work progressed, Hirt's co-worker Bickenbach became likewise concerned that Hirt might claim all the credit for the research, and sought support from Brandt. Rostock later recalled that he was present when Brandt promised Bickenbach aid.[179]

Brandt's involvement in Bickenbach's experiments resulted from internal infighting and distrust among SS scientists. Brandt first helped Bickenbach to obtain the necessary animals and establish a new laboratory in the vicinity of Strasbourg. At the beginning of 1944, Bickenbach sought to establish closer relations with Brandt. Like Dohmen, Bickenbach approached Brandt on his own initiative in order to obtain the necessary approval for his experiments. On 2 February, after a meeting with Bickenbach in Karlruhe, Sievers recorded in his diary: 'Met Prof. Bickenbach in Karlsruhe, and he advises that he has put his research work under the control of General Commissioner Prof. Dr. Brandt.'[180] Sievers also learned that Brandt had visited Natzweiler together with Bickenbach, and that this had undermined Hirt's research:

> Prof. Dr. Bickenbach, without instructions from Hirt or Prof. Stein, contacted General Commissioner Prof. Dr. Brandt concerning the phosgene experiments and was in Natzweiler with him. Commission is to be withdrawn, for our part Natzweiler is to be closed.[181]

Bickenbach's research ambitions were the primary motive for transferring the supervision of the experiments from the SS to Brandt. Brandt may also have realized that Bickenbach's research would allow him to control yet another key area of military medical research.

In the meantime, Brandt received a request from the German Red Cross for the provision of gas masks that were needed for the rising demands in anti-aircraft protection, fire fighting and rescue work.[182] After discussing the matter in February 1944 with SS-Brigadeführer Walter Schieber from the Armaments Supply Office, himself involved in human experiments at Mauthausen concentration camp, Brandt realized that Germany's defensive capability against a potential chemical warfare attack was in a 'disastrous' state of readiness.[183] Walter Mielenz, a chemist from the Reich Air Ministry, described the situation as 'totally inadequate'.[184] The civilian population, including women and children, were left without any form of protective equipment against Allied gas attacks. Depending on the region, between 10 and 70 per cent of the civilian population could be supplied with gas masks. On average, the figure was about 32 per cent, for children only about 7 per cent.[185] At the same time, rumours were circulating that the Western Allies were planning a massive gas attack. Germany's intelligence agencies had also received reports that the Allies had stored large quantities of 'poison gas ammunition' at Tunis and Dakar, ready to be used against the Axis powers.[186] Brandt later recalled that on his way back from the conference to Führer headquarters, he met with Göring and informed him about the situation. Realizing that the war would be all but over after a massive gas attack on Germany, Göring immediately informed Hitler. Twenty-four hours later, Brandt conferred with Hitler and Göring. According to Brandt, he was asked whether his office for planning and economics would take over responsibility for the production of gas masks. Brandt suggested the creation of a parallel office, which not only gave him control over gas masks, but which put him in charge of gas and gas production itself.[187]

On 1 March 1944, Hitler expanded Brandt's already extensive powers by putting him in charge of chemical warfare.[188] There is conflicting evidence, however, whether Brandt's power extended to the whole of the chemical warfare field or whether his power was limited, at least at the beginning, to the defensive side of operations. On 8 March, Brandt sent the top-secret Führer order to Himmler, asking him to circulate copies of it only among the leading personalities in his sphere of influence.[189] Alike Krohne, Brandt's secretary, recalled that she had dispatched the order and had corresponded with Schieber from the Armaments Supply Office about it.[190] No copy of the order seems to have survived. However, Mielenz remembered the wording of the order as follows:

> I have ordered my Commissioner General for the Medical and Health Services (Prof. Dr. Brandt) to take a major part in all matters concerning protection against chemical warfare (of the army and the civilian population) and to issue orders to the stations (military and civilian) established for this purpose. In questions of the protection of the civilian population against chemical warfare, he must obtain in advance the approval of the Reich Air Minister and Commander-in-Chief of the Luftwaffe.[191]

Copies of the order were forwarded to Grawitz and Sievers, who had previously worked on chemical warfare matters, and to Oswald Pohl, head of the SS Finance and Administration Head Office, and to Hans Jüttner, chief of the SS Operational Head Office.[192] Brandt asked Himmler to 'induce those men on their part to get in touch with' him so that he could 'settle the matter with the greatest expediency'.[193] Brandt did not want to write to the officials himself, and explain his new role and responsibility, because he was concerned about getting into 'contact with subordinate agencies who might think they had something to do with it, but who actually did not'.[194] The statement shows that Brandt consciously kept his professional distance from subordinate agencies and officials. By strictly compartmentalizing his areas of responsibility, Brandt granted access to information, and to himself, only to those officials whose professional responsibility or assignment was directly relevant for a particular field of activity. Brandt later stated that his jurisdiction 'extended to pharmaceutical products to treat gas wounds' which included research into the most effective methods of medical treatment.[195] According to Rudolf Brandt, however, Brandt was charged with encouraging 'medical research in connection with gas attacks'.[196]

As Hitler's Special Plenipotentiary for Chemical Warfare, Brandt first wanted to talk to the leading chemical warfare scientists and technical experts, explain his role and responsibility, and become acquainted with the field. Either Otto Ambros, director of the IG Farben company and head of Committee C (*Sonderausschuss 'C'*) for poison gas in Speer's Armaments Ministry, or Karl Quasebarth, in charge of gas mask production in the same ministry, advised Brandt to get in touch with Walter Hirsch, head of the Gas Protection Department (Wa Prüf 9). The department had been established as a cover to conduct research into various poison gases. From March 1943, Hirsch was also chairman of the *Blitzableiter* committee to develop defensive measures against biological warfare.[197] He was also an expert on mustard gas, and liaised on a monthly basis with Colonel Otiai, a Japanese technical attaché, on foreign chemical warfare intelligence.[198] Brandt later recalled that in the middle of March 1944 he met Hirsch, who 'readily gave him the information that other "super" gases existed naming Tabun and Sarin'.[199] A couple of days later, Brandt reported his findings to Goebbels in order to coordinate the extent to which the German public should be informed about gas warfare. On 25 March, Goebbels recorded in his diary:

> Professor Brandt visits me and reports to me about our preparations for gas warfare. These are very poor. There is a lack of gas masks, and there is also a lack of information for the population. The Führer now has ordered a large programme for the production of gas masks, according to which there shall be a monthly production of seven million gas masks from next month onwards … We would then be out of the woods in four to five months. Gas warfare has, God help us, not yet been introduced. What Professor Brandt tells me about the possibilities of gas warfare is truly horrible. But I really believe it to be possible that the modern civilised humanity resorts to this instrument to destroy itself. Anyway, it would be irresponsible if we were not to prepare ourselves for such an eventuality. It is a difficult question, whether one should now already inform the population about gas warfare. I don't think that is opportune … I therefore order that a sufficient number of gas masks should be produced first; we can then also begin with the propaganda against gas warfare.[200]

Brandt was acutely aware that Germany, at this point, would have been unable to withstand a coordinated attack with chemical agents. After the war, he remarked: 'If chemical warfare agents had been used it would have been impossible for us to have lasted even for weeks. After the first attack with chemical warfare agents the war would have been over for us.'[201] A couple of months later, Brandt learned that there existed an even deadlier nerve gas, called Soman, which was still at the laboratory stage. It also transpired that the existing respirators for civilians (Type M.44) only offered limited protection against these types of gases. They had to assume that the Allies had similar nerve agents, particularly those of the Tabun type, and were prepared to use them. The meetings with Hirsch and others had brought the scale of the crisis home to Brandt. On 1 April 1944, Germany was put on a 'state of alert' with regard to chemical warfare. As far as Brandt and the German authorities were concerned, the so called 'warfare agent case' (*Kampfstoff-Fall*), the moment at which hostilities with chemical warfare agents would commence, had already begun.

Speer recalled that soon after a meeting with Hitler on 9 April 1944, during which the issue of German chemical warfare operations was discussed, Hitler 'entrusted Brandt with the direction of the entire CW field including the offensive side'.[202] It appears that Hitler officially charged Brandt with the production of gas masks in March, and, perhaps more informally, with the whole field of chemical warfare one month later.[203] Post-war testimonies by leading chemical scientists seem to confirm Speer's recollection. Some time in April 1944, Brandt summoned Otto Ambros from the IG Farben company and his deputy, Jürgen von Klenck, to a meeting in Munich.[204] Ambros had been instrumental in developing one of the most deadly nerve agents on earth: Sarin. At the end of 1938, he had been part of a group of scientists who had synthesized the organophosphorus compound and had named it in honour of those involved in the discovery: Schrader, Ambros, Rüdiger and van der Linde.[205] The potential of these deadly new agents as weapons of mass destruction was soon realized by the German military authorities. Brandt told Ambros and von Klenck that German nurses and other health officials were without gas masks, and that Hitler had 'asked him to take charge of the production of gas masks, and later also of the active side of production of chemical warfare substances'.[206] According to von Klenck, Brandt's ideas about gas warfare were as follows:

> We know of the enemy's superiority in manufacturing facilities and in stocks of war gases and we must create a new and more efficient defence (the increased production of gas masks served this purpose). It is essential to increase the production of decontaminating agents and charcoal. At the same time the offensive side must be considered, even if it is only to prevent the initiation of gas warfare by the enemy, which he [the enemy] might be inclined to start if we stop production.[207]

Brandt agreed with Ambros and von Klenck that the production of chemical warfare agents should be concentrated on 'the most effective materials such as mustard gas, Tabun and Sarin'.[208] Whether they also discussed the future production of the 'N-agent' (N-Stoff), an incendiary agent that had properties akin to poison gas, is unclear, but likely, given that the IG Farben company and the SS were engaged in a battle about the ownership and control of the substance.[209] Brandt told the two chemists that, because of his influence with Hitler, he was in a position to procure raw materials and personnel for the production of poison gas more easily than Ambros from the IG Farben company or Schieber from the Armaments Supply Office. If von Klenck's recollections are true, it would suggest that Brandt was determined to centralize and control the production of chemical warfare agents within his own office of the General Commissioner in order to create a more efficient chemical warfare industry.

The three men apparently did not discuss the effects of chemical warfare agents on humans, at least not explicitly, but Brandt told them that he had 'witnessed one of [Wolfgang] Wirth's tests with Sarin and that the results had been very impressive'.[210] Although Brandt spoke only of 'guinea pigs', von Klenck believed that Brandt actually referred to experiments on humans. 'Judged by the manner in which the results were described [by Brandt]' he concluded 'that human beings had been the subjects, not animals'.[211] According to a British intelligence report from 1945, the testing of chemical warfare agents on human volunteers was not uncommon in Germany at the time:

> There was extensive testing of German CW [chemical warfare] on human volunteers – experiments to test skin decontamination agents, the miotic action of Tabun, possible protective suits, eye, nose and throat irritants, etc. Observers were given small financial rewards. They were mainly officers, clerks, employees, labourers and occasionally students of institutions like the Gas Protection Laboratory, Spandau. At the Army Experimental Station, Raubkammer, suits were worn with 10 × 10 centimetre windows

cut into them. Sometimes no protective clothing was worn apart from rubber shorts to protect genitals.[212]

Given that Brandt had met Hirsch and other military experts in March, and had probably been introduced to Wolfgang Wirth, the toxicologist from the Military Medical Academy, it is quite plausible that Brandt might have witnessed a demonstration of the effects of Sarin exposure on man.[213] In general, the chemical warfare field saw a greater emphasis on solving defensive problems, and an intensification of experimental work on Tabun and the Sarin group.

In the summer of 1944, Brandt travelled to Heidelberg to visit Richard Kuhn, director of the Kaiser-Wilhelm Institute for Chemistry and the president of the German Chemical Society. Kuhn and his team of scientists had synthesized the extremely toxic nerve agent Soman in spring 1944. According to Brandt, they discussed the 'treatment of Tabun and Sarin poisoning (not Soman)' because it was believed that the United States had developed a nerve gas of this type.[214] After the war, Allied investigators realized that Kuhn and his co-workers had been at the forefront of German chemical warfare research, especially with regard to the 'mechanisms of action and pharmacological properties' of nerve gases, and that their data was of great significance for British scientists working at Porton Down in Wiltshire.[215] In September 1944, the work of Kuhn and his team was cut short when the German army ordered the transfer of all documents and notebooks to Rüdesdorf, east of Berlin, and the total destruction of all laboratory facilities.[216]

Brandt's discussion with Kuhn and other experts highlighted the fact that Germany needed to accelerate the output of articles for defensive chemical warfare operations. One of the problems, however, was that those working in the industry, often forced and slave labourers, worked under appalling conditions and received inadequate medical attention. After the outbreak of war, German scientists had produced fifty tonnes of Tabun in a pilot plant in a suburb of Münster. By 1942, the production of Tabun and Sarin had started at a large production facility in Dyhernfurth, forty kilometres north of Breslau. The factory, code-named 'Hochwerk', was able to produce up to 3,000 tonnes of the nerve agent Tabun per month.[217] By June 1944, the plant had produced a total of 12,000 tonnes of Tabun.[218] The handling and production of these new substances was extremely dangerous. From early on, German scientists and the military knew that the toxic agents were 'lethal when applied to the skin'.[219] In 1945, Schrader told investigators that there had been a number of cases where plant workers had developed convulsions, but that there had only been a 'single human fatality', when a worker died within two minutes of being exposed to 300 cubic centimetres of Tabun.[220] Plant workers, and forced and slave labourers, however, reported that they had suffered multiple and severe injuries, including a number of fatalities. In general, 'the effects upon man were observed whenever it was possible to do so; the accidents in factories, laboratories, etc. offered the opportunity to study the effects as well as the proper treatment'.[221] Military officials later conceded that there had been

324 'minor accidental casualties' over a five-year period, and 'a total of 10 fatal cases' after nerve gas production had got under way at Dyhernfurth.[222] At another facility in Gendorf, which produced mustard gas, workers were similarly exposed to serious health risks.

During one of their meetings, Ambros, as the director (*Betriebsführer*) of Dyhernfurth and Gendorf, told Brandt that he was having major staff problems. The medical services, in particular, were understaffed in chemical warfare factories because personnel had been drafted into the army. In the summer of 1944, Brandt visited the two plants to investigate the problem. It is likely that Brandt's visit to Dyhernfurth coincided with his visit to Breslau to inspect the state of Germany's penicillin production, and meet up with some of the scientists attending the Breslau conference on hepatitis research. According to Ambros, Brandt wanted to 'become generally acquainted with the nature of the poison-gas itself'.[223] He told Ambros that he was taking an active interest in 'chemical warfare agents and counter-measures'.[224] Although Brandt's main concern was the organization of supplies and materials for the production of gas masks, the enormous health risks to the plant workers were all too apparent. Brandt recalled that he 'saw the plant for Tabun production [at Dyhernfurth], talked to Dr Mertens, medical officer of the factory, and saw certain workers with the characteristic small pupils of Tabun poisoning'.[225] Brandt also witnessed how plant workers who had been contaminated were thrown into a decontaminating bath of an alcoholic solution of bleaching powder as a first-aid measure.[226] If nothing else, Brandt was well informed of the risks to which workers were exposed in Germany's chemical warfare industry. His subsequent approach to Himmler's SS also demonstrates that he knew that the industry employed forced and slave labourers.

On 9 June 1944, Brandt asked Himmler whether it was possible to increase the productivity in the chemical warfare industry by improving the living conditions of forced and slave labourers. He told Himmler that 'prisoners are employed, with best results, in several *Kampfstoff* [warfare] factories, and in plants producing chemical warfare protection articles. I inspected the camps on several occasions and was, on the whole, favourably impressed by them.'[227] Brandt was concerned, however, that the security precautions, which he described as 'a double or triple, partly electrified fence', could slow down production and cause unnecessary delay. He did not explain how or why the fence 'slowed down production', but one must assume that prisoners who tried to escape from the camps got seriously injured or died as a result. Given the evidence, Brandt can hardly pretend ignorance of the conditions in some of the slave labour camps, and of the way in which prisoners were exploited by the German war industry. In responding to Brandt's letter, Pohl made it clear that the SS was not responsible for the accommodation of prisoners, but the companies that were contracting them from the SS.[228] Although Himmler did not permit any changes in the security system, Pohl was willing to look into individual cases and examine whether certain improvements could be made by talking to the relevant companies. Brandt never responded to Pohl's letter. On 16 August, Pohl told Rudolf Brandt that one could throw the correspondence with

Brandt 'into the bin! Your namesake has still not been in touch with us.'[229] Brandt, it seems, was unwilling to engage in further debate about the issue.

After the war, Brandt claimed that, as far as chemical warfare agents were concerned, he had initiated experiments only on animals. According to Schieber, Brandt had told him in the summer of 1944 that he was having problems in procuring 'animals which were needed for test purposes concerning the effect of the top chemical warfare agents and for which he had requests from testing officials'. Schieber also remembered that 'the problem was how to convert the production of chemical warfare agents on account of raw-material shortage for the production of the top chemical warfare agent Sarin, the effect of which could not yet be finally determined'.[230] As a result of Brandt's request, Schieber dispatched one of his assistants to Spain to obtain the necessary animals. It may well be true that Brandt organized the procurement of animals for testing through his connections with Speer's Armaments Ministry, and thus established certain facts which would have allowed him to 'plausibly deny' his involvement in human experiments with chemical warfare agents. Evidence to the contrary, however, does exist. During cross-examination in 1947, Brandt conceded that 'the effectiveness of these new gases was not quite clear and special experiments were certainly necessary'.[231]

By 1944, Brandt was in regular communication with a number of leading SS personalities, including Grawitz, Sievers, Jüttner and Pohl. All these men were asked to contact Brandt to coordinate German chemical warfare research. For example, on 31 March, Sievers reported to Brandt at Beelitz about the ongoing Natzweiler experiments.[232] At Nuremberg, Brandt admitted that he had received Sievers' report which documented the fact that Hirt had been conducting human experiments at Natzweiler since November 1942. The report distinguished between 'heavy, medium and light wounds' that had been caused by the exposure to mustard gas. Hirt had conducted mustard gas experiments on approximately 220 camp inmates, of whom 50 later died, and none had volunteered.[233] Brandt also admitted that he had talked to Hirt about the findings of the report at the end of April 1944, but had apparently not realized that it detailed experiments on humans: 'I was at Hirt's place at the end of April 1944, and I did not gain the impression that we were concerned with experiments on some concentration camp inmates carried [out] in camps.'[234] Brandt's visit to Strasbourg also included, in all likelihood, a joint meeting with Hirt and Bickenbach.[235] Brandt wanted to mediate between Hirt and Bickenbach to ensure that their collaborative work would continue. Hirt's experiments, classified by Rostock as 'urgent', continued throughout the summer of 1944. Given the available evidence, it stretches credibility to its limits to assume that Brandt was unaware of Hirt's concentration camp experiments. At best, he must have ignored the fact that Hirt had been performing criminal experiments on camp inmates which had resulted in fatalities. Brandt's testimony suggests that he was primarily interested in the research results and paid little attention to how the data was obtained.[236]

Brandt's credibility is further undermined by the fact that he sponsored another set of human experiments which Bickenbach and his assistants, Helmut Rühl and Friedrich Letz from Alsace, carried out at Natzweiler in the summer of 1944. This time, four experimental subjects died as a result of the experiments. Bickenbach later attributed the fatalities to the 'defective condition of the individuals concerned'.[237] Other subjects suffered serious pulmonary oedema, a swelling and fluid accumulation in the lungs which impairs breathing and can lead to respiratory failure. Bickenbach's post-war defence not only rehearsed the argument that he had merely followed orders, but he also implicated Brandt in the experiments. According to Bickenbach, Brandt had told him in Strasbourg that Himmler had insisted on the experiment, and that he, Bickenbach, was prohibited from conducting an experiment on himself. He also told the court that he recognized that the experiments had been unethical, but that he had performed them in order to protect the German population from the horrors of gas warfare: 'I thought it my duty to do everything to ensure this protection and to save the lives of thousands of Germans, especially the children and women; also, because I had to obey Himmler's orders. I had always been assured that my discovery [hexamethylentetramin] was the only means of protection; Professor Brandt himself had told me so.'[238]

Bickenbach's testimony has to be treated with caution, given that he probably wanted to shift responsibility for the experiments onto Brandt and the SS, but Brandt can hardly claim to have been ignorant about the criminal nature of the experiments. In, or around, August 1944, Bickenbach's assistant, Letz, informed Brandt about the progress of the experiments. He told Brandt that they had carried out experiments on '40 prisoners on the prophylactic effect of hexamethylentetramin [urotropin] in cases of phosgene poisoning'.[239] All the research subjects were probably Russian prisoners of war. Twelve subjects were given urotropin orally, twenty intravenously and eight persons were used as a 'control group' without any form of protection. All of the experimental subjects were middle-aged men, 'almost all in a weak and underfed condition'.[240] Two of the research subjects, J. Rei. and A. Rei., their names abbreviated, were suffering from localized tuberculosis.[241] Whereas all of the intravenously protected subjects survived, all of the unprotected subjects who were used as 'controls' fell ill. The above-mentioned J. Rei. and two further control subjects died from phosgene poisoning. Their abbreviated names were A. Eck. and A. Ho. A fourth research subject, named in the record as Z. Re., also died from the experiment. He had been protected with urotropin, but found himself in the group that was exposed to the highest level of phosgene poisoning.[242] At the end of the report, Letz told Brandt that the 'dosis letalis minima [minimum lethal dose] based on these experiments cannot yet be determined with certainty'.[243] In an experiment that had been carried out under the auspices of Brandt, four people had been killed without yielding any conclusive results. 'This document completely destroys the credibility of the defendant Brandt,' the US prosecution remarked in 1947.[244]

One of the few witnesses of the experiments, Willy Herzberg, recalled that he had seen four persons being carried out of the gas chamber:

> They had brown foam at the mouth, which also came through the ears and nose ... After we were led into the gas chamber, the professor [probably Bickenbach] stood in the

entrance and had two glass ampoules which looked like Dr. Oetkers aroma bottles. The professor [probably Bickenbach] encouraged us once again to move swiftly, and inhale strongly ... Then he threw the two ampoules against the wall and rapidly closed the door ... Approximately 10 minutes after the experiment had begun, I heard a noise with a thud, like someone clapping hands with the hands curved. This noise was the bursting lungs of two of the prisoners, who then fell on the ground, and who manifested the foam on mouth, nose and ears I described earlier.[245]

We know that Brandt and Bickenbach visited the Natzweiler concentration camp and that Brandt was shown Bickenbach's experimental set-up.[246] Brandt later claimed seeing only animal experiments at Natzweiler. This may have been true, given that Bickenbach also exposed cats to phosgene poisoning, and reported to Brandt about the experiments.[247] Yet on balance, it seems unlikely. A series of progress reports which Bickenbach and his researchers sent to Brandt in 1944 show that they were experimenting on humans, and that some of the research subjects had died as a result of the experiments.[248] Brandt's defence lawyers also floated the idea that Brandt might never have received the reports, and if he had received them, might never have read them. Again, this is possible. However, on the face of the evidence, it is difficult to imagine that Brandt was unaware of the experiments, or that he knew of only those experiments which were harmless, or in which none of the subjects suffered any injuries or death. At the end of 1944, Bickenbach was still conducting research on chemical warfare agents under the supervision of Brandt, after it had been granted priority status at a conference in Beelitz in August 1944, which Brandt had attended.[249] On 11 November, Sievers informed a member of Himmler's personal staff: 'Prof. Bickenbach is carrying out research on a warfare agent [*Kampfstoffauftrag*] on the order of the General Commisioner SS-Gruppenführer Prof. Dr. Brandt.'[250]

As late as December 1944, when Germany was on the verge of military collapse, Brandt and Wolfgang Wirth, the Military Medical Academy toxicologist, initiated yet another series of human experiments. Wirth had previously inspected Bickenbach's institute to see whether his experiments would yield useful results to the German army.[251] On 31 March 1945, officials from the Reich Institution for Water and Air Purification reported on water decontamination experiments that had been performed on human subjects at the Neuengamme concentration camp: 'A third series of experiments was carried out with an agent of the Lost group, the asphyxiating gas Lost, in accordance with the suggestion made by Obertstabsarzt Dr Wirth at the conference on 4 December [1944] with Reichkommissar [sic] Dr Brandt.'[252] Those present at the conference were representatives from the air ministry, including Walter Mielenz, and from the army and the anti-aircraft services.[253] The fact that the German military and civilian research community saw Brandt as the leading medical authority, who by 1944 could initiate, support and sanction human experiments in concentration camps, confirms his overall level of responsibility in Nazi medical experimentation. The Sachsenhausen and Natzweiler experiments, as well as those conducted at Ravensbrück, Neuengamme and elsewhere, show that Brandt took an active role in human experimentation. At times, he sponsored, supported or supervised specific research projects; at others he initiated particular series of experimental tests. Despite the apparent rivalry between Himmler's SS and Brandt's agency, Brandt could rely on Himmler's willingness to place camp inmates at the disposal of German researchers.

VIII. SPICES FROM DACHAU

Brandt and Himmler respected each other's position of power. From 1944 onwards, Brandt also received frequent visits from Grawitz, Himmler's right-hand man in all medical matters for the SS, and discussed the use of human experiments with him.[254] In the spring of 1944, Brandt had a small favour to ask of Himmler. His request was promptly executed. On 24 April 1944, Himmler instructed the head of the SS Finance and Administration Head Office to send a box of spices (*Gewürzkasten*) to Brandt as a birthday present for his wife, Anni Brandt.[255] On 1 May, SS-Hauptsturmführer Vogt from the SS Herbal Medical Centre at Dachau (*SS-Heilkräuterkulturen* Dachau) reported back to Himmler's personal secretary Rudolf Brandt: 'In fulfilment of … your letter, I am sending you today through the adjutant of the RFSS in Munich a box of spices, which would you please pass on to the wife of SS-Gruppenführer Prof. Dr. Brandt.'[256] Four days later, another letter was sent. Himmler's field command post (*Feld-Kommandostelle*) reported back to Brandt at Führer headquarters: 'Dear Gruppenführer! I am referring to our telephone conversation on 4 May this year, and send you on behalf of the RFSS a spice box for your wife. For the refilling of empty sprinklers (*Streudosen*), refill packs can be obtained from the SS Herbal Medical Centre at Dachau.'[257] While Germany was being laid to ashes by the ongoing bombing campaign of the Western Allies, and while millions of Jews and other victim groups were being persecuted and killed in an unprecedented genocidal programme, the SS bureaucracy continued to function with orderly precision. The box and the spices arrived in time. On 25 August 1944, it was Anni Brandt's fortieth birthday. Karl Brandt, her husband, now had a wonderful surprise: a spice box. The present and its contents had been produced in the concentration camp at Dachau, another place in the German *Gulag Archipelago* in which criminal experiments had been performed on hundreds of human subjects.

9

Medical Supremo

I. BRANDT *VERSUS* BORMANN

Ever since his appointment as General Commissioner, Brandt had wanted to establish a German health ministry, with himself as minister of health. It would give him an important institutional base, a *Hausmacht*, which would allow him to shape German medicine. A ministry of health with Brandt at its helm would also increase Speer's power base, and thus weaken the role of the party at the centre of government. These objectives did not escape a group of powerful operators, men such as Bormann, Himmler and Goebbels. The attempt of an 'outsider', one who was not an 'old fighter', to assume executive powers met with suspicious jealousy amongst the party faithful. Although Brandt gave party leaders the impression that Conti was a troublemaker, people soon realized that Hitler's doctor was carefully constructing his own promotion. On 7 December 1943, for example, Brandt reported to Goebbels about the 'great difficulties' which Conti was causing for the organization of first-aid measures for Berlin and other cities vulnerable to air raids. As chair of the Inter-Ministerial Committee for Air Raid Damage, Goebbels decided to give one of Brandt's representatives, a Dr Löllke, 'special powers' which would allow him to overrule Conti. Goebbels himself was anxious not to get involved in the dispute: 'At least I don't want to get embroiled in the conflict (*Ich möchte diese Schwierigkeiten wenigsten nicht auf meinem Rücken austragen lassen*).'[1] Six weeks later, Goebbels was already aware of the urgent need to curb Brandt's almost unstoppable rise to power.

Brandt recalled after the war that he had been 'friends' with Bormann in 1942/43. For most of the time, however, their relationship remained distant, even hostile. Bormann's rise had begun in 1934 after he had taken over the management of the Obersalzberg complex. He had been a party treasurer before he became the secretary of Rudolf Heß, Hitler's deputy. When the transformation of Haus Wachenfeld began, Bormann was originally given the task of supervising the building work, but the project quickly exploded into a major logistical and financial operation which increased Bormann's power base in the Berchtesgaden region. Hitler saw Bormann as a 'small man' and did not realize his own dependence on this unobtrusive and industrious party treasurer, whose insatiable ambition turned him into one of the most powerful men in the Reich. Bormann, not unlike Brandt, had made himself increasingly indispensable to Hitler. He would write down all Hitler's comments and wishes on white index cards, and then issue them as party instructions (*Parteianordnungen*).[2] This could mean little additional services to his master: if Hitler mentioned a book over dinner, for example, it would be ordered immediately and sent to the Berghof by courier so that Hitler could give a copy to his guests at the end of the evening. If Hitler mentioned the name of an old party comrade, Bormann would rush off and find out how that person was by radio or telecommunication.[3] But Bormann's services also could have fundamental implications for German society. Every remark made in passing by Hitler, every wish he expressed, every innuendo or allusion to a matter of interest could immediately become government policy, with sometimes disastrous consequences for those affected.

The more power Bormann amassed, the more he exploited his role as the gatekeeper at the centre of power. For many areas of government, the flow of vital information to and from the centre went through Bormann. This meant that he could control and manipulate the channels of communication. Agencies of the state and the party were sometimes totally dependent on their relationship with Bormann, as the only form of communication with Hitler. Brandt later recalled: 'Reports to the Führer about events, and in turn, the transmission of Führer directives to the outside world, were undertaken by Martin Bormann who acted as a filter.'[4] In general, Bormann issued all instructions as Führer directives which he then countersigned. This meant that the directives had to be carried out unquestioned. His position allowed him to issue orders which had almost the same force as if Hitler had given the orders himself. State and party functionaries feared the grey eminence in Hitler's shadow, whom they described as the 'uncrowned King'. To have Bormann as an enemy could be life-threatening. Even men like Himmler and Goebbels took great care to avoid conflicts with Bormann.[5] Hitler, on the other hand, could run his government from the armchair of his tea-house. Reacting to Hitler's every whim, his secretary and other servants were shaping a form of government which was characterized by personal rule and arbitrariness. It was a form of absolutism totally remote from reality. What is more, Hitler could always deny responsibility.

After the war, most witnesses described Bormann as ruthless and brutal in personal and professional relationships. Short, but strong, he had no moral inhibitions about using physical violence to teach his four-year-old son not to run away from a dog. Later, he prided himself on having cured his son's fear of dogs, though in the event, it turned out that the son was concussed. He had also no qualms about sending his wife, with their three-month-old infant, from Berchtesgaden to their apartment in Munich in the middle of the night, when he realized that something was missing in his laundry.[6] In professional relationships, Bormann showed an extraordinary degree of calculated strategic planning, terminating relationships with real and perceived opponents from one minute to the next. One of Bormann's adjutants suggested that Bormann – who had been a farmer – had forgotten that he was dealing with human beings, but instead was using people as if 'he had harnessed livestock in front of his plough'.[7] Feared by many, hated by all – except, perhaps, by his submissive wife – Bormann was a factor no one dared to underestimate at court.

From 1943, powerful personalities in the vicinity of Hitler including Bormann tried, with partial success, to curb Brandt's almost unstoppable rise to power. In January 1944, a journalist from the magazine *Das Reich* published an unusually perceptive portrait of the General Commissioner in anticipation of Brandt's fortieth birthday. The report might have been censored, perhaps even tailored, to reassure the German public that the government remained in control. Behind the linguistic pathos, the article provides insight into how Brandt appeared to other people at the pinnacle of his professional power:

> … in the style of a secret which hides the many complicated ingredients at a chemist's in a simple and dignified manner behind the labels of bottles – this is the impression made by this tall man, just forty years old. The elegance here says less than the cold indifference conveyed by some physicians. Their whole being seems to be stretched tightly, like a swimming cap or a rubber glove: any effort is masked by their relaxed air. Such is Karl Brandt, the escort physician of the Führer. His dark eyes are completely calm, though large, and with a penetrating gaze. In the slim face the straight nose is almost tough, and the mouth is made of a more robust substance than flesh – both are hard and as precise as tools. The thin head is turned rapidly, but the wiry promptness is not so much athletic discipline as a tenacity of a different kind.[8]

The person described here was conscious of his superior position. Brandt conveyed and represented an image of power. Since the signing of the second Führer decree in September 1943 Brandt had been confident that he was the man in charge of German medicine. Leading Nazi physicians were beginning to sense change at the highest level of the medical hierarchy. Given that he had almost no access to Hitler any more, Conti's power base appeared seriously dubious. On 17 January 1944, Nitsche responded to Rüdin's enquiry about who was actually in charge of German medicine: 'I cannot answer your query at this point about whether one now has to approach C.[onti] or Br.[andt] in general medical questions. Yet it seems to be certain that Professor Brandt is superior to C. and holds the power in all medical matters in his hands. Apart from this, the foundations of the whole institutional structure are not yet fully developed.'[9] Nitsche had hit the nail on the head. In the amorphous, highly personalized power structures of the Third Reich, those with ready access to Hitler could amass substantial powers independent of their institutional or professional position, and it would be in the interest of those on the receiving end to work towards those who appeared to have the support of the Führer. The system resembled that of a medieval court.

At the end of January 1944, Hitler's court became increasingly nervous after a number of journals, such as the *Illustrierter Beobachter*, had published leading articles about Brandt's key role in the German health system. His fortieth birthday had undoubtedly given him a lot of publicity. On 24 January, Goebbels enquired from Bormann whether Brandt would soon be promoted to minister of national health. Others were concerned about Brandt as well, but for somewhat more selfish reasons. The same evening, Morell told Bormann that he was worried about Brandt because he had 'taken the chemical industry with its production of pharmaceuticals "under his wing", with the assistance of Comrade Speer'.[10] Then, on the morning of 25 January, Ley rang to ask Bormann the same question Goebbels had asked twenty-four hours previously.[11] There was obviously something afoot. Bormann immediately saw an opportunity to curb Brandt's increasing influence. On 25 January, he told his wife: 'At long last various people realise Brandt's very obvious aim, which he admittedly camouflaged quite cleverly at the beginning. *Here* we see Brandt rarely nowadays, one might say, only when he wants a rest; he is entrenching and installing himself in Berlin!'[12] Goebbels was so concerned about Brandt's ambitions that he decided to have a word with Hitler. On 25 January, he noted in his diary:

> I report to the Führer that Professor Brandt intends to establish a health ministry. I believe this to be quite premature. Brandt first has to win his spurs. He is a very ambitious boy, but his performance stands diametrically opposed to his wishes. There will be no talk about the health ministry in the foreseeable future, because of my intervention. I also do not believe it to be right that Dr. Brandt just outstrips Conti. Conti is really not very skilled in his tactics, but a great expert, and, in particular, a very reliable and good party member.[13]

Brandt's plan to establish a health ministry was shelved for the time being. How far the plan had advanced is difficult to say, but Brandt's meteoric rise to power seems to have warranted Goebbels' personal intervention. Brandt knew that his position as General Commissioner continued to carry a lot of weight. Perhaps it would be possible to persuade the Führer to grant him ministerial powers at a later date, especially if he kept a low profile for some time. The consolation prize was also not negligible. On 15 March 1944, Hitler handed Brandt a cheque from the Reich bank for over 50,000 Reichsmark for his duty to Führer and fatherland. The money was exempt from income tax.[14] About a month later, on Hitler's birthday, Brandt was promoted to the rank of SS-Gruppenführer and General Lieutenant of the Waffen-SS.[15] Some of Hoffmann's photographs show Brandt, wearing a decorative armband with the inscription 'Adolf Hitler', with his wife Anni, clearly enjoying the birthday celebrations.[16]

Around the same time, Bormann planned another attack on Brandt. On 19 February, he wrote yet another letter of complaint to the head of the Reich Chancellery.[17] He told Lammers that in Baden a Dr Weyrauch was conducting control examinations (*Kontrolluntersuchungen*) in the name of Brandt's representative for special tasks in the war industry, the SS-Untersturmführer and internal medicine specialist, Willy Gutermuth. In 1943, Brandt had put Gutermuth in charge of the Aktion Brandt hospital in Köppern, near Bad Homburg, and had given him the special task of reducing the number of sick in the war industry. Weyrauch's attempt to give workers a clean bill of health had stirred up the feelings of many party faithful. Bormann was particularly concerned that Weyrauch, who was examining up to 150 workers per day for an extra two Reichsmark per head, was misdiagnosing many of them. The mood among the workers had subsequently soured as a result, he told Lammers. According to Bormann, it was also unacceptable that the medical opinions of physicians whose political reliability was unquestionable were subordinate to those of Brandt's representatives, who apparently did not possess the necessary expertise. Weyrauch was also criticized for conducting his examinations without consulting the regional physicians, and without notifying the Office for People's Health, the Chamber of Physicians or the civil administration in the region of Baden-Alsace. Last but not least, party officials, including Bormann, were concerned that one of Brandt's representatives was earning additional money.[18]

On 4 March, Lammers discussed the matter with Bormann. They agreed that the issue did not warrant the involvement of the Reich Chancellery, but that Hitler should be asked on another occasion whether he condoned Brandt's increasingly obvious attempts to establish a health ministry. Bormann also told Lammers, in confidence, that Brandt had referred to the Chief of Army Medical Services, Handloser, as his head of department (*Abteilungsleiter*).[19] By joining forces with the Reich administration, Bormann, as the representative of the Nazi Party, was hoping to contain, if not curtail, Brandt's power ambitions in the long run. Days later, on 7 March, Bormann wrote another letter to Lammers which further fuelled the ongoing power struggle over conflicting areas of responsibility. He had discovered that Rostock, as Brandt's representative for medical science and research, had invited a number of relevant government ministers, including the Reich Minister for the Interior and the Reich Health Leader, to a conference to discuss the future of medical research. The conference was about to take place three days later, on 10 March. Conti had already informed Bormann, as well as Brandt, that he would neither attend the meeting, nor would he send a representative 'because the subject area clearly belonged in his area of responsibility'.[20] Bormann thought that Brandt had once again violated Hitler's administrative brief:

> Even if Professor Brandt believes, based on his general instruction, that he needs to create an active momentum in this direction, he still has to do this through the Reich Health Leader … In any event, Professor Brandt should have consulted the Reich Health Leader.[21]

While Hitler was holding talks at the palace of Kleßheim to bully the Hungarian government into submission, and occupy the country by military force, some of the leading officials of the regime were debating whether or not Hitler's doctor had breached the administrative code by sending out an invitation without their prior consultation. In his telex of 9 March, Lammers advised Bormann to request a decision from Hitler on whether he was prepared to 'suspend' Brandt's range of activities. Although Hitler agreed, it was nonetheless a hollow victory for Bormann, given that the conference was only postponed. Five months later, in August 1944, Brandt convened the conference after it had become clear that Hitler would promote him to the position of Reich Commissioner.

While Brandt was struggling to remain in control of his power, Speer, his closest ally and long-term friend, was facing a palace revolt in his ministry after he fell seriously ill at the beginning of 1944. On 18 January, Speer was rushed to the Hohenlychen hospital, north of Berlin, with a badly swollen leg.[22] Brandt had advised Speer to consult Gebhardt, the director of the Hohenlychen hospital, believing that his friend would receive expert treatment. Little did Brandt know that Gebhardt not only misdiagnosed Speer's illness – he was probably suffering from the early stages of an embolism on arrival at the clinic – but also was colluding with Himmler to rid Germany of the Minister of Armaments. A whole range of leading Nazi officials, including Bormann, Göring, Himmler and Ley, were using the opportunity to depose Speer. Himmler seems to have gone so far as to instruct Gebhardt to let Speer die. Himmler visited Hohenlychen around 7 or 8 February, and was told about Speer's deteriorating health. He told Gebhardt: 'Well, then he's dead.'[23] Gebhardt tried to query the implications of what he had heard, but was cut short: 'That's enough,' Himmler told him. 'The less said, the better.'[24] Having overheard the conversation, Speer's secretary, Annemarie Kempf, who had noticed 'a curious minimum of treatment for an obviously very sick man', immediately informed Speer's wife, who contacted Brandt. Alerted to the fact that Speer was in grave danger, Brandt instructed Gebhardt to hand over Speer's treatment to Friedrich Koch, one of his friends and professor of internal medicine at the University of Tübingen. Shortly after Koch had arrived at Hohenlychen on 10 February, Speer's health further deteriorated, his pulse shot up to 120, his skin colour turned blue and he haemorrhaged several times. Speer's wife was told that she had to prepare herself for the worst. Despite Gebhardt's continued interferences, Koch managed to stabilize the patient, and by mid-February he had miraculously recovered. Brandt, who visited Speer two or three times during these dramatic days, must have realized that power was a double-edged sword in Nazi Germany.[25] Those who possessed it, and could not defend it, were likely to pay with their lives.

Throughout the spring and summer of 1944, leading officials of the Nazi Party and the Reich administration continued their criticism of Brandt's style of governance. At the heart of the argument stood the historically undefined relationship between the state and the party. One of the recurring topics of discussion was Gutermuth and Poschmann's alleged attempts to subordinate the 'factory physicians' (*Betriebsärzte*) in the war industry to their command, in the name of Brandt's office, establish their own parallel organization, and exclude the influence of the party from as many organizations in the health system as possible. At the beginning of June, the head of the German Labour Front, Robert Ley, had reached the end of his tether after Brandt had not responded to his attempts to resolve the matter.[26] On 30 May, Brandt had simply sent Ley a telex, stating that he had not instructed Poschmann to subordinate the physicians, and that, as far as he knew, Poschmann had made no such attempts. Brandt was either not well informed about the activities of some of his officials, which may well have been true, given that it would correspond to his level of ignorance of the 'euthanasia' programme, or, and this is perhaps more plausible, he consciously denied having any knowledge, thus forcing Ley to prove his allegations. It was a strategy which Brandt also employed during the Nuremberg Doctors' Trial. Ley, however, could back up his claims.

On 1 June, he told Brandt that Poschmann had either used Brandt's name on his own initiative and for his own benefit, or had lied to Brandt.[27] According to Ley, Poschmann could not be trusted. For example, having been instructed to purchase important drugs from Italy for millions of Reichsmark, Poschmann had returned with hundreds of bottles of *Schnaps*. In the subsequent inquiry, he had alleged that he had been instructed by Brandt, a fact which Brandt later vehemently denied in front of Speer. *Gauleiter* Eigruber from the Upper Donau region described Poschmann as a 'puffed-up and power-hungry' personality, who was not prepared to recognize leadership from the region or from any other organization of the Nazi Party or the state. As a result, Poschmann had been advised, for his own safety, to avoid the region.[28] Sources close to him, Ley argued, had also informed him that Poschmann and Gutermuth had made 'political comments' which suggested that Brandt was planning to establish a parallel organization, with the ultimate aim of excluding the party from the German health system. Dozens of reports and directives that had been issued to the fighter command (*Jägerstab*) and other war industries in Dessau, Lüneburg, Steiermark and Berlin left no doubt that Poschmann was attempting to 'extract physicians in the industry from the control of the German Labour Front and create an "Operation Brandt" [*Einsatz Brandt*]'.[29] Criticizing the manner in which Brandt's officials were operating was only the opening shot. Ley also had issues with Brandt's style of leadership. If Brandt felt that it was necessary to become involved in fighter command, and in other areas of production, Ley argued, why had he never consulted or contacted him? '[M]y department for Health and People's Protection, including thousands of doctors, would have been available to you.'[30] The available evidence seems to suggest that the number of sick in the war-important industries was as low as 1 or 2 per cent, whilst production output had steadily increased. According to Ley, Brandt's persistent interferences had led to such a level of 'disquiet and dissatisfaction' in the factories that he was no longer able to guarantee the government peaceful labour relations in the industries:

> If others are to be permitted to interfere, in rather obvious and careless ways, in the sensitive political system of a factory, and to behave like a bull in china shop, then I have to decline to take any responsibility.[31]

At first, it seemed that Ley's letter had the desired effect. During June and July Brandt engaged in negotiations with Ley about their mutual areas of responsibility, but no agreement could be reached. On 29 June, Klopfer informed State Secretary Kritzinger of the Reich Chancellery about the ongoing talks. A week later, on 6 July, Bormann told Lammers that the matter had not only become totally confusing, but was raising fundamental questions about the relationship between the Nazi Party and the state. Bormann first wanted to write to Brandt, outlining the position of the party and laying down the administrative and judicial limits of the two Führer decrees, but he was prepared to report the matter to Hitler if Brandt continued with his 'reckless practice.'[32]

In a draft letter to Brandt of July 1944, Bormann told Brandt that his interpretation of the nature and scope of the two Führer decrees was wrong, that his work touched upon the 'fundamental position of the Party' and that his position did not permit the establishment of his own organization.[33] Brandt did not have the power to issue instructions to Nazi Party organizations, which included the German Labour Front, because his role only involved the agencies of the state. That is why the two Führer decrees made no mention of the party, Bormann argued. To use any of the resources or personnel of the Nazi Party, Brandt was obliged to consult with the Party Chancellery or with the Reich Health Leader as the representative of the party in all medical matters. In theory, he was also required to collaborate with Conti in all areas which touched upon the medical matters of the party and the state, because of Conti's dual responsibilities as Reich Health Leader and State Secretary in the RMdI. Bormann stressed the enormous discrepancy between Brandt's official orders and the way in which he carried them out in practice. According to Bormann, the Reich Health Leader had to keep an overview of the actual planning at all times, and 'under no circumstances should the impression arise in the factories that there is a complete confusion of the powers of authority'.[34] Rather than clarifying the issue, Bormann's letter exposed a chaotic administrative structure in which the agencies of the party and the state competed for power and control over the German health system.

The correspondence of Ley, Lammers and Bormann shows that powerful opposition to Brandt's managerial style was yet again gaining momentum. At around the same time, Himmler told Brandt that he was unwilling to antagonize Bormann 'for the sake of doctors'.[35] From the correspondence between Himmler and Brandt it becomes clear that the Reichsführer-SS did not hold physicians in particularly high regard anyway. When it transpired that Brandt had suggested to Hitler that young men should be permitted to start their medical studies during the war, Himmler intervened, telling Brandt that his proposal would attract a 'guard of shirkers of the most unfavourable kind'. According to Himmler, it could not be 'the wish of a profession to bring together the moral waste (*moralischer Abhub*) of a nation'.[36] Although Himmler agreed with Brandt's plans to reform the health system, he was unwilling to support Brandt in his dispute with Conti. Brandt recalled Himmler telling him that he would have to see for himself how he 'would get along with Conti or even with Bormann'.[37]

Brandt was certainly willing to fight his corner alone, given that he continued to enjoy the ear of the Führer. He had spent the best part of the last four months with Hitler in his alpine retreat at the Obersalzberg before flying back with him to *Wolfsschanze* on the morning of 14 July. Hitler had increasingly withdrawn from the world, rarely inviting any outside guests. On the evening before departing to Rastenburg, Hitler kissed the hand of Anni Brandt, perhaps to bid farewell, not just to her, but to the Berghof as well.[38] It would be the last time that he saw the Berghof before committing suicide in the bunker in Berlin.[39] Twenty-four hours later, Hitler, and by default, Brandt as well, cheated death once again by a tiny margin. A photograph, taken on 15 July 1944, shows Brandt in conversation with Hitler in the woods of the *Wolfsschanze* in East Prussia to which Hitler had just returned.[40]

The only witness to the conversation was Hitler's Alsatian. Unknown to both men was the fact that Colonel Claus Schenck Graf von Stauffenberg, chief of staff of Colonel-General Friedrich Fromm, in command of the reserve army, was planning an assassination attempt on Hitler's life during one of the three situation briefings that afternoon.[41] The idea was to kill Hitler and Himmler simultaneously. When it transpired that Himmler was absent, Stauffenberg telephoned Berlin to receive further instructions. In the end, the plot was cancelled.

Five days later, on 20 July, the group around Stauffenberg made another attempt on Hitler's life. This time the bomb went off. For a moment, there was total pandemonium in the conference room, but Hitler was alive, and left the wooden barracks almost unscathed.[42] Hitler's almost paranoiac fear of assassination attempts had been the reason why Brandt had been employed in the first place, but as it happened, Brandt was not at Führer headquarters that day. Heinz Linge, Hitler's valet, immediately summoned Hitler's other escort physician, Hanskarl von Hasselbach, to the Führer's bunker to provide first aid. Von Hasselbach remembered Hitler sitting on a sofa looking 'very much upset but not unconscious'. His trousers and jacket were badly torn, the hair on the back of his neck was heavily singed. Apart from a few scratches on his lower legs and a haemorrhage under the skin of his left hand and on the right elbow, Hasselbach detected no serious injuries. Almost all of Hitler's injuries were superficial in nature, yet von Hasselbach had to remove hundreds of small wooden splinters which had penetrated through the skin of Hitler's legs.[43] Hitler could not hear well, which was understandable, given the noise of the blast, but he was clearly able to speak. He told von Hasselbach that he was 'glad that the attempt was undertaken, for now he would be able to get his enemies and now it would be possible to persecute them, to wipe them out'.[44] Attempting to explain the assassination away, Hitler said: 'All these months I have felt that something is going on and now I know it and it is possible to make an end of this.'[45] It was little more than a case of self-fulfilling prophecy. Rushing to Hitler's room, Morell also diagnosed a badly swollen right forearm and some burn injuries on his left hand. After Hitler had recovered from the first shock, he welcomed Mussolini, who arrived later that day, and showed him the room where he had brushed with death.

Having been informed of the attempt on Hitler's life, Brandt raced back to Rastenburg. He later stated that Hitler had suffered injuries to one arm and leg as well as haemorrhages in both middle ears.[46] Significantly, Brandt noticed that the tremor on Hitler's left leg had disappeared, but reappeared a couple of weeks later. At first, however, Hitler was delighted, telling Jodl: 'The miracle is that the shock got rid of my nerve complaint almost entirely … not that I would recommend this kind of remedy.'[47] Brandt later told interrogators that he believed that the tremor 'must have been due to Parkinson's disease, or may have been of psychogenic origin'.[48] Brandt was particularly concerned about the blood which was seeping out of Hitler's ears. In consultation with Morell, it was decided to call Carl von Eicken, director of the ENT-clinic in Berlin, who had removed a vocal polyp from Hitler in 1935. However, von Eicken was attending the wedding of his daughter in

South Germany. As an alternative, Brandt summoned von Eicken's assistant, the ENT-specialist Erwin Giesing, who was on duty in the nearby army reserve hospital in Lützen, and ordered him to conduct an ear examination.[49] Upon arriving at the Wolf's Lair on 22 July, Giesing found Hitler in a poor state of health. Hitler's facial expressions at the time of the examination were 'fatigued, exhausted, with [the] appearance of senility'.[50] Von Eicken arrived the next day. Together with Morell, he examined Hitler and diagnosed bruising on the right upper arm and forearm, and burn injuries on his right and left thighs. Both of Hitler's eardrums were ruptured and his right ear was full of blood. As a consequence, he had difficulties in keeping his balance. Brandt was in the meantime attending to the officers who had been injured in the blast. Eleven of the wounded men had immediately been transferred to the nearby hospital, but within forty-eight hours, three of them had succumbed to their injuries. On 23 July, Annelise Schmundt, the wife of Rudolf Schmundt, Hitler's army adjutant, noted in her diary: 'Three professors – Brandt, Hasselbach and Wustmann – are working around the clock to keep Rudolf alive.'[51] To perform emergency surgery was what Brandt had been trained to do, but in the end Schmundt died as well. Four weeks later, on 18 August, von Eicken was in a position to tell Hitler that both eardrums had healed.

Having miraculously survived the assassination attempt, and suffered only minor injuries, Hitler unleashed a terrible vengeance.[52] The conspirators and their families were arrested or killed in an unprecedented bloodbath which the regime unleashed after Hitler had pledged that he would 'wipe out and eradicate' each and every one of them.[53] Within weeks, about 200 men and women who were directly implicated in the plot were killed, and another 5,000 rounded up and imprisoned by Himmler's ruthless police forces.[54] Brandt, on the other hand, accompanied Hitler to the military field hospital Carlshof, where he visited some of the soldiers who had been seriously injured by the blast. To exploit the occasion for propaganda purposes, Hoffmann captured Hitler's care for the wounded for public consumption. With Brandt, Hitler visited Karl-Jesko von Puttkamer, his naval adjutant, and Major General Scherff, who had suffered major burn injuries to his face and hands.[55] Brandt's loyalty to one of the most brutal dictators of modern times remained unquestioned. Feeling isolated and deeply betrayed by the military high command, Hitler turned to those in his vicinity in a last-ditch attempt to avert military disaster. It provided Brandt with a unique opportunity to persuade Hitler to bestow on him even greater political powers.

II. THE THIRD FÜHRER DECREE

A first indication that Hitler might be won over by Brandt surfaced at the beginning of August 1944. About three weeks after the assassination attempt, Hitler must have had an open mind about Brandt's arguments on how to run the German health system. This time, Brandt used Conti's attempts to prohibit members of his staff from collaborating with his office as a pretext to ask Hitler for greater powers. On Sunday 8 August 1944, Brandt talked to Conti on the phone about the matter. Given that Conti kept a memo of the conversation, we have a fairly good idea what was discussed. Brandt was certainly in no mood for compromise:

Brandt: I hear that you have prohibited Dr [Heinrich] Grote from attending a meeting with me?

Conti: I have agreed that I would immediately come to you with Dr Grote.

[Repeated question by Professor Brandt: Have you prohibited Dr Grote from coming to see me? – followed by my same reply as above].

Brandt: But I don't wish to talk to you, I want to talk to Dr Grote alone. If you come out to Beelitz, I shall feel sorry for you, because I would not meet you, but I will talk to Dr Grote alone.

Conti: Does that mean that you don't want to talk to me under any circumstances about matters that concern the German Association of Medical Insurers [*Kassenärztliche Vereinigung Deutschlands*, KVD] for which I am responsible?

Brandt: I won't give you an answer to this. I wish to have an answer from you. I don't wish to talk to you, but only with Dr Grote.

Conti: The matter is absolutely clear. I am ready at any time to come to you together with Dr Grote.

Brandt: I regard it as self-evident that you and Dr Grote come to see me if I wish that. But I don't wish [to see] you, I wish [to see] Dr Grote alone.

Conti: But you will have to accept that I am present at the conference, because it concerns matters for which I am responsible and for which Dr Grote is merely my representative.

Brandt: I will find a way to talk to Dr Grote alone.

[Professor Brandt hangs up with the German greeting which is followed by my German greeting].[56]

Furious about Conti's audacious demands, Brandt raced to Führer headquarters and told Hitler that Conti's interferences damaged the Geilenberg programme that had been set up to rebuild fuel factories that had been damaged in air raids. Exploiting, perhaps, Hitler's momentary physical and mental weakness, Brandt managed to persuade Hitler to grant him total power over the German health system. On 7 August, twenty-four hours after the telephone conversation between Brandt and Conti, the first draft of the third Führer decree was ready.[57] Two days later, on 9 August, Lammers informed Frick about a third Führer decree which would promote Brandt to Reich Commissioner and his office to a superior Reich Office. This news spread like wildfire down the chain of command. Within hours, senior members of the state and party machinery were fully aware of it. Travelling back from Berlin to Munich in a sleeper, one of Conti's staff members met officials from the Party Chancellery, who told him that Bormann had strongly objected to Himmler about the decree, and that Brandt had already been given permission for the decree by Hitler. 'Even if this information is being questioned by the Party Chancellery, I do actually think that this matter cannot now be resolved without a Führer decision,' he told Conti the next day. Conti was now on high alert. One day later, on 11 August, State Secretary Wilhelm Stuckart told Himmler that Brandt would have a more senior position than other Reich ministers if Hitler granted him the power to issue directives to all relevant health agencies in the German territory.[58] Bormann was particularly concerned that another Führer decree would undermine the power and independence of the party. On the morning of 14 August, Hitler asked Bormann about the decree, and ordered that the decree be immediately presented to him for signature. In the evening, Bormann told his wife that it had been such a 'black day' that he had offered Hitler his resignation:

I am greatly reproaching myself because for years I have considered Brandt to be a decent man, i.e. a man with an unselfish mind. It was I who proposed him for the Badge of Honour; shortly afterwards it was brought home to me that Brandt was behaving in the most repulsive, unpleasant manner towards Conti. After he had been given plenary powers – to get them, Brandt had largely exploited my own credulousness – he not only failed to support Conti as a National Socialist should, but blackened his reputation and, through an incredibly subtle campaign, prevented him from seeing the Führer. At the same time Brandt followed a boldly conceived plan to achieve his ambitious personal ends, assisted, of course, by Speer, Saur and Co! And now he is going to be granted new extraordinary powers – Brandt and Saur put it to the Führer that such powers were necessary in the present difficult circumstances.

Today I tried my best to get Conti a hearing with the Führer – so that Conti should not be slaughtered without being able to speak up for himself at least once! – and to give a true picture of the situation, which is by no means such as Brandt and his admiring associates – a mutual admiration society – painted it. To my great distress, the Führer, who believes that every good thing he has been told of and about Brandt and every bad thing he has been told about Conti is the gospel truth, got very annoyed with my lack of understanding. I told the Führer that so far, wanting to spare him, I had not reported all complaints against Brandt; that Brandt had woven his web deliberately, with the greatest subtlety, and that it was an injustice to represent Conti as *completely* unqualified and inefficient or to exaggerate his weaknesses. A man who was the first physician to work in Red Berlin did not deserve to be removed in this way by a climber like Brandt and by his collaborators of the years 1933 and 1937. *Audiatur et altera pars!*

The Führer thought differently; he spoke with high praise of Brandt – Speer's and Saur's paeans of praise had had the intended effect – and he, the Führer, to whom I wish to give only pleasure, was upset about my denseness and lack of understanding! I had to tell him that I would at once acclaim Brandt – indeed, would have done so long ago – if I believed him truly efficient and a National Socialist. I said that in my eyes Brandt was an ambitious climber and intriguer, and I would not like to sit down at the same table as him. So I asked the Führer repeatedly to release me and let me join the army at the front. Unfortunately the Führer refused, though I asked his permission urgently several times.

This outcome has left me completely shaken, which is saying a lot in my case, as you well know. Admittedly, in real life it isn't honesty which overcomes dishonesty; in the hard struggle of existence it is the steelier, stronger capacity to succeed which wins the day every time – and yet, it is a bitter thing if that capacity is based on intrigue and a burning ambition as in the present case. The other day, in Berlin, Funk, too, expressed himself in very strong terms on Brandt's burning ambition which 'almost tore him in two.' Just imagine how loathsome I find Brandt!

And on top of it I, of all people, who want to serve the Führer and his sub-leaders with honesty and sincerity, *I* have had to upset the Führer – without in the least intending to – for the sake of that intriguer! Never again let yourself be taken in by Brandt! He is one of the cleverest cheats I know.[59]

The next day, Bormann told Conti that his objections to the forthcoming decree had not made any difference: 'The Führer replied that under the current difficult circumstances, which might become even more difficult, he was not in a position to accept my reservations.'[60] A week later, on 23 August, Goebbels noted that Brandt had 'talked the Führer over' to giving him general responsibilities for the whole of the German health system: 'Brandt wants to enforce a Führer decree which would give his department the character of a Reich ministry, directly subordinate to the Führer. The Führer has already let himself be talked round to the plans of Professor Brandt, which I think is disastrous.'[61] What Goebbels feared was not so much Conti's potential resignation, but the loss of Nazi Party influence over German medical affairs. Although he and others launched a last-ditch attempt to prevent the decree, Goebbels saw that defeat was inevitable. On the same day, he noted: 'Brandt is a pretty ambitious boy, who knows no consideration, and by constantly influencing the Führer, he manages more or less to realise his far-reaching plans.'[62]

Goebbels had hit the nail on the head. Despite having no health ministry, Brandt was now in total control, and he wanted to make sure that the leading experts in Germany knew this immediately. On Thursday 24 August 1944, one day before Brandt's official appointment as Reich Commissioner, and days before the actual signing of the decree, Brandt chaired a conference to identify and support medical science research projects important to the war effort.[63] The meeting had originally been scheduled to take place in March, but had been cancelled at the last minute because of Bormann's intervention.[64] Research considered to be of less importance for the war effort was to receive no further funding from the government. The conference took place in Rostock's office in Beelitz, and was attended by Brandt and Rostock, by Blome and Schreiber from the Reich Research Council, by Paul Würfler, head of the Army Medical Inspectorate, by the psychiatrist Hans Luxenburger and by Dr Joedicke, Dr Helpap, Dr Ebel and Dr Teller. Dr Becker-Freyseng from the High Command of the German Air Force, himself involved in the Dachau sea-water experiments on Gypsies, was also present at the meeting. Brandt later alleged that he had met Becker-Freyseng for the first time during the Nuremberg Doctors' Trial.[65] Conti, Sauerbruch and Menzel did not attend.[66] In his opening remarks, Brandt stated that the aim of the meeting was not to test the necessity of every project. Medical research had to continue, he told the delegates; the current need to save on personnel should not detract from the potential damage which could be caused if research work was to be curtailed. Brandt also told the conference that it was his intention to defend this position vis-à-vis Goebbels. The task was to direct all available manpower and resources to those areas of research which possessed the highest military priority. Once this was achieved, more long-term projects could be envisaged.[67]

Following the conference, Rostock was asked to compile a register of institutes that were conducting 'war decisive' research work. He came up with a total of forty-five institutes which conducted work on typhus, malaria, hepatitis, brain pathology, tuberculosis, nutrition, blood circulation, oxygen deficiency, penicillin, virus research and, above all, chemical warfare research. Research on various chemical warfare agents was carried out, among others, at the pharmacological institutes in Giessen (Hildebrandt) and Marburg (Gremels), the physiological chemistry institute in Heidelberg (Fischbeck), the chemical institute in Prague (Walschmidt-Leitz), the medical clinic in Strasbourg (Bickenbach) and at the anatomical institute in Strasbourg (Hirt).[68] Researchers wanting to consult foreign-language literature on any of these subjects were asked to contact Rostock. A memorandum about the conference also recorded that no further army medical research (*Wehrmedizinische Forschung*) should be conducted in the history of medicine and anthropology, and in the fields of racial science and eugenics. Significantly, someone later crossed out the paragraph.[69]

Of four drafts which Lammers hastily prepared, and which included a number of counter-proposals, Hitler selected the one which gave Brandt the greatest possible leverage.[70] In practice, however, the third Führer decree did little more than codify the power relations that had been prevailing in the medical system for some time. Brandt had waited for the opportunity since the beginning of the year, when Goebbels had ruined his plans to establish a health ministry. However, having managed to persuade Hitler to sign the decree, Brandt did not realize the extent to which his conduct at the heart of the regime was met with jealousy and open hostility by the party faithful. It was the combination of Brandt's 'insidious policy of intrigue', Goebbels claimed, and the aim to establish an agency that was subordinate to Hitler alone, which infuriated many. On 24 August, he noted: 'This we know: it is those who plan to play with the apparatus of the state and the party who want to be dependent only on the Führer.'[71] Continuing his quest for power, Brandt was alienating ever more of those who were determined to defend their parallel empires. On the day Brandt's wife, Anni, was celebrating her fortieth birthday, Brandt was officially appointed to 'Reich Commissioner of the Führer for Health and Sanitation'. The decree was dated 25 August 1944, but it was probably signed on or around 31 August 1944.[72] The decree stated:

I hereby appoint the General Commissioner for Health and Sanitation, Professor Dr Brandt, at the same time to Reich Commissioner for Health and Sanitation for the duration of this war. In this capacity his office ranks as highest Reich authority. The Reich Commissioner for Health and Sanitation is authorised to issue instructions to the offices and organisations of the State, Party and Wehrmacht which are concerned with the work of the medical and health care system.[73]

Brandt's promotion formally elevated him to the position of highest medical authority of the German Reich at a time when the German occupied territories, and the Reich itself, were seriously under threat from Allied military forces. One day before his official appointment, on 24 August, the French capital had been liberated by a French division; two days later, a mass of jubilant crowds cheered the leader of the Free French, Charles de Gaulle, along the Champs-Elysées. The days of the regime were clearly numbered. Germany now needed all available medical resources to cope with an increasingly desperate military situation. Brandt was authorized to give orders to all Reich agencies, whether those of the state, the party or the army. It was not only a far-reaching and all-empowering decree, which Brandt had tailored to his own needs, but it meant the total loss of power and prestige for Conti. Work became almost impossible for him. On 30 August, Himmler told him: 'I know how difficult your situation is. After weighing up all the pros and cons, the Führer has decided. However hard it is for you, now only one thing counts: clear obedience with respect to the Führer's order.'[74] Bormann, on the other hand, was relieved that Hitler held no grudge against him, telling his wife: 'In spite of our difference about Herr Brandt, the Führer is touchingly kind to me.'[75] Goebbels was nonetheless furious about the outcome. On 31 August, he wrote in his diary: 'Dr Brandt got his decree by hanging around long enough (*Dr Brandt hat ihn sich richtig im Vorzimmer ersessen*).'[76] Trying to mediate between the conflicting parties a week later, Goebbels realized that only threats might deter Brandt from wanting to accumulate even more power. On 1 September, after taking a firm line with Brandt, he noted:

> Brandt has the ear of the Führer, while Conti has not been able to give a report to the Führer for years. But Brandt cannot exploit this advantage to press Conti into the corner. I leave Brandt in no doubt that his conduct has given rise to the most serious criticism in the party. That in fact seems to impress him so deeply that he promises me to make the attempt to come to terms with Conti.[77]

Goebbels' threats had the desired effect. On the same day that Goebbels talked tough with Brandt, the latter was scheduled to meet Conti to discuss the 'basic consequences' of the decree. Brandt had ordered Conti on 31 August to see him the next day in Beelitz. It amounted to nothing less than Conti's walk to Canossa. Demoted and humiliated, Conti was forced to endure Brandt's show of dominance. Several times during the meeting, Conti pleaded to be released from his position. Then the telephone rang. Gebhardt was on the line to say that Himmler would not oppose Conti's resignation. It was another nail in the coffin. Brandt was reluctant to agree, however. He probably realized that it was strategically unwise to run the health system by himself and shoulder all the blame for any potential shortcomings. He told Conti that he did not want to 'run the machinery alone'. The meeting was adjourned. Three weeks later, Brandt met Conti at 74 Wilhelmstraße for another discussion about the matter. He now told Conti that he had decided that he actually wanted to 'parade the doctor' (den Arzt herauskehren), and that the Führer was happy about his decision. He would keep his office in the clinic to hold conferences. His postal address would remain, however, because it gave him greater status. Brandt no longer had any need to run down his position and power in the regime.

Combining his position as Hitler's accompanying doctor, professor at the surgical clinic in Berlin, SS-Gruppenführer, General Lieutenant of the Waffen-SS and Reich Commissioner, Brandt had accumulated extensive political, military and civil powers. After the war, the Allies quickly realized that Brandt had been a leading official in the regime. One of the interrogators told Brandt: '[After August 1944] your position ... was absolutely clear for the most stupid and persistent. You were what Goebbels was for propaganda or what Speer was in questions of armaments or previously Göring in the area of the air force. On 25 August 1944 you held the highest Reich Office and had the right to issue instructions.'[78] Brandt strongly disagreed; it would have meant that he had to shoulder the same amount of responsibility as Speer or Goebbels. He saw himself as a 'differential' (Differential), a kind of 'mediator' (Vermittler) between the various civil and military agencies, a concept which sounded too good to be true.[79] Although the various decrees could be interpreted in this way, Brandt knew that, in practice, things had been different. Allied interrogators had every reason to doubt Brandt's interpretation of the events:

Q: You had de facto the rights of a health ministry, although you were de jure not a health minister?

A: That's correct. I have given a radio interview in January 1944. There I was asked the question: 'So you are the top?' And I said: 'I am not the top, but I and my office are the differential for civil and army [services].'

Q: ... The gentlemen I have interviewed with regard to this point are men who for years have been in closest touch with you; I am not saying they were your staff, but they were people with whom you dealt on a professional basis, such as Handloser, Conti before he committed suicide, and others. From August 1944 everyone said 'Brandt is our boss', how one would say in America.

A: I was the boss, yes.

Q: ... Conti has told me and you really must believe me that after 25 August 1944 he was never again unsure about his position and his relation to you. He said: 'From then on Brandt is my boss.' At least you could be his boss, if you wanted it, you had the power to do so.[80]

The third Führer decree clarified the relation between Brandt and Conti unequivocally. Shortly after the war, Brandt had told his interrogators: 'As these things then still ran alongside one another and there was no clear right of command assigned to anyone, this new post of Reich Commissioner was instituted in 1944. Then things were cleared up.'[81] It was Brandt's way of saying that he was in total control. Zeitler later remarked that 'during 1944 and 1945 Brandt was truthfully an absolute dictator over all health and medical matters for the German nation.'[82] After considering resigning and taking up the position of Reich Sport Leader – which might have suited him – Conti was persuaded by Bormann and Himmler to stay. Both feared that the influence of the Nazi Party on the health system might otherwise further decrease, but they were also not willing to support him any longer. When, in October 1944, Walther Gross, the head of the Race Political Office (*Rassenpolitisches Amt*, RPA) of the Nazi Party, requested the Chancellery of the Führer to clarify the position, it turned out that the party had no further use for Conti and that Bormann had 'dropped Dr. Conti entirely'.[83] The ongoing power struggle between Brandt and Conti had left doctors and health officials uncertain about the leadership situation and was beginning to sap morale within the health care system more generally. On 7 October 1944, Kauffman told Brandt that when the press had announced his promotion to Reich Commissioner, it had failed to mention Conti's name. Brandt was probably 'unable to imagine what consequences such an announcement ... would have outside on the periphery because he was living on Olympus'.[84] Having achieved his goal, Brandt was willing to listen to criticism. However, his subsequent proposal to ask Hitler for a decree which would have given Conti the powers to intervene – under Brandt's overall supervision – in all matters of civilian health and welfare, and control the social security system, never went much beyond a draft stage. The collapse of the Third Reich made any further changes in the hierarchy of the regime pointless.[85]

Brandt never had time to enjoy his success. As often in history, hubris is followed by nemesis: those who overreach their zenith, if they are over-confident and inattentive to other forces, can easily be engulfed by a downward spiral. It was Brandt's fate that he failed to spot that he was the target of intrigue such as he himself had cultivated. On 1 September 1944, Goebbels began to ally himself with Bormann against the 'newcomers' at court, particularly against Brandt, Speer and Saur, whom Bormann described as 'an efficient mutual admiration society'.[86] Two days later, Goebbels told Bormann about the ongoing negotiations between Brandt and Conti. His attempts to mediate had so far failed. Both agreed that Brandt had to be punished for having been disloyal to Conti, and for having acted against the interests of the party. Goebbels' undisguised threat was a dark foreboding of what was to come. On 3 September, he confided to his diary: '[Brandt] either must be brought back under the discipline of the Party, or we declare war against him.'[87]

III. FALLING FROM GRACE

In September 1944, after years of tensions, Brandt attempted, but failed disastrously, to rid Hitler's court of Theodor Morell, Hitler's personal physician. As a result,

Brandt lost his position as Hitler's accompanying physician. Morell, whose personal habits seem to have left a great deal to be desired, had acquired one of the worst reputations among the medical men in the vicinity of the Führer. Brandt and others could not wait to see the back of a man whom they considered to be a fraud, but they underestimated Hitler's personal attachment to Morell. Hitler might also have felt that criticism of his personal physician was criticism of himself. Moreover, the constant air raids and medical emergencies made the existing administrative chaos in the health and welfare system more and more apparent. On 21 September, Goebbels remarked: 'Even the appointment of Professor Brandt has not put an end to the organisational mess. On the contrary, he has only added another new [organisation] to the many existing organisations.'[88] By the beginning of October 1944, Brandt's star was waning.

The post-war evidence surrounding the 'doctors' conflict' is not always reliable and sometimes rather questionable.[89] Those involved in the conflict, Brandt, Morell, Hasselbach, Giesing and others, certainly each had a vested interest in giving a biased account of the incident after the war. As a consequence, they told very different stories. The group around Brandt, Hasselbach and Giesing, the three doctors who launched the attack on Morell, painted the most unfavourable picture of Hitler's personal doctor. In particular, they accused him of poisoning Hitler with strychnine. They argued that it had been their medical duty to inform Hitler about the continued intake of overdoses of a common drug. According to their testimonies, however, the time had passed where Hitler would listen to reason. All three physicians were subsequently dismissed from their positions.

The existing evidence about the 'doctors' conflict' has to be treated with considerable caution. In 1945, when most of the interrogations took place, Morell was the ideal person to blame. He was not only totally discredited by large parts of the German medical establishment, but was a mentally and physically broken man who had made a poor impression on Allied interrogators. Most regarded him as a quack. Whilst sharing a prison cell with Brandt, Morell had told him with tears in his eyes: 'I wish I weren't I.'[90] The protocols of the investigation into Hitler's health became a central part of the literature; rarely did scholars challenge the credibility of post-war accounts by Brandt, Giesing and Hasselbach.[91] To understand what might have happened, however, we need to examine those sources that were written at the time of the incident itself, including Morell's personal notes.[92] His diary entries have the advantage of having been written during the hectic days when Brandt and others at Hitler's court had attempted to oust Morell.

The crisis occurred at the beginning of October 1944, but it had been in the making for weeks, if not months. Hans Killian, professor of surgery at Breslau, recalled that Brandt had discussed Hitler's health with him during a visit to his penicillin laboratory at the beginning of June 1944. While both men were walking back from the pathological institute to Killian's surgical clinic, Brandt told him that he had discovered that Morell was 'almost poisoning' the Führer with strychnine. Brandt suggested that Hitler's poor health, his shaking hands, in particular, were connected with Morell's prescription of stimulants and strychnine pills.[93] The subsequent discovery that Morell's penicillin ampoules, which he produced in a pharmaceutical company in Olmütz, did not contain penicillin added to the impression among leading German medical officials that Morell was a fraud.

Other evidence suggests that Brandt and his colleagues discovered that Hitler was being given large amounts of strychnine after Stauffenberg's failed assassination attempt on 20 July 1944. The ENT specialist Erwin Giesing made the potentially explosive discovery when he examined Hitler in the aftermath of the plot. Giesing first saw Hitler on 22 July to assess his eardrum which had been ruptured from the bomb explosion.[94] Fearing competition, Morell told Giesing that he alone was responsible for Hitler's health, and that no other physician was permitted to examine Hitler without his authorization. It may well be that the dispute between the two doctors started the crisis in the first place. Two days later, on 24 July, Giesing removed some of the pills from Hitler's breakfast table and interviewed Linge about them. It turned out that for at least two years Morell had been giving Hitler a proprietary drug known as 'Dr. Koesters Antigas Pills', which contained compounds of strychnine and belladonna. The dose which Hitler had been taking was way above the norm, apparently two to four pills with every meal, yet the maximum dose was said to be eight pills per day. Morell had given the pills to Linge, who gave them to Hitler on demand and without any medical supervision.

Giesing first told Hasselbach about his discovery, and he raced hotfoot to Brandt. All agreed that Morell's treatment was gradually poisoning Hitler with strychnine, and that his pills were responsible for causing constant stomach pains and a progressive discoloration of the skin. To confirm their theory, Brandt, Hasselbach and Giesing attempted to get hold of a blood and urine sample from Hitler. They knew that if the sample showed traces of strychnine poisoning, Morell's career would be at an end. Morell managed, however, to prevent any examination of Hitler's blood or urine. When, at the end of September 1944, Hitler fell critically ill, the three doctors feared that they might be held responsible and, perhaps in total panic, launched their strike to rid German medicine of the man almost everyone deplored for his greediness and lack of culture.

Since 1943, Hitler's health had been rapidly declining. In September 1944, he became increasingly unwell at the East Prussian headquarters of Rastenburg. In general, he could only force himself to the daily situation conference. With his phobias multiplying, Hitler began refusing to go out into the open air. He feared exercise and was beginning to suspect danger everywhere. In addition, he suffered from severe stomach cramps, general weakness, and nervous unrest in his left leg and hands. At the end of September, after a series of bad news about the military situation may have further weakened his general condition, Hitler suffered one of the worst trembling fits ever.[95] Weeks after the assassination attempt, Hitler was suddenly on the brink of collapse.[96] On 27 September 1944, he was laid to bed with a jaundice infection.

In a country like Germany under the Third Reich, the news that Hitler was gravely ill was a total catastrophe. Goebbels later noted that the country could

not have continued the war any further 'without the Führer'.[97] Total confusion
was rampant throughout the highest levels of government. Many, including
Göring, blamed Morell for the current crisis. Brandt raced to Führer headquarters
in order to monitor the situation over the next five days. Rumours of Hitler's
imminent death were spreading far and wide. To ensure that blame would fall upon
Morell, Brandt denounced him to Himmler, who had been intercepting Morell's
private correspondence for some time. At the same time, the Gestapo questioned
Morell's assistant in Berlin, asking whether he believed that Morell was capable
of systematically poisoning the Führer. The answer was negative: Morell was
characterized as too much of a coward.[98] By linking the strychnine of the Antigas
pills with Hitler's current illness, Brandt and others hoped to discredit Morell at
Führer headquarters. That strychnine could not cause jaundice, and that Hitler
had probably contracted infectious jaundice, which is not uncommon among
troops, was conveniently overlooked. This was not a rational debate among medical
scientists, rather a group of court physicians attempting to find a convenient person
to blame, in case Hitler were to die. They knew that for each of them the slightest
suggestion of poisoning Hitler would destroy their professional career. The 'doctors'
conflict' was a pre-emptive strike to divert attention from themselves.

On the evening of 3 October 1944, Brandt accused Morell of having attempted to
poison Hitler. He claimed that Hitler's current sickness was the result of strychnine
poisoning which had occurred as a result of taking sixteen pills a day over a couple
of months.[99] Morell defended himself by stating that he had not ordered the
exaggerated intake of pills, and that he had heard about it only recently. Brandt
also claimed that Hitler's condition had improved only because he had not taken
any more pills. Although Hitler had told Brandt on the same day that he himself
had decided to take the high dosage of pills, because he had believed they were like
charcoal tablets, Brandt continued to point the finger at Morell:

> Dr. Brandt then painted the devil on the wall and spoke of the responsibility which I had
> even though I had not prescribed the pills. He said: 'Do you think that anybody would
> believe your claim that you had not authorised these orders? Do you think that Himmler
> would have treated you differently from anybody else? So many are being hanged now
> – do you think your case would have been treated with sentimentality, rather than in
> a cold-blooded manner? If anything had happened to the F. can you imagine what
> would have followed? They would not have made v. Hasselbach responsible but you and
> probably even me. It is therefore best if I always be kept informed about what is going
> on here. I have the proof in my hands that this is a case of strychnine poisoning beyond
> any doubt. The strychnine trace must be seen in the urine. I frankly tell you that I have
> stayed here these last five days only because of the F.'s sickness.[100]

Morell knew that he had to act fast in order to save his skin. He told Hitler that
Brandt and some of the other escort physicians had accused him of negligence
because he had done neither an X-ray nor an examination of Hitler's stomach
contents. Hitler's response was one of furious rage. He told Morell that 'such

gentlemen' should come and see him, because he would tell them that Morell had suggested such examinations many times, but he had always refused.[101] Given Hitler's dislike of medical examination, together with his prudishness about showing his naked body, Morell's narrative seems plausible. Over the next two days, Morell continued to criticize the group of doctors in front of Hitler. On 5 October, shortly after midnight, he finally asked Hitler for a written statement that he had never given any prescriptions to take Antigas pills in great quantity per day, that he had advised him to have an X-ray and an examination of his stomach, and that Hitler had not given his permission. Hitler promised to write a letter to Morell:

> Concerning the utterances of Dr. Brandt, I remembered that he asserted that he could present proof of the presence of strychnine. Since he spoke of the eight tablets which had been taken with every meal, this remark did not strike me as important. Later he mentioned also one could show the presence of strychnine in the urine. (if str[ychnine] was in any medicine it is self-evident that one gets a positive result). Apparently Brandt had the urine sample which I sent to the Hospital Revier for examination … analysed for strychnine. While discussing these statements of Brandt's, the F. blew up: if Br. really maintained that I had ordered the taking of Antigas pills, since HE had already told him that he took them at his own decision. I answered: no, but I would be grateful if I had a statement from you for my own security.[102]

Morell's notes suggest that Brandt, Hasselbach and Giesing tried to relieve Morell from his post by exaggerating the toxicity of the Antigas pills. Wielding his new powers as Reich Commissioner, Brandt probably got hold of a urine sample which showed that Hitler was suffering from strychnine poisoning. Evidence also suggests that Hitler had believed that the pills had been charcoal tablets, and that he himself was responsible for the exaggerated intake. But by telling Morell that he could prove a case of strychnine poisoning, Brandt had given his game away. Now the tables could be turned, and Brandt be exposed as conspiring behind Morell's back. On 4 October 1944, Bormann was still complaining to his wife that Brandt was 'building up his Health Ministry to his heart's content' while Hitler was gravely ill.[103] A week later, Brandt was no longer Hitler's doctor.

On Sunday 8 October 1944, Hitler told Morell that Hasselbach had been sent back to Berlin, and that Brandt had been released from his duties at Führer headquarters.[104] From now on Brandt was to concentrate on his job as Reich Commissioner. Two days later, on 10 October, Bormann gleefully signed the document which released Brandt and Hasselbach from their duties as escort physicians of the Führer.[105] On the same day, he told his wife that Brandt would no longer act as Hitler's personal doctor.[106] It is safe to assume that Bormann and Goebbels felt a sense of *Schadenfreude*.[107] Bormann, in particular, was not prepared to concern himself any longer with either Brandt or Conti. 'To treat with kindness every Mächler, every Brandt or Conti, or others of that ilk – no, that's a terrible thought!' he told his wife.[108] Pleased with the outcome of the conflict, Goebbels remarked: 'The Führer has expressed his unlimited trust in Professor Morell. Now Brandt can do nothing else but focus on his work as General [sic]

Commissioner. He will soon realise how difficult it is, if he cannot constantly lean on the Führer.'[109]

IV. ON DEATH ROW

Brandt now experienced what it meant to be outside Hitler's inner circle. He knew that by being removed from Hitler's court he was being cut off from his patron and benefactor. After more than ten years of service, the unexpected dismissal as Hitler's doctor must have come as shock. Weeks before the war came to an end, Brandt was still bitter about the whole experience when he described Morell to one of Hitler's test pilots as an unhygienic, obnoxious, unprofessional and greedy quack.[110] Coupled with the disappointment of having misjudged Hitler's loyalty was the realization that his entire position depended entirely on Hitler's goodwill. Moreover, the barbaric nature of the regime could hardly be ignored any longer. Manfred von Brauchitsch, one of the most famous racing drivers of the 1930s, recalled meeting Brandt and Gebhardt late in the evening in a fashionable pub in Berlin in October 1944. The two men were apparently in a fatalistic mood, throwing the dice to see whether they would survive the war. 'And the prospects are bad', von Brauchitsch remembered Brandt saying.[111] Brandt's loyalty to the idea of National Socialism and his devotion to the Führer remained unchanged, however. Although Hitler had distanced himself from him, Brandt was not yet in a position to reflect on his relationship with the man whom he had followed for most of his adult life.

In late 1944, Brandt's situation turned from bad to worse. After a dispute with Goebbels in November, Brandt was left exposed to severe criticism from leading party officials. Goebbels told Brandt that the Nazi Party, who regarded him as a 'young swerver' (*junger Schlenker*), was unhappy with his performance, and that he would have to expect party political interferences in the future. Almost all the *Gauleiters*, Goebbels told Brandt, and Bormann too, were not only opposed to him but were waiting for revenge. Brandt later recalled that Goebbels left him in no doubt about his exposed position: 'I should be in no doubt that my appointment as Reich Commissioner for Health and Sanitation had happened against the will of Martin Bormann; Martin Bormann and all the Gauleiter were therefore against me. I would only have Hitler on my side and … that is very thin.'[112] Shortly afterwards, Brandt and his office were placed under surveillance by the regime.

By December 1944, the situation for medical supplies and pharmaceuticals had reached catastrophic proportions. As a last-ditch attempt to avoid the imminent collapse of the health system, Brandt began releasing the six-month strategic reserve which the industry had been obliged to store since the beginning of 1943.[113] The so-called 'Brandt Contingency' could only be released on his personal approval.[114] During the first three months of 1945, further releases were made. By the beginning of April 1945, the situation was becoming critical. Existing medical supplies could only last for another two to four months. The production of drugs and instruments had already collapsed. On 2 April 1945, Brandt travelled to the Führer bunker in Berlin to report to Hitler directly. Bormann, Morell and Goebbels were also present at the meeting. He told Hitler that 'more than 20 per cent of all essential medical items were totally depleted, that another 40 per cent of essential items would last two months and that the remainder would last four months', but only if the following three conditions were met: first, the transportation system were restored; second, sufficient guards were placed in front of storage depots to prevent looting, and ensure an equitable distribution of materials to the army, SS and civilians; finally, no additional requirements would be made on the existing stocks.[115] Hitler and his closest allies listened to Brandt in silence. No comments were made, and Brandt withdrew from the conference room. The moment the conference was over, however, the three men accused Brandt of defeatism. This time, Hitler was willing to listen.[116]

In the early hours of Monday 16 April 1945, Brandt was driven by an SS man from his apartment in Beelitz, sixty-five kilometres from Berlin, to the flat of SS-Gruppenführer Heinrich Müller, the head of the German secret police.[117] Hitler had ordered his arrest.[118] There, near the Wannsee, Brandt waited for hours. At 8 a.m., he was told that Müller was still waiting for documents. Two hours later, at 10 a.m., Brandt cancelled his appointments for the day. Müller told Brandt on the phone that there had been complaints against him, and that he would be asked to respond once he had received all the relevant documentation from the Reich and Party Chancelleries. Müller hoped that the matter could be resolved expeditiously. At this stage, Brandt was not yet concerned. At noon, Müller finally turned up and gave his apologies. He told Brandt that he had waited to receive a direct report from the Führer. From the interview which followed, and from the documents that were placed in front of him, it became apparent to Brandt that the accusations were extremely serious. He was accused of not having moved his office back to Berlin from Thuringia after the American military had occupied the region. He was also accused of having moved his family to Thuringia to ensure that they would be captured by the Americans. His frequent travels to the front were seen as a plan to defect to the Allies. In short, Hitler had lost trust in Brandt.[119]

It also transpired that Brandt and his office had been under police surveillance for months. At first, Brandt suspected another intrigue by Goebbels, Bormann or Morell. He defended himself by pointing out that his office had developed apart from most of the party agencies, and referred to some of the recent disputes between himself and Goebbels or Bormann. He also stressed the difficulties in establishing his office. Brandt's written report was immediately sent by special courier to the Führer bunker, where Hitler was waiting for an answer. After a brief delay, Müller returned in the afternoon, having received further instructions from Hitler and Bormann. Another interrogation followed about Brandt's contacts with the opposition, especially with those involved in the assassination attempt on Hitler's life. A second 'special report' was compiled, and Brandt was informed that Hitler had refused to accept the first. The situation was becoming increasingly serious. When Brandt mentioned in passing that he had discussed these conflicts with Rostock, Müller realized that there might be a witness on behalf of Brandt. Further cross-examinations continued long into the evening.[120]

The next morning, Brandt was told that Hitler had also rejected the second report. Müller now regarded his case as 'hopeless'. At noon it turned out that Hitler had convened a court martial, presided over by none other than Goebbels himself. The place and time of the court martial was fixed for 5 p.m. at Goebbels' private flat in Hermann-Göring-Straße. It all must have sounded rather grotesque to Brandt.[121] When he turned up at Goebbels' flat, most members of the 'court' were already present. These included SS-Obergruppenführer and head of the SS Head Office Gottlob Berger, Reich Youth Leader Arthur Axmann, SA-Obergruppenführer Grenz, and an unknown lawyer, dressed in civilian clothes. A representative of Bormann's Party Chancellery later joined the court martial. It transpired that Berger represented Goebbels as president of the court, and that he would conduct the trial in 'his way'.[122] Those present received Brandt's two reports which Hitler had marked with his personal comments such as 'lies', 'traitor' or 'pig'.[123] According to Brandt's post-war recollection, the following conversation then took place:

Berger: You have conducted your travels to the front to find somehow a hole [i.e. an opportunity to defect], did you not?

Brandt: If that is assumed, I believe that you might have to look at my previous work in the last months and years more closely.

Berger: Why?

Brandt: I believe that I have tried to fulfil my duty to the best of all my available energies.

Berger: (to the lawyer) This sentence will be taken into the protocol. If you, Mr. Brandt, are of the opinion that you have fulfilled your duty, I can tell you only that this is entirely untrue.

Brandt: Why?

Berger: The Führer is such a great man that no one can ever claim … to have done enough. If you now claim to have done your duty, then this shows that in reality your duty, which in regard to the Führer can never be fulfilled, has never been fulfilled. That also means, at the same time, that you actually did not know your assignment.

Brandt: This is where my comprehension stops. I refuse to make any further answer.[124]

Brandt's narrative has to be treated with caution. Was he really as rational and relaxed as he wanted to appear in retrospect? The literature about the last days of the Third Reich seems to suggest, however, that the regime was spiralling out of any control, and that Hitler was increasingly becoming delusional, highly irrational and erratic in his decision-making. After the hearing was over, Brandt was brought back to Gestapo headquarters at the Prinz-Albrecht-Straße. Speer seems to have attempted a last-minute intervention, but without any success. In the meantime everyone, including Goebbels, had voted for the death sentence after receiving the report of the court martial, and after Hitler had confirmed the sentence by putting his signature under the order of execution. The decision was relayed by telephone to Müller at the Gestapo. A copy of the execution order was also sent by courier to Himmler, who had set up his headquarters in his train 'Steiermark' at Hohenlychen.[125] On 18 April, Brandt was taken to the Gestapo prison in Potsdam. After Müller had handed him the verdict, Brandt was told that he would be shot the next morning, 19 April 1945. Lammers from the Reich Chancellery had already published the order for his execution which had been authenticated by the state secretary, Kritzinger. According to some witnesses, Goebbels even announced Brandt's imminent execution for high treason over the radio.[126]

The next day, Brandt's execution was put on hold for one day. For some unknown reason, it had been decided that Rostock had to be heard as a witness.[127] Meanwhile, Rostock was on his way to Garmisch-Partenkirchen. Given that almost the entire German communication systems were by now destroyed, he could not be contacted by telephone, telegram or radio. Consequently, the execution of Brandt's death sentence was postponed from one day to the next. Finally, on 22 April 1945, Müller told him that Hitler had issued a special order to find Rostock, and that he would soon be on his way to Berlin. At the same time, hundreds of Nazi officials decided that the game was up. The following days saw a whole wave of suicides, among them men like de Crinis, and Grawitz who killed himself in his house in Babelsberg. The Russians were now closing in from the south of Berlin. To avoid capture, the Gestapo office was relocated to Schwerin in the north of Germany. Brandt was transferred to Schwerin as well.[128]

Speer's version of events differs quite significantly from Brandt's narrative. According to Speer, Himmler had told him that Rostock had first to be interrogated before the execution could be carried out, but had added ominously: 'This witness is not going to be found.'[129] Klopfer also told Speer that the arrest had been masterminded by Bormann, and was meant as a blow against Speer. On Speer's notorious last trip to Berlin on 22 April, where Hitler was, by then, hiding deep beneath the Reich Chancellery, he stopped at Sigrön, an estate near Wilsnack, which he had built for friends years earlier. There he met with one of Brandt's assistants, who told him that Brandt was being held as a prisoner in a villa near the Wannsee. His idea, Speer later claimed, was to use his authority and liberate Brandt in the confusion which reigned in Berlin. When he eventually phoned Berlin from Kyritz, it turned out that Himmler had transferred Brandt to Northern Germany.[130]

The existing evidence suggests, however, that it was Speer, rather than Himmler, who had a vested interest in Brandt staying alive. Speer's line of argument as outlined in *Inside the Third Reich* needs to be treated with care. We know that on 22 April 1945 the south-west of Berlin was on the brink of surrender to the advancing Russian forces, and that the Gestapo office was hastily evacuated to Schwerin. Brandt was kept there for about a week. Then, on 28 April 1945, Bormann sent a radio signal, ordering that Brandt was to be transferred further north, to the Gestapo prison in Kiel, for execution. According to Brandt it was on the same day that the Gestapo office received a telephone call from Speer, who 'on behalf of Himmler' countermanded the previous order, instructing the officers that the execution order should under no circumstance be carried out.[131] Himmler does not seem to have been informed about Speer's intervention. When given two conflicting orders, the general procedure for Gestapo officers was to carry out the orders of their direct superior, and that was Himmler. In the confusion, they decided to take Brandt wherever they went, whilst waiting to receive further instructions. Travelling first to Lübeck and later to a place near Rendsburg, Brandt remained with this group of Gestapo men until 2 May 1945. By then Hitler had been pronounced dead.

Why Speer might have altered his story in retrospect is difficult to say. He may simply have misremembered. Another possibility is that he did not wish to be associated too closely with Himmler, and seem to have been able to give orders 'on behalf of Himmler' during the last days of the regime. Be this as it may, the fact remains that a number of leading Nazi politicians, Himmler and Speer included, were under the impression that Brandt could be of use to them in the future. On the whole, Brandt seems to have had extraordinary luck. The collapse of the Third Reich had unfolded so fast that no real coordination had been possible any more.

The psychological stress of life on death row must have been tremendous for Brandt. The experience left him extremely bitter. He also felt 'seriously humiliated' (*schwere Kränkung*), he later told Alexander, one of his interrogators. It was apparently the only humiliation he ever experienced in his entire life.[132] To die for the nation and the fatherland might have been one thing for Brandt, but to be sentenced to death because he had tried to ensure the continued production of medical supplies was another matter.[133] At least this is how Brandt wanted to see his role after the war. Rather late in the day, he was also beginning to question Hitler's murderous regime. A couple of months later, he told Allied interrogators that from 'that afternoon' onwards, after he had been sentenced to death, life was pleasant, 'just to be alive another day and to enjoy the sun, birds etc.'[134]

On 2 May 1945, an SS officer from the 'Dönitz government', which had established its headquarters in Flensburg, appeared in Rendsburg with a letter from Speer who ordered the immediate release of Brandt. Travelling to Flensburg, Brandt joined the remaining members of the Nazi government. For a couple of days, he stayed on board the S.S. *Patria*, and later Speer provided him with lodgings at Castle Glücksburg. On arrival, he learned that his office of Reich Commissioner had been dissolved and integrated into parts of the civil and military administration. Shortly after his arrest, Hitler had issued an order to draft a law to dissolve the office of Reich Commissioner. Signed and sealed by State Secretary Kritzinger in the absence of Lammers, the law was announced on 20 April 1945, Hitler's last birthday. For Brandt, this was proof that it had all been a conspiracy against him personally. Months later he was still deeply disappointed: '[Because of this senseless decision, and] after so much sacrificial effort, my office, my work and even my staff were put out of operation without any sense and plan.'[135]

In the meantime, Dönitz and his ministers were living an illusion. On 8 May Germany had unconditionally surrendered. At first the British, who controlled

North Germany, did not know what to do with the Dönitz government, and decided to leave it for the time being. While Speer was attending his daily 'cabinet meetings', and discussing the 'non-existent plans for a non-existent country' on brightly coloured chairs around a brightly coloured table in a former schoolroom, American interrogators from the US Strategic Bombing Survey began questioning him about his role in the Nazi regime in the afternoons and evenings. Their assignment was to find out as much strategic and military intelligence as possible. Brandt's role, at this point, seems to have been negligible, both for the German government and for the Allies. He was neither allowed to attend the phoney 'cabinet meetings', nor had he been identified as an important member of Hitler's government. On the morning of 23 May 1945, the Allied governments ended the surreal situation and arrested the entire Dönitz government, Brandt included. The Third Reich had ceased to exist.

10

Nuremberg

For a long time the question of what to do with Germany after the war was left open.[1] It was not until the Casablanca Conference in January 1943 that the Allies declared that nothing short of Germany's unconditional surrender was acceptable, and began to formulate a concerted policy of occupation; they planned to assume supreme authority to prevent a repetition of the failure to punish German war criminals after the First World War.[2] Since 1942, the punishment of war crimes had been a major war aim, formulated and endorsed by the representatives of nine governments in exile, in the St James's Declaration. Its novel force lay in making not only those who had committed the crimes responsible, but in laying ultimate responsibility on those who had governed, ordered, supervised or commanded those who had carried out the crimes. The Declaration was a major warning to the Germans that international action was envisaged to bring war criminals and the Nazi leadership to account. How this goal would be achieved remained unclear. No comprehensive lists of names of alleged war criminals and no investigative or judicial machinery to put such pledges into action existed at that stage.

In early November 1943, the three Allied Foreign Ministers reached agreement in Moscow to punish Nazi atrocities by holding war crimes trials in and by the countries where the atrocities had been committed. In the Declaration of Moscow, the Allies committed themselves to the decision that the major Axis criminals whose crimes had no particular geographical location would be judged by 'joint declaration' by the Allied governments, while those responsible for specific massacres and executions would be sent back 'to the countries in which their abominable deeds were done in order that they may be judged and punished according to the laws of those liberated countries'.[3]

The Moscow Declaration became the theoretical cornerstone for Allied war crimes policy after the war. Its powerful rhetoric was also intended to send a warning signal to the German soldier in the field. But what exactly it meant, whether wholesale shooting of some ten thousand officers, as suggested by Stalin, drumhead court martials, summary executions, a series of show trials, or a political indictment and executive action by the international community, remained open to question. Another option was to do nothing at all, to take the moral high ground, and wait until those who had suffered under the regime took the law into their own hands and lynched the war criminals. For lynching was what many, including the Allied soldiers liberating the camps, expected – and feared – would be the mass instinct after the war.[4]

By the end of the war, the Allied governments had not progressed much beyond the St James's and Moscow Declarations. Apart from two vaguely defined categories of criminals, minor and major, the question as to how the major criminals were to be punished, and on what kind of evidence, continued to be ignored. War crimes had relatively low priority in the complex political battles over the shape of the post-war world, especially over Allied occupation of Germany, which included contentious issues of massive social restructuring, demilitarization and dismemberment. This changed rapidly when the US and other armies advanced further into German territory, captured the concentration camps, and discovered that hundreds of thousands of people had been worked, starved or gassed to death. The mass murder of an entire people, of children, women and the elderly, had been planned and calculated. Jews, Gypsies and Slavs, prisoners of war, soldiers and civilians had been killed, not in the heat of war, but systematically, in a concerted and bureaucratically organized fashion.[5] Masses of documents chronicled the organized plunder of whole nations, slave labour, and wholesale barbarities of previously unseen and unimaginable proportions. Tens of thousands of handicapped patients had been killed in places such as Hadamar near Limburg, Hartheim near Linz, Grafeneck near Munsingen, Sonnenstein near Dresden, Bernburg near Halle, and in Brandenburg on the Havel. From every corner of the former Reich, details of atrocities left both investigators and soldiers in total shock. But there were few revelations which outraged the American public as much as the news of the Malmedy massacre, the murder of seventy-two unarmed American soldiers at a road crossing in the Belgian town of Malmedy in December 1944 during the Ardennes offensive. Those responsible for this cold-blooded killing spree were members of the 1st SS-Tank-Division 'Leibstandarte Adolf Hitler', who were sworn to total secrecy over these acts: a fact which made it extremely difficult for investigators to find out what had actually happened. The public demand for justice to be exacted for such horrific crimes carried substantial political weight, and it was therefore hardly surprising that forty-three out of seventy-three defendants were later sentenced to death.[6] It was the efficiency of cold-blooded mass murder which many felt made swift and international action paramount.

While journalists and newsreel crews alerted the world to slave labour and the horrors of the camps, Western governments were suddenly waking up to the immediacy of the war crimes problem. Following the liberation of Buchenwald in April 1945, at the time when Brandt was being tried by Hitler's court martial, newspapers were reporting on piles of corpses, gassing facilities and the mass murder of mental patients. Investigations into the 'euthanasia' programme were being stepped up. Eyewitness accounts and testimonies from survivors gave graphic details of torture and degradation to a public struggling to comprehend the extent and brutality of the crimes. The first photographs of the conditions in the camps were believed to have been manipulated for propaganda purposes. Survivors were thought to be exaggerating. But after weeks of sustained and broad press coverage, the US House of Representatives called for the United Nations War Crimes Commission (UNWCC), which previously had little status and was almost impotent, to speed up its work. Specially arranged tours of Bergen-Belsen, Buchenwald and Dachau for newspaper editors, and visits by senators and congressmen, further strengthened public sentiment. By the beginning of May, *Life* reported under the headline 'Atrocities' that the capture of German concentration camps piled up 'evidence of barbarism that reaches the low point of human degradation'.[7]

The camps also revealed chilling evidence of some of the most gruesome medical experiments. At Dachau, physicians, such as the notorious Sigmund Rascher, had conducted cold-water experiments to test the survival time for German fighter pilots shot down over the English Channel, and to establish what kinds of protective clothing and rewarming methods were most effective. In other experiments, prisoners were placed in pressure chambers to see how the body would react when pilots had to bail out at high altitude, and to document their survival rates. At Auschwitz, physicians had experimented with mass sterilization by means of X-rays, to find our whether it would be possible to sterilize two to three million Jews earmarked for German factory work. In Ravensbrück, Karl Gebhardt and Fritz Fischer had performed sulphonamide drug experiments to prove that the drugs could not prevent sometimes fatal gas gangrene infections.[8] In Buchenwald and Dachau, prisoners were infected with typhus and malaria, and in other camps maltreated with biological and chemical warfare agents.[9] Despite such irrefutable evidence, all twenty-three defendants, including Brandt, later pleaded 'not guilty' at the Nuremberg Doctors' Trial.

The mass of evidence pouring out of Germany left Allied military officials with little choice but to face the realities of German occupation. They had to decide what to do with the major war criminals once they had been apprehended or had surrendered themselves. They also had to investigate the crimes, and collect as much hard evidence as possible to mount war crimes trials. One of the central preconditions was gathering and interrogating the leaders of the regime.

Finding the accused turned out to be a daunting task. Allied prosecutors were looking for needles in a haystack. British intelligence traced war criminals under the code-names 'Operation Fleacomb' and 'Operation Haystack'.[10] Whereas some doctors, such as the notorious Josef Mengele, had gone into hiding, the passage of time made it more likely that others might escape the net of criminal prosecution by being released from prisoner of war camps. Some of the major criminals accused of medical crimes had committed suicide or were thought to be dead. To dispose of vital evidence, Himmler had ordered the execution of Sigmund Rascher shortly before the end of the war.[11] The rate of suicides in the weeks leading up to Germany's defeat had also been high. Many ordinary Germans and party functionaries had decided to end their lives. At the end of April 1945, Grawitz had killed himself by detonating a bomb in his house in Berlin-Babelsberg. Maximinian de Crinis, head of the psychiatric clinic at the Charité and one of the organizers of the 'euthanasia' operation, shot himself on the outskirts of Berlin. Even in custody, some of the doctors with blood on their hands decided to escape prosecution. In October 1945, Leonardo Conti, the Reich Health Leader, hanged himself in his cell at Nuremberg.[12] All three would have been defendants in the Doctors' Trial. Some

US newspapers called them the 'missing defendants'.[13] It is therefore not surprising that those in the dock, including Brandt, later attempted to shift responsibility onto them.

Others physicians were fortunate enough to escape attention, at least for a time. Doctor Fritz Fischer, for example, who had experimented with sulphonamide drugs on young Polish girls at the Ravensbrück camp, was overlooked while Allied investigators arrested his namesake, the historian Dr Fritz Fischer, the future world-famous author of *Griff nach der Weltmacht*. It took Fischer, the historian, a considerable amount of time and effort to convince the authorities that his identity had actually been mistaken. A month later, on the evening of 4 August 1945, the 5th Counter Intelligence Corps arrested the Ravensbrück Doctor Fischer in Rosche, near Uelzen.[14] Fischer was first transferred to Neumünster, then to Nuremberg to serve as a witness in the trial of the major war criminals, the International Military Tribunal (IMT). By September, he told his wife that he was 'under arrest to answer for actions' which he had carried out during the war 'on orders from above'. This became his standard line of defence. He was in good spirits and lectured her about God, humanity and purity as the basis for the education of their children.[15] Brandt later told an investigator: 'I have been together with Fischer in a camp for several weeks this year and I can only say that he is a marvellous person'.[16]

Fischer was part of the Hohenlychen Group. This group included the head of the SS sanatorium in Hohenlychen and Fischer's superior, Karl Gebhardt, who was arrested on 16 May in Flensburg-Mürwick and brought to Nuremberg as a witness in the IMT. His staff member and assistant in the criminal experiments was Herta Oberheuser. On the evening of 20 July 1945, she was arrested by the British Secret Service in Stocksee, near Ploen, and brought to Bad Oeynhausen, where the British had established their war crimes headquarters. She also appeared as a witness at the IMT before being charged with multiple crimes, the only woman in the Doctors' Trial.

Two months earlier, on 20 May, the American Counter-Intelligence Corps (CIC) arrested a man called Hermann Ober, near Stuttgart.[17] In June, Ober was discharged from a prisoner of war camp, but again taken into custody in Traunstein and later in Moosburg, where his identity was eventually established: he was Victor Brack, a bicycle enthusiast with no medical expertise whatsoever, and one of the leading figures in the organization of the 'euthanasia' programme, when he had used the pseudonym 'Jennerwein'. Using expertise he had gathered in the 'euthanasia' programme, Brack had proposed to Himmler in 1942 that two to three million out of the ten million Jews consigned to death should be sterilized and used as slave labourers. He had every reason to disguise his identity and lie about his involvement in the murder of hundreds of thousands.

On the same day that Brack, alias Ober, was captured, the 3rd Counter-Intelligence Group arrested Rudolf Brandt in Bremervörde, North Germany.[18] Brandt was chief of Himmler's personal staff and the coordinating link in some of the most atrocious medical experiments. The fact that Himmler's right-hand man had almost the same name and position in the SS hierarchy as Karl Brandt cost them both dear. It meant that Allied intelligence was particularly suspicious and vigilant whenever the name Brandt cropped up.

Then there was the air force group. They were physicians who had initiated, supervised and participated in various Dachau medical experiments, such as the director of the Berlin-based Research Institute for Aviation, Siegfried Ruff, his assistant researcher and collaborator in the experiments, Hans-Wolfgang Romberg, Hermann Becker-Freyseng and the Austrian doctor Wilhelm Beiglböck. Beiglböck had been arrested by the British during March in Linz and was about to be put on trial in Graz when the Nuremberg war crimes authorities became aware of his existence.[19] Romberg was arrested in October 1945 at his home in Gilzum near Braunschweig, but Ruff and Becker-Freyseng enjoyed their freedom and considerable status as aviation scientists until shortly before the trial. Both were employed by the US army air force at the Aero-Medical Centre in Heidelberg until the authorities became aware of this potential embarrassment.[20] In mid-September 1946, the CIC finally arrested both of them and brought them to Nuremberg.[21] Another physician imprisoned as one of the first suspects responsible for the Dachau experiments was August Weltz. On 21 June 1945, he was arrested by CIC in Munich and detained in the same prison complex in Dachau where the subjects of their experiments had once suffered.

There was at least one group of potential defendants that was easy to find: the members of the last German government under Admiral Dönitz, which had established its headquarters in the North German town of Flensburg in Schleswig-Holstein, near the Danish border. Within a week of taking office, Dönitz had offered Germany's unconditional surrender,[22] but throughout most of May his government was allowed to exist, despite having no territory or function. Although military government had been imposed around 10 May in Flensburg in the north of Germany,[23] the Supreme Headquarters Allied Expeditionary Forces – SHAEF for short – had a conceptual problem: how did one handle the surrender of a government that had ceased to exist as a consequence of its unconditional surrender? On 14 May, Churchill told the Foreign Office that he neither knew nor cared about Dönitz, except that he was 'a useful tool' to the Allies. This would have to be written off against his war crimes: 'The question for us is has he any power to [make] the Germans lay down and hand over weapons quickly without any more loss of life? We cannot go running round into every German slum and argue with every German that it is his duty to surrender or we will shoot him.' Five days later this position had become untenable. Public pressure and Russian fears that the British might collaborate with the Germans forced Churchill to change tack. On 19 May, he gave the go-ahead to arrest the so-called German government: 'All this should be very popular with the papers right now. It seems a notable step in making sure we have no one to deal with in Germany.'[24]

Among those arrested by the British forces were Lutz Graf Schwerin von Krosigk, the former Reich Finance Minister, Wilhelm Stuckart and Leonardo Conti, both state secretaries in the RMdI, and Karl Brandt, the future chief defendant at the Nuremberg Doctors' Trial. Brandt had reported to General Hucks of the Allied

Commission in Flensburg and had found accommodation with his friend Albert Speer in a luxurious sixteenth-century waterside castle in Glücksburg.[25] Speer had accepted an invitation from the Duke of Mecklenburg and Holstein to reside for the time being at his magnificent home, a few miles outside Flensburg and in close proximity to Dönitz's headquarters. Throughout May, Speer was comprehensively interrogated by members of the US Strategic Bombing Survey (USSBS).[26] On the morning of 23 May, a unit of British soldiers armed with anti-tank guns finally surrounded Glücksburg Castle to arrest Speer and his staff. Whether Brandt was arrested inside the castle or in his nearby living quarters is not known, but his detention report lists the same time of arrest as that of Speer: 9.30 a.m.[27] After a brief and confusing search, Speer was found shaving in the bathroom, looking 'unhappy and tired': American interrogators had interviewed him all night about Hitler's last days.[28] Both Brandt and Speer were taken into custody and brought to Flensburg prison, where all prisoners were thoroughly strip-searched for poison capsules, a treatment some of the former high-ranking ministers later described as 'undignified'. Three of Brandt's main staff members and colleagues – Paul Rostock, head of the surgical clinic at the Charité, Siegfried Handloser, Chief of Army Medical Services, and Kurt Blome, Deputy Reich Health Leader – had already been arrested several days earlier in Garmisch, Flensburg and Munich respectively.[29] Later, all found themselves in the dock at Nuremberg.

The first weeks after his arrest in the spring of 1945 must have been deeply depressing for Brandt. He had fallen from presiding over German medicine to being a pawn in the game of international politics, and faced the prospect of being charged as a war criminal. Together with the Dönitz government, Brandt was first flown to Luxembourg and then whisked to Mondorf to be reunited with the leading politicians, diplomats and military men of the Third Reich in the prison camp sardonically called 'Ashcan'.[30] A photograph taken shortly after his arrest shows Brandt with Dönitz and Speer as they are boarding the plane.[31] Brandt's registration number was 31G 350020, his position being recorded as 'Reich Commissioner of Sanitation and Health and Hitler's personal surgeon'.[32] The Allies had selected the small town of Mondorf near the River Mosel on the border with Germany for security reasons. Located on a plateau, the town was strategically well placed to be controlled and guarded by the army against all kinds of unwelcome visitors. Made up of vineyards and patches of woodland, the surrounding countryside could be observed from almost every position in the town. Military planners anticipated attacks from hardline SS fanatics, including suicide squads, and feared that released concentration camp victims might go on the rampage and take revenge on their former tormentors. Every possible scenario to free or kill the top prisoners, including Brandt, was carefully considered, including rescue missions by air or tunnel.

As a spa resort, Mondorf also provided good housing for the military in comfortable villas and half a dozen small hotels. Before the war its guests had been mainly middle-class Luxembourgeois and Belgians, and some French. Now it was full of Americans. It was a town with nice shady streets and a beautiful park. Most importantly, though, it provided the perfect accommodation for the former Nazi leadership: the Grand Hotel. Formerly a centre for thermal cures for rheumatism and liver complaints, the hotel was rapidly transformed into a prison camp. It was a long, graceless, boomerang-shaped white building on six floors, combining architectural features of art deco with a plain stucco facade; at the front stood a waterless fountain and a pool with a water-nymph in the middle. Access could be easily restricted by blocking the only road leading to the hotel. Slopes on three sides offered perfect conditions to overlook all activities in the hotel grounds and in the adjacent park. Before Brandt and the other top prisoners arrived, any fading luxury was replaced by camp beds, straw mattresses (except for Göring, who was bedridden) and straight-backed chairs, and the windows were fitted with shatterproof glass and bars.[33] Sixteen booths provided spaces for interrogation. The prison was under the command of Colonel Burton C. Andrus, a meticulous, dark-haired, bespectacled and unobtrusive go-by-the-book officer, who was detested by many of the defendants for his unwillingness to recognize their former rank and status.[34] His main objective was to be fair and treat all of the defendants in the same way. He later became Commandant of Nuremberg prison. For Andrus, Mondorf was a powder-keg from the security point of view, and might go off at any given moment.[35] He immediately ordered floodlights, an electric alarm system and new, trained guards. An airstrip was built and top-security teleprinters were installed. Surrounded by a double stockade of barbed-wire fence fifteen to twenty feet high, covered with a greenish-yellow camouflage cloth, and four watchtowers armed with machine guns, the Grand Hotel became under Andrus's direction a high-security complex.[36] Once the sergeant on duty told an applicant for admission that he needed 'a pass from God, and someone to verify the signature'.[37] For John Kenneth Galbraith from the USSBS it was one of those rare prisons which it was 'far easier to leave than to enter'.[38]

Here were the leaders of the former Reich. Angry, arrogant, cold and fearsome, these men had dominated German politics for years. Apart from 'technicians' like Brandt and Speer, the Allies had imprisoned politicians including Robert Ley, the head of the *Arbeitsfront*, who looked like a frightened groundhog,[39] and Joachim von Ribbentrop, the Foreign Minister, who, according to Goebbels, had bought his name, married his money and swindled his way into politics. Ribbentrop was utterly devoid of intellect or eloquence, and his performance later in court was uniformly regarded as very poor.[40] Then there were the military men in their uniforms, men like Field Marshal Wilhelm Keitel and Colonel General Alfred Jodl, the 'nodding donkeys', as Speer would later call them, because they had carried out or passed on whatever monstrous orders Hitler had given them. All ribbons, decorations or insignia of rank had been peeled off their once-impressive uniforms, leaving unfaded blotches and holes where once symbols of status and power had hung. After his arrest, Jodl had commented bitterly: 'Formerly when we lost a war we laid down our swords, traded you a province and were friends. Now you seek to destroy us.'[41] Grand Admiral Karl Dönitz and Field Marshal Albert Kesselring, the last commander of the Western Front, and Julius Streicher, the country's fanatical anti-Semite, were there too. The latter appeared to suffer from the 'occupational disease of a professional Nazi'.[42] He would walk normally with the others for an hour and then, without warning, suddenly turn around to the railing, stiffen to attention and throw out his arm in the Nazi salute. After a few minutes, once the imagined SS battalion had stomped by, he would relax, lower his arm, and walk away, leaving his prison companions – and some of the guards – feeling uneasy.[43]

Most of the future Nuremberg defendants were not what one could call bookish people, rather they were organizers and men of military and political power. Stripped of their positions, they quickly lost their sense of purpose, often drowning in feelings of self-pity, depression or plain boredom. Göring had not only arrived with a whole army of monographed suitcases, a red hatbox, red fingernails and toenails, but also with 20,000 paracodeine tablets to fight his morphine addiction.[44] He also brought three hidden cyanide capsules, two of which remained hidden until he used them after his trial in October 1946.[45] For Allied investigators he proved nonetheless 'a most useful guide' to plundered works of art.[46] Hans Frank, the former governor of Poland, wearing 'only lace panties', was deep in melancholia and needed constant attention after his abortive suicide attempt.[47] Others looked rather shabby and repellent: unshaven, without belts, neckties, watches or shoelaces to prevent them from committing suicide. On arrival, each prisoner was stripped naked and given a complete physical examination by the prison doctor. Suicide weapons had been sewn into uniforms or concealed in the heels of shoes; some had razor blades fixed with tape to the soles of their feet.

When General Ivone Kirkpatrick and General Thorne, Commander-in-Chief in Norway, came to visit Mondorf, they found the leadership of the Third Reich sunbathing in cane chairs on the large veranda.[48] Their arrival sparked off a sudden interest among the 'hotel guests', except for Dönitz, who sat huddled and sulking in his chair. 'Get up, that man!' roared one of the nearby corporals, and the last leader of the Reich shuffled to his feet. Talking to von Ribbentrop about his role in Hitler's Germany, Kirkpatrick found the former Foreign Minister boasting of his one-time influence. 'I was a man of considerable importance,' he said, although at Nuremberg he tried to prove at great length his insignificance in the Third Reich.[49] He was probably right in the second instance. Leaving aside the theatrical scenery, Kirkpatrick felt that the oppressive atmosphere matched that of a 'criminal lunatic asylum'.[50] Others expressed similar views. Galbraith, for one, shared the opinion of his escorting pilot, a young second lieutenant. 'Who'd have thought', the latter mused while piloting the plane back to Eisenhower's headquarters in Frankfurt, 'that we were fighting this war against a bunch of jerks?'[51]

In the immediate aftermath of the war, many Allied officials were curious to catch a glimpse of the top Nazis. For Victor Cavendish-Bentinck, chairman of the British Joint Intelligence Committee, 'Ashcan' showed the Germans 'at their worst'.[52] After his visit with Kirkpatrick in June, it was decided to allow the defendants to have their ties, braces and shoelaces back. In rather robust terms, Cavendish-Bentinck stated the reason for this temporary change in prison policy: 'Personally, I cannot understand why elaborate precautions should be taken to prevent these people committing suicide. It will save us a great deal of trouble and maybe eventual ridicule, if all the inmates of "Ashcan" were to commit mass suicide.'[53] For certain quarters of the British establishment, mass suicide at 'Ashcan' would have solved one of their most pressing problems; throughout the war men like Cavendish-Bentinck had been extremely reluctant to deal with the war crimes issue effectively. As late as 1943, he was of the opinion that the Jews were exaggerating Nazi atrocities 'in order to stoke us up'.[54] Now he was 'puzzled' as to whether posterity would view some of the defendants as criminals, and uncertain whether a case against others, for instance Göring, could be established. Andrus had also told Allied officials that he regarded all the inmates as 'nuts', a view Cavendish-Bentinck certainly shared: 'What is really mortifying is that such nasty and in every respect third-rate creatures should have caused so much trouble for five years,' he told the Foreign Office.[55]

Until August 1945, a total of fifty-two prominent Nazi figures were interned at 'Ashcan'. Fifteen of them would eventually be tried at the IMT. Of the twenty-three defendants in the subsequent Doctors' Trial, Brandt was the only one who had been interned at 'Ashcan'. Here, extraordinary scenes took place between the officials of the former Nazi regime, especially between Göring and Dönitz, both of whom claimed formal succession to the leadership. Major conflicts could only be avoided by keeping the two physically apart. They had to be prevented from entering a room at the same time. During dinner they would preside at different tables. In such a charged atmosphere, it was not surprising that Brandt was sometimes involved in the tension. One day, when he was casually talking about the mountains and how sad he was that he had lost his house there, Göring snapped at him over the table: 'Oh, come on, don't you talk! What possible reason can you have to complain when you had so little? But I, who had so much, think what it means to me.'[56] Dönitz sitting nearby only murmured to his neighbour: 'Yes, and all stolen.'[57]

To understand Brandt's reaction to Allied custody, and later at Nuremberg, we need to turn our attention to the events of spring 1945. Within a short period of time, less than six weeks, almost all the elements of Brandt's former value system had totally disintegrated. Three weeks before the collapse of Nazi Germany, Brandt was personally sentenced to death by Hitler for not having done his duty to the Führer ('traitor to the Führer'), for having spent time at the front in order to defect ('traitor to the Fatherland') and for having left his family at a place where they would be captured by the enemy ('traitor to the family'). Such accusations, however false or absurd, together with the subsequent show trial and death sentence, hammered home the message that Hitler had irrevocably distanced himself from him. The feeling of deep disappointment and pain, coupled with fury at having been sentenced to death after almost eleven years of loyal service, were crucial factors in Brandt's beginning to distance himself emotionally from Hitler. In their first interview with Brandt, Allied interrogators noted that 'since that afternoon' he had lived only to enjoy each passing hour and day: 'The death sentence as a reward for his attempt to re-establish German medicine on a professional level was extremely bitter, far more than to die.'[58] At the same time, Brandt was trying to cope with feelings of guilt about his family, trying to re-establish relations with his wife and son, and to justify his role in the regime. Brandt's first priority was to show that he had not committed a treasonable act towards his family or towards the nation as a whole.

The weeks following his arrest offered little hope. Almost the entire leadership of the state, including Hitler, had committed suicide and thus, in Brandt's view, shirked responsibility for the endless misery their politics had caused.[59] While unimaginable crimes of unseen proportions were revealed day after day, there was little left that the regime could be given credit for in retrospect. What is more, Brandt knew that he was likely to be indicted by the Allies because he had been a member of the Nazi government, especially if his links with the murders of the handicapped were discovered. Brandt had a limited number of choices: He could commit suicide, an option which he regarded as cowardice. Remaining loyal to the regime and defending its policies was no real option, because the Nazi state had obviously been barbarous and criminal, and had sentenced him to death. For the second time within weeks, Brandt now faced the prospect of standing trial for his life. The only viable alternative Brandt saw was to take responsibility for the 'ideal' of National Socialism and the 'ideal' of euthanasia, while at the same time denying any involvement in the execution of these policies.

What triggered Brandt to position himself as a fundamental idealist in post-war Germany were the events of spring 1945, rather than cool reflection about some of Hitler's outrageous policy decisions. Hitler's death sentence on him and the Führer's subsequent suicide allowed Brandt to distance himself emotionally from his patron but to believe in the righteousness and purity of his ideal. This included Hitler's apparently idealistic intentions.

Relying solely on Brandt's statements about 'euthanasia', made between 1945 and 1948 during Allied interrogations or while being questioned at Nuremberg, can easily lead to a distorted view of his role in the killing programme. Brandt had never intended to disclose anything about it. By drawing particular attention to his work as Reich commissioner he intended to keep his involvement in, and responsibility for, the killing operation secret.

For Speer it may have been 'a moment's pleasure' to find Brandt in Mondorf, but it soon became clear that the latter was anything but optimistic about the future. When walking with Speer in the hotel grounds, Brandt confided to his friend that if the Americans found out what he had been involved in, 'It'll all be over for me.'[60] 'I don't think a death penalty was in anybody's mind then,' Speer told the journalist Gitta Sereny years later, but then added, 'or, now that I remember Brandt's voice, *did* he perhaps think of it?'[61] In September 1945, British interrogators only sensed that Speer was evasive about Brandt, when he told them in a rather patronizing manner: 'I realise that he is in your bad books, but I consider him a very decent man. We have been good friends and I should like to discuss him with you for half an hour.'[62] But there was no time to talk about Brandt. Speer was asked to write down what he knew about him, but then had second thoughts and wrote a report on underground storage instead. He knew that this information was of great interest to Allied technical intelligence and shifted attention away from his friend. For the moment, Brandt was able to cover his tracks by emphasizing his involvement in the creation of hospitals and emergency care during the war. The 'euthanasia' programme and criminal medical experiments played no significant role in the early interrogations, not least because those who conducted them were less interested in investigating war crimes than in gathering scientific and strategic intelligence information about Germany's infrastructure.

Interrogations provided a welcome break from the dull daily routine of playing chess or Monopoly, or walking aimlessly up and down the veranda, alone or in pairs. Breakfast was at 7.30 a.m. (cereal, soup and coffee), lunch at midday (pea soup, beef hash and spinach) and supper at 6.30 p.m. (powdered eggs, potatoes and tea).[63] Interrogations were enjoyed by many: they provided a chance to relive former power and status and win old battles or arguments. At the same time, the prison inmates had to be on guard in case questions were framed to implicate them in any crimes. They were all hermetically cut off from the outside world. There was no radio and no newspaper. They were forbidden to receive any visitors or letters. Some took advantage of the English lessons provided by the prison staff, others attended lectures on Shakespeare (by Schwerin von Krosigk, the former Finance Minister), the benefits of paper currency (by Walther Funk, the successor to Hjalmar Schacht as President of the Reichsbank), or on plans to reconstruct Germany by means of private enterprise by Robert Ley, formerly one of the greatest advocates of state-controlled business enterprises. Almost all the early interrogations were conducted by high-profile experts from the US Strategic Bombing Survey, who screened the German scientific and technical elite for clues on how to conduct the air campaign against Japan more effectively.

On 17 and 18 June 1945, Lieutenant-Colonel R. L. Meiling and his staff from the USSBS conducted one of the first interrogations of Brandt.[64] Meiling not only questioned Brandt about his upbringing, medical studies, professional career and military duties, but also about his contacts with members of Hitler's entourage and involvement in German medical and public health affairs. By shifting the focus of discussion to his work as Reich Commissioner – which was probably what the officers were interested in – Brandt managed to talk at great length about the administration of hospitals, medical personnel and training, and industrial medicine. He discussed aerial warfare and the medical problems caused by Allied bombing, the role of public morale, his impression of the Russian health system, and his own earlier trial and death sentence. He also commented on Hitler's health and gave an assessment of the future of German medicine. It was a comprehensive interview about almost all aspects of Brandt's life and professional duties during the final years of the war, surpassed only by a series of highly penetrating interrogations in September and October 1945.[65] Not a single word was mentioned of his role in the 'euthanasia' programme or in human experimentation.

Only a couple of days later, on 24 June, another debriefing session of 'Ashcan' inmates took place. It was conducted by Major Ivo von Giannini, in the presence of two of the most senior people from the British intelligence community: Cavendish-Bentinck and his assistant.[66] They had established their office in a small room in the Grand Hotel with straight-backed chairs and a table across which the subject faced them. Each person was asked how many Jews were left in Germany. Most claimed that they had no idea, except for those Jews whom *they* had helped to get out of Germany. The mere mention of the words 'concentration camp' evoked tense responses and a flood of verbose self-justification. It was an absolutely taboo subject which brought any interview at any time to an abrupt end. When Belsen was mentioned, Lammers thought that he would be dispatched to the camp and immediately fell into 'unmistakable despair'. The interrogators felt that they 'could hardly have been in less sociable company'. At the end, all of them were 'very far from sorry to leave Ashcan'.[67]

After Otto Meißner, the former head of the Presidential Chancellery and Brandt's neighbour in Berlin, had given an appalling performance, resembling 'a sick and broken old man', it was Brandt's turn. The results of the interview were laid down in the report 'Karl Brandt: His Career, his Position as Reich Commissioner for Health and Medical Services'. This time Brandt skipped the entire period from 1939 to 1941, which coincided exactly with the first phase of the killing programme. Trying to muddy the issue, he pretended that he had had nothing to do with the programme at all, when asked about it for the first time:

> [Brandt] stated that euthanasia cropped up in one way or another before the war and that various radical Gauleiters were constantly advocating it. A legal formulation of this principle was rejected because of the difficulty of controlling it. In 1940 Hitler prohibited euthanasia. In 1944, however, [Brandt] received a notice from the Gestapo that there was a surprisingly high death rate in an insane asylum in Pomerania. [Brandt] requested information from the Gauleiter there and was told that he was misinformed. He passed this information on to the Gestapo. He has no further information.[68]

This statement demonstrates Brandt's ability to manipulate events to mislead his interrogators. Here, he first shifted responsibility for the 'euthanasia' programme away from Hitler (and himself) to the Nazi Party and an unspecified 'radical Gauleiter'. Though he drew attention to a group of people obviously implicated by Nazi politics and propaganda, they had in fact relatively little to do with the actual introduction and planning of the killing programme. According to Brandt, a law on 'euthanasia' was rejected because the government (and therefore also Brandt) knew that such an operation could easily get out of hand. Brandt also stated that 'euthanasia' was prohibited in 1940, which was simply untrue.[69] Both statements taken together were meant to imply that the German government had handled the matter responsibly. Brandt then jumped four years in his narrative to a point when his star in the Nazi hierarchy was waning, leaving him with little influence or responsibility for events. He stated that the only 'euthanasia' he had known of had taken place outside his jurisdiction as Reich Commissioner. The whole statement shows a carefully constructed lie designed to shift responsibility away from Hitler and government agencies to known Nazi fanatics.

If Brandt's tale was true, why had he remained conspicuously passive on hearing about cases of euthanasia? Major Ivo von Giannini, Brandt's interrogator from the US intelligence branch G-2, does not seem to have picked up on such inconsistencies in the summer of 1945. It was probably not a priority area for his superiors, who were more interested in population and disease statistics.[70] As a consequence, Brandt almost escaped the net of investigations set up to catch suspected war criminals. On 1 July, a secret cable from SHAEF to the commandant of 'Ashcan' requested information about any further interrogations of Brandt that were pending; once these were completed, Brandt was scheduled to be transferred to another detention centre, and likely to be released in the near future.[71] At this point, Brandt seems to have regained his ingenuity. When asked the next day by a Captain Hamilton whether he knew anything about the 'horrors' carried out in mental asylums, he denied all knowledge, because, as he later stated at Nuremberg, 'It was one of about thirty general questions for information and I did not want to trivialize the problem by generalising it "in between" in such a way.'[72] Pressed on the issue during cross-examination, he admitted that the interrogation was made at a time 'when only partly true statements were made [by me]'.[73]

At the beginning of July, Brandt and other members of the German government, including his friend Speer, were transferred to 'Dustbin', the VIP debriefing centre for scientists and technicians, located at Kransberg Castle in the Taunus Mountains near Frankfurt am Main.[74] The castle had once been Göring's air force headquarters, and had been refurbished and decorated according to Speer's architectural designs.[75] For Göring's large staff of servants, Speer had added the two-storey wing which now served to house most of the prisoners. It must have given Speer an odd feeling of familiarity being held prisoner in one of 'his own' buildings. Except for Speer, almost all of the prisoners had to share a room; they were free to walk around in the prison complex, chat, play games and listen to music. They also enjoyed the same food as the Americans. In the morning, Brandt and the other inmates would do gymnastics. His prison companions included the designer-engineer and industrialist Ernst Heinkel, who by 1943 had been in control of more than 50,000 slave labourers for his plane production plants, and had collaborated with Brandt in what was called the 'Fighter Emergency Programme'.[76] Others were the head of the Security Service of the Reich Security Main Office (RSHA), Otto Ohlendorf, who was responsible for the murder of 90,000 civilians in Russia, the physicist Walter Gerlach, the ageing Director General of the German railway, Julius Dorpmüller,[77] the engineer Ferdinand Porsche and the rocket scientist, Werner von Braun, who was later whisked off to America under the codename 'Project Paperclip' to launch the US space programme.[78] It was a truly distinguished group of 'technicians' who kept Brandt company in the late summer of 1945.

Eager to make a good impression, Brandt supplied the Allies with technical and administrative intelligence about the German medical system, including a handwritten memorandum on hospital planning.[79] He also produced a flood of brief memoranda on topics such as 'Aviation Medicine', 'Nurses', 'Sanitary Measures' and 'General Public Health Conditions'.[80] It was certainly something that British and other Allied experts were interested in. Even more, they wanted to find out about the personality of the dictator himself. The British intelligence officer and

Oxford historian Hugh Trevor-Roper had been detailed to investigate the last days under the Reich Chancellery and establish without doubt whether Hitler was in fact dead, or whether he had escaped or gone underground. Any accurate information about the life of Hitler, his eating and sleeping habits, his illnesses or his mistress Eva Braun, was suddenly of great interest, especially to the media.[81] At the end of July, *Life* reported that there was evidence recovered from Hitler's bunker which suggested that Hitler and Eva Braun had committed suicide there.[82] Dozens of witnesses were cross-examined to reconstruct what had happened during the final months of the regime. The report concluding that the dictator was dead was submitted on 1 November 1945 and later published in the acclaimed account *The Last Days of Hitler*.[83]

Brandt supplied what he thought the Allies wanted. Another report by him, written on 7 July, was entitled 'Problem Hitler'.[84] This was followed by 'Problem Hitler No. 2',[85] written on 24 July, a report on 'Women Around Hitler',[86] based on an interview with Colonel Pratt on 6 August, and a report about 'The Hitler Legend' on 17 August.[87] On 21 August, he gave a comprehensive assessment of the role of Martin Bormann at Hitler's court, and on 30 August he was asked to give evidence on 'Hitler as Seen by His Doctors'.[88] Like many high-ranking Nazi officials, Brandt produced hundreds of pages full of implicit self-justification in the summer of 1945. Although unsophisticated, wooden and biased, Brandt's brief report 'Problem Hitler' constitutes one of the first post-war insights into Hitler's complex personality. Stating that the report was based on his personal memories and on observation over a prolonged period, Brandt made it plain that his assessment of 'Hitler's multiple and yet all-inclusive personality' could only be a partial view, which would need to be complemented by other writers in the future. Brandt's report was strongly coloured by his own fascination with Hitler and with National Socialism. His reflections reveal a deep-rooted bond between himself and his patron: a combination of emotional dependence and gratitude.

Brandt stressed that Hitler had understood his importance in world history from very early on. Only two other politicians from this period were judged to be of importance by Hitler: Mussolini and Stalin. Hitler described the latter as a 'true colossus' and a 'giant' of world history. There was little that was original in Brandt's account of Hitler's appeal:

> Within the powerful influences of external events of his time, Hitler adopted the 'intuition' – his expression of the explanation of his idea of God – and with a logical deduction held within himself the conviction that he had been chosen to fulfil this 'intuition.' With that he was being entrusted with the task to rouse the German people, to secure their political and cultural place, and to become their 'Leader' in the fight between views and developments of power in our time. The rest is National Socialism, born out of world-war comradeship, and moulded by Hitler. To this also belonged his idea that a generation which had lost a war had the duty to make good the burden caused by its own failure, and that it could not leave that burden as a heritage to their children and their children's children.[89]

Hitler was described as the 'chosen one', the national redeemer, who would rectify the humiliation of Versailles and lead Germany and its people to international strength. To achieve this task required, according to Brandt, 'Hitler's whole ability and thinking, his time and energy, his proven endurance, and his unshakeable faith'. Such a positive understanding of Nazism distanced Hitler from his government of fear and suppression, from the politics of discrimination, segregation and racial hatred, and from the countless murders of men, women and children which his regime had unleashed throughout Europe. Brandt presented Hitler's political decisions as coming from someone who was striving towards an ideal, which was essentially centred around the greater good of Germany:

> For those living in his time, there appeared enthusiasm, in a fascinating interchange which seemed to have the force of a physical law: people would give hours of increased service, willingness, and gratitude to the 'Leader', and they perceived that he gave the same to them. Hitler spoke in a sovereign and often superhuman manner. The individual as well as the crowd felt, when facing this man, that his thoughts and acts were the fruit of genius, and this from the very beginning precluded any discussion. The broad flow of his vocabulary, and memory, which never seemed to fail, gave him extraordinary power. But also his external behaviour created an impression, and his directness was decisive, and overcame all doubts and arguments. His authority, established over the years by his numerous successes, and therefore accepted by all, inspired trust and confidence and dispelled any fear or panic. It became unquestioned that 'Any wish of the Leader is an order' – indeed over time this acquired the force of law.[90]

By shifting Hitler's form of government to a level where the actions of its participants were judged according to their intentions, Brandt was directing responsibility away from himself. He was also portraying himself as an idealist, who had only followed his leader's great vision, and he stressed the external and internal factors which had prevented this ideal from becoming reality. But for those mapping out plans for a post-war world, including a comprehensive denazification and war crimes programme for Germany, these arguments hardly constituted a convincing defence.

According to the Moscow Declaration of October 1943, war criminals were to be tried by those countries where their crimes had been committed.[91] The Moscow agreement, however, excluded those criminals whose crimes were not restricted to a defined geographical area. Those criminals were to be tried on the basis of the 'London Agreement on the Punishment of the Major War Criminals of the European Axis' of August 1945, which established the legal basis for the International Military Tribunal (IMT).[92] Allied legislation was further defined by Control Council Law No. 10, operational from 20 December 1945, which introduced a uniform legal basis in Germany for the prosecution of war criminals, except for those dealt with by the IMT.[93] The Control Council law changed the political and legal situation, and opened up various possibilities for future Allied trials. It was the essential legal instrument in charging men like Brandt with war crimes and crimes against humanity.[94] Before this legislation was introduced it was unclear whether Brandt would stand trial in front of an American military tribunal, whether he would be extradited to another country, to Czechoslovakia, for example, or whether he would be tried by the British in the scheduled Ravensbrück trial. By December 1946, various options had been discussed.

Although Allied intelligence was in possession of unconfirmed reports about the killing of handicapped children and adults, hard evidence was first gathered and evaluated in the spring and early summer of 1945 by specially assigned war crimes investigators. Having distanced himself from the actual killing operations, Brandt was almost never mentioned when witnesses testified about the systematic murder of tens of thousand of patients. Those implicated at first were doctors and nurses, asylum directors and regional government officials, rather than those in charge of overall direction of the programme. One of the first and most substantial investigations into the 'euthanasia' programme was conducted in the spring of 1945 by the Austrian neurologist Leo Alexander, who later served as the medical expert at the Doctors' Trial. Alexander, who had emigrated first to China and later to the United States, returned to Germany as part of extensive US intelligence operations from 23 May to 26 June, to investigate the extent of criminal human experiments conducted in Nazi concentration camps. Among Alexander's seven Combined Intelligence Objectives Sub-Committee Reports (CIOS Reports) was a 173-page assessment of 'Public Mental Health Practices in Germany'. This provided US and British authorities with substantial information about the methods and procedures used in the 'euthanasia' programme. Brandt's name, however, was totally absent.[95]

The first suspicions about Brandt arose in the late summer and autumn of 1945, when the United Nations War Crimes Commission listed him among potential war criminals wanted for trial by various national and military authorities.[96] Charges included mass murder, massacre and medical atrocities. In these early investigations, two factors worked against Brandt. He was constantly confused, for the next two years,[97] with the other Brandt: Dr Rudolf Brandt, chief of Himmler's personal staff and high up on the list of wanted criminals by various Allied agencies. The first US intelligence report on the Dachau cold-water experiments, for example, written by Alexander and widely distributed among British and US military agencies and publicized during the IMT,[98] mentioned an 'Obersturmbannführer Dr Brandt' who, it was assumed, was Karl Brandt.[99] The fact that Rudolf Brandt carried almost the same SS and military rank, and was equally involved in criminal medical experiments, turned against Karl Brandt. Special scrutiny was exercised whenever his surname came up. One British intelligence report devoted a whole section to the 'Identification of Karl Franz Friedrich Brandt', and tried to establish links between the two men.[100] Secondly, by April 1946, Brandt had been listed four times in the Central Registry of War Criminals and Security Suspects (CROWCASS), whether as a security suspect, a witness of crimes, or actually wanted for trial by other nations, including Czechoslovakia. Even if some of the charges were unfounded, the sheer amount of evidence beginning to appear at this point made it increasingly unlikely that he would escape trial.

In August 1945, the list of major war criminals was published. Brandt was not among them. The defendants before the IMT were Göring, Ribbentrop, Heß, Kaltenbrunner, Rosenberg, Frank, Bormann (*in absentia*), Papen, Sauckel, Dönitz and Speer. Two months later they were served with their indictments at Nuremberg. The *Glasgow Herald* poignantly commented that 'of all these men, who but a year ago enjoyed wide influence or supreme power, not one could find a refuge in a continent united in hate against them'.[101] On 20 November, after many obstructive attempts and doubts, the first session of the IMT began.[102] The courtroom was packed with the world's press, which was astonished by the appearance of these once powerful men. All the defendants looked much smaller than everyone had imagined. People knew these men from Nazi newsreels, where the flattering camera angle and lighting had given them stature. 'They are so insignificant you wouldn't notice them on the tube' was the general reaction. But Robert Jackson's opening speech for the prosecution graphically displayed the defendants' callousness, brutality and arrogance in pursuing their aggressive power politics: they were the planners of mass murder and atrocities on a scale previously unimaginable, 'men who know how to use lesser folk as tools'. The accused at the IMT were the first national leaders of a defeated nation to be prosecuted, but they were also the first to be given the chance to defend themselves, 'a favour which these men when in power rarely extended to their fellow countrymen'. Their crimes had been intentional, premeditated and systematically carried out. 'The privilege of being the first trial in history for crimes against peace of the World imposes grave responsibilities,' Jackson stated. 'The wrongs which we seek to condemn and punish have been so calculated, so malignant, and so devastating, that civilisation cannot tolerate their being ignored because it cannot survive their being repeated. That four great nations, flushed with victory and stung with injury, stay the hand of vengeance and voluntarily submit their captive enemies to the judgement of the law is one of the most significant tributes that Power has ever paid to Reason.'[103] Those hundreds of thousands of Germans who had sworn an oath of absolute obedience to Hitler and his regime had, in the eyes of the prosecution, abdicated their 'personal intelligence and moral responsibility'.[104] The fundamental issue at the IMT and all other war crimes trials was one of individual moral responsibility. 'The very idea that states commit crimes', Jackson said, 'is a fiction. Crimes are always committed by persons.'[105] Those men who exercised great power would not be allowed to shift their responsibility to some abstract idea of the state 'which cannot be produced for trial, cannot testify, and cannot be sentenced'. They were not alone in their guilt, nor would they be alone in their punishment; lesser men would appear before other tribunals. Men like Brandt.

The documentary evidence introduced by the prosecution shocked the world. Even some of the defendants saw the material as 'concentrated political madness'. The ruthless and aggressive planning for war, most commentators hoped, would for ever after undermine any propaganda myths that Germany was forced into a war of self-defence. When the prosecution showed a film of the concentration camps, as they had been discovered by the Allied armies, outrage and shock turned into sickened revulsion. Not one of those present in the courtroom on that day ever forgot the film. Most spectators preferred to watch the reaction of the accused rather than watching the film, but few of them could watch it either. When the screening ended, there was total silence in the courtroom. Then the judges left without uttering their usual words of adjournment. A journalist was overheard saying, 'Why can't we shoot the swine now?' In the dock, Göring was wiping his sweaty palms; in the evening he told the prison psychiatrist that the film had ruined the whole morning when the prosecution had placed him centre stage: 'Everyone was laughing with me and then they showed that awful film and it just spoiled everything.' Funk sobbed, 'Horrible! Horrible!' The military men denied any knowledge of what they had seen. Speer showed no emotion whatsoever and declared that he was now determined to take collective responsibility in order to exculpate the German people from guilt.[106] On 3 January 1946, his counsel announced in court that his client had actually attempted to assassinate Hitler in February 1945. The announcement cut a first decisive rift between the defendants and left the defence divided. It was a tactic which eventually paid off for Speer. He was sentenced to twenty years in prison but escaped the gallows.

As Brandt had been apprehended by the British, the Deputy Judge Advocate General (DJAG), BAOR, was in the meantime preparing a case against him, albeit permitting Allied prosecution teams to question him as a witness in conjunction with the start of the IMT.[107] A British intelligence report from the end of August had raised serious suspicions about Brandt. Major A. Kingscote and Major L. B. Gill from the Royal Signals, Scientific and Technological Branch, interviewed Brandt on 21 August 1945 at Kransberg Castle about German medical science, in order to gather evidence about the country's chemical and biological warfare programme. They found Brandt to be a 'nice looking and intelligent and, to the outward eye ... a pleasing personality'. But the moment they touched on the issue of chemical warfare 'an almost impenetrable smoke-screen was found'. When attention was shifted to one of Himmler's SS branches, which, Brandt hastened to explain, was only 'theoretically' under the Chief of Army Medical Services (and thus connected to himself), 'a cloud came over the hitherto sunny scene and, with righteous indignation, Brandt complained we had led him to suppose [our] interest was German medical science and now it was really on the SS and their doings'.[108] Both interrogators thought that this confrontational approach showed a certain cleverness but that it would have been cleverer if Brandt had not mentioned it and adjusted his tactics accordingly. They were surprised by Brandt's 'remarkable ignorance' for a man in his position, especially when he denied knowledge of Keitel's order that the army should not conduct experiments on human beings. Brandt also denied that the army or the air force had ever commissioned the SS to undertake such research:

> When faced with the fact, known to us, that prisoners had been frozen by the SS to test remedies for high flying accidents, these experiments being requested by the GAF [German Air Force], he said it must have been before his time ... Asked if he approved

[of] such experiments, he evaded an answer by constantly repeating that human beings were unnecessary, as animals would do as well. He finally, however, admitted that he would condemn experiments well outside the usually accepted medical tenets of decency; but, when asked as an obvious corollary, if he would therefore assist [in bringing] the perpetrators to justice, a typical flood of verbiage was unleashed.[109]

Both interrogators got the impression that, according to 'Brandt's theory', no war criminals should be punished at all. They thought it 'a little curious' that Brandt had not adopted a more plausible attitude than promising help, but regretting that SS secrecy had kept all facts from him. They concluded that Brandt's 'voluble argument' had probably been prepared for some emergency. This suggested that 'Brandt himself may have been more closely connected with such experiments – probably with poison gases – than we can yet prove, and had prepared his defence in advance.'[110] At the end of their conversation, Brandt asked them whether Rostock could be brought to Kransberg to 'assist him' in answering questions about his organization. The interrogator's comment made it clear that Brandt was now considered a major war crimes suspect: 'Perhaps [it is] a genuine reason – perhaps not.'[111]

At the end of September, Brandt was transferred to Nuremberg prison. Here the US Office of Chief of Counsel for War Crimes began a comprehensive investigation into Brandt's involvement in medical crimes, including the 'euthanasia' programme, medical experiments and chemical warfare research. Brandt was comprehensively interrogated on 29 September, twice on 1 October, on 3 October, and throughout the morning of 18 October 1945.[112] He vigorously denied any knowledge of the murder of Jews and political prisoners in 'Aktion 14f13', and claimed that he was ignorant of criminal medical experiments on children and other inmates in concentration camps. It was only during the IMT that it transpired that Brandt had been one of the men entrusted with the organization of the 'euthanasia' operation. The investigation was closing in on Brandt.

Whilst Brandt was being interrogated in October, the Americans opened their first major 'euthanasia' trial in Wiesbaden.[113] The accused were seven staff members of the notorious Hadamar asylum, near Wiesbaden. The chief administrator, the doctor, three nurses and two clerical employees were charged with the murder of more than four hundred Polish and Russian men, women and children as part of the 'euthanasia' operation. As the victims were Allied nationals, these acts were undeniable war crimes, though little reference was made to the more than 10,000 German patients who had lost their lives at the killing centre. The issue of euthanasia, though, now received additional attention from Allied war crimes investigators, prosecutors and the press alike. The three senior employees were hanged, the other four received long prison sentences.[114]

Parallel to the IMT, British preparations for charging doctors with war crimes at the Ravensbrück concentration camp were taking shape.[115] The camp was approximately one hundred kilometres north of Berlin, at Fürstenberg near Lake Schwedt, and the Russians had taken it over at the end of April 1945.[116] The British government had anticipated that the Russians would follow up the Ravensbrück cases, as the concentration camp was located in their zone of occupation.[117] After the opening of the IMT in November 1945, however, British officials realized that the Russians were not going to deal with the cases, probably because most of the potential defendants had escaped to the western zones of occupation and were in British custody, making it difficult for the Russians to establish a substantial case. As a result, legal experts advised the British government to take over the Ravensbrück trial. Brandt was among the potential defendants.

At the end of 1945, British agencies discussed the possibility of charging Brandt with war crimes committed at the concentration camp of Sachsenhausen-Oranienburg. The coordination between the various British and Allied departments was characterized, however, by confusion over general policy direction and a lack of political commitment.[118] In April 1946, Brandt was scheduled to be released after having been transferred from Nuremberg to Dachau, where the American Third Army had established an extensive prison camp for thousands of alleged war criminals. Brandt later recalled that his treatment in Dachau, where he slept in one of the bunkers, was 'beneath criticism' because some of the guards hurled expletives at the inmates.[119] At Dachau, war crimes trials were held against 1,672 defendants, 426 of whom were sentenced to death or imprisoned in Landsberg am Lech.[120] Brandt's release was stopped only at the last minute when the Belgian member of the War Crimes Commission, M. de Baer, who happened to be at Dachau for the trial of Mauthausen camp officials, discovered that the detaining authorities had not been furnished with the Commission's list of war crimes suspects. This list named Brandt as one of their most wanted men. The authorities had apparently 'been unable to find anything with which to charge him and he would probably have been released'.[121] Baer immediately informed the American commandant that Brandt was wanted as a war criminal by one or two nations which had charged Brandt and submitted a wanted report to CROWCASS.[122]

It was only after the announcement of the Control Council Law No. 10 in December 1945 that Britain began to take a firm stance on Brandt.[123] In the spring of 1946, further investigations were launched into his part in medical crimes and chemical warfare research.[124] In a final appraisal, the British investigator recorded Brandt's change in attitude and his apparent lack of openness when talking about issues related to medical crimes, stating that some of his answers had been given 'somewhat tersely and negatively'. Though unaware of the full extent of his complicity, interrogators noticed frequent shifts in the way in which he volunteered information, and concluded that he was trying to keep certain aspects secret:

> Brandt could not be confused in his replies by repeated questioning, and in general proved a convincing interrogee in most matters. The investigators were left with the impression however that his connection with experiments and killings in concentration camps was not entirely confirmed to be nil, but that definite evidence of complicity will be needed to destroy his negatory statements.[125]

British investigators now had their eyes fixed firmly on Brandt. When in August 1946 the Czechoslovakian government requested extradition of Brandt for war crimes, the response by the British government was firm: 'Brandt is wanted by us and cannot be handed to the Czechs.'[126] In September, the Political Intelligence Department of the Foreign Office produced a comprehensive ninety-nine-page report on the 'Killing of Asylum Inmates', which included major accusations against Brandt.[127] Hitler's doctor now also became the focus of American lawyers seeking to establish war crimes proceedings against the German professional elite.

One of those involved in pursuing Brandt was Alexander Hardy, who later became part of the US prosecution team at the Nuremberg Doctors' Trial. In May 1946, while Brandt was still in custody in Dachau, Hardy drafted a comprehensive report on the 'Individual Responsibility of Prof. Dr Karl Brandt'.[128] Having carefully studied the bulk of interrogations, Hardy realized that Brandt had 'been very evasive, in an effort to create the general impression that his "hands are clean" in crimes that were committed by medical organisations'.[129] Stressing that his connection with the SS was only theoretical, Brandt had rehearsed the myth of the 'empire within an empire', in which secrecy had allegedly prevented him from knowing anything about the SS and its crimes. Hardy simply did not believe this, concluding that Brandt was probably more closely connected with criminal experiments on humans than it was possible to prove at the time. He believed that further interrogations of Brandt and his subordinates, together with documentary analysis, would 'place Brandt in an unhealthy position', and in all probability 'establish Brandt's guilt for war crimes'.[130]

Hardy was right. When questioned about the 'euthanasia' programme a fortnight before the Doctors' Trial commenced, Brandt began a major climb-down:

> That was in 1939/40, after some kind of preliminary discussions in which I had not participated, and which had been conducted with the Ministry of the Interior and in which Minister Lammers probably took part. The discussions did not come to any conclusion, so that in the autumn – at least as I recall after the Polish campaign – on the basis of newly submitted documents the Führer wanted a decree, and in this decree he gave the order to Mr. Bouhler and me to authorise doctors to perform euthanasia for the incurably ill, after the most critical assessment of the illness.[131]

Though this statement was a simplistic version of a complex lie, Brandt had made some major concessions during the previous year. He no longer denied participation in the 'euthanasia' programme, but stressed that there was no link whatsoever between the killing of mental patients and the extermination of human beings in concentration camps.[132] He flatly denied knowing that his staff had been involved in anything other than the killing of incurables, and insisted that he knew nothing about the extermination of Jews and others in the East; he also pretended that he had never heard of the *Gemeinnützige Stiftung für Anstaltspflege*, the charitable foundation which represented T-4 in its dealings with party or government agencies. Brandt justified what he termed 'mercy killings' by saying that the victims were better off when put out of their misery. According to Brandt, only those doctors who had ordered the death of the mentally ill could and should be charged with responsibility. He went into great detail about how the chain of command worked before the decision was taken that an individual patient should be killed. Apparently, doctors acted individually, and on their own responsibility. He also stated that he had been unable to monitor the administration of the killing operation because he was constantly in the company of Hitler and at his court, a statement which was called into question by subordinates, who reported having seen Brandt as often as three or four times a week in the KdF.[133] Documentary evidence suggested that the programme had been carried out very differently from the way Brandt and T-4 officials wanted the Allies to believe it had been. The interrogators had by this point also gradually realized the importance of Brandt's position as Reich Commissioner and his far-reaching influence in Hitler's regime.

By August 1946, it had been decided to put Brandt at the top of the list of defendants in the forthcoming Doctors' Trial. After Conti had committed suicide in October, it became clear that Brandt would be the key defendant, lending his name to the title of the trial: *United States of America* versus *Karl Brandt*.[134] To establish further evidence against him, James McHaney, one of the US prosecutors, compiled a list of questions for defendants and witnesses in the medical field:

> Did you know Dr Karl Brandt, Reichskommissar for Health and Sanitation? Was he not the *Führer* [leader] of the German medical profession? Are you familiar with the decrees of Hitler which placed Brandt in the position of supreme Reich authority? Do you know what other doctors thought of Brandt's position and authority?[135]

Other questions involved Brandt's relationship to high-ranking officers in civil and military medicine, for example:

> In the field of civilian health, Dr Leonardo Conti was the leader and Dr Siegfried Handloser in the field of the Armed Forces, were they not? These decrees of the Führer, particularly the first one, made Dr Karl Brandt superior to both Conti and Handloser, did they not?[136]

Besides establishing Brandt's pivotal role within the Nazi medical hierarchy, new evidence suggested that he had also been involved in human experimentation on concentration camp inmates:

> Did Dr Karl Brandt have knowledge of the medical experiments on human beings performed by German doctors? Had he not authority to intervene into any of these medical matters and stop them if he saw fit? To your knowledge did Karl Brandt ever participate in any of the medical experiments on human beings?[137]

Such questions, phrased to stand up in a court of law, were meant to reveal whether Brandt had directly or indirectly participated in, initiated or consented to criminal activities, which, if proved beyond doubt, meant that he would serve a long prison sentence, or be condemned to death. McHaney made his robust line of investigation crystal clear: 'It is my desire to place him as top man on the Totem pole as of the earliest possible date.'[138]

By the autumn of 1946, the US Office of Chief of Counsel for War Crimes (OCCWC) indicted twenty German doctors and three bureaucrats for crimes against peace, war crimes and crimes against humanity. The Americans thereby signalled that they intended to go ahead with the first of the subsequent Nuremberg proceedings, the Doctors' Trial.[139] General Telford Taylor was in charge of the subsequent proceedings. He had succeeded the Chief American Prosecutor, Supreme Court Justice Robert Jackson, at the end of March 1946. During the war, Taylor had worked as Chief of the Military Intelligence Service, Special Branch, in London, and he served as Chief of Counsel in Nuremberg until April 1949. He had quickly realized that the quality of his legal staff, with few exceptions, was poor and that the available evidence in the US on medical war crimes was insufficient to secure the conviction of the accused. He therefore needed British and French support at the trial. At the beginning of September, he officially approached British war crimes investigators to ask for their cooperation in extraditing German doctors to the American zone for trial: 'In the event that the extradition of the prisoners to us is agreed upon, we plan to join Brandt with Sievers, Mrugowsky, Haagen, Bouhler, Brack, the "Hohenlychen Group" [Karl Gebhardt, Fritz Fischer, Herta Oberheuser][140], and perhaps Rudolf Brandt and Field Marshal Milch.'[141] Out of a total of twenty-one defendants listed by the US in September 1946, twelve were in British custody.[142] Taylor also wanted to have access to British intelligence information and assistance from British investigators. Although the British government departments had been reluctant to help with extradition requests from countries such as Poland or Czechoslovakia, London was certainly willing to comply with American wishes. The entire Hohenlychen Group, including Karl Brandt, as well as substantial documentary evidence, files and expert reports, were placed at the disposal of the US prosecution team. On the eve of the Cold War, US demands were given high priority in London.

When, in the late autumn of 1946, preparations for the Doctors' Trial were being put into place, the US prosecution invited Leo Alexander to Nuremberg. Alexander was one of its key medical war crimes investigators and had gathered medical intelligence for SHAEF a year earlier. His information and medical expertise proved of immense value in the subsequent trial proceedings. A medical consultant to the US Office of Chief of Counsel for War Crimes, Alexander's assignment was to report on the medical, psychological and ethical dimensions of the 'euthanasia' programme, and on human experiments, and to brief the US prosecution about the potential defence strategies of the defendants. At the beginning of November 1946, he was asked to produce meticulous protocols of all conversations and interviews with the defendants for the 'Interrogation Unit'.[143] On 18 November, after an exhausting five-day trip, Alexander arrived at Nuremberg, where he was introduced to the US prosecution staff. His first impression, which he later recorded in his diary, was not particularly optimistic: 'Went right to work. Found them short of documents, called for my microfilm.'[144] Less than two weeks later, Alexander had interviewed each of the twenty-three defendants at the forthcoming trial, and had produced general assessments of their individual involvement and responsibility for medical crimes. His extensive analysis of the motives and psychological profiles of some of the perpetrators was passed on to Taylor, who made extensive use of this material in his opening speech on 9 December 1946.[145] Brandt was interviewed many times by Alexander throughout the next ten months.

On 26 November 1946, Brandt met Alexander for the first time. They were almost the same age, both had studied medicine in Germany in the 1920s and both were German-speakers, which facilitated their mutual and sometimes frank conversations. 'It is perfectly clear', Brandt agreed with Alexander, 'that on the basis of one's profession one can talk about many things differently and understand each other differently than when this is not the case and explaining is very difficult.'[146] Alexander was particularly interested in finding out about how Brandt intended to justify his role in the 'euthanasia' programme. One of their conversations began after Alexander had asked Brandt why the killing operation had also included the mentally ill and epileptics, some of whom seemed to have been curable:

> *Brandt*: [They] were the terminal cases. The things which I am [charged with], the documents which are with the prosecution somewhere, all this does not correspond [to] those things [that] we were interested in. It was the pure idea of Euthanatos, and in fact seen from the medical perspective. Therapeutic measure[s] which are known and achievable could not help these patients any more. It was therefore also not possible to achieve a standstill in the development of the disease. The condition itself was agonising. That is a term ['euthanasia'] to deliver these humans from this condition.
>
> *Alexander*: That was somehow the idealistic perspective?
>
> *Brandt*: That was not the idealistic perspective.
>
> *Alexander*: How did it happen that the term was somehow extended to Russian and Polish prisoners of war?
>
> *Brandt*: I can only say [that] I do not know that. In 1941/42 – I cannot be sure of the date – essentially because – no not essentially, *also* because of the opposition from the churches the operation was halted, that means it was stopped. There may have been some other cases, but that this was somehow extended to prisoners of war or to conditions which did not correspond to what I previously outlined in general terms I don't know; it did not occur with my approval, nor with my knowledge and against all ideas which I personally hold, also not from Bouhler's agencies, who had the whole administrative apparatus.
>
> *Alexander*: It can happen that this looks very beautiful from the green table, and be distorted in practice.
>
> *Brandt*: Yes, without my knowledge.
>
> *Alexander*: Did you make inspections?
>
> *Brandt*: No, that was not my assignment; my assignment was to inform the Führer. I accompanied him during the war.
>
> *Alexander*: It was not your assignment to convince yourself that the things were carried out according to your guidelines?

Brandt: No.

Alexander: Those are somehow the difficulties of the administration. I am convinced that if you had inspected these things you would have found many faults.

Brandt: I don't know how, for example, Polish prisoners of war or anyone else … should have been included.

Alexander: I can say, I came from the working camp in Hadamar; there was a special block.

Brandt: I've also heard about the procedure in Hadamar, I think in 1944 or 1943.

Alexander: I forget when it was, but this apparatus was used for that [killing of prisoners of war].

Brandt: It is simply a question by whom. I can only testify about something as long as this decree was in existence and involved Herr Bouhler and myself; according to the decree, all personnel matters were Bouhler's responsibility; he had the whole apparatus.

Alexander: I mean the practical effects of this thing, whether you would have necessarily agreed with them. There were, for example, epileptic children with birth defects whom one could have operated on. Euthanasia has been over-simplified.

Brandt: It depends when this happened and under what conditions and directed by whom. You see, I cannot, if a Gauleiter – three times have I found this out from the Gaue, from the Gauleiter, anyway, in an area of the Gaue, the question was dealt with independently, 1944, 1945 – I cannot state the exact time – I received information from some official of the Reich Chancellery that euthanasia was carried out there, twice in the Gau of Saxony and once in the Gau of Pomerania. I had no knowledge, it did not occur as a result of my orders, and I did everything possible to slow it down. It was the only thing I could do, because I did not know anything beforehand or it occurred at a time when the programme had been halted and where I, because it had been halted, had nothing to do with this problem any more. I can imagine that some have claimed that Brandt was there; now we don't have anyone else and Brandt must have done it. More than stopping it, if I heard something that was not right, I could not do.[147]

Apart from the naivety which Brandt sometimes exhibited, and which to some degree may have been genuine, we find him again insisting that the programme had been based on the idea of providing a 'good death' for terminally ill patients, delivering them from unspeakable agony, and that it had been planned and performed from an ideal and medical perspective. He either did not know of, did not approve of, or had attempted to prevent any transgressions of this ideal.

Such a withdrawal to the high ground of idealism made it difficult for Allied interrogators to press him on his responsibility, because as far as he was concerned he had never been responsible for the actual introduction and organization of the programme. He seemed to argue that he was merely in charge of the ideal. Yet this line of defence allowed the US prosecution to catch him out on a relatively minor point over 'euthanasia', not with regard to what he had done but what he had not done: the question of negligence. Having officially been in charge of a government programme, and assuming that its ideal had really been its aim, it should have been Brandt's duty to supervise, oversee, check, confer and control the proper introduction of the programme. If nothing else, Brandt was guilty of negligence. It was a minor point, but one which played a major role throughout his trial as well as in the final judgement.

11

Trial

During the preparations for the International Military Tribunal (IMT), the question arose as to where the trials of the major war criminals should take place.[1] Berlin and Munich were overcrowded with Allied forces and completely destroyed. General Lucius Clay, Deputy Military Governor of the US zone of occupation, suggested Nuremberg, because the courtroom in the Palace of Justice had miraculously survived the sustained bombing campaign on the city. It was located on the Fürtherstrasse, the main traffic artery leading to the nearby city of Fürth in Bavaria, and on to Würzburg and Frankfurt am Main. It was a large building complex, stretching along three blocks, which had served as the Court of Appeal for the Nuremberg region. Behind it ran the River Pegnitz.[2] There was also sufficient space for up to 1,200 prisoners in the adjacent prison complex, and adequate housing facilities for the large number of trial staff, legal experts and journalists who were expected to attend this historic event. Crucially, though, the city had significant symbolic meaning. For over a decade, it had hosted Hitler's infamous Nazi rallies and had witnessed the promulgation of the Nuremberg Race Laws, one of the cornerstones of the Nazi racial programme. It was a fitting place to hammer home to the Germans that the regime had been wholly reprehensible and its moral value system criminal. On a more practical level, Nuremberg was in the American zone of occupation, where food rations were better, and materials and equipment were more easily accessible than in other zones. The Americans had the money and the organizational know-how to stage such a major event. Not surprisingly, the Russians were not in favour of the idea. Berlin, therefore, became the 'permanent seat of the Tribunal' where the judges first met, before travelling to Nuremberg to hold the trials. It was one of many peculiar compromises in inter-Allied power politics at the dawn of the Cold War.[3]

All twelve subsequent Nuremberg trials, which involved 184 defendants, were American trials, rather than four-power trials.[4] They were established on the basis of Control Council Law No. 10. As a result of mounting tension with the Russians, a second International Military Tribunal proved impractical. In response, the Americans decided to establish a Military Tribunal at Nuremberg in order to hold a series of war crimes trials independent of the other nations. On 25 October 1946, Military Tribunal I was established under General Order No. 68, issued by the command of the United States Military Government for Germany. It was the first of several tribunals which the United States eventually established in their zone of occupation. The trial against the Nazi doctors was Case 1 of Tribunal No. I. The Tribunal was made up of four judges, who seem to have been proposed by the War Department, together with the Military Governor of the US zone of occupation. The authorities were anxious to select at least one judge from the East Coast of the United States and one from the West, thereby striking a geographical balance. On 25 October, the day that the indictment was filed against Brandt and his co-defendants, General Clay appointed the following as the designated Judges of Military Tribunal I: Walter Beals, justice of the Supreme Court of the State of Washington, Harold L. Sebring, justice of the Supreme Court of Florida, Johnson T. Crawford, former justice of the Oklahoma District Court in Ada, and Victor C. Swearingen, alternate member and former assistant attorney general of Michigan from Detroit.[5] Their appointment was confirmed by executive order No. 9813, signed by President Harry S. Truman on 20 December 1946.[6]

The courtroom, located on the second floor of the Palace of Justice in the easternmost wing, provided space for about six hundred people, mostly Allied military officials, trial observers, journalists, film crews and specially vetted members of the German public, who were seated in the gallery. Its entrance was heavily guarded by well-armed American soldiers, who thoroughly checked everyone's credentials, sometimes in a rather brusque fashion. The building and courtroom needed major refurbishment and enlargement. For the subsequent Nuremberg trials, the rooms 196, 295, 319 and 581 were to be transformed into courtrooms. The army worked day and night to install the communication and simultaneous translation facilities necessary for hundreds of lawyers and their staff, interpreters, defence counsel and the press. Air, rail or motor transport had to be organized, and telephones and other means of communication to national governments had to be installed. A total of 124 miles of telephone wire was installed in the courthouse alone. The press had to have access to special signal equipment in order to be able to forward their news reports on time. 240 seats were reserved in the courtroom to provide constant news coverage. A hospital and dispensary was provided for prisoners and courtroom staff. All the rooms had to be repainted, and all the woodwork, including the wooden panelling, needed to be restored and polished.[7] The total cost was estimated at around 12,000 dollars, which was in addition to the cost of refurbishing the building at the start of the IMT.

Life in the Nuremberg prison was markedly different from what Brandt and the other accused had experienced in 'Ashcan' or 'Dustbin', where they had been free to visit each other, chat and attend lectures. Prison procedure required that they be kept in solitary confinement in order to prevent the defendants from preparing and coordinating their lines of defence. For some that rule was later relaxed. Colonel Andrus, the prison commandant, allowed no privileges on the basis of former status or rank. No German military rank was recognized by the Allies, otherwise it would have become necessary to apply the Geneva Convention to the treatment of prisoners of war, and then none of the prisoners could have been kept in solitary confinement.[8] The number of letters the defendants were permitted to write was restricted both in number and in length. Parcels were forbidden. The prison building consisted of five wings radiating out from a central rotunda, and was connected to the courthouse by a wooden passageway. Each wing had three floors of cells. All the cells were roughly the same size, about thirteen feet by six and a half. All had uneven stone-flagged floors and rough brick walls with patches of damp.[9] In the wall opposite the door was a small window, barred, and fitted with wire mesh since Conti had hanged himself with a towel tied to the bars; later, in the cold winter of 1945, opaque glass was fitted, though this prevented the prisoners from seeing the sky. Every cell was furnished with a simple wooden chair, a rickety table – to prevent suicides – and an iron bed with a straw mattress and grey US army blankets. By the door, in one of the corners, was the only space which could not be monitored from the hatch: the lavatory. For many this became the only escape from constant surveillance. It was difficult for the defendants to get enough sleep because of the sound of whistling guards, talking or stamping their feet up and down the corridor. Some of the prisoners found shelving where they could store the modest belongings which they were allowed to have with them in their cells; only a few had anticipated a long stay and some had literally been captured in their nightgowns. Here, in one of the wings, on the third floor was cell No. 373. It belonged to Karl Brandt.

Hermann Giesler, Hitler's architect, later recalled that Brandt attempted to give his fellow prison inmates a sense of hope and perspective, but also express their common sense of pain and loss. Outside, on the wall above his cell, Brandt wrote in pencil:

> The infinite Gods give everything,
> To their Loved once, completely,
> All the joy, the infinite,
> All the pain, the infinite, completely.[10]

At Nuremberg, Brandt's and his co-defendants' lives were governed by routine. Early in the morning, the changing of the guards signalled the beginning of the day. Water for washing was passed through the hatch. At 7.00 a.m. they had breakfast (cereal, biscuits and coffee, sometimes scrambled eggs), followed by mopping and cleaning out the cells, a menial task many regarded as beneath their social status. In 1945/46 coal and food were in scarce supply and usually the accused received the same amount of food as was handed out to the German population. The basic restricted diet didn't do some of them any harm. After having a bath or a shower (twice a week), they would then visit the barber, the nearby dentist, or discuss some of their mental or physical health problems with the prison doctors. At midday they were brought out into the prison yard for fresh air and exercise. The exercise yard measured 137 feet by 97 and was surrounded by high prison walls and barbed wire. It was the only time of the day when they had the opportunity to chat to each other and exchange information. After half an hour they were brought back into their cells to wait until lunch (usually soup, meat and vegetables) was served. Supper, served at 6 p.m., was the same as breakfast.[11] Day after day they would endure long hours in their cells; later on they were permitted to play cards or engage in conversation in a specially designated room. Of special interest were those days when they could see their wives and children, albeit through a metal grill. After they had been served with the indictment on 5 November 1946, their lives became less arduous. They began to study the charges, write memos for their lawyers, make notes in their diaries, and think about their best line of defence. This also meant that they could leave their cells to discuss strategies with their counsel in the Defendants' Visiting Room. Shortly before the indictment was served, the number of interrogations had increased significantly, because the US prosecution feared that the accused would be less willing to speak afterwards. They could, at this point, refuse to talk, if they felt that this would better serve their interests, although not all the defendants were informed of this right.[12] Brandt was further interrogated on 9 October, 18 October and 4 and 5 November 1946.[13] A year earlier, at the IMT, the British had taken the opposite approach. They had stopped interrogating the defendants altogether, because they feared this would reveal how the prosecution was intending to tackle the case. It was during this time that Brandt began to write down his thoughts in what was to become his trial diary.

Sitting in his Nuremberg prison cell, Brandt mulled over what he had heard since his arrest, about his supposed role in the Nazi system, and about the information he had heard from fellow prison inmates or from US and British war crimes investigators. He began to reflect on all the unspeakable crimes which had been committed in the name of Hitler's regime, and about his own role in the mass killings. He now openly admitted his involvement in the 'euthanasia' programme, as far as Hitler's official decree on 'euthanasia' was concerned. There were just too many records and affidavits which directly linked him to the killing operation. But there were also allegations that he had been actively involved in other crimes, such as criminal human experimentation, and the murder of the Jews. Such allegations, if sustained, Brandt knew, would mean severe punishment, probably death. While Brandt now knew that he was likely to be convicted, he hoped to at least avoid a death sentence. Any allegations linking him to other crimes committed by the T-4 personnel in charge of 'euthanasia' came as a shock to him. At the same time, he hoped that his decision to remain ignorant at the time when the crimes had been committed might now pay off: he could genuinely pretend that he had not known of such crimes. For some of the crimes, that may in fact have even been true.

Shortly before the start of the Doctors' Trial, Brandt began writing down his thoughts about the coming weeks and months in what became a kind of diary for his family.[14] This book was intended to express his feelings, and as a kind of self-justification in the face of history. After having received the indictment on 5 November 1946, Brandt realized that he needed to find a means of communicating his thoughts and ideas during the forthcoming trial. Instead of writing a protocol about the trial, he recorded his thoughts for the benefit of his wife and his eleven-year-old son, Karl-Adolf. He wanted them to participate in his daily prison life, giving mutual support to each other in these difficult hours. Using post or telephone as a means of communication was virtually impossible: the number of letters he was permitted to write was limited to two sheets of paper per month.[15]

The facilities he had for preparing himself for his trial were also meagre: he had neither chair nor table in his cell, just a plank bed with a mattress and some blankets. Although he engaged in sustained activity in order to provide his defence lawyer, whom he had not yet met, with substantial material and information to be used in his defence, Brandt was not at all optimistic about the outcome of the trial. There seemed to be too much evidence which could potentially be turned against him. He also felt that his guilt had somehow been decided in advance by the military authorities, making him feel that the situation somehow resembled his 'Berlin experiences', Hitler's court martial in April 1945, when he had been sentenced to death.

Addressing himself in the third person, Brandt began to assess the situation:

> It is ... clear. Someone in the environment of AH who has made [out of it a successful] career can only have achieved this through his link with the party – this is the line of thought. Also: If he was with AH for such a long time, then he has to be a pig, or at least has to be declared as one.[16]

Brandt was also greatly concerned at having been earmarked as the key defendant in the trial. By this stage, some of the main perpetrators were dead, men like Bouhler, Grawitz, de Crinis and Conti, each of whom had been equally likely to stand trial – 'yes, and now everything is concentrating on me'.[17] Added to this was, of course, the 'euthanasia' programme, where Brandt found himself accused as the only key decision-maker, apart from underlings such as Brack or Sievers. He was well aware that though the killing operation was administered and organized by Bouhler, the prosecution would attempt to shift responsibility onto his shoulders. What is more, he now fully grasped the extent to which the Control Council Law No. 10 had established binding legal principles for future war crimes trials in Germany. This meant that challenging the jurisdiction of the court was futile. His state of mind increasingly darkened:

> I concentrate and think, but whichever way I look at things, I fail at the Control Council Law No. 10. With that everything just stops. From euthanasia judgements [in] Berlin and Vienna I could see today how it is applied. Yes, and there everything just stops. Power is right. [Brandt underlined the letter 'r' as an orthographic joke. The word *recht* in German means not only both 'good' and 'correct', but – with an initial capital – also 'the law'. By spelling the word *Recht* with a small 'r,' Brandt wanted to stress that where power determines the law, the quality of the law becomes 'small'. Though the joke was rather simplistic, it seems to have made the day for Brandt and his fellow inmate, Fischer.][18]

Brandt's reflections suggest that he was realistic about the likely outcome of the trial, admitting to himself that he had seen it coming for months, if not years. His immediate reaction was a combination of stubbornness and pride, but also of hopelessness.

On 18 November 1946, about three weeks before the trial started, Brandt met his lawyer, Robert Servatius, who had represented Fritz Sauckel, the Plenipotentiary for Labour Mobilization, at the IMT. It was the latter who in 1944 had boasted that out of the five million foreign workers in Germany 'not even 200,000 came voluntarily'.[19] In retrospect, it seems quite extraordinary that Brandt had not talked to a lawyer before, but then again we must remember the speed with which the American authorities mounted the Doctors' Trial, and its improvised nature.[20] It was only on 5 November that Brandt had received the indictment, leaving him with little more than a month to prepare his defence before the opening of the trial. Brandt's first impression of Servatius was anything but positive. For him, Servatius represented the skilled technician (which he was), trained in the art of twisting and turning the rules of law, of finding loopholes in legal texts, of propaganda strategies and backroom deals. This was not Brandt's strategy of defence, because he anticipated that his case would, in any event, be lost. What Brandt wanted was to make one final and lasting impression. He wanted to go down in history as the one holding the flag.

Throughout the diary there are several different voices, a conspicuous dichotomy in tone and content, frequent notions of a 'soft' and 'caring' Brandt, and then, in sharp contrast, a man who is almost boiling with rage, fear and aggression. Whenever he is directing his attention to his wife or son, Brandt writes in a soft and sometimes even upbeat mode.[21] At other times, when reflecting on the trial itself, we can detect an underlying current of outrage over the fact that he finds himself in a situation where he is supposed to shoulder all responsibility for the crimes committed in connection with the 'euthanasia' programme. On the evening of 8 December, on the eve of the trial, he noted the link between the 'euthanasia' programme and the extermination of the European Jews in a mixture of despair and self-motivation:

> They [the coming weeks] will be dreadful. From files etc. I can now also see that Bouhler has obviously of his own accord pursued the extermination of the Jews. Today (!) I find this out. How shall I now be able to separate that from honest euthanasia? I have no witnesses, no papers, nothing! Now, be it as it may, I will see it through. Such news like the piece [of news] today is in fact a shock, but it means for me at the same time a strengthening of my conscience. And that must be my best companion – apart from you of course![22]

The whole process of writing, the very act of putting down his thoughts on paper, of what he perceived as 'opening his mind and heart', was of utmost importance to Brandt in making him *feel* better. It served as a form of relaxation, a kind of therapy to wind down and reduce the tensions which had been building up throughout the day: 'That is the irony of this book. If something is written there [in the diary], then I think, the matter has solved itself for all of us!'[23] His notes were not only meant to reassure his family about his innocence at some later and unspecified date but, most of all, himself. Brandt needed to constantly reassure himself of his 'better self', the one who felt he had done nothing but his duty to Germany and the health of the population, as opposed to the one who had given veiled hints to go ahead with the killing of patients and initiated medical experiments. Those supporting his case, such as his family and friends, gave him the feeling that there was more to him than just Brandt the 'Euthanasia Doctor'. In his diary he noted: 'But I am also just a human being and satisfied, if the image of me becomes balanced.'[24]

We must be careful not to leap to conclusions and follow Brandt's line of argument too readily, for complex psychological processes were at work. This is not to say that Brandt attempted to manipulate his future reader or consciously distort events, but we need to see the specific function of the diary in creating a 'private image'. Brandt was fully aware of his role as the key defendant in the trial, the one who would have to shoulder responsibility for crimes he claimed he had neither committed nor initiated. He also knew that his 'family' expected an explanation as to why he had first been accused by Hitler and then, shortly afterwards, by the Allies. This was coupled with feelings of guilt at having been a bad father and husband, who had almost never been at home, and had been involved in unlawful acts. His family needed something which explained his position during the trial, and in case he was hanged.

There seem to have been two major principles which determined the direction of Brandt's line of argument, both privately in his diary and publicly throughout the trial. Brandt wanted to continue to believe and argue in favour of an ideal. He had always been a devoted follower of an ideal. An ideal was what motivated him to shape the direction of Nazi medicine; it had determined almost all his decisions. Yet he wanted to purify the ideal, to cleanse it from the 'taint' which had become attached to it as a result of the monstrosities of the Third Reich. Over the last two years of his life, Brandt, whilst in detention, on trial and on death row, aimed to leave the world with a good conscience.[25] Like terminally ill patients, who know that they are going to die, Brandt wanted to clarify and explain the many open questions his actions had raised before leaving the land of the living. The diary, in particular, seems to have been a kind of confession, which was to enable his family to make some sense of what had happened after his death, and to continue to live with Brandt's memory. It enabled Brandt to create a 'private image' of himself. The trial, on the other hand, provided him with a platform to construct a 'public image' for posterity.

On one level, the diary was an attempt to clarify his own position, on another, it projected guilt and responsibility away from himself. The absent and intangible family served as a screen onto which he was able to project the 'good' and 'sensitive' Brandt, the caring and loving husband and father, the witty and energetic surgeon, the one who, as a result of fate, had had to endure misery and trial, but who would be brave and strong until the end. Bearing in mind the horrors and untold misery that Brandt had witnessed, and in part initiated, and his reluctance to take responsibility for some of these policies, one comes to the conclusion that Brandt showed signs of a split personality. One cannot help but feel that Brandt was speaking to himself, to his other self. To counter-balance the one side of his self which was now accused of having planned and organized medical atrocities, he needed to promote his other self, the doctor and loving husband worried about what his family and relatives were going through.

Careful analysis of some of the passages corroborates the assumption that Brandt was, if not suicidal, at least in danger of losing his self-control. All his mental and physical energy was geared towards preventing this from happening, by nurturing the loving husband/father, his 'family self', and by giving meticulous attention to his outer appearance, his 'outer self', which sparked comments from trial observers about his arrogant expression. In fact, it wasn't arrogance at all. It was Brandt's survival strategy, not in practical and legal terms but in mental and psychological terms. Brandt's apparent expression of arrogance throughout the trial allowed him to walk a fine line between accepting responsibility for the ideal of 'euthanasia', while at the same time refusing to accept any responsibility for the reality this ideal had produced. In this sense, the diary created a new and more positive image of himself, one which helped him to deny any involvement in crimes and removed any sense of guilt.

What is more, the concept of 'plausible deniability' now bore fruit, not only with regard to the limited evidence which implicated Brandt directly in medical crimes (most of the evidence was in fact circumstantial), but also, and more importantly, psychologically. It facilitated a process whereby Brandt was genuinely able to believe that he was innocent. Passages in his diary are, in fact, strikingly convincing and carry an aura of authenticity. He had anticipated the potential implications of the deed itself on one level, although denying at the time that it was a crime on another, and had detached himself from the crime scene and its participants on yet another level, and all this now helped him to distance himself further from any feelings of guilt or responsibility. Nurturing the side of his personality which *wanted to believe* that he had not known, turned him into that personality. Brandt presented the events as he would have liked them to have happened, and himself as he would have liked himself to have been. It provided him with the confidence and mental strength to face the trial, while at the same time leaving those he loved in the belief that he had been the victim of external influences and power politics.

The Doctors' Trial was the first in a series of twelve war crimes tribunals which the American military authorities mounted against specific professional groups in the Nazi regime.[26] It was meant to expose and punish twenty-three physicians and administrators for their participation in a common design or conspiracy, war crimes, crimes against humanity, and membership of an organization declared to be criminal by the IMT. On 25 October 1946, the Chief of Counsel for War Crimes filed the indictment against the defendants. It listed the accused according to the position that they had held in the Nazi medical hierarchy: Karl Brandt, Reich Commissioner for Health and Sanitation; Siegfried Handloser, Medical Inspector of the Army and Chief of the Medical Services of the Armed Forces; Paul Rostock, Chief of the Department for Medical Research and Science under the Reich Commissioner for Health and Sanitation; Oskar Schröder, Chief of the Medical Service of the Air Force; Karl Genzken, Chief of the Medical Department of the Waffen-SS; Karl Gebhardt, Chief Surgeon of the Staff of the Reich Physician-SS and Police and President of the German Red Cross; Kurt Blome, Deputy Reich Health Leader and Plenipotentiary for Cancer Research in the Reich Research Council; Rudolf Brandt, Personal Administrative Officer to Reichsführer-SS Himmler and Ministerial Counsellor and Chief of the Ministerial Office in the Reich Ministry of the Interior; Joachim Mrugowsky, Chief Hygienist of the Reich Physician-SS and

Police and Chief of the Hygiene Institute of the Waffen-SS; Helmut Poppendick, Chief of the Personal Staff of the Reich Physician-SS and Police; Wolfram Sievers, Reich Manager of the 'Ahnenerbe' Society and Director of its Institute for Military Scientific Research and Deputy Chairman of the Managing Board of Directors of the Reich Research Council; Gerhard Rose, Vice President, Chief of the Department for Tropical Medicine and Professor of the Robert-Koch-Institute and Hygienic Adviser for Tropical Medicine to the Chief of the Medical Service of the Air Force; Siegfried Ruff, Director of the Department for Aviation Medicine at the German Experimental Institute for Aviation; Hans-Wolfgang Romberg, Doctor on the Staff at the Department for Aviation Medicine at the German Experimental Institute for Aviation;[27] Victor Brack, Chief Administrative Officer in the Chancellery of the Führer of the NSDAP; Hermann Becker-Freyseng, Chief of the Department for Aviation Medicine of the Chief of the Medical Service of the Air Force; Georg August Weltz, Chief of the Institute for Aviation Medicine in Munich; Waldemar Hoven, Chief Doctor of the Buchenwald Concentration Camp; Wilhelm Beiglböck, Consulting Physician to the Air Force; Herta Oberheuser, Physician at the Ravensbrück Concentration Camp and Assistant Physician to the defendant Gebhardt at the SS-Hospital in Hohenlychen; and Fritz Fischer, Assistant Physician to the defendant Gebhardt at the SS Hospital in Hohenlychen.[28]

When, on 21 November 1946, exactly one year after the opening of the IMT, Military Tribunal I convened for the first time, all the accused entered a plea of 'not guilty' to all charges lodged against them. Not one of them thought that they had done anything wrong. It was this denial of individual moral responsibility which shocked national and international observers. The *Augusta Chronicle* reported that the doctors had given human beings no higher value than the life 'of a dog, a cat or a rat' and that the latest Nuremberg trial would give startling insight into the philosophy of Nazism 'which denies the dignity of men, and glorifies sadism and cruelty'.[29]

The trial started on Monday 9 December 1946. The procedure set down on the first morning remained the same throughout the next 139 trial sessions. The defendants were the first to enter the courtroom, always ten minutes before the opening of each session. At the back of the dock, a panel in the wall opened to one side, and three or four defendants came in at a time, squeezing their way through to their allocated seats. Brandt had been given the highly symbolic seat No. 13 in the front left-hand corner of the defendants' box (looked at from the front), precisely the same place where Göring had sat a year earlier. The accused were brought up in small groups in a lift from the prison complex. The lift was fitted with a closed section for the defendants at the back, and sufficient room for their escorting military police at the front. All the defendants had been sent to the barber the day before and had been properly dressed to ensure that they would not 'inspire pity'. The theatrical atmosphere nevertheless resembled that of the opening of the IMT. The courtroom was packed with dozens of journalists and newsreel crews, the public, and military observers from around the world. Before the proceedings started, press photographers and film crews were allowed to take pictures of the courtroom and of individual defendants. During the trial sessions, filming was restricted to cameras permanently installed in soundproof booths. After the defendants the prosecution and defence staff came in, edging their way to the tables. Finally the judges, led by the presiding judge Walter Beals, entered the courtroom. Once all were seated, at 10 a.m., the marshal of the court declared: 'Military Tribunal No. I is now in session. God save the United States of America and this honourable Tribunal. There will be order in the court.'[30]

The trial began with the presentation of evidence to sustain the charges contained in the indictment. In the Doctors' Trial, the head of the US counsel for trials of war criminals at Nuremberg, Brigadier General Telford Taylor, delivered the opening statement for the whole of the first day before handing over to James M. McHaney, the chief prosecutor for Case 1.[31] The latter had been one of the key figures in pushing for a trial against Brandt and his co-defendants, and was highly qualified to undertake the prosecution. Taylor began by outlining the framework and responsibility of the trial. The defendants were charged with murder, torture and multiple atrocities in the name of medical science. Their victims numbered hundreds of thousands. Only a few were still alive and some later gave evidence to the court. The representatives of the United States, judges and prosecutors alike, had grave and unusual responsibilities towards the victims, to the parents and children of the victims, the 'nameless dead'. Taylor referred to the victims of Nazi medical experiments, the '200 Jews in good physical condition, 50 Gypsies, 500 tubercular Poles, or 1000 Russians', who numbered among the anonymous millions of victims of Nazi mass murder. Among the victims were countless Germans and nationals of countries overrun by Germany, prisoners of war, and Jews of many nationalities. Taylor made it plain that the 'mere punishment of the defendants, or even of thousands of others equally guilty, can never redress the terrible injuries which the Nazis visited on these unfortunate peoples'. One of the central aims of the trial was to establish these events by clear and public proof 'so that no one can ever doubt that they were fact and not fable; and that this court, as the agent of the United States and as the voice of humanity, stamps these acts, and the ideas which engendered them, as barbarous and criminal'.[32] The prosecution also had other responsibilities:

> We cannot rest content when we have shown that crimes were committed and that certain persons committed them. To kill, to maim, and to torture is criminal under all modern systems of law. These defendants did not kill in hot blood, nor for personal enrichment. Some of them may be sadists who killed and tortured for sport, but they are not all perverts. They are not ignorant men. Most of them are trained physicians and some of them are distinguished scientists. Yet these defendants, all of whom were fully able to comprehend the nature of their acts, and most of whom were exceptionally qualified to form a moral judgement in this respect, are responsible for wholesale murder and unspeakable cruel torture.[33]

The accused were charged with murder, Taylor said, but this was not merely a murder trial. 'It is our deep obligation to all people of the world to show why and how these things happened. It is incumbent upon us to set forth with conspicuous clarity the ideas and motives which moved these defendants to treat their fellow men as less than beasts.'[34] He was convinced that the trial also offered an opportunity for the German people to see and understand the causes of their current misery, the destruction of their cities and industry. The 'bold and lucid consummation' of these proceedings would also be of great importance in helping other nations to understand the 'sinister doctrines' of Nazism. It was the ideology of Nazism which 'sealed the fate of Germany, shattered Europe, and left the world in ferment'. The actual policy of mass extermination, Taylor argued, 'could not have been so effectively carried out without the active participation of German medical scientists'.[35] As to the organization of the German medical services and the role of each of the accused within the system, Taylor pointed out that only one of the defendants was directly responsible to Adolf Hitler himself: Karl Brandt.[36] He was the supreme medical authority in the Reich. None of the others accused had enjoyed such a direct and intimate relationship with the centre of power.

Taylor then addressed each of the experiments in turn: the high altitude, freezing and sea-water experiments, the malaria and mustard gas experiments, the sulphonamide drug experiments at the Ravensbrück concentration camp, the epidemic jaundice experiments, the sterilization, typhus and poison experiments, the incendiary bomb experiments, the Jewish skeleton collection at the University of Strasbourg and the 'euthanasia' programme.[37] It was a long list of unspeakable human degradations and stomach-churning horrors. All the defendants had shown 'a callous lack of consideration and human regard for, and an unprincipled willingness to abuse their power over the poor, unfortunate, defenceless creatures'.[38] The experimental subjects had been deprived of their rights and dignity by a ruthless regime. All the accused had violated the Hippocratic medical tradition, including the fundamental principle never to do harm – *primum non nocere*.[39] One of them, Kurt Blome, had actually boasted in his autobiography, entitled *Arzt im Kampf,* that he had chosen a medical career because it would enable him to become 'master over life and death'.[40]

Finally, Taylor turned to the question of medical ethics, the most fundamental issue of the trial. Regardless of what they may have agreed to or signed at the time, none of the victims had been volunteers. Most of the victims hadn't been condemned to death, and those who had been weren't criminals, 'unless it be a crime to be a Jew, or a Pole, or a Gypsy, or a Russian prisoner of war'.[41] But most importantly, there had been no voluntary and informed consent prior to the experiments:

> Whatever book or treatise on medical ethics we may examine, and whatever expert on forensic medicine we may question, [they] will say that it is a fundamental and inescapable obligation of every physician under any known system of law not to perform a dangerous experiment without the subject's consent. In the tyranny that was Nazi Germany, no one could give such a consent to the medical agents of the State; everyone lived in fear and acted under duress.[42]

All the accused had departed from 'every known standard of medical ethics', so that it would be cynical to detail the gulf between these atrocities and serious medical research. For the prosecution, the case against the doctors was 'one of the simplest and clearest', but it was also one of the most important, because it epitomized Nazi thinking and the Nazi way of life, the noxious merger of the German militarized state with Nazi racial policies.[43] Germany's leaders had failed to stand firm against the destructive forces of Hitler's party; their failure was the outcome of 'that sinister undercurrent of German philosophy that preaches the supreme importance of the state and the complete subordination of the individual'. It was this sort of philosophy that Brandt had inculcated and advocated from early on; he was absolutely convinced that the supreme importance of the state in the Nazi philosophy would exculpate all people from individual moral responsibility. In his concluding statement, Taylor remarked that a nation in which the individual means nothing, will find few leaders courageous and able enough to serve its best interests.[44]

Taylor's wholesale condemnation of the Nazi regime and its corrupt moral value system was widely acknowledged by American, German and French newspapers as an impressive example of legal rhetoric, in which judicial and moral argument had skilfully been woven together with graphic examples.[45] The *Philadelphia Record*, for example, noted that the prosecution had outlined its case 'in sharp, bitter tones', and asserted that Nazi Germany had 'died of its own poison'.[46] Some observers also commended the thoroughness of the proceedings and the dispassionate way in which the prosecution was handling its material. Others made a mockery of the defendants' line of defence. On 11 December, the French papers *L'Ordre* and *L'Époque* reported that Brandt had objected through his attorney that he was never Hitler's personal physician. 'You will prove in a short time,' retorted the prosecutor to Servatius, 'that he was only his driver.'[47]

Brandt was well aware that the trial had suddenly made him the subject of global attention, but he deplored the moral high ground taken by the prosecution. 'The United States of America "as the voice of humanity" against Karl Brandt and fellows! I am hardly able to say more,' Brandt noted with consternation on the opening day of the trial.

> The line of argument, however, is clear. On the basis of some organisational plan, to which we are connected as members of some kind of association, the prosecution will show the conspiracy. With regard to the experiments, I will be assigned responsibilities which I did not have, but which I should have used to terminate them, and concerning euthanasia one will dispute the power which was given. In between I can juggle with details![48]

Brandt and his fellow defendants also protested at the way in which the trial was conducted: they were being tried before the world's press. The whole trial atmosphere was difficult for men who for years had worked in secrecy, who had given their orders to kill through hints made in passing, and who had attempted to camouflage their involvement and cover up their tracks. 'The external picture,' Brandt noted, 'the presentation and so forth is colourful, bright cinema.'[49]

On the first day, the presiding judge had announced that the trial would be 'a public trial, not one behind closed doors'.[50] Newsreel companies such as Pathé and Gaumont began regular coverage of the Doctors' Trial.[51] The German newsreel *Welt im Film* noted that the trial revealed the extent to which medical authority had degenerated and been abused during the Third Reich. Of great importance were witness testimonies from survivors of the concentration camps. 'This Polish woman', *Welt im Film* reported in December,

> was used for gas gangrene experiments in the Ravensbrück camp. She was brutally forced to undergo two operations, and as a consequence has suffered permanent mutilation of her right leg. However, this woman is considered a so-called 'light case'. Still, the number of those who did not survive the experiments, or did so only as human shells, has not even been roughly established.[52]

Observers were particularly shocked by the examination of Walter Neff, first a prisoner, and then a male nurse at the Dachau camp. Neff described in great detail the freezing experiments and the experiments with poison and salt water which had been conducted at Dachau. In dozens of cases, the subjects had died as a result of the experiment. George C. Putnam from the UNWCC described the opening of the trial as 'showdown time' for the men of medicine who had ruled in Hitler's name: 'Tales of deliberately wanton killings, of so-called "mercy killings" by torture – they're all on the record tonight.'[53] On 12 December, the *New York Times* informed readers about a fifty-page report on cold-water experiments using human subjects, which was introduced as evidence by the prosecution, as being 'the most startling and succinct report on murder in the history of criminology'.[54] These accounts shaped the public image of the otherwise insignificant-looking men and the one woman in the dock.

News coverage of the trial was not restricted to Allied media. About two dozen German correspondents regularly reported the latest news from Nuremberg, including representatives of the German news agencies from all four zones. The United States zone radio station broadcast fifteen-minute commentaries on the progress of the trial, and occasionally the odd Nazi would pay tribute to the former medical elite.[55] By the beginning of March 1947, the Sunday edition of the *New York Times* carried the headline 'Nazi Medical Horrors Revealed at New Trials': 'Nearly 100 German spectators observe the Nuremberg trials daily. They are checked only for criminal record before admission.'[56] Frequent requests by medical students for passes were generally granted as part of the ongoing denazification effort. The German medical profession also sent a group of official observers to the trial. Led by the Heidelberg psychologist Alexander Mitscherlich, the group's objective was to report on the extent of medical misconduct during the war.

Many people were somewhat disconcerted when they first saw the defendants. The majority wore civilian clothes and those in uniform had had their decorations or insignia of rank removed. Countess Alice von Platen, one of the three German trial observers, observed 'with horror the ordinary faces'. She had difficulty in understanding that 'no external features distinguished these twenty-three people from us ... The whole event would be easier to understand, if these were notorious sadists or psychopaths, but on the contrary they are men who for years filled the most responsible positions.'[57] The only woman on trial, Herta Oberheuser, attracted particular attention.[58] For many observers, it was difficult to grasp that a woman could have been involved in such heinous and brutal acts. Other spectators were plainly outraged that not a single one of the accused had pleaded guilty to the charges – something that many felt was nothing other than 'shameless and incredible arrogance'.[59] Such comments were not confined to German commentators. One American doctor let off steam in a letter to the editor of the New York Times, expressing his anger over the lack of compassion and moral stature of the German doctors: 'Not a single word of protest or of indignation was heard from the so-called outstanding men at the head of the German universities nor from the German Medical Association. Nothing of that sort is heard even today. They probably have the nerve to claim they did not know anything about it.'[60] For David Willis from the UNWCC, the demand to condemn the men as murderers was therefore an 'eminently reasonable proposal'.[61]

For many of the defendants such publicity was humiliating, especially for those who called the legitimacy of the court into question. Those who, like Karl Brandt and Joachim Mrugowsky, saw themselves as soldiers, demanded to be tried by a military court, not by an American military tribunal of the occupying forces. Others, such as Paul Rostock, could hardly bear the 'language' of the accusations of the chief prosecutor.[62] Taylor had said that they were not ignorant men, but trained physicians who were fully able to comprehend the nature of their acts, doctors exceptionally qualified to form a moral and professional judgement, but responsible for wholesale murder and unspeakably cruel tortures.[63] The actual content of the accusations seems not to have concerned Brandt, or to have provoked him into anything other than defiance, but he commented on the appearance and apparent character of the tribunal members: 'The prosecutor General Taylor is relatively young, not unsympathetic. The judges respectable and civilised. Such is my first impression.'[64]

The first days and weeks of the trial were awful for Brandt and for the other doctors accused of having committed the most unspeakable brutalities. Some of the crimes they may genuinely not have known of, others they had preferred not to know of or not to have been involved in, whereas there were others in which they had actually participated and collaborated. Before their eyes some of their own victims now gave poignant testimony of how they had been beaten, tortured and otherwise maltreated before and after the experiments. Outside the courtroom there were small intrigues, with some of the defendants jockeying for position to blame others for certain crimes. Victor Brack, a notorious liar, was nevertheless frequently used as a key witness by later historians.[65] He attempted to shift responsibility to Brandt by stating that the latter had given his express approval to the extermination of Jews in Poland as an integral part of the 'euthanasia' programme. Though it is true that the 'euthanasia' operation was expanded, and later involved the killing of prisoners in concentration camps in 'Aktion 14f13', it is highly unlikely that Brandt would have admitted his involvement to Brack. By the time the killings began, Brandt was fully aware of the potential danger of such a statement. Assuming that Brandt had had knowledge that such killings were carried out, he may only have given his silent approval to Bouhler, who may have communicated this to Brack, who stated it as fact in the trial. Although all of this is speculative, Brandt's outrage at Brack's evidence carries the ring of truth:

> I have just had an awful day. Viktor Brack has given an affidavit which is the most mendacious thing one can think of. I will grant him the benefit of stupidity, but such stupidity is dangerous. Previously I never would have believed this. But it is like that. Such stupidity is as unpredictable as madness! This man has testified and underwritten that the euthanasia problem is linked to the extermination of Jews in Poland and that this extermination was carried out with my approval. I still cannot find the right words. One – and especially I – have to be prepared for quite a lot, and every day there are little problems. But I was not quite prepared for such heavy stuff. Now I have spoken with S.[ervatius]. Brack knows that his affidavit is false. His lawyer came to me and to S. in order to state this officially. But what is said cannot be unsaid. First it goes into the world! And I can never quite capture it again![66]

This suggests that Brack had distorted the facts, and it also reveals the extent to which Brandt continued to try to control his public image, and to manipulate the course of events. Hostile evidence from other participants in the T-4 operation could ruin his carefully constructed strategy of plausible deniability. Brack's statement, though later withdrawn and admitted to be false, was perfect ammunition for the prosecution in challenging him on his having remained ignorant of what was happening in Germany, undermining the essential part of his defence strategy. It also seriously undermined his ability to create a public image for posterity, portraying him as an idealist and a believer in the pure and uncontaminated idea of euthanasia, which had nothing to do with any of the other crimes. Brandt had every reason to be furious with Brack.

Brandt's mood darkened by the hour. He knew that he was going to face the past, his past. His exact role in the killing of the handicapped was going to be thoroughly scrutinized during cross-examination. Referring to medical ethics and the 'euthanasia' programme, Brandt noted on 21 December 1946:

> I am awaiting these days in horror in which I now after all must once again address this problem, and deal with it. But there is no way round it, and I must reach into that open jaw![67]

Brandt was realistic in his assessment of his predicament. Almost none of the other defendants gave him a chance of survival. One of them, his colleague and friend Rostock, even predicted the outcome of the trial of each of the defendants after each trial section. An 'O' meant acquittal, a '/' meant a prison sentence, a '|' meant a life sentence and a '+' meant a death sentence. After cross-examination, and after hearing the final statements by the counsel for the defence and prosecution, as well as in the actual sentencing, Brandt's box was always marked with a '+'.[68]

For a sentimental character such as Brandt, to be alone in a prison cell over Christmas, accused of the most heinous crimes (of which he claimed that he was ignorant), was very hard. His thoughts were with his family and his son, and what Karl-Adolf would think of his father. And there was Brack's affidavit. The prosecution used it to produce an organizational plan which placed Brandt right in the centre of Nazi medicine, from where he had apparently given his deadly orders.[69] Such an understanding of Nazi medical machinery underestimated the nature of the regime, in which real power was limited by a combination of organizational chaos and overlapping competencies. Brandt had never had a ministerial machinery at his disposal: he had always had to liaise, confer and collaborate with other government agencies. His rise to 'Minister of Health' had been nipped in the bud by Goebbels. Even after the August 1944 decree – when most of the experiments had already been carried out – Brandt had not been granted a Reich ministry. He had been a minister without a ministry. Brandt was neither all-powerful, as the prosecution wanted the court to believe, nor did his part in Nazi policy correspond to the image which Brandt portrayed of himself as Hitler's idealistic, and somehow innocent, surgeon. Through remaining close to Hitler, Brandt had been able to have real influence over policy decisions, informally and inconspicuously. To draw too much attention to his formal position, necessary in the legal context to secure conviction, would overlook how Brandt and some of the other Nazi leaders had, in fact, operated.

In January 1947, Brandt tried to recover from Brack's denunciation. Over and over again, it was his public and private image which caused him concern, and how the world would view him after this or that revelation. What his family and friends thought of him. What the children in the playground would say about Karl-Adolf's father. Would they bully his son? How would they speak of Karl Brandt? As a murderer? What concerned Brandt was his image, not the accusations, and certainly not the hundreds of thousands of victims. Late in the evening on 9 January, he wrote:

> For the next weeks I am standing in front of the world with a face which, once looked at, is nothing but dreadful. I must withdraw into myself *very* much to appear freely! Even Brack's defence lawyer came to me and said that he will do what he can. But how little does this mean afterwards! Tomorrow [the news] races throughout the world that I am standing in the middle of it all, with a really devilish and grotesque face. That is disgusting. Brack himself has said that 'he had become soft' when he signed the report! Is this now consolation? It is quite dreadful how humans can lose control of themselves for pomposity![70]

At this point, Brandt was at the end of his tether. The idea of suicide seems to have been in his mind. He could not bear the idea of how he was being presented to the world and the fact that he had lost control of both his public and private image. After the close of one of the trial days, he commented:

There I have no words any more. Because I am integrated into all this and powerless! I am feeling like I wrote three pages earlier, if I am accused in front of the world that I had starved children to death! I then feel as if I would hear this from Karl-Adolf. It revolts inside so that I could explode – and then exhausted I let my arms hang and fall: powerless! I am just powerless ... We all are. At such times you have to reach inside yourself, otherwise there is only one way out. So I reach into myself, and there I find a word of comfort, a feeling, a wish! If I nurture it, it comes to life – and so I find I can fight through and find myself again.[71]

Brandt was right. The press had drawn exactly the conclusion he had feared, presenting him as the man in charge of German medicine and research. One US article was entitled 'The Face of the Beast', with pictures of Brandt, Handloser and Oberheuser. Adding to this was the occasional crude joke. For several nights into January someone had pencilled a gallows on the woodwork of Brandt's seat No. 13 with remarks such as 'Hitler's alive' and 'I'm coming'.[72] Court officials first believed that Brandt had been doodling, but on entering the court on 8 January, he excitedly called the officer of the guard. Pointing to a new series of doodles, Brandt snapped: 'It wasn't me', like a schoolboy unjustly accused of misdemeanour.[73] Cleaning material was hurriedly procured and the sketches removed. Such incidents nonetheless fuelled Brandt's already depressed mood. There seemed nothing left but to remain firm in his position, however indefensible it seemed. At least it gave him the feeling of consistency and stability.

On the day that the trial had opened, the *New York Times* had commented that 'Karl Brandt ... will take Hermann Goering's corner seat in the dock in the same court where the international trials were held'.[74] Now, after twenty-eight trial days, on the morning of Monday 3 February 1947, Brandt settled into the witness box just as Göring had done a year earlier and given testimony in chief as the first of the defendants. Security precautions inside and outside the courthouse had been stepped up for fear of rescue attempts or bomb attacks. Brandt's testimony followed a period of heightened tension in the American zone of occupation after a number of bomb attacks on denazification tribunals in Frankfurt am Main and in Nuremberg had put the security forces on high alert. In February, General Clay informed the German Council of States that 'more and stronger subversive activity' was to be expected in the future.[75]

The session started at 9.30 a.m. with a brief dispute over the question as to why the prosecution had not been given due warning that Brandt would be called as a witness. For a moment, Brandt looked slightly nervous, but then calmed down when he raised his hand to take the oath. Straightening his pitch-black hair Brandt waited for his counsel, Dr Robert Servatius, to lead him through his carefully prepared statement for the whole of the morning and afternoon, and the whole of the next morning. His questions and Brandt's answers were concise and to the point and, despite occasional objections from the prosecution, the Tribunal was satisfied with Servatius' examination.[76]

Brandt started off by establishing his expert credentials, listing his education and specialized medical training, his professional career as a surgeon and his multiple duties as Hitler's personal physician. His specialized assignments for Hitler followed naturally, one after another, up to the point where he was appointed as a kind of health minister without a ministry. A vivid description of his disputes with party fanatics like Conti, Himmler and Bormann was meant to present Brandt as a conscientious personality, a man of character, who had attempted to keep moral and scientific standards high.[77] Key to Brandt's statement was the precise definition and understanding of his office and his official position, first as General Commissioner and later as Reich Commissioner for Health and Sanitation. He portrayed the role of his office as that of an 'enabler' (*Differential*), who had coordinated the demands of various military and civilian agencies. From this argument all others followed: that he had not actually been in a position to initiate or order certain policies and crimes or had not had the actual staff to enable him to carry them out. His approach was to stress those elements which were indisputable, such as his official rank and position, but to play down their importance and influence, deny any knowledge of those crimes and experiments which had led to multiple deaths, and admit 'some' knowledge of those which had not caused any significant harm or had been ordered and carried out for 'a superior state of interest'.[78] He alleged that he had not been involved in any of the experiments directly, that is to say in a clinical sense (which was probably true), and had learned of nearly all of the experiments during the interrogation, in the indictment, or in Nuremberg for the first time. 'I knew nothing about them before' was his typical reply.[79]

To speed up the proceedings, the prosecution largely ignored Brandt's jibes at his adversaries and the employment of *tu quoque* arguments, for example that US medical scientists had conducted similar 'unethical' medical experiments. But, after the first recess, McHaney jumped to his feet and objected that Brandt was reading his statement almost literally from notes which he had brought into the witness box. The objection, and a request to be furnished with copies of these papers, was overruled by the Tribunal, after Servatius had stressed that the defendants in the IMT had been permitted to use similar notes to make a 'fluent and sensible' statement.[80] It was one of many incidents which showed that the Tribunal wanted to conduct the hearing in a fair and impartial atmosphere.

Once Brandt's lack of knowledge of specific experiments had been established, he turned to his co-defendants to point out the limited contact between them in the past. Of twenty-two co-defendants, Brandt had apparently met nine for the first time at Nuremberg (Ruff, Romberg, Becker-Freyseng, Weltz, Schäfer, Hoven, Beiglböck, Pokorny, Oberheuser), three he allegedly knew only by name (Poppendick, Fischer and Rudolf Brandt), and with the other seven (Mrugowsky, Schröder, Gebhardt, Blome, Rose, Genzken and Sievers) he had had only brief and occasional contact. Except for Rostock, Handloser and Brack, the head of German medicine appeared not to have known the other people in the dock.[81]

Finally, on the morning of 4 February, Brandt answered the most difficult charge against him: the 'euthanasia' programme.[82] He was extremely careful not to give the impression that he had had any dealings with the programme directly, and

37. Karl Brandt treating wounded soldiers in Hitler's plane, August 1941. (BSB, Fotoarchiv Hoffmann, hoff-37397)

38. Hitler's Reichstag speech, 1 September 1939. Karl Brandt sits on the right hand side. (BSB, Fotoarchiv Hoffmann, hoff-27225)

39. Leonardo Conti and Karl Brandt. (BSB, Fotoarchiv Hoffmann, hoff-321)

40. Karl Brandt with his son Karl-Adolf Brandt, c. 1942/43. (Source: Karl-Adolf Brandt)

41. Karl Brandt with a member of Hitler's Leibstandarte at the palace of Kleßheim, Salzburg, 16–17 April 1943. (BSB, Fotoarchiv Hoffmann, hoff-47776)

42. Hitler with the children of his entourage, including Brandt's son, Karl-Adolf Brandt, 20 April 1943. (BSB, Fotoarchiv Hoffmann, hoff-47834)

43. Hitler's entourage celebrating Hitler's birthday, 20 April 1944. From left to right: Otto Dietrich, Eva Braun, Herta Schneider, Hans-Karl von Hasselbach, Gretl Fegelein, Karl Brandt, Anni Brandt, Heinrich Hoffmann. (BSB, Fotoarchiv Hoffmann, hoff-53550)

44. Karl Brandt and Karl Gebhardt, c. 1943–44. (Source: Karl-Adolf Brandt)

45. Hitler and Karl Brandt at Führer headquarters Wolfsschanze, 15 July 1944. (BSB, Fotoarchiv Hoffmann, hoff-53867)

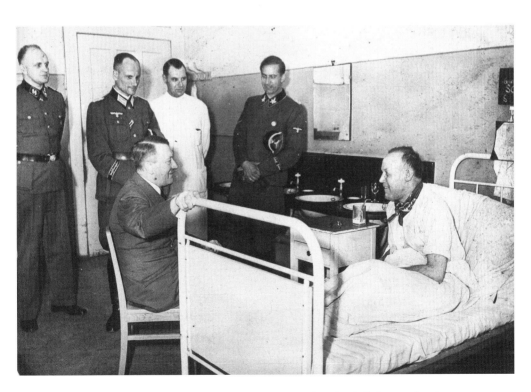

46. Hitler and Karl Brandt visiting wounded soldiers after the failed assassination attempt on Hitler's life, *c.* end of July 1944. (BSB, Fotoarchiv Hoffmann, hoff-53942)

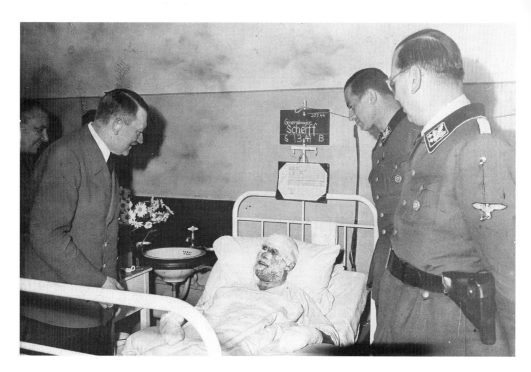

47. Hitler and Karl Brandt visiting wounded soldiers after the failed assassination attempt on Hitler's life, *c.* end of July 1944. (BSB, Fotoarchiv Hoffmann, hoff-53929)

48. Transport of Brandt, Dönitz and Speer after their arrest in Flensburg by the British Army, 23 May 1945. (Source: IWM)

49. Karl Brandt being interrogated by a member of the prosecution team, Nuremberg, Germany, 1945–46. (Source: NARA)

50. The defendants in the Nuremberg Doctors' Trial, Germany, 1946–7. (Source: NARA)

51. *Left:* Karl Brandt swearing an oath at the Nuremberg Doctors' Trial, 1946–7. (Source: Ray D'Addario)

52. *Below:* Karl Brandt, Hitler's doctor, being sentenced to death, Nuremberg, Germany, 20 August 1947. (Source: NARA)

was usually quick in shifting responsibility for the execution of the operation to departments or other officials, for example to the head of state, Hitler, to Bouhler and the KdF, or to the doctors carrying out 'euthanasia'. According to Brandt, 'every individual doctor' had been responsible for his or her involvement in the programme:

> The chief expert was also responsible, and the doctor at the observation institution, as well as the doctors in the euthanasia institution, [they] were also responsible. It must not be assumed that the doctor involved in these measures would have been obliged to carry out euthanasia if he did not agree on the basis of his own decision. He had the right and the duty, if he did not approve, to refuse to carry out euthanasia.[83]

Brandt himself had allegedly never visited T-4 headquarters, nor had he ever inspected any of the killing centres; Bouhler appeared to have been solely in charge of the administrative side of the operation. He dodged sensitive areas, such as the question of consent or the obvious shortcomings of the programme, for example when relatives had received two urns by mistake. He dismissed them as 'regrettable instances' which had occurred because Hitler had ordered the programme to be carried out in secrecy, but affirmed that they did 'not affect the principle'. He was convinced that 'if this Hippocrates were alive today he would formulate his oath differently'.[84]

For Brandt it was important that the head of state had given him the assignment of implementing 'euthanasia' and was therefore responsible. He stretched credibility to the limits by arguing that he 'certainly could not expect' that he had been given such a decree for any criminal action.[85] Considering what was known of the regime by 1939, how hints and orders from Hitler and his acolytes developed their own dynamism to fulfil the projected wishes of the Führer, such a statement was hard to believe. For Brandt and his circle 'everything was done as if everything was in order, and it was in order as far as we were concerned'.[86]

As far as the morality of operation was concerned, Brandt was convinced that what he and others had done was right. He told the court that those wanting to judge the 'euthanasia' programme should visit an 'insane asylum' and stay there for a couple of days with the 'sick people'. The person should then ask two questions: 'The first would be whether he himself would like to live like that, and the second, whether he would ask one of his relatives to live that way – perhaps his child or his parents.'[87] Brandt accepted that the execution of the operation had not been 'very pleasant' and that the death of humans was horrible. 'But everything in life that is biological is not pleasant,' Brandt said.[88] His defence stressed the idealistic intentions behind the programme. To understand the programme, Brandt said, one should not look at the reality of the operation, but at the ideal which the Nazi leadership had in mind.

In October 1945, Brandt had made it plain to his interrogators that the mentally ill, especially those pictured in the film 'Existence without Life' ('Dasein ohne Leben'), were ugly to look at:

I think that everybody who has any imagination will turn away shudderingly [sic] from the misdevelopment of nature. These people live under cruel imagination and persecution manias, partly without any consciousness, and one can safely say that every one of these people if they for one clear moment would be able to see their real condition would be very grateful to be dead.[89]

Believing that the handicapped would wish to die, if only they could reflect upon their mental and physical condition, was largely a rehearsal of Binding and Hoche's arguments on euthanasia from the 1920s. Brushing aside racial, eugenic or economic factors, Brandt argued that the only rationale for the 'euthanasia' programme had been to free handicapped and incurably ill patients from suffering:

I do not feel that I am incriminated. I am convinced that I can bear the responsibility for what I did in this connection before my conscience. I was motivated by absolutely humane feelings. I never had any other intention. I never had any other belief than that those poor miserable creatures – that the painful lives of these creatures were to be shortened. The only thing that I regret in this connection is that external circumstances brought it about that pain was inflicted on the relatives. But I am convinced that these relatives have overcome this sorrow today and that they themselves feel that their dead relatives were freed from suffering.[90]

Only a few in the courtroom would have been prepared to question Brandt's sincerity and strong belief in the moral righteousness of euthanasia. He had managed to paint himself as a wholehearted idealist, who wanted to stand up for the ideal in which he believed, a position which earned him a certain respect from the court.

After he had finished his statement, he was examined by almost all of the defence counsel in turn. Most of the defendants were given the chance to develop a suitable line of defence, which demonstrated that effectively none of them, including Brandt himself, could exercise real influence or authority in Germany and, therefore, none could be responsible for the crimes which had been committed. Siegfried Handloser, Chief of Army Medical Services, like Brandt, was allegedly unable to issue orders to any members of the armed forces unless he did so through Hitler. Brandt apparently never discussed questions of medical experimentation, or anything else, with his immediate subordinates and colleagues. He neither 'hinted' at specific experiments, nor did he inform others of his authority in the 'euthanasia' operation. Secrecy was a 'fundamental part' which meant that people were only informed on a need-to-know basis. 'I had to keep this thing to myself and to only inform those who were immediately affected by [the orders]. That was a directive which we always strictly complied with, and which applied to all of those who were in the close circle around the Führer,' Brandt said.[91]

On the morning of 5 February, Brandt's cross-examination began. Brandt had given more than nine hours of evidence, an impressive mental as well as physical achievement, if nothing else. He had spoken with few interruptions, and the bench had only rarely intervened, even when his answers were becoming long-winded and cumulative. For the prosecution, it was essential to pull Brandt away from his broad generalizations and to pin him down to those specific charges in the indictment. James McHaney, the prosecutor, went straight onto the offensive in his examination. He quickly discredited Brandt's expert credentials in the 'euthanasia' programme, and undermined his smokescreen of lofty moral and scientific ideals. Alexander, the medical expert for the prosecution, noted in his diary: 'Testimony [of Brandt] continued. McHaney really shook him to his foundations when he began the cross-examination today.'[92]

Brandt had neither training as a psychiatrist, nor had he any expert knowledge in the field of psychiatry. He had never visited any mental asylums for observation or study. He was unable to state the average time a mentally ill person spent in an asylum, but would swear that the 'insane died at an early stage in their life', were generally unhappy and suffered from pain. Bouhler was likewise no expert, not even a medical doctor. Brandt and his staff did not take any precautions to ensure that proper medical examinations of patients were carried out at the killing centres. The whole programme relied on questionnaires to determine whether or not a person was 'incurably ill', after Brandt had been 'assured' that a proper questionnaire would be filled out by a specialist.[93] He believed that the approval of parents in the children's 'euthanasia' programme was 'absolutely necessary', but he did not know whether it had ever been given, nor whether it had been given in writing or orally.[94] What Brandt saw as a medical procedure full of 'safeguards' was a system open to total arbitrariness, abuse and administrative chaos.

Although Hitler's decree explicitly stated that both Brandt and Bouhler should 'authorise' physicians by name, Brandt could not remember a single name, nor was he prepared to accept responsibility for these appointments. 'I am curious to know', McHaney hammered his point home,

> why a man in your position with the responsibility to designate these men with authority to perform euthanasia could not remember the names of ten or fifteen men who were actually doing it. You recalled only yesterday that two to four per cent of the people sent to a euthanasia station were rejected and weren't killed. I can't understand in the face of such remarkable memory that you wouldn't remember the names of ten or fifteen men?[95]

Brandt was unable to answer that question, but was 'quite sure' that none of these men had been sent to the East 'with my knowledge' to exterminate the Jews or commit other crimes. Brandt would not admit to anything on this day, even when exposed.

When the questions became too sensitive, Brandt would avoid answering them or talk about different matters. He was certainly a skilled and stubborn witness who would not be pressured into admissions. At one point McHaney questioned: 'I take it that you deny responsibility for the operation, the functioning of the "euthanasia" programme on the assumption that it was criminal: yes or no?' Brandt replied, 'We who participated in that programme, considered it as absolutely legal so that the execution of a crime during its execution cannot be considered.'[96] Regarding the mass terror and discrimination suffered by the Jews, he knew, of course, nothing, except 'that certain groups of Jews' were given a 'distinguishing mark'. Later it became known that 'they had been settled in certain areas. Outside of this I did not know anything.'[97] After another series of dodged questions, McHaney snapped: 'Herr Brandt, I am not in the least bit of a hurry. I will keep you on this stand for three days if necessary to get responses to my questions.'[98] The bench even became slightly impatient with Brandt's pretended ignorance and constant evasion. Finally, Judge Sebring stepped in and fired a round of sharp and concise questions to establish Brandt's moral and legal belief system:

> *Sebring*: Witness, … let us assume that it would have been highly important to the Wehrmacht to ascertain, as a matter of fact, how long a human being could withstand exposure to cold before succumbing to the effects of it. Do you understand that? Let's assume secondly that human subjects were selected for such freezing experiments without their consent. Let's assume thirdly that such involuntary human subjects were subjected to the experiments and died as a direct or indirect result thereof. Now, would you be good enough to inform the Tribunal what your view of such an experiment is – either from the legal or from the ethical point of view?

> *Brandt*: In this case I am of the opinion that, when considering the circumstances of the situation of war, this state institution [government] which has laid down the importance in the interest of the state at the same time takes the responsibility away from the physician if such an experiment ends fatally and such a responsibility has to be taken by the state.

> *Sebring*: Now, does it take away that responsibility from the physician, in your view, or does it share that responsibility jointly with the physician?

> *Brandt*: This responsibility is taken away from the physician because, from that moment on, the physician is merely an instrument, maybe in the same sense as it would be in the case of an officer who receives an order at the front and leads a group of three or four soldiers into a position where they have to meet death.[99]

Now Brandt was on the ropes. 'The Tribunal has one further question,' Sebring said mildly, before going for the kill:

> Would an order which authorised or directed a subordinate medical officer or subordinate medical group to carry out a certain medical experiment … without delineating or specifying in detail the exact course of those experiments – would you conceive that such an order would authorise the medical officer to whom the order was addressed to select subjects involuntarily and subject them to experiments, the execution of which that officer absolutely knew or should have known would likely result in death to the subject?[100]

'May I have your last sentence repeated?' Brandt was trying to buy some time. 'This question is extremely difficult to answer,' he said, before giving a number of examples which he hoped would show him a way out. Eventually Brandt expressed his moral belief system, for the first time, perhaps: 'In this case … the personal feeling and the feeling of a special professional, [the] ethical obligation has to stop behind the totalitarian nature of war.'[101] A moment later he expressed this view in even clearer terms:

> This authoritarian leadership interfered with the personality and the personal feeling of the human being. At the moment *as* [when] a personality is dissolved in the concept of a *collective body* [body politic], every demand which is put to that *personality* [person] has to be dissolved in the concept of a collective system. Therefore, the demands of society are put above every individual human being ... and this individual ... is completely used in the interest of that society ... At that moment everything was done in the interest of humanity and so that the individual person had no meaning whatsoever.[102]

What Brandt was effectively saying was that the physician, once he became a soldier, had to subordinate any of his medical or ethical views which might be in conflict with a military order from a higher authority. It was a position which the American judge could not accept. 'Dr Brandt,' Sebring inquired rhetorically,

> is it not true that in any military organisation, even one of an authoritarian State, there comes a point beyond which the officer receiving an order subjects himself to individual responsibility, at least in the eyes of civilised society, for carrying out any military orders, particularly if the order is unlawful or transcends the limits of an extreme military necessity?[103]

Sebring had finally got to the bottom of the Nazi moral belief system in which individual responsibility and morality had been totally abandoned or corrupted. Within Nazi medical research, 'the point' at which decent human beings would say 'stop' and disobey an order, had almost never come. This debate was based on the assumption that certain experiments had been ordered. But in most cases, Nazi research was initiated by the scientists themselves, and sanctioned retrospectively by the respective state representatives.

Brandt's cross-examination had been planned for a long time. The prosecution employed the well-proven technique of luring Brandt into making false statements and denials, before battering him in quick succession with irrefutable evidence which contradicted what he had said. On the afternoon of 6 February, and on the morning of 7 February, McHaney assailed Brandt with a flood of damning documents from the Himmler files. They showed that he had had substantial knowledge of human experiments in the camps, and that he had initiated a number of experiments himself. By this time, Brandt showed signs of mental fatigue, after having been on the stand for almost three days. His evasions became even less convincing when the prosecution introduced the best of its material, and thus secured a number of 'near admissions' from him.[104]

Brandt had to correct himself and admit that he had visited concentration camps more than once and that he had known of, and had not prevented, the Ravensbrück sulphonamide drug experiments. He had given a group of doctors a *carte blanche* to conduct experiments with poisonous gases and water on camp inmates: 'It is quite possible that something of this sort was said ... On the basis of this document it appears that special tests were carried out in the camp at Hamburg-Neuengamme following the discussion. Yes,' an admission he probably would not have made on the previous day.[105] Brandt seems to have used the same style as Hitler, giving his subordinates or colleagues broad and vague suggestions as to how he imagined certain orders should be fulfilled. He was adamant that he had not given 'precise suggestions', and if the prosecution could prove him to be wrong, he claimed that he had only passed on an order from Hitler. In January 1943, Brandt had asked Himmler's adjutant, Karl Wolff, whether 'it is possible to carry out relevant nutritional experiments in concentration camps'.[106] Now Brandt claimed that at the time he 'did not consider this anything special, and besides, I had forgotten about it. Under other circumstance it would have been called a troop experiment.'[107] If nothing else, it was an admission of ignorance, coupled with callousness.

Next, McHaney produced as evidence a teletype from February 1944 in which Rudolf Brandt stated that 'Brandt called up and requested the approval of the SS-Reichsführer that ten prisoners from Oranienburg should be made available as of tomorrow for two days, to test a certain drug. Nothing would happen to them.'[108] During cross-examination Brandt only replied: 'According to the teletype message here, I did that, assuming that this is authentic.'[109] Four days later, on 8 February 1944, Himmler had communicated his approval through Glücks, the head of the concentration camps. Brandt, by now entangled in a web of contradictions, immediately seized on the name 'Glücks', whom he had allegedly never met and did not know. 'Well, Herr Brandt,' McHaney was closing in, 'whether or not you knew Glücks, you knew where to go when you needed concentration camp inmates for experiments, didn't you?' whereupon Brandt replied: 'If there had been anything like that I addressed Wolff ... and here apparently through the same channels an appeal went to Himmler.'[110] It was one of the few instances where Brandt probably told the truth. For McHaney, summing up his case, it showed that Brandt had consistently tried to mislead the Tribunal, that he had been in contact with the SS and had tried to obtain prisoners, for whatever purposes, although he had previously vehemently denied such contact. The cross-examination greatly undermined Brandt's credibility in the eyes of the Tribunal and left the image of the idealistic and morally sound doctor in tatters.

Behind the scenes, however, Brandt's defence staff and family were mobilizing all contacts and channels of influence. Late in the evening of 24 January, Servatius had tried, but failed, to establish a telephone connection with Paul Diepgen, professor of medical history at Berlin University, to brief him on the latest developments in the trial, and secure his support for Brandt.[111] His call triggered a frenzy of activity; Brandt's name still carried weight in the higher echelons of the medical faculty. The content of Servatius's call was immediately relayed by the official on duty to the head of the faculty, the eminent gynaecologist Walter Stoeckel, who suggested calling Diepgen at his home in the Teutonenstrasse in Berlin-Nikolassee. Diepgen had expected the call and was willing to offer his support. Among those supporting Brandt were Oberstabsarzt Victor Müller-Heß, the former head of the

Institute for Military Forensic Medicine of the Military Medical Academy,[112] and the distinguished Hamburg psychiatrist, Hans Bürger-Prinz. On 12 February, a week after Brandt's cross-examination, British intelligence intercepted a telephone conversation between a female member of staff at Servatius's office in Nuremberg and Annemarie Bürger-Prinz, wife of the Hamburg professor.[113] The conversation revealed that the text of Bürger-Prinz's affidavit was not written by himself, but that Servatius's office was drafting its exact wording. The caller dictated to Frau Bürger-Prinz a statement of the numerous alleged good deeds that Brandt had performed while in active service. Brandt was supposed to have saved the lives of several defendants at the notorious People's Court (*Volksgerichtshof*), in particular that of a physician who had refused to swear the oath to Hitler.[114] He also sent convoys of cars to Hamburg to evacuate major cities before and after air raids. These hospitals were evacuated, and no distinction was made between the patients whether they were Jews, foreigners or Germans, the caller was overheard to say. Finally Frau Bürger-Prinz received detailed instructions about having the declaration confirmed by a notary and sent to Nuremberg.[115] To what extent the prosecution was provided with this kind of information about defence strategy remains unclear. It would certainly have enabled them to prepare their rebuttal in advance. It is more likely, though, that the intelligence agencies were primarily interested in the network of contacts that high Nazi officials like Brandt had, in order to monitor the security situation in post-war Germany.

By April, after most of Brandt's defence witnesses had been cross-examined, the *Süddeutsche Zeitung* published its observations on the trial in an editorial entitled 'Hippocrates as a Warning Signal', written by W.E. Süßkind.[116] Süßkind's article dealt extensively with Brandt, seen as an 'undoubtedly strong, if cold and unapproachable intelligence', whose views on medical ethics and the Hippocratic tradition were of general interest in understanding Nazi medicine and the future of medical education. For Brandt, the Hippocratic oath, Süßkind noted, was nothing but a professional code of conduct for doctors, and subject to change throughout history. With regard to 'euthanasia', Brandt had argued that Hippocrates would have modified the code if he had been a contemporary. Claiming to be 'absolutely rational', Brandt assigned total priority to the state over absolute medical ethics. For Brandt, 'this simple and old-fashioned sounding declaration that one should pass one's knowledge on, and never apply it to the harm of a patient' was a principle which was not always valid in practice. However the individual cases might turn out, and disregarding the personal guilt of the defendants, Süßkind concluded that the trial had plainly shown that fundamental moral principles had been broken and abused.

Taking Brandt's argument to its logical conclusion and viewing it in isolation, Alexander argued, years later, it could appear almost unassailable.[117] 'Nothing has brought home to me more clearly the key importance of the concept of the inviolable dignity of the individual than my many and varied conversations with Dr Karl Brandt,' Alexander stated. In some of their more informal conversations, Brandt had argued that American doctors, or doctors anywhere else in the world, would not hesitate to destroy several million cancer cells if these were considered harmful to the patient, or rid the individual of any disfigurement, because it was believed the person would be better off without it.

> We German physicians look upon the state as an individual to whom we owe prime allegiance, and we therefore do not hesitate to destroy an aggregate of, for instance, a trillion cells in the form of a number of individual human beings if we believe they are harmful to the total organism – the state – or if we feel that the state will thrive without them.[118]

It is doubtful that Herbert Spencer anticipated such a line of argument when he introduced the concept of the 'Social Organism' into academic debate at the end of the nineteenth century.[119]

The months following Brandt's cross-examination saw a minor victory for the defendants after the Defence Counsel submitted evidence of US human experiments on prison inmates and conscientious objectors, something which was anything but welcome to the prosecution, but was eventually allowed as evidence.[120] The most embarrassing example was evidence of large-scale malaria experiments on 800 American prisoners, many of them black, who had been selected from Federal penitentiaries in Atlanta, the Illinois State Penitentiary and New Jersey State Reformatory. Human experiments had been conducted with malaria tropica, one of the most dangerous of the malaria strains, to aid the war effort in South-East Asia. In June 1945, the magazine *Life* had given the story wide publicity in an article entitled 'Prison Malaria', which revealed, among other things, that the research was organized by the Office of Scientific Research and Development.[121] The journal noted that 'the experimenters ... have found prison life ideal for controlled laboratory work with humans'.[122] Brandt was quick to stress that 'a certain number of fatalities had to be taken into account from the start when infecting eight hundred people with malaria'.[123] Further evidence of poison experiments on condemned prisoners in other countries, or cholera and plague experiments on children, raised considerable doubts regarding the research practices of Allied medical researchers. It forced the US prosecution to fly in a second medical expert, Andrew Ivy, whose task was to explain the differences in medical ethics between German and US medical experiments. Interestingly, Ivy himself had been involved in the malaria experiments at the Illinois State Penitentiary. It was this intense debate about the definition of volunteers and of informed consent which led the prosecution to draft written principles for permissible experiments on humans, later adopted by the judges in their final judgement.[124]

What infuriated Brandt and the other defendants most was the moral high ground that the US prosecution took, especially since there was evidence which raised questions about the voluntary nature of some of the experiments carried out in the United States during the war. Furthermore, the prosecution's attempt to make it seem that there had been 'written' medical ethics guidelines in the United States prior to the trial was exposed as untrue.[125] In his testimony in June 1946, which lasted for more than four days, Ivy stated that the United States had specific research standards for research on humans, which were laid down in the American Medical Association (AMA) guidelines. It turned out, however, that Ivy had studied the prosecution evidence before the start of the trial and had reported his views on the ethics of human experimentation to the American Medical Association's trustees. Ivy's 'Principles of Ethics Concerning Experimentation on Human Beings' included the need for 'voluntary consent', prior animal experiments, and proper protection and management of the experiment.[126] During cross-examination, the defence easily discovered the lack of published international ethics standards on human experimentation. Ivy had to admit that the principles had been published by the AMA on 28 December 1946, nineteen days after the opening of the trial. No such published principles had existed for American research before. What is more, the publication of the AMA principles on medical ethics in human experimentation had been made in anticipation of Ivy's testimony in the trial:

Ivy: I submitted to them [AMA] some ethical principles and asked them to take action regarding, or to make a statement regarding the ethical principles of the American Medical Association in regard to the question of human beings as subjects in medical experiments on the basis of their principles of medical ethics.

Defence: This was December 1946?

Ivy: Yes.

Defence: Did that take place in consideration of this trial?

Ivy: Well, that took place as a result of my relation to the trial, yes.

Defence: Before December of 1946 were such instructions in printed form in existence in America?

Ivy: No. They were understood only as a matter of common practice[127]

But coming back to the issue of individual moral responsibility, Ivy maintained 'that there is no state or politician under the sun that could force me to perform a medical experiment which I thought was morally unjustified'.[128] The whole incident was nonetheless a considerable embarrassment for the US prosecution; they were forced to pull together their expert testimonies into a set of ethical principles that could be used by the judges in their final judgement. These principles served as the basis for the Nuremberg Code.

Despite such short-lived victories, the defence could not alter the fact that German doctors had largely violated their own medical ethics standards as laid down in government directives from 1931 and legally in force until 1945. According to German law, most of the concentration camp experiments constituted crimes. The discrepancy between existing codes of medical practice and actual behaviour by German doctors also raised the question of the almost non-existent effect of formal ethical regulations in Germany. And it raised the fundamental issue of medical training and ethical education in Germany.[129] The general disregard for ethical issues and patient rights in medicine ranged from overt violations of human and civil rights by camp physicians to more sophisticated forms of circumvention and mere formal obedience. But it also became apparent in ordinary doctor–patient relationships and medical paternalism, in daily medical examinations and tests, in medical records, in the use of discriminatory language, and also in medical films.[130] The handicapped, the sick and frail no longer enjoyed the same degree of respect and sympathy as their fellow healthy Aryan citizens; tolerance and behaviour towards human beings had become dependent on whether the person was seen as a valuable member of society, or as a burden or threat to the health of the nation. For the pragmatic Nuremberg prosecutors, the issue was even simpler: any use of involuntary subjects in a medical experiment constituted a crime, one which resulted in death being a crime of murder. On 14 July the prosecution demanded the death sentence for Brandt.

Days earlier, on 8 July, writing to reassure his family that he had known nothing about the reality of the 'euthanasia' operation, Brandt reflected about the extent to which the prosecution would place the responsibility of the 'euthanasia' programme onto his shoulders; he was not only convinced that he would have to shoulder the blame for some of the crimes in the Eastern territories, but believed that he could not have prevented any of these, even if he had known about them:

> Why I did not know anything, well, the answer lies in the matter itself. The implementation was just none of my business. For this Bouhler had his organisation. He signed for it. However, the prosecution will now attempt to make me responsible, because only I am now here. Moreover, the prosecution will try to blame me for all the killings in the concentration camps and in Poland. I don't know how they propose to prove this ... In any case, I would like to give you once more the inner reassurance [innere Beruhigung] that I was in no way informed about these things and that I in no way ever initiated anything even remotely of this nature. In retrospect, I have to add: what would have happened, if I had known? Could I have influenced it? Could it have been prevented? Not through me, I believe. Even my channels would have been limited: AH [Adolf Hitler], Bormann, Bouhler – I could not have approached anyone else. So today I must say – whether it was for good or bad – that fate protected me from having to make difficult choices.[131]

On 19 July, Brandt gave his closing speech. Standing next to the microphone in the middle of the defendants' box, his speech combined notions of idealism with a discourse about medical ethics in human experimentation and practice. Brandt's whole defence came down to arguing that he had done nothing wrong except in obeying the orders of the head of state. It was a defence which the bench had to endure many more times. 'There is a word which seems so simple,' he said, 'and that is the word order, and yet how atrocious are its implications, how immeasurable are the conflicts which hide behind the word. Both affected me, to obey and to give orders, and both are responsibility. I am a doctor and before my conscience there is this responsibility as the responsibility towards men and towards life.'[132] Brandt believed that it was 'immaterial for the experiment' whether it was conducted 'against the will' of the experimental subject, thereby assigning a value to the human experiment itself, without considering the human subjects involved. The value of the experiment apparently was 'much deeper' than the life of the individual:

> Can I, as an individual, remove myself from the community? Can I be outside and without it? Could I, as a part of this community, evade it by saying I want to thrive in this community, but I don't want to sacrifice anything for it, not bodily and not with my soul? I want to keep my conscience clear. Let them try how they can get along.[133]

For Brandt such a position was clearly untenable. He believed that he and the community were 'somehow identical'. Continuing his rhetoric, he asked the court to have sympathy with both his action and inaction:

> Would you believe that it was a pleasure to me to receive the order to start euthanasia? For fifteen years I had laboured at the sick-bed and every patient was to me like a brother, every sick child I worried about as if it had been my own. And then that hard fate hit me. Is that guilt? Was it not my first thought to limit the scope of euthanasia? Did I not, the moment I was included, try to find a limit as well as finding a cure for the incurable? Were not the professors of the Universities there? Who could there be who was more qualified?[134]

Brandt defended himself against the charge of 'inhuman conduct'. He certainly did not want to be seen as being on the same level as some of the SS murderers from the occupied eastern territories. Against such a charge, he felt he had the 'right to human treatment'. He wanted the court to believe that he had not aspired to take charge of the 'euthanasia' programme, but that the head of state had ordered him to implement the operation:

> With the deepest devotion I have tortured myself again and again, but no philosophy and no other wisdom helped here. There was the decree and on it there was my name. I do not say that I could have feigned sickness. I do not live this life of mine in order to evade fate if I meet it. And thus I affirmed Euthanasia. I realise the problem is as old as man, but it is not a crime against man nor against humanity. Here I cannot believe like a clergyman or think as a jurist. I am a doctor and I see the law of nature as being the law of reason. From that grew in my heart the love of man and it stands before my conscience.[135]

Finally, Brandt repeated his deep conviction of the moral justification of the 'euthanasia' programme. His simplistic view of this complex problem must have been hard to stomach for some spectators after eight months of sustained and appalling evidence:

> I am deeply conscious that when I said 'Yes' to euthanasia I did so with the deepest conviction, just as it is my conviction today, that it was right. Death can mean relief. Death is life – just as much as birth. *It was never meant to be murder* [emphasis added]. I bear this burden but it is not the burden of crime. I bear this burden of mine, though,

with a heavy heart as my responsibility. Before it, I survive and prevail, and before my conscience, as a man and as a doctor.[136]

Brandt's closing speech made it clear that he had genuinely believed in the right-eousness of the killing operation. His arguments were nevertheless unconvincing: neither did he give any explanation as to why he had accepted a commission from someone who was governing a regime which was obviously barbarous and criminal, nor explain why he believed that it had not been necessary to supervise an unprecedented government programme which aimed at killing part of the country's population. It may not have been meant to be murder, but it was de facto murder beyond any reasonable doubt.

The weeks leading up to the judgement in the Doctors' Trial were marked by heightened tension among the members of the court. The defendants had produced voluminous closing briefs, which needed to be translated before the judgement was prepared. Becker-Freyseng's brief came to a total of 203 pages, Beiglböck's 206 pages, while Brandt had three books with a total of 246 pages. All of Brandt's material was translated and handed to the office of the Secretary General by 1 August, although Brandt later alleged that the material had not been given to the judges prior to the day when judgement was handed down.[137] The translation of the judgement was carried out in total secrecy and under guard of the United States armed forces. It was of utmost importance that the verdict should not be leaked before it was actually read out in court. The date when the judgement was translated was only known to a few senior officials, and to those involved in the actual trial. Judge Beals personally swore to secrecy each person who might have access to the contents of the document. When parts of the judgement were received for translation by the language division on 15 August, the translators and clerical personnel were placed incommunicado with all other people, and thus they had to remain for four days. The last part of the judgement was received on 18 August, one day before it was delivered.

Amounting to 248 pages, the judgement had taken the judges more than two weeks to draw up. It constituted a significant document of linguistic precision, objectivity and impartiality.[138] On Tuesday 19 August, while the region was suffer-ing from an oppressive heatwave, it was read out to a packed court for about eight and a half hours by Beals and two of the senior judges, each taking turns. Judge Swearingen listened intently; he remained content 'where circumstances had put him'. All the defendants had dressed for the occasion, 'less sloppy than usual'.[139] The atmosphere before the reading began reminded some of the moment before the start of a religious service. Each case was examined at great length before the judges gave their verdict. The actual reading was a solemn procedure, conducted in the deepest silence in the courtroom. During the four court recesses, each lasting for about ten minutes, the public remained seated, stunned by what they had heard. Hardly any comments were exchanged. If people talked at all, it was about the unbearable heat. At 6.30 p.m., the reading of the judgement was finished, followed by the announcement that sentences would be delivered the next day. Fifteen of the twenty-three defendants were found guilty of war crimes and crimes against humanity; seven were found not guilty and acquitted. One of them, Poppendick, was acquitted of the charges, but found guilty of membership of an organization declared criminal by the IMT.

Though engaging with the idealistic intentions claimed by Brandt, the Tribunal had not lost sight of the crimes which had been committed, real crimes by real people such as Brandt. Overall, they accepted the view of the prosecution that Brandt had 'held a position of the highest rank directly under Hitler. He was in a position to intervene with authority on all matters; indeed, it appears that such was his positive duty. It does not appear that at any time he took any steps to check medical experiments upon human subjects.'[140] As to the issue of 'euthanasia', the judges had come to the same conclusion. Without going into further debate about the legality of euthanasia if sanctioned by the state, they found him guilty on the weakest points of his defence: on negligence and the proven inclusion of foreign nationals in the 'euthanasia' programme. One foreign national killed in the 'euthanasia' programme would have sufficed. On 20 August 1947, the judges announced their verdict:

Karl Brandt admits that after he had disposed of the medical decision required to be made by him with regard to the initial program which he maintains was valid, he did not follow the program further but left the administrative details of execution to Bouhler. If this be true, his failure to follow up a programme for which he was charged with special responsibility constituted the gravest breach of duty. A discharge of that duty would have easily revealed what now is so manifestly evident from the record; that whatever may have been the original aim of the program, its purposes were prostituted by men for whom Brandt was responsible, and great numbers of non-German nationals were exterminated under its authority.

We have no doubt but that Karl Brandt – as he himself testified – is a sincere believer in the administration of euthanasia to persons hopelessly ill, whose lives are burdensome to themselves and an expense to the state or to their families. The abstract proposition of whether or not euthanasia is justified in certain cases of the class referred to, is no concern of this Tribunal. Whether or not a state may validly enact legislation which imposes euthanasia upon certain classes of its citizens, is likewise a question which does not enter into the issues. Assuming that it may do so, the Family of Nations is not obligated to give recognition to such legislation when it manifestly gives legality to plain murder and torture of defenceless and powerless human beings of other nations.

The evidence is conclusive that persons were included in the program who were non-German nationals. The dereliction of the defendant Brandt contributed to their extermination. That is enough to require this Tribunal to find that he is criminally responsible in the program.

We find that Karl Brandt was responsible for, aided and abetted, took a consenting part in, and was connected with plans and enterprises involving medical experiments conducted on non-German nationals against their consent, and in other atrocities, in the course of which murders, brutalities, cruelties, tortures and other inhumane acts were committed. To the extent that these criminal acts did not constitute War Crimes they constitute Crimes against Humanity.

    ... Military Tribunal I finds and adjudges the defendant Karl Brandt guilty, under Counts Two, Three, and Four, of the Indictment.[141]

The next day the *New York Times* carried a brief article under the headline 'Hitler's Doctor, Fourteen Others Guilty in Medical Experimentation Trial'. Brandt, described as 'sallow, lean and youthful', led the list of the accused by virtue of his 'almost unlimited influence with Hitler ...'[142]

For the pronouncement of sentences, secrecy was even tighter. No one, except the four judges, had prior knowledge of the sentences. They were read out and translated extemporaneously on the floor of the court on 20 August 1947.[143] Since the early hours, the courtroom had been filling up with official Allied and German observers, journalists and public spectators. All hotel rooms in Nuremberg and the surrounding areas had been booked for weeks in advance. By 9.45 a.m., all seats were occupied. For the last time the courtroom was packed in silence, 'almost meditative', as one commentator noted. The seats and the door of the dock had been removed to ensure an expeditious procedure. The session opened half an hour later than usual, at 10 a.m. sharp. At 10.04 a.m., the President ordered the guards to bring in the first defendant: Karl Brandt. The official film record shows Brandt being led in by a guard to the centre of the dock where he stood motionless, at attention, between two military policemen, facing Walter Beals and the other judges. He picked up the headphones and heard:

> Karl Brandt, Military Tribunal I has found and adjudged you guilty of War Crimes, Crimes against Humanity, and membership in an organisation declared criminal by the judgement of the International Military Tribunal, as charged under the indictment heretofore filed against you. For your said crimes, on which you have been, and now stand convicted, Military Tribunal I sentences you, Karl Brandt, to death by hanging. And may God have mercy on your soul.[144]

'Not a muscle of his face moves, not a wink, not a respiratory motion more rapid than the precedent one, completely insensitive, he seems to listen to a sentence which does not concern him and which strikes a stranger,' one commentator remarked.[145] Brandt remained motionless for a number of seconds, waiting for the translation to come through. 'The Officer of the Guards will remove the defendant Brandt,' Judge Beals finally said. Before leaving the courtroom, he briefly turned to look at the cameras, for the last time, and smoothed out a strand of his pitch-black hair. In the shadow of the elevator, the figures of the two guards who took possession of the condemned became visible. Then the automatic door closed in silence. 'It is perhaps the most poignant moment and it seems to everyone that the condemned already no longer belongs to the world of human beings, that he has disappeared definitively, for ever ...,' one observer said.[146] The incident had lasted one minute and forty seconds.

Five of the defendants were sentenced to life imprisonment, later commuted to fifteen or twenty years.[147] Herta Oberheuser, the only woman on trial, was sentenced to twenty years' imprisonment, but released in the mid-1950s. Rostock, Blome, Ruff, Romberg, Weltz, Schäfer and Pokorny were acquitted and freed. Like Brandt, six others of the accused were sentenced to death by hanging: Brack, Sievers, Gebhardt, Hoven, Mrugowsky and Rudolf Brandt. At 10.33 a.m., the last of the defendants, Fritz Fischer, sentenced to life imprisonment, disappeared into the dark through the sliding door in the courtroom wall. The final drama had lasted twenty-nine minutes. At 10.35 a.m., Walter Beals lifted the gavel and, with a brief rap, the session was adjourned. Military Tribunal I, Case 1, had completed its mission.

'Outside, no gatherings,' Charles Sillevaerts reflected on his way back to Belgium after having reported for nine months from Nuremberg:

> It seems to me that the German public is not very interested by these judgements; life is hard, very hard; bread good or bad is hard to earn. One has no time to lose, everybody for himself. The past does not matter, neither does the future, provided that one can live, half decently, in the present.[148]

12

Under Sentence of Death

At the beginning of September 1947, Brandt was moved to the old fortress at Landsberg am Lech, where Hitler had written *Mein Kampf* after his 1923 Munich putsch attempt. Landsberg, Hitler had once told Hans Frank, later Governor General in occupied Poland and condemned to death by the IMT, was his 'university paid for by the state'.[1] It was here that Hitler, Germany's would-be redeemer, had held court to 500 visitors in his comfortable prison cell overlooking the Bavarian landscape. Now, almost twenty-five years later, the prison was to become a poignant reminder that any remnants of the former regime were to be rooted out. Here Hitler's most loyal and guiltiest servants were to be hanged. Landsberg am Lech was itself a small and picturesque town about forty miles west of Munich, but its name is forever linked with Hitler's ascendancy to supreme leadership of the *völkisch* movement.

In the memory of the people of Landsberg, the 'War Crimes Prison No. 1' formed a major part of the post-war reconstruction period and this placed a heavy burden on the overall atmosphere and character of the town.[2] The first condemned war criminals to enter the prison complex came in December 1945 after the conclusion of the first of the Dachau trials. One year later, the prison was officially taken over by the US military government. The guards were mostly Polish soldiers, often former Displaced Persons (DPs), who had been recruited into the US Army. They wore blue uniforms and could be easily distinguished from their American comrades. Over the years, the identification of the town with prison affairs steadily increased. Doctors from the town hospital provided basic medical care for the imprisoned men. Council officials organized accommodation for relatives who wanted to visit or say farewell for the last time. Whenever a prisoner was hanged, the local council issued the death certificate, and journalists reported on the executions in the local press. Sometimes the head of the local police would act as a witness. A nearby slope gave would-be spectators a view into the prison courtyard where the hangings took place. Rumours about new prisoners and imminent executions spread far and wide, leading to a series of petitions by the Landsberg women to Eleanor Roosevelt and General Clay, in which they asked for clemency for the condemned men. At Christmas and at other religious holidays, the Landsberg youth choir gave a concert for the prisoners as a sign of sympathy. It was not so much the enormity of the crimes of the prison inmates which mattered to the town officials and the public alike, but the prospect of gaining a reputation and image as the 'town of executions'. In the political struggle against the executions, the hundreds and thousands of Nazi victims, some of them clearly visible in the Jewish DP camp on the outskirts of Landsberg, were of little concern to the German authorities.

The first reactions from Brandt's friends and colleagues reached Anni Brandt days after the verdict. On 24 August, Werner von Bargen told her that the verdict had turned Brandt, against 'all his expectations', into the prime culprit responsible for experiments on concentration camp inmates.[3] In a note of protest to the President of the Tribunal, Rostock declared that the verdict was a 'miscarriage of justice'. Another letter came from one of the heads of the special hospitals built under the code name 'Aktion Brandt'. Although he had only met Brandt once in his life, Hans Rink of the Marienheide hospital felt obliged to register his protest against the judgement. The existence of the hospital alone was 'obvious proof', in Rink's opinion, that Brandt had had a 'deep feeling of responsibility towards society'.[4] In his concluding paragraph he criticized the trial procedure by implying that the verdicts had been biased. Moreover, he linked the alleged injustice of the Nuremberg trials with the violation of laws and justice in the Nazi regime, a frequently employed tactic in the forthcoming political battle over German war criminals: 'How easily do all of us Germans (whose sense of justice was apparently badly violated) gain the impression that the classification of a defendant as No. 1 in a trial implies a heavily-weighted bias in the judgement.'[5] Rink was effectively saying that Brandt had been condemned to death before the trial had started and that the judges had been biased, an unfounded and offensive assumption.

In Landsberg, Brandt was placed in solitary confinement. The long hours in the prison cell were only interrupted when his counsel Servatius or his friends and relatives came to visit him. They would sit opposite each other and talk through a hatch while a guard watched them. Apparently, during one of these visits, Brandt was offered poison to avoid the humiliating death by hanging. His response was reported to be: 'A Brandt does not kill himself. They shall have their pleasure of hanging me.'[6] It is doubtful whether there is much credibility in the story, but Brandt seems to have entertained all sorts of ideas in the immediate aftermath of the trial. Despite his conviction, he was uncompromising in his belief that most of the experiments carried out had been for the good of mankind. He launched his counter-attack the day after being sentenced to death. After months of passivity, this was an opportunity to regain the initiative. On Thursday 21 August, he asked the US authorities to use his body in a medical experiment with no chance of survival:

> In order to raise the significance of this death sentence above the level of mere execution of a judicial principle to the level of a deliberate act in the interest and to the benefit of mankind, I am of my free will willing to submit myself to a medical experiment offering no chance of survival. Being convinced that some of my colleagues sentenced together with me will join in my plea, there will not only be the possibility of a single experiment, but that of a collective one. I appeal to the public of the whole world not only to support my request but to demand compliance with it.[7]

Brandt hoped to expose America and American medical science as hypocritical if the authorities granted his request, but the whole idea was rejected without being given serious consideration.

Before his transfer from Nuremberg to Landsberg, Brandt saw one last official interrogator from the Department of Conservation of the American Military Government. On the afternoon of 3 September, Mr Lehmann-Haupt explained the reason for the unusual interview:

> Our task is to establish order in this chaos of transferred art. As you know, a lot of property and massive amounts of art and cultural possessions were moved to other places for reasons of security and misappropriation ... The *Ahnenerbe* played a major part in securing and appropriating art treasures, not so much for reasons of art, but for scientific reasons.[8]

More than two years after the war, Brandt was still being confused with Rudolf Brandt, who had had strong links with Himmler's Research Foundation, Ancestral Heritage ('*Ahnenerbe*' for short). Apart from some art treasures which were located in the Führer building in Munich, and in the bunker of the Reich Chancellery in Berlin, Karl Brandt really could not help him.

What Brandt did not tell him, however, was about his own art treasures, some of which he had received from Hitler as recognition for long-standing loyalty and service. Paintings, sculptures and other art treasures had indeed played a significant role in some of the early investigations, when it transpired that Brandt had had considerable debts.[9] During cross-examination, it turned out that Hitler had given Brandt 50,000 tax-free Reichsmarks to pay his debt and continue his luxurious lifestyle. 'At that time I got into debt and the Führer knew about it. Consequently, I received this sum of money,' Brandt told the prosecution.[10] Such a large payment suggested a certain degree of corruption, since government funds had been used to finance the private lives and hobbies of Hitler's acolytes. There were also payments in kind. Among Brandt's other paintings was a landscape with an inn, painted by a Sudeten German and given to Brandt as a present by Hitler. He had never received the painting because it was exhibited in one of the exhibitions on German Romanticism in the 'House of Art'. Hitler took particular pride in selecting monumental kitsch, not only for his staff to own, but for the German public to see. Another 'Führer present' was a painting of a zither player, given to him by Hoffmann, probably as a birthday present. Brandt also owned a number of still lifes from the eighteenth and nineteenth centuries, one of which he had received as a present from his Munich acquaintance, Marion Schönemann. His art treasures were exhibited to the medical and political elite, who visited Brandt in his apartment in Bellevue Palace, an eighteenth-century palace in the centre of Berlin. Paintings by Stuck, Froehlich, Chasserdeux, Buchner, Thoma and Lessing were poignant reminders that Brandt was a man of taste and culture. Sculptures by Thorak and Breker were also part of the atmosphere. As he was a condemned war criminal, all Brandt's property was confiscated by the Control Council of Germany.[11]

The court meanwhile received numerous petitions from influential physicians and colleagues of Brandt, and from his co-defendants.[12] His lawyer also tried everything possible to commute the death sentence to life imprisonment, submitting one plea for clemency after another to the US military government.[13] The list started with an application to the Military Governor and a petition to the Supreme Court on 28 August, followed by a plea for clemency to the Judge Advocate General on 4 September. German church leaders had been approached in advance by Brandt's wife and lawyers to secure their support 'in case it became necessary'.[14] On 11 August, one week before the promulgation of judgement, Eugen Gerstenmaier, a leader of the German Protestant Church and a member of the newly founded CDU, asked the Bodelschwingh asylum near Bielefeld whether it was inclined to support a clemency petition for Brandt.[15] Gerstenmaier was himself 'indebted to Professor Brandt', who had apparently made Gerstenmaier's RSHA police record available to his 'friends' at 'a particularly difficult moment'. He had thus been able 'to gain important information for [his] own defence' during the prosecution of those suspected of participating in the assassination attempt on Hitler's life. Gerstenmaier was adamant that euthanasia should not be viewed as a war crime, 'so that the Nuremberg court should be seen as having no jurisdiction over Brandt'.[16] Conflating different issues, namely whether or not the Nazi 'euthanasia' programme was criminal, and whether or not the Nuremberg Tribunal was legally justified in putting Brandt on trial, became one of the strategies of Gerstenmaier and other church leaders in mounting a concerted campaign against the trials.

The response from R. Hardt, acting director of the Bodelschwingh asylum, made it clear that the institution was willing to support Brandt's case, although there was some rather incriminating material which the late von Bodelschwingh had collected about Brandt and the 'euthanasia' programme: 'I still have in my possession a number of written notes from the hand of Pastor von Bodelschwingh which would not be suitable for the defence of Prof. Brandt, but which could provide a sufficient basis to support a plea for clemency.'[17] On 17 September, the petition by the Bodelschwingh asylum implied that 'Dr Brandt had suffered under the order he had been given', and that Hitler's 'order had been a heavy burden'. Lifting the encounter between Brandt and von Bodelschwingh in 1941 and 1943 onto an almost metaphorical plane, Hardt's usage of religious rhetoric was intended to soften the views of the authorities as well as shaping a post-war myth about von Bodelschwingh and the Bodelschwingh institution. Two years after the war, the process of rewriting German history was in full swing:

> In hour-long personal struggles, Pastor von Bodelschwingh was able to gain a deep insight into the innermost condition of Brandt's soul. He tried to keep the voice of his conscience awake and received a response. In fact, in the course of the negotiations with Dr Brandt in our asylums not a single patient was killed and in the whole of West Germany the 'euthanasia' programme was discontinued.[18]

Another petition came from Julia von Bodelschwingh, whose husband had developed an amicable relationship with Brandt.[19] In an emotive appeal, Julia von Bodelschwingh requested 'insistently and from the bottom of [my] heart before God and mankind: spare his life!' She told the authorities that she had sometimes been party to the talks between von Bodelschwingh and 'this erring man who, however, erred in all sincerity'.[20]

A more politically coloured petition came from Britain on the eve of the Cold War. On 25 September 1947 a Mr A. B. Chittick from Hammersmith in London, a frequent writer of clemency petitions on behalf of condemned criminals, wrote to the Commander-in-Chief of the American Forces in Germany. Chittick feared that the hangings of Brandt and other Germans would send the wrong signal, and might fuel support for the Communist cause. Apparently the hangings by the Communists in Bulgaria had 'roused indignation' in Britain: 'If Dr Brandt is doomed to die, it is only the Communists not only in England, but all over the Earth, who will celebrate and blatantly proclaim another victory, as they always do when anybody they deem an enemy is killed. They have not considered murder as being beneath their dignity to resort to.' Chittick continued his anti-communist diatribe by stating that 'their literature is openly hostile to the Constitution of the United States'.[21] All these interventions had no impact.

On 7 October 1947, Rostock wrote to Brandt that this time his notorious pessimism had been justified: 'I was correct in my judgement of the opposition.' He also passed on the latest gossip after having met members of the prosecution and the bench who had been friendly and helpful. As he was unemployed, the presiding judge had apparently recommended Rostock to the US government. At the end of his letter he struck a rather sombre note:

> For what lies ahead of you, my dear Brandt, I wish you courage and energy and the exemplary attitude which you have always displayed, especially last year. Some day the world will think differently about it. That can be seen already. On us rests a nightmare, which we old ones will not get rid of any more. May the coming generation and Karl-Adolf one day have it better than we have had.[22]

On the same day he wrote to Anni:

> What can one really write? The one possible outcome, often considered in mutual talks with Karl, which we had all hoped would pass, has become reality. Those who have looked the prosecution and the judges in the eye (*Wer in das Gesicht der Männer der Gegenseite gesehen hat*) had to anticipate this [outcome]. And Karl has done this from the very beginning, even before we all saw these faces.[23]

Meanwhile Brandt's lawyers were far from ready to give up. Even otherwise highly critical voices, such as Alexander Mitscherlich, now held the view that one should support a plea of clemency for Brandt.[24] One of the more spectacular petitions came from twenty-six notable German medical scientists, signed amongst others by the Nobel laureate Gerhard Domagk (whom Hitler had prevented from accepting the award), and seven leading medical professors: Carl von Eicken, Robert Rössle, Ferdinand Sauerbruch, Walter Stoeckel, Wilhelm Toennis, Paul Uhlenhuth and Werner Wachsmuth.[25] Domagk felt that Brandt should be given the opportunity 'to sacrifice himself for other human lives which are endangered instead of hanging him for the destroying of lives'.[26] Stoeckel stressed that he had made the personal acquaintance of Brandt when Anni Brandt had given birth to their son, Karl-Adolf, in Stoeckel's Gynaecological Clinic in 1935. He had gained the impression of 'a serious, modest and sensitive man living up to his duty'.[27] Only one out of the twenty-six scientists addressed the issue of culpability. For Sauerbruch, there was 'no doubt that Herr Brandt has more than once become guilty in his activities as a physician and as a soldier'.[28] He believed, however, that Brandt had committed the offences not out of 'bad motives', but was forced to do so by Hitler and his gang.[29] In a concerted move, the petitions were submitted to the Secretary of the Army at the end of February 1948.

Reports from other prisoners suggest that the general treatment of the Landsberg prisoners, especially those sentenced at the Nuremberg trials as opposed to those in the Dachau trials, was satisfactory, and in compliance with American prison standards at the time. Landsberg prisoners, unlike other condemned prisoners, could receive parcels and did not have to work.[30] Rostock and other colleagues ensured that Brandt and his fellow prisoners were kept up to date with the latest specialist medical literature; some of them were even allowed to practise medicine in the hospital wing of the prison. Brandt was particularly interested in surgical books.[31] When, in 1950, the Clemency Board was established under the direction of the US High Commissioner for Germany (HICOG), John J. McCloy, it was found that Landsberg offered 'ideal prison conditions'.[32] Commissioner Frederick A. Moran, Chairman of the New York Board of Parole and an authority on prison administration, conducted an intensive inspection and interviewed the prisoners. He and the board were satisfied that the care, treatment and attention given to the prisoners complied with the 'highest standards' in prison administration.

Mounting criticism from high-ranking German church officials against the legality and conduct of the trials, and the conditions in which the condemned were held, bore fruit. In the aftermath of the war, the Western Allies had welcomed the contribution of one of the few apparently uncompromised elite groups. This had led the representatives of the Catholic and Protestant faiths to conduct a concerted campaign in support of Germans accused of war crimes. Following the end of the IMT and the Doctors' Trial, their activities in favour of individual defendants became increasingly enmeshed in wider political issues and a general opposition to Allied war crimes policy. The founding of the Federal Republic also consolidated effective structures of influence and power. As early as 1946, the chairman of the Protestant Church of Germany (EKD), the Württembergian state Bishop Theophil Wurm, one of the most outspoken opponents of the trials, had told the President of the IMT, Sir Geoffrey Lawrence, that 'the Germans could not understand why the Nuremberg proceedings only addressed their share in the aggressive war against Poland', implying that the Soviet Union apparently bore equal responsibility for the horrors in Poland.[33] In January 1948, he had suggested to Robert Kempner, the deputy chief of counsel, that many Nazi officials, such as Ernst von Weizäcker, for example, 'were forced now and then to participate in things and to say things which were to produce an impression of national-socialist reliability'. Wurm was effectively saying that all these men had been part of the resistance movement and should not be put on trial. Likewise, the Dachau trials, with more than 1,500 defendants, became increasingly the target of legal and moral criticism. By drawing attention to crimes committed by other nations and by conflating different contentious issues in the war crimes programme, including political denazification and criminal justice, bureaucratic responsibility and physical acts of violence, the old German elite hoped to blur, discredit and ultimately stop any further war crimes trials.

Their protest found unexpected support in February 1948, when subsequent Nuremberg proceedings, and thereby all cases tried up to that point, suffered a severe blow. Shortly before departing to America, the judge in the Hostage Case, Charles F. Wennerstrum, Justice at the Supreme Court of Iowa, gave an interview to one of the most outspoken opponents of the proceedings, the German-friendly *Chicago Tribune*, which sent shockwaves through the American military government. Wennerstrum alleged that, had he known seven months earlier what he knew now, he would never have come to Nuremberg. Not only had the trial procedure allegedly been flawed, but the concept of the prosecution was supposedly based on vengeance and personal ambitions. His comments also included some thinly disguised anti-Semitic remarks, amongst others that it was 'significant' that many members of the prosecution had only recently been naturalized as American citizens. Those members were 'rooted in the prejudices and feelings of hate against Europe', and thus prevented justice from being done to the Germans on trial. For Wennerstrum this was also evident in the non-existence of a board of appeal.[34] The furious knee-jerk reaction by the head of OCCWC, General Taylor, which reached the press before the interview was printed in the *Chicago Tribune*, described the critique as 'absolutely unfounded, evil and subversive', and as an expression of a 'psychopathic defect'.[35] His comments not only fanned suspicions that tensions between different factions among the American authorities had increased, but exposed the US headquarters to the charge of having a serious information leak. The whole affair played into the hands of an increasingly organized group of the German ruling elite, whose objective was to overturn the war criminal verdicts, especially in the cases of those sentenced to death.

At the beginning of 1948, Brandt fell ill with endocarditis and was transferred to the hospital wing of Landsberg, where he received medical treatment from his co-defendant Beiglböck and was X-rayed by Fischer.[36] At Christmas 1947, he had already indicated to Rostock that he was beginning to lose all hope and was ready to face death: 'What you said in N. [Nuremberg], that was all correct; it really could not have been different. Be convinced of that; who would know this better than me!'[37] Anni Brandt, who had visited her husband over Christmas, told friends that Brandt was composed, knowing 'that he had wanted the best for humanity'.[38] On 16 February, the US Supreme Court denied the final writ of habeas corpus.[39] By March, it had become clear that almost all petitions had been rejected, and that Washington would not exercise clemency. Although Gebhardt's wife clung to the idea that the death sentences would not be enforced, Rostock remained pessimistic.[40] On 19 April, a friend of his reported that the mood among the defendants was 'below zero', and that Servatius was apparently conducting 'some frantic efforts' which, according to Brandt, were 'pretty hopeless.'[41] The next day,

Rostock repeated his dire warning that 'whoever had looked with an open mind into the eyes of the other side, also into those of Clay, must know what is at stake'.[42] One of the Nuremberg prosecutors, Robert Kempner, also told Brandt's lawyer that the case of Brandt worsened the more one tried to support it.[43] All further petitions to the office of the President of the United States were referred back to the relevant military authorities. The final decision on the execution therefore lay in the hands of the most senior American military commander, General Lucius Clay. He saw his duty of reviewing the evidence in order to approve the sentence as a 'solemn responsibility', but had made it clear that he would not allow an appeal, and would go ahead once the stop on the execution order was lifted. On 10 May, he told another of the many petitioners that

> regardless of what inner conviction Dr Brandt may have held, he was directly responsible for much of the suffering and death caused to the unfortunate concentration camp victims chosen to be used as subjects in the brutal medical experiments. In justice to these persons who underwent torture and death, I am unable to grant clemency in this case.[44]

Four days later, on 14 May, he issued the order for the execution of the sentences in the Doctors' Trial.[45]

At the same time, the American authorities were confronted with a full-blown attack against the Nuremberg proceedings led by the leaders of the German Church in the American zone. On 20 May, its representative, Bishop Wurm, submitted their petition to Charles M. LaFollette, head of the military government in Württemberg-Baden. The latter was asked to forward the petition to Clay. Using inside information, which they had received from the Nuremberg defence lawyers, the church leaders cited the 'handicap of the defence against the prosecution', the 'coercion of witnesses', the 'general obligations of international law', the 'discrepancy of name and character of the Tribunals' and the 'lack of opportunity to have the Nuremberg judgements reviewed by an independent court'.[46] Significantly, the working conditions and wages of the defence lawyers figured high on the list of complaints. The tone of the Protestant church leaders was almost aggressive. They complained that the appointment of civilians as judges to a military court which tried German officers was a departure from 'customary practice laid down in the statutes of international law'. The last time that officers had been stripped of their rank and tried against international conventions, they said, had its 'historic precedent in the treatment of the German officers of 20 July 1944 by Adolf Hitler'. The creation of an appeal procedure and a review of judgements was seen as an 'imperative demand'.[47] In their final analysis, the church leaders warned that the Nuremberg trials would have a 'detrimental influence' on the 'recovery of sound public opinion'.[48] Underlying this robust line of argument was the threat of 'a new wave of nationalism in the German people', one which 'does not consider members of another nation as brothers'.[49] LaFollette was incensed by the petition, and advised Clay to read between the lines. The timing of the petition was no coincidence, when prominent industrialists such as Farben and Krupp and really big militarists such as the general staff generals and really important political figures such as Weizäcker are facing the end of their trials. The people previously convicted, although prominent in their fields, almost uniformly belonged to a class not previously revered by the German people. That is to say, they were doctors or lawyers or civil servants or people from the middle classes … In other words, there is a possibility now of people being convicted who comprise those elements in Germany which have always made it militaristic and nationally arrogant. We cannot forget that the Protestant Church of Germany was always the state church of Prussia and certainly unless we are blind we can see a connection between this sudden rushing of the church to the defence of those with whom it had such close ties in the past.[50]

Despite LaFollette's justified caution, the petitions had a considerable impact. On the eve of the Cold War, any policies which could potentially alienate the German public from the Western alliance were carefully weighed against the moral responsibility of putting Nazi war criminals behind bars. Although Clay issued a robust reply to the church leaders, telling them that 'never in history has evidence so convicted those in high places for their actions', and that it was difficult to see how a review of the cases 'could provide a basis for sentimental sympathy for those who brought suffering and anguish to untold millions', a change of policy was beginning to take shape behind the scenes.[51] At the highest level of US government, the question of German war criminals and the creation of a review board was discussed in a series of top secret exchanges at the end of May. The board was to make recommendations as to whether or not death sentences should be commuted to life imprisonments. But for Brandt time was running out.

In addition to being flooded with protests from all sections of German society against the execution of the 'red jackets' (*Rotjacken*) at Landsberg, so-called because the condemned men wore red jackets on their way to the gallows, Clay's initiative was actually triggered by a mistake. On 24 May 1948, he sent a top-secret cipher to Under Secretary William Draper in Washington, requesting advice on the handling of, as he believed, more than 500 death sentences which had accumulated due to delays in review and stay of sentences pending possible appeal to the Supreme Court. Clay was anxious that this 'mass execution' might give the appearance of cruelty by the United States, although there was no question in his mind that 'the crimes committed fully justify the death sentence'.[52] Taking further into account the time which had elapsed since the crimes had been committed, Clay was 'somewhat inclined to consider the commutation of these death sentences to life imprisonment in substantial measure'. Washington suggested the appointment of a clemency board which, Clay confirmed, was 'badly needed'. He pressed for its immediate selection. 'Problem is urgent and final action on sentences is necessary as soon as possible,' he cabled back from London on 26 May.[53] The clemency board would have meant a last chance for Brandt and might have put his imminent execution on hold. But on 31 May, two days before Brandt's execution, the urgency of the problem was significantly scaled down when it transpired that Clay had got the figures wrong: 'I must apologise for my figure 550 under death sentence. [It] should read 150 … The smaller number makes Clemency Board unnecessary as I can handle this here'.[54] Hence, there was no need to intervene in the execution of the first seven of the 150 prisoners on death row twenty-four hours later.[55]

In the meantime, Pastor von Bodelschwingh, Hardt's successor and von Bodelschwingh's nephew, launched a last-ditch attempt to delay Brandt's execution. He now made use of contacts who, in turn, had connections amongst the highest levels of politics in the Federal Republic and military government. On 29 May, he wrote to Hellmut Becker, one of Ernst von Weizäcker's lawyers. Von Weizäcker had been a high-ranking Foreign Office diplomat in the Third Reich and was the father of Richard von Weizäcker, subsequently president of Germany in the 1980s. Becker was a high-flying thirty-something barrister from an aristocratic Prussian background who was unscrupulous in exploiting every potential channel in politics and the media, whether direct or indirect, to mobilize support for his client. Hence, ultimately, the Weizäcker case became a catalyst for politicizing the war criminals issue.[56] It was this contact, Pastor von Bodelschwingh hoped, who might rescue the situation at the eleventh hour. He told Becker that Anni Brandt had told him from an 'unknown source' that a board of review was being established at the beginning of July to review the existing death sentences. From whom Anni Brandt received this information remains unclear. Overall, Brandt's lawyers and family were extremely well informed about almost every move of the Allied authorities, which suggests that they had inside informants. Pastor von Bodelschwingh asked Becker to 'pave the way for Mrs Brandt to Mr Maggee', Weizäcker's influential American lawyer, who was mobilizing support for his client in the United States. Pastor von Bodelschwingh concluded his letter by sending kind regards to 'Mr von Weizäcker'.[57] The old German elite was closing ranks in what became a first test case as to whether or not there was room for leniency after the conclusion of the IMT.

Twenty-four hours later, Pastor von Bodelschwingh approached Bishop Wurm of Württemberg, asking him to 'call for the power of mercy' at this late hour: 'If you are therefore willing and able to say a word in this matter at the highest level, I ask you to do this also in the name of my late uncle and the Bethel institution.'[58] He reiterated the news of the plan to create a review board, but warned in no uncertain terms that there was the likely danger that the Americans would want to 'terminate a number of especially strenuous cases before the start of the negotiations, by means of a rapid execution of the sentences'.[59] Wurm's objective, therefore, had to be to ensure that the future review board would be considered, and that no further executions should take place before then. Pastor von Bodelschwingh had made an accurate assessment. Before any official review of sentences could take place, Clay's aim was to dispose of the worst offenders. Any intervention on behalf of Brandt, therefore, had no chance of success.

On 24 May, the same day that Clay had secretly discussed the war crimes issue with Washington, another friend of the family had written to Rostock that 'the thing is apparently now so pressing, based on information from a leaked office report, that one can't see which way to turn'.[60] He was asked to intervene immediately because it was feared that within days the stop to the execution order might be lifted. At this point, Brandt seems to have been ill, as a friend told Rostock: 'Karli is very very ill; if there is no decision soon, it is the end. As you will probably know, Karli's lung is now also part of the equation.'[61] On 27 May, Rostock replied: 'The drama of Landsberg will now probably come to an end. You know that I have never expected another outcome. How greatly it affects me you will sense. I don't like to talk about it.'[62]

The next day, on 28 May 1948, Brandt wrote his last letter to Rostock:

> Dear *Vati* [Dad] Rostock, … now we are standing at the end and I know it. I am not angry. I get along without the world and without humans. That is not the problem and I have no further words to waste. If they do not want me, if they do not need me, that's OK … Preserve your friendship with Anni and stay at her side; it will also help the son.[63]

A final visit was scheduled for 31 May. Karl-Adolf was given the chance to see his father but preferred to stay at home.

The night before the hanging, the prison authorities sealed off the section in which the condemned were spending their final hours. Brandt was given a red shirt and led to a specially designed cell where he could say goodbye to whoever wished to see him. Anni had already travelled on 30 May to Landsberg, where she met other close friends who had come to say goodbye.[64] Waltraut von Hasselbach, the wife of Hanskarl von Hasselbach, Hitler's second escort physician and Brandt's deputy at Führer headquarters, was one of them. Von Hasselbach and Brandt had been close friends since they had become part of the notorious circle of Nazi doctors in Bochum who surrounded Georg Magnus. For Waltraut von Hasselbach, the last visit was a 'shocking experience'.[65] She sat opposite Brandt and exchanged a number of words. Then they laid their hands on the wire mesh and said farewell.

Another person who kept Brandt company in these dark hours was the prison doctor and former member of the Nazi Party, Rudolf Boeckh, the son of a priest, who not only had close connections with von Bodelschwingh and the Bethel asylum, where he had worked as a senior physician (*Oberarzt*) from 1925 to 1936, but who was himself involved in the deportation of mental patients as part of the 'euthanasia' programme.[66] There was certainly a lot Brandt and Boeckh could talk about. Boeckh had been detailed to serve at Landsberg prison since the beginning of 1948. During the preceding months, Brandt had often shared his daily thoughts with Boeckh, who tried to give solace to the condemned. One of the topics which particularly interested Brandt, and which he frequently discussed with Boeckh, was Albert Schweitzer's ethic of respect for life. The topic may well have struck a chord with Boeckh, who had worked as a missionary doctor in China before his employment in Bethel.[67] In some way, Brandt's life had come full circle. Brandt, it seems, must have believed that he himself had followed Schweitzer's ethic, and that the aim of his life had been to show the greatest respect for life. By persuading Boeckh of his overall good intentions, Brandt managed to convince himself that he had done nothing wrong and that he was free from any sense of guilt. For Brandt it was of utmost importance that his conscience was, and remained, clear. Until shortly before Brandt died, Boeckh remained with him. On 1 June, the night before the hanging, Brandt expressed his deep gratitude to Boeckh in one of his last letters. He thanked Boeckh for the fact that their conversations had been based on 'mutual understanding and attempts to understand'.[68] He also expressed the hope that Boeckh would remain a friend of the family and visit his wife at times, and sent his regards to Julia von Bodelschwingh. 'We do have it in us (*In uns ist alles*),' Brandt concluded his letter, 'to have experienced that with you and in you, time and time again, that is a great hope. Yours Karl Brandt.'[69]

On 2 June, at 10.10 a.m., Brandt was hanged as the first of the seven men condemned to death in the Doctors' Trial.[70] They were the first to be hanged of twenty-five prisoners sentenced to death at the Nuremberg trials. It was a rainy and chilly day. No visitors or relatives were allowed to be present during the execution. A number of journalists, guards and prison officials filled the wet courtyard of the prison, where two black gallows had been erected. They exhibited grim symbols: thirteen steps to the scaffold; thirteen coils in the knot of the noose. Brandt was the only one of the condemned men who refused religious aid at the scaffold. Instead, he made a long and agitated speech. Held at the elbows by two assistant hangmen, Brandt denounced the United States and described his sentence as nothing other than an 'act of political vengeance' and 'political murder'. It was one last desperate and incoherent attempt to vent his anger against the former enemy.

> How can the nation which holds the lead in human experimentation in any conceivable form, how can that nation dare to accuse and punish other nations which only copied their experimental procedures? And even euthanasia! Only look at Germany, and the way her misery has been manipulated and artificially prolonged. It is, of course, not surprising that the nation which in the face of the history of humanity will forever have to bear the guilt for Hiroshima and Nagasaki, that this nation attempts to hide itself behind moral superlatives. She does not bend the law: Justice has never been here! Neither in the whole nor in the particular. What dictates is power. And this power wants victims. We are such victims. I am such a victim.[71]

Brandt remained proud of having served his fatherland with all his energy: 'The gallows of Landsberg is the symbol of the inner duty of all upright and honest men.'[72] Finally, addressing his relatives, he said: 'My old parents and my courageous son do not need to be ashamed of me. I am close to them and linked in unshakeable confidence. In love I think of my wife: I am ready.'[73]

Newspapers reporting on the execution, such as the *Florida Times Junior*, suggest that Brandt delivered only part of the speech because it was too long. The American hangman, when Brandt ignored his admonitions to cut it short, threw the black hood over Brandt's head in mid-sentence, tied it around his neck and fastened the noose beneath his chin. Then he stepped back, pulled the lever, the trap sprang and Brandt fell. For those who witnessed the speech, it showed that Brandt had remained unrepentant to the end. Next came Mrugowsky, chief hygienist of the SS, who shouted defiantly from the scaffold: 'I die as a German officer sentenced by a brutal enemy and conscious that I never committed the crimes charged against me.' Karl Gebhardt, the head of the SS hospital at Hohenlychen and the last President of the German Red Cross, exclaimed: 'I die without bitterness, but regret there is still injustice in the world.' He was followed by Sievers, Brack, Hoven, and finally, Rudolf Brandt, personal adjutant to Himmler. After criticism about the time it had taken the prisoners of the IMT to die, some as long as sixteen minutes, the authorities were happy to report that the condemned men had died 'without a hitch'. Others, however, have suggested that the hangman's job in Landsberg was worse than in Nuremberg. Apparently some of the executed had to be suffocated with cotton wool which was pushed into their noses and mouth by American soldiers standing underneath the gallows.[74] Newspapers reported that the executions had lasted sixty-two minutes.[75]

In the meantime, Brandt's parents and his wife were at Boeckh's flat. He had offered them hospitality during these long days. 'An unforgettable time,' he remarked almost thirty years later.[76] In the afternoon, at 3 p.m., after the hanging of the seven men had been completed, Brandt's body was brought to the nearby cemetery of the Landsberg prison. Allied authorities at this point were less concerned with burial ceremony or any kind of formality. In their eyes, Brandt was a condemned war criminal who deserved nothing better than a speedy burial in an anonymous grave. The corpse was driven in a lorry to the grave, but it turned out that the grave was too short. After all, Brandt was 184 cm tall. Workmen were called in to lengthen the grave while the army captain supervising the work stood nearby smoking a cigarette. For the relatives and friends of the family this was nothing short of an act of desecration. Anni Brandt allegedly refused to be present under these circumstances and watched the burial from a nearby building. Only after the American GIs had left did a brief burial ceremony take place with the relatives and closest friends of the family. An Army priest called Lonitzer gave a brief speech in the name of Brandt's army comrades, and the prison doctor Boeckh delivered a farewell speech in the name of the Landsberg inmates:

I have to take an oath: the death of this man places all of us under an obligation – not for revenge or retaliation – that would not be his way, no, but to look forward and live his life. His death places us under an obligation in a rather different sense: health and happiness! That is how he greeted me with his sparkling eyes on 17 March, your wedding anniversary, which we celebrated with Professor Beiglböck in his cell in the building over there. That is how he wrote in his farewell letter to me: 'health and happiness, take this further!'

Yes, health! Isn't that our medical calling, but also in a deeper sense: the inner healing of our poor German people and fatherland, which he loved so much, for whom he gave his life?

And happiness? What is the relevance of happiness in this hour, here at the grave of the dear man? Yes, that is his legacy to us: forward-looking happiness, courage and confidence!

Recently I talked with Karl Brandt about Albert Schweitzer's ethic of respect for life.

Wasn't this respect for life the content of his life? Didn't he teach it to us and wasn't he a model in this for us German doctors and German youth?

Karl Brandt, you were truly a doctor in the spirit of Paracelsus: doctor and priest, researcher and helper. You dedicated your life to your profession until the last hour. In the building over there, where so many valuable human beings, truly German men, share a common destiny, you have followed this priestly medical calling [*priesterlichem Arzttum*] until the last moment, [you were the] focal point and model for us all.

I myself, an insignificant German doctor, call upon the German doctors and German youth to take on this legacy of Karl Brandt as an obligation and as a responsibility, to preserve his memory faithfully and follow his life. That we promise to you – thank you, Karl Brandt![77]

As a sign of gratitude, Anni Brandt shortly afterwards gave her bridal veil to Boeckh's daughter, who married in the same year.[78] Passing on the veil also carried strong symbolic weight as a romantic notion of marriage and reproduction, as a metaphor meant to hold the families of Hitler's inner circle and their children together. All together were his 'family'. At the beginning of the twenty-first century, some of them were still in contact with each other.

The next day the American newspaper *Stars and Stripes* reported that the hanged men had

> paid an eye for 10,000 eyes, a tooth for 10,000 teeth. In a chilling rain, they died unfrightened … A new-type knot developed by the Americans at Landsberg brought death quickly. It was over in an hour. All were found criminally responsible for horrible medical experiments conducted on helpless concentration camp inmates under the guise of scientific research.

On 4 June, Irmgard Günther, a friend, told Rostock in great fury that she had not believed that the sentence would ever be carried out. 'So our mutual friend did have to undertake this difficult journey,' she said before assigning to Brandt the virtues of a martyr: 'I heard from colleagues who were there that he walked his way proud and upright, without a muscle of his face moving, as we know him from the trial.' Two days after his death, the shaping of Brandt's image was already in full swing. At the end she cursed the Allies for this act: 'One day there will be vengeance, I am sure of that. Maybe it will take a couple of years, but it is coming. How must the poor wives feel; I have such great pity for them. And all the children, horrible!'[79] No such overflowing feelings of compassion and sympathy had been expressed when hundred of thousands of men, women and children had been murdered by the Nazis years earlier. To the horrors of the past and the ongoing suffering of Nazi victims, most Germans responded, as McCloy later pointed out, with 'abysmal ignorance'.

The graves of those sentenced to death in Nuremberg had to remain unmarked to prevent the spread of any kind of martyrdom or worshipping of former high-ranking Nazi officials. No cross was permitted. Only a number of smaller and bigger white stones surrounded the grave. At the foot of the grave stood a small metal plate which enabled relatives to identify the grave of the condemned person. Two weeks after it was all over, as family and friends were getting over the intense emotional stress, Anni wrote to Rostock from their house in Marienheide, near Gummersbach, where the family would live for the next thirty years: 'The boy, who is so completely the son of his father, is now my holy duty.'[80]

At the beginning of the 1950s, the remaining Landsberg prisoners fuelled a heated political debate across party political boundaries and strained American–German relations on the eve of German rearmament.[81] The foundation of the Federal Republic of Germany had boosted the self-confidence of the former ruling elite. In the hope of reintegrating and attracting large numbers of the German people, West Germany's founding fathers had abolished the death sentence as part of the constitution. The longer the hangings continued, the more forceful, right-wing and national conservative circles of Germany protested and demanded an end to them. Whereas there was a strong feeling of sympathy and support for the war criminals among the German public, in Landsberg, in particular, the general population cared little about the actual victims of Nazi mass murder. Right on the outskirts of Landsberg was a large Jewish DP camp, a place hardly ever visited by any of the townspeople. In January 1951, during a gathering of some three thousand demonstrators who demanded an end to the hangings, about three hundred Jews staged a counter-demonstration. The mayor of Landsberg responded by telling the cheering crowd that the 'time for silence was over', and that the Jews should go wherever they came from.[82] Stirred up by questionable support groups such as the 'Association for World Reconciliation', and the 'Working Committee for Truth and Justice' headed by the Princess of Isenburg, who believed that the case of a mass murderer such as Otto Ohlendorf had been distorted by 'evil propaganda', the public mood was close to fever pitch at the beginning of 1951. At one point, extremists terrorized the family of High Commissioner McCloy with death threats. On 31 January, he finally published a comprehensive report in which he commuted the death sentences of twenty-one out of twenty-eight condemned prisoners to life imprisonment or less, but did not mince his words over the appalling attitude of large sections of the German public on this issue. In response to a letter by President Heuss, McCloy wished that 'the German government and the German people had a wider concept of the crimes which are represented by many of those at Landsberg. I find from my mail the most abysmal ignorance of both the offences and the character of the proof of the guilt which prevails in respect to them.'[83]

It is possible, though highly unlikely, considering the politically balanced character of the commutations by the High Commissioner, that Brandt's death sentence might have been turned into life imprisonment. There were some crimes of such proportions that McCloy and the board felt unable to recommend any commutation: 'Clemency, where any grounds can be found for exercising charitable instincts, may be an encouraging example, but a mistaken tenderness toward the perpetrators of mass murder would be a mockery. It would undo what Nuremberg has accomplished, if in the end we were guided entirely by considerations of sympathy or generosity.'[84] As to the execution of death sentences in the Doctors' Trial, the only comment made by the High Commissioner was that 'the worst offenders in this category of crimes have already been dealt with'.[85]

Karl Brandt was of no concern to anyone any more. Neither were academics interested in him, taking at face value most of what he had said during the trial, which appeared to suggest that he had been little more than an idealist, a decent Nazi, who erred, nor was he a controversial and much discussed figure in any of the post-war debates on European fascism, totalitarianism and National Socialism. It was not until the beginning of the 1980s that doctors and medical historians stressed the need for research into the origins of Nazi medical policy. A vast amount of literature then began to appear on German and international eugenics and racial medicine. Libraries were filled with endless volumes on almost every aspect of Hitler's murderous regime. The life of Karl Brandt, Hitler's doctor, however, was neglected for half a century, as were the precise mechanisms of society, politics and science which had made him and his master possible. At the turn of the twenty-first century, we are beginning to understand some of these mechanisms in greater detail, though we are far from grasping them conclusively. We must recognize that we probably never will. To strive towards greater understanding, though, will be a daunting task for future historians. Whatever may be said by a saturated public, complacent politicians and a cynical media industry to turn our attention to new and more exciting shores lurking beyond the virtual horizon, we cannot allow this history to be ignored, because we cannot survive its repetition.

Notes

Notes to Chapter 1: Prologue

1 Brandt Diary, 10 November 1946. I am grateful to Brandt's son for having sent me a selection of excerpts of his father's Nuremberg diary and trial notebook, and for granting me permission to quote from them. I have not had access to the diary as a whole. Excerpts of Karl Brandt's Nuremberg diary and trial notebook have previously been published in a three-part television series *Doctors under the Swastika* (*Ärzte unterm Hakenkreuz*), produced by Ulrich Knödler and Christian Feyerabend in 2004.

2 Ibid.

3 Ibid., 14 November 1946.

4 Ibid.

5 Ibid., 17 November 1946. Quoted from Shakespeare, Vol. IV, *The Tragedies and The Poems, Antony and Cleopatra*, Act V, Sc ii, p. 243.

6 Brandt Diary, 8 December 1946.

7 Ibid.

8 Ibid.

9 Ibid.

10 The existing body of literature on Nazi medicine and the 'euthanasia' programme has grown substantially in size and quality over the last two decades. Whereas almost all institutions and layers of the 'euthanasia' programme have been examined, and continue to be researched, the literature on Karl Brandt and Phillipp Bouhler, the two architects of the killing operation, is at best limited. For some of the literature on the 'euthanasia' programme see, for example, Nowak 1984; Müller-Hill 1984; Aly 1985; Klee 1986; Schmuhl 1987; Müller-Hill 1988; Proctor 1988; Aly 1989; Dörner 1989; Kater 1989; Hohendorf 1990; Frei 1991; Klee 1991; Aly 1994; Burleigh 1994; Friedlander 1995; Kaminsky 1995; Burleigh 1997; Hochmuth 1997; Faulstich 1998; Dahl 1998; Platen-Hallermund [1948] 1998; Süß 2000; Frewer and Eickhoff 2000; Schmidt 2002; Süß 2002; Süß 2003; Schmidt 2004; Hinz-Wessels *et al.* 2005.

11 Contemporary sources also refer to Brandt as 'General Commissioner of the Führer for the Health System', as 'Commissioner General for the Medical and Health Services', as 'General Commissioner of Sanitation and Health', and as 'General Commissioner for Health and Medical Services'. In quotations, I have left references to Brandt as they stand in the original source.

12 For the Nuremberg Doctors' Trial see Schmidt 2004; see also Grodin 1992.

13 For some of the existing literature which includes sections on Brandt see, for example, Lifton 1986; Sereny 1995; Trevor-Roper 1995; Schmidt 2001; Süß 2002; Süß 2003; Schmidt 2004.

14 Herbert 1998, pp. 16f.

15 Wildt 2002; see also Smelser and Syring 2000.

16 See Wiegrefe 2005, pp. 74–86.

17 By far the best and most thorough analysis of Brandt has been written by Winfried Süß from the Ludwig-Maximilians University in Munich, Germany, in his book *Der 'Volkskörper' im Krieg. Gesundheitspolitik, Gesundheitsverhältnisse und Krankenmord im nationalsozialistischen Deutschland 1939–1945*, published in 2003; see also Faulstich 1998, pp. 587–633 and Süß 2002, pp. 197–223. See also the three-part television series 'Doctors under the Swastika' (*Ärzte unterm Hakenkreuz*), produced by Ulrich Knödler and Christian Feyerabend, which painted Brandt as an idealist. The series was screened on 13, 14 and 15 April 2004. The programme was criticized for its apologetic character and lack of historical context. For a critique of the programme see, for example, Benzenhöfer 2004.

18 Lifton 1986, pp. 114–17; Michael Burleigh described Brandt as an aristocratic 'medical idealist'; Burleigh 1994, p. 275.

19 Lifton 1986, pp. 114–16.

20 Ibid., p. 117.

21 Trevor-Roper 1995, pp. 53f; for Morell see also Irving 1983a; Irving 1983b; Irving 1990.

22 Trevor-Roper 1995, p. 53.

23 Platen-Hallermund [1948] 1998, p. 13; see also Platen 1947a, p. 29.

24 Lifton 1986, p. 115; also TNA, WO 208, 2178.

25 Lifton 1986, p. 115.

26 NDT-Documents, frames 4/2538f.

27 Hamann 2002, p. 558.

28 Lifton 1986, p. 116.

29 NDT-Documents, frames 4/2535–7, here frame 4/2536; see also frames 4/1853f.

30 Lifton 1986, p. 115.

31 NDT-Records, frames 2/11504–11507.

32 Schmidt 2001, p. 395.

33 Ernst Klee, for example, described Brandt as the 'most powerful medical official of the Nazi period' and as the 'highest-ranking Nazi medical official'. Winfried Süß suggested that from the summer of 1943 onwards, Brandt was 'the most important centre of gravity within increasingly fluid health and political power structures'; Klee 1997, pp. 141ff; Klee 2003, p. 70; Süß 2002, p. 197.

34 See also Eckart 2006.

35 See, for example, Schmuhl 1987; Proctor 1988; Weindling 1989; Proctor 1999; Frewer 2000; Frewer and Neumann 2001.

36 StaNü, Handakten Dr. Fröschmann No. 20.

37 Letter Karl Brandt, 8 July 1947.

38 See also NARA, M 1270, Roll 2, Interrogation Karl Brandt, 1 October 1945, frame 334.

39 NDT-Records, frames 2/11504f.

40 See also Koonz 2005.

41 For a study on Nazism as an 'irrational' political religion and a form of totalitarianism see, for example, Burleigh 2000.

42 For Conti see Kater 1985; sources relating to Conti are also in BAB, R18 and NARA, RG 238, Entry 200, Box 5 prison file Leonardo Conti. Hans-Walter Schmuhl is in possession of some of Conti's private papers; for Grawitz see Wicke 1999; for Bouhler see Noakes 1989; Noakes 1998. For a study of the psychiatrist Maximinian de Crinis see Jasper 1991.

43 For the phenomenon of 'strategic recollections' by the German officer corps in their autobiographies see Gerstenberger 1995, pp. 620–33.

44 Herbert 1996; Kershaw 1998; Kershaw 2000; Cesarani 2004.

45 See also Kershaw 1997, pp. 209ff.

46 Süß 2002, p. 223.

47 Dörner and Ebbinghaus 1999. The micro-fiche edition contains the trial transcripts of the Nuremberg Doctors' Trial (in the following referred to as: NDT-Records), as well as prosecution and defence documents and background material (in the following referred to as: NDT-Documents). Whenever the German version of the trial transcripts has been used, the footnote refers to: NDT-Records (German). For the 'Guide to the Microfiche-Edition' see Dörner and Ebbinghaus 2001. See also Heiber and Longerich 1983–1992; Ebbinghaus and Dörner 2001. The University of Harvard has begun to digitalize the documents and transcripts of all 12 Nuremberg war crimes trials and is making the material publicly available on the Internet. A significant proportion of documents from the Nuremberg Doctors' Trial are now accessible through the Internet: see www.nuremberg. law.harvard.edu; for documents and debates relating to the Nuremberg Doctors' Trial see also Mitscherlich and Mielke 1947; Mitscherlich and Mielke 1949a and 1949b; Mitscherlich and Mielke 1960; Peter 1994; Tröhler and Reiter-Theil 1997; Frewer and Wiesemann 1999; Schmidt 2004; Weindling 2004.

48 See, for example, Süß 2003.

49 To reconstruct Brandt's childhood and youth, as well as his years as a student, I conducted archival and library research, for example, at the Archives de la Ville de Mulhouse in France, the City and District Archive in Schmalkalden, the Schmalkalden City Council, the Saxon State Archive in Dresden, the City Archive in Dresden, the City Archive in Chemnitz, the Thuringian University and State Library in Jena, the Archive of the Humboldt University in Berlin, the Archive of the Ludwig-Maximilians University in Munich, the Archive of the Albert-Ludwigs University in Freiburg, the Archive of the Ruhr University in Bochum, the City Archive in Bochum, the Bergmannsheil clinic in Bochum, the

German Swimming Association in Kassel and the City Archive in Velbert. I also researched the particular relationship between Karl Brandt and Alfred Hoche, one of the leading proponents of euthanasia during the 1920s, and explored as far as was possible the suggestion that Brandt was in contact with Albert Schweitzer.

50 BSB, Fotoarchiv Hoffmann.

51 Welch 2003, p. 99.

52 See also Herz 1994.

53 Schmidt 2004.

54 Herbert 1996, p. 23.

55 The scarcity of sources which exist for Brandt's office as General Commissioner for Health and Sanitation is likewise part of the clue to understanding how Hitler's special commissars functioned outside the traditional bureaucracy; see Süß 2002, p. 198, footnote 5.

56 Herbert 1996, pp. 23f; see also Glover 1999, pp. 317–97.

57 StaNü, KV-Verteidigung, Handakten Rostock No. 8.

58 Schmidt 2001b, pp. 374–404.

59 Noakes and Pridham 1994, vol. 2, p. 196.

60 Ibid.

61 Süß 2002, pp. 198f; Süß 2003, pp. 76f.

62 Kershaw 1987; see also Welch 2003, pp. 93f.

63 Süß 2003, pp. 76f.

64 See Overy 2004.

65 HBAB, file 2/39–189, Meeting with Professor Brandt, 13 February 1943.

66 See also Welch 2003, pp. 93–117.

67 Kershaw 1998, pp. 527–91; also Kershaw 1993; for the concept of cumulative radicalization and the uniqueness of Hitler's form of government see Kershaw 1995; Kershaw 1997a; Kershaw 1997b; see also the edited volume by McElligott and Kirk 2003, p. 7.

68 Kershaw 1998, p. 530; McElligott and Kirk 2003, pp. 6f.

69 Welch 2003, p. 107.

70 StaNü, IMT, vol. 32, ND 3063-PS, 13 February 1939; see also Evans 2005, pp. 580ff. I would like to thank Richard Evans for having drawn my attention to this source.

71 Süß calls this process the 'deinstitutionalisation of rational critieria in order to turn ideology into reality and a decreasing ability to coordinate differentiated systems of society'; Süß 2002, p. 222.

72 BAB, R18, 3809, Note of a meeting between Kaufmann, Brandt and Rostock in Beelitz, 7 October 1944.

73 BAK, All. Proz. 2/FC 6069 P, Vernehmung Karl Brandt, 1 March 1947.

Notes to Chapter 2: The Ambitious Idealist

1 Bayle 1950, p. 64. The translation from the French original is my own.

2 See also Harvey 2001, pp. 86–129.

3 Commune de Mulhouse. Archives de la ville de Mulhouse. File Karl Julius Brandt.

4 Stadtverwaltung Schmalkalden, Standesamt, death certificate of Carl Berhard Johannes Lehnebach, 21 January 1901. He was the son of Georg Friedrich Lehnebach and his wife Maria Lehnebach, née Dehnert.

5 Stadt- und Kreisarchiv Schmalkalden, Königlicher Kreisarzt, CIII/12-6, Medizinpersonal.

6 HUA, personal file Karl Brandt 379. Also Stadtverwaltung Schmalkalden, Standesamt, death certificate of Maria Luise Lehnebach, 10 April 1888.

7 Stadt- und Kreisarchiv Schmalkalden. The Schmalkalder Tageblatt from 1902 contains the following entry: 'In 1886 Herr Syrowy sold the pool to a consortium of Schmalkalder notabilities, headed by Dr Lehnebach. The consortium sold it in the autumn of 1898 to Herrn Gustav Rößler, who enlarged and improved it through installations and new halls.'

8 Stadt Steinbach-Hallenberg, Stadtverwaltung, Standesamt, birth certificate of Catherina Emilie Elisabeth Brandt, née Lehnebach, 25 April 1879. Brandt's mother died on 22 December 1956 in Wipperfürth.

9 Steinbach-Hallenberg, Taufbuch der reformierten Kirche, p. 108, Franz Friedrich Lehnebach, born 4 June 1873. I am grateful to Hans-Joachim Scholz for having supplied me with this information.

10 Steinbach-Hallenberg, Taufbuch der reformierten Kirche, p. 112, Karl Lehnebach, born 15 November 1874.

11 Ibid., p. 119, Georg Richard Lehnebach, born 30 January 1877.

12 BAK, All. Proz. 2/FC 6069 P, Vernehmung Karl Brandt, 1 March 1947.

13 Stadtverwaltung Schmalkalden, Standesamt, death certificate of Carl Berhard Johannes Lehnebach, 21 January 1901.

14 Commune de Mulhouse. Archives de la ville de Mulhouse, birth certificate Karl Brandt, 11 January 1904.

15 See also Harvey 2001, p. 80.

16 Ibid., p. 89.

17 Ibid., p. 100.

18 Harp 1998, pp. 60–62.

19 Ibid., pp. 62, 89.

20 Ibid., p. 16.

21 NDT-Records, frame 2/2378.

22 Schweitzer 1996, pp. 28ff; for Schweitzer see also Bähr 1987; Günzler 1996; Lenk 2000; Bentley 2001; Bähr 2003; Steffahn 2004.

23 StaNü, Handakten Rostock, File 5.

24 BAK, All. Proz. 2/FC 6069 P, Vernehmung Karl Brandt, 13 August 1947.

25 Ibid., 1 March 1947; for Leo Alexander see Schmidt 2001a; Schmidt 2001b; Schmidt 2004.

26 BAK, All. Proz. 2/FC 6069 P, Vernehmung Karl Brandt, 1 March 1947.

27 Ibid.; NARA, SS personal file Karl Brandt.

28 BAK, All. Proz. 2/FC 6069 P, Vernehmung Karl Brandt, 1 March 1947.

29 Ibid.

30 'Selbstbildnis eines "Kriegsverbrechers"' 1962, p. 5.

31 Address register Mülhausen, 1913.

32 Harvey 2001, p. 114.

33 Curtius 1920, p. 243.

34 Harvey 2001, p. 115.

35 BAK, All. Proz. 2/FC 6069 P, Vernehmung Karl Brandt, 1 March 1947.

36 Quoted from Harvey 2001, p. 127.

37 NDT-Records, frame 2/2378.

38 Stadt- und Kreisarchiv Schmalkalden, Heimatkalender 1918.

39 Heckert and Scholz (no date), pp. 8f.

40 After divorcing Eva Rade in the early 1920s, perhaps because their marriage was childless, Gottfried Rade remarried and emigrated with his Jewish wife to the small village of Seewis, Switzerland, after the Nazi takeover of power in 1933; Hans-Joachim Scholz to author, 13 February 2006; telephone conversation with Peter Rade, 17 February 2006.

41 'Selbstbildnis eines "Kriegsverbrechers"' 1962, p. 5.

42 Ibid.

43 BAK, All. Proz. 2/FC 6069 P, Vernehmung Karl Brandt, 1 March 1947.

44 Stadtarchiv Eisenach, Jahresbericht des Realgymnasiums zu Eisenach, Ostern 1920. I am grateful to Reinhold Brunner for having sent me the document.

45 'Selbstbildnis eines "Kriegsverbrechers"' 1962, p. 6.

46 Ibid.

47 NDT-Records (German), frame 2/2312.

48 BAK, All. Proz. 2/FC 6069 P, Vernehmung Karl Brandt, 1 March 1947.

49 Süß 2003, p. 79; also BAK, All. Proz. 2/FC 6069P, Interrogation Brandt, 1 March 1947.

50 Landeshauptstadt Dresden, Stadtarchiv, Akten der Stadtverordneten zu Dresden, betreffend die Landesschule, 1920, No. 237.

51 See also BAK, All. Proz. 2/FC 6069 P, Vernehmung Karl Brandt, 1 March 1947.

52 Sächsisches Hauptstaatsarchiv Dresden, Ministerium for Volksbildung, Landesschule Dresden, Reifeprüfungen, No. 21368, Abiturzeugnis Karl Brandt 1923. I am grateful to Markus Henneke for providing me with this source.

53 Sächsisches Hauptstaatsarchiv Dresden, Ministerium for Volksbildung, Landesschule Dresden, Reifeprüfungen, No. 21368, Abiturzeugnis Karl Brandt 1923.

54 A police officer and major, C. Julius Brandt, probably Brandt's father, was registered in the Wormser Straße 3 in Dresden from 1923 to 1925; Stadtarchiv Dresden, Hoppe to Henneke, 15 August 2001.

55 NDT-Records (German), frame 2/2312.

56 BAK, All. Proz. 2/FC 6069 P, Vernehmung Karl Brandt, 1 March 1947.

57 See also NDT-Documents, frames 4/2538f.

58 StaNü, Handakten Rostock, File 5.

59 BAK, All. Proz. 2/FC 6069 P, Vernehmung Karl Brandt, 1 March 1947.

60 NDT-Records, frame 2/2378.

61 NDT-Records (German), frame 2312.

62 Sächsisches Hauptstaatsarchiv Dresden, Ministerium for Volksbildung, Landesschule Dresden, Reifeprüfungen, No. 21368, Abiturzeugnis Karl Brandt 1923.

63 BAK, All. Proz. 2/FC 6069 P, Vernehmung Karl Brandt, 1 March 1947.

64 Süß 2003, p. 79; also BAK, All. Proz. 2/FC 6069P, Interrogation Brandt, 1 March 1947.

65 BAK, All. Proz. 2/FC 6069 P, Vernehmung Karl Brandt, 1 March 1947.

66 NDT-Records, frame 2/2378. The English has been slightly edited in order to make the text more fluent; see also BAK, All. Proz. 2/FC 6069 P, Vernehmung Karl Brandt, 1 March 1947; also Süß 2003, p. 92, footnote 245.

67 NDT-Records, frame 2/2378.

68 Ibid.

69 Schmidt 2002, p. 97.

70 NDT-Records, frame 2/2382; StaN, KV-Anklage, Interrogations, Karl Brandt, No. B154; also Albert-Ludwigs-Universität Freiburg, Universitätsarchiv, Abgangszeugnis Karl Brandt (B44/110/34).

71 HUA, Student file Karl Brandt, 27 October 1925 to 12 March 1926.

72 NDT-Records, frame 2/2378 and frame 2/2382.

73 Ludwig-Maximilian-Universität, Universitätsarchiv, Student file Karl Brandt, 29 April 1926 to 6 October 1926.

74 See also NDT-Records, frame 2/2378.

75 NDT-Records (German), frame 2/2315.

76 Schmidt 2004, p. 92.

77 Quoted from Burleigh 1994, p. 40.

78 An attempt to corroborate the incident failed because Aziz used a pseudonym for the doctor whom he interviewed in 1972 and because he provided no footnotes in his book. It was also not possible to ask Aziz because he died shortly before this book was written; Aziz 1976, p. 16.

79 See also Cornelia Essner's work on the Nuremberg race laws. She describes Brandt as a 'radical anti-Semite', who in January 1935 not only launched into a diatribe about the Jews as blood-sucking parasites, but who apparently promoted the cleansing of the 'German blood stream from Jewish blood'. It is quite possible that Essner's sources refer to Rudolf Brandt and not to Karl Brandt; Essner 2002, pp. 34f; 69f; see also Longerich, who seems to confuse Karl Brandt with Rudolf Brandt; Longerich 1998, p. 237.

80 HUA, personal file Karl Brandt 379.

81 Ibid.

82 Ibid.

83 NDT-Records, frame 2/2382; see also Albert-Ludwigs-Universität Freiburg, Universitätsarchiv, Promotionsakte Karl Brandt (B54/3350).

84 Hoche 1936, p. 124.

85 Ibid.

86 Hoche 1937, p. 230.

87 Binding and Hoche 1920.

88 Ibid., p. 27.

89 Ibid.

90 Ibid., pp. 31f.

91 Dahl 1998, p. 15.

92 Schmuhl 1987, p. 119.

93 Hoche 1937, p. 178.

94 Hoche 1936, pp. 289f.

95 NARA, M 1270, Roll 2, Interrogation Karl Brandt, 1 October 1945, frame 333.

96 Albert-Ludwigs-Universität Freiburg, Universitätsarchiv, Promotionsakte Karl Brandt (B54/3350). The title of his dissertation was 'Angeborener Verschluss der Gallenausfuhrgänge'.

97 Albert-Ludwigs-Universität Freiburg, Universitätsarchiv, file Karl Brandt (D29/36/969).

98 Brandt's knowledge of his supervisor may explain why Noeggerat was later summoned to the Chancellery of the Führer and asked to implement the children's 'euthanasia' programme in Freiburg, Klee 2003, p. 438.

99 Albert-Ludwigs-Universität Freiburg, Universitätsarchiv, Promotionsakte Karl Brandt (B54/3350).

100 Photo album of Karl Brandt entitled: 'Examen Freiburg i/Br. März–Juni 28. (26.6.28) K.'. I was unable to locate Brandt's exam record of 26 June 1928 at the Albert-Ludwigs-Universität Freiburg.

101 For the hospital Bergmannsheil see Bergbau-Berufsgenossenschaft Bochum 1990, pp. 37–83.

102 NDT-Records, frame 2/2379.

103 Brandt 1933.

104 Ibid.

105 NDT-Records, frame 2/2380. The text has been quoted from the English translation of the Nuremberg trial transcripts.

106 NDT-Records, frame 2/2502.

107 StaNü, Handakten Rostock, File 5.

108 HUA, personal file Karl Brandt 379.

109 Ibid.

110 Ibid.

111 NDT-Records, frame 2/2383.

112 StaNü, Handakten Rostock, File 5. The English has been slightly edited in order to make the text more readable.

113 StaNü, KV-Anklage, Dokumente, L11, interrogation of Fritz Bleich, 22 March 1945.

114 Trevor-Roper 1995, p. 53.
115 Bähr 2003, p. 21.
116 Schmidt 2001b, pp. 401f; Alexander 1955, pp. 88f; also Proctor 1999; Weindling 2000.
117 Proctor 1999, p. 114; Bumke 1952, p. 145.
118 NDT-Records, frame 2/2474.
119 Ibid., frame 2/2501.
120 Ibid., frame 2/2511.
121 Bähr 1987, p. 97.
122 The Albert Schweitzer Archive in Günsbach was less than helpful in supporting a research project which wanted to investigate the relationship between Karl Brandt and Albert Schweitzer. The archive is run by a former student of Schweitzer and administered by the son-in-law of this student, hardly a situation which enhances scholarship on Albert Schweitzer's life. Perhaps the private papers of Albert Schweitzer should be deposited in an archive to which the general public and scholars have full and unrestricted access.
123 StaNü, KV-Anklage Interrogations, No. B154, Interrogation Karl Brandt, 26 November 1946; also BAK, All. Proz. 2/FC 6069 P, Vernehmung Karl Brandt, 26 November 1946.
124 NDT-Records (German), frame 2/2314; NDT-Records, frame 2/2380.
125 Aziz 1976, p. 17.
126 Schweitzer 2004, p. 183.
127 Aziz 1976, p. 17.
128 NDT-Documents, frames 4/2538f.; see also BAK, All. Proz. 2/FC 6069 P, Vernehmung Karl Brandt, 1 March 1947; for the friendship between Sutz and Bonhoeffer see Schlingensiepen 2006.
129 NDT-Documents, frames 4/2538f.
130 Ibid.
131 Welch 2003, pp. 99ff; see also Burleigh 2000.
132 BDC, personal file Karl Brandt.
133 Fröhlich 1987, part I, vol. 1, p. 191, 6 July 1926.
134 Brandt worked at the Weimar city hospital for six weeks in March and April and during August and September 1926; HUA, personal file Karl Brandt 379.
135 NDT-Records (German), frame 2/2321; NDT-Records, frames 2/2387f. The German and the English transcript differ from one another. Compared with a literal translation of the German transcript, in which Brandt states that 'the wish to become a member

of the Party was not great for me', he states in the English transcript that 'the decision to become a member of the Party was not very difficult'. Whereas Brandt's statement in the German transcript is ambiguous, the meaning of the English transcript is unambiguous. However, given that Brandt spoke in German, the German transcript is probably closer to what he actually said at Nuremberg. There are two ways of reading his statement in the German transcript. Brandt may have wanted to say that he was not particularly keen to join the Nazi Party because of his family connections and because of the professional context in which he was working. Or, alternatively, and taking into account that his German grammar was often poor and his language ambiguous, Brandt may have wanted to say that his family connections to the Naumann circle and his work as a doctor in the Ruhr region had made it 'not difficult' for him to decide whether or not to join the Nazi Party. Admittedly, it is difficult to reconstruct exactly what Brandt wanted to say in this instance. The latter interpretation appears to me to be the more plausible one.
136 Kershaw 1998, p. 135.
137 Lewerenz 1994, p. 223.
138 Krey 2000, pp. 115–47.
139 Brandt's NSDAP membership number was 1009017. Working for the local air-safety service in Bochum he became the regional expert for gas- and air-safety of the SA-Group Westfalen in February 1933; HUA, personal file Karl Brandt 379; BDC, personal file Karl Brandt.
140 StaNü, KV-Anklage, Dokumente, NO-333; Sereny 1995, p. 194.
141 BAK, Kl. Erw. 525.
142 NDT-Records (German), frame 2/2321; see also Süß 2003, p. 79, footnote 175.
143 Schirach 1983, p. 152.
144 Julius Rehborn was the son of the baker Wilhelm Julius Rehborn, who was born on 1 August 1845 and who died on 28 November 1904 in Elberfeld, and his wife Johanna, née Löwenstein, born on 6 June 1842 in Frücht. She died on 19 February 1918 in Remscheid; Stadtarchiv Bochum, BO 11/174, Personalakte Julius Rehborn.
145 Stadtarchiv Velbert, Bürgerrolle Langenberg Julius Rehborn. I am grateful to the archivist,

Mr Schotten, for having supplied me with the relevant sources.

146 Schirach 1983, p. 152.
147 Ibid.
148 BSB, Fotoarchiv Hoffmann, hoff-313.

Notes to Chapter 3: Becoming Hitler's Doctor

1 According to some later testimony, Hitler's niece, also called Angela Raubal ('Geli'), was supposedly in the car. The problem with the testimony is that Hitler's niece 'Geli' had killed herself in Hitler's apartment in mid-September 1931. Brandt further stated that Hitler's sister had been in the car. This is also not possible as Ida Hitler, Hitler's only sister, had died in 1888. Brandt probably did not know that Angela Raubal was only Hitler's half-sister. According to Hanskarl von Hasselbach, one of the other women in the car was called Stork. She owned a shop for fishing supplies in Munich; StaNü, KV-Anklage, Dokumente, NO-332, NO-333; also KV-Anklage Interrogations, No. B154, interrogation Karl Brandt by Walther H. Rapp, 9 October 1946; BAK, Kl. Erw. 525 'Hitler as Seen by his Doctors'; also Schlie 1999, p. 226; and Kater 1985, p. 315.
2 Sereny 1995, p. 194.
3 See Möller *et al.* 2001, pp. 54f.
4 StaNü, KV-Anklage, Dokumente, NO-332, NO-333.
5 Ibid., NO-333.
6 Lammel 1994, pp. 578ff. Whether there is a link between Brandt's medical intervention in the summer of 1933 and Magnus' appointment in November 1933, as Lammel has suggested, is difficult to establish with certainty; see also Lammel 1993, pp. 63–75.
7 BSB, Fotoarchiv Hoffmann, hoff-45776, 45777, 45778.
8 Lammel 1994, pp. 568–91.
9 Brandt was promoted to Oberarzt on 1 April 1934; HUA, personal file Karl Brandt 379.
10 Sereny 1995, p. 194.
11 Hitler once told Speer: 'I was looking for a young architect to whom I would be able to entrust my building plans one day. He had to be young because, as you know, these plans extended far into the future'; Sereny 1995, p. 105.

12 Görlitz and Quint 1952, p. 336.
13 StaNü, KV-Anklage, Dokumente, NO-332, NO-333.
14 Von Below 1980, p. 30.
15 StaNü, KV-Anklage, Dokumente, NO-332.
16 Ibid., NO-333.
17 Ibid.
18 Zoller 1949, p. 120; Görlitz and Quint 1952, p. 336.
19 StaNü, KV-Anklage, Dokumente, NO-202, SS personal file Karl Brandt.
20 After the war, Brandt claimed that he was obliged to join the SS in order to be a member of Hitler's staff of bodyguards and chauffeurs. His claim is technically correct, but it does not correspond to the events in 1934, because Brandt applied for SS membership before his first assignment as Hitler's escort physician in June 1934. It is likely that members of Hitler's entourage may have suggested to him that he should join the SS in case he wanted to stand a chance of joining Hitler's entourage or, and this is also probable, that he himself made the decision to place himself in the best possible position in case Hitler suddenly needed a doctor; BAB, BDC, personal file Karl Brandt; also StaNü, KV-Anklage, Dokumente, NO-202, SS personal file Karl Brandt.
21 Sereny 1995, p. 118.
22 Möller *et al.* 1999, p. 66.
23 Ibid., p. 67.
24 Plaim and Kuch 2005, p. 32.
25 Schenck 1989, p. 95.
26 Heiber 2001, p. 61.
27 Ibid., p. 118.
28 Sereny 1995, p. 120.
29 Heiber, 2001, p. 13.
30 Herz 1994, pp. 242–259, esp. pp. 250f.
31 BSB, Fotoarchiv Hoffmann, hoff-322.
32 Ibid., hoff-11377.
33 Welch 2003, p. 100.
34 Möller *et al.* 1999, pp. 59–61.
35 Heiber 2001, pp. 43f.
36 See also Proctor 1999.
37 Noakes 1998, pp. 15–16.
38 For the role of *Gauleiters* as 'Viceroys of the Reich' see Noakes 2003, pp. 118–52.
39 Wiedemann 1964, p. 84.
40 StaNü, KV-Anklage Interrogations, No. S 35, Interrogation Julius Schaub, 8 September 1945.

41　Staatsarchiv München, Spruchka. Ka.
　　1894, Wagner, Winifried, Eidesstattliche
　　Versicherung Karl Brandt, 31 March 1947.
42　For Hitler's secretaries see TNA, FO 1031,
　　102; also Schlie 1999, pp. 231ff.
43　Heiber 2001, p. 119.
44　TNA, FO 1031, 102, Karl Brandt, 'Women
　　around Hitler'.
45　Fröhlich 1987, part I, vol. 2, pp. 647f, 24 July
　　1936 and 26 July 1936.
46　Sigmund 1998, p. 8.
47　HUA, personal file 379, Rostock to University
　　administration, 19 January 1935.
48　Sereny 1995, p. 119.
49　Ibid.
50　TNA, FO 1031, 102, Karl Brandt, 'Women
　　around Hitler'.
51　StaNü, KV-Anklage, Dokumente, NO-778;
　　BAB, R-43-II, 986.
52　Heiber 2001, p. 105.
53　BAK, All. Proz. 2/FC 6069 P, Vernehmung
　　Karl Brandt, 1 March 1947.
54　Schlie 1999, p. 225.
55　Möller et al. 1999, p. 62.
56　Heiber 2001, p. 38.
57　Ibid.
58　Fox 2000, p. 124.
59　TNA, FO 1031, 102, Karl Brandt, 'Women
　　around Hitler'.
60　Sereny 1995, p. 436.
61　Von Below 1980, p. 57.
62　Ibid., p. 97.
63　NARA, RG 238, Entry 188/190/191, Box 2,
　　Biographical Report Karl Franz Friedrich
　　Brant, May 1946.
64　Ibid.
65　Personal conversation with Karl-Adolf
　　Brandt, 14 April 1999.
66　Sereny 1995, p. 123.
67　Ibid., p. 124.
68　Schlie 1999, p. 226.
69　Sigmund 1998, p. 12.
70　Ibid.
71　Plaim and Kuch 2005, p. 98.
72　Heiber 2001, p. 63.
73　Schlie 1999, pp. 230–34.
74　TNA, FO 1031, 102, Karl Brandt, 'Women
　　around Hitler'.
75　Ibid.
76　Ibid.
77　Ibid.
78　Ibid.
79　Kershaw 1998, pp. 12f.

80　Proctor 1999, p. 179, p. 189.
81　TNA, FO 1031, 102, Karl Brandt, 'Women
　　around Hitler'.
82　Ibid.
83　Ibid.
84　Hugh Trevor-Roper Papers, Detailed
　　Interrogation Report, Special Detention
　　Center 'Ashcan', Dr Karl Brandt: Reply to CI
　　Questionnaire, 15 June 1945. I am grateful
　　to the late Hugh Trevor-Roper, Lord Dacre,
　　who supplied this document to me during a
　　long evening at his house in Oxfordshire in
　　January 2000.
85　Sigmund 1998, p. 177.
86　Plaim and Kuch 2005, p. 39.
87　BSB, Fotoarchiv Hoffmann, hoff-316.
88　Sigmund 1998, p. 166.
89　Schlie 1999, p. 228.
90　TNA, FO 1031, 102, Karl Brandt, 'Women
　　around Hitler'.
91　Sigmund 1998, pp. 184f.
92　Linge 1980, p. 74.
93　Sereny 1995, p. 193.
94　TNA, FO 1031, 102, Karl Brandt, 'Women
　　around Hitler'.
95　Ibid., also Schlie 1999, p. 227.
96　Ibid.
97　Heiber 2001, p. 27.
98　Padfield 1995, p. 268.
99　Kershaw 1998, pp. 536f.
100　Heiber 2001, p. 81.
101　StaNü, KV-Anklage, Dokumente, NO-332.
102　For Werner Haase and Hanskarl von
　　Hasselbach see Lammel 1994, pp. 578f;
　　StaNü, KV-Anklage, Dokumente, NO-333;
　　for Haase see also Gussatschenko et al. 1996,
　　pp. 161ff.
103　HUA, personal file 379, Karl Brandt; for
　　Magnus' biography see HUA, personal file,
　　Georg Magnus; Magnus' appointment over
　　the heads of the medical faculty was probably
　　politically motivated, as he had been for
　　some time an outspoken Nazi supporter; see
　　Lammel 1994, p. 578.
104　Klemperer 1998, p. 91.
105　Sereny 1995, p. 9.
106　Von Below 1980, p. 121.
107　On 24 July 1934, Rostock wrote to the clinic
　　administration: 'The letter addressed to
　　Herr Oberarzt Dr. Brandt of 21.7.34 … can
　　currently not be answered as Herr Oberarzt
　　Dr. Brandt is accompanying the Führer on
　　a journey. It is not yet known when Herr

Oberarzt Dr. Brandt will return'; HUA, personal file 379; Schlie 1999, p. 238.
108 TNA, WO 309, 469.
109 Heiber 2001, p. 47.
110 Ibid., pp. 44–49, p. 48.
111 Kershaw 1998, pp. 529f.
112 Speer 2000, p. 109.
113 Ibid., p. 110.
114 Welch 2001, pp. 147–59; Welch 2002, pp. 114–15.
115 BSB, Fotoarchiv Hoffmann, hoff-31523.
116 HUA, personal file 379.
117 BSB, Fotoarchiv Hoffmann, hoff-310 and hoff-311.
118 Ibid., hoff-11250, hoff-11251, hoff-11252.
119 Ibid., hoff-10521; see also hoff-11368 where Brandt is pictured with Hitler attending a military exercise by the German navy on the Baltic Sea at the end of August 1935.
120 BSB, Fotoarchiv Hoffmann, hoff-11166.
121 Brandt trial notebook, Euthanasia, II/9 (11), p. 35 (pagination by US); also Knödler and Feyerabend 2004, part II.
122 Platen-Hallermund, p. 35; Schmuhl 1987, p. 169.
123 Gruchmann 1983, pp. 418–23.
124 Burleigh 1994, p. 97; see also HHStAW, Abt. 631a Nr 301, interrogation of Hans Heinrich Lammers, 21 March 1961, p. 2.
125 For racial propaganda films see Burleigh 1994, pp. 183–219.
126 NDT-Records (German), frames 2/2413ff; Mitscherlich and Mielke's edited version of the document has led to some minor, but significant errors in the way Brandt's statement has been read by scholars in the past, especially by those who, like Burleigh, have translated from Mitscherlich's edited version, rather than from the original. In the original trial transcript Brandt says that *he has to assume* that the Führer was of the opinion, and that Hitler *is supposed* to have told Wagner. These caveats are almost entirely lost in Mitscherlich's text of 1960 as well as in Burleigh's account of 1994, which suggest that Brandt recalled the events as facts. As it happened, Brandt was significantly more vague about the event, and made it clear that he had not been party to the conversation; see Mitscherlich and Mielke 1960, p. 184; Burleigh 1994, p. 97.
127 Platen-Hallermund [1948] 1998, p. 34.
128 Kühl 1997, pp. 54–67.

129 Lifton 1986, p. 52.
130 Schmidt 2002.
131 Benze 1935, pp. 8f.
132 Peiffer 1997, p. 25.
133 Schenck 1989, pp. 300f.
134 Heiber 2001, p. 100.
135 Schenck 1989, pp. 216f.
136 Ibid., pp. 215ff.
137 Fröhlich 1987, part I, vol. 2, p. 488, 29 April 1935.
138 Hugh Trevor-Roper Papers, Detailed Interrogation Report, Special Detention Centre 'Ashcan', Dr Karl Brandt: Reply to CI Questionnaire, 15 June 1945.
139 Schenck 1989, pp. 316f; also StaNü, KV-Anklage, Dokumente, NO-332. The medical analysis was conducted by Professor Rössle from the pathological institute at the Charité in Berlin. Two years later Rössle was still disappointed, because he felt that he had not been sufficiently rewarded for his work. In October 1937, Rössle told Werner Haase, Brandt's deputy at Führer headquarters, that he had expected to receive a 'picture of the Führer'; Heiber 2001, pp. 51f.
140 Schenck 1989, p. 316.
141 Heiber 2001, p. 25.
142 Schenck 1989, p. 255.
143 Heiber 2001, pp. 51f.
144 Schenck 1989, p. 317.
145 Heiber 2001, p. 80.
146 Schenck 1989, p. 308.
147 Kershaw 2000, p. 37.
148 BAK, All. Proz. 2/FC 6069 P, Vernehmung Karl Brandt, 1 March 1947.
149 Trevor-Roper 1995, p. 54.
150 Schenck 1989, p. 479.
151 US Strategic Bombing Survey, APO 413, Subject: Prof. Dr. med. Karl Brandt, 17–18 June 1945.
152 Schlie 1999, p. 231.
153 TNA, WO 309, 469.
154 See Schmidt 2005.

Notes to Chapter 4: Hitler's Envoy
1 Wiedemann 1964, p. 203.
2 Plaim and Kuch 2005, pp. 24ff.
3 For the regional newspapers the story was headline news, especially after it transpired that the woman wanted to sue Hitler's manager for compensation. Although Döring had driven into the cyclist, and was thus

liable, the court decided in favour of Hitler's manager; Plaim and Kuch 2005, p. 27.

4 Jasper 1991, p. 131.

5 See, for example, Meyer 1986, pp. 134f.

6 BAB, NS 10/125, vol 1, Diensttagebuch der persönlichen Adjutantur, geführt von Max Wünsche, 16 June 1938 until 20 November 1938, pp. 110–83, here p. 112.

7 BSB, Fotoarchiv Hoffmann, hoff-20063, hoff-20047.

8 For Brandt's involvement in the cancer scandal see Goebbels' diary entries in July 1936; Fröhlich 1987, part I, vol. 2, p. 647, 23 July 1936; p. 647, 24 July 1936; p. 648, 26 July 1936; StaNü, KV-Anklage Interrogations, No. B154, interrogation Karl Brandt by Walther H. Rapp, 9 October 1946; also BAB, R18, 3782; for the meaning of the case in the context of Nazi cancer research see Proctor, pp. 254ff; also Stroink 1986, pp. 522–24; also in Aziz 1976, pp. 31f.

9 NDT-Records (German), frame 2/2316.

10 BAB, R 43 II/1226, p. 38.

11 NDT-Records (German), frame 2/2317.

12 Fröhlich 1987, part I, vol. 2, p. 646, 22 July 1936.

13 Ibid., 23 July 1936.

14 Ibid., 24 July 1936.

15 Ibid., p. 648, 26 July 1936. In 1935 Streicher helped von Brehmer to establish the Tumor Research Institute at the Theresien Hospital in Nuremberg; see Proctor 1999, p. 255.

16 Fröhlich 1987, part I, vol. 2, p. 648, 26 July 1936.

17 Schmidt 2002, p. 81.

18 Hockerts 2002, p. 892.

19 In 1942, after he had been appointed General Commissioner for Health and Sanitation, Brandt made yet another representation on behalf of Chaoul to ensure that he would become the head of the X-ray Institute of the University of Berlin which Hitler wanted to establish after the war; Hockerts 2002, p. 892.

20 After Paul Rostock had been provisionally appointed head of the clinic in Berlin Ziegelstraße in 1936, Brandt was appointed 'first surgeon' of the surgical clinic; StaNü, KV-Anklage Dokumente, NO-333; see also Lammel 1994, pp. 578ff; also StaNü, KV-Prozesse, Fall 1, Spezialia Karl Brandt H 1, affidavit of Netty Germann.

21 StaNü, KV-Anklage, Dokumente, L11, interrogation of Fritz Bleich, 22 March 1945;

see also NARA, RG 153, 100–767, Box 62.

22 BAK, All. Proz. 2/FC 6069 P, Vernehmung Karl Brandt, 1 March 1947.

23 See Petrakis 2005.

24 Fröhlich 1987, part I, vol. 2, p. 648, 27 July 1936.

25 Ibid., p. 665, 22 August 1936 and p. 667, 26 August 1936.

26 Ibid., p. 680, 18 September 1936.

27 BSB, Fotoarchiv Hoffmann, hoff-14110

28 Fröhlich 1987, part I, vol. 2, p. 682, 21 September 1936.

29 BSB, Fotoarchiv Hoffmann, hoff-14149.

30 Ibid., hoff-14147 and hoff-14148.

31 Fröhlich 1987, part I, vol. 2, p. 682, 22 September 1936.

32 Ibid., p. 683, 22 September 1936.

33 BSB, Fotoarchiv Hoffmann, hoff-13934, hoff-13935, hoff-13936.

34 Fröhlich 1987, part I, vol. 2, p. 685, 24 and 26 September 1936; also BSB, Fotoarchiv Hoffmann, hoff-13862, hoff-13932, hoff-14011, hoff-14012, hoff-14057.

35 BSB, Fotoarchiv Hoffmann, hoff-14057.

36 Ibid., hoff-14077ff.

37 Ibid., hoff-14082ff.

38 Ibid., hoff-14094.

39 Fröhlich 1987, part I, vol. 2, p. 688, 28 September 1936.

40 Ibid.

41 BAB, BDC, personal file Karl Brandt.

42 Schirach 1983, pp. 153f.

43 Ibid.

44 BAB, NS 10/125, vol 1., Diensttagebuch der persönlichen Adjutantur, geführt von Max Wünsche, 16 June 1938 until 20 November 1938, pp. 110–83, here p. 112.

45 Ibid., here p. 143.

46 StaNü, KV-Anklage Interrogations, No. B154, interrogation Karl Brandt by Herbert Meyer, 4 November 1946; for the history and development of Nazi art see Petropoulos 2000.

47 Wolbert 1982, pp. 218–21.

48 See also Welch 2003, pp. 100ff.

49 Brandt Diary, 21 December 1946. I have used Lloyd-Jones 1994 to translate Brandt's text passage from Sophocles' play *Ajax* from the German language into English. I am grateful to Anna Miller and Jason Harper from the Templeman Library, Canterbury, for their support.

50 Glover 1999, pp. 317–97.

51 NARA, SS personal file Karl Brandt.
52 Ullstein Bild, Database, Image Number, 00018290.
53 BSB, Fotoarchiv Hoffmann, hoff-14812.
54 'Der Grosse Bauherr Unterwegs' 1937, pp. 319f.
55 Ibid., p. 319.
56 BSB, Fotoarchiv Hoffmann, hoff-14957-62, hoff-14987, hoff-15004-7, hoff-15018-20.
57 Ibid., hoff-15021-22.
58 Ullstein Bild, Database, Image Number, 00018455.
59 Hugh Trevor-Roper Papers, Detailed Interrogation Report, Special Detention Center 'Ashcan', Dr Karl Brandt: Reply to CI Questionnaire, 15 June 1945.
60 BSB, Fotoarchiv Hoffmann, hoff-38729.
61 NDT-Records, frame 2/2391; NDT-Records (German), frame 2/2324.
62 BSB, Fotoarchiv Hoffmann, hoff-317.
63 Schenck 1989, pp. 32f; see also Proctor 1999 for German research on the link between smoking and lung cancer in the 1930s and 1940s.
64 Schirach 1983, pp. 153f.
65 Sereny 1995, pp. 104ff; Kershaw 2000, pp. 503f.
66 HUA, personal file Karl Brandt 379.
67 Ibid.
68 BAK, All. Proz. 2/FC 6069 P, Vernehmung Karl Brandt, 1 March 1947.
69 Brandt 1939, p. 187.
70 Ibid.
71 Ibid., p. 188.
72 Brandt's appointment was instigated by Hitler's deputy, Rudolf Heß, who recommended his nomination to the minister of education, Bernhard Rust; HUA, personal file Karl Brandt 379.
73 Welch 2003, p. 107; see also Geyer 1982, Kershaw 1989.
74 Quoted from Welch 2003, p. 107.
75 Quoted from Kershaw 1998, p. 590.
76 BSB, Fotoarchiv Hoffmann, hoff-12799.
77 Ibid., hoff-12804, hoff-12808 and hoff-12812. See also hoff-12800, an image of Hitler and his supporters, including Brandt, standing in front of the old Reich Chancellery on 29 March 1936.
78 BSB, Fotoarchiv Hoffmann, hoff-12804, hoff-12808.
79 'Der Große Sieg' 1936, p. 539.
80 BSB, Fotoarchiv Hoffmann, hoff-12812.
81 Ibid., hoff-12804, hoff-12808.
82 See Süß 2002, p. 197; Süß 2003, p. 76.
83 Welch 2002, pp. 204–08, here p. 206; see also p. 33; also Kershaw 2000, pp. 37f.
84 Welch 2002, p. 207.
85 Ullstein Bild, Database, Image Number, 00075464.
86 BSB, Fotoarchiv Hoffmann, hoff-18833.
87 Ullstein Bild, Database, Image Number, 00061528; see also Kershaw 2000, pp. 80ff.
88 BSB, Fotoarchiv Hoffmann, hoff-31556.
89 Ibid., hoff-20920.
90 For an excellent account of the 'Crystal Night' (*Reichskristallnacht*) and its implications for the Jewish community in Germany see Evans 2005, pp. 580–610.
91 Kershaw 2000, p. 137.
92 BSB, Fotoarchiv Hoffmann, hoff-21610.
93 Von Below 1980, p. 135.
94 BAK, Scherl Bilderdienst, No. 14772/38, Brandt, Dr Karl, 45/1648.
95 Döscher 1988, p. 64.
96 Ibid.
97 Ibid., p. 74.
98 Quoted from Bräutigam 1968, p. 344.
99 Evans 2005, p. 581.
100 Von Below 1980, pp. 135f.
101 Quoted from Kershaw 2000, p. 138.
102 Quoted from Evans 2005, p. 589.
103 Ibid.
104 Ibid., pp. 582f.
105 Kershaw 2000, p. 140.
106 Evans 2005, p. 587.
107 StaNü, IMT, vol. 32, ND 3063-PS, 13 February 1939; see also Evans 2005, p. 582.
108 See, for example, Gellately 2001; Süß 2003.
109 StaNü, IMT, vol. 32, ND 3063-PS, 13 February 1939, p. 21; see also Evans 2005, p. 582.
110 StaNü, IMT, vol. 32, ND 3063-PS, 13 February 1939, p. 26.
111 Ibid.
112 Ibid.
113 Ibid., p. 29.
114 Ibid.
115 Ibid.
116 Ibid., p. 27.
117 BSB, Fotoarchiv Hoffmann, hoff-22164, hoff-22165.
118 Kershaw 2000, p. 142.
119 Quoted from Bräutigam 1968, p. 345.
120 BAK, All. Proz. 2/FC 6069 P, Vernehmung Karl Brandt, 1 March 1947.

121 HUA, personal file Karl Brandt 379; StaNü, KV-Anklage Interrogations, No. B154, interrogation Karl Brandt by Herbert Meyer, 4 November 1946.

122 Klee 1986, p. 63.

Notes to Chapter 5: The 'Euthanasia' Doctor

1 See Klee 1991, pp. 77f; Schultz 1985, pp. 107–24, pp. 118f; Schmuhl 1987, pp. 182ff; Proctor 1988, pp. 185ff; Burleigh 1994, pp. 93ff; Friedlander 1995, pp. 39ff; Dahl 1998, pp. 26–32; Schmidt 1999a; Schmidt 2000b.

2 For the Chancellery of the Führer only a single relevant file exists at the Federal Archive in Berlin; BAB, 62 ka1, Kanzlei des Führers, 242, Reichsausschuß zur wissenschaftlichen Erfassung von erb- und anlagebedingten schweren Leiden, Reichsbeihilfen für den Reichsausschuß, 1940–1945; for the Children's Clinic at the University of Leipzig, the patient files are thought to be lost. According to the archive of the Children's Clinic at the University of Leipzig, all patient files and finding aids of the 1930s and 1940s have been destroyed. The only remaining finding aid is a so-called 'coded card index' (*Verschlüsselungskartei*) which dates back to the beginning of the 1950s and provides references to files stored in what the archivist calls the 'bunker'.

3 Benzenhöfer 1998a, p. 955; see also Benzenhöfer 1998b; Benzenhöfer 1999; Benzenhöfer 2000; Benzenhöfer 2003.

4 Until recently, scholars have assumed that this infant was called Knauer and that the case had occurred around the end of 1938 or at the beginning of 1939. It has now been established that the family's name was not Knauer and that the case occurred much later, in the summer of 1939; see Benzenhöfer 1998a; Schmidt 1999a; also Schmidt 2000b.

5 It is difficult to clarify who exactly petitioned the Chancellery of the Führer since the individual testimonies differ substantially from one another. Most of the times those involved testified that it was the father or the parents, sometimes also the uncle or the grandmother. Moreover, the letter requesting that the child should die has never been discovered; see Schmuhl 1987, p. 430.

6 Burleigh 1994, p. 93.

7 NDT-Records, frame 2/2475.

8 For Brack see Friedlander 2000.

9 HHStA, Abt. 631a/79, GStA Frankfurt. Anklage Heyde, Bohne und Hefelmann, Js 17/59 (GStA), 22 May 1962, pp. 47–49.

10 Ibid.

11 Burleigh 1994, p. 93.

12 Brandt trial notebook, Euthanasia, II/9 (16), pp. 73f (pagination by US); also Knödler and Feyerabend 2004, part II.

13 Burleigh 1994, pp. 96ff; for Helmut Kohl see Schultz, p. 118.

14 Friedlander 1995, p. 312.

15 HHStA, Abt. 631a/79, GStA Frankfurt. Anklage Heyde, Bohne und Hefelmann, Js 17/59 (GStA), 22 May 1962, p. 50.

16 Quoted from Burleigh 1994, pp. 94ff; see also NDT-Records, frame 2/2476.

17 Kershaw 2000, p. 253; see also Gruchmann 1990.

18 Quoted from Burleigh 1994, p. 96; see also NDT-Records, frame 2/2476.

19 Aziz 1976, p. 14.

20 Ev.-Luth. Pfarramt Pomßen mit Großsteinberg und Grethen, Hauptstraße 31, 04668 Pomßen, church register (Begräbnisbuch) for the year 1939.

21 Ibid.; The children were killed separately; usually they were given an overdose of the sedative luminal (Phenobarbitone) and veronal (sleeping tablets), which caused congestion of the lungs. As a result, the children generally contracted pneumonia, bronchitis or other breathing deficiencies which eventually resulted in death. The second choice was morphium-scopolamine, the third death by starvation. The children did not die of poisoning, but from the medical complications caused by the overdose of a common medicine; see also Burleigh 1994, p. 103; Friedlander 1995, pp. 54f.

22 NARA, M 1270, Roll 2, Interrogation Karl Brandt, 1 October 1945, frame 324.

23 Brandt trial notebook, Euthanasia, II/9 (16), pp. 74f (pagination by US); also Knödler and Feyerabend 2004, part II.

24 NARA, RG153, 100–767, Box 62, Report of an Interview with Dr. Karl Brandt, 26 June 1945.

25 HHStA, Abt. 631a/79, GStA Frankfurt. Anklage Heyde, Bohne und Hefelmann, Js 17/59 (GStA), 22 May 1962, p. 50.

26 BAK, All. Proz. 2/FC 6069 P, Vernehmung Karl Brandt, 1 March 1947.

27 Süß 2002, pp. 204f.

28 Kater 1985, pp. 308f; Süß 2002, pp. 203ff; for Ley see also Smelser 1989.

29 Peiffer 1997, p. 25.

30 Herbert Linden (1899–1945) remains an obscure figure and relatively little is known about him. He received his medical licence in 1925. In the same year he became a member of the NSDAP (23 November 1925). He apparently did not join the SA and the SS. On 27 April 1945, he committed suicide to escape arrest by the Allies; Friedlander 1995, pp. 40ff.

31 Friedlander 1995, pp. 40ff.

32 Klee 1991, pp. 78f. In 1936–37 Gütt wanted to establish a 'Reich Hereditary Health Court', which was meant to serve as the highest court of appeal in sterilization cases. Although this court was never set up, a secret 'Reich Committee for Hereditary Health Questions' did materialize. It was this committee which was renamed to serve as a cover for the killing of infants; Burleigh 1994, p. 98.

33 Friedlander 1995, p. 44.

34 Burleigh 1994, p. 100.

35 Engel 1974, p. 56.

36 Schmidt 2002, pp. 137f.

37 Engel 1974, p. 56.

38 StaNü, KV-Anklage, NO-3008.

39 Schmuhl 1987, p. 191.

40 Klee 2001, pp. 84f.

41 BAK, All. Proz. 2/FC 6069 P, Vernehmung Karl Brandt, 5 November 1946.

42 StaNü, KV-Anklage, NO-3008.

43 Peiffer 1997, p. 26.

44 For Heinze see Kersting 1996, pp. 351f; for Wentzler see Schmidt 2002, pp. 244–49, pp. 270f.

45 Friedlander argues that Brack's post-war testimony, and that of other witnesses, suggests that these talks had occurred months earlier, and says that the evidence supports the earlier date without actually mentioning it. The fact is that Brack, as Friedlander will know, is a rather unreliable source, especially during the Nuremberg Doctors' Trial, at which he was several times proved to have distorted events or lied through his teeth. For all the other witnesses, who were interrogated twenty years later, two general observations should be taken into account. First, the likelihood that people do not remember dates precisely increases rather than decreases with time; second, none of the witnesses was ever involved in these talks and had received their information only from second or third hand or hearsay. On the other hand, those closely involved in the talks, such as Lammers and Brandt, were interviewed shortly after the war and had little reason to shift the time of these talks to some earlier or later date. Of all existing sources, Lammer's recollection seems to me the most reliable; his notion that the talks occurred at Führer headquarters is also another indication that they probably took place after the outbreak of war at the end of September or beginning of October. My account therefore follows primarily his testimony; StaNü, KV-Prozesse, Fall 1, No. 2-H, affidavit Hans-Heinrich Lammers, 30 January 1947; see also Friedlander 1995, pp. 62ff; Burleigh 1994, pp. 111f.

46 StaNü, KV-Prozesse, Fall 1, No. 2-H, affidavit Hans-Heinrich Lammers, 30 January 1947.

47 Ibid.

48 Ibid.

49 Brandt trial notebook, Euthanasia, II/9 (14), p. 66 (pagination by US).

50 Ibid., p. 58.

51 Ibid., p. 56.

52 Ibid., p. 57.

53 Ibid., p. 55.

54 Quoted from Burleigh 1994, p. 97; NDT-Records, frame 2/2473; see also National Archives and Records Service, Records of the United States Nuremberg War Crimes Trials. United States of America v. Karl Brandt et al. (Case 1) November 21, 1946 – August 20, 1947 (Washington, 1974), pp. 2396ff.

55 Brandt trial notebook, Euthanasia, II/9 (16), pp. 84f (pagination by US); also Knödler and Feyerabend, part III.

56 Ibid., p. 85.

57 Ibid., pp. 86f.

58 Ibid., pp. 85f.

59 NDT-Records, frame 2/2473; StaNü, Records of the United States Nuremberg War Crimes Trials. United States of America v. Karl Brandt et al. (Case 1) 21 November 1946–20 August 1947, pp. 2396ff; see also StaNü, KV-Anklage Interrogations, No. B154, Interrogation Karl Brandt, 26 November 1946.

60 See also StaNü, Interrogation of Fritz Wiedemann by Philipp H. Fehl, 23 December 1946.

61 Schlie 1999, pp. 28f.
62 Linge 1980, p. 113.
63 Kershaw 1998, pp. 527–91.
64 NARA, M 1270, Roll 2, Interrogation Karl Brandt; also StaNü, KV-Verteidigung, Handakten Rostock No. 6.
65 Engel 1974, p. 64.
66 Brandt trial notebook, Euthanasia, II/9 (47), p. 259 (pagination by US).
67 Ibid., II/9 (16), p. 83.
68 StaNü, KV-Anklage, No. 426, affidavit of Viktor Brack, 12 October 1946.
69 After the war, Brandt stated that upon his request they added a sentence such as 'to the best of my knowledge' because in his view euthanasia was a biological matter where one could never be one hundred per cent certain. What he meant was the phrase 'on the basis of human judgement' in the actual decree, which apparently was to function as a 'safety factor' against potential claims of negligence if mistakes were made in the selection of patients. Brandt wanted to present himself as a caring and responsible physician to his interrogators, something that worked only as long as his role in the programme had not been fully exposed; BAK, Kl. Erw. 525.
70 NDT-Records, frames 2/2473f; StaNü, Records of the United States Nuremberg War Crimes Trials. United States of America v. Karl Brandt et al. (Case 1) November 21, 1946 – August 20, 1947, pp. 2396f; see also NARA, M 1270, Roll 2, Interrogation Karl Brandt, 1 October 1945, frame 348; also Brandt trial notebook, Euthanasia, II/9 (16), p. 86 (pagination by US).
71 NDT-Documents, Exhibit 330, 630 PS, frame 3/1112.
72 Brandt trial notebook, Euthanasia, II/9 (17), p. 99 (pagination by US).
73 Ibid., II/9 (16), pp. 94f.
74 Ibid., II/9 (18), p. 101.
75 Engel 1974, p. 65.
76 Ibid.
77 Schmidt 2000b, pp. 133f.
78 Brandt trial notebook, Euthanasia, II/9 (23), pp. 136f; pp. 156f (pagination by US).
79 Ibid., pp. 136f.
80 Ibid., p. 138.
81 For individual biographies of the staff of the 'euthanasia' programme see Friedlander 1995, pp. 68ff.

82 Brandt trial notebook, Euthanasia, II/9 (24), p. 162 (pagination by US).
83 StaNü, KV-Anklage, No. 426, affidavit of Viktor Brack, 12 October 1946.
84 Friedlander 1995, pp. 68f.
85 Ibid., p. 69.
86 StaNü, KV-Anklage, No. 426, affidavit of Viktor Brack, 12 October 1946.
87 Burleigh 1994, p. 113.
88 For the various roles of the cover organizations see Friedlander 1995, pp. 73ff.
89 Friedlander 1995, p. 71.
90 Sächsisches Hauptstaatsarchiv Dresden, 11120 Staatsanwaltschaft beim Landgericht Dresden, No. 2529, Anklageschrift gegen Paul Nitsche u.a., 7 January 1947.
91 Friedlander 1995, pp. 86ff. According to Brandt, the killing method had not been decided by the time Hitler signed the authorization; Brandt trial notebook, Euthanasia, II/9 (38), p. 228 (pagination by US).
92 NARA, M 1270, Roll 2, Interrogation Karl Brandt, 1 October 1945, frame 333.
93 Ibid. The source has been edited to improve the fluency of the text.
94 Brandt trial notebook, Euthanasia, II/9 (38), pp. 230ff (pagination by US); permission to use the source was granted on the condition that one part of it would be omitted.
95 NARA, M 1270, Roll 2, Interrogation Karl Brandt, 1 October 1945, frame 334.
96 Brandt was not the only one involved in the 'euthanasia' programme to have made such off-putting remarks. One of the technical engineers involved in the killing operation looked at his interrogators with surprise when asked about his rationale for using gas to kill human beings: 'What are you talking about, it works'; Friedlander 1995, p. 86.
97 Friedlander 1995, pp. 87f.
98 Gauck-Behörde, interrogation with Richard von Hegener, 17 March 1949.
99 Klee 1991, pp. 110ff.
100 Süß 2002, p. 203.
101 Kershaw 2000, p. 294.
102 Ibid.
103 Sereny 1995, p. 217.
104 BSB, Fotoarchiv Hoffmann, hoff-29909.
105 Ibid., hoff-30184, 30282, 30458.
106 Ibid., hoff-30530, 30565, 30566, 30596.
107 Ibid., hoff-30596.

NOTES TO PAGES 142–150

108 Ibid., hoff-30811, 30832, 30835, 30837, 30838, 30839, 30841, 30842, 30843, 30877, 30879.

110 Ibid., hoff-30999, 31000, 31001, 31002, 31004, 31040, 31047, 31049, 31056, 31061, 31065, 31067, 31077, 31078.

111 NARA, T 253, Roll 62, Morell papers.

112 Ibid.

113 BSB, Fotoarchiv Hoffmann, hoff-31305, 31306, 31393, 31396.

114 Ibid., hoff-31282, 31283, 31302, 31303, 31394, 31436.

115 Ibid., hoff-31795, 31797, 31799, 31851.

116 Ibid., hoff-31933, 31937.

117 Ibid., hoff-31961, 31970, 31971.

118 Ibid., hoff-32116, 32121, 32122, 32124, 32127, 32133, 32137, 32139, 32140.

119 Breker 1972, p. 153.

120 See also Breker 1972, pp. 154f.

121 BSB, Fotoarchiv Hoffmann, hoff-32143, 32169, 32175, 32176, 32189, 32190, 32193, 32194, 32195, 32206, 66072.

122 Ibid., hoff-32209, 32210, 32211, 32212, 32216, 32219, 32220, 32221, 32222, 32227.

123 Ibid., hoff-32340, 32353, 32354.

124 Ibid., hoff-32355, 32357, 32358.

125 Ibid., hoff-32431, 32434, 32435, 32438, 32441, 32463, 32464, 32465.

126 Ibid., hoff-32484, 32485, 32498, 32507, 32523, 32524, 32525, 32525, 32529, 32530, 32545, 32546.

127 Ibid., hoff-32630.

128 StaNü, KV-Prozesse, Fall 1, NO. 2-H, affidavit Hans-Heinrich Lammers, 30 January 1947.

129 Ibid.

130 Ibid.

131 Maastricht is en route from Brussels to Bonn. This may corroborate the assumption that Bouhler was coming from Brussels, where on 28 May 1940 Lammers was signing the unconditional surrender of Belgium with the Belgian King, Leopold III.

132 NARA, T 253, Roll 62, Morell papers.

133 Denkschrift 1957, 194–98; Sereny 1995, p. 213.

134 Denkschrift 1957, 197.

135 Lammers received one of the few copies of Himmler's memorandun; see Denkschrift 1957, 195.

136 Denkschrift 1957, 196.

137 StaNü, KV-Prozesse, Fall 1, NO. 2-H, affidavit Hans-Heinrich Lammers, 30 January 1947.

138 Friedlander 1995, pp. 120f.

139 Schmuhl 1987, p. 299; also Friedlander 1995, pp. 120f; see also NDT-Records 4/2162.

140 Friedlander 1995, p. 121.

141 Sächsisches Hauptstaatsarchiv Dresden, 11120 Staatsanwaltschaft beim Landgericht Dresden, No. 2529, Anklageschrift gegen Paul Nitsche u.a., 7 January 1947.

142 Ibid.

143 Rost 1987, p. 102.

144 Klee 1986, pp. 162ff.

145 Friedlander 1995, p. 113.

146 TNA, FO 371, 26508, 26509, 26510, 26518, 26526, 26534; FO 371, 26513, 1941: Reported killing of aged, infirm and insane persons and abnormal children, and seriously maimed casualties: possible utilization for experiments on effect of poison gas: suggested utilization for British whispering campaign; FO 371, 24392, 1940: Reported destruction of mentally defective and infirm persons; also FO 371, 24376; see also Nowak 1984.

147 TNA, FO 371, 26508.

148 Ibid., 24392.

149 Ibid.

150 Ibid., 26534.

151 Ibid., 26513.

152 StaNü, KV-Anklage, Dokumente, NO. 3059.

153 Ibid.

154 Ibid.

155 Ibid.

156 Ibid., NO. 1658.

157 For the role of Friedrich von Bodelschwingh and the Bethel asylum during the 'euthanasia' programme see, for example, HBAB, 2/39–188; 2/39–189; 2/39–191; 2/39–192; 2/39–193; also Hochmuth 1979; Klee 1991, pp. 317ff, pp. 421ff; Schmuhl 1987, pp. 327ff; Kühl 1990; Burleigh 1994, pp. 166ff; Benad 1997a; Benad 1997b; Hochmuth 1997; Kühl 1997, pp. 54–67; Schmuhl 1997, pp. 101–17; Walter 1997, pp. 137–52; Faulstich 1998, pp. 588f; for Braune see Cantow and Kaiser 2005.

158 Von Bodelschwingh established his contact with Brandt through von Oeynhausen and not through Göring. On 10 December 1940, von Oeynhausen informed von Bodelschwingh of Brandt's forthcoming visit to Bethel; Hochmuth 1997, pp. 317f; also Brandt trial notebook, Euthanasia, II/9 (20) (21), pp. 120f; p. 129 (pagination by US).

159 StaNü, KV-Anklage, Dokumente, NO-895.
160 Ibid.; Schmuhl 1987, p. 330.
161 Schmuhl 1987, p. 331.
162 Ibid., p. 332.
163 TNA, FO 371, 26508.
164 Schmuhl 1987, p. 338; Matthias Benad estimates that approximately twenty patients from the Bethel asylum were eventually killed; Benad 1997a, pp. xxxiif.
165 HBAB, 2/39–188, Von Bodelschwingh to Göring, 6 January 1941.
166 Ibid.
167 Ibid., 29 January 1941.
168 The exact size of the medical commission can be deduced from a letter which Bodelschwingh sent to Brandt in April 1941; HBAB, 2/39–188, Bodelschwingh to Brandt, 25 April 1941. See also Hochmuth 1997, p. 107, who has identified sixteen members of the commission by name.
169 HBAB, 2/39–188, Besuch der Ärztekommission, 19 February 1941.
170 Ibid.
171 Hochmuth 1979, p. 31.
172 HBAB, 2/39–188, Summary about the conversation between v. Bodelschwingh and Brandt, 19 February 1941.
173 Kühl argues that Bethel's rejection of the 'euthanasia' programme is not identical with a clearly defined opposition to the killing operation, and that one can only talk of 'opposition' and 'resistance' in this context, if the Bethel doctors had refused to collaborate with the T-4 commission, and if Bethel's leadership had openly opposed the programme in the event that patients were to be transferred to one of the killing centres. Kühl's view lacks, I believe, the necessary appreciation of the power relationship between the Bethel institution and the Nazi regime in 1941. As far as the 'euthanasia' programme was concerned, von Bodelschwingh took a distinctly pragmatic approach to save as many of Bethel's patients as possible. If that meant negotiating with Brandt and some of the leading members of the regime, and perhaps even becoming culpable in remaining silent, then that was a price which von Bodelschwingh was willing to pay to ensure that Bethel would largely be excluded from the killing operation. I am doubtful whether von Bodelschwingh would have shown greater moral courage if Bethel had publicly opposed the killings, and if, as a result, more of Bethel's patients had been included in the 'euthanasia' programme. In 1963, Friedrich [III] von Bodelschwingh remarked about his uncle Fritz von Bodelschwingh: 'For him it was more important to save a limited, even if practically the greatest possible number of human lives, and thereby to become a compromise-seeking negotiator [kompromißlerischen Verhändlers] than to acquire the fame of an uncompromising attitude, but to accept a complete failure in the practical success'; see Benad 1997a, p. xxxiv. I also do not think, as Schmuhl suggests, that it was 'luck' that the Bethel institution remained largely unaffected by the 'euthanasia' programme. It is important to acknowledge von Bodelschwingh's diplomatic activity, which may have been a less visible and public form of 'resistance', but an altogether effective way of saving the majority of Bethel's patients; see Schmuhl 1997, p. 117; see also Klee 1991; Schmuhl 1987; Kühl 1990.
174 Hochmuth 1997, pp. 110f.
175 HBAB, 2/39–188, Notes about meeting in Minden, 28 February 1941; see also Hochmuth 1997, pp. 113f.
176 Kühl 1990, p. 59.
177 Witte 1999, pp. 107f.
178 Ibid., p. 141 and p. 157.
179 NARA, T-1021, Roll 12, frames 127398–127400.
180 Ibid., frame 127400.
181 Fröhlich 1987, part I, vol. 4, p. 485, 31 January 1941.
182 NARA, T-1021, Roll 12, frames 127398–127399.
183 Ibid., frame 127398.
184 Ibid., frame 127399.
185 BSB, Fotoarchiv Hoffmann, hoff-34291, 34293.
186 NDT-Documents, frames 3/2896–2956, Closing brief for the United States of America against Karl Brandt, 16 June 1947, frame 3/2953.
187 When asked after the war to name any of the ten or fifteen physicians whom he and Bouhler had charged with implementing the 'euthanasia' programme, Brandt was unable to do so. Brandt never examined their medical credentials, nor had he himself any

expert knowledge in psychiatry; NDT-Documents, frames 3/2896–2956, Closing brief for the United States of America against Karl Brandt, 16 June 1947, frame 3/2930.

188 For Bouhler's presence during the meeting see HBAB, 2/39–188, Bodelschwingh to Brandt, 23 May 1941; for Oeynhausen's presence see Brandt trial notebook, Euthanasia, II/9 (20) (21), pp. 129f. (pagination by US).

189 It is likely, but not certain, that Brandt visited the nursing home during his visit in March 1941. He could also have visited it in February 1941, but the later date is more likely. For von Bodelschwingh's suggestion to visit the *Hermannsheide* see HBAB, 2/39–188, Bodelschwingh to Brandt, 29 March 1941.

190 NDT-Records (German), frames 2/2443; also NDT-Records, frames 2/2507f; see also HBAB, file 2/39–189, Meeting with Professor Brandt, 13 February 1943. The document confirms Brandt's visit to one of the children's wards. See also BAK, All. Proz. 2/FC 6069 P, Vernehmung Karl Brandt, 13 August 1947.

191 Brandt trial notebook, Euthanasia, II/9 (20) (21), pp. 128f; also p. 108 (pagination by US).

192 HBAB, file 2/39–189, Meeting with Professor Brandt, 13 February 1943.

193 NARA, M 1270, Roll 2, Interrogation Karl Brandt, 1 October 1945, frame 325.

194 HBAB, 2/39–188, Bodelschwingh to Brandt, 25 April 1941.

195 Ibid.

196 BSB, Fotoarchiv Hoffmann, hoff-35330, 35366

197 Ibid., hoff-35408, 35414, 35418, 35428.

198 Ibid., hoff-35509, 35510, 35542, 35543, 35544, 35549, 35550, 35571.

199 HBAB, 2/39–188, Bodelschwingh to Brandt, 23 May 1941.

200 BSB, Fotoarchiv Hoffmann, hoff-35796.

201 Ibid., hoff-36541, 36542, 36543, 36554, 36555, 36558, 36559, 36560, 36567, 36579, 36581, 36589, 36875, 36892, 36897, 36958, 36965, 36972, 36988, 37171, 37172, 37211, 37213, 37214.

202 Ibid., hoff-37483; see also Faulstich 1998, pp. 282f.

203 BSB, Fotoarchiv Hoffmann, hoff-37576, 37621, 37644, 37698, 37789, 37790, 37851, 37853, 37854, 37855, 37856, 37857, 37882, 37883, 37884, 37920.

204 Streit 1995, pp. 80f.

205 BSB, Fotoarchiv Hoffmann, hoff-37393, 37394, 37396, 37397, 37398, 37410.

206 Kershaw 2000, p. 397.

207 Ibid., p. 396.

208 HBAB, 2/39–188, Bodelschwingh to Brandt, 28 August 1941.

209 Ibid.

210 Ibid.

211 Ibid.

212 Ibid.

213 HBAB, 2/39–188, Meeting with Professor Brandt, 13 February 1943.

214 Faulstich 1998, pp. 271–88.

215 Burleigh 1994, p. 178.

216 NARA, M 1270, Roll 2, Interrogation Karl Brandt, 1 October 1945, frame 341.

217 StaNü, KV-Anklage, Dokumente, NO-1702; affidavit Kurt Blome, 17 January 1946.

218 Sereny 1988, p. 76.

219 See Faulstich 1998, pp. 271–88.

220 NARA, M 1270, Roll 2, Interrogation Karl Brandt, 1 October 1945, frame 332.

221 Reuth 1999, 15 August 1941, pp. 1652f; for the film 'I accuse' (*Ich klage an*) see Burleigh 1994, pp. 205ff; Hachmeister 1998; Schmidt 2002, p. 28; for the suggestion that Brandt was involved in the decision-making to produce the film see Riess 1956, pp. 652ff.

222 Reuth 1999, 19 August 1941, pp. 1653f.

223 Faulstich 1998, p. 287.

224 Reuth 1999, 19 August 1941, pp. 1658f; for the role of the German army in the killing of tens of thousands of civilians, and in the Holocaust, see Heer 2005, pp. 57–77; also Heer and Naumann 2005.

225 Roseman 2002, p. 57.

226 Ibid., p. 67.

227 Faulstich 1998, p. 285.

228 Ibid.

229 Witte 1999, p. 198.

230 Faulstich 1998, p. 590.

231 BAB, R18, 737b, Brandt to Bormann, 24 August 1941; quoted from Faulstich 1998, p. 590; see also Süß 2003, p. 281.

232 BSB, Fotoarchiv Hoffmann, hoff-38083, 38215, 38219, 38230, 38243, 38249, 38250, 38265, 38267, 38269, 38283.

233 Quoted from Faulstich 1998, pp. 590f.

234 Faulstich 1998, p. 591.

235 Ibid.

236 Witte 1999, p. 195; Gerlach 1999, pp. 571ff.

237 Witte 1999, pp. 196f.

238 Quoted from Süß 2003, p. 315.
239 Roseman 2002, p. 52; Gerlach 1999, p. 647.
240 Burleigh 1994, pp. 220ff.
241 Quoted from Roseman 2002, p. 73.
242 Roseman 2002, p. 72.
243 In 1939 Bleich was employed by the Reich Academy for Sport, where he produced plaster models for anatomical studies. From November 1939 he worked as a civilian in the OKW War Graves Commission, Berlin. In February 1940 he joined Brandt's staff for the first time. In 1942, whilst stationed in Russia with the O.T., he fell ill with spotted fever and returned to Brandt's office. In July 1942 Bleich was again conscripted for three months with the medical reserve and education department. In October he began full duties as a civilian clerk in the offices of T-4 and, when this work was finished, he transferred to Brandt's personal staff in his office in Beelitz. In June 1944 he was again called up and captured by the Allies in March 1945; StaNü, KV-Anklage, Dokumente, L11, Interrogation of Fritz Bleich, 22 March 1945; see also StaNü, KV-Anklage Interrogations, B95, Interrogation Fritz Bleich, 4 January 1946, 4 December 1946; NARA, RG 238, Entry 188/190/191, Box 2, Individual Responsibility of Prof. Dr. Karl Brandt, May 1946; also Entry 185, Box 1, Interrogation Summary Fritz Bleich, 4 December 1946; also RG 153, 109–1, Box 94, Report on interrogation of PW LD 563 San Soldat Fritz Bleich, 1 April 1945.
244 Sereny 1988, p. 86.
245 Witte 1999, p. 290.
246 Ibid.
247 NDT-Documents, frames 3/2896–2956, Closing brief for the United States of America against Karl Brandt, 16 June 1947, frame 3/2936.
248 StaNü, KV-Anklage, Dokumente, L11, Interrogation of Fritz Bleich, 22 March 1945.
249 The letter was addressed directly to Brandt and made no mention in the letterhead of either 'Kdo Stab RFSS' (Commando Unit Reich Leader SS) or 'Pers Stab RFSS' (Personal Unit Reich Leader SS); StaNü, KV-Anklage, Dokumente, L11, Interrogation of Fritz Bleich, 22 March 1945.
250 StaNü, KV-Anklage, Dokumente, L11, interrogation of Fritz Bleich, 22 March 1945.
251 NARA, RG 238, Entry 188/190/191, Box 2, Individual Responsibility of Prof. Dr. Karl Brandt, May 1946.
252 StaNü, KV-Anklage, Dokumente, L11, interrogation of Fritz Bleich, 22 March 1945; also Sereny 1988, pp. 82–90.
253 Most of the trucks that were used were produced in Switzerland by the company Saurer in Arbon, and were modified at a small Berlin-based company for the specific killing purposes in the East. Saurer trucks were especially suited because they could deal with the bad roads and weather conditions in Poland during the winter. The bodies were then either burnt on site or buried in mass graves which the victims often had to dig themselves. The company has never fully examined this part of its history.
254 StaNü, KV-Anklage, Dokumente, L11, interrogation of Fritz Bleich, 22 March 1945.
255 Brandt Diary, 16 December 1946; also Knödler and Feyerabend 2004, part I.

Notes to Chapter 6: The General Commissioner

1 BAK, All. Proz. 2/FC 6069 P, Vernehmung Karl Brandt, 9 October 1946.
2 NDT-Records (German), frame 2328; the English version of the transcript suggests that the reports turned out to be incorrect, which is not what Brandt actually said; see NDT-Records, frame 2/2395.
3 NDT-Records, frames 2/2395f; NDT-Records (German), frame 2/2328.
4 NDT-Records, frames 2/2396f; NDT-Records (German), frames 2/2328f.
5 One of Hoffmann's photographs shows Brandt at Führer headquarters on 18 January 1942; BSB, Fotoarchiv Hoffmann, hoff-43997, 43998.
6 StaNü, Interrogation of Brandt by Walther H. Rapp, 9 October 1946.
7 Fröhlich 1995, part II, vol. 3, p. 142, 20 January 1942.
8 Burleigh 1994, pp. 231f; Süß 2003, p. 315, footnote 20.
9 Burleigh 1994, p. 255.
10 Ibid., pp. 220–37.
11 Fröhlich 1995, part II, vol. 3, p. 220, 30 January 1942.
12 See also Jaehn 1985; Jaehn 1991; Kümmel 2001; as well as Bruns and Frewer 2005.

13 HUA, Institut für Geschichte der Medizin, Diepgen to Brandt, 29 August 1941. I am grateful to Florian Bruns and Andreas Frewer for having drawn my attention to the source, and to Dr W. Schultze from the Humboldt-University Archive in Berlin for sending me a copy. For an analysis of the origins and history of Nazi medical ethics see especially Proctor 1988; Frewer 2000; Bruns and Frewer 2005; Bruns [in preparation].

14 Schmidt 2004, p. 143, p. 197, p. 212, p. 229, pp. 259–61.

15 HUA, Institut für Geschichte der Medizin, Diepgen to Brandt, 29 January 1942.

16 Ibid., Brandt to Diepgen, 4 February 1942.

17 See especially Proctor 1988; Proctor 1999; Frewer 2000; Frewer and Neumann 2001; Frewer and Roelcke 2003; Frewer and Bruns 2003; Bruns and Frewer 2005.

18 Quoted from Bruns and Frewer 2005, p. 150; see also Proctor 1988, pp. 284f.

19 NDT-Records (German), frames 2401f.

20 BAK, All. Proz. 2/FC 6069 P, Vernehmung Karl Brandt, 1 March 1947.

21 BAK, Kl. Erw. 441, No. 3, Karl Brandt, Das Problem Hitler, No. 2, 27 September 1945, p. 5; also Süß 2003, p. 94.

22 There is some evidence which suggests that Brandt knew of the Wannsee conference and the planned extermination of the European Jews. Shortly before the end of the war, he apparently told one of Hitler's test pilots that certain criminals in Hitler's vicinity, Heydrich and Eichmann included, were pursuing the extermination of the Jews without limits. The credibility of the source has to be treated with some caution, however; Perlia 1999, p. 196.

23 See, for example, BAK, All. Proz. 2/FC 6069 P, Vernehmung Karl Brandt, 26 November 1946; NDT-Records, frame 2/2516.

24 NARA, RG 153, 100–767, Box 62, US Strategic Bombing Survey, Interview with Prof. Dr. med. Karl Brandt, 17–18 June 1945.

25 Süß 2003, pp. 192ff.

26 See, for example, Proctor 1988, pp. 154ff.

27 BAK, All. Proz. 2/FC 6069 P, Vernehmung Karl Brandt, 18 October 1946.

28 NARA, RG 153, 100–767, Box 62, US Strategic Bombing Survey, Interview with Prof. Dr. med. Karl Brandt, 17–18 June 1945.

29 Ibid.

30 See also NARA, M 1270, Roll 2, Interrogation of Karl Brandt, 29 September 1945.

31 Staatsarchiv München, SpKA K, No. 1832, Affidavit Karl Brandt, 6 August 1947.

32 Ibid.

33 BSB, Fotoarchiv Hoffmann, hoff-42914, 42915.

34 Trevor-Roper 1954, pp. 103f, M. Bormann to G. Bormann, 8–9 September 1944.

35 Ibid., pp. 78–80, M. Bormann to G. Bormann, 14 August 1944.

36 Ibid.

37 NDT-Documents, frame 3/22.

38 Süß 2003, pp. 254–68; see also Süß 2002, pp. 205ff.

39 BAB, R18, 3810, Conti memo about Brandt, 26 January 1944.

40 Ibid.

41 Süß 2003, p. 160.

42 Ibid., footnote 174.

43 NDT-Documents, frame 3/22.

44 NDT-Records, frame 2/2397.

45 NDT-Documents, frame 3/22.

46 Ibid., frames 3/22f; see also RGBl. 1942, I, pp. 515f, Erlaß des Führers über das Sanitäts- und Gesundheitswesen; NDT-Documents, Exhibit 004, NO-475, frames 3/18ff, affidavit Karl Brandt, 25 October 1946; Aly 1989, pp. 168–82.

47 BAK, Kl. Erw. 512–2, p. 156, Hitler to Brandt, 20 August 1942.

48 BSB, Fotoarchiv Hoffmann, hoff-44803, 44804, 44984; Kershaw 2000, p. 527.

49 Fröhlich 1995, part II, vol. 5, p. 481, 11 September 1942; Fröhlich 1996, part II, vol. 6, p. 250, 7 November 1942.

50 StaNü, Interrogation of Brandt by Walther H. Rapp, 9 October 1946.

51 BAK, All. Proz. 2/FC 6069 P, Vernehmung Karl Brandt, 1 March 1947.

52 BAB, R18, 3810, Kaufmann to Conti, 8 June 1943; also BAB, R18, 3810, Conti memo about Brandt and the origin of the first Führer decree, 26 January 1944; see also Süß 2003, p. 160.

53 Der Angriff, No. 209, 28 September 1942.

54 BAB, R18, 3810, Conti memo about Brandt and the origin of the first Führer decree, 26 January 1944.

55 BAB, R18, 3811, note by Conti about a meeting with Lammers, 16 February 1943.

56 Fröhlich 1995, part II, vol. 5, p. 481, 11 September 1942.

57 Süß 2003, p. 87; StaNü, KV-Anklage, Dokumente, L11, interrogation of Fritz Bleich, 22 March 1945.

58 StaNü, KV-Anklage Interrogations, No. B154, Interrogation Karl Brandt, 18 October 1946.

59 Süß 2003, pp. 76–94, pp. 160–68; also Süß 2002, pp. 214f.

60 Süß 2002, p. 210.

61 BAK, Kl. Erw. 512–1, pp. 46f; Brandt to Gossel, 18 February 1945.

62 Süß 2003, p. 161.

63 Ibid., pp. 204ff.

64 NARA, RG 153, 100–0, Book 1, Box 1, Interview by US Strategic Bombing Survey with Captain Heinz Gluck, 15 June 1945.

65 Süß 2003, p. 206.

66 BAB, R18, 3809, Brandt to Conti, 22 December 1942; Conti to Brandt, 30 December 1942.

67 StaNü, Interrogation of Brandt by Walther H. Rapp, 9 October 1946.

68 Fröhlich 1996, part II, vol. 6, p. 250, 7 November 1942.

69 Schaub 2005, p. 256.

70 Breker 1972, pp. 292f.

71 At the end of October 1941, the special corps (*Sonderkommando*, SK) 4a, a unit of the *SS-Einsatzgruppe C*, which accompanied the Sixth Army through the Ukraine, reported that the total number of executions had exceeded 55,000; Boll and Safrian 2005, pp. 269ff.

72 Breker 1972, p. 293.

73 For the various attempts by Conti to obstruct the work of Brandt see especially IfZ, MB 15, 29, affidavit of Carl-Heinz Grabe.

74 Brandt to Görnnert, 7 September 1942, printed in Hamilton 1984, p. 139.

75 StaNü, Interrogation of Brandt by Walther H. Rapp, 9 October 1946. Other sources suggest that in 1942 Brandt's office had eighteen members of staff. A planned increase of personnel to 169 members of staff never materialized before the end of the war; Süß 2002, p. 214, footnote, 63.

76 Bleich described Geist as shrewd and egoistic with a duelling scar on the right cheek; StaNü, KV-Anklage, Dokumente, L11, interrogation of Fritz Bleich, 22 March 1945.

77 NARA, M 1270, Roll 2, Interrogation Karl Brandt, 29 September 1945.

78 StaNü, KV-Anklage, Dokumente, NO-860.

79 StaNü, KV-Anklage, B95 Interrogation Fritz Bleich by Mr de Vries, 27 November 1946.

80 Ibid.

81 StaNü, KV-Anklage, Dokumente, L11, interrogation of Fritz Bleich, 22 March 1945; see also StaNü, KV-Anklage Interrogations, B95, Interrogation Fritz Bleich, 4 January 1946, 4 December 1946; NARA, RG 238, Entry 188/190/191, Box 2, Individual Responsibility of Prof. Dr. Karl Brandt, May 1946; also Entry 185, Box 1, Interrogation Summary Fritz Bleich, 4 December 1946.

82 StaNü, KV-Anklage, Dokumente, NO-860.

83 StaNü, KV-Anklage Interrogations, B95 Interrogation Fritz Bleich by H. Meyer on 4 January 1946.

84 StaNü, B95 Interrogation Fritz Bleich by H. Meyer on 4 January 1946.

85 StaNü, KV-Prozesse, Fall 1, Spezialia Karl Brandt H 1.

86 StaNü, KV-Anklage, Dokumente, L11, interrogation of Fritz Bleich, 22 March 1945.

87 Ibid., B95 Interrogation Fritz Bleich by H. Meyer on 4 January 1946.

88 Ibid., NO-426.

89 Ibid., B95 Interrogation Fritz Karl Albert Bleich by Mr Iwan de Vries and Mr Hochwald on 4 December 1946.

90 See also BAB, R18, 3809, Conti memo about a conversation with Brandt, 20 September 1944.

91 NARA, M 1270, Roll 2, Interrogation Karl Brandt, 29 September 1945.

92 StaNü, KV-Prozesse, Fall 1, Spezialia, Karl Brandt H 6, Affidavit Carl-Heinz Grabe.

93 For Conti's biography see Kater 1985, pp. 299–325; also Zentrum für Sozialpolitik Bremen (ZeS), File Conti; also Conti papers (in possession of Hans-Walter Schmuhl).

94 The film was discovered by the author in one of Goebbels' former film bunkers in Berlin-Babelsberg, where during the war cameramen from the RMfVuP had recorded the views of leading Nazi officials. This film was located for more than fifty years in one of the bunkers of the former State Film Archive of the German Democratic Republic and only became accessible after German unification; see also the film *Homo Sapiens 1900*, directed by Peter Cohen, released in 1999.

95 BAFA, Archiv der Persönlichkeiten, Leonardo Conti, 35 mm (black and white).

96 NARA, RG 238, Entry 185, Box 1, Interrogation Summary Fritz Bleich, 4 December 1946.
97 Lifton 1986, p. 38.
98 Schlie 1999, p. 31; Sereny 1995, p. 307.
99 BAB, R43-II, 745a, Führererlaß, 30 November 1942, p. 39; also Lammers to Brandt, 20 April 1943; see also Süß 2003, p. 163.
100 BAB, R18, 3811, Conti memo about meeting with Lammers, 22 April 1943.
101 BAB, R43-II, 745a, Lammers to Brandt, 4 June 1943.
102 Ibid.
103 NARA, SS personal file Karl Brandt.
104 BAB, R18, 3809, Meeting between Brandt and Conti, 10 February 1943.
105 BSB, Fotoarchiv Hoffmann, hoff-47283, 47284.
106 Kershaw 2000, pp. 660ff.
107 BSB, Fotoarchiv Hoffmann, hoff-49660, 49661, 49662, 49663.
108 BAB, R43-II, 745a, Lammers to Brandt, 20 April 1943.
109 BAB, R18, 3810, Lammers to Conti, 1 April 1943.
110 BAB, R18, 3811, Conti memo about meeting with Göring, 22 April 1943; Conti memo about meeting with Lammers, 22 April 1943; Conti memo about meeting with Bormann, 22 April 1943.
111 BAB, R18, 3811, Conti memo about meeting with Göring, 22 April 1943.
112 Ibid., Conti memo about meeting with Bormann, 22 April 1943.
113 BAB, R43-II, 745a, Lammers to Brandt, 4 June 1943.
114 BAB, R18, 3811, Conti memo about lunch with the Führer, 12 May 1943.
115 Ibid.
116 Ibid.
117 Ibid.
118 NARA, RG 153, 100–0, Book 1, Box 1, Interview with First Lieutenant Zeitler, no date.
119 BAB, R18, 3811, Conti memo about lunch with the Führer, 12 May 1943.
120 Ibid.
121 Süß 2003, p. 84; also BAK, Kl. Erw. 512–2, p. 143, Führererlaß, 20 May 1943; also Süß 2002, p. 210.
122 Süß 2003, p. 84; also BAK, Kl. Erw. 512–2, p. 146, Aufstellung der im Rahmen des Führerauftrages durchzuführenden Maßnahmen, 21 May 1943.
123 BAB, R43-II, 745a, Lammers to Brandt, 4 June 1943.
124 On 30 May, for example, Brandt was invited to join the 'Air Raid Damage Committee' (Luftkriegsschädenausschuss) and supervise the central planning of all hospital beds; BAB, R18, 3808, Berndt (RMfVuP) to Brandt, 30 May 1943.
125 StaNü, KV-Anklage, Dokumente, NO-3881, Brandt to Conti, 29 May 1943.
126 Ibid.
127 Ibid., Conti to Brandt, 1 June 1943.
128 BAB. R18, 3811, Conti memo about meeting with Brandt on 18 June 1943; see also BAB, R 43-II, 745a, Lammers to Brandt, 4 June 1943.
129 BAB, R 43-II, 745a, Lammers to Brandt, 4 June 1943; Süß 2003, p. 164.
130 BAB, R43-II, 745a, Lammers to Brandt, 4 June 1943.
131 BAB, R18, 3809, Kauffmann to Conti, 8 June 1943.
132 Fröhlich 1993, part II, vol. 8, p. 453, 10 June 1943.
133 BAB, R18, 3810, Conti about meeting on 18 June 1943; R18, 3811, Conti memo about meeting on 18 June 1943; BAB, R 43 II/1609a and b, Diensttagebuch Lammers, Friday, 18 June 1943, p. 149.
134 BAB, R18, 3811, Conti memo about meeting on 18 June 1943.
135 Ibid.
136 Ibid.
137 Fröhlich 1993, part II, vol. 9, p. 27, 1 July 1943. For Frick's complaints about Brandt see BAB, R18, 3809, Brandt to Lammers, 30 June 1943; Lammers to Frick, 30 June 1943.
138 BAB, R18, 3810, Conti to Bormann, 23 June 1943.
139 BAB, R18, 3811, Conti memo about meeting on 22 June 1943; see also R18, 3810, Bormann to Conti, 3 August 1943.
140 BAB, R18, 3811, Conti memo about meeting on 22 June 1943.
141 BAB, R18, 3810, Conti to Bormann, 23 June 1943.
142 BAK, Kl. Erw. 512–1, p. 140, Brandt to Reich Minister of the Interior, Chief of the Supreme Command of the Armed Forces, and the head of the Party Chancellery, Bormann, 17 June 1943; see also Süß 2002, p. 210.
143 BAK, Kl. Erw. 512–1, p. 147, draft letter Lammers to Frick, 6 July 1943.

144 Walter 1996, p. 758; see also BAB, R96I, 18, Rüdin to Nitsche, 22 September 1943; Nitsche to Rüdin, 17 January 1944.

145 BAB, R96, 18, Rüdin to Nitsche, 22 September 1943; Nitsche to Rüdin, 17 January 1944.

146 Conti was not informed of these policy changes; BAB, R18, 3809, Brandt to RMdI and OKW, 21 June 1943, note by Conti about meeting with Brandt on 22 June 1943.

147 BAB, R18, 3809, Brandt to Lammers, 30 June 1943.

148 BAB, R18, 3810, Lammers to Frick, 30 June 1943.

149 BAB, R18, 3810, Bormann to Conti, 3 August 1943.

150 Ibid.; Süß 2003, pp. 164f.

151 Fröhlich 1993, part II, vol. 9, p. 245, 9 August 1943.

152 Ibid., p. 259, 10 August 1943.

153 StaNü, KV-Anklage, Dokumente, NO-3882, draft letter by Conti, 16 August 1943; also BAB, R18, 3809-II, draft letter by Conti, 20 September 1943.

154 NARA, RG242, Box No. 13, Item 1, Heinz Linge, Record of Hitler's Daily Activities 11 August 1943 – 30 December 1943, p. 6, 16 August 1943.

155 Fröhlich 1993, part II, vol. 9, p. 317, 20 August 1943.

156 Ibid.

157 Kershaw 2000, pp. 599f.

158 Trevor-Roper 1954, pp. 15f, M. Bormann to G. Bormann, 26 July 1943.

159 NARA, RG242, Box No. 13, Item 1, Heinz Linge, Record of Hitler's Daily Activities 11 August 1943 – 30 December 1943, p. 14, 24 August 1943.

160 BAB, R18, 3810, Lammers to Brandt, 7 September 1943.

161 BAB, R18, 3809, Klopfer to Conti, 25 August 1943.

162 Ibid., Conti to Bormann, 27 August 1943.

163 See also BAB, R18, 3810, Conti note about second Führer decree, c. 7 September 1943.

164 See also BAB, R18, 3809, Conti to Bormann, 27 August 1943.

165 NDT-Documents, frame 3/24; also BAK, Kl. Erw. 512–2, p. 152, Führer decree of 5 September 1943.

166 BAB, R18, 3810, Lammers to Brandt, 7 September 1943. The letter by Lammers had no official or modifying function for the second Führer decree, because it could not be published for fear that the conflicts at the top of the regime would become apparent. Brandt therefore could ignore the letter.

167 BAB, R18, 3809, Kaufmann to Conti, 11 September 1943; Fröhlich 1993, part II, vol. 9, p. 512, 15 September 1943.

168 Fröhlich 1993, part II, vol. 9, p. 512, 15 September 1943.

169 BAB, R18, 3809, Conti memorandum for a discussion with Brandt, ca. September 1943.

170 Ibid., Kaufmann to Conti, 11 September 1943.

171 Ibid., broadcast by the Deutsche Volkssender which had been intercepted by the RMfVuP, 17 September 1943.

172 Ibid., Conti to Hitler, 25 September 1943.

173 BAB, R18, 3810, Bormann to Conti, 27 September 1943.

174 BAB, R18, 3809, Kauffmann to Conti, 20 October 1943; also Süß 2002, p. 216; Süß 2003, p. 165.

175 Süß 2002, p. 204.

176 Süß 2003, pp. 280ff.

177 BAK, All. Proz. 2/FC 6069 P, Vernehmung Karl Brandt, 18 October 1946.

178 HUA, Institut für Geschichte der Medizin, Brandt to Diepgen, 25 September 1943; Diepgen to Brandt, 5 October 1943; see also Diepgen to von Brunn, 16 September 1943.

179 Süß 2003, p. 86.

180 StaNü, KV-Anklage, Dokumente, NO-3883, Copy of Hitler's second decree, 5 September 1943; also Fröhlich 1993, part II, vol. 9, p. 512, 15 September 1943.

181 NARA, M 1270, Roll 2, Interrogation Karl Brandt, 29 September 1945, frames 298f.

182 Ibid., frame 299.

183 Ibid.

184 Sereny 1995, p. 406.

185 BAB, R43-II, 719, Brandt to Lammers, 15 October 1943.

186 Ibid.

187 Ibid., 12 January 1944.

188 Fröhlich 1993, part II, vol. 8, p. 98, 12 April 1943; also Kershaw 2000, p. 571.

189 Kershaw 2000, p. 572.

190 Fröhlich 1993, part II, vol. 7, p. 454, 2 March 1943; see also Kershaw 2000, p. 570.

Notes to Chapter 7: Detached Leadership

1 Süß 2003, pp. 269–91; also BAK, Kl. Erw. 441, No. 3, Brandt about 'Sanitary Measures', 16 August 1945.

2 See, for example, Friedlander 1995, pp. 162f.

3 See especially Süß 2003, p. 311; Faulstich 1998, p. 582.

4 Kaminsky 2000, pp. 68f.

5 Uwe Kaminsky provides a good overview of the debate; Kaminsky 2000, pp. 68–83; for the different interpretations of the 'Aktion Brandt' see Schmuhl 1987; Daub 1992; Wunder 1994; Kaminsky 1995; Walter 1996; Harms 1997; Faulstich 1998; Süß 2002; Süß 2003; also Hinz-Wessels *et al.* 2005.

6 Roseman 2002, p. 66.

7 BA, R18, 5576, Rundschreiben des Reichsbeauftragten für die Heil- und Pflegeanstalten, 5 August 1942, pp. 269f; see also Süß 2003, p. 285.

8 NARA, T1021, Roll 12, frames 128145–152.

9 Ibid., frame 127429.

10 Ibid., frames 127428f; frames 127723–26.

11 Ibid., frame 128247, Linden to Nitsche, 20 August 1942.

12 See also the establishment of a research department in Wiesloch in 1942; NARA, T1021, Roll 12, frame 127118, frames 127434–8, frames 127441f.

13 NARA, T1021, Roll 12, frame 127060.

14 Ibid., frame 127061.

15 RGB, No. 121, Verordnung über die Bestellung eines Reichsbeauftragten für die Heil- und Pflegeanstalten vom 28 October 1941.

16 NARA, T1021, Roll 12, frames 127863f.

17 Ibid., frame 128206.

18 See especially NARA, T1021, Roll 12, frame 127415, Nitsche to Müller, 18 June 1942; frame 128232, Schulz to Nitsche, 16 August 1942.

19 Aly 1989, p. 169.

20 The conference in September/October 1942 was attended by Kurt Borm (T-4), Valentin Falthauser (Kaufbeuren-Irsee), Otto Hebold (Eberswalde), Hans Heinze (Görden), Rudolf Lonauer (Linz), Friedrich Mennecke (Eichberg), Robert Müller (T-4), Paul Nitsche (T-4), Hermann Pfannmüller (Eglfing), Victor Ratka (Tiegenhof), Curt Runckel (T-4), Curt Schmalenbach (T-4), Ernst-Adolf Schmorl (Heidelberg), Carl Schneider (Heidelberg), Gustav Schneider (T-4), Alfred Schulz (Großschweidnitz), Horst Schumann (T-4), Theodor Steinmeyer (Pfafferode), Erich Straub (T-4) and Gerhard Wischer (Waldheim). NARA, T1021, Roll 12, frames

128222f; frame 128226; also Süß 2003, p. 353, footnote 203.

21 NARA, T1021, Roll 12, frames 128224f.

22 Ibid., frame 128224.

23 Ibid.

24 Ibid., frame 127350.

25 Ibid., frame 127158, frames 127347–52; frames 127160–70; see also Burleigh 1994, pp. 197–202; Schmidt 2002, pp. 264–67.

26 Süß 2003, p. 322.

27 Ibid.

28 Ibid., pp. 319f.

29 Klee 1986, pp. 289f.

30 Ibid.

31 KV-Prozesse, Fall 1, Spezialia Karl Brandt H 6.

32 Ibid., Spezialia Karl Brandt H 3 und 4.

33 NARA, M 1270, Roll 2, Interrogation Karl Brandt, 29 September 1945, frame 297.

34 Süß 2003, p. 281.

35 NARA, T1021, Roll 12, frame 128074; also Süß 2003, p. 354, footnote 207. In preparation for the meeting with Conti, and probably Linden as well, Nitsche drafted a memorandum in collaboration with Heinze, Carl Schneider, Rüdin and de Crinis. The memorandum is almost identical with the memorandum which Nitsche and de Crinis gave to Brandt in June 1943; NARA, T1021, Roll 12, frames 128079f; frames 128236–44.

36 HBAB, file 2/39–189, Ministry of the Interior to Bodelschwingh, 10 November 1942. Bodelschwingh received the letter on 10 December 1942; see Bodelschwingh to Brandt, 2 January 1943; also Hochmuth 1997, pp. 147f.

37 HBAB, file 2/39–189, Neil to Bodelschwingh, 17 December 1942.

38 Kühl 1990, p. 67; also HBAB, file 2/39–189.

39 HBAB, file 2/39–189, Bodelschwingh to Brandt, 2 January 1943. Three weeks later, on 23 January 1943, Bodelschwingh approached the Reich Minister of the Interior about the same issue; Bodelschwingh to Reich Minister of the Interior, 23 January 1943.

40 HBAB, file 2/39–189, Meeting with Professor Brandt, 13 February 1943.

41 Ibid., Brandt to Bodelschwingh, 21 January 1943.

42 BAK, All. Proz. 2/FC 6069 P, Vernehmung Karl Brandt, 26 November 1946.

43 Fröhlich 1993, p. 161, 23 January 1943.

44 NDT-Documents, Exhibit 447, NO-1419; see also NDT-Records (German), frame 2660.

45 Fröhlich 1993, p. 336, 13 February 1943; it is not entirely clear to whom Goebbels is referring with regard to the 'young hooligans'.

46 HBAB, file 2/39–189, Bodelschwingh to Brandt, 28 January 1943.

47 Ibid., Brandt to Bodelschwingh, 5 February 1943.

48 NARA, M 1270, Roll 2, Interrogation Karl Brandt, 1 October 1945, frame 342.

49 HBAB, file 2/39–189, Meeting with Professor Brandt, 13 February 1943.

50 Ibid.

51 NDT-Records (German), frames 2442f; also HBAB, file 2/39–189, Bodelschwingh to Brandt, 29 March 1941.

52 HBAB, file 2/39–189, Meeting with Professor Brandt, 13 February 1943.

53 Ibid.

54 Ibid.

55 Ibid.

56 Ibid.

57 The meeting between Bodelschwingh and Goebbels does not seem to have taken place. With regard to Goebbels' views about Bishop Wurm and von Galen see, for example, Fröhlich 1996, part II, vol. 1, p. 232, p. 258, p. 266, p. 299. p. 504, p. 514; Fröhlich 1996, part II, vol. 2, p. 362, p. 397, p. 506; Fröhlich 1995, part II, vol. 3, p. 111, p. 376, p. 545.

58 HBAB, file 2/39–189, Meeting with Professor Brandt, 13 February 1943.

59 Aly 1989, p. 170; for Mennecke see also Burleigh 1994, pp. 221–50.

60 Ibid, p. 171.

61 Ibid.

62 BSB, Fotoarchiv Hoffmann, hoff-47460, 47517, 47521, 47523, 47524, 47525, 47536, 47542, 47565, 47569, 47577, 49668, 49669, 49670.

63 Reuth 1999, 9 April 1943, p. 1920.

64 Süß 2003, pp. 335f.

65 Süß 2002, p. 211, footnote 50.

66 Süß 2003, p. 337.

67 BSB, Fotoarchiv Hoffmann, hoff-47603.

68 Kershaw 2000, p. 582.

69 Ibid., pp. 582f.

70 BSB, Fotoarchiv Hoffmann, hoff-47776.

71 BAB, R18, 3810, Brandt to Conti 16 April 1943.

72 BSB, Fotoarchiv Hoffmann, hoff-47822, 47824, 47825, 47826, 47827, 47829, 47833,

73 Ibid., hoff-47837, 47839, 47840, 49802, 49803, 49804.

74 Ibid., hoff-47816, 47817, 47834; see also hoff-47818.

75 Faulstich 1998, pp. 623f.

76 See also Schmidt 2002.

77 Süß 2003, p. 318.

78 Streit 2005, p. 88.

79 Süß 2003, p. 285.

80 See also Lynch and Bogen 1996, pp. 1–56.

81 NARA, RG153, 100–767, Box 62, Report of an Interview with Dr. Karl Brandt, 26 June 1945.

82 Kershaw 1998, pp. 527–91.

83 Süß 2003, p. 220.

84 Faulstich 1998, pp. 627f.

85 Süß 2003, p. 358, footnote 227.

86 Ibid., p. 366, footnote 257.

87 BAK, Kl. Erw. 512–1, pp. 140ff; see also BAB, R18, 3791, circular by the Supreme Command of the Army, 19 July 1943.

88 Faulstich 1998, pp. 310f; also Süß 2003, p. 356.

89 Walter 1996, p. 758.

90 NARA, T1021, Roll 12, frames 127764–98.

91 See also Linden's views from February 1943 about the value of patients as long as they were able to work; NARA, T1021, Roll 12, frames 127840f.

92 Hochmuth 1979, p. 27; Kühl 1990, p. 69; Hochmuth 1997, p. 156.

93 HBAB, file 2/39–189, Brandt to Bodelschwingh, 2 March 1943; Bodelschwingh to Brandt, 3 April 1943; Brandt to Bodelschwingh, 9 April 1943; Bodelschwingh to Brandt, 16 April 1943; BSB, Fotoarchiv Hoffmann, hoff-47776.

94 HBAB, file 2/39–189, Brandt to Bodelschwingh, 20 April 1943

95 Ibid., Bodelschwingh to Brandt, 27 April 1943.

96 BAB, R18, 3810, Conti to Bormann, 23 June 1943.

97 NDT-Documents, frames 4/1809–11; also StaNü, KV-Prozesse, Fall 1, Spezialia Karl Brandt H 1.

98 AHtA, EA-108-3, 2, Bodelschwingh to Braune, 15 June 1943.

99 HBAB, file 2/39–189, Bodelschwingh to Nell, 16 February 1943; see also the carefully worded correspondence between von Bodelschwingh and Nell from January and February 1943, in which they used the letter 'B' to refer to von Bodelschwingh's negotiations with 'Brandt' and the Reich

Ministry of the Interior in 'Berlin';
Hochmuth 1997, pp. 151f.

100 StaNü, KV-Verteidigung, Handakten Rostock,
closing statement of Brandt, 19 July 1947;
also Brandt trial notebook, Euthanasia, II/9
(20) (21), pp. 125–28 (pagination by US).

101 HBAB, file 2/39–189, Meeting with Professor
Brandt, 13 February 1943.

102 Brandt trial notebook, Euthanasia, II/9 (20)
(21), pp. 124f (pagination by US).

103 Brandt recalled that the conversations with
Bodelschwingh were 'serious and based on
greatness and the ethical value of the subject';
Brandt trial notebook, Euthanasia, II/9 (20)
(21), p. 124 (pagination by US).

104 Von Bodelschwingh was certainly aware that
certain issues pertaining to the 'euthanasia'
programme should not be recorded on paper;
HBAB, file 2/39–189, Bodelschwingh to Nell,
18 January 1943; Hochmuth 1997, p. 151.

105 Hochmuth 1997, p. 157. Rach remembered
that Bodelschwingh once said publicly 'that
his institutions had been spared this kind of
access [to their patients]'; StaNü, KV-
Prozesse, Fall 1, Spezialia Karl Brandt H 1.

106 BDC, Personal File Nitsche; see also NARA,
T1021, Roll 10.

107 BAB, R96 I, 18, Nitsche to Rüdin, 25 August
1943.

108 Shortly after the meeting, Brandt was sent
a hard copy of the memorandum, together
with information about the various authors.
He was thus well informed with regard to
the 'I. Aktion', which Nitsche and Rüdin had
initiated with the Reich Health Leader on
5 June 1943 to boost the image of German
psychiatry; see BAB, Personal File Nitsche,
Nitsche to de Crinis, 25 August 1943; for the
memorandum see NARA, T1021, Roll 10,
frame 126418, frames 126420–427; also Roll
12, frames 128011–018; frames 128019–127;
also frames 128236–44 for the original
memorandum which was drafted for Conti
at the beginning of 1943; also BAB, R96 I, 18,
meeting between Conti, Nitsche and Rüdin,
5 June 1943; R96 I, 18, Nitsche to Rüdin,
25 August 1943; Aly 1985, pp. 41–48; Thom
1989, p. 152; Hinz-Wessels et al. 2005,
pp. 99f.

109 The memorandum was composed by
Maximinian de Crinis, Paul Nitsche, Ernst
Rüdin, Carl Schneider and Hans Heinze; also
Proctor 1992, p. 24.

110 BAB, R96I, 18, Rüdin to Nitsche 22
September 1943; Nitsche to Rüdin,
17 January 1944.

111 NARA, T1021, Roll 12, p. 128015.

112 Ibid.; Faulstich 1998, p. 296; Hinz-Wessels et
al. 2005, p. 89 and p. 99; also Schmuhl 1987,
pp. 224ff.

113 BAB, R96 I, 18, Nitsche to de Crinis,
30 October 1943.

114 Faulstich 1998, p. 629; see also Sächsisches
Hauptstaatsarchiv Dresden, 11120
Staatsanwaltschaft beim Landgericht
Dresden, No. 2529, Anklageschrift gegen Paul
Nitsche u.a., 7 January 1947.

115 BAB, R96 I, 18, De Crinis to Nitsche, 26 May
1944; BAB, R96 I, 18, Nitsche to de Crinis,
20 April 1944.

116 BAB, R18, 3811, note by Conti about meeting
with Brandt, Lammers, Bormann, and
Klopfer at Berchtesgaden on 18 June 1943.

117 BAB, R96 I, 18, De Crinis to Nitsche, 26 May
1944.

118 Ibid., 31 August 1943; Nitsche to de Crinis,
20 April 1944; De Crinis to Nitsche, 26 May
1944.

119 BAB, R18, 3791, memo Cropp, 24 June 1943.

120 Ibid.

121 Linden told the Cure and Nursing Home
in Giessen, for example, that the Charitable
Foundation for the Transport of Patients,
Ltd., the organization which had transported
the patients to the killing centres during
the 'euthanasia' programme, would transfer
twenty-five men and fifty women to the
institution in the next couple of days; BAB,
R18, 3791, Linden to Cure and Nursing
Home Giessen, 25 June 1943; R18, 3810,
telephone conversation between Conti and
Bormann, 26 June 1943.

122 BAB, R18, 3791, Cropp to Linden, 5 July
1943.

123 BAB, R18, 3810, telephone conversation
between Conti and Bormann, 26 June 1943.

124 Süß 2003, p. 342.

125 Klee 1991, p. 425.

126 BAK, All. Proz. 2/FC 6069 P, Vernehmung
Karl Brandt, 1 March 1947.

127 BAB, NS 51/39, Schaub to Treulinde, 21 June
1943.

128 BAB, R18, 3809, Brandt to Lammers, 30 June
1943.

129 BAK, All. Proz. 2/FC 6069 P, Vernehmung
Karl Brandt, 26 November 1946.

130 NARA, RG 153, 100–767, Box 62, US Strategic Bombing Survey, Interview with Prof. Dr. med. Karl Brandt, 17–18 June 1945.

131 BAK, All. Proz. 2/FC 6069 P, Vernehmung Karl Brandt, 26 November 1946.

132 NARA, RG 153, 100–767, Box 62, US Strategic Bombing Survey, Interview with Prof. Dr. med. Karl Brandt, 17–18 June 1945.

133 Friedrich 2002, pp. 113ff.

134 Bürger-Prinz 1973, p. 115.

135 NDT-Records (German), frame 2/2665; NDT-Records, frame 2/2727; NDT-Documents, Exhibit 449, NO-1620, frames 3/2093f; see also Padfield 1990, p. 461.

136 Heinz Gluck, the chief pharmacist of the Hamburg area, recalled that the bombing raid left the town without medical supplies, dextrose solutions and baby foods for five weeks; NARA, RG 153, 100–0, Book 1, Box 1, Interview by US Strategic Bombing Survey with Captain Heinz Gluck, 15 June 1945. See also NARA, RG 153, 100–0, Book 1, Box 1, Interview with First Lieutenant Zeitler, no date. For Brandt's personal experience of the bombing raid see StaNü, KV-Anklage, Dokumente, NO-332; also NARA, RG 153, 100–767, Box 62, US Strategic Bombing Survey, Interview with Prof. Dr. med. Karl Brandt, 17–18 June 1945.

137 See also BAK, All. Proz. 2/FC 6069 P, Vernehmung Karl Brandt, 1 March 1947.

138 BAB, R18, 3810, Conti memo, 24 July 1943.

139 BAB, R18, 3809, Kauffmann to Conti, 30 July 1943.

140 Fröhlich 1993, part II, vol. 9, p. 245, 9 August 1943.

141 NARA, T1021, Roll 12, frames 128136–38; see also Hinz-Wessels et al. 2005, pp. 90f; for the Hartheim killing centre see Kepplinger 2003, pp. 53–109.

142 NARA, T1021, Roll 12, frame 128137.

143 Ibid., frame 128138.

144 Ibid., frame 128028; also Klee 1986, p. 426.

145 NARA, T1021, Roll 12, frame 128028.

146 Faulstich 1998, p. 629.

147 BAB, R96 I, 18, Nitsche to de Crinis, 30 October 1943.

148 Faulstich 1998, p. 629; Schmuhl 1987, p. 233.

149 HBAB, file 2/39–189, Meeting with Professor Brandt, 13 February 1943.

150 BSB, Fotoarchiv Hoffmann, hoff-48384.

151 NARA, RG242, Box No. 13, Item 1, Heinz Linge, Record of Hitler's Daily Activities 11 August 1943 – 30 December 1943, p. 6, 16 August 1943.

152 Fröhlich 1993, part II, vol. 9, p. 317, 20 August 1943.

153 Süß 2003, p. 314.

154 Ibid.

155 Ibid., pp. 316f.

156 NDT-Records, frame 2/2515.

157 Sächsisches Hauptstaatsarchiv Dresden, 11120 Staatsanwaltschaft beim Landgericht Dresden, No. 2529, Anklageschrift gegen Paul Nitsche u.a., 7 January 1947; see also Süß 2003, p. 357, footnote 219.

158 See NDT-Documents, Exhibit 330, 630 PS, frame 3/1112.

159 Süß 2003, p. 353, footnote 203; see also NARA, T1021, Roll 12, frames 128224f; frame 127890.

160 The quality of the existing evidence that these T-4 psychiatrists attended the meeting varies to a certain degree. The evidence is quite strong for the psychiatrists from Saxony, for Schulz, Wischer and Beese, in particular. Both Schulz and Wischer had attended the meeting in May and September 1942, and stated after the war that they had received the authorization in August 1943. The asylum of Großschweidnitz, in which Schulz was director, also received the necessary drugs to kill the patients in 1944. Moreover, in September 1943, only weeks after the meeting, Wischer, who had attended all three T-4 conferences in May, September and October 1942, corresponded with Nitsche about the progress in killing patients, which makes it very likely that he attended the meeting. According to Süß, there is also good evidence that Beese, the director of Uchtspringe, attended the meeting. The evidence is also strong for Heinze and Ratka. Heinze, who had attended the conference in May and September 1942, was not only known as an ardent supporter of the 'euthanasia' programme, but corresponded with Nitsche in January 1944, a couple of months after the meeting in August, about some of the problems which they encountered in having resumed the 'euthanasia' programme. The Görden asylum, of which he was the director, also received the necessary drugs in 1944 to kill the patients. Ratka, on the other hand, had attended all three T-4 conferences in May, September and

October 1942, and his asylum later received the necessary drugs to kill the patients. It is also likely that Falthauser, Pfannmüller and Steinmeyer attended the conference. All three had attended the T-4 conference in May and September 1942, and Steinmeyer had attended both conferences in September and October 1942. All three were committed T-4 psychiatrists, and possessed significant expertise. Given that the asylums of Ansbach, Kalmhof/Idstein and Meseritz-Obrawalde later received the necessary drugs for the killing of patients, there is a possibility that the directors of these asylums, Schuch, Weber and Wernicke, may also have attended the meeting. Süß argues, however, that one cannot infer a participation of those asylum doctors in the meeting whose asylums received the necessary drugs to kill patients, because the asylums received the drugs in 1944. For the T-4 conferences in May, September and October 1942 see NARA, T1021, Roll 12, frame 128206, frame 128223, frames 128224f; see also Süß 2003, p. 353, footnote 203. For the asylums which received the necessary drugs, see Süß 2003, p. 358, footnote 226. For Wischer and Beese see Süß 2003, p. 358, footnote 226. For Wischer and Heinze's correspondence with Nitsche see BAB, R96 I, 18, Wischer to Nitsche, 13 September 1943, 4 November 1943, 29 December 1943 and Heinze to Nitsche, 20 January 1944.

161 BAB, R96 I/4, Nitsche to Schneider, 14 January 1944; see also Schmuhl 1987, pp. 232f.

162 Süß 2003, p. 349.

163 Ibid., p. 346, footnote 172.

164 Ibid., p. 359, footnote 229.

165 Ibid., p. 359.

166 Süß, for example, alleges that the health department of the Saxon Ministry of the Interior authorized Schulz and Wischer to kill patients by means of drugs. His assumption is based, however, on the post-war statements of those involved in the operation. It is quite likely that they wanted to shift the responsibility for the operation onto the regional government, rather than admitting that they had acted upon Nitsche's general authorization, which in itself was based on a rather vague and general authorization by Brandt. So far, no evidence has been discovered which shows that Nitsche passed the authorization which he had received from Brandt to the Saxon Ministry of the Interior, and that the Ministry then authorized the relevant asylum directors in the region; see Süß 2003, pp. 345ff; see also Sächsisches Hauptstaatsarchiv Dresden, 11120 Staatsanwaltschaft beim Landgericht Dresden, No. 2529, Anklageschrift gegen Paul Nitsche u.a., 7 January 1947.

167 NARA, T1021, Roll 12, frame 128028, frame 127988.

168 Ibid., frame 128224.

169 Ibid., frame 127988; see also Hinz-Wessels *et al.* 2005, footnote 33.

170 Klee 1991, p. 205; Schmuhl 1987, p. 470; Schmuhl 1997, p. 117. A report from February 1944 lists a total of eleven expert referees who processed the relevant forms for the continued 'euthanasia' programme. The expert referees were as follows: Wischer, Kihn, Ratka, Falthauser, Schneider, Pfannmüller, Müller, Schulz, Steinmeyer, Hefter, Hebold; NARA, T1021, Roll 12, frame 127959.

171 BDC, Personalakte Nitsche, Nitsche to De Crinis, 25 August 1943; also BAB, R96 I, 18, De Crinis to Nitsche, 31 August 1943; Nitsche to De Crinis, 30 October 1943; also BDC, Personal File De Crinis; Aly 1989, p. 172; also NARA, T1021, Roll 12, frames 127997–128000.

172 BAB, R96 I, 18, De Crinis to Nitsche, 31 August 1943.

173 Ibid., Nitsche to De Crinis, 30 October 1943; BDC, Personal File De Crinis, Personal File Nitsche; Aly 1989, p. 172.

174 Kershaw, 1998, p. 471.

175 See also Rüdin's letter to Nitsche about the confusion among leading psychiatrists in September 1943, most of whom did not know any longer who was actually in charge of German medicine; BAB, R96 I, 18, Rüdin to Nitsche, 22 September 1943.

176 Klee 1991, p. 427.

177 IWM, H/28/18–20, Brandt to Himmler, 22 September 1943; also Padfield 1995, p. 476; also quoted in Bayer 1979, p. 119. See also Klee 1991, p. 427; see in this context also Brandt's correspondence with SS-Obersturmbannführer Rudolf Brandt about the future use of the Eichberg asylum, IWM, H/28/1–7, K. Brandt to R. Brandt, 28 October 1943.

178 IWM, H/28/18–20, Brandt to Himmler, 22 September 1943.

179 Ibid., Rudolf Brandt to Reichssicherheitshauptamt, c. October 1943.

180 Ibid.

181 IWM, H/28/18–20, Rudolf Brandt to Ernst Kaltenbrunner, 3 November 1943; also Padfield 1995, p. 476; also quoted in Bayer 1979, p. 120.

182 BAB, R96 I, 18, Wischer to Nitsche, 13 September 1943.

183 Ibid., 4 November 1943.

184 Süß 2003, p. 346, footnote 172.

185 BAB, R96 I, 18, Nitsche to Allers, 2 December 1943; Nitsche to Allers, 6 December 1943.

186 NARA, T1021, Roll 12, frames 127894f.

187 BAB, R96 I, 18, Wischer to Nitsche, 29 December 1943.

188 NARA, T1021, Roll 12, frames 127971f.

189 Ibid., frames 127878–85; see also Schmidt 2002a, 264–70

190 BAB, R96 I, De Crinis to Nitsche, 9 November 1943.

191 BAB, R96 I/4, Nitsche to Schneider, 14 January 1944; see also Schmuhl 1987, pp. 232f.

192 BAB, R96 I/1, Allers to Nitsche, 15 January 1944; NARA, T1021, Roll 12, frames 127963f; also Klee 1991, p. 439.

193 BAB, R96 I, 18, Heinze to Nitsche, 20 January 1944.

194 Ibid., Nitsche to de Crinis, 20 April 1944.

195 Ibid., Steinmeyer to Nitsche, 7 February 1944.

196 Faulstich 1998, p. 631.

197 Klee 1991, p. 443.

198 One month earlier, in February 1944, Mennecke had praised himself in a letter to Blankenburg for having been one of the first asylum directors who had placed himself in the 'service of the Aktion' and who had enthusiastically pursued the aims of 'our special tasks'; NARA, T1021, Roll 12, frames 127954f.

199 StaNü, KV-Prozesse, Umdrucke englisch, NO-924.

200 Ibid.

201 BAB, R96 I, 18, De Crinis to Nitsche, 26 May 1944.

202 BAB, NS 19/862, Himmler to Brandt, 9 June 1944; see also Heiber 1970, p. 337.

203 Faulstich 1998, p. 631; Klee 1991, p. 444.

204 NARA, T1021, Roll 12, frames 127926–29; Faulstich 1998, pp. 651f.

205 Ibid., frame 127927.

206 Ibid., frame 127928.

207 Süß 2003, p. 364.

208 BAB, R96 I, 18, Nitsche to Brandt, 10 July 1944; see also Nitsche to Brandt, 24 August 1944.

209 NARA, T1021, Roll 12, frames 127919–23; Runckel memorandum about meeting with Brandt, 20 July 1944; frames 127916f, Runckel to Nische, 24 July 1944; also Süß 2003, p. 363. See also Schmuhl 1987, p. 442, who erroneously believes that the proposals were made by Brandt.

210 NARA, T1021, Roll 12, frame 127919–23; Runckel memorandum about meeting with Brandt, 20 July 1944.

211 Süß 2003, p. 318, p. 340; see also Faulstich 1998, p. 628.

212 See also NARA, M 1270, Roll 2, Interrogation Karl Brandt, 1 October 1945, frame 335.

213 NARA, T1021, Roll 12, frames 127916f, Runckel to Nische, 24 July 1944; BAB, R96 I, 7, Runckel to Nitsche, 24 July 1944.

214 BAB, R96 I, 18, Brandt to Nitsche, 26 July 1944.

215 NARA, T1021, Roll 12, frames 127924f; Nitsche to Blankenburg, alias Brenner, 30 July 1944.

216 BAB, R96 I, 18, Nitsche to Brandt, 24 August 1944; see also NARA, T1021, Roll 12, frames 127924f; Nitsche to Blankenburg, alias Brenner, 30 July 1944.

217 NARA, M 1270, Roll 2, Interrogation Karl Brandt, 1 October 1945, frame 335.

218 NARA, M 1270, Roll 2, Interrogation Karl Brandt, 1 October 1945, frame 359.

219 See NARA, T-1021, Roll 12, frames 127963f; Klee 1991, p. 439.

220 For the recent literature on 'Nazi conscience' see Koonz 2003; for the role of conscience in other dictatorial regimes, for example in Soviet Russia, see Boobbyer 2005.

221 BAK, All. Proz. 2/FC 6069 P, Vernehmung Karl Brandt, 26 November 1946.

222 NDT-Records, frame 2/2516; see also NARA, M 1270, Roll 2, Interrogation Karl Brandt, 1 October 1945, frame 333.

223 See also Gerstenberger 2005, pp. 626f.

224 NDT-Records, frame 2/2516.

225 Speer 1973, p. 26.

226 KV-Prozesse, Fall 1, Spezialia Karl Brandt H 3 und 4.

227 The 'Salvatorian Order', also called the Order of Saint Saviour or the Order of the Most

Holy Saviour of Saint Bridget, is an order for monks and nuns which was founded in 1346 by Saint Bridget of Sweden at Vadstena, and approved by Pope Urban V as a branch of the Augustinians. Members of the order, also called Brigittines, engage in the translation and interpretation of religious texts.

228 KV-Prozesse, Fall 1, Spezialia Karl Brandt H 3 und 4.

229 Welch 2001, pp. 147–59; Welch 2002, pp. 114–15.

230 StaNü, KV-Anklage, Dokumente, NI-9113.

Notes to Chapter 8: Human Experimentation

1 NARA, M 1270, Roll 2, Interrogation Karl Brandt, 29 September 1945, frame 301.

2 Ibid.

3 Brandt later expanded his arguments in a five-page report on 'Experiments'; see BAK, All. Proz. 2/FC 6069 P, Prof. Dr Karl Brandt, Betrifft: Versuche, 15 February 1947.

4 See also the edited collections on human experimentation in the twentieth century; Roelcke and Maio 2004; Eckart 2006.

5 NARA, M 1270, Roll 2, Interrogation Karl Brandt, 29 September 1945, frame 302.

6 Ibid., frame 304.

7 Ibid.

8 Ibid., frame 305.

9 NDT-Records (German), frames 2/2628f.

10 NDT-Records, frame 2/2692.

11 NDT-Documents, frame 3/1030.

12 Quoted from Kershaw 2000, p. 529.

13 BAB, NS 51/39, Schaub to Treulinde, 1 December 1942.

14 Quoted from Kershaw 2000, p. 548.

15 Fröhlich 1993, p. 161, 23 January 1943.

16 StaNü, KV-Anklage, Dokumente, NO-1418; see also Padfield 1995, p. 394.

17 Kershaw 2000, p. 527.

18 StaNü, KV-Anklage, Dokumente, NO-1418.

19 NDT-Documents, Exhibit 447, NO-1419, frame 3/2531; see also NDT-Records (German), frame 2660.

20 NDT-Records (German), frames 2661f.

21 Ibid., frame 2661.

22 Ibid.

23 BAK, All. Proz. 2/FC 6069 P, Vernehmung Karl Brandt, 1 March 1947.

24 StaNü, KV-Anklage, Dokumente, NO-1422.

25 Ibid.

26 Ibid.

27 Klee 1997, p. 182.

28 Ibid., p. 183.

29 Ibid.

30 Ibid., p. 189; Alexander Neumann refers to 164 experimental subjects, who died from the nutrition experiments or were subsequently killed; Neumann 2006, p. 160.

31 Klee 1997, p. 189.

32 NDT-Records, frame 2/2702.

33 Neumann 2006, pp. 154f.

34 For some of the sources and literature on the Ravensbrück medical experiments see Mitscherlich and Mielke 1960; Ebbinghaus 1987; Klier 1994; Martin 1994a; Martin 1994b; Ebbinghaus and Dörner 2001; Schmidt 2001b; Schmidt 2004; Schmidt 2005.

35 Schmidt 2005.

36 TNA, WO 309, 469.

37 Ibid.

38 Ibid.

39 Ebbinghaus 1987, pp. 256–59.

40 TNA, WO 309, 469.

41 NARA, M 1270, Roll 2, Interrogation Karl Brandt, 29 September 1945, frame 316f.

42 NDT-Documents, Closing Brief for the United States of America against Karl Brandt, 16 June 1947, 3/2896–2956, here frame 3/2908.

43 NDT-Records, frame 2/2702.

44 NDT-Documents, frame 3/2909.

45 Martin 1994a, p. 108.

46 Klee 1997, p. 201.

47 In 1944, the camp physician Stumpfegger, for example, published a detailed account of bone transplantations which he had conducted on Ravensbrück inmates. The experiments described in his article showed a striking similarity with testimony given two years later by some of the mutilated witnesses; TNA, WO 309, 1791; see also Stumpfegger 1944, 495.

48 NARA, M 1270, Roll 2, Interrogation Karl Brandt, 29 September 1945, frames 305–320.

49 Leyendecke and Klapp 1989, pp. 263f.

50 Ibid., p. 273.

51 Ibid., p. 272.

52 NDT-Records, frames 2/2803ff; see also NDT-Records, frames 2/2773–2780; also Leyendecker papers, Statement Arnold Dohmen, 26 August 1974.

53 See Brigitte Leyendecker, 'Deutsche Hepatitisforschung im Zweiten Weltkrieg.

Die Arbeitsgruppe um Kurt Gutzeit'
(forthcoming).

54 Dohmen papers, Dohmen to Gutzeit, no date
(c. end of December 1943); I am grateful to
Brigitte Leyendecker for supplying me with
key documents from the Dohmen papers.
The Dohmen papers are located in the
archive of the Gedenkstätte Sachsenhausen,
Germany.

55 Ibid. For Waetzoldt see Hühn 1989, pp. 185ff.

56 Dohmen papers, Report by the Medical
Officer Dr Dohmen about the Investigation
on the Etiology of Hepatitis Epidemica,
30 April 1943, p. 4.

57 Ibid., Dohmen to Gutzeit, no date (c. end of
December 1943).

58 Ibid.

59 Süß 2003, p. 84; also BAK, Kl. Erw. 512-2,
p. 143, Führererlaß, 20 May 1943.

60 NDT-Documents, frame 3/1029.

61 [Rudolf] Brandt to Pohl, 2 August 1943; Pohl
to [Rudolf] Brandt, 16 August 1943.

62 NDT-Documents, frame 3/1029.

63 Ibid., Closing Brief for the United States
of America against Karl Brandt, 16 June
1947, 3/2896–2956, here frame 3/2903; also
NDT-Documents, Exhibit 39, 002-PS, frames
3/112ff.

64 Ibid., Exhibit 447, NO-1419, frame 3/2531;
see also NDT-Records (German), frame
2/2660; NDT-Records, frames 2/2722f.

65 BA-MA, H20/508, Report by the Medical
Officer Dr Dohmen about the Investigation
on the Etiology of Hepatitis Epidemica,
30 April 1943. See also RH12–23/v.117,
Tagebuch des Beratenden Internisten,
30 April 1943.

66 BA-MA, H20/508, Report by the Medical
Officer Dr Dohmen about the Investigation
on the Etiology of Hepatitis Epidemica,
30 April 1943, p. 4.

67 Ibid.

68 BA-MA, RH12–23/v.117, Tagebuch des
Beratenden Internisten, 17 May 1943.

69 Dohmen papers, Dohmen to his mother, no
date (date of postmark, 4 June 1943).

70 Ibid.

71 BA-MA, H20/508, Bericht des Stabsarztes
Dr Dohmen über die Kommandierung ins
Führerhauptquartier am 20 May 1943 und
den Vortrag beim Generalkommandeur
des Führers für das Sanitäts- und
Gesundheitswesen gemäß Verfügung OKH

Chef H Rüst u.BdE 49 b (m) S.In.Pers. (Ic)
6106/43.

72 Ibid.

73 NDT-Documents, Exhibit 187, NO-010,
frames 3/597f; Mitscherlich and Mielke
1962, p. 128; see also Brandt's attempt to
explain Grawitz's letter in one of the post-war
interrogations; BAK, All. Proz. 2/FC 6069 P,
Vernehmung Karl Brandt, 19 October 1946.

74 NDT-Documents, Exhibit 187, NO-010,
frames 3/597f; Mitscherlich and Mielke 1962,
p. 128.

75 Ibid.

76 Ibid., pp. 128f.

77 Ibid., frame 3/599; Mitscherlich and Mielke
1962, p. 129.

78 Institute für Zeitgeschichte, 4749/72, F19/4,
Heinz Linge and Hans Junge: Record
of Hitler's Daily Activities, 22 March
1943–20 June 1943, transcribed by David
Irving, 1968, 17 June 1943.

79 Leyendecker and Klapp 1989, p. 276.

80 Padfield 1995, p. 440.

81 Leyendecker papers, testimony Max
Rosmarin, 29 September 1973.

82 Ibid.

83 Ibid.; for the names and date of birth of the
children see Leyendecker and Klapp 1989,
pp. 276f.

84 Ibid.; Leyendecker and Klapp 1989, p. 276.

85 Oren-Hornfeld 2005, p. 108.

86 Ibid.; see also Leyendecker and Klapp 1989,
pp. 276f.

87 Franz Ballhorn seems to have realized that
Wolf Silberglet was younger than he had told
fellow prisoners, although his estimate was
not entirely correct.

88 Oren-Hornfeld 2005, pp. 110f.

89 Ibid., p. 114.

90 Leyendecker papers, testimony Max
Rosmarin, 29 September 1973.

91 Ibid.

92 Ibid.; Oren-Hornfeld 2005, pp. 113f.

93 Dohmen papers, Dohmen to Gutzeit, no date
(c. end of December 1943).

94 Leyendecker and Klapp 1989, pp. 278f.

95 This assumption is further corroborated
through Dohmen's post-war statement of
1974 in which he declared that the particular
conditions of the war and the expansion
of the hepatitis epidemic 'created the idea
in military circles to inoculate humans'
with hepatitis in order to demonstrate that

the material which he had discovered 'was the causal agent of hepatitis epidemica'. Leyendecker papers, statement Arnold Dohmen, 26 August 1974.

96 NDT-Documents, frame 3/602.

97 NDT-Records, frames 2/2799ff.

98 Ibid., frame 2/2815; frame 2/9616.

99 Ibid., frame 2/6505.

100 Ibid., frame 2/3128.

101 Ibid., frames 2/2797ff; frames 2/9725 and 2/9753.

102 See also NDT-Documents, frame 3/605, frame 3/608.

103 Killian 1972, p. 34.

104 NDT-Documents, frame 3/3309; NDT-Records, frame 2/2799.

105 Klee 1997, p. 262.

106 BA-MA, RH 12–23/1137; Invitation of the Reich Commissioner to the conference in Beelitz, 16 August 1944; also NDT-Documents, Exhibit 457, NO-692, frames 3/2132f, List of medical institutes working on problems of research which were designated as urgent by the discussion on research on 26 August 1944 in Beelitz, 14 September 1944. The date which is listed in the latter document is an error. The meeting took place on 24 August 1944.

107 BA-MA, H20, 860, 2.

108 BA-MA, RH 12–23/1137; also Klee 1997, p. 262.

109 See also Dohmen's post-war justification for carrying out the experiments at this point; Leyendecker papers, statement Arnold Dohmen, 26 August 1974.

110 Oren-Hornfeld 2005, pp. 131f; see also Leyendecker and Klapp 1989, pp. 280–85; Klee 1997, pp. 267f.

111 I am grateful to Dr Leyendecker for this information. She has extensively researched the individual cases of the children and has interviewed some of them in Israel; personal correspondence with Dr Leyendecker, 29 November 1999.

112 NARA, M 1270, Roll 2, Interrogation Karl Brandt, 29 September 1945, frame 295.

113 Rostock stated during the Nuremberg Doctors' Trial that he had never been in charge of, supervised or controlled any of the Kaiser-Wilhelm-Institutes; StaNü, Handakten Rostock, File 2.

114 Friedrich 2002, p. 474.

115 Süß 2003, p. 279.

116 NDT-Records (German), frame 2/2668.

117 Friedrich 2002, p. 115.

118 Trevor-Roper 1954, pp. 17f, M. Bormann to G. Bormann, 2 August 1943.

119 Ibid., pp. 28f, M. Bormann to G. Bormann, 14 August 1943.

120 NDT-Records (German), frame 2/2665; NDT-Records, frame 2/2727; NDT-Documents, Exhibit 449, NO-1620, frames 3/2093f; see also Padfield 1990, p. 461.

121 Ibid., frame 2/2667; NDT-Records, frame 2/2729; NDT-Documents, Exhibit 449, NO-1620, frame 3/2094.

122 Ibid., frame 2/2666.

123 Ibid., frame 2/2664; NDT-Records, frame 2/2726.

124 Kershaw 2000, p. 549.

125 Brandt later recalled that Buchenwald was a suitable location because some of the prisoners had suffered from phosphorous burns after Allied air attacks; NDT-Records (German), frame 2/2668.

126 NDT-Documents, frame 3/936.

127 Ibid., frames 3/2464ff; see also NDT-Documents, frames 3/2363ff.

128 Ibid., frame 3/2466.

129 Ibid., frames 3/903, 3/936, 3/1791; Klee 1997, p. 334. See also the report on the findings of 2 January 1944 on a skin medicament called R 17 for phosphorous-caoutchouc burns; NDT-Documents, frames 3/2360ff.

130 Klee 1997, p. 334.

131 NDT-Documents, frame 3/1791.

132 NDT-Records (German), frame 2/2641.

133 Ibid., frame 2/2668.

134 Geißler 1999, p. 672; see also Hansen 1993, pp. 8f, pp. 126f. After 1945, Brandt claimed that he had persuaded Hitler not to use chemical warfare agents in the last days of the war; see Gellermann 1986, pp. 178f.

135 Ibid., pp. 341–78; p. 672.

136 Ibid., p. 359.

137 Friedrich 2002, p. 474.

138 Geißler 1999, p. 379; for Blome see also Moser 2006.

139 Ibid., p. 380.

140 Ibid., p. 382.

141 Hansen 1993, p. 137.

142 Geißler 1999, pp. 341–412.

143 Ibid., p. 388.

144 NDT-Documents, frame 3/2525; see also Geißler 1999, p. 369.

145 NDT-Documents, frame 3/1020; see also Friedrich 2002, p. 105.

146 NDT-Documents, frame 3/2526; for Blome's role in conducting human experiments see Moser 2006, p. 144.

147 Geißler 1999, pp. 369f.

148 Brandt himself recalled that in 1944 he received secret intelligence reports about biological warfare preparations by enemy forces, for example about the use of foot and mouth disease by the Allies; Geißler 1999, p. 499; see also Moser 2006, pp. 145f.

149 Geißler 1999, pp. 579ff; also Moser 2006, footnote 67.

150 Geißler 1999, p. 583.

151 Ibid.

152 Ibid., p. 593.

153 NDT-Documents, frame 3/1019.

154 Ibid.

155 NDT-Records, frame 2/2696.

156 Ibid.

157 NDT-Documents, frame 3/1019.

158 Ibid.

159 NDT-Records, frame 2/2695.

160 NDT-Documents, frames 3/2849f.

161 Geißler seems to be more certain about Brandt's overall knowledge and involvement in biological warfare research; Geißler 1999, p. 407.

162 For a comprehensive study on chemical warfare research under National Socialism see, most recently, Schmaltz 2005; see also Schmaltz 2006a, Schmaltz 2006b, Schmaltz 2006c.

163 StaNü, Handakten Rostock, File 2, biography of Paul Rostock.

164 BAK, All. Proz. 2/FC 6069 P, Vernehmung Karl Brandt, 19 October 1946.

165 StaNü, KV-Anklage, Dokumente, L11, interrogation of Fritz Bleich, 22 March 1945; for a map of the Beelitz complex see NARA, RG 153, 109–1, Box 94.

166 Henneke papers, Brandt's poem entitled 'To Beelitz' (An Beelitz), no date: 'To Beelitz/Since I am far away/and separated from time but now also/from the smell and odour of pines/which once surrounded me, black and golden, and dark red/since I am now far away/remembrance grows./A silent shining,/ as real as everything,/softens with the soul my/smile and my tear drop/Nothing, that has disappeared,/neither glance nor breath or doing./Only lighter it appears to me today,/ and in remembering,/oh, so full of sunlight' (translation by US). The German version of

the poem reads as follows: 'An Beelitz/Da fern ich bin/und abgesetzt in Zeit nun auch/von Duft und Rauch der Kiefern/meiner Wälder/ die schwarz und golden, feurig rot/mich einst umstanden/da ich nun fern bin/wächst Erinnerung auf./Ein stiller Glanz,/so Gegenwart wie alles,/betaut in überseeligem Sinn mir/das Lächeln wie die Träne/Nichts, das versunken,/nicht Blick noch Hauch und Tun./Nur leichter scheints mir heute,/und im Erinnern,/ach, so durchsonnt'. Markus Henneke obtained the document from Gerd Heidemann, a journalist best known for his role in the publication of the 'Hitler Diaries' which turned out to be forgeries. According to Henneke, Heidemann received the document from Kurt Schultze, Brandt's pilot. The authenticity of the document could not be verified.

167 KV-Prozesse, Fall 1, Spezialia Karl Brandt H 1.

168 StaNü, KV-Prozesse, IMT, No. Y5, Speer Dokument 60, Beantworteter Fragebogen des Zeugen Karl Brandt, 28 May 1946.

169 NDT-Documents, frame 3/3114.

170 Ibid., frames 3/1037f.

171 Ibid., frame 3/2641.

172 Ibid., frame 3/1038.

173 NDT-Records (German), frames 2/2662f; NDT-Documents, Exhibit 448, NO-1382, frames 3/2091f.

174 Ibid., frame 2/2663; NDT-Documents, Exhibit 448, NO-1382, frames 3/2091f.

175 For Bickenbach's biography see NDT-Documents, frames 3/1831ff; see also Schmaltz 2006, pp. 139–56.

176 NARA, RG 153, 109–7, Box 100.

177 For Hirt's experiments see NDT-Documents, frames 3/1048–1082; also frames 3/2198–2201.

178 Klee 1997, pp. 364f.

179 NDT-Documents, frame 3/3307.

180 Ibid., frame 3/409; also Closing brief for the United States of America against Karl Brandt, 16 June 1947, frame 3/2915.

181 Ibid.; also Klee 1997, p. 382.

182 BIOS, Final Report, No. 542, Item No. 8, Interrogation of Certain German Personalities Connected with Chemical Warfare, 1946, p. 21.

183 NDT-Records, frame 2/2410.

184 NDT-Documents, frame 4/2058.

185 Ibid. Brandt's figures differ slightly; see BIOS, Final Report, No. 542, Item No.

8, Interrogation of Certain German Personalities Connected with Chemical Warfare, 1946, p. 22.

186 NDT-Documents, frame 4/2058; see also BAK, All. Proz. 2/FC 6069 P, Vernehmung Karl Brandt, 1 March 1947.

187 NDT-Records, frame 2/2411.

188 NDT-Documents, frames 3/1084–1086.

189 Ibid., frame 3/1083.

190 Ibid., frames 4/1801f.

191 Ibid., frame 4/2057; see also Süß 2003, p. 86.

192 Ibid., frames 3/1084–1086; see also NDT-Documents, frame 3/1038.

193 Ibid., frame 3/1083. On 17 March 1944, Grawitz received a copy of Hitler's order and immediately got in contact with Brandt; NDT-Documents, frame 3/1087.

194 NDT-Records, frame 2/2412.

195 NDT-Documents, frame 3/3305.

196 Ibid., frame 3/1038.

197 Geißler 1999, pp. 341–78.

198 CIOS, Item No. 8, Chemical Warfare Installations in the Munsterlager Area, 23 April–3 June [1945], p. 3.

199 BIOS, Final Report, No. 542, Item No. 8, Interrogation of Certain German Personalities Connected with Chemical Warfare, 1946, p. 22.

200 Fröhlich 1994, part II, vol 11, p. 548, 25 March 1944.

201 BAK, All. Proz. 2/FC 6069 P, Vernehmung Karl Brandt, 1 March 1947.

202 FIAT, Control Commission for Germany (B.E.), Report on Chemical Warfare, based on Interrogation and written Reports of Jürgen E. von Klenck, Speer, and Dr E. Mohrhardt, 6 December 1945, p. 20.

203 Hans Kehrl, the head of the Department for Raw Materials and director of the Planning Department in the Ministry for Armaments and War Production, recalls that he received a detailed plan from Brandt in September 1944 for the increased production of gas masks for the entire German population, including special tents to protect infants and babies against gas warfare; Kehrl 1973, pp. 415ff. In 1949, Kehrl was sentenced to fifteen years' imprisonment in one of the Nuremberg trials for his involvement in exploiting the occupied territories for Germany's war effort.

204 FIAT, Control Commission for Germany (B.E.), Report on Chemical Warfare, based on

Interrogation and written Reports of Jürgen E. von Klenck, Speer, and Dr E. Mohrhardt, 6 December 1945, p. 20.

205 BIOS, Final Report, Item No. 8, Examination of various German Scientists, 29 August–1 September 1945.

206 FIAT, Control Commission for Germany (B.E.), Report on Chemical Warfare, based on Interrogation and written Reports of Jürgen E. von Klenck, Speer, and Dr E. Mohrhardt, 6 December 1945, p. 20.

207 Ibid., p. 8.

208 Ibid.

209 FIAT, Control Commission for Germany (B.E.), Report on Chemical Warfare, based on Interrogation and written Reports of Jürgen E. von Klenck, Speer, and Dr E. Mohrhardt, 6 December 1945. In November 1944, Grawitz requested the use of concentration camp inmates for experiments with 'N-substance' on and through the human skin. Whether Brandt had knowledge of these experiments is not known; NDT-Documents, frames 3/448f; frames 3/845f; frames 3/1092f; frames 3/2087f; frames 3/3050f.

210 FIAT, Control Commission for Germany (B.E.), Report on Chemical Warfare, based on Interrogation and written Reports of Jürgen E. von Klenck, Speer, and Dr E. Mohrhardt, 6 December 1945, p. 21; for recent work on Wolfgang Wirth see Kopke and Schultz 2006, pp. 113–29.

211 FIAT, Control Commission for Germany (B.E.), Report on Chemical Warfare, based on Interrogation and written Reports of Jürgen E. von Klenck, Speer, and Dr E. Mohrhardt, 6 December 1945, p. 21.

212 BIOS, Final Report No. 138, Item No. 8, Interrogation of German CW Medical Personnel, August/September 1945.

213 See also Fröhlich 1994, part II, vol. 11, p. 548, 25 March 1944.

214 BIOS, Final Report, No. 542, Item No. 8, Interrogation of Certain German Personalities Connected with Chemical Warfare, 1946, p. 29.

215 Kuhn's team had developed a chemical method to estimate the degree of nerve gas exposure from the level of cholinesterase (an enzyme) inhibition; BIOS, Final Report, No. 542, Item No. 8, Interrogation of Certain German Personalities Connected with Chemical Warfare, 1946, pp. 4–17; also

BIOS-Report, Final Report No. 782, Item No. 8, Interrogation of Professor Ferdinand Flury and Dr Wolfgang Wirth on the Toxicology of Chemical Warfare Agents. No date; for human experiments which were conducted at Porton Down during the Cold War see Schmidt 2006, pp. 366–80.

216 It is believed that Kuhn's reports were later discovered by the Russians, and transferred to the Karpov Institute in Moscow; BIOS, Final Report, No. 542, Item No. 8, Interrogation of Certain German Personalities Connected with Chemical Warfare, 1946, pp. 6f.

217 CIOS-Report, Item No. 80, A New Group of War Gases, 23 April 1945; see also CIOS-Report, Item No. 4 & 8, German CW Charging Station and CW Dump at Espelkamp, 19 April 1945.

218 BIOS-Report, Final Report No. 41, Item No. 8, Interrogation of German CW Personnel at Heidelberg and Frankfurt. By the end of the war, the German air force had 130,000 Tabun-filled bombs alone. The bombs had a total weight of 11,050 tonnes; BIOS, Final Report No. 9, Item No. 28, Interrogation of German Air Ministry (OKL) Technical Personnel, Luftwaffe Lager, Near Kiel, 17 July and 2 August 1945; also Bryden 1989, p. 181.

219 CIOS-Report, Item No. 80, A New Group of War Gases, 23 April 1945.

220 Ibid.

221 CIOS, Item No. 8, Chemical Warfare Installations in the Munsterlager Area, 23 April–3 June [1945], p. 3.

222 BIOS-Report, Final Report No. 41, Item No. 8, Interrogation of German CW Personnel at Heidelberg and Frankfurt. No date; also BIOS-Report, Final Report No. 782, Item No. 8, Interrogation of Professor Ferdinand Flury and Dr Wolfgang Wirth on the Toxicology of Chemical Warfare Agents. No date.

223 NDT-Documents, frame 4/2051.

224 Ibid.

225 BIOS, Final Report, No. 542, Item No. 8, Interrogation of Certain German Personalities Connected with Chemical Warfare, 1946, p. 24.

226 Ibid.

227 NDT-Documents, frame 3/1089.

228 Ibid., frame 3/1091; also NARA, SS-file Oswald Pohl.

229 NARA, SS-file Oswald Pohl.

230 NDT-Documents, frame 4/1824.

231 NDT-Records, frame 2/2709.

232 NDT-Documents, frame 3/1088.

233 Ibid., frame 3/2914.

234 NDT-Records, frame 2/2690.

235 Klee 1997, p. 382.

236 NDT-Records, frames 2/2706f.

237 NDT-Documents, frame 3/1836.

238 Ibid.

239 NDT-Documents, frame 3/2125.

240 Ibid., frame 3/2127.

241 Ibid., frame 3/2126.

242 Ibid., frame 3/2130.

243 Ibid., frame 3/2128.

244 Ibid., frame 3/2916.

245 Klee 1997, pp. 383f.

246 See also the testimony by Fritz Leo, a former internee of Natzweiler concentration camp, who saw Brandt visiting the Natzweiler camp some time in 1943/44; CIOS, Item No. 8, Chemical Warfare Installations in the Munsterlager Area, 23 April – 3 June [1945], p. 8.

247 NDT-Documents, frame 3/2124.

248 Ibid., frames 3/2110–2130.

249 NARA, RG 153, 86-3-1, Book 3, Box 10, Verzeichnis medizinischer Institute, welche Forschungsaufgaben bearbeiten, die in der Forschungsbesprechung vom 26 August 1944 [sic] in Beelitz als vordringlich bezeichnet wurden; also NDT-Documents, frames 3/2132–2135; also Klee 1997, pp. 262ff.

250 Klee 1997, p. 384.

251 NDT-Documents, frame 3/3114.

252 Ibid., frame 3/2088; see also BAK, All. Proz. 2/FC 6069 P, Vernehmung Karl Brandt, 5 November 1946. Contrary to Wolfgang Woelk's suggestion that Wolfgang Wirth 'was at no time involved in medical crimes', it appears that he proposed and sanctioned concentration camp experiments on humans and, as Christoph Kopke and Gebhard Schultz have shown, he was generally well informed about camp experiments because of his leading position in the army. At one point, he visited the Sachsenhausen concentration camp to inspect the effects of mustard gas exposure on human subjects and he may well have visited other camps, for example Natzweiler; see Woelk 2003; also Kopke and Schultz 2006.

253 NDT-Documents, frame 4/2060.

254 NARA, RG 238, Entry 185, Box 1, Interrogation Summary Fritz Bleich, 4 December 1946.
255 BAB, BDC, personal file Karl Brandt.
256 Ibid.
257 Ibid.

Notes to Chapter 9: Medical Supremo
1 Fröhlich 1994, part II, vol. 10, p. 435, 7 December 1943.
2 TNA, FO 1031, 102, Dr Karl Brandt, 21 August 1945.
3 Ibid.
4 Ibid.
5 Ibid.
6 Ibid.
7 Ibid.
8 HUA, personal file Karl Brandt 379.
9 BAB, R96 I, 18, Nitsche to Rüdin, 17 January 1944.
10 Trevor-Roper 1954, p. 44, M. Bormann to G. Bormann, 25 January 1944.
11 Ibid.
12 Ibid.
13 Fröhlich 1994, part II, vol. 11, p. 170, 25 January 1944.
14 StaNü, KV-Anklage, Dokumente, NO-778; BAB, R 43-II, 986.
15 BAB, BDC, personal file Karl Brandt.
16 BSB, Fotoarchiv Hoffmann, hoff-53548, 53550, 53559, 53580.
17 BAB, R43-II, 745a, Bormann to Lammers, 19 February 1944.
18 Ibid.
19 Ibid., note about General Commissioner Dr Brandt, 4 March 1944.
20 Ibid., Bormann to Lammers, 7 March 1944.
21 BAB, R43-II, 745a, Bormann to Lammers, 7 March 1944.
22 Sereny 1995, pp. 409–30.
23 Ibid., p. 415.
24 Ibid.
25 BAK, All. Proz. 2/FC 6069 P, Vernehmung Karl Brandt, 9 October 1946.
26 BAB, R43-II, 745a, Ley to Brandt, 1 June 1944.
27 Ibid.
28 Ibid.
29 Ibid.
30 Ibid.
31 Ibid.
32 Ibid., Bormann to Lammers, 6 July 1944.

33 Ibid., Bormann to Brandt, July 1944.
34 Ibid.
35 TNA, FO 1031, 102, Dr Karl Brandt, 21 August 1945.
36 BAB, R18, 3810, Himmler to Brandt, 13 July 1944.
37 TNA, FO 1031, 102, Dr Karl Brandt, 21 August 1945.
38 Kershaw 2000, p. 651.
39 See Kershaw 2005.
40 BSB, Fotoarchiv Hoffmann, hoff-53867.
41 For some of the ideology and future political plans of the German resistance against Hitler see Mommsen 2003, pp. 246–59.
42 For Hitler's health after the assassination attempt on 20 July 1944 see, for example, NARA, Headquarters United States Forces European Theater, Military Intelligence Service Center, Consolidated Interrogation Report, 'Hitler as seen by his Doctors', 15 October 1945; also Consolidated Interrogation Report, 'Hitler as seen by his Doctors', 29 October 1945; also Irving 1983b, pp. 167ff; Schenck 1989, pp. 250ff, pp. 301f, pp. 317f.
43 Schenck 1989, p. 301; see also Irving 1983b, p. 168.
44 DUPA, Interrogations of Hitler Associates. A Subcollection of the Michael A. Musmanno Collection, Series 1, Box 1, No. 18, Interrogation of Hans Karl von Hasselbach, Regensburg Internment Camp, 14 April 1948.
45 Ibid.
46 NARA, RG 153, 100–767, Box 62, US Strategic Bombing Survey, Interview with Prof. Dr. med. Karl Brandt, 17–18 June 1945.
47 Irving 1983b, p. 169.
48 NARA, Headquarters United States Forces European Theater, Military Intelligence Service Center, Consolidated Interrogation Report, 'Hitler as seen by his Doctors', 15 October 1945.
49 NARA, RG 153, 100–767, Box 62, US Strategic Bombing Survey, Interview with Prof. Dr. med. Karl Brandt, 17–18 June 1945; also NARA, Consolidated Interrogation Report, 'Hitler as seen by his Doctors', 29 October 1945.
50 NARA, Headquarters United States Forces European Theater, Military Intelligence Service Center, Consolidated Interrogation Report, 'Hitler as seen by his Doctors',

15 October 1945; also Irving 1983b, p. 171; see also Schenck 1989, pp. 317ff.

51 Irving 1983b, p. 178.

52 For the injuries which Hitler suffered as a result of the assassination attempt on 20 July 1944 see NARA, Headquarters United States Forces European Theater, Military Intelligence Service Center, Consolidated Interrogation Report, 'Hitler as seen by his Doctors', 15 October 1945.

53 Kershaw 2000, p. 688.

54 Ibid., pp. 691ff.

55 BSB, Fotoarchiv Hoffmann, hoff-53928, 53929, 53934, 53935, 53942, 53945.

56 BAB, R18, 3812, Conti memo about telephone conversation with Brandt, 6 August 1944.

57 Ibid., Draft of third Führer decree, 7 August 1944.

58 Süß 2003, p. 166.

59 Trevor-Roper 1954, pp. 78–80, M. Bormann to G. Bormann, 14 August 1944; Süß erronously locates Bormann's letter to his wife in the period *after* the signing of the third Führer decree; Süß 2003, pp. 167f.

60 BAB, R18, 3812, Bormann to Conti, 15 August 1944.

61 Fröhlich 1995, part II, vol. 13, p. 297, 23 August 1944.

62 Ibid.

63 BA-MA, RH 12–23/1137.

64 BAB, R43-II, 745a, Bormann to Lammers, 7 March 1944.

65 NDT-Records, frame 2/2466.

66 BA-MA, RH 12–23/1137; see also NDT-Documents, frame 3/3306.

67 BA-MA, RH 12–23/1137.

68 NARA, RG 153, 86-3-1, Book 3, Box 10, Verzeichnis medizinischer Institute, welche Forschungsaufgaben bearbeiten, die in der Forschungsbesprechung vom 26 August 1944 [sic] in Beelitz als vordringlich bezeichnet wurden; also NDT-Documents, frames 3/2132–2135; also Klee 1997, pp. 262ff.

69 BA-MA, RH 12–23/1137.

70 See also BAB, R18, 3812, Lammers to Conti, 27 August 1944.

71 Fröhlich 1995, part II, vol. 13, p. 305, 24 August 1944.

72 Ibid., p. 371, 31 August 1944.

73 NDT-Documents, frame 3/25.

74 BAB, R18, 3812, Himmler to Conti, 30 August 1944.

75 Trevor-Roper 1954, pp. 86f, M. Bormann to G. Bormann, 26 August 1943.

76 Fröhlich 1995, part II, vol. 13, p. 371, 31 August 1944.

77 Ibid., p. 380, 1 September 1944.

78 StaNü, KV-Anklage Interrogation, Vernehmung von Brandt by Walther H. Rapp, 9 October 1946.

79 Ibid.

80 Ibid.

81 NARA, M 1270, Roll 2, Interrogation of Karl Brandt, 29 September 1945.

82 NARA, RG 153, 100–0, Book 1, Box 1, Interview with First Lieutenant Zeitler, no date.

83 StaNü, KV-Anklage, Dokumente, NO-451; see also Süß 2003, p. 168.

84 BAB, R18, 3809, Note of a meeting between Kaufmann, Brandt and Rostock in Beelitz, 7 October 1944.

85 BAB, R18, 3812, Meeting between Brandt, Himmler and Gebhard to discuss the proposed decree to appoint Conti to 'Chief of the Civilian Health System', 1 November 1944. For the wording of the proposed decree see Süß 2003, p. 168.

86 Trevor-Roper 1954, p. 104, M. Bormann to G. Bormann, 8–9 September 1944.

87 Fröhlich 1995, part II, vol. 13, p. 397, 3 September 1944.

88 Ibid., p. 534, 21 September 1944.

89 For some of the sources on the 'doctor conflict' in 1944 see NARA, T 253, Morell papers, Roll 62; StaNü, KV-Anklage, Dokumente, NO-331, NO-332, NO-333; BAK, Kl. Erw. 525 (Irving collection), Dr. Karl Brandt, His Career, His Position as Reich Commissioner for Health and Medical Services; for secondary literature see Trevor-Roper 1995, pp. 58ff; Schenck 1989, pp. 238ff, pp. 477–511; Irving 1983b, pp. 167–213.

90 Schenck 1989, p. 484, p. 493.

91 See also Schenck 1989 and Irving 1983b.

92 NARA, T 253, Morell papers, Roll 62.

93 Killian 1972, pp. 34f.

94 Schenck 1989, p. 493, p. 507.

95 On 26 September Himmler had apparently given Hitler a dossier entitled 'Treason since 1939' which revealed that Admiral Canaris and some army officers had passed on vital military intelligence to the Allies. Around the same time the German Luftwaffe was engaged in a major showdown. Both aspects

may have further destabilized Hitler's by then fragile mental and physical condition; see also Irving 1983b, p. 52, p. 190.

96 Trevor-Roper 1995, pp. 58ff.

97 Fröhlich 1996, part II, vol. 14, p. 80, 11 October 1944.

98 Irving 1983b, p. 199.

99 Ibid.

100 NARA, T 253, Morell papers, Roll 62.

101 Ibid.

102 Ibid.

103 Trevor-Roper 1954, pp. 130f, M. Bormann to G. Bormann, 4 October 1944.

104 NARA, T 253, Morell papers, Roll 62.

105 Ibid.

106 Trevor-Roper 1954, p. 137, M. Bormann to G. Bormann, 10 October 1944.

107 NARA, T 253, Morell papers, Roll 62; see also Irving 1983b, p. 211.

108 Trevor-Roper 1954, pp. 142f, M. Bormann to G. Bormann, 27 October 1944.

109 Fröhlich 1996, part II, vol. 14, pp. 79f, 11 October 1944.

110 Perlia 1999, p. 196.

111 Von Brauchitsch 1967, pp. 160f.

112 TNA, FO 1031, 102, Dr Karl Brandt, 21 August 1945; see also BAK, Kl. Erw. 441–3, pp. 54–59, Brandt report, 21 September 1945, p. 2; also BAK, All. Proz. 2/FC 6069 P, Vernehmung Karl Brandt, 26 November 1946.

113 NARA, RG 153, 100–767, Box 62, US Strategic Bombing Survey, Interview with Prof. Dr. med. Karl Brandt, 17–18 June 1945.

114 BAK, Kl. Erw. 441, No. 3, Brandt about 'Sanitary Measures', 16 August 1945; see also BAK, All. Proz. 2/FC 6069 P, Vernehmung Karl Brandt, 26 November 1946.

115 NARA, RG 153, 100–767, Box 62, US Strategic Bombing Survey, Interview with Prof. Dr. med. Karl Brandt, 17–18 June 1945.

116 StaNü, KV-Anklage, Dokumente, NO-332.

117 The following sequence of events is largely based on a six-page report which Brandt wrote about the events following his arrest in April 1945. The report has no title and is dated 21 September 1945; BAK, Kl. Erw. 441–3, pp. 54–59; StaNü, KV-Anklage Interrogations, No. B154, Interrogation Karl Brandt, 9 October 1946 and 27 November 1946; also KV-Anklage, Dokumente, NO-332.

118 StaNü, KV-Anklage, Dokumente, NO-332.

119 BAK, Kl. Erw. 441–3, pp. 54–59, Brandt report, 21 September 1945, p. 1.

120 Ibid., pp. 1–3.

121 BAK, All. Proz. 2/FC 6069 P, Vernehmung Karl Brandt, 9 October 1946.

122 BAK, Kl. Erw. 441–3, pp. 54–59, Brandt report, 21 September 1945, p. 4.

123 StaNü, KV-Anklage, Dokumente, NO-332; see also Brandt papers, Brandt report, 21 September 1945, p. 4.

124 BAK, Kl. Erw. 441–3, pp. 54–59, Brandt report, 21 September 1945, pp. 4f.

125 StaNü, KV-Anklage Interrogations, No. B154, Interrogation Karl Brandt, 9 October 1946.

126 StaNü, KV-Anklage, Dokumente, NO-332.

127 BAK, All. Proz. 2/FC 6069 P, Vernehmung Karl Brandt, 9 October 1946.

128 BAK, Kl. Erw. 441–3, pp. 54–59, Brandt report, 21 September 1945, p. 6.

129 Speer 2000, p. 465.

130 Ibid., pp. 476ff.

131 BAK, Kl. Erw. 441–3, pp. 54–59, Brandt report, 21 September 1945, p. 6; see also Speer's account of the events; Sereny 1995, pp. 524ff.

132 BAK, All. Proz. 2/FC 6069 P, Vernehmung Karl Brandt, 1 March 1947.

133 StaNü, KV-Anklage, Dokumente, NO-332.

134 Ibid.

135 BAK, Kl. Erw. 441–3, pp. 54–59, Brandt report, 21 September 1945, p. 6.

Notes to Chapter 10: Nuremberg

1 Sections of this chapter have previously been published in Schmidt 2004.

2 Of 901 men charged with war crimes, 880 were eventually acquitted, the rest released after brief sentences, or allowed to escape; Tusa and Tusa 1995, pp. 17–20.

3 Breitmann 1998, p. 215.

4 See, for example, Abzug 1987, pp. 89–103; see also AP, Alexander calendar (1945), note on Dachau concentration camp.

5 Davidson 1997, pp. 7ff.

6 Frei 1996, pp. 141f.

7 'The German Atrocities' 1945, pp. 32–37.

8 Schmidt 2005.

9 Mitscherlich and Mielke 1960; Caplan 1992; Annas and Grodin 1992, pp. 94–104.

10 TNA, 'Operation Fleacomb,' WO 309, 476–77, 1458, 1460, WO 311, 650; 'Operation Haystack,' WO 309, 1606; see also Schmidt 2005.

11 For Josef Mengele see, for example, Cefrey 2001; Lifton 1985; Lifton 1986; Müller-Hill 1988; Posner and Ware 2000; for Rascher see Benz 1988, pp. 190–214.

12 For Conti's suicide on 6 October 1945 see NARA, RG 238, entry 200, box 5, prison file Leonardo Conti; see also Kater 1985, pp. 299–325; for de Crinis see Jasper 1991; for Grawitz see BA-BDC, Personal File Ernst Robert Grawitz; also Wicke 1999.

13 NARA, RG 238, entry 28, box 3, War Crimes News Digest, 22 January 1947.

14 After the International Military Tribunal (IMT) Fischer was transferred to Hersbruck, before eventually being detained in the PoW camp in the American zone in Plattling, near Deggendorf. From here he was released in July 1946 and transferred to a civilian detention centre before being included in the group of doctors accused at Nuremberg; see NARA, RG 238, entry 200, box 8, prison file Dr phil. Fritz Fischer (born 5 March 1908); also NARA, RG 238, entry 200, box 8, prison file Dr. Fritz Fischer (born 5 October 1912); see also Schmidt 2001b, pp. 381–89.

15 NARA, RG 238, entry 200, box 8, prison file Dr. Fritz Fischer (born 5 October 1912).

16 StaNü, KV-Anklage Interrogations, No. B154, Interrogation Karl Brandt, 26 November 1946.

17 NARA, RG 238, NM-70, entry 200, box 3, Detention Report Viktor Brack.

18 Ibid., box 4, Detention Report Rudolf Emil Hermann Brandt.

19 Ibid., box 2, Detention Report Wilhelm Beiglboeck.

20 See also 'The Wrong Stuff', Channel 4 series, screened on 2 April 2001.

21 NARA, RG 238, NM-70, entry 200, box 2, Detention Report Becker-Freyseng.

22 See also 'The Germans Sign the Surrenders' 1945, pp. 25–31.

23 TNA, WO 171, 8017.

24 TNA, FO 371, 46914.

25 Annas and Grodin 1992; BAK, Kl. Erw. 441–3, pp. 54–59, Brandt report, 21 September 1945, also StaNü, KV-Anklage, Dokumente, NO-332; also KV-Anklage Interrogations, No. B154, Interrogation Karl Brandt, 9 October 1946; Steiner 1967, p. 145.

26 Ball 1982, pp. 51–68; see also Schlie 1999.

27 NARA, RG 238, NM-70, entry 200, box 4, Detention Report Karl Brandt.

28 Ball 1982, p. 58.

29 NARA, RG 238, NM-70, entry 200, Detention Report Paul Rostock. Blome was arrested on 16 May by members of the American Counter Intelligence Corps in Munich; NARA, RG 238, NM-70, entry 200, box 3, Detention Report, Kurt Blome.

30 Galbraith 1945, pp. 17–24.

31 IWM, BU 6724, Transport of Brandt, Dönitz and Speer from Flensburg after their arrest by the British armed forces in May 1945.

32 TNA, WO 208, 3153.

33 See also New York Times, 25 July 1945; Andrus 1969, pp. 22ff.

34 Taylor 1992, p. 230; see also Andrus 1969, pp. 22ff.

35 Andrus 1969, p. 24.

36 Tusa and Tusa 1995, pp. 42ff.

37 Galbraith 1945, p. 18.

38 Galbraith 1981, p. 192; also Galbraith 1945, pp. 17f.

39 Galbraith 1945, p. 22.

40 Tusa and Tusa 1995, pp. 299f.

41 Galbraith 1945, p. 24.

42 Ibid., p. 18.

43 Galbraith 1981, p. 195.

44 Andrus 1969, pp. 29f.

45 Taylor 1992, pp. 618ff.

46 TNA, FO 371, 46914.

47 New York Times, 25 July 1945.

48 Kirkpatrick 1959, pp. 193ff; also TNA, FO 371, 46778.

49 Davidson 1997, p. 165.

50 Tusa and Tusa 1995, p. 46.

51 Galbraith 1945, p. 24; also Galbraith 1981, p. 195.

52 TNA, FO 371, 46778.

53 Ibid.

54 Breitmann 1998, p. 9.

55 TNA, FO 371, 46778.

56 Sereny 1995, p. 558; also Speer 2000, p. 502.

57 Sereny 1995, p. 558.

58 StaNü, KV-Anklage, Dokumente, NO-332.

59 StaNü, KV-Anklage Interrogations, No. B154, Interrogation Karl Brandt, 26 November 1946.

60 Sereny 1995, p. 558.

61 Ibid.

62 TNA, WO 208, 2178.

63 Tusa and Tusa 1995, pp. 44f.

64 StaNü, KV-Anklage, Dokumente, NO-332.

65 NARA, M 1270, Roll 2, Interrogation Karl Brandt.

66 StaNü, KV-Anklage, Dokumente, NO-333; TNA, FO 371, 46778.

67 TNA, FO 371, 46778.

68 StaNü, KV-Anklage, Dokumente, NO-333; see also NARA, RG 238, entry 185, box 1, Interrogation Summary Karl Brandt, 5 November 1946.

69 On the side of the page in which Brandt stated that the 'euthanasia' programme had stopped in 1940, a Foreign Office official also noted in pencil '? It certainly continued'; TNA, FO 371, 46778.

70 TNA, FO 371, 46778.

71 Following Brandt's release, 'Ashcan' was about to receive Conti from the 21st Army Group; StaNü, KV-Anklage, Dokumente, NO-333.

72 Brandt trial notebook, Euthanasia, II/9(53), p. 286 (pagination by US).

73 NDT-Records, frame 2/2693.

74 StaNü, KV-Anklage, Dokumente, NO-333.

75 Sereny 1995, p. 559.

76 See also Heinkel 1953.

77 TNA, WO 219, 1330.

78 Bower 1987; see also Bower 1982; Bower 1995.

79 NARA, M 1270, Roll 2, Interrogation Karl Brandt.

80 BAK, Kl. Erw. 441–3.

81 Schenk 1989; Schlie 1999.

82 'Berlin' 1945, 19–27.

83 Trevor-Roper 1995.

84 NARA, M 1270, Roll 2, Karl Brandt: 'Problem Hitler', 7 July 1945, frames 382–87.

85 BAK, Kl. Erw. 441–3.

86 Schlie 1999, pp. 217–41; see also TNA, FO 1031, 102.

87 BAK, Kl. Erw. 441–3.

88 For the assessment of Bormann see TNA, FO 1031, 102; also BAK, Kl. Erw. 525, HQ, US Forces European Theater, MI Service Center, CIR, 'Hitler as Seen by his Doctors'; Interview Karl Brandt on 30 August 1945 at 'Dustbin'. The document can also be found in NARA, RG 319, Box 2031.

89 NARA, M 1270, Roll 2, Karl Brandt: 'Problem Hitler', 7 July 1945, frame 383.

90 Ibid., frame 384. The source has been edited to improve the fluency of the text.

91 Trials of War Criminals, i, pp. viiif.

92 Ibid., pp. ix–xvi.

93 Ibid., pp. xvi–xx; also Annas and Grodin 1992, pp. 317–21.

94 Annas and Grodin 1992, pp. 317–21.

95 Leo Alexander, Public Mental Health Practices in Germany: Sterilisation and Execution of Patients Suffering from Nervous or Mental Diseases, CIOS, item 24, Medical, Combined Intelligence Objectives Sub-Committee, G-2 Division, SHAEF (Rear), APO 413, 19 August 1945. For Alexander see Schmidt 2004.

96 TNA, FO 371, 57576.

97 StaNü, KV-Anklage Interrogations, No. B154, Vernehmung Karl Brandt, 3 September 1947.

98 Taylor 1992, p. 171.

99 Leo Alexander, The Treatment of Shock from Prolonged Exposure to Cold, Especially in Water, CIOS, target No. 24, Medical, Combined Intelligence Objectives Sub-Committee, G-2 Division, SHAEF (Rear), APO 413, 10 July 1945.

100 BIOS, Final Report No. 542, Interrogation of Certain German Personalities Connected with Chemical Warfare, 1946.

101 Tusa and Tusa 1995, p. 94.

102 Ibid., p. 146.

103 Ibid., p. 155.

104 Ibid.

105 Ibid.

106 Gilbert 1962, pp. 50ff; also Tusa and Tusa 1995, p. 243.

107 TNA, FO 371, 57576; also WO 309, 468.

108 TNA, WO 208, 2178.

109 Ibid.

110 Ibid.

111 Ibid.

112 NARA, M 1270, Roll 2, Interrogation Karl Brandt, 29 September 1945, 1 October 1945, 3 October 1945, 18 October 1945, frames 284–381.

113 Taylor 1992, p. 271.

114 Ibid.

115 Schmidt 2005.

116 Schindler-Saefkow 1995, pp. 137–208.

117 For post-war trials in the Russian zone of occupation and in the German Democratic Republic (GDR) on some of the Ravensbrück camp wards see Eschebach 1997, pp. 65–74.

118 TNA, FO 371, 57576.

119 BAK, All. Proz. 2/FC 6069 P, Vernehmung Karl Brandt, 1 March 1947.

120 For the statistics of the American, British, French and Russian war crime trials see Frei 1996, p. 143.

121 TNA, FO 371, 57596/U4040.

122 Ibid.; see also Bauer 1995, p. 250.

123 TNA, FO 371, 57576; also WO 309, 468.
124 BIOS, Final Report No. 542, Interrogation of Certain German Personalities Connected with Chemical Warfare, 1946.
125 Ibid., p. 30.
126 TNA, WO 309, 418.
127 Ibid., 762.
128 NARA, RG 238, entry 188/190/191, box 2, Individual Responsibility of Prof. Dr Karl Brandt, May 1946.
129 Ibid.
130 Ibid.
131 StaNü, KV-Anklage Interrogations, No. B154, Interrogation Brandt, 26 November 1946.
132 See Friedlander 1995.
133 NARA, RG 238, entry 188/190/191, box 2, Individual Responsibility of Prof. Dr Karl Brandt, May 1946; StaNü, KV-Anklage Interrogations, B95, Interrogation Fritz Bleich, 4 January 1946.
134 For archival sources about Conti's suicide at Nuremberg prison on 6 October 1945 see NARA, RG 238, entry 200, box 5, prison file Leonardo Conti.
135 NARA, RG 238, entry 186, box 1, Attention Interrogation Branch, 19 August 1946.
136 Ibid.
137 Ibid.
138 Ibid.
139 TNA, WO 309, 468. The British War Office informed the UNWCC on 6 September 1946 about the American plans to mount a trial against German doctors. The US proposed that the trial should either be held by Anglo-American Military Government Courts under Law No. 10, or by American Military Courts in the American zone; for the term 'subsequent proceeding' see also Taylor 1992.
140 This group of doctors from the SS sanatorium at Hohenlychen had been in charge of criminal human experiments at the Ravensbrück concentration camp.
141 TNA, WO 309, 468.
142 Ibid.
143 Duke University Archives, box 4, folder 27, Travel Orders from 8 November 1946: 'Dr Leo Alexander, Expert to the Secretary of War, $40 per day, is hereby directed to proceed by air on or about 14 November 1946 from Washington, DC, to Nurnberg, Germany, on temporary duty for approximately three (3) months, and upon completion thereof to return to Washington, DC US-ET-3-25123-WDP-NOV.'
144 Duke University Archives, 'Alexander Tagebuch'.
145 Ibid.; see also AP, Leo Alexander to Phyllis Alexander, 7 December 1946.
146 StaNü, KV-Anklage Interrogations, No. B154, Vernehmung Karl Brandt, 26 November 1946.
147 Ibid.; also BAK, All. Proz. 2/FC 6069 P, Vernehmung Karl Brandt, 26 November 1946.

Notes to Chapter 11: Trial

1 Sections of this chapter have previously been published in Schmidt 2004.
2 Taylor 1992, p. 129, p. 230.
3 Tusa and Tusa 1995, pp. 83ff.
4 Annas and Grodin 1992; Taylor 1992, p. 611.
5 For the press coverage about the establishment of further Nuremberg trials see, for example, NARA, RG 238, Entry 28, Box 3 Daily Press Review, *Baltimore Sun*; *St. Louis Dispatch*, 25 October 1946; *Michigan Times Dispatch*, 26 October 1946.
6 Supreme Court Historical Society Tallahassee, Florida, Sebring papers; I am indebted to Nancy Dobson, Executive Director of the Florida Supreme Court Historical Society, for her support and hospitality during my research trip to Tallahassee in March 1998.
7 Davidson 1997, p. 21; Tusa and Tusa 1995, pp. 109f; TNA, FO 371, 57576.
8 Davidson 1997, p. 21.
9 Tusa and Tusa 1995, pp. 125ff.
10 Giesler 1977, p. 40.
11 Tusa and Tusa 1995, pp. 127f.
12 StaNü, KV-Anklage Interrogations, No. B154, Interrogation Karl Brandt, 26 November 1946.
13 Ibid.
14 Brandt Diary, 10 November 1946.
15 See also StaNü, KV-Anklage Interrogations, No. B154, Interrogation Karl Brandt, 13 August 1947.
16 Brandt Diary, 14 November 1946; also Knödler and Feyerabend 2004, part I.
17 Ibid.
18 Ibid., 8 December 1946.
19 Tusa and Tusa 1995, pp. 378ff.
20 Annas and Grodin 1992; see also Schmidt 2004.

21 Brandt Diary, 8 December 1946.
22 Ibid.; also Knödler and Feyerabend 2004, part I.
23 Ibid.
24 Ibid.
25 BAK, All. Proz. 2/FC 6069 P, Vernehmung Karl Brandt, 26 November 1946.
26 Annas and Grodin 1992; Taylor 1992.
27 For Romberg see Schmidt 2001b.
28 For Fischer see Schmidt 2001b.
29 NARA, RG 238, entry 28, box 3 Daily Press Review; *Augusta Chronicle*, 24 November 1946; *Washington Post*, 21 November 1946; see also *Denver Post*, 27 November 1946.
30 NDT-Records, frame 2/50.
31 Ibid., frames 2/61–124.
32 Annas and Grodin 1992, p. 68.
33 Ibid.
34 Ibid.
35 Ibid., p. 71.
36 NDT-Records, frames 2/64f.
37 Annas and Grodin 1992, pp. 71–86.
38 Ibid., p. 87.
39 Ibid.
40 Ibid.; see also Blome 1942.
41 Annas and Grodin 1992, p. 89.
42 Ibid.
43 *New York Times*, 10 December 1946.
44 NDT-Records, frame 2/118.
45 NARA, RG 238, entry 28, box 3 Daily Press Review; *Philadelphia Record*; *Baltimore News Post*; *Philadelphia Bulletin*, 9 December 1946. *Minneapolis Times Dispatch*; *Dallas Morning News*; *Baltimore Sun*; *Philadelphia Record*; *Washington Post*; *Chicago Sun*; *New York Herald Tribune*, 10 December 1946. *Frankenpost*; *Fränkischer Tag*; *Badische Neuste Nachrichten*, 11 December 1946. *Darmstädter Echo*; *Fränkische Nachrichten*; *Mittelbayrische Zeitung*; *Frankfurter Rundschau*, 12 December 1946. *Die Neue Zeitung*; *Main Post*; *Frankenpost*, 13 December 1946. *Fränkische Landeszeitung*; *Weser Kurier*; *Stuttgarter Nachrichten*; *Fränkischer Tag*, 14 December 1946. *Libération*; *Le Figaro*; *L'Epoque*; *La Dépêche de Paris*; *L'Humanité*; *Paris Matin*; *L'Aurore*; *L'Aube*, 17 December 1946.
46 NARA, RG 238, entry 28, box 3 Daily Press Review; *Philadelphia Record*, 9 December 1946.
47 Ibid.; *L'Ordre*; *L'Epoque*, 11 December 1946.
48 Brandt Diary, 9 December 1946; see also NDT-Records, frames 2/65ff.
49 Brandt Diary, 9 December 1946.

50 NDT-Records, frame 2/60.
51 Grinberg Film Library, New York; see also IWM, newsreels of the Doctors' Trial.
52 IWM, *Welt im Film*, newsreel, 1946/47.
53 NARA, RG 238, entry 28, box 3 Daily Press Review.
54 It was also revealed that the French authorities were beginning to collaborate with the Military Tribunal I by arresting Otto Ambros, the IG Farben expert for poison gas, and sending him to Nuremberg. Ambros had previously been employed by the French to run the IG Farben plant at Ludwigshafen; *New York Times*, 12 December 1946.
55 FCLM, Beecher papers, box 11, folder 79.
56 Ibid.
57 Von Platen 1947a, pp. 29–31.
58 *New York Times*, 10 December 1946.
59 StaNü, KV-Prozesse, Generalia, P318, DANA papers, 9 December 1946; NARA, RG 238, entry 28, box 3 Daily Press Review, 11 December 1946 and 13 December 1946.
60 FCLM, Beecher papers, box 11, folder 79.
61 NARA, RG 238, entry 28, box 3 Daily Press Review.
62 Annas and Grodin 1992, p. 68.
63 See Annas and Grodin 1992, pp. 67ff.
64 Brandt Diary, 9 December 1946.
65 See, for example, Friedlander 1995, pp. 63ff.
66 Brandt Diary, 16 December 1946; also Knödler and Feyerabend 2004, part I.
67 Ibid. and 21 December 1946.
68 StaNü, KV-Verteidigung, Handakten Rostock No. 10.
69 StaNü, KV-Anklage, Dokumente, NO-645; also Knödler and Feyerabend 2004, part I.
70 Brandt Diary, 9 January 1947.
71 Ibid.
72 NARA, RG 238, entry 28, box 3 Daily Press Review, *Daily Express*, 8 January 1947.
73 Ibid.
74 *New York Times*, 9 December 1947.
75 Ibid., 5 February 1947, 8 February 1947.
76 NDT-Records, frames 2/2447f.
77 Ibid., frames 2/2382ff and frames 2/2389ff.
78 Ibid., frame 2/2459.
79 Ibid., frame 2/2444.
80 Ibid., frame 2/2395.
81 Ibid., frame 2/2466.
82 See also Brandt's discussion about the problems related to euthanasia, which he wrote down in a seven-page report two weeks after having given evidence in court on the

subject; BAK, All. Proz. 2/FC 6069 P, Prof. Dr Karl Brandt, Betrifft: Euthanasie, 15 February 1947.

83 NDT-Records, frames 2/2501f.

84 Ibid., frames 2/2511f.

85 Ibid., frame 2/2503.

86 Ibid., frame 2/2503.

87 Ibid., frame 2/2514.

88 Ibid.

89 NARA, M 1270, Roll 2, Interrogation of Karl Brandt, 1 October 1945, frame 328.

90 NDT-Records, frames 2/2516f; NDT-Records (German), frame 2/2453; also Burleigh 1994, p. 275; see also NARA, M 1270, Roll 2, Interrogation Karl Brandt, 1 October 1945, frames 325f.

91 NDT-Records, frame 2/2524.

92 DUMC, Alexander papers, box 4, folder 33, Alexander diary (1946/47), p. 187.

93 NDT-Records, frame 2/2598.

94 Ibid., frame 2/2621.

95 Ibid., frame 2/2558.

96 Ibid., frame 2/2570.

97 Ibid., frame 2/2611.

98 Ibid., frame 2/2576.

99 Ibid., frame 2/2647.

100 Ibid., frame 2/2648.

101 Ibid., frame 2/2649.

102 Ibid., frames 2/2651f.

103 Ibid., frame 2/2653.

104 Ibid., frame 2/2716, frame 2/2720, frame 2/2722, frames 2/2725–2730.

105 Ibid., frames 2/2716–2720.

106 Ibid., frame 2/2722.

107 Ibid.

108 Ibid., frame 2/2725.

109 Ibid.,

110 Ibid.

111 HUA, personal file Karl Brandt 379.

112 Klee 1997, pp. 196f; pp. 204ff.

113 TNA, WO 309, 420.

114 See also NARA, RG 238, entry 212, box 1; plea for clemency for Brandt by Julius Meyer-Boekhoff, 8 October 1947.

115 TNA, WO 309, 420.

116 StaNü, KV-Verteidigung, Handakten Rostock No. 8.

117 Alexander 1955, pp. 81–99.

118 Ibid., p. 89.

119 Weindling 1981, pp. 99–155.

120 StaNü, KV-Verteidigung, Handakten Rostock No. 2.

121 'Prison Malaria' 1945, pp. 43–46.

122 Ibid., p. 43.

123 NDT-Records, frame 2/2649.

124 Grodin 1992, pp. 121–44; Shuster 1997, pp. 1436–40.

125 Grodin 1992, pp. 134ff.

126 NDT-Records, frames 2/9309ff.

127 Ibid., frames 2/9337f.

128 Ibid., frame 2/9398.

129 For medical training and ethics education in Nazi Germany see Kater 1985; Kersting 1996; Schmidt 2000c; Schmidt 2002a.

130 Schmidt 2002a.

131 Letter Karl Brandt, 8 July 1947.

132 NDT-Records, frames 2/11504–11507.

133 Ibid., frame 2/11505.

134 Ibid., frames 2/11505f.

135 Ibid., frame 2/11506.

136 Ibid., frame 2/11507.

137 NARA, RG 238, entry 146, box 1, affidavit Thomas K. Hodges, Director, Language Division, and Chief of Translation Branch.

138 Sillevaerts 1947.

139 Ibid.

140 NDT-Records, frame 2/11583.

141 Ibid., frames 2/11589f.

142 FCLM, Beecher papers, box 11, Folder 79.

143 NARA, RG 238, entry 146, box 1, affidavit Thomas K. Hodges, Director, Language Division, and Chief of Translation Branch.

144 NDT-Records, frame 2/11728.

145 Sillevaerts 1947.

146 Ibid.

147 Annas and Grodin 1992, pp. 105ff.

148 Sillevaerts 1947.

Notes to Chapter 12: Under Sentence of Death

1 Kershaw 1998, p. 240.

2 Eder 1998, pp. 80–84; see also Frei 1996, pp. 133–233.

3 StaNü, KV-Verteidigung, Handakten Rostock, file 5, Von Bargen to Anni Brandt, 24 August 1947.

4 Ibid., Rink to Beals, 1 September 1947.

5 Ibid.

6 'Arzt unterm Galgen' 1952, pp. 29–31.

7 StaNü, KV-Verteidigung, Handakten Rostock, file 5.

8 StaNü, KV-Anklage Interrogations, No. B154, Interrogation Karl Brandt, 3 September 1947.

9 Ibid., 4 November 1946.

10 NDT-Records, frame 2/2685.

11 NDT-Documents, frame 4/2470.

12 By October, the military governor had received four letters for Rudolf Brandt, eight letters for Karl Brandt, thirteen letters for Viktor Brack, eleven letters and a hundred telegrams for Karl Gebhardt, one letter and one telegram for Waldemar Hoven, two letters for Joachim Mrugowsky, one letter for Gerhard Rose and five letters for Wolfram Sievers; Burman 1985, pp. 209f.

13 For some of the many petitions on behalf of Brandt see StaNü, KV-Verteidigung, Handakten Rostock, file 5; also NARA, RG 238, entry 212, box 1; see also Meier 1996, pp. 73–85.

14 HBAB, file 2/39–192, Gerstenmaier to Hardt, 11 August 1947; see also Anni Brandt to von Bodelschwingh, 10 October 1947; Anni Brandt to von Bodelschwingh, 8 November 1947.

15 HBAB, file 2/39–192, Gerstenmaier to Hardt, 11 August 1947.

16 Ibid.

17 Ibid., Hardt to Gerstenmaier, 18 August 1947.

18 Ibid., Hardt to General Secretary of Military Tribunal I, 17 September 1947.

19 StaNü, KV-Verteidigung, Handakten Rostock, file 5, Julia von Bodelschwingh to Secretary of the Army, 10 March 1947.

20 NDT-Documents, frame 4/2533; see also the petition by Dr Meyer-Boeckhoff; NDT-Documents, frames 4/2543ff; see also NARA, RG 238, entry 212, box 1, Julia von Bodelschwingh, 30 October 1947.

21 NARA, RG 238, entry 212, box 1; A.B. Chittick to Headquarters European Command, 25 September 1947.

22 StaNü, KV-Verteidigung, Handakten Rostock, file 5, Rostock to Brandt, 7 October 1947.

23 Ibid., Rostock to Anni Brandt, 7 October 1947.

24 HBAB, file 2/39–192, Haering to von Bodelschwingh, 2 January 1948; see also von Bodelschwingh to Haering, 7 January 1948.

25 NDT-Documents, frames 4/2485f and frames 4/2494f. The twenty-six medical scientists were W. Achelis (1 December 1947), H. Buerkle de la Camp (7 December 1947), H. Coenen (1 December 1947), P. Diepgen (13 December 1947), G. Domagk (30

December 1947), H. Domrich (19 January 1948), K. von Eicken (18 December 1947), E. K. Frey (12 December 1947), W. Heubner (undated), F. Jaeger (29 November 1947), K.W. Joetten (13 January 1948), W. Nonnenbruch (8 January 1948), K. Quasebart (3 December 1947), E. Freiherr v. Redwitz (2 December 1947), V. Reichmann (6 December 1947), R. Roessle (31 December 1947), F. Sauerbruch (11 December 1947), W. Schulemann (28 November 1947), H. Siegmund (29 November 1947), W. Stoeckel (20 December 1947), A. Stoermer (9 January 1948), W. Toennis (6 January 1948), P. Ulenhuth (12 January 1948), W. Wachsmuth (28 November 1947), W. Zabel (8 December 1947), L. Zukschwerdt (4 January 1948); StaNü, KV-Verteidigung, Handakten Rostock, file 5; also NARA, RG 238, entry 146, box 1.

26 NDT-Documents, frame 4/2500.

27 Ibid., frame 4/2516.

28 Ibid., frame 4/2513.

29 Ibid., frame 4/2513.

30 TNA, FO 371, 104148.

31 StaNü, KV-Verteidigung, Handakten Rostock, file 5, Karlstetter to Rostock, 28 February 1948.

32 United States Office of the High Commissioner for Germany 1951, p. 17; also Meier 1996, pp. 73–85.

33 Frei 1996, pp. 138f.

34 Ibid., pp. 139ff.

35 Ibid., p. 140.

36 StaNü, KV-Verteidigung, Handakten Rostock, file 5, Brandt to Rostock, 7 March 1948.

37 Ibid., Brandt to Rostock, Christmas 1947.

38 HBAB, file 2/39–192, Haering to von Bodelschwingh, 2 January 1948.

39 Burman 1985, p. ii.

40 StaNü, KV-Verteidigung, Handakten Rostock, file 5, Rostock to Karlstetter, 3 March 1948.

41 Ibid., Karlstetter to Rostock, 19 April 1948.

42 Ibid., Rostock to Karlstetter, 20 April 1948.

43 'Arzt unterm Galgen' 1952, pp. 29–31.

44 StaNü, KV-Verteidigung, Handakten Rostock, file 5, Clay to Theisen, 10 May 1948.

45 NARA, RG 238, entry 145–46.

46 Ibid., entry 213, Box 4, NM-70, Memorandum by the Evangelical Church in Germany on the Question of War Crimes Trials before American Military Courts (Waiblingen-Stuttgart, 1949), pp. 24f.

47 Ibid., p. 25.

48 Ibid.

49 Ibid., p. 3.

50 LaFollette to Clay, 8 June 1948; quoted from Frei 1996, pp. 146f.

51 Frei 1996, p. 147.

52 Smith 1974, document 403, pp. 658f.

53 Ibid., document 404, pp. 659f.

54 Ibid., document 409, pp. 661f.

55 The Clemency Board was eventually established in January 1950 under the leadership of John J. McCloy; see United States Office of the High Commissioner for Germany 1951.

56 Frei 1996, pp. 178f.

57 HBAB, file 2/39–192, von Bodelschwingh to Becker, 29 May 1948.

58 Ibid., Bodelschwingh to Wurm, 30 May 1948.

59 Ibid.

60 StaNü, KV-Verteidigung, Handakten Rostock, file 5, Ungerin to Rostock, 24 May 1948.

61 Ibid.

62 Ibid., Rostock to Ungerin, 27 May 1948.

63 Ibid., Brandt to Rostock, 28 May 1948.

64 HBAB, file 2/39–192, von Bodelschwingh to Wurm, 30 May 1948.

65 Conversation with Waltraut von Hasselbach, 19 August 2000.

66 Schmuhl 1997, p. 112.

67 Ibid., pp. 116f.

68 HBAB, 2/39–193, Brandt to Boeckh, 1 June 1948.

69 Ibid.

70 Telegram by Anni Brandt to Rostock on 3 June 1948: 'Urteil 10 Uhr 10 vollstreckt = Anni Brandt'; StaNü, KV-Verteidigung, Handakten Rostock, file 5, Anni Brandt to Rostock, 3 June 1948.

71 For a copy of the speech see StaNü, KV-Prozesse, case 1, Spezialia Karl Brandt H24/25; see also Oscar 1950, pp. 10–12.

72 StaNü, KV-Prozesse, case 1, Spezialia Karl Brandt H24/25.

73 Ibid.

74 Maser 1979, p. 255; for the executions in the IMT see also Duff 1948, pp. 55f.

75 'Seven Hanged for Brutality in Nazi Camps' 1948.

76 HBAB, 2/39–193, Boeckh to the head of the Bethel-Kanzlei, 29 December 1977.

77 Oscar 1950, pp. 13f.

78 HBAB, Boeckh to Ms Imort, 7 January 1978.

79 StaNü, KV-Verteidigung, Handakten Rostock, file 5, Günther to Rostock, 4 June 1948.

80 Ibid., Anni Brandt to Rostock, 16 June 1948.

81 For a comprehensive and excellent account about the politics surrounding the issue of war criminals at Landsberg see Frei 1996, pp. 133–233.

82 Frei 1996, p. 211.

83 Ibid., p. 214.

84 United States Office of the High Commissioner for Germany 1951, pp. 17f.

85 Ibid., p. 5.

Bibliography

'13 Stufen'. *Der Spiegel*, 5 June 1948.

Abzug, R. H. (1985), *Inside the Vicious Heart. Americans and the Liberation of Nazi Concentration Camps*. Oxford: Oxford University Press.

Alexander, L. (1945a), *Public Mental Health Practices in Germany: Sterilisation and Execution of Patients Suffering from Nervous or Mental Diseases*. CIOS, Item 24, 19 August 1945.

Alexander, L. (1945b), *The Treatment of Shock from Prolonged Exposure to Cold, especially in Water*. CIOS Target No. 24, Medical, CIOS, G-2 Division, SHAEF (Rear), APO 413, 10 July 1945.

Alexander, L. (1955), 'Moralisms and Morality from the Viewpoint of the Psychiatrist', in I. Galdston (ed.), *Ministry and Medicine in Human Relations*. New York: International Universities Press, pp. 81–99.

Aly, G. (1985), 'Der saubere und der schmutzige Fortschritt', in G. Aly *et al.* (eds.), *Reform und Gewissen. 'Euthanasie' im Dienst des Fortschritts*. Berlin: Rotbuch, pp. 9–78.

Aly, G. (1989), 'Die "Aktion Brandt" – Bombenkrieg, Bettenbedarf und "Euthanasie"', in G. Aly (ed.), *Aktion T4, 1939–1945: Die 'Euthanasie'-Zentrale in der Tiergartenstraße 4*. Berlin: Hentrich, pp. 168–82.

Aly, G. (ed.), (1989), *Aktion T4 1939–1945: Die 'Euthanasie'-Zentrale in der Tiergartenstraße 4*. Berlin: Hentrich.

Aly, G. *et al.* (eds.), (1985), *Reform und Gewissen. 'Euthanasie' im Dienst des Fortschritts*. Berlin: Rotbuch.

Aly, G. *et al.* (eds.), (1994), *Cleansing the Fatherland. Nazi Medicine and Racial Hygiene*. Baltimore, London: Johns Hopkins University Press.

Andrus, B. C. (1969), *I was the Nuremberg Jailer*. New York: Coward-McCann.

Annas, G. J. and Grodin, M. A. (eds.), (1992), *The Nazi Doctors and the Nuremberg Code. Human Rights in Human Experimentation*. New York, Oxford: Oxford University Press.

Arendt, H. (1963), *Eichmann in Jerusalem. A Report on the Banality of Evil*. London: Faber & Faber.

'Arzt unterm Galgen'. (1952), *Wochenend*, 45, 29–31.

Aziz, P. (1976), *Doctors of Death*, vols 1–4. Geneva: Ferni Publishers.

Baader, G. and Schultz, U. (eds.), (1983), *Medizin im Nationalsozialismus. Tabuisierte Vergangenheit – ungebrochene Tradition?* Berlin: Verlags-Gesellschaft Gesundheit.

Bähr, H. W. (ed.), (1987), *Albert Schweitzer. Leben, Werk und Denken 1905–1965. Mitgeteilt in seinen Briefen*. Heidelberg: Lambert Schneider.

Bähr, H. W. (ed.), (2003), *Die Ehrfurcht vor dem Leben. Grundtexte aus fünf Jahrzehnten*. Munich: Beck.

Baker, R. and McCullough, L. B. (eds.), (2007), *A History of Medical Ethics*. Cambridge, New York: Cambridge University Press.

Ball, G.W. (1982), *The Past has another Pattern: Memoirs*. New York, London: Norton.

Bar-On, D. (2003), *Die Last des Schweigens. Gespräche mit Kindern von NS-Tätern*. Hamburg: Edition Körber Stiftung.

Bauer, T. and Süß, W. (eds.), (2000), *NS-Diktatur, DDR, Bundesrepublik. Drei Zeitgeschichten des vereinigten Deutschlands. Werkstattberichte*. Neuried: Ars Una.

Bayer, I. (ed.), (1979), *Ehe alles Legende wird*. Baden-Baden: Signal Verlag.

Bayle, F. (1950), *Croix Gammée contre Caducée. Les Expériences Humaines en Allemagne pendant la Deuxième Guerre Mondiale*. Berlin: Commission Scientifique Française des Crimes de Guerre.

Becker, P. E. (1988), *Zur Geschichte der Rassenhygiene. Wege ins Dritte Reich*. Stuttgart: Thieme.

Below, N. von. (2001), *At Hitler's Side. The Memoirs of Hitler's Luftwaffe Adjutant, 1937–1945*. London: Greenhill Books.

Benad, M. (1996), 'Widerstand als beharrliche Einrede – Kampf gegen Euthanasie'. *Der Ring. Zeitschrift der v. Bodelschwinghschen Anstalten Bethel*, pp. 6–12.

Benad, M. (1997a), 'Einleitung', in A. Hochmuth, *Spurensuche: Eugenik, Sterilisation und Patientenmorde und die v. Bodelschwinghschen Anstalten Bethel 1929–1945*. Bielefeld: Bethel Verlag, pp. xv–xxxvi.

Benad, M. (ed.), (1997b), *Friedrich v. Bodelschwingh d.J. und die Betheler Anstalten. Frömmigkeit und Weltgestaltung*. Stuttgart, Berlin, Cologne: Kohlhammer.

Bentley, J. (2001), *Albert Schweitzer. Eine Biographie*. Düsseldorf: Patmos.

Benz, W. (1988), 'Dr. med. Sigmund Rascher. Eine Karriere', in B. Benz and B. Diestel (eds.), *Medizin im NS-Staat. Täter, Opfer, Handlanger*. Dachau: Deutscher Taschenbuch Verlag, pp. 190–214.

Benz, W. and Diestel, B. (eds.), (1988), *Medizin im NS-Staat. Täter, Opfer, Handlanger*. Dachau: Deutscher Taschenbuch Verlag.

Benze, R. (1935), *Rasse und Schule. Grundzüge einer lebensgesetzlichen Schulreform*. Braunschweig: Appelhans.

Benzenhöfer, U. (1998a), 'Der Fall "Kind Knauer"'. *Deutsches Ärzteblatt*, 95 (1998), 19, 954–55.

Benzenhöfer, U. (1998b), 'Ohne jede moralische Skrupel'. *Deutsches Ärzteblatt*, 97 (1998), 42, 2352–55.

Benzenhöfer, U. (1999), *Der gute Tod? Euthanasie und Sterbehilfe in Geschichte und Gegenwart*. Munich: Beck.

Benzenhöfer, U. (2000), *'Kinderfachabteilungen' und 'NS-Kindereuthanasie'*. Wetzlar: GWAB-Verlag.

Benzenhöfer, U. (2003), 'Genese und Struktur der "NS-Kinder und Jugendlichen-euthanasie"'. *Monatschrift Kinderheilkunde*, 10 (2003), 1012–19.

Benzenhöfer, U. (2004), '"Ärzte unterm Hakenkreuz": Fesselnde Bilder, aber kein Gesamtbild'. *Deutsches Ärzteblatt*, 101 (2004), 18, A-1222, B-1008, C-980.

'Berlin'. *Life*, 19 (1945), No. 4, pp. 19–27.

Binding, K. and Hoche, A. (1920), *Die Freigabe der Vernichtunng lebensunwerten Lebens. Ihr Mass und ihre Form*. Leipzig: Meiner.

Bleker, J. and Jachertz, N. (eds.), (1993), *Medizin im Dritten Reich*. Cologne: Deutscher Ärzteverlag.

Blome, K. (1942), *Arzt im Kampf: Erlebnisse u. Gedanken*. Leipzig: Barth.

Bock, G. (1986), *Zwangssterilisation im Nationalsozialismus. Studien zur Rassenpolitik und Frauenpolitik*. Opladen: Westdeutscher Verlag.

Böhme, K. and Lohalm, U. (eds.), (1993), *Wege in den Tod. Hamburgs Anstalt Langenhorn und die Euthanasie in der Zeit des Nationalsozialismus*. Hamburg: Ergebnisse Verlag.

Boll, B. and Safrian, H. (2005), 'Auf dem Weg nach Stalingrad. Die 6. Armee 1941/42', in H. Heer and K. Naumann (eds.), *Vernichtungskrieg. Verbrechen der Wehrmacht 1941–1944*. Hamburg: Hamburger Edition, pp. 260–96.

Boobbyer, P. (2005), *Conscience, Dissent and Reform in Soviet Russia*. London, New York: Routledge.

Bower, T. (1982), *The Pledge Betrayed: America and Britain and the Denazification of Post-War Germany*. New York: Doubleday.

Bower, T. (1987), *The Paperclip Conspiracy: The Battle for the Spoils and Secrets of Nazi Germany*. London: Joseph.

Bower, T. (1995), *Blind Eye to Murder. Britain, America and the Purging of Nazi Germany – A Pledge Betrayed*. London: Little Brown.

Brandt, K. (1933), 'Ergebnisse bei Oberschenkelbruchbehandlung'. *Deutsche Zeitschrift für Chirurgie*, 239, (1933), 294–331.

Brandt, K. (1939), 'Die Schließung der Bierschen Klinik', in P. Diepgen and P. Rostock (eds.), *Das Universitätsklinikum in Berlin. Seine Ärzte und seine wissenschaftliche Leistung 1810–1933*. Leipzig: Barth, pp. 183–88.

Brauchitsch, M. von. (1967), *Ohne Kampf kein Sieg*. Berlin: Verlag der Nation.

Bräutigam, O. (1968), *So hat es sich zugetragen … Ein Leben als Soldat und Diplomat*. Würzburg: Holzner.

Breitman, R. (1992), *The Architect of Genocide: Himmler and the Final Solution*. London: Grafton.

Breitman, R. (1999), *Official Secrets. What the Nazis Planned, what the British and Americans Knew*. London: Allen Lane.

Breker, A. (1972), *Im Strahlungsfeld der Ereignis. Leben und Wirken eines Künstlers. Porträts, Begegnungen, Schicksale*. Preußisch Oldendorf: Schütz.

Browning, C. (1998), *Der Weg zur 'Endlösung'. Entscheidungen und Täter*. Bonn: Dietz.

Browning, C. (2001), *Ordinary Men. Reserve Battalion 101 and the Final Solution in Poland*. London: Penguin.

Browning, C. (2005), *The Origins of the Final Solution. The Evolution of Nazi Jewish Policy, September 1939–March 1942*. London: Arrow Books.

Bruch, R. v. (2000), *Friedrich Naumann in seiner Zeit*. Berlin, New York: De Gruyter.

Bruns, F. [in preparation]. 'Medizinethik und Arzttum im Nationalsozialismus. Entwicklungen und Protagonisten in Berlin (1939–1945)', Diss. med., Hannover [in preparation].

Bruns, F. and Frewer, A. (2005), 'Fachgeschichte als Politikum: Medizinhistoriker in Berlin und Graz im Dienst des NS-Staates', in *Jahrbuch Medizin, Gesellschaft und Geschichte*, 24 (2005) pp. 147–76.

Bumke, O. (1952), *Erinnerungen und Betrachtungen: Der Weg eines deutschen Psychiaters*. Munich: Pflaum.

Bürger-Prinz, H. (1973), *Ein Psychiater berichtet*. Munich: Droemer Knaur.

Burleigh, M. (1994), *Death and Deliverance: 'Euthanasia' in Germany, 1900–1945*. Cambridge, New York: Cambridge University Press.

Burleigh, M. (1997), *Ethics and Extermination. Reflections on Nazi Genocide*. Cambridge, New York: Cambridge University Press.

Burleigh, M. (2000), *The Third Reich. A New History*. Basingstoke, Oxford: Macmillan.

Burman, W. P. (ed.), (1985), *The First German War Crimes Trial. Chief Judge Walter B. Beals' Desk Notebook of the Doctors' Trial*. Chapel Hill: Documentary Publications.

Burrin, P. (1994), *Hitler and the Jews. The Genesis of the Holocaust*. London, New York, Sydney, Auckland: Arnold.

Cantow J. and Kaiser, J-C. (eds.), (2005), *Paul Gerhard Braune (1887–1954). Ein Mann der Kirche und Diakonie in schwieriger Zeit*. Stuttgart: Kohlhammer.

Caplan, A. L. (ed.), (1992), *When Medicine Went Mad*. Totowa NJ: Humana Press.

Cefrey, H. (2001), *Doctor Josef Mengele: the Angel of Death*. New York: Rosen Publishing Group.

Cesarani, D. (2004), *Eichmann. His Life and Crimes*. London: William Heinemann.

Cornwell, J. (2003), *Hitler's Scientists. Science, War and the Devil's Pact*. London: Viking.

Curtius, F. (1920), *Deutsche Briefe und Elsässische Erinnerungen*. Frauenfeld: Huber.

Dahl, M. (1998), *Endstation Spiegelgrund. Die Tötung behinderter Kinder während des Nationalsozialismus am Beispiel einer Kinderfachabteilung in Wien 1940 bis 1945*. Vienna: Erasmus.

Dahl, M. (2000), 'Die Tötung behinderter Kinder in der Anstalt Am Spiegelgrund 1940 bis 1945', in E. Gabriel and W. Neugebauer (eds.), *NS-Euthanasie in Wien*. Vienna, Cologne, Weimar: Böhlau Verlag, pp. 75–92.

Daub, U. (1992), 'Krankenhaus-Sonderanlage Aktion Brandt in Köppern im Taunus. Die letzte Phase der "Euthanasie" in Frankfurt am Main. Zur politischen und historiographischen Rezeption der "Aktion Brandt"'. *Psychologie und Gesellschaftskritik*, 16 (1992) 2, 39–68.

Davidson, E. (1997), *The Trial of the Germans*. Columbia, London: University of Missouri Press.

'Denkschrift Himmlers über die Behandlung der Fremdvölkischen im Osten (Mai 1940)'. *Vierteljahreshefte für Zeitschichte*, 5 (1957), 194–98.

'Der Grosse Bauherr Unterwegs'. *Illustrierter Beobachter*, 16 (1937), 319f.

'Der Große Sieg'. *Illustrierter Beobachter*, 15 (1936), 539.

Diepgen, P. and Rostock, P. (eds.), (1939), *Das Universitätsklinikum in Berlin. Seine Ärzte und seine wissenschaftliche Leistung 1810–1933*. Leipzig: Barth.

Dörner, K. (ed.), (1989), *Der Krieg gegen die psychisch Kranken*. Frankfurt: Mabuse-Verlag.

Dörner, K. and Ebbinghaus, A. (eds.), (1999), *The Nuremberg Medical Trial 1946/47. Transcripts, Material of the Prosecution and Defense, Related Documents*. Microfiche-Edition, Munich: Saur.

Dörner, K. and Ebbinghaus, A. (eds.), (2001), *The Nuremberg Medical Trial 1946/47. Transcripts, Material of the Prosecution and Defense, Related Documents*. Guide to the Microfiche-Edition, Munich: Saur.

Döscher, H.-J. (ed.), (1988), *"Reichskristallnacht": die Novemberpogrome 1938*. Frankfurt a.M., Berlin: Ullstein.

Duff, C. (1948), *A Handbook on Hanging*. London: Freedom Press.

Ebbinghaus, A. (ed.), (1987), *Opfer und Täterinnen*. Nördlingen: Greno.

Ebbinghaus, A. and Dörner, K. (eds.), (2001), *Vernichten und Heilen: Der Nürnberger Ärzteprozeß und seine Folgen*. Berlin: Aufbau-Verlag.

Eberle, H. and Uhl, M. (2005), *The Hitler Book. The Secret Dossier Prepared for Stalin*. London: John Murray.

Eckart, W. U. (1998a), 'Generaloberstabsarzt Prof. Dr. med. Siegfried Handloser', in G. Ueberschär (ed.), *Hitlers militärische Elite*, vol. 2. Darmstadt: Primus Verlag, pp. 87–92.

Eckart, W. U. (1998b), 'SS-Gruppenführer und Generalleutnant der Waffen-SS Prof. Dr. med. Karl Brandt', in G. Ueberschär (ed.), *Hitlers militärische Elite*, vol. 2. Darmstadt: Primus Verlag, pp. 12–19.

Eckart, W. U. (1998c), 'SS-Obergruppenführer und General der Waffen-SS Prof. Dr. med. Ernst Grawitz', in G. Ueberschär (ed.), *Hitlers militärische Elite*, vol. 2. Darmstadt: Primus Verlag, pp. 63–71.

Eckart, W. U. (ed.), (2006), *Man, Medicine and the State: the Human Body as an Object of Government-Sponsored Medical Research*. Stuttgart: Steiner.

Eckart, W. U. and Neumann, A. (eds.), (2006), *Medizin im Zweiten Weltkrieg. Militärmedizinische Praxis und medizinische Wissenschaft im 'Totalen Krieg'*. Paderborn, Munich, Vienna, Zurich: Schöningh.

Eder, A. (1998), *Flüchtige Heimat: Jüdische Displaced Persons in Landsberg am Lech 1945 bis 1950*. Munich: Uni-Druck.

Elkeles, B. (1996), *Der moralische Diskurs über das medizinische Menschenexperiment im 19. Jahrhundert*. Stuttgart, Jena, New York: Fischer.

Engel, G. (1974), *Heeresadjutant bei Hitler: 1938–1943. Aufzeichnungen des Majors Engel*. Stuttgart: Deutsche Verlags-Anstalt.

Eschebach, I. (1997), "'Ermittlungskomplex Ravensbrück'. Das Konzentrationslager in den Akten des Ministeriums für Staatssicherheit', in S. Jacobeit (ed.), *Forschungsschwerpunk Ravensbrück. Beiträge zur Geschichte des Frauen-Konzentrationslagers*. Berlin: Hentrich, pp. 94–114.

Essner, C. (2002), *Die 'Nürnberger Gesetze' oder die Verwaltung des Rassenwahns 1933–1945*. Paderborn, Munich, Vienna, Zurich: Schöningh.

Evans, R. J. (2003), *The Coming of the Third Reich*. London: Allen Lane.

Evans, R. J. (2005), *The Third Reich in Power*. London: Allen Lane.

Faulstich, H. (1998), *Hungersterben in der Psychiatrie 1914–1949: mit einer Topographie der NS-Psychiatrie*. Freiburg im Br: Lambertus-Verlag.

Fest, J. (1999), *Speer. Eine Biographie*. Berlin: Alexander Fest Verlag.

Fox, J. (2000), *Filming Women in the Third Reich*. Oxford, New York: Berg.

Frei, N. (1987), *Der Führerstaat. Nationalsozialistische Herrschaft 1933–1945*. Munich: Deutscher Taschenbuch Verlag.

Frei, N. (ed.), (1991), *Medizin und Gesundheitspolitik in der NS-Zeit*. Munich: Oldenbourg.

Frei, N. (1996), *Vergangenheitspolitik. Die Anfänge der Bundesrepublik und die NS-Vergangenheit*. Munich: Beck.

Frei, N. (2001), *Karrieren im Zwielicht. Hitlers Eliten nach 1945*. Frankfurt a.M., New York: Campus.

Frewer, A. (2000), *Medizin und Moral in Weimarer Republik und Nationalsozialismus. Die Zeitschrift 'Ethik' unter Emil Abderhalden*. Frankfurt a.M., New York: Campus.

Frewer, A. and Eickhoff, C. (eds.), (2000), *'Euthanasie' und die aktuelle Sterbehilfe-Debatte. Die historischen Hintergründe medizinischer Ethik*. Frankfurt a.M., New York: Campus.

Frewer, A. and Neuman, J. N. (eds.), (2001), *Medizingeschichte und Medizinethik. Kontroversen und Begründungsansätze 1900–1950*. Frankfurt a.M., New York: Campus.

Frewer, A. and Schmidt, U. (eds.), (2007), *Standards der Forschung*. Frankfurt a.M., New York: Olms.

Frewer, A. and Siedbürger, G. (eds), (2004). *Medizin und Zwangsarbeit im Nationalsozialismus. Einsatz und Behandlung von 'Ausländern' im Gesundheitswesen*. Frankfurt a.M., New York: Campus.

Frewer, A. and Wiesemann, C. (eds.), (1999), *Medizinverbrechen vor Gericht. Das Urteil im Nürnberger Ärzteprozeß gegen Karl Brandt und andere sowie aus dem Prozeß gegen Generalfeldmarschall Milch*. Erlangen, Jena: Palm & Enge.

Frewer, A., Schmidt, U. and Wolters, C. (2004), 'Hilfskräfte, Hausschwangere, Untersuchungsobjekte. Der Umgang mit Zwangsarbeitenden in der Universitätsfrauenklinik Göttingen', in A. Frewer and G. Siedbürger (eds.), *Medizin und Zwangsarbeit im Nationalsozialismus. Einsatz und Behandlung von 'Ausländern' im Gesundheitswesen*. Frankfurt a.M., New York: Campus, pp. 341–62.

Frewer *et al.* (2001), 'Zwangsarbeit und Medizin im 'Dritten Reich': Ein Desiderat historischer Forschung. *Deutsches Ärzteblatt*, (2001), A-2866–70.

Friedlander, H. (1995), *The Origins of Nazi Genocide. From Euthanasia to the Final Solution*. Chapel Hill, London: University of North Carolina Press.

Friedländer, S. (1997), *Nazi Germany and the Jews. vol. 1. The Years of Persecution, 1933–1939*. London: Weidenfeld & Nicolson.

Friedlander, H. (2000), 'Victor Brack. Parteimann, SS-Mann und Mordmanager', in R. Smelser and E. Syring (eds.), *Die SS. Elite unterm Totenkopf. 30 Lebensläufe*. Paderborn, Munich, Vienna, Zurich: Schöningh, pp. 88–99.

Friedrich, J. (2002), *Der Brand. Deutschland im Bombenkrieg 1940–1945*. Munich: Propyläen.

Fröhlich, E. (ed.), (1987), *Die Tagebücher von Joseph Goebbels, Sämtliche Fragmente, part I, Aufzeichnungen 1923–1941*, vols 1–4. Munich: Saur.

Fröhlich, E. (ed.), (1993–1996), *Die Tagebücher von Joseph Goebbels, part II Diktate 1941–1945*, vols 1–15. Munich: Saur.

Fulbrook, M. (ed.), (1997), *German History since 1800*. London: Arnold.

Füllberg-Stolberg, C. *et al.* (eds.), (1994), *Frauen in Konzentrationslagern Bergen-Belsen, Ravensbrück*. Bremen: Edition Temmen.

Gabriel, E. and Neugebauer, W. (eds.), (2000), *NS-Euthanasie in Wien*. Vienna, Cologne, Weimar: Böhlau Verlag.

Galbraith, J. K. (1945), 'The Effects of Strategic Bombing on the German War Economy. The United States Strategic Bombing Survey'. n. p.

Galbraith, J. K. (1981), *A Life in Our Times: Memoirs*. Boston: Deutsch.

Geißler, E. (1999), *Biologische Waffen – nicht in Hitlers Arsenalen. Biologische und Toxin-Kampfmittel in Deutschland von 1915 bis 1945*. Münster: LIT Verlag.

Gellately, R. (2001), *Backing Hitler. Consent and Coercion in Nazi Germany*. Oxford: Oxford University Press.

Gellermann, G. W. (1986), *Der Krieg, der nicht stattfand. Möglichkeiten, Überlegungen und Entscheidungen der deutschen Obersten Führung zur Verwendung chemischer Kampfstoffe im Zweiten Weltkrieg*. Koblenz: Bernard & Graefe.

Gerlach, C. (1998), *Krieg, Ernährung, Völkermord. Forschungen zur deutschen Vernichtungspolitik im Zweiten Weltkrieg*. Hamburg: Hamburger Edition.

Gerlach, C. (1999), *Kalkulierte Morde: die deutsche Wirtschafts- und Vernichtungspolitik in Weißrußland 1941 bis 1944*. Hamburg: Hamburger Edition.

Gerlach, C. (2004), *Das letzte Kapitel. Der Mord an den ungarischen Juden 1944–1945*. Frankfurt a.M: Fischer.

Gerstenberger, F. (1995), 'Strategische Erinnerungen. Die Memoiren deutscher Offiziere', in H. Heer and K. Naumann (eds.), *Vernichtungskrieg. Verbrechen der Wehrmacht 1941–1944*. Hamburg: Hamburger Edition, pp. 620–33.

Geyer, M. (1982), 'Review of "Der Hitler Mythos: Volksmeinung und Propaganda im Dritten Reich" (by Ian Kershaw)'. *The Journal of Modern History*, 54, (1982) 4, 811–12.

Giesler, H. (1977), *Ein anderer Hitler. Bericht seines Architekten. Erlebnisse, Gespräche, Reflexionen*. Leoni am Starnberger See: Druffel-Verlag.

Gilbert, G. M. (1962), *Nürnberger Tagebuch*. Frankfurt a.M: Fischer Bücherei.

Glover, J. (1999), *Humanity. A Moral History of the Twentieth Century*. London: Jonathan Cape.

Goliszek, A. (2003), *In the Name of Science: A History of Secret Programs, Medical Research, and Human Experimentation*. New York: St Martin's Press.

Görlitz, W. and Quint, H. A. (1952), *Hitler. Eine Biographie*. Stuttgart: Steingrüben-Verlag.

Gruchmann, L. (1983), '"Blutschutzgesetz" und Justiz. Zu Entstehung und Auswirkung des Nürnberger Gesetzes vom 15. September 1935'. *Vierteljahreshefte für Zeitgeschichte*, 3 (1983), 418–42.

Gruchmann, L. (1990), *Justiz im Dritten Reich 1933–1940. Anpassung und Unterwerfung in der Ära Gürtner*. Munich: Oldenbourg.

Günzler, C. (1996), *Albert Schweitzer. Einführung in sein Denken*. Munich: Beck.

Gussatschenko, W., Dwornitschenko, O. and Sawjakow, S. (eds.), (1996), *Unbekannte Kapitel des Zweiten Weltkrieges. Hitler. Dokumente aus den Geheimarchiven des KGB*. Darmstadt: Progress.

Gütt, A., Rüdin, E. and Ruttke, F. (eds.), (1936), *Gesetz zur Verhütung erbkranken Nachwuchses vom 14. Juli 1933 mit Auszug aus dem Gesetz gegen gefährliche Gewohnheitsverbrecher und über Maßnahmen der Sicherung und Besserung vom 24. November 1933*. Munich: Lehmann.

Hachmeister, S. (1992), *Kinopropaganda gegen Kranke. Die Instrumentalisierung des Spielfilms 'Ich klage an' für das nationalsozialistische 'Euthanasieprogramm'*. Baden-Baden: Nomos-Verlags-Gesellschaft.

Hamann, B. (1999), *Hitler's Vienna. A Dictator's Apprenticeship*. Oxford, New York: Oxford University Press.

Hamann, B. (2002), *Winifred Wagner oder Hitlers Bayreuth*. Munich: Piper.

Hamilton, C. (1984), *Leaders and Personalities of the Third Reich. Their Biographies, Portraits, and Autographs*. San Jose, California: R. J. Bender Publishing.

Hansen, F. (1993), *Biologische Kriegsführung im Dritten Reich*. Frankfurt a.M., New York: Campus.

Harms, I. (1997), '"Aktion Brandt" und die Asylierung Tuberkulöser. Die Räumung der Bewahr- und Pflegeanstalt Blankenburg und der Umbau zum "Sonderkrankenhaus Aktion Brandt"', in *Beiträge zur nationalsozialistischen Gesundheits- und Sozialpolitik*, 15, pp. 149–78.

Harp, S.L. (1998), *Learning to be Loyal. Primary Schooling as Nation Building in Alsace and Lorraine, 1850–1940*. De Kalb: Northern Illinois University Press.

Harvey, D.A. (2001), *Constructing Class and Nationality in Alsace 1830–1945*. De Kalb: Northern Illinois University Press.

Hastedt, H. (1998), *Der Wert des Einzelnen. Eine Verteidigung des Individualismus*. Frankfurt a.M: Suhrkamp.

Heckert, P. and Scholz, H.-J. (n. d.), 'Kirche im Steinbacher Grund. Auszüge aus den großen, ausführlichen "Steinbach-Hallenberger Chroniken"' (unpublished manuscript).

Heer, H. (2005), 'Killing Fields. Die Wehrmacht und der Holocaust', in H. Heer and K. Naumann (eds.), *Vernichtungskrieg. Verbrechen der Wehrmacht 1941–1944*. Hamburg: Hamburger Edition, pp. 57–77.

Heer, H. and Naumann, K. (eds.), (1995), *Vernichtungskrieg. Verbrechen der Wehrmacht 1941–1944*. Hamburg: Hamburger Edition.

Heiber, H. (1970), *Reichsführer! …: Briefe an und von Himmler*. Munich: Deutscher Taschenbuch Verlag.

Heiber, H. (ed.), (2001), *Der ganz normale Wahnsinn unterm Hakenkreuz. Triviales und Absonderliches aus den Akten des Dritten Reiches*. Munich: Herbig.

Heiber, H. and Longerich, P. (eds.), (1983–1992), *Akten der Partei-Kanzlei der NSDAP. Rekonstruktion eines verlorengegangenen Bestandes*. Munich: Saur.

Heinkel, E. (1953), *Stürmisches Leben*. Stuttgart: Mundus-Verlag.

Herbert, U. (1996), *Best. Biographische Studien über Radikalismus, Weltanschauung und Vernunft, 1903–1989*. Bonn: Dietz.

Herf, J. (1984), *Reactionary Modernism. Technology, Culture, and Politics in Weimar and the Third Reich*. Cambridge, New York: Cambridge University Press.

Herz, R. (1994), *Hoffmann & Hitler. Fotographie als Medium des Führer-Mythos*. Munich: Fotomuseum im Münchner Stadtmuseum.

Hinz-Wessels, A. *et al.* (2005), 'Zur bürokratischen Abwicklung eines Massenmords. Die "Euthanasie"-Aktion im Spiegel neuer Dokumente'. *Vierteljahreshefte für Zeitgeschichte*, 1, 79–107.

Hirschfeld, G. and Jersak, T. (eds.), (2004), *Karrieren im Nationalsozialismus. Funktionseliten zwischen Mitwirkung und Distanz*. Frankfurt a.M., New York: Campus.

Hitler, A. (1936), *Mein Kampf*. Munich: Zentralverlag der NSDAP.

Hitler, A. (1939), *Mein Kampf*. London: Hurst & Blackett.

Hoche, A. (1936), *Jahresringe. Innenansicht eines Menschenlebens*. Munich, Berlin: Lehmann.

Hoche, A. (1937), *Aus der Werkstatt*. Lehmann: Berlin.

Hochmuth, A. (1997), *Spurensuche: Eugenik, Sterilisation und Patientenmorde und die v. Bodelschwinghschen Anstalten Bethel 1929–1945*. Bielefeld: Bethel Verlag.

Hochmuth, A. (ed.), (1979), *Bethel in den Jahren 1939–1943. Eine Dokumentation zur Vernichtung lebensunwerten Lebens*. Bethel near Bielefeld: Verlagshandlung der Anstalt Bethel.

Hockerts, H. G. (ed.), (1998), *Drei Wege deutscher Sozialstaatlichkeit. NS-Diktatur, Bundesrepublilk und DDR im Vergleich*. Munich: Oldenbourg.

Hockerts, H. G. (ed.), (2002), *Akten der Reichskanzlei: Regierung Hitler 1933–1945*, vol. 3, 1936. Munich: Oldenbourg.

Hohendorf, G. and Magull-Seltenreich, A. (eds), *Von der Heilkunde zur Massentötung*. Heidelberg: Wunderhorn.

Hohmann, J. S. (1993), *Der "Euthanasie"-Prozeß Dresden 1947. Eine zeitgeschichtliche Dokumentation*. Frankfurt a.M.: Lang.

Hühn, M. (1989), 'Psychiatrie im Nationalsozialismus am Beispiel der Wittenauer Heilstätten', in G. Aly (ed.), *Aktion T4, 1939–1945. Die"Euthanasie"-Zentrale in der Tiergartenstraße 4*. Berlin: Hentrich, pp. 183–97.

Irving, D. (1970), *Die Tragödie der Deutschen Luftwaffe. Aus den Akten und Erinnerungen von Feldmarschall Milch*. Frankfurt a.M.: Ullstein.

Irving, D. (1979), *Rommel. Eine Biographie*. Hamburg: Hoffmann und Campe.

Irving, D. (1983a), *Die geheimen Tagebücher des Dr. Morell. Leibarzt Adolf Hitlers*. Munich: Goldmann.

Irving, D. (1983b), *Morell, Theodor Gilbert, 1886–1948. The secret diaries of Hitler's doctor*. New York: Macmillan.

Jacobeit, S. (ed.), (1995), *'Ich grüße Euch als freier Mensch'. Quellenedition zur Befreiung des Frauen-Konzentrationslagers Ravensbrück im April 1945*. Berlin: Hentrich.

Jacobeit, S. (ed.), (1997), *Forschungsschwerpunk Ravensbrück. Beiträge zur Geschichte des Frauen-Konzentrationslagers*. Berlin: Hentrich.

Jaehn, T. (1985), 'Zur Rolle Paul Diepgens, Direktor des Instituts für Geschichte der Medizin und der Naturwissenschaften von 1930–1947, in den internationalen Beziehungen des Instituts von 1930–1945'. Med. Diplomarbeit, Berlin.

Jaehn, T. (1991), 'Der Medizinhistoriker Paul Diepgen (1878–1966). Eine Untersuchung zur methodologischen, historiographischen und zeitgeschichtlichen Problemen und Einflüssen im Werk Paul Diepgens unter besondere Berücksichtigung seiner persönlichen Rolle in Lehre, Wissenschaftspolitik und Wissenschaftsorganisation während des Dritten Reiches'. Diss.med., Berlin.

Jansen, C., Niethammer, L. and Weisbrod, B. (eds.), (1995), *Von der Aufgabe der Freiheit: Politische Verantwortung und bürgerliche Gesellschaft im 19. und 20. Jahrhundert. Festschrift für Hans Mommsen zum 5. November 1995*. Berlin: Akademischer Verlag.

Jasper, H. (1991), *Maximinian de Crinis (1889–1945). Eine Studie zur Psychiatrie im Nationalsozialismus*. Husum: Matthiesen.

Johnson, E. A. (1999), *Nazi Terror. The Gestapo, Jews, and Ordinary Germans*. London: John Murray.

Junge, T. (2002), *Bis zur letzten Stunde. Hitlers Sekretärin erzählt ihr Leben*. Munich: Claassen Verlag.

Jütte, R. (ed.), (1997), *Geschichte der deutschen Ärzteschaft*. Cologne: Deutscher Ärzte Verlag.

Kaminsky, U. (1995), *Zwangssterilisation und 'Euthanasie' im Rheinland. Evangelische Erziehungsanstalten sowie Heil- und Pflegeanstalten 1933–1945*. Cologne: Rheinland-Verlag.

Kaminsky, U. (2000), '"Aktion Brandt" – Katastrophenschutz und Vernichtung', in Sandner, P. (ed.), *Arbeitskreis zur Erforschung der nationalsozialistischen "Euthanasie" und Zwangssterilisation. Protokoll der Herbsttagung 19. bis 21. November 1999 in Gießen*. Ulm: Klemm und Oelschläger, pp. 68–83.

Kater, M. H. (1985), 'Doctor Leonard Conti and his Nemesis: The Failure of Centralized Medicine in the Third Reich'. *Central European History*, 18 (1985), 299–325.

Kater, M. H. (1989), *Doctors under Hitler*. Chapel Hill, London: University of North Carolina Press.

Katz, J. (1972), *Experimentation with Human Beings*. New York: Russel Sage Foundation.

Katz, J. (1992), 'The Consent Principle of the Nuremberg Code: Its Significance Then and Now', in G. J. Annas and M. A. Grodin (eds.), *The Nazi Doctors and the Nuremberg Code. Human Rights in Human Experimentation*. Oxford, New York: Oxford University Press, pp. 227–39.

Katz, J. (1993), 'Ethics and Clinical Research Revisited – A Tribute to Henry K. Beecher'. *Hastings Center Report*, 23 (1993) 31–39.

Kehrl, H. (1973), *Krisenmanager im Dritten Reich. 6 Jahre Frieden – 6 Jahre Krieg. Erinnerungen*. Düsseldorf: Droste.

Kepplinger, B. (2003), 'Die Tötungsanstalt Hartheim 1940–1945', in T. Oelschläger (ed.), *Erforschung der nationalsozialistischen 'Euthanasie' und Zwangssterilisation. Beiträge zur NS-'Euthanasie'-Forschung 2002*. Ulm: Klemm und Oelschläger, pp. 53–109.

Kershaw, I. (1987), *The 'Hitler Myth': Image and Reality in the Third Reich*. Oxford: Clarendon.

Kershaw, I. (1991), *Hitler. Profiles in Power*. London: Longman.

Kershaw, I. (1993), '"Working towards the Führer": Reflections on the Nature of the Hitler Dictatorship'. *Journal of Contemporary European History*, 2 (1993), 103–18.

Kershaw, I. (1995), '"Cumulative Radicalisation" and the Uniqueness of National Socialism', in C. Jansen, L. Niethammer and B. Weisbrod (eds.), *Von der Aufgabe der Freiheit: Politische Verantwortung und bürgerliche Gesellschaft im 19. und 20. Jahrhundert. Festschrift für Hans Mommsen zum 5. November 1995*. Berlin: Akademischer Verlag, pp. 323–36.

Kershaw, I. (1997a), 'Hitler and the Nazi Dictatorship', in M. Fulbrook (ed.), *German History since 1800*. London: Arnold, pp. 318–38.

Kershaw, I. (1997b), *The Nazi Dictatorship. Problems and Perspectives of Interpretation*. London: Arnold.

Kershaw, I. (1998), *Hitler. 1889–1936: Hubris*. London: Allen Lane.

Kershaw, I. (2000), *Hitler. 1936–45: Nemesis*. London: Allen Lane.

Kershaw, I. (2005), *Death in the Bunker*. London: Penguin.

Kersting, F.-W. (1996), *Anstaltsärzte zwischen Kaiserreich und Bundesrepublik. Das Beispiel Westfalen*. Paderborn, Munich, Vienna, Zurich: Schöningh.

Killian, H. (1972), 'Waren Morell und Bormann Komplizen'. *Die deutsche Nation in Geschichte und Gegenwart. Zeitschrift für historische Wahrheitsfindung*, 20 (1972) 2/3, 34–5.

Kirkpatrick, I. (1959), *The Inner Circle: Memoirs of Ivone Kirkpatrick*. London: Macmillan.

Klee, E. (1986), *Dokumente zur 'Euthanasie'*. Frankfurt a.M: Fischer.

Klee, E. (1991), *'Euthanasie' im NS-Staat. Die 'Vernichtung lebensunwerten Lebens'*. Frankfurt a.M: Fischer.

Klee, E. (1997), *Auschwitz. Die NS-Medizin und ihre Opfer*. Frankfurt a.M.: Fischer.

Klee, E. (2001), *Deutsche Medizin im Dritten Reich. Karrieren vor und nach 1945*. Frankfurt a.M: Fischer.

Klee, E. (2003), *Das Personenlexikon zum Dritten Reich. Wer war was vor und nach 1945?* Frankfurt a.M: Fischer.

Klemperer, V. (1998), *I shall Bear Witness. The Diaries of Victor Klemperer 1933–41*. London: Phoenix.

Klier, F. (1994), *Die Kaninchen von Ravensbrück*. Munich: Droemer Knaur.

Kolb, S. and Seithe, H. (eds.), (1998), *Medizin und Gewissen. 50 Jahre nach dem Nürnberger Ärzteprozeß – Kongreßdokumentation*. Frankfurt a.M: Mabuse Verlag.

Koonz, C. (2005), *The Nazi Conscience*. Cambridge, Mass., London: Belknap Press.

Kopke, C. and Schultz, G. (2006), 'Die Menschenversuche mit dem Kampfstoff Lost im KZ Sachsenhausen (1939) und die Debatte über die Rolle des Wehrmachtstoxikologen Wolfgang Wirth', in W. U. Eckart and A. Neumann (eds.), *Medizin im Zweiten Weltkrieg. Militärmedizinische Praxis und medizinische Wissenschaft im 'Totalen Krieg'*. Paderborn, Munich, Vienna, Zurich: Schöningh, pp. 113–29.

Krey, U. (2000), 'Der Naumann-Kreis: Charisma und politische Emanzipation', in R. v. Bruch (ed.), *Friedrich Naumann in seiner Zeit*. Berlin, New York: De Gruyter, pp. 115–47.

Krieg, M. (ed.), (1990), *100 Jahre Bergmannsheil*. Bochum: Bergbau-Berufsgenossenschaft.

Kühl, S. (1990), 'Bethel zwischen Anpassung und Widerstand. Die Auseinandersetzung der von Bodelschwinghschen Anstalten mit der Zwangssterilisation und den Kranken- und Behindertenmorden im Nationalsozialismus' (unpublished manuscript).

Kühl, S. (1994), *The Nazi Connection. Eugenics, American Racism, and German National Socialism*. Oxford, New York: Oxford University Press.

Kühl, S. (1997a), *Die Internationale der Rassisten. Aufstieg und Niedergang der internationalen Bewegung für Eugenik und Rassenhygiene im 20. Jahrhundert*. Frankfurt a.M., New York: Campus.

Kühl, S. (1997b), 'Eugenik und "Vernichtung lebensunwerten Lebens": Der Fall Bethel aus einer internationalen Perspektive', in M. Benad, (ed.), *Friedrich v. Bodelschwingh d.J. und die Betheler Anstalten. Frömmigkeit und Weltgestaltung*. Stuttgart, Berlin, Köln: Kohlhammer, pp. 54–67.

Kümmel, W. F. (2001), 'Geschichte, Staat und Ethik: Deutsche Medizinhistoriker 1933–1945 im Dienste "nationalsozialistischer Erziehung"', in A. Frewer and J. N. Neumann (eds.), *Medizingeschichte und Medizinethik. Kontroversen und Begründungsansätze 1900–1950*. Frankfurt a.M: Campus, pp. 167–203.

LaFleur, W. R., Boehme, G. and Shimazono, S. (eds.), (2007), *Dark Medicine. Rationalizing Unethical Medical Research in Germany, Japan, and the United States*. Bloomington: Indiana University Press.

Lammel, H.-U. (1993), 'Tradition auf Abruf. Zur Personalpolitik an der Berliner Chirurgischen Universitätsklinik in der Ziegelstraße zwischen 1933 und 1945', in G. Grau and P. Schneck (eds.), *Akademische Karrieren im "Dritten Reich". Beiträge zur Personal- und Berufungspolitik an Medizinischen Fakultäten*. Berlin: Institut für Geschichte der Medizin, pp. 63–75.

Lammel, H.-U. (1994), 'Chirurgie und Nationalsozialismus am Beispiel der Berliner Chirurgischen Universitätsklinik in der Ziegelstraße', in W. Fischer *et al.* (eds.), *Exodus von Wissenschaften aus Berlin*. Berlin, New York: De Gruyter, pp. 568–91.

Lederer, S. (1995), *Subjected to Science. Human Experimentation before the Second World War*. Baltimore, London: Johns Hopkins University Press.

Lenk, H. (2000), *Albert Schweitzer – Ethik als konkrete Humanität*. Münster: LIT Verlag.

Lewerenz, O. (1994), *Zwischen Reich Gottes und Weltreich. Friedrich Naumann in seiner Frankfurter Zeit*. Sinzheim: Pro Universitate Verlag.

Ley, A. (2001), 'Wissenschaftlicher Fortschritt, äußerer Druck und innere Bereitschaft. Zu den Bedingungen verbrecherischer Menschenversuche in der NS-Zeit', in A. Ley and M.M. Ruisinger (eds.), *Gewissenlos – Gewissenhaft. Menschenversuche im Konzentrationslager*. Erlangen: Specht Verlag, pp. 35–51.

Ley, A. and Ruisinger, M. M. (eds.), (2001), *Gewissenlos – Gewissenhaft. Menschenversuche im Konzentrationslager*. Erlangen: Specht Verlag.

Leyendecker, B. and Klapp, B. F. (1989), 'Deutsche Hepatitisforschung im Zweiten Weltkrieg', in C. Pross and G. Aly (eds.), *Der Wert des Menschen. Medizin in Deutschland 1918–1945*. Berlin: Hentrich, pp. 261–93.

Liere, K.-P. (1980), 'Aus den Akten der Reichskanzlei: Über Krankenhäuser, Krankenanstalten und Bäderwesen im Deutschen Reich von 1921–1945 mit dem Versuch einer Darstellung der "Aktion Brandt", d.h. der Errichtung von Ausweichkrankenhäusern durch das Reich im letzten Kriege'. Diss. Med. Bochum.

Lifton, R. J. (1985), *Mengele: What made this Man?* New York: *New York Times*.

Lifton, R. J. (1986), *The Nazi Doctors. Medical Killing and the Psychology of Genocide*. New York: Basic Books.

Linge, H. (1980), *Bis zum Untergang. Als Chef des persönlichen Dienstes bei Hitler*. Munich, Berlin: Herbig.

Lloyd-Jones, H. (ed.), (1994), *Sophocles*. Cambridge, Mass., London: Harvard University Press.

Longerich, P. (1998), *Politik der Vernichtung*. Munich, Zurich: Piper.

Longerich, P. (2003), *The Unwritten Order. Hitler's Role in the Final Solution*. Stroud: Tempus.

Longerich, P. (2006), *'Davon haben wir nichts gewusst!'. Die Deutschen und die Judenverfolgung 1933–1945*. Munich: Siedler.

Lynch, M. and Bogen, D. (1996), *The Spectacle of History: Speech, Text, and Memory of the Iran-Contra Hearings*. Durham: Duke University Press.

McElligott, A. and Kirk, T. (2003), *Working towards the Führer*. Manchester, New York: Manchester University Press.

Maio, G. (2002), *Ethik der Forschung am Menschen: Zur Begründung der Moral in ihrer historischen Bedingtheit*. Stuttgart-Bad Cannstatt: Frommann-Holzboog.

Marien-Lunderup, R. (1993), 'Die Verlegungen in die Lübecker Heilanstalt Stecknitz', in K. Böhme and U. Lohalm (eds.), *Wege in den Tod. Hamburgs Anstalt Langenhorn und die Euthanasie in der Zeit des Nationalsozialismus*. Hamburg: Ergebnisse Verlag, pp. 233–58.

Martin, D. (1994a), 'Menschenversuche im Krankenrevier des KZ Ravensbrück', in C. Füllberg-Stolberg *et al.* (eds.), *Frauen in Konzentrationslagern Bergen-Belsen, Ravensbrück*. Bremen: Edition Temmen, pp. 99–112.

Martin, D. (1994b), 'Versuchkaninchen – Opfer medizinischer Experimente', in C. Füllberg-Stolberg *et al.* (eds.), *Frauen in Konzentrationslagern Bergen-Belsen, Ravensbrück*. Bremen: Edition Temmen, pp. 113–22.

Maser, W. (1979), *Nuremberg. A Nation on Trial*. London: Allen Lane.

Meier, C. (1996), 'Die Gnade der späten Verurteilung. Eine kurze Geschichte der Gnadenentscheidungen zu den zwölf Nürnberger Prozessen'. *1999*, 4, 73–85.

Meissner, H.-O. (1988), *Junge Jahre im Reichspräsidentenpalais. Erinnerungen an Ebert und Hindenburg 1919–1934*. Munich: Bechtle.

Meyer, E. (1986), *Menschen zwischen Weser und Ems 1933–1945. Wie sie lebten, was sie erlebten*. Oldenburg: Holzberg.

Michejda, K. (1947), 'Operacje Doswiadczalne w obozie koncentracyjnym Ravensbrück'. *Biuletyn Glownej Komisji Badania Zbrodni Hitlerowskich w Polsce*, 2 (1947) 123–75.

Mitscherlich, A. and Mielke, F. (eds.), (1947), *Das Diktat der Menschenverachtung. Der Nürnberger Ärzteprozeß und seine Quellen*. Heidelberg: Schneider.

Mitscherlich, A. and Mielke, F. (eds.), (1949a), *Doctors of Infamy. The Story of the Nazi Medical Crimes*. New York: Schuman.

Mitscherlich, A. and Mielke, F. (eds), (1949b), *Wissenschaft ohne Menschlichkeit. Medizinische und eugenische Irrwege unter Diktatur, Bürokratie und Krieg. Mit einem Vorwort der Arbeitsgemeinschaft der westdeutschen Ärztekammern*. Heidelberg: Schneider.

Mitscherlich, A. and Mielke, F. (eds.), (1960), *Medizin ohne Menschlichkeit*. Frankfurt a.M: Fischer-Bücherei.

Moll, A. (1902), *Ärztliche Ethik. Die Pflichten des Arztes in allen Beziehungen seiner Thätigkeit*. Stuttgart: Enke.

Möller, H., Dahm, V. and Mehringer, H. (1999), *Die tödliche Utopie. Bilder, Texte, Dokumente, Daten zum Dritten Reich*. Munich: Institut für Zeitgeschichte.

Mommsen, H. (2003), 'Beyond the Nation State: the German Resistance against Hitler, and the Future of Europe', in A. McElligott and T. Kirk (eds.), *Working towards the Führer*. Manchester, New York: Manchester University Press, pp. 246–59.

Moreno, J. D. (1996), '"The Only Feasible Means": The Pentagon's Ambivalent Relationship with the Nuremberg Code'. *Hastings Center Report*, 26 (1996), 11–19.

Moreno, J. D. (1997), 'Reassessing the Influence of the Nuremberg Code on American Medical Ethics'. *Journal of Contemporary Health Law and Policy*, 13 (1997), 347–60.

Moreno, J. D. (1999), *Undue Risk. Secret State Experiments on Humans*. New York: Freeman.

Moser, G. (2006), '"Forschungen für die Abwehr biologischer Kriegsmethoden" und Krebsforschung im Zweiten Weltkrieg: Die Forschungsarbeiten beim "Reichsbevollmächtigten für Krebsforschung", Kurt Blome, 1943–1945', in W. U. Eckart and A. Neumann (eds.), *Medizin im Zweiten Weltkrieg. Militärmedizinische Praxis und medizinische Wissenschaft im 'Totalen Krieg'*. Paderborn, Munich, Vienna, Zurich: Schöningh, pp. 131–50.

Müller-Hill, B. (1984), *Tödliche Wissenschaft. Die Aussonderung von Juden, Zigeunern und Geisteskranken 1933–45*. Reinbek near Hamburg: Rowohlt.

Müller-Hill, B. (1988), *Murderous Science. Elimination by Scientific Selection of Jews, Gypsies, and Others, Germany 1933–1945*. Oxford, New York: Oxford University Press.

Neumann, A. (2006), 'Ernährungphysiologische Humanexperimente in der deutschen Militärmedizin 1939–1945', in W. U. Eckart and A. Neumann (eds.), *Medizin im Zweiten Weltkrieg. Militärmedizinische Praxis und medizinische Wissenschaft im 'Totalen Krieg'*. Paderborn, Munich, Vienna, Zurich: Schöningh, pp. 151–70.

Niven, B. (ed.), (2006), *Germans as Victims. Remembering the Past in Contemporary Germany*. Basingstoke: Palgrave.

Noakes, J. (1989), 'Philipp Bouhler und die Kanzlei des Führers der NSDAP. Beispiel einer Sonderverwaltung im Dritten Reich', in D. Rebentisch and K. Teppe (eds.), *Verwaltung contra Menschenführung im Staat Hitlers*. Göttingen: Vandenhoeck und Ruprecht, pp. 209–36.

Noakes, J. (1998), 'In Search of Unconditional Obedience: Favourites, Power-Brokers and Body Servants at Hitler's Court'. *The Times Literary Supplement*, 2 (1998), 15–16.

Noakes, J. (2003), '"Viceroys of the Reich"? Gauleiters 1925–45', in A. McElligott and T. Kirk (eds.), *Working towards the Führer*. Manchester, New York: Manchester University Press, pp. 118–52.

Noakes, J. and Pridham, G. (1983–1998), *Nazism 1919–1945: A Documentary Reader*, 4 vols. Exeter: University of Exeter Press.

Nowak, K. (1984), *'Euthanasie' und Sterilisierung im 'Dritten Reich': Die Konfrontation der evangelischen und katholischen Kirche mit dem Gesetz zur Verhütung erbkranken Nachwuchses und der 'Euthanasie'-Aktion*. Vienna, Cologne, Weimar: Böhlau Verlag.

Oren-Hornfeld, S. (2005), *Wie brennend Feuer. Ein Opfer medizinischer Experimente im Konzentrationslager Sachsenhausen erzählt*. Berlin: Metropol Verlag.

Oscar, F. [alias Friedrich Olmes] (1950), *Über Galgen wächst kein Gras. Die fragwürdige Kulisse der Kriegsverbrecherprozesse im Spiegel unbekannter Documente*. Braunschweig: Erasmus-Verlag.

Overy, R. (2004), *The Dictators. Hitler's Germany and Stalin's Russia*. London: Allen Lane.

Padfield, P. (1995), *Himmler: Reichsführer SS*. London: Papermac.

Peiffer, J. (1997), *Hirnforschung im Zwielicht: Beispiele verführbarer Wissenschaft aus der Zeit des Nationalsozialismus. Julius Hallervorden – H.J. Scherer – Berthold Ostertag*. Husum: Matthiesen.

Perlia, R. (1999), *In geheimer Mission. Memoiren eines Testpiloten unter Hitler*. Augsburg: Bechtermünz-Verlag.

Peter, J. (1994), *Der Nürnberger Ärzteprozeß im Spiegel seiner Aufarbeitung anhand der drei Dokumentensammlungen von Alexander Mitscherlich und Fred Mielke*. Münster, Hamburg: Literatur-Verlag.

Petrakis, M. (2005), *The Metaxas Myth. Dictatorship and Propaganda in Greece*. London: I. B. Tauris.

Petropoulos, J. (2000), *The Faustian Bargain. The Art World in Nazi Germany*. New York: Allen Lane.

Plaim, A. and Kuch, K. (2005), *Bei Hitlers. Zimmermädchen Annas Erinnerungen*. Munich: Knaur.

Platen, A. von. (1947a), 'Ärzteprozeß Nürnberg'. *Hippokrates*, 1 (1947), 29–31.

Platen, A. von. (1947b), 'Der Nürnberger Ärzteprozeß II'. *Hippokrates*, 17 (1947), 199–202.

Platen-Hallermund, A. [1948] (1998), *Die Tötung Geisteskranker in Deutschland*. Frankfurt a.M: Psychiatrie-Verlag. Reprint.

Posner, G. L. and Ware, J. (2000), *Mengele: The Complete Story*. New York: Cooper Square Press.

Prinz, M. and Zitelmann, R. (eds.), (1991), *Nationalsozialismus und Modernisierung*. Darmstadt: Wissenschaftliche Buchgesellschaft.

'Prison Malaria: Convicts Expose Themselves to Disease so Doctors Can Study it'. *Life*, 18 (1945), 23, 43–46.

Proctor, R. N. (1988), *Racial Hygiene. Medicine under the Nazis*. Cambridge, Mass. Harvard University Press.

Proctor, R. N. (1992), 'Nazi Doctors, Racial Medicine, and Human Experimentation', in G. J. Annas and M. A. Grodin (eds.), *The Nazi Doctors and the Nuremberg Code. Human Rights in Human Experimentation*. Oxford, New York: Oxford University Press, pp. 17–31.

Proctor, R. N. (1999), *The Nazi War on Cancer*. Princeton: Princeton University Press.

Pross, C. and Aly, G. (eds.), (1989), *Der Wert des Menschen. Medizin in Deutschland 1918–1945*. Berlin: Hentrich.

Read, A. (2004), *The Devil's Disciples. The Lives and Times of Hitler's Inner Circle*. London: Pimlico.

Rebentisch, D. (1989), *Führerstaat und Verwaltung im Zweiten Weltkrieg. Verfassungsentwicklung und Verwaltungspolitik 1939–1945*. Stuttgart: Steiner.

Rebentisch, D. and Teppe, K. (eds.), (1989), *Verwaltung contra Menschenführung im Staat Hitlers*. Göttingen: Vandenhoeck und Ruprecht.

Reuth, G. (ed.), (1999), *Joseph Goebbels. Tagebücher 1924–1945*, 5 vols. Munich, Zurich: Piper.

Riess, C. (1956), *Das gab's nur einmal. Das Buch der schönsten Filme unseres Lebens*. Hamburg: Verlag der Sternbücher.

Rimmele, E. (1996), *Sprachenpolitik im Deutschen Kaiserreich von 1914. Regierungspolitik und veröffentlichte Meinung in Elsaß-Lothringen und den östlichen Provinzen Preußens*. Frankfurt a.M.: Lang.

Roelcke, V. and Maio, G. (eds.), (2004), *Twentieth Century Ethics of Human Subject Research – Historical Perspectives on Values, Practices, and Regulations*. Stuttgart: Steiner.

Rose, O. (2005), *Julius Schaub – In Hitlers Schatten. Erinnerungen und Aufzeichnungen des Chefadjutanten 1925–1945*. Stegen: Druffel und Vowinckel.

Roseman, M. (2002), *The Wannsee Conference and the Final Solution. A Reconsideration*. New York: Metropolitan Books.

Rost, K. L. (1987), *Sterilisation und Euthanasie im Film des 'Dritten Reiches'*. Husum: Matthiesen.

Schenck, E. G. (1989), *Patient Hitler: Eine Medizinische Biographie*. Düsseldorf: Droste.

Schindler-Saefkow, B. (1995), 'Die Befreiung des Konzentrationslagers Ravensbrück durch die Rote Armee und die erste Beweisaufnahme von Verbrechen', in S. Jacobeit (ed.), *'Ich grüße Euch als freier Mensch'. Quellenedition zur Befreiung des Frauen-Konzentrationslagers Ravensbrück im April 1945*. Berlin: Hentrich, pp. 137–208.

Schirach, H. von. (1983), *Frauen um Hitler*. Munich, Berlin: Herbig.

Schlie, U. (ed.), (1999), *Albert Speer. 'Alles, was ich weiß'. Aus unbekannten Geheimprotokollen vom Sommer 1945*. Munich: Herbig.

Schlingensiepen, F. (2006), *Dietrich Bonhoeffer 1906–1945*. Munich: Beck.

Schmaltz, F. (2005), *Kampfstoff-Forschung im Nationalsozialismus. Zur Kooperation von Kaiser-Wilhelm-Instituten, Militär und Industrie*. Göttingen: Wallstein.

Schmaltz, F. (2006a), 'Neurosciences and Research on Chemical Weapons of Mass Destruction in Nazi Germany'. *Journal of the History of Neurosciences*, 15 (2006), 186–209.

Schmaltz, F. (2006b), 'Otto Bickenbach's human experiments with chemical warfare agents and the concentration camp Natzweiler', in W. U. Eckart (ed.), *Man, Medicine and the State: The Human Body as an Object of Government-Sponsored Medical Research*. Stuttgart: Steiner, pp. 139–56.

Schmaltz, F. (2006c), 'Pharmakologische Nevengasforschung an der Militärärztlichen Akademie und an den Universitäten Marburg, Danzig und Leipzig im Zweiten Weltkrieg', in W. U. Eckart and A. Neumann (eds.), *Medizin im Zweiten Weltkrieg. Militärmedizinische Praxis und medizinische Wissenschaft im 'Totalen Krieg'*. Paderborn, Munich, Vienna, Zurich: Schöningh, pp. 171–94.

Schmidt, U. (1997), 'German Medical War Crimes, Medical Ethics and Post-War Justice: A Symposium held at the University of Oxford to Mark the 50th Anniversary of the Nuremberg Medical Trial, 14 March 1997'. *German History*, 15 (1997), 385–91.

Schmidt, U. (1998), 'Reform Psychiatry and Society between Imperial and Nazi Germany. Review of *Anstaltsärzte zwischen Kaiserreich und Bundesrepublik* (Kersting) and *Psychiatrie und Gesellschaft in der Moderne* (Walter)'. *Social History of Medicine*, 11 (1998), 336–37.

Schmidt, U. (1999a), 'Reassessing the Beginning of the "Euthanasia" Programme'. *German History*, 17 (1999), 541–48.

Schmidt, U. (1999b), 'The History of the Kaiser-Wilhelm-Society During National Socialism. Observations on a Three-Day Working Conference organised by the Max-Planck-Society in Berlin, 10–13 March 1999'. *German History*, 17 (1999), 549–55.

Schmidt, U. (2000a), '"Der Blick auf den Körper": Sozialhygienische Filme, Sexualaufklärung und Propaganda in der Weimarer Republik', in M. Hagener (ed.), *Geschlecht in Fesseln*.

Sexualität zwischen Aufklärung und Ausbeutung im Weimarer Kino 1918–1933. Munich: Edition Text und Kritik, pp. 23–46.

Schmidt, U. (2000b), 'Kriegsausbruch und "Euthanasie": Neue Forschungsergebnisse zum Knauer Kind im Jahre 1939', in A. Frewer and C. Eickhoff (eds.), *Euthanasie und die aktuelle Sterbehilfe-Debatte. Die historischen Hintergründe medizinischer* Ethik. Frankfurt a.M., New York: Campus, pp. 120–37.

Schmidt, U. (2000c), 'Sozialhygienische Filme und Propaganda in der Weimarer Republik', in D. Jasbinski (ed.), *Gesundheitskommunikation. Medieninhalte und Mediennutzung aus Sicht der Public Health-Forschung*. Wiesbaden: Westdeutscher Verlag, pp. 53–82.

Schmidt, U. (2001a), 'Der Ärzteprozeß als moralische Instanz? Der Nürnberger Kodex und das Problem "zeitloser Medizinethik", 1946/47', in A. Frewer and J. N. Neumann (eds.), *Medizingeschichte und Medizinethik 1900–1950*. Frankfurt a.M., New York: Campus, pp. 334–73.

Schmidt, U. (2001b), 'Die Angeklagten Fritz Fischer, Hans W. Romberg und Karl Brandt aus der Sicht des medizinischen Sachverständigen Leo Alexander', in K. Dörner and A. Ebbinghaus (eds.), *Vernichten und Heilen: Der Nürnberger Ärzteprozeß und seine Folgen*. Berlin: Aufbau Verlag, pp. 374–404.

Schmidt, U. (2001c), 'Discussing Slave Labourers in Nazi Germany: Topography of Research or Politics of Memory?' *German History*, 19 (2001), 408–17.

Schmidt, U. (2002a), *Medical Films, Ethics and Euthanasia in Nazi Germany*. Husum: Matthiesen.

Schmidt, U. (2002b), 'Medicina e Nazismo'. *Sistema Salute*, 5 (2002), 9–18.

Schmidt, U. (2004), *Justice at Nuremberg. Leo Alexander and the Nazi Doctors' Trial*. Basingstoke: Palgrave.

Schmidt, U. (2005), 'The Scars of Ravensbrück: Medical Experiments and British War Crimes Policy, 1945–1950'. *German History*, 23 (2005), 1, 20–49.

Schmidt, U. (2006), 'Cold War at Porton Down: Informed Consent in Britain's Biological and Chemical Warfare Experiments'. *Cambridge Quarterly for Healthcare Ethics*, 15 (2006), 4, 366–80.

Schmidt, U. (2007a), 'Medicine and Nazism', in R. Baker and L. B. McCullough (eds.), *A History of Medical Ethics*. Cambridge, New York: Cambridge University Press.

Schmidt, U. (2007b), 'Medical Ethics and Human Experimentation at Porton Down: Informed Consent in Britain's Biological and Chemical Warfare Experiments', in U. Schmidt and A. Frewer (eds.), *History and Theory of Human Experimentation. The Declaration of Helsinki and Modern Medical Ethics*. Stuttgart: Steiner.

Schmidt, U. (2007c), 'The Nuremberg Doctors' Trial and the Nuremberg Code', in U. Schmidt and A. Frewer (eds.), *History and Theory of Human Experimentation. The Declaration of Helsinki and Modern Medical Ethics*. Stuttgart: Steiner.

Schmidt, U. and Frewer, A. (eds.), (2007a), *History and Theory of Human Experimentation. The Declaration of Helsinki and Modern Medical Ethics*. Stuttgart: Steiner.

Schmidt, U. and Frewer, A. (2007b), 'History of Research Ethics. The Twisted Road to Helsinki. An Introduction', in U. Schmidt and A. Frewer (eds.), *History and Theory of Human Experimentation. The Declaration of Helsinki and Modern Medical Ethics*. Stuttgart: Steiner.

Schmidt, U. and Frewer, A. (2007c), 'Nuremberg Code of Medical Ethics. Geschichte und Ethik des Ärzteprozesses', in A. Frewer and U. Schmidt (eds.), *Standards der Forschung*. Frankfurt a.M., New York: Olms.

Schmuhl, H.-W. (1987), *Rassenhygiene, Nationalsozialismus, Euthanasie. Von der Verhütung zur Vernichtung 'lebensunwerten Lebens', 1890–1945*. Göttingen: Vandenhoeck & Ruprecht.

Schmuhl, H.-W. (1991), 'Reformpsychiatrie und Massenmord', in M. Prinz and R. Zitelmann
    (eds.), *Nationalsozialismus und Modernisierung*. Wissenschaftliche Buchgesellschaft:
    Darmstadt, pp. 239–66.

Schmuhl, H.-W. (1997), 'Eugenik und "Euthanasie" – Zwei Paar Schuhe? Eine Antwort auf
    Michael Schwartz'. *Westfälische Forschungen*, 47 (1997), 757–62.

Schultz, U. (1985), 'Dichtkunst, Heilkunst, Forschung: Der Kinderarzt Werner Catel', in G. Aly
    et al. (eds.), *Reform und Gewissen. 'Euthanasie' im Dienst des Fortschritts*. Berlin: Rotbuch,
    pp. 107–24.

Schwartz, M. (1996), 'Rassenhygiene, Nationalsozialismus, Euthanasie?' *Westfälische
    Forschungen*, 46 (1996), 604–22.

Schwartz, M. (1998), '"Euthanasie"-Debatten in Deutschland (1895–1945)'. *Vierteljahreshefte
    für Zeitgeschichte*, 46 (1998), 617–65.

Schweitzer, A. (1990), *Kultur und Ethik*. Munich: Beck.

Schweitzer, A. (1996), *Aus meiner Kindheit und Jugendzeit*. Munich: Beck.

Schweitzer, A. (2004), *Aus meinem Leben und Denken*. Frankfurt a.M.: Fischer.

'Selbstbildnis eines "Kriegsverbrechers"'. *Deutsche Hochschullehrer-Zeitung*, 10 (1962), 1, 5–9.

Sereny, G. (1988), *Into that Darkness. From Mercy Killing to Mass Murder*. London: Pimlico.

Sereny, G. (1995), *Albert Speer: His Battle with Truth*. London: Picador.

Sereny, G. (2000), *The German Trauma. Experiences and Reflections, 1938–2000*. London: Allen
    Lane.

'Seven Hanged for Brutality in Nazi Camps'. *Florida Times-Union*, 3 June 1948.

Shuster, E. (1997), 'Fifty Years Later: The Significance of the Nuremberg Code'. *The New
    England Journal of Medicine*, 337 (1997), 1436–40.

Shuster, E. (1998a), 'The Nuremberg Code: Hippocratic Ethics and Human Rights'. *Lancet*, 351
    (1998), 974–77.

Shuster, E. (1998b), 'The Significance of the Nuremberg Code'. Letter to the Editor, *New
    England Journal of Medicine*, 338 (1998), 995–96.

Sigmund, A. M. (1998), *Die Frauen der Nazis*. Vienna: Ueberreuter.

Sigmund, A. M. (2000), *Die Frauen der Nazis II*. Vienna: Ueberreuter.

Sillevaerts, C. (1947), 'The Nurnberg Trial'. *Bruxelles Médical*, 31 August 1947.

Smelser, R. (1989), *Robert Ley: Hitlers Mann an der 'Arbeitsfront'. Ein Biographie*. Paderborn,
    Munich, Vienna, Zurich: Schöningh.

Smelser, R. and Syring, E. (eds.), (2000), *Die SS. Elite unterm Totenkopf. 30 Lebensläufe*.
    Paderborn, Munich, Vienna, Zurich: Schöningh.

Smith, J. E. (1974), *The Papers of General Lucius D. Clay: Germany, 1945–1949*. Bloomington:
    Indiana University Press.

Speer, A. (1976), *Spandau. The Secret Diaries*. New York: Macmillan.

Speer, A. (2000), *Inside the Third Reich: Memoirs*. New York: Phoenix (first published in 1970).

Spotts, F. (2003), *Hitler and the Power of Aesthetics*. London: Pimlico.

Stargardt, N. (2005), *Witnesses of War. Children's Lives under the Nazis*. London: Jonathan Cape.

Steffahn, H. (2004), *Albert Schweitzer mit Selbszeugnissen und Bilddokumenten*. Reinbek bei
    Hamburg: Rowohlt.

Steinert, M. G. (1967), *Die 23 Tage der Regierung Dönitz*. Düsseldorf: Econ-Verlag.

Sterkowicz, S. (n. d.), 'Medizinische Untersuchungen in dem Konzentrationslager Ravensbrück'
    (typescript manuscript).

Streit, C. (1995), 'Das Schicksal der verwundeten sowjetischen Kriegsgefangenen', in H. Heer
    and K. Naumann (eds.), *Vernichtungskrieg. Verbrechen der Wehrmacht 1941–1944*. Hamburg:
    Hamburger Edition, pp. 78–91.

Stroink, H. (1986) 'Borst and the Von Brehmer Incident'. *American Journal of Dermatology*, 8 (1986), 522–24.

Stumpfegger, L. (1944), 'Die freie autoplastische Knochentransplantation'. *Zeitschrift für Chirurgie*, 259 (1944), 495ff.

Süß, W. (1998), 'Gesundheitspolitik', in H. G. Hockerts (ed.), *Drei Wege deutscher Sozialstaatlichkeit. NS-Diktatur, Bundesrepublilk und DDR im Vergleich*. Munich: Oldenbourg, pp. 55–100.

Süß, W. (2000), 'Krankenmord. Forschungsstand und Forschungsfragen zur Geschichte der nationalsozialistischen "Euthanasie"', in T. Bauer and W. Süß (eds.), *NS-Diktatur, DDR, Bundesrepublik. Drei Zeitgeschichten des vereinigten Deutschlands. Werkstattberichte*. Neuried: Ars Una, pp. 47–86.

Süß, W. (2002a), 'Der beinahe unaufhaltsame Aufstieg des Karl Brandt: Zur Stellung des "Reichskommissars für das Sanitäts- und Gesundheitswesen" im gesundheitspolitischen Machtgefüge des "Dritten Reiches"', in W. Woelk and J. Vögele (eds.), *Geschichte der Gesundheitspolitik in Deutschland. Von der Weimarer Republik bis in die Frühgeschichte der 'doppelten Staatsgründung'*. Berlin: Duncker & Humblot, pp. 197–223.

Süß, W. (2002b), 'Von der Gesundheitspolitik zum Krankenmord. Medizin im Zeichen der Rassenhygiene', in C. Vollnhals (ed.), *Sachsen in der NS-Zeit*. Leipzig: Kiepenheuer, pp. 155–69, pp. 269–73.

Süß, W. (2003), *Der 'Volkskörper' im Krieg. Gesundheitspolitik, Gesundheitsverhältnisse und Krankenmord im nationalsozialistischen Deutschland 1939–1945*. Munich: Oldenbourg.

Szöllösi-Janze, M. (ed.), (2001), *Science in the Third Reich*. Oxford, New York: Berg.

Taylor, T. (1992), *The Anatomy of the Nuremberg Trials*. New York: Knopf.

'The German Atrocities'. *Life*, 18 (1945), 19, 32–37.

'The Germans Sign the Surrenders'. *Life*, 18 (1945), 21, 25–31.

Thom, A. and Catagorodcev, G. I. (eds.), (1989), *Medizin unterm Hakenkreuz*. Berlin: VEB Verlag Volk und Gesundheit.

Trevor-Roper, H. (1995), *The Last Days of Hitler*. London: Papermac.

Trevor-Roper, H. (ed.), (1954), *The Bormann Letters*. London: Weidenfeld & Nicolson.

Tröhler, U. and Reiter-Theil, S. (eds.), (1997), *Ethik und Medizin: 1947–1997. Was leistet die Kodifizierung von Ethik?* Göttingen: Wallstein.

Tröhler, U. and Reiter-Theil, S. (eds.), (1998), *Ethics Codes in Medicine. Foundations and Achievements of Codification since 1947*. Aldershot: Ashgate, Brookfield.

Tusa, T. and Tusa, J. (1995), *The Nuremberg Trial*. London: BBC Books.

United States Office of the High Commissioner for Germany, (ed.), (1951), *Landsberg: A Documentary Report*. Frankfurt a.M.: United States Office of the US High Commissioner for Germany.

Vat, D. van der, (1998), *The Good Nazi. The Life and Lies of Albert Speer*. London: Phoenix.

Vogeler, K. (1941), *August Bier. Leben und Werk*. Munich: Lehmann.

Vollnhals, C. (ed.), (2002), *Sachsen in der NS-Zeit*. Dresden: Kiepenheuer.

Walter, B. (1996), *Psychiatrie und Gesellschaft in der Moderne. Geisteskrankenfürsorge in der Provinz Westfalen zwischen Kaiserreich und NS-Regime*. Paderborn, Munich, Vienna, Zurich: Schöningh.

Walter, B. and Benad, M. (1997), 'Zwangssterilisation und Planwirtschaft im Anstaltswesen. Die Konfrontation der v. Bodelschwinghschen Anstalten in Bethel mit den rassenhygienischen Maßnahmen des NS-Regimes', in M. Benad (ed.), *Friedrich v. Bodelschwingh d.J. und die Betheler Anstalten. Frömmigkeit und Weltgestaltung*. Stuttgart, Berlin, Köln: Kohlhammer, pp. 137–52.

Webster, C. (ed.), (1981), *Biology, Medicine and Society 1840–1940*. Cambridge, New York: Cambridge University Press.

Weindling, P. J. (1981), 'Theories of the Cell State in Imperial Germany', in C. Webster (ed.), *Biology, Medicine and Society 1840–1940*. Cambridge, New York: Cambridge University Press, pp. 99–155.

Weindling, P. J. (1989), *Health, Race and German Politics between National Unification and Nazism, 1870–1945*. Cambridge, New York: Cambridge University Press.

Weindling, P. J. (2000), *Epidemics and Genocide in Eastern Europe, 1890–1945*. Oxford, New York: Oxford University Press.

Weindling, P. J. (2004), *Nazi Medicine and the Nuremberg Trials: From Medical War Crimes to Informed Consent*. Basingstoke: Palgrave.

Weingart, P., Kroll, J. and Bayertz, K. (1996), *Rasse, Blut und Gene. Geschichte der Eugenik und Rassenhygiene in Deutschland*. Frankfurt a.M.: Suhrkamp.

Welch, D. (2001), *Propaganda and the German Cinema 1933–45*. Oxford: I. B. Tauris.

Welch, D. (2002), *The Third Reich. Politics and Propaganda*. London, New York: Routledge.

Welch, D. (2003), '"Working towards the Führer": Charismatic Leadership and the Image of Adolf Hitler in Nazi Propaganda', in A. McElligott and T. Kirk (eds.), *Working towards the Führer*. Manchester, New York: Manchester University Press, pp. 93–117.

Weyers, W. (2003), *The Abuse of Man. An Illustrated History of Dubious Medical Experimentation*. New York: Ardor Scribendi.

Wicke, M. (1999), 'Arzt und Mörder'. *Berliner Zeitung*, 16/17 January 1999.

Wiedemann, F. (1964), *Der Mann der Feldherr werden wollte. Erlebnisse und Erfahrungen des Vorgesetzten Hitlers im 1. Weltkrieg und seines späteren Persönlichen Adjutanten*. Velbert: Blick + Bild.

Wiegrefe, K. (2005), 'Der charmante Verbrecher'. *Der Spiegel*, 18 (2005), 74–86.

Wiesemann, C. and Frewer, A. (eds.), (1996), *Medizin und Ethik im Zeichen von Auschwitz. 50 Jahre Nürnberger Ärzteprozeß*. Erlangen, Jena: Palm & Enke.

Wildt, M. (2002), *Generation des Unbedingten. Das Führungskorps des Reichssicherheitshauptamtes*. Hamburg: Hamburger Edition.

Witte, P. *et al.* (eds.), (1999), *Der Dienstkalender Heinrich Himmlers 1941/42*. Hamburg: Christians.

Woelk, W. (2003), 'Der Pharmakologe und Toxikologe Wolfgang Wirth (1898–1996) und die Giftgasforschung im Nationalsozialismus', in W. Woelk *et al.* (eds.), *Nach der Diktatur. Die medizinische Akademie Düsseldorf nach 1945*. Essen: Klartext.

Woelk, W. *et al.* (eds.), (2003), *Nach der Diktatur. Die medizinische Akademie Düsseldorf nach 1945*. Essen: Klartext.

Wolbert, K. (1982), *Die Nackten und die Toten des Dritten Reiches: Folgen einer politischen Geschichte des Körpers in der Plastik des deutschen Faschismus*. Giessen: Anabas.

Wunder, M. (1994), 'Die Spätzeit der Euthanasie', in K. Böhme and U. Lohalm. (eds.), *Wege in den Tod. Hamburgs Anstalt Langenhorn und die Euthanasie in der Zeit des Nationalsozialismus*. Hamburg: Ergebnisse Verlag, pp. 397–400.

Zoller, A. (1949), *Hitler privat. Erlebnisbericht seiner Geheimsekretärin*. Düsseldorf: Droste.

Index